MANDELSTAM

[Osip Emilievich]

THE COMPLETE CRITICAL PROSE AND LETTERS

Edited by Jane Gary Harris
Translated by Jane Gary Harris and Constance Link

ARDIS  ANN ARBOR

The manuscript of this book was edited for publication by
Carl R. Proffer, copy-edited by Fred Moody and William Kalvin.
The typeset text was proof-read and corrected by Thais Houtteman,
Sydney Schultze, and Nancy Beveridge. The Index was prepared by
Fred Moody.

Osip Emilievich Mandelstam

The Complete Critical Prose and Letters

Translation by Jane Gary Harris and Constance Link
Introduction and Notes by Jane Gary Harris
Copyright © 1979 by Ardis.
ISBN 0-88233-163-9
LC Catalog Card No.: 78-64999
Published by Ardis, 2901 Heatherway,
Ann Arbor, Michigan 48104

CONTENTS

IV. REVIEWS (1923)

V. MEMOIRS, VIGNETTES, REPORTAGE (1922-1923)

VI. ESSAYS, SKETCHES, POLEMICS, FOREWORDS (1926-early 1930s)

VII. INTERNAL REVIEWS (late 1920s-early 1930s)

VIII. MAJOR PROSE WORKS OF THE 1930s

IX. LETTERS (Translated by Constance Link)

Other Letters

THE COMPLETE CRITICAL PROSE AND LETTERS

PREFACE

> For the sheer joy of it, take from my hands
> A bit of honey and a bit of sun,
> As Persephone's bees once commanded.
> (November, 1920)

This book is offered as a humble gift to all my Soviet friends, colleagues, and correspondents who, for nearly two decades, have lavished on me gifts of love, friendship, and poetry inspired by that spirit of moral and esthetic commitment informing the work of Osip Emilievich Mandelstam.

The translations, annotations and introductory essay comprising this volume are consequently intended, first, for those who know no Russian—to convince them to want to read the original; second, for those who fear they do not know enough Russian—to help them gain the courage to try; and, last but not least, for those who know Russian but welcome new insights or interpretations as part of the vital, ongoing discussion of Mandelstam's immortal gift to all of us, "the reader in posterity."

Special thanks and grateful acknowledgements are due to the many persons who offered me their kind help and support during the various stages of this project: to Connie Link who worked so tirelessly and with such undaunted enthusiasm on the translations; to Walter Arndt for his generous and invaluable suggestions on translating *Journey to Armenia*; to George Kline for his inspiring comments and suggestions on translating "On the Nature of the Word"; to my family, friends, colleagues and students for their countless suggestions, enthusiastic comments, selfless help, interest and time—to them I am obliged for more than they perhaps realize; to the American Council of Learned Societies and the American Philosophical Association for their much-needed financial assistance in the formative stages of this project; and, last but hardly least, to the editors of the three-volume *Collected Works* (cited as *SS* in the annotations), without whose efforts this volume would never have been possible, and to all the dedicated students, friends and devotees of Mandelstam and his *oeuvre* whose comments are solicited and whose works are cited with gratitude in the annotations.

Jane Gary Harris
University of Pittsburgh
June, 1978

THE COMPLETE CRITICAL PROSE AND LETTERS

[A poet's] lines continue to live on long after they were written, as events, not merely as tokens of an experience which has passed.

On the Addressee, 1913

Human lips, that have no more to say,
Preserve the form of the last uttered word,
The hand continues to feel the full weight
even after the jug
    has splashed itself half empty
      on the way home.

What I'm saying now isn't said by me.
It's dug out of the ground like fossilized grains of wheat.

The Horseshoe Finder, 1923

Only through metaphor is it possible to find a concrete sign to represent the instinct for form creation . . .

I should hope that in the future [scholars] will study the coordination of the impulse and the text.

Conversation about Dante, 1933

INTRODUCTION:
THE IMPULSE AND THE TEXT

For Mandelstam, the wonder of "the word" springs from "the instinct for form creation," from the "impulse" to preserve the eternal verities for us, "the reader in posterity." For us, Mandelstam's "love of the word" never ceases to invite wonderment. Indeed, we may attribute to a miracle of poetic justice the very fact that the poet's words have been preserved through the unselfish love of the word and the selfless love of the poet's widow and friends.

In one of his earliest essays, "On the Addressee," the young Mandelstam distinguishes between prose and poetry by calling attention to the poet's "addressee" as the "reader in posterity," while the prose writer's audience is viewed as "the dynamic representatives of his age." Taken to its extreme, the dichotomy states: poetry preserves, prose instructs. The principle that the poet speaks only to the future, to the "reader in posterity," while the prose writer speaks directly to his contemporaries, was a concept inherited from an earlier tradition, mainly from the Romantics, but revitalized by the Symbolists. Mandelstam was to struggle with it for at least

3

a decade before recognizing that his own ideological and esthetic impulse derived more readily from the Classical tradition, which obliged the poet to devote equal attention to the impulse and the text. In contrast to the Romantic tradition in which the poet views himself primarily as a seer or visionary, Classical esthetics demand that the poet perceive himself as the interpreter of truth and take cognizance of the reader. Consequently, while the Romantic tradition emphasized the dichotomy between the intuitive and interpretive mind, the Classical vision served as an inspiration to "the mind seeking unities and connections."

As Mandelstam matured, the bonds between his poetry and prose gradually tightened. Not only did the themes of his essays influence his poems, but by 1923, the major turning point in his life and literary career, the verbal fabric of his poetry found expression in his literary prose. Not only did the earlier distinction between the "addressee" of poetry and the "addressee" of prose give way, but the artificial dichotomy between the poet and the intellectual yielded to the perception of the essential bond or "connection" between the poet and the reader. The story of the young poet's intellectual quest for the esthetic bond uniting his intellectual and artistic vision is to be found in Mandelstam's early essays. Indeed, these essays may be read as the poet's intellectual autobiography or even as the "notebooks" for his poetry and literary prose.

On the other hand, Mandelstam's literary prose, begun in 1922-1923, may be read as a series of autobiographical syntheses in which the autobiographical impulse mediates between the intellectual and esthetic impulses, transforming extra-literary genres into texts of literary prose. In these works, the poet subtly reveals esthetic solutions to artistic, intellectual and moral problems, solutions which emerge from the poet's unique "philological" focus—from his literal, Mandelstamian "love of the word" (*philia + logos*), from his "insatiable hunger for thought," and from his quest to determine "what is perceptible to the mind seeking unities and connections."

Mandelstam's first substantial piece of literary prose, his masterpiece of autobiographical fiction, *The Noise of Time*[1], was simultaneously the culmination of the first phase of his life as a poet—his artistic *rite de passage*— and an esthetic declaration of intellectual maturity.

While the first phase (up to 1923) may be said to have been dominated by Mandelstam's quest to understand the relationship between his poetic and intellectual identity, the second phase (1923-1930s) may be said to be dominated by his quest for the proper expression of that identity. Indeed, in the first phase, themes of intellectual identity—the image of the poet, the role of the poet in society, the relationship of freedom and morality, the identification of audience, the nature and source of poetry and the poetic impulse— were subject to vacillation, ambiguous interpretation, and contradictory judgments, while problems of style were regarded primarily as "craft," and therefore relatively easily accessible to the self-confident, young Acmeist (see the essays "François Villon," "Morning of Acmeism," and "On the Addressee"). Furthermore, the relatively rigid distinction between themes proper for lyric poetry and themes whose proper domain was prose—made finding expressions for particular ideas or values relatively uncomplicated. The poetic impulse led directly to the poetic text; the intellectual impulse inspired the critical essay.

In the early 1920s, however, when Mandelstam recognized the "category of obligation" as inherent to Classical poetry, when he pondered over the "union of the mind and the furies," and when, finally, he defined his ultimate subject as "philology," literally as "love of the word" which he gradually came to distinguish from "Literature," problems of poetic expression, concern with genre, and experimentation with new forms became paramount: the results may be seen in his meditative poetry of 1921-1925, and in his literary prose, critical essays, and polemics of the 1920s and 1930s. The creative impulse—the "instinct for form creation"—sought new modes of expression, new forms, new texts.

Osip Mandelstam, the son of a prosperous, Jewish leather merchant with an all-consuming passion for German philosophy, and a civic-minded, intellectual mother who took pride in her perfect accentless Russian and in the securing of proper French governesses for her three sons, was born in Warsaw in 1891, but raised in the culturally eclectic atmosphere of St. Petersburg's bourgeois intelligentsia at the turn of the century. After graduating from the Tenishev Commercial School in 1907, he travelled abroad and continued his education for a year (1909-10) at the University of Heidelberg studying Old French Literature.

However, at the same time that he exhibited a deep interest in French literature and European culture (see "François Villon," 1910, "Remarks on Chénier," conceived in 1914-15, and his Letters), young Mandelstam was attempting to come to terms with his Russian cultural heritage (see "Peter Chaadaev," 1915, "Pushkin and Scriabin," fragments begun in 1915) and to ascertain his identity as a poet and as an intellectual, as a European and as a Russian.

Although Mandelstam may still have been a Symbolist protegé of Vyacheslav Ivanov in 1909, sending the older poet his first poetic efforts from abroad (see Letters, No. 2-10), by the following year, in his essay "François Villon," he was already expressing the basic tenets of a new movement in Russian poetry, the Symbolist heresy headed by Nikolai Gumilev and known subsequently as Acmeism. By 1911, upon his return to Russia, Mandelstam enrolled in the Department of History and Philology of the University of St. Petersburg and joined Nikolai Gumilev's Guild of Poets.[2]

François Villon, the subject of Mandelstam's first extant essay, was not only a popular cult figure with the French Romantics and the anti-Romantic école romane, but was honored by the Symbolists, and, subsequently, by

Nikolai Gumilev as one of the forefathers of Acmeism. Indeed, the publication of Mandelstam's essay in the third issue of *Apollon* for 1913, accompanied as it was by Gumilev's translation of fragments from the *Grand Testament* and by a carefully chosen group of outstanding Acmeist poems, may be regarded as Mandelstam's first *printed* Acmeist manifesto.[3]

"François Villon" is remarkable for containing in embryonic form so many thematic and stylistic elements of Mandelstam's future poetry and prose. Specifically, this essay raised most of the intellectual and esthetic dilemmas confronting the young poet between 1910 and the early 1920s, namely: 1) the image and role of the poet, 2) the nature and source of poetry and the poetic impulse, 3) the relationship of art to society or, on a more cosmic scale, the relationship of art to history or Time, and 4) the problem of audience, and the relationship between the poet and the reader.

This essay is also of major interest in foreshadowing Mandelstam's literary prose. The fact that it contains far more biographical and historical details than his subsequent essays seems to substantiate its origin as a student paper in Heidelberg; however, the accumulation of such details assumes a prominent stylistic role in his later literary prose; indeed, autobiographical and historical references assume major structural functions in the prose of the 1920s-1930s.

Mandelstam, the nineteen-year-old student and would-be poet, is captivated above all by Villon's dynamism both as a poet and as a human being. He attributes Villon's dynamism (and amorality), at least in part, to his being a transitional figure in both space and time: a homeless vagabond only superficially bound by the restraints of the Middle Ages, but not yet the son of the Renaissance. "The blood of the Middle Ages flowed in Villon's veins. He was obliged to the Middle Ages for his integrity, his temperament, for the source of his spiritual values." However:

> Villon, last-born child of the Middle Ages, epigone of the feudal disposition, proved unreceptive to its ethical aspect, to its mutual guarantee! Gothic stability and morality were completely alien to him. On the other hand, greatly attracted by its dynamics, he elevated the Gothic to the heights of amoralism.

It is in this essay that Mandelstam first ponders the question of the image and role of the poet. Although he raises the issue of poetic freedom clearly and distinctly, in ethical terms, it is raised merely in passing, "Might there not be some inverse ratio between the moral and the dynamic development of the soul?" In 1910, Mandelstam's major concern is with understanding the impulse behind Villon's human and poetic vitality, "I think that Villon was captivated not by the demonic, but by the dynamics of criminal life." Indeed, Mandelstam rather bluntly distinguishes between Villon's not very profound "spiritual experiences" and the vitality of his "human relationships."

If, for all their originality, Villon's spiritual experiences are not distinguished by particular profundity, his human relationships, his intricate network of acquaintances, connections and reckonings, represent a composite of brilliant complexity . . . How precise he was, how detailed! Villon's *Testaments* captivate the reader simply by the mass of precise information they communicate. The reader can imagine himself using the data, and can experience the life of the poet's contemporaries. The passing moment can thus endure the pressure of centuries and preserve itself intact, remaining forever the same "here and now." You need only know how to extract that "here and now" from the soil of Time without harming its roots, or it will wither and die. Villon knew how to extract it.

The young Mandelstam was thus as fascinated by Villon's human experiences as by his poetic craft. He is essentially rejecting the Symbolist emphasis on the profound nature of the "spiritual experience" for Villon's romanticization of the vital details of the human experience. Villon's craft appealed to him as an example of poetry which allows the reader to relive the poet's human experiences vicariously, making the "passing moment . . . endure the pressure of centuries."

Another Romantic ideal which the Symbolists also accepted as a major characteristic of the poet's image—self-confidence or "the consciousness of being right"—is explicitly established in Mandelstam's Acmeist essays of 1913. Indeed, in these essays, the issue of poetic freedom and morality is not even mentioned in passing. What is more, in the essay "Pushkin and Scriabin" (begun in 1915, but completed only in the early 1920s), Mandelstam goes even further, asserting that the poet's "consciousness of being right" is a fundamental characteristic of the "Christian artist" whom he defines as a free spirit, absolutely unburdened by questions of "necessity."

In direct contrast, however, Mandelstam's essays on Chaadaev and Chénier (dating from about the same period, 1914-15) indicate the young poet's profound concern with intellectual and moral issues, his abiding interest in the problem of freedom and morality, and his serious concern over the question of the relationship of the artist to society. These essays provide us with an extraordinary insight into Mandelstam's image of himself as a poet, foreshadowing the metaphor of the *raznochinets-pisatel'* (intellectual-author or "philological nihilist") which he finally applies to himself in 1922-1923.

"Peter Chaadaev" is particularly significant in that it implicitly associates Mandelstam's incipient image of the poet as *raznochinets-pisatel'* to Russia itself. In this essay, Mandelstam focuses on establishing the image of Chaadaev as a metaphor for Russia's national idealism, interpreted as moral nationalism. In identifying "moral freedom" as the essence of Russian national identity and individuality, Chaadaev (according to Mandelstam) established it as one of the vital impulses determining every subsequent Russian writer's world view.

In Mandelstam's view, the very fact that Chaadaev dared to admit that Russia was cut off from the West and therefore had nothing to offer history but its own essence, allowed him to perceive Russia in a new and positive light, as a "free" entity—free from the West's legacy of stagnation, free from its petrified forms and ideas, indeed, morally and spiritually free to accept the necessity of choosing its own path of development: "moral choice" or "moral freedom."

Furthermore, in Mandelstam's opinion, Chaadaev's journey to the West and his independent decision to return home to Russia, was an unprecedented act of moral commitment, indicating his perception of Russia's significance in world culture, and recognizing the "moral" essence of Russia's national identity. Mandelstam thus perceived Chaadaev's consciousness as a metaphor for Russia's cultural legacy: "moral freedom."

Chaadaev was the first Russian who had actually lived in the West ideologically, and found the road back. His contemporaries . . . could point to him with superstitious respect, as they once pointed to Dante: "He was there, he saw—and he returned."

For Chaadaev, Russia had only one thing to offer: moral freedom, the freedom of choice.

. . . moral freedom, the gift of the Russian earth, its finest flower. This freedom is worth the majesty petrified in architectural forms, it is as valuable as everything the West has created in the realm of material culture, and I see that the Pope himself . . . has arisen to greet this freedom.

Having endowed us with inner freedom, Russia offers us a choice, and those who make this choice are true Russians, no matter what they affiliate themselves with.

Equally significant, Mandelstam was intrigued by the stimulus Chaadaev's writings offered him to define his own intellectual conception of the connection between freedom and morality, an issue raised merely in passing in "François Villon" and virtually ignored in the early Acmeist essays. After "Peter Chaadaev," the issue of poetic freedom and morality is pursued once again, in more depth, although from opposite points of view, in "Pushkin and Scriabin" and in "Remarks on Chénier."

"Pushkin and Scriabin" is a fascinating, if rather confusing essay,[4] as well as the most mystical of Mandelstam's writings. It would appear, at least on one level, that this essay is a response to the pamphlet, "Pushkin

8

and Christianity," published in Petrograd in 1915 by his former Tenishev School teacher, mentor and fellow poet, V. V. Gippius (see Letters, No. 1). Reflecting one of the dominant intellectual-esthetic trends of the day—the endeavor to synthesize the esthetic and cultural principles of Antiquity and Christianity—Gippius characterizes Pushkin's "Christianity" as pre-Christian "tragic pathos," maintaining that the Christian nature of his poetic soul is evident in his essentially Hellenistic aspiration toward grace:

> If I were asked to define Pushkin's soul as it was expressed in his poetry, it would be necessary to define it as a Christian soul in its most fundamental aspect,—sin aspiring toward sanctity . . . The depth of [Pushkin's] sinfulness was in his sensuality and, insofar as his sensuality was that of a suffering man, it was the passion of the Christian experience. The Greeks understood the relationship of sensuality and passion in just this way, in their tragic consciousness which identified passion and suffering as Pathos . . . The highest expression of Pushkin's passion was artistic—the tragic pathos.

Mandelstam continues Gippius's argument by referring to the Russian Symbolist composer, Scriabin, as a "mad Hellene," that is, not yet the recipient of Christian Grace, and therefore incapable of expressing "joy," defined by Mandelstam as the basic tenet of the Christian esthetic—"the joyous communion with God." Likewise, Scriabin is incapable of comprehending Mandelstam's conception of Christian freedom, "the divine illusion of redemption":

> ... Scriabin whose sun-heart burns above us, but alas!—his is not the sun of redemption but the sun of guilt.

> Scriabin is the next stage of Russian Hellenism after Pushkin, the most extreme revelation of the Hellenistic nature of the Russian spirit possible. Scriabin's great value for Russia and for Christianity derives from his being a "mad Hellene."

Above all, this essay provides us with Mandelstam's highly personal definition of Christianity, a concept which seems to grow out of his attempts to characterize Christian art as not much more than a unique call for artistic freedom and "art for art's sake" clothed in Christian terminology, and based on a purely esthetic conception of the Redemption: "the divine illusion of the redemption." According to Mandelstam, by offering mankind divine grace, Christ relieved him of all "necessity," thus permitting him to live, henceforth, the free, joyous and unrestrained life of the child or primitive man. According to Mandelstam, the Christian artist alone is capable of celebrating this state of "joy," for he alone is "free" to experience it. In

9

this essay, Mandelstam rejoices in the idea that Christian art is free from the "tragic pathos" of pre-Christian art, for

> It is "art for art's sake" in its fullest meaning. No necessity of any kind, not even the highest, darkens its bright inner freedom, for its prototype, that which it imitates, is the very redemption of the world by Christ. Thus, neither sacrifice nor redemption in art, but rather the free and joyous imitation of Christ is the keystone of Christian esthetics . . .

> What remains? Joyous communion with God, like some game played by the Father and his children, some blindman's buff or hide-and-seek of the spirit!

Scriabin does not express this Christian esthetic, but emerges rather closer to Gippius's view of Pushkin. Mandelstam states, "Scriabin's chiliasm expresses a purely Russian passion for salvation; the madness with which he expressed this passion is his legacy from the Ancient world." Pushkin, we might guess from the fragments of this essay, is Mandelstam's ultimate reference, a completely free and independent spirit, and the defender of "art for art's sake."

The attempt in this essay to characterize the poet as a free "Christian" spirit, that is, in Mandelstam's definition, as free from all "necessity," runs completely counter to the essay on Chaadaev. Indeed, Christian freedom is in no way associated here with "moral freedom" or morality, rather it is presented as the "final triumph of individuality," as freedom from all forms of restraint.

Furthermore, in this essay Mandelstam contrasts "Christian" and Classical art, stating that while the ancient Greeks placed numerous demands on the artist, Christianity demands absolutely nothing. This is expressed in the differing attitudes of the State and Religion toward music:

> Christianity adopted a completely free relationship to art which no human religion either before or since was able to do.

> In the ancient world, music was considered a destructive element . . . The distrust of music as some dark and suspicious element was so great that the state took music under its own supervision, making it a state monopoly. And musical harmony became synonymous with eunomy.

While this Romantic extremism did not hold Mandelstam very long, as a moment in his intellectual autobiography, "Pushkin and Scriabin" represents a major development. It is both his clearest and most extreme defense of artistic freedom and "art for art's sake." It also reflects his attempt to restate in Christian terms the quest of the early Acmeist essays

10

for a satisfactory image of the poet and a more precise understanding of the artist's relationship to society. It also seems to indicate a concerted effort to avoid, respectively, the purely esthetic or philosophical approach characterizing the essays on Villon and Chaadaev, and to transcend the early Acmeist statements in which the poet views himself entirely as an artisan and defines his role almost entirely in terms of his craft.

The essay, "Remarks on Chénier," evolves as a kind of intellectual counterpoint to "Pushkin and Scriabin." Indeed, both essays use Pushkin as an ultimate reference. While in the latter, Pushkin emerges as a completely free and independent spirit, as the defender of "art for art's sake," in the essay "Remarks on Chénier" (echoing "Peter Chaadaev"), morality is recognized as an essential element in Pushkin's esthetic vision (expressed here through his admiration for André Chénier, the poet of the French Revolution). Chénier, we know, expressed the belief that the writer must be a free individual aware of his own capacity as an artist as well as a social being responsive to his society.

Indeed, it could very well have been the 1914 republication of Chénier's *Essai* on literature and society (in Abel Lefranc, *Oeuvres inédites*) which sparked Mandelstam's own essay on Chénier, conceived, if not completed, as early as 1914-15, when it was "proposed for publication" in *Apollon*.

Chénier's *Essai* contains, among other things, the theory that only free men living in a free society can create great literature. However, Chénier was careful not to allow his view of art and society to limit his sense of history. He envisioned the artist as an active force in society, both opposing and reflecting social values and institutions. Nevertheless, like Mandelstam, Chénier held a somewhat exaggerated idea of the power of "the word," believing that the health (or corruption) of society was balanced by the moral consciousness of its artists. According to Chénier, literature was an integral part of life in young societies, but as soon as the social structure began to weaken, the writer was put on the defensive. Hence, courage to protest also became the sign of a great writer.

Similar ideas emerge time and again in Mandelstam's essays and literary prose, in particular in *The Noise of Time* and "Fourth Prose," in which he asserts the poet's right to challenge temporal values in the name of "the word," a theme also expressed in the meditative poems of the 1920s and in his work of the 1930s.

In "Remarks on Chénier," Mandelstam juxtaposes a polemic against what he sees as the artificiality and false values of the eighteenth century philosophers and the consequent abstraction of fundamental values into meaningless rhetorical principles or clichés with his celebration of the "absolute character of Classical morality" perceived as "pure," "naive," and "hygenic," seemingly an echo of various thoughts expressed in Chénier's poetry and in his *Essai*. However, the most significant aspect of Mandelstam's

11

appraisal of Chénier is his revelation that, "Chénier ingeniously found the middle road between the Classical and Romantic manner." This rejection of absolutes and concomitant striving towards a meaningful "middle road" characterizes Mandelstam's attempt at synthesis which he achieves in 1922-23. For instance, in the essay, "On the Nature of the Word" (1922), Mandelstam broadens his definition of Acmeism to encompass appropriate elements from both the Romantic and Classical traditions:

> The wind of Acmeism turned the pages of the Classicists and the Romantics, opening them to just that page which most appealed to the age. Racine was opened to *Phèdre,* Hoffmann to *The Serapion Brothers.* Chénier's *Iambes* were discovered along with Homer's *Iliad.*

Finally, in the essays of the early 1920s, in his continuing endeavor to ascertain the image and role of the "contemporary poet," Mandelstam once more raises the issue of poetic freedom and posits the necessity for both esthetic and extra-esthetic restraints on the artist/poet. He concludes that the poet is not, and cannot, be entirely free from social and moral obligations. On the other hand, in the early 1920s, he attempts to redefine social obligation and civic poetry.

Moral commitment is clearly accepted as a necessity, but Mandelstam defines it both as the poet's "social obligation" and as an act of individual heroism—as a "heroic feat." While previously, in "François Villon" (1910), he had noted that the "heroism" of Medieval man stemmed from the social pressures of his daily existence, he had perceived the poet as an exception. Villon's "amorality," his freedom from the social restraints and obligations of feudal society, were not seen to detract from his dynamism as a poet.

In "The Word and Culture" (1921), on the other hand, Mandelstam depicts the poet as a new kind of "hero." Indeed, his heroism derives from a kind of perverse "social obligation." Here Mandelstam's image of the poet takes on Biblical dimensions, for he is presented as both a second Joshua of Nun and in a priestly role:

> Whosoever shall raise the word on high and confront Time with it, as the priest displays the Eucharist, shall be a second Joshua of Nun . . . To show compassion for the State which denies the word shall be the contemporary poet's social obligation and heroic feat.

By 1921, Mandelstam recognized that all men, including the poet, were obliged to the State for their material culture. He even entertained the highly "poetic" idea of the State's being dependent on the poet, in that only the compassion of the poet or the poet's "word" might immortalize the State. However, Mandelstam regarded the feasibility of mutual "feudal obligations" between the poet and the State most uneasily. "Compassion for the State" (a genuinely Christian concept) might lead to Martyrdom; mutual feudal obligations might reduce the "life of the word" to mere civic poetry.

The life of the word has entered a heroic era. The word is flesh and bread. It shares the fate of bread and flesh: suffering. People are hungry. The State is even hungrier. But there is something still hungrier: Time. Time wants to devour the State. . . .

Today the State has a unique relationship to culture that is best expressed by the term *tolerance*. But at the same time a new type of organic interrelationship is beginning to appear, one which connects the State with Culture in a way not unlike that which once linked appanage princes to the monasteries. The princes maintained monasteries for *counsel*. This explains everything. The isolation of the State insofar as cultural values are concerned makes it fully dependent on culture. Cultural values ornament the State, endowing it with color, form, and if you will, even gender. Inscriptions on State buildings, tombs and gateways insure the State against the ravages of Time.

Hence, it is not surprising to find that Mandelstam carefully modified both his ideas of civic obligation and civic poetry one year later in "On the Nature of the Word." He pointed out that the poet's duty to the State is not the highest form of moral commitment; the poet's highest duty is to confront Time itself, in the name of "the word." Consequently, the poet's obligation is first to educate his fellow "Men," not merely to support the State by educating its "citizens." Indeed, we must constantly remind ourselves that the impulse behind Mandelstam's conception of moral obligation is esthetic. That is, it may not be politically or even philosophically justified. Morality is perceived as one of the eternal verities which it is the poet's role to uncover, reveal, celebrate and, ultimately, preserve: it is one of the basic impulses behind the text.

Acmeism is a social as well as a literary phenomenon in Russian history. With Acmeism a moral force was reborn in Russian poetry. . . . Until now the social inspiration of Russian poetry has reached no further than the idea of "citizen," but there is a loftier principle than "citizen," there is the concept of "Man."

As opposed to the civic poetry of the past, modern Russian poetry must educate not merely citizens, but "Men."

Furthermore, it is with this essay that Mandelstam began to give proper attention to the problem of audience—his fellow "Men"—and, consequently, to the concept of the ideal reader or interpreter of poetry. Although he virtually never granted his audience the right to make demands on the poet, Mandelstam perceived the poet as obliged to educate. In return, he demanded an educated reading public.[5] His ideal reader he conceived as an interlocutor sharing the same poetic consciousness or "love of the word" as the poet. Even more significant, Mandelstam esteemed his ideal reader as *no less* essential to society and history than the poet.

The first model for Mandelstam's image of the ideal reader is Vasily Rozanov, whose attitudinal portrait is presented in the essay, "On the Nature of the Word" (1922); the second model is V.V. Gippius whose *persona* is developed as young Mandelstam's teacher and mentor, "the molder of souls and teacher of remarkable people," in the autobiographical novella, *The Noise of Time* (1923).

The "philological nature of his soul" defines Rozanov. Mandelstam's literal definition of "philology" (*philia* + *logos*) as the immediate, intense, direct "love of the word" is presented as the only genuine and fully conscious response to poetry, history and life:

> Rozanov's attitude toward Russian literature was most unliterary. Literature is a social phenomenon, while philology is domestic, intimate. Literature is a lecture, the street; philology is a university seminar, the family. . . . Philology is the family because every family clings to its own intonations, its personal references, and to its own special meanings of words defined in parenthesis. The most casual utterance within a family takes on a nuance of its own. Moreover, such perpetual, distinctive, and purely philological nuancing defines the atmosphere of family life. I would derive Rozanov's attraction to the domestic quality of life, which so powerfully defined the entire structure of his literary activity, from the philological nature of his soul. . . .
>
> That anarchistic, nihilistic spirit recognized only one authority: the magic of language, the power of the word. . . .

In *The Noise of Time*, Mandelstam ascribes similar characteristics to V.V. Gippius:

> Beginning as early as Radishchev and Novikov, V.V. [Gippius] had established personal relations with Russian writers, splenetic and loving liaisons filled with noble envy, jealousy, with jocular disrespect, grievous unfairness—as is only natural between family members.

V.V. Gippius and the young Osip Mandelstam are first presented in *The Noise of Time* in a teacher-pupil relationship: the young poet is seen as the apprentice of the genuine "philologist," studying to "love the word" in the manner of his mentor. In the final chapter or epilogue, written from the post-revolutionary perspective of 1923, the relationship changes, the young poet has matured and his apprenticeship has ended. The young poet has finally come to terms with his own identity and role, as an intellectual and as a poet. Indeed, the adult author, Mandelstam, refers to his autobiographical *persona* for the first time in hyphenated form as a *raznochinets-pisatel'*, an "intellectual-author," and he defines his creative impulse as "philological," literally, the impulse of one who "loves the word." Thus, a mature authorial consciousness is revealed at the conclusion of this autobiographical novel, an author in control of his materials and master of his identity.

Teacher and pupil are now on an equal footing as "companions." Their equality is based on a shared "love of the word." Both are characterized as philological nihilists (on the model of Rozanov) and as hyphenated *raznochintsy*. The former teacher is now graced with the metaphorical title, *raznochinets-literator;* the former pupil, *raznochinets-pisatel'*. And both share the same esthetic vision of philological nihilism termed "literary savagery" *(literaturnaia zlost')* in this work.

The *raznochinets* metaphor thus functions to associate the creative poetic consciousness of the poet and the creative consciousness or "creative cognition" ("Journey to Armenia") of the ideal reader. The two complementary voices merge for all intents and purposes into the single voice of the controlling authorial consciousness which, in the post-revolutionary year 1923, looks back at the experience of "philological" apprenticeship from the distance of a new age, a new time, and a new esthetic. Moreover, the use of the *raznochinets* metaphor for the ideal poet, ideal reader, and, indeed, for poetic consciousness itself, concludes Mandelstam's attempts in the early essays to resolve the dilemmas of the image and role of the poet in society, the relationship of morality to poetic dynamism, and to define the image and role of the ideal reader or audience.

The various characteristics of Mandelstam's image of the poet and the poet's role in society raised in the essays of the 1910s and early 1920s are established. The ideal poet as well as the ideal reader is characterized as dynamic and vital, morally and socially conscious, self-confident and capable of moral protest. The poet's freedom to transcend history or Time is seen to derive from his "obligation" to his fellow Man in the name of "the word" or the higher poetic or, indeed, "philological" consciousness. Mandelstam's early essays thus culminate in his first autobiographical act.

Mandelstam's autobiographical novella may thus be read as the "story" of the origins and destiny of the poet's "love of the word." It tells of the apprenticeship of the poetic or "philological" consciousness. What is more, it treats the origins of "philology" in accord with the theoretical discussions aired in the essays of the early 1920s. The relationship of language and history, of genuine poetry and critical reading, and of Bergsonian conceptions of space and time were originally raised in the essay, "On the Nature of the Word" (1922). These discussions are closely associated with the themes of "literary genesis" and "historical sensitivity" voiced in "Badger Hole" (1922).

15

In his endeavors to reach an intellectual understanding of the "nature" and "source" of "the word," of the impulse(s) behind the text, Mandelstam virtually equated the Russian language with Russian history. In "On the Nature of the Word" he says of the Russian language: " . . . so highly organized, so organic a language is not merely a door into history, but is history itself." And he tells us why he perceives the Russian language as "historical": "The Russian language is historical by its very nature, since in its totality it is a turbulent sea of events, a continuous incarnation and activation of rational and breathing flesh." These passages would suggest that in the very process of shaping poetry out of the raw materials of language, the poet simultaneously gives order to, or interprets history; that just as random words in the Russian language serve the poet as raw materials, as impulses, for his lyric poems, so historical and autobiographical data serve him as raw materials or impulses for his works of literary prose. In his capacity to intuit "the word," the poet thus connects the seemingly unconnected details of history just as he connects the unconnected units of everyday speech, making history "intelligible" to "the mind seeking unities and connections," "synthesis and internal structure."

Insofar as his "love of the word" is also a love of history, Mandelstam's "philology" is both the study (read: "love") of "the word" and of history. The poet's role is viewed as intuitive, interpretive, and cognitive, for he intuits the essence of the raw materials of history—the "noise of Time," its dynamic impulses—and orders them, shapes and transforms them into meaningful forms "intelligible to the human mind." Similarly, in his literary prose, Mandelstam exhibits "historical sensitivity" through the artistic ordering of historical details just as he exhibits emotional sensitivity in shaping his lyric poems.

Mandelstam's love of history *cum* literary or philological history is perhaps best expressed in "Badger Hole," his fine tribute to Blok on the first anniversary of the older poet's death. In expressing his common bond with Blok, this essay furthers Mandelstam's own personal views on history and literary biography:

Establishing the literary genesis of the poet, his literary sources, his *ancestry* and origin, brings us at once to solid ground. A critic does not have to answer the question: what did the poet want to say, but he is obliged to answer the question: where did the poet come from. . . .

This passage, written about a year before *The Noise of Time*, indicates Mandelstam's fundamental intellectual desire to establish his own "literary genesis," or autobiography, his own impulses to literary creation.

Equally illuminating are Mandelstam's statements about Blok's "historical love" and "historical sensitivity." Mandelstam's "historical love" was intimately connected with his "love of the word," since he equated Russian history with the Russian language:

> Blok possessed historical love, historical objectivity toward that domestic period of Russian history which existed under the sign of the intelligentsia and populism. . . .

> Blok's historical sensitivity is astonishing. Even long before he implored us to listen to the music of the revolution, Blok heard the subterranean music of Russian history, where the most attuned ear caught only a syncopated pause. Kostomarev, Soloviev, and Klyuchevsky gaze at us from every line of Blok's poetry about Russia. It is Klyuchevsky, the benevolent genius, the domestic spirit, the patron of Russian culture, under whose aegis no ordeals and no trials are terrifying.

Mandelstam also "possessed historical love, historical objectivity" toward that period of Russian history from which he emerged (the 1890s, as opposed to Blok's 1880s). Not only was he sensitive to history, but he was also able to discern the "two poles . . . of all Russian culture of the modern age," to perceive the "deep spiritual fissure in Russian society."

In his earlier essay, "Peter Chaadaev," Mandelstam discerned "moral freedom" as Russia's unique contribution to modern European history. In "The Nineteenth Century" (1922), he both condemned and condoned Russia's past, recognizing, like Blok's mentor, Klyuchevsky, that "no ordeals and no trials are terrifying," if they are understood in the context of history (see also Letter No. 84).

This poetic perception of Russian history, of the nature or origins of the Russian language and "the word," helps to illuminate the concluding passages of *The Noise of Time*, wherein the author posits the right of the poet to challenge history, but simultaneously envisions history as an elemental autonomous force:

> And in this wintry period of Russian history, literature taken at large, strikes me as something patrician, which puts me out of countenance. . . . In this no one is to blame and there is nothing to be ashamed of. A beast must not be ashamed of his furry hide. Night furred him. Winter clothed him. Literature is a beast. His furriers are night and winter.

What is more, throughout *The Noise of Time* history is perceived through the vehicle of language, in linguistic or philological metaphors, in the physiological and psychological transference of language from generation to generation, and in the ideas and values contained in and conveyed by that language, however confused, ornate or abstract:

17

The speech of the father and the speech of the mother—does not our language feed throughout its long life on the confluence of these two?

My father had absolutely no language; his speech was tongue-tied and languagelessness. . . . A completely abstract, counterfeit language, the ornate and twisted speech of an autodidact, where normal words are intertwined with the ancient philosophical terms of Herder, Leibnitz and Spinoza, the capricious syntax of a Talmudist. . . .

In essence, my father transferred to me a totally alien century and distant, although completely un-Jewish, atmosphere.

The elemental force of history bequeathed to the poet through his linguistic and ideational inheritance is complemented and supplemented by the creative inspiration of the teacher of "philological" consciousness, V.V. Gippius. The "philologist's" capacity for intuiting and interpreting "the word" is sharply juxtaposed to the superficiality and artificiality of the Literary Fund meetings held to commemorate dead poets or living idols in the Tenishev School auditorium by the intellectuals of the 1890s, to the literature of the Andreyevs, the "traffickers in life and death" of the 1900s, and to the mechanical response of pedantic Pushkin scholars to the card catalogue in lieu of poetry itself.

The pupil, young Mandelstam, is essentially guided by his "philologist" teacher out of the historic past into the new age with little more than his "love of the word" to keep him warm. But teacher and pupil emerge as equals—"companions"—with a shared esthetic vision to face the historic future, unafraid, acceptant, and even optimistic with regard to the destiny of "the word": "Literature is a beast. His furriers are night and winter." And for them "literary savagery" is the only esthetic possible.

Literary savagery! If not for you, what should I eat the salt of the earth with?

You are the seasoning for the unleavened bread of understanding, you are the joyful consciousness of injustice, you are the conspiratorial salt which is transmitted with a malicious bow from decade to decade, in a cut-glass saltcellar, with a serving cloth!

"Literary savagery" is presented as that natural, direct and essential response of the poetic or "philological" consciousness to history. It is a response of wit and wisdom, not of naiveté. It combines the conscious and the unconscious, the cognitive and the instinctual response to life, emerging as it does from Mandelstam's fundamental esthetic impulses of "astonishment" and "sweet recognition" so evident in his lyrics.

18

The Novgorodians and Pskovians used to be depicted as raging on their ikons; the laity stood in tiers on each other's heads, to the right and left, disputing and scolding, in astonishment turning their wise peasant heads on short necks toward the event. The beefy faces and hard beards of the disputants were turned toward the event with malign amazement. I think I can discern in them the archetype of literary savagery.

As the Novgorodians voted spitefully with their beards on the Ikon of the Last Judgment, so literature rages for a century and glowers at the event with the ardent slant-eyed gaze of a *raznochinets* and chronic failure, with the spite of a lay brother . . . dragged in to be a witness in the Byzantine court of history.

The genre of autobiographical reminiscences which Mandelstam chose for his first substantial experiment in literary prose offered him a structural and ideological framework through which to combine and reshape his exceptionally broad range of interests, his Bergsonian as well as Marxian perceptions, his philological metaphors, and his cultural, historical and esthetic impulses.

What is more, autobiography provided Mandelstam with a medium through which he might supercede the purely intellectual confines of the critical essay as well as the lyric restrictions of the meditative poem to present the poet's experience of the self with regard to the phenomena of space, time, consciousness and memory. He was able to consider these themes from the inner perspective of a prospective poetic consciousness as well as from the distance of a mature poet and critical reader.

Instead of the more traditional family chronicle or reminiscences of childhood on the order of Aksakov or Tolstoi, in which relatively clear causal relationships are established between the formative experiences of childhood and the emerging adult consciousness by means of a coherent and continuous narrative structure, Mandelstam attempts a completely new form. *The Noise of Time* is structured around fragments or vignettes involving recurrent poetic images and a density of references and associations, unified by the autobiographical impulse and ordered "according to their spatial extension." The genre of autobiography provides the illusion of a frame within which the fragments, images and associations are enclosed; it provides the suggestion of external narrative structure.

The images out of which *The Noise of Time* is constructed are conveyed on one level as merely partial images or metonymies representing explicit historical events, periods, or biographical *personae*. On another level, they are presented as complete in and of themselves, thus giving a fragmented feeling to the work. Indeed, the separate units or "fragments" can be read as fascinating autobiographical and historical sketches or vignettes, like the majority of Mandelstam's excursions into literary prose in the 1920s: "Sukharevka,"

19

"Cold Summer," "Mensheviks in Georgia," "Kiev," "Mikhoels," among others.

These "fragments" are united spatially, like stanzas in a poem, through their peculiar juxtaposition in the novella, rather than temporally or causally. The author consciously avoids emphasizing causal or chronological relationships. The rationale for this technique is given in the essay, "On the Nature of the Word":

> To preserve the principle of unity amidst the vortex of changes and the unceasing flood of phenomena, contemporary philosophy in the person of Bergson . . . offers us a theory of the system of phenomena. Bergson does not consider phenomena according to the way they submit to the law of temporal succession, but rather according to their spatial extension. He is interested exclusively in the internal connection among phenomena. He liberates this connection from time and considers it independently. Phenomena thus connected to one another form, as it were, a kind of fan whose folds can be opened up in time; however, this fan may also be closed up in a way intelligible to the human mind.
>
> To compare phenomena united in time to form such a fan emphasizes only their internal connection. Thus, instead of the problem of causality . . . [Bergson] poses the problem of the connection alone, purged of any admixture of metaphysics, and therefore more fruitful for scientific discoveries and hypotheses.
>
> A science based on the principle of connection rather than on the principle of causality saves us from the bad infinity of evolutionary theory, not to mention its vulgarized corollary—the theory of progress.
>
> The movement of an endless chain of phenomena having neither beginning nor end is precisely that bad infinity which has nothing to offer the mind seeking unities and connections. Such a concept hypnotizes scientific thought with a simple and easily accessible evolutionism, which, to be sure, gives an appearance of scientific generalization, but only at the cost of renouncing all synthesis and internal structure.

The Noise of Time thus appears as the culmination of the first phase of Mandelstam's life and work. While on one level, it may be read simply as autobiographical reminiscences, on a deeper level Mandelstam's theoretical statements, hypotheses and ideas about the poet, poetry, "philology," and esthetics are sifted through a peculiar new syntax which transforms autobiography and criticism into literary prose. Indeed, the fundamental structure of the work evolves out of the esthetic and philological formulations conceptualized in the essays but transformed into poetic prose through the mediation of the autobiographical impulse. The origins of Mandelstam's poetic or "philological" consciousness are established, and the future destiny of "philology" or Mandelstam's "love of the word" is reaffirmed.

20

After 1923, Mandelstam continued to experiment with prose genres, concentrating on first person, extra-literary forms. Taken as a whole, this literary prose may be regarded as the autobiographical act of a modern Russian "philologist," with each individual work seen as a new chapter expanding on the initial autobiographical impulse.

Stylistically, *The Noise of Time* begins a new phase in the poet's creative consciousness in that Mandelstam recognizes his autobiography for the first time as basic poetic material. Indeed, he begins treating his autobiography as he would the lyrical *persona* of his poems, as both subject and object simultaneously. It may be that by 1923 prose offered him more of an opportunity to experiment with several voices than lyric poetry. This, at least, was one of the directions he had been pursuing since 1920. Indeed, in "The Slate Ode" (No. 137, 1923), we already find such complex passages as:

Only the voice will teach us
What was clawing and fighting there.
And we will guide the callous slate
As the voice leads us.
I break the night, burning chalk
for the firm notation of the moment.
I exchange noise for the singing of arrows.
I exchange order for the fierce drumming of a grouse.
what am I? . . . . .
I am a double-dealer, with a double soul. . . .
                    (Translation by Clarence Brown and W.S. Merwin)

In chronological order, following *The Noise of Time*, Mandelstam's four major works of literary prose include: "The Egyptian Stamp," "Fourth Prose," "Journey to Armenia," and "Conversation about Dante." The work receiving the most critical attention thus far has been "The Egyptian Stamp."[6] The later texts, unfortunately, have been virtually disregarded with respect to their place in Mandelstam's *oeuvre* or with respect to the poet's persistent concern with literary prose and with the autobiographical impulse.

Each of the above pieces is an autobiographical act juxtaposing memory and the perception of that memory through two or more consciousnesses, one of which consistently belongs to the author. The ultimate subject in each instance continues to be "philology"; the "hero" remains the poet, while the "plot" revolves primarily around the emergence of the poet's voice—the controlling consciousness of the work—which grows louder and clearer as the work moves toward its conclusion. Other voices prominent in these texts may include the author's alter ego as "hero," his narrator, or interlocutor.

The subject of "philology" is slowly revealed in each work through layers of autobiographical and historical data serving several functions, as the raw verbal material of the work, as the means for creating an illusion of reality,

21

as references to other genres more dependent on chronology for their narrative structure or plot, and as the basis for moral commentary on topical events directed toward the contemporary reader.

Most significant is the expression of the philologist's "love of the word" which informs these pieces and provides their ultimate meaning. Their message might be read simply as "philology preserves," or as "the text preserves its own impulse." They are thoroughly modernist works in which "memory" rather than "inquiry" dominates, indeed, historical, autobiographical and philological memory is perpetually invoked to preserve the impulse behind the text: "the instinct for form creation."

Furthermore, after 1923, certain secondary or even tertiary motifs in Mandelstam's earlier writings emerge as dominant autobiographical themes. These include, among others, the theme of the creative consciousness in an alien environment reflected especially in "The Egyptian Stamp," "Fourth Prose," and "Journey to Armenia"; the Jewish theme poignantly expressed in the Kievan sketches, "The Egyptian Stamp" and "Fourth Prose"; the theme of the creative process, discussed primarily as an organic phenomenon in "Journey to Armenia" and as "performance" in "Conversation about Dante"; the theme of the reader in the polemical essays of the late 1920s, "Journey to Armenia" and "Conversation about Dante"; the theme of death and immortality in all the literary prose works of the 1930s.

The autobiographical impulse behind these themes is emphasized by the choice of genre in which the poet's voice resounds clearly. The autobiographical mode allows for "random reminiscences" and auto-reminiscences, objective and subjective commentary, allusions, advice, revelations, emotional overtones, all interspersed with continuous narrative. Simultaneously, the autobiographical impulse provides a rationale for the poet's direct appeal to his reader/interlocutor as both "the reader in posterity" and the contemporary reader.

As in *The Noise of Time*, the author of "The Egyptian Stamp" attempts to create the atmosphere of a particular historical era[7] which shaped his philological consciousness. He attempts to identify it, order it, and give it form so as to achieve an esthetic as well as a psycho-socio-historical perspective on himself and the epoch, or, as he put it so succinctly some years later in "Journey to Armenia": "[to locate] that truth which helps us form some sense of our own selves in tradition."

The tranquil atmosphere and harmonious life of the nineteenth century is viewed in the last chapter of *The Noise of Time* as "settled weather" from the perspective of the post-Revolutionary year 1923, a "wintry period in Russian history." In direct contrast, "the Kerensky summer of 1917" is perceived in "The Egyptian Stamp" as a "wintry period" from the perspective of its date of composition, 1927. Hence Mandelstam's choice of style. The latter work is approached through the vehicle of an alien, anxiety-ridden nightmare rather than through nostalgic reminiscences.

22

The surrealistic nightmare vision of "The Egyptian Stamp" treats the awkward, frustrating and terrifying experience of the young writer vainly struggling to grasp the past as it vanishes in the turmoil of the present by imagining himself in the shoes of his hero, Parnok. "The Kerensky summer of 1917" is marked by insecurity, instability, incomprehension, fear, and unfathomable demands which could only be rendered through the nightmare vision and surrealistic prose style enveloping the humble and humiliated hero of this work.

Parnok's ambiguous activities as well as his vacillations, inner struggle, and terror are perceived and commented upon by the third-person narrator (who ultimately reveals himself as the first-person author) as if through a persistent, terrifying nightmare. The reality of the dream is too close to offer the author the satisfaction and pleasure of esthetic distance assured by the traditional novel or poem. Esthetic distance is achieved only through form, through the "objective" stance of third-person narration. However, Parnok's "story" seemingly cannot be written; hence, it is interspersed with autobiographical explanations, reminiscences, digressions, imaginary rewrites, wishes, and thoughts couched in various future-oriented tenses (the subjunctive, the future, and even the imperative).

Mandelstam's concern with the proper grammatical tense is further developed in "Fourth Prose," in which lyrical digressions representing the poet's escape from the present, from "reality," are mainly cast in the past or future. Indeed, in "Journey to Armenia," Mandelstam clearly identifies the tense of his fantasy existence as he engages in the following internal dialogue with himself:

What tense would you choose to live in?
"I want to live in the imperative of the future passive participle—in the 'what ought to be.' "
I like to breathe that way. That's what I like. It suggests a kind of mounted, bandit-like equestrian honor. . . .

In "The Egyptian Stamp," however, the author sees himself as so involved in his hero's life that he fears to be identified with him: "Lord! Don't make me like Parnok! Give me the strength to distinguish myself from him."

"The Egyptian Stamp" may thus be perceived as Mandelstam's second effort to tell the tale of the poet's or "philologist's" life, a second autobiographical act, or the response to a second autobiographical impulse. Only this time he concentrates on the terrifying prospects lying ahead for the mature creative consciousness in an alien environment, rather than on the reminiscences of formative childhood experiences: "It is terrifying to think that our life is a tale without a plot or hero, made up out of desolation and glass, out of the feverish babble of constant digressions, out of the delirium of the Petersburg influenza."

The form of the surrealistic nightmare allows the narrator-author to tell the tale of the would-be Petersburg poet who "received back all the streets and squares of Petersburg in the form of rough galley proofs, [who] composed the prospects, stitched the gardens"; of the would-be Petersburg "philologist" who:

To calm himself consulted a certain small, unwritten dictionary—or rather, a register of little homey words that had gone out of use. He had long ago composed it in his mind for use in case of misfortune or shock:

"Horseshoe." That was the name for a poppy-seed roll.

"Fromuga"—his mother's name for the large, hinged dormer window, which slammed shut like the lid of a grand piano.

"Don't botch it." This was said about life.

"Do not command." One of the commandments.

Parnok remains one of Petersburg's humble and humiliated youths who, when considering his future, dreams of overcoming his hallucinations, of regaining consciousness, so that he might act like an ordinary person: "recover, become like all other people, even—perhaps—get married. . . . It was time to put an end to his lap-dog youth."

Although Parnok has a very vivid imagination ("he can metamorphose the streetcar rattle of life into events of consequence"), he remains humble, anxious, and terrified of life, one of Mandelstam's "doubles," perhaps, but hardly Mandelstam, the controlling authorial consciousness of "The Egyptian Stamp."

Like his hero, Mandelstam enjoyed escaping reality through his powerful imagination. However, while Parnok suffered silently, concealing his thoughts in his small "unwritten dictionary," the power of the pen allowed Mandelstam to cope with the idea that life is "both terrifying and beautiful!" His pen makes anything possible:

My pen sketches a beautiful moustached Greek woman and someone's fox-like chin.

It is thus that arabesques spring up in the margins of first drafts and live independent, gorgeous, and perfidious lives.

Little men shaped like violins drink the milk of the paper. . . .

This surrealistic autobiographical tale is told in "my dear prosaic delirium" by an author who rejoices in the esthetic freedom and catharsis engendered by the autobiographical act itself: "What a pleasure for the narrator to switch from the third person to the first!"

While attempting to tell Parnok's "story," Mandelstam thus juxtaposes his own attitudes as a writer, his own feelings, responses and values to those of his hero. Parnok's life becomes a kind of foil for identifying certain of his own responses to life, in particular, for identifying the role of the poet or of the creative imagination floundering in an alien environment. But whereas Parnok finds himself in countless impossible and, indeed, humiliating situations, the object of outright deception, entertaining incredible "false memories" which he barely surmounts only by resorting to his imagination, Mandelstam composes literary prose.

Indeed, "The Egyptian Stamp" is more than a semi-autobiographical piece of surrealistic fiction in which a terrified narrator begs to be disassociated from his hero. It is also a work of meta-fiction, an author's "handbook," as well as a personal testimony directed toward those who desire to transcend reality through art and the imagination:

> Destroy your manuscript, but save whatever you have inscribed in the margins out of boredom, out of helplessness, and, as it were, in a dream. These secondary and involuntary creations of your fantasy will not be lost in the world but will take their places behind shadowy music stands, like third violins in the Mariinsky Theatre, and out of gratitude to their author will strike up the overture to *Lenore* or the *Egmont* of Beethoven.

The style of this tale differs radically from that of *The Noise of Time*. Its essence is foreshadowed in the poet's essays on literary prose, in particular, "The End of the Novel," and "Literary Moscow: The Birth of Plot"; in Mandelstam's very hostile critique of Andrei Bely's prose expressed in his review of *Diary of an Eccentric*; and in the author-narrator's continuous commentary on prose composition in "The Egyptian Stamp" itself. In a certain sense, this work is a realization of several of Mandelstam's theoretical ideas about prose and the creative process, just as *The Noise of Time* is a fictional realization of his ideas about poetry, "the word," literary interpretation, and history.

"The End of the Novel" contains Mandelstam's most explicit statement about the function, or lack thereof, of biography (in contradistinction to autobiography) in modern prose fiction. A major difference between nineteenth and twentieth century literary prose grows out of the proposition that there is "a connection between the fate of the novel and the status at any given time of the problem of the individual's fate in history." In discussing the nineteenth-century novel, Mandelstam accounts for its structure and existence in terms of the relationship between the extra-textual and textual functions of biography:

> It is clear that when we entered the epoch of powerful social movements and organized mass actions, both the actions of the individual in history and the influence and power of the novel declined, for the generally accepted role of the individual in history serves as a monometer indicating the pressure of the social atmosphere. The measure of a novel is human

25

biography or a system of biographies. . . .

In discussing twentieth-century literary forms, Mandelstam predicts: "The future development of the novel will be no less than the history of the atomization of biography as the form of personal existence, even more, we shall witness the catastrophic ruin of biography."

However, it was only in 1927, with the composition of "The Egyptian Stamp," that Mandelstam fictionalized this idea. His would-be author makes an abortive attempt to write a nineteenth-century novel—a biographical novel. In the end, the third-person narrator expresses his relief at being able to switch from third person to first. The autobiographical consciousness takes over: "The measure of the novel" as "human biography" is no longer sufficient. Two years later, when Mandelstam began "Fourth Prose," he no longer even considered the objective approach of the novel or biography as appropriate.

Aspects of the style of "The Egyptian Stamp" are continued in modified form in "Fourth Prose," "Journey to Armenia," and "Conversation about Dante." For instance, "Fourth Prose" alternates first-person and third-person narration, while juxtaposing tenses to distinguish between the realms of fantasy and reality; "Journey to Armenia" alternates description with autobiographical reminiscences and critical commentary on numerous topics, including organic growth and the creative process; and "Conversation about Dante" is virtually a commentary "in process" on creative cognition "in performance" mediated by the autobiographical impulse in the form of digressions and asides to the interlocutor.

If in "The Egyptian Stamp" Mandelstam may be said to imagine himself in his humble hero's shoes experiencing the terrifying reality of a nightmare, from which he, nevertheless, extricates himself by awakening and composing a literary masterpiece, in "Fourth Prose" he may be said to imagine himself as Parnok's perverse antithesis. In the latter work, the protagonist emerges triumphant as an established poet, although a social outcast, cognizant of his rights as a poet and as a human being in an environment demanding his destruction. Indeed, he triumphs over all forms of death and destruction, physical and psychological, individual and cultural, historical and political.

If "The Egyptian Stamp" is illuminated by reading it in conjunction with Mandelstam's essays on prose genres such as "The End of the Novel," "Fourth Prose" should be read in conjunction with the essays of 1928-29 which focus on the poet's polemic with the literary establishment over such problems as editing, publishing and translating, as well as problems of audience—namely, the reader and the reviewer. On at least one level, "Fourth Prose" may be read as Mandelstam's attempt to canonize this polemic in fictional form. By carefully juxtaposing the polemical tone of the essayist to the lyrical voice of the poet, Mandelstam successfully manipulates tone, diction and syntax, voice and tense, to reinforce the metaphorical and thematic structures of this unique work.

The "dear prosaic delirium" and the "secondary and involuntary creations of fantasy" of "The Egyptian Stamp" are continued in "Fourth Prose," but they are renewed and invigorated by the esthetic of "philological nihilism" or "literary savagery," originally enunciated in "On the Nature of the Word" and *The Noise of Time*, and here called upon to scourge the enemy. The passive surrealistic dream and the abortive novel give way to the potency of perverse literary exorcism.

"Fourth Prose" is organized or structured around the juxtaposition of the polemical and the lyrical on several levels, the most general level being the musical paradigm of the "Theme and Variations." "Fourth Prose" resembles a prose poem rather than a traditional genre of literary prose. Its sixteen prose vignettes are arranged like stanzas in the manner of a Theme and Variations. Its major theme is Man's response to the Old Testament Commandment: "Thou shalt not kill." The variations are many and include the most personal autobiographical responses as well as highly abstract political, social and fictional responses and value judgments. These responses are relieved periodically by lyrical digressions celebrating life, truth, justice, freedom, human dignity and genuine art.

The musical paradigm allows for voice modulations, alternating various levels of moral outrage and lyrical fantasy. Simultaneously, the polemical diction of the feuilleton is contrasted to the more poetic diction of the lyrical digression. Thus, the various responses to the moral imperative of the Old Testament Commandment are presented as "variations" on the major "theme," reinforcing the power of its statement.

The work develops in intensity, climaxing in the exorcism of the twelfth vignette. The two central paragraphs read:

> I insist that the writer's profession as it has developed in Europe and, in particular, in Russia, is incompatible with the honorable title of Jew, in which I take great pride. My blood, burdened with the heritage of sheep breeders, patriarchs and kings, rebels against the shifty Gypsy character of the writers' tribe. . . .
>
> The race of professional writers emits a repugnant odor from its skin and exhibits the filthiest habits of food preparation. It is a race that camps and sleeps in its own vomit, is expelled from cities and persecuted in villages, but is forever close to the authorities who find its members shelter in the red-light districts. . . . For literature is forever fulfilling a single assignment: it helps the rulers keep their soldiers at bay and it helps the judges carry out reprisals against the condemned.

The last four vignettes act virtually as an epilogue, containing a past-tense flashback to the ultimate nightmare in his life; a declaration of moral responsibility and moral innocence; a reiteration of the right to perversity—a right accepted through the ages by the poet and the Jew; and a concluding statement rephrasing the eternal verities and reaffirming Mandelstam's faith in Life (associated with genuine art and "the word") as opposed to the international Death Trust (the literary establishment and the death of "mother philology").

The imagery of death and destruction permeates all the vignettes except the lyrical digressions. This imagery includes autobiographical references to such terrifying acts as character assassination (in charges of plagiarism levelled against Mandelstam), cases of mob rule, and crimes of murder and suicide permitted for the sake of social or political expedience.

In contrast, the voice of genuine poetry is associated with the refusal to kill, with the victim and victimized, and ultimately with the image of the Jew, and by implication, the Old Testament Commandment: "Thou shalt not kill," the subtext whose force infuses the entire work as an esthetic imperative.

The Jew and the genuine poet are further associated with the field of images connected with Life and "the life of the word": escape, freedom, the Promised Land, the south, Armenia, creature comforts, fantasy, imagination, dreams, genuine literature, happiness, free verbal expression (including nonsense language and children's ditties), human dignity, justice, truth, pride and perversity.

The contrasting imagery of fantasy and reality is also cleverly intertwined with the use of grammatical tenses. The conditional, the future, and the past tenses are most often used to convey fantasies and dreams, including nightmares, while the present tense is most commonly used to convey reality: the world of facts as well as the world of false premises. A good example is the seventh vignette, Mandelstam's delightful lyrical digression on his would-be journey to Armenia, termed in this work "the younger sister of the Jewish nation." The journey is obviously associated with the traditional pilgrimage to the Promised Land and ultimate spiritual freedom. The entire vignette is presented in the conditional and future moods.

I am a Chinaman, no one understands me. Higgledy-Piggledy! Let's go to Alma-Ata where the inhabitants have raisin eyes, where the Persian has eyes like fried eggs, where the Sart had the eyes of a sheep.

Higgledy-Piggledy! Let's go to Azerbaijan!

Once I had a patron, Mravian-Muravian, the Peoples' Commissar of the Armenian nation, younger sister of the Jewish nation. He sent me a telegram.

My patron died, the Peoples' Commissar, Mravian-Muravian. . . .

Higgledy-Piggledy! Let's go to Azerbaijan!

I had a letter for the Peoples' Commissar Mravian. I handed it to the secretaries at the Armenian residence on the cleanest, most ambassadorial

28

street in Moscow. I was just about to depart for Erevan. . . .

Had I traveled to Erevan, I would have spent three days and three nights eating black caviar sandwiches at the huge railway station buffets.

Higgledy-Piggledy!

On the way, I would have read Zoshchenko's best book and exulted like a Tatar running off with a hundred stolen rubles.

Higgledy-Piggledy! Let's go to Azerbaijan!

I would have taken courage with me in my yellow straw basket piled high with fresh, clean-smelling linen, and my fur coat would have danced on a golden hook. I would have descended at the Erevan station, bearing my winter coat in one hand, and my walking stick—my Jewish crozier—in the other.

Autobiographical and historical details function variously in Mandelstam's literary prose; in "Fourth Prose" they provide the necessary authentification to transform this work into literary exorcism. While in *The Noise of Time* such details act to create a sense of intellectual distance and esthetic perspective on the relationship of art to time, and in "The Egyptian Stamp," the mediation of auto-reminiscences functions to encourage an esthetic perspective on the theme of the creative consciousness in an alien environment, in "Fourth Prose" autobiographical references allow Mandelstam to transform both factual and imaginary experiences in order to gain esthetic distance on the meaning of life in the abstract as well as in concrete political and moral terms—focussing on the very specific issue of taking a life. The Old Testament says "Thou shalt not kill"; the new society allows for killing, encourages individual and mass killing, and provides its members with the instruments for murder. Under the circumstances, to refuse to kill (Esenin's line, cited in the eighth vignette, "I did not shoot the wretched in the dungeons") or to intercede for someone condemned to death (Isaiah Benediktovich's, alias Mandelstam's, incredible interference in State policy in the first vignette) can only be understood as acts of treachery, rebellion, or at best, as the perverse acts of an outsider—of a Jew or a poet.

Hence Mandelstam's triumphant mocking tone, his delight in acts of perversity, his esthetic of "philological nihilism" or "literary savagery"; hence his glorification of the poet, his celebration of the Jew, and his sardonic apostrophe to the literary establishment in which he implicates the Writer's Union in his attempts to gain intellectual distance and an esthetic (or "objective") perspective on himself. He begins:

My dear Gypsies of Tverskoi Boulevard, we have written a novel together of which you have not even dreamed. I love to come across my name among official papers. . . . There my name takes on a completely objective ring: a rather new sound for my ears. . . . I am often curious myself to find out what sort of a bird is that Mandelstam, who for so many years was supposed to have done such and such, but always managed, the rogue, to evade it?

The alternation of triumphant mockery and sardonic self-mockery with poignant self-pity jolt the reader back to reality, forcing him to recall the autobiographical person behind the fictional *persona*. A tension is developed between the autobiographical reality and the authorial consciousness:

I'm a man who is growing old; with the bitten stump of my heart I scratch the master's dog. But it's not enough. . . . Russian writers stare at me with the tenderness of their dog's eyes imploring me: drop dead!

However, the dominant tone is literary irony. The controlling impulse is the esthetic of "philological nihilism" or "literary savagery," revitalized and newly formulated on the solid moral foundation of the Old Testament Commandment, "Thou shalt not kill!" The authorial consciousness thus ultimately controls the emotions of the autobiographical person. Genuine poetry and a Modernist esthetic allow Mandelstam to obtain intellectual and esthetic distance both with regard to his own individual life and to contemporary history.

The concluding vignette contains the poet's final *apologia* for "philology," his perverse affirmation of his "calling." Perversity is both justified and glorified through the images of the poet and the Jew who, from time immemorial, have always championed the eternal verities to challenge temporal values:

No matter how hard I work, whether I carry a horse slung across my shoulders, whether I turn millstones, no matter what I do I shall never become a worker. My work, regardless of its form, is considered mischief, lawlessness, mere accident. But I like it that way, and I agree to my calling. I'll even sign my name with both hands.

Thus, the intentional blurring of the boundaries of art and life, which Mandelstam first attempted in *The Noise of Time*, becomes an essential part of the structure of "Fourth Prose"; the autobiographical act facilitates not only the fictionalization of the poet's life but of the esthetic process itself, forcing the reader to recognize the poet's affirmation of the esthetic process as a moral, intellectual and cognitive act.

Mandelstam's Jewish consciousness reaches its peak in his autobiographical "Fourth Prose," climaxing in the twelfth vignette in which the image of the Jew is presented as the direct antithesis to the universal forces of death and destruction represented by the "Gypsies of Tverskoi Boulevard" or the Literary Establishment. Here "Jew" and poet are synonymous, reinforcing, broadening, and universalizing the moral and esthetic power of the earlier image of the "intellectual-writer" or *raznochinets-pisatel'*. Simultaneously, the moral passion of Old Testament prophecy reinforces the esthetic of "philological nihilism" or "literary savagery." The Mosaic law: "Thou shalt not kill," is elevated to a moral and esthetic imperative which informs the exorcism or scourge whose literary expression is "Fourth Prose." This exorcism of the forces of death and destruction frees Mandelstam once again to reformulate his esthetic vision: to establish once and for all the bond between the ideal of art as moral wisdom and the ideal of art as celebration.

The Jewish theme in Mandelstam's prose is a fascinating one, in that it is closely associated not only with the moral passion of the Old Testament (the Biblical heritage) and with the realm of fantasy and imagination (the world of Chagall), but also with Classicism and Hellenism. The latter are associated in Mandelstam's esthetic imagination with the origins of human spirituality and compassion for the earth; geographically, they are associated with the South, the Promised Land, the Caucasus, Armenia, Italy, Greece and Palestine. While many of these associations are vague, they are too numerous to be ignored in both Mandelstam's poetry and prose.[8]

The year 1926, documented as it is by numerous letters to his wife, Nadezhda Yakovlevna, indicates a fairly clear turning point in Mandelstam's personal life, in which the poet gradually rediscovers his Jewish consciousness and seeks a suitable esthetic expression for his awakened interest. However, until "Fourth Prose," he does not fully realize the positive esthetic value of his Jewish consciousness. In "The Egyptian Stamp," as in *The Noise of Time*, the Jewish theme still persists in negative form. Only in "Fourth Prose" does he associate the ideal image of poet and Jew, recognizing his Jewish consciousness as the moral imperative, indeed, moral impulse, behind his poetic or "philological" consciousness.

In February 1926, Mandelstam writes to Nadezhda Yakovlevna in Yalta that he now feels comfortable only "with Jews" (Letter No. 34). In other letters dating from February and March of the same year, he specifies a group of Jewish writers and editors who help him not only to survive physically, by finding him work, but spiritually, by encouraging him to believe that he is still able to write and publish.

In May of the same year, Mandelstam finally joins his wife in Kiev, where he writes his Kievan sketches, including an essay on the "Ukrainian-Jewish-Russian city [which] breathes a triple breath," and a brief but poignant piece on the extraordinary Jewish actor, Solomon Mikhoels.

"Kiev" is revealing for the sheer number of remarks about Jewish life in that city. This vignette appears at least partially as an attempt on Mandelstam's part to identify those aspects of his Jewish consciousness which might have esthetic meaning for him. Mandelstam's comments upon stumbling across a basement synagogue, for instance, are indicative:

I hear some sort of muttering just below my feet. Is it a *cheder*? No . . . a basement synagogue. A hundred venerable old men in striped *talesim* are seated like schoolchildren behind narrow yellow desks. No one pays any attention to them. If only Chagall were here!

It would appear that Mandelstam is aware of the esthetic potential of his new discovery but does not yet know quite how to use it: "If only Chagall were here!"

"Mikhoels," written a short time later, is another matter, for it expresses the overwhelming impression that Mikhoels made on Mandelstam. Indeed, this was the first time Mandelstam had even deigned to attend one of the Jewish actor's performances. Mandelstam's response can only be described as a new understanding of his "Jewish consciousness." He states:

Both the plasticity and power of Judaism come from its having managed to develop and perpetuate down through the ages a feeling for form and movement. . . . I have not taken it into my head to justify on esthetic grounds the ghetto or village life style. Rather, I am speaking about the inner plasticity of the ghetto, about that immense artistic power which is surviving the ghetto's destruction and which shall emerge completely only after the ghetto is destroyed.

He goes so far as to associate Mikhoels's artistic power with the power of Classical esthetics, finally recognizing the esthetic potential of Judaism in his own creative vision. He says:

Mikhoels's face takes on an expression of world-weariness and mournful ecstasy in the course of his dance as if the mask of the Jewish people were drawing nearer to the mask of Classical antiquity, becoming almost indistinguishable from it.

The dancing Jew now resembles the leader of the ancient Greek chorus. All the power of Judaism, all the rhythm of abstract ideas in dance, all the pride of the dance whose single motive is, in the final analysis, compassion for the earth,—all this extends into the trembling of the hands, into the vibration of the thinking fingers which are animated like articulate speech.

Never before had Mandelstam spoken of Judaism and the Jewish consciousness so openly and so eloquently, nor recognized its esthetic potential. His lyrical celebration of the Jewish actor's "compassion for the earth," seen in terms of the heritage of "immense artistic power" which will survive the ghetto, is a far cry from the ambiguous associations evoked in the "Judaic chaos" section of *The Noise of Time* or in the experiences of the humble and humiliated Jewish hero, Parnok, in "The Egyptian Stamp." In his poignant

32

depiction of Mikhoels, Mandelstam recognizes his Jewish consciousness as having esthetic value within his own creative vision, and links it to his major theme of the artist's relationship to Time.

Armenia, to which Mandelstam lovingly refers in "Fourth Prose" as the "younger sister of the Jewish nation," comes to symbolize his Promised Land. Indeed, Armenia comes to symbolize everything meaningful in human life, both that which is "promised" and that which is realized. As the cradle of human civilization, the birthplace of "philology," the geological and archaeological preserve of the eternal verities, Armenia is associated with human passion and endeavor, freedom and happiness, creative cognition and the realm of the imagination.

In "Fourth Prose," Armenia is still a "promised land," a distant mythological homeland, a realm of fantasy and dreams, and thus subject for lyrical digression. Shortly after its composition, Mandelstam was aided by his political mentor, Nikolai Bukharin, to actually travel there, and "Journey to Armenia" was written a year later. "Journey to Armenia" is Mandelstam's literary response to both the "promise" and the realization of his journey. It is anything but a descriptive account of a journey, however; its genesis as a "lyrical digression" in the earlier work is of major significance in understanding it as a literary genre.

In terms of genre, "Journey to Armenia" combines materials based directly on Mandelstam's journals (see "Addenda" to "Journey to Armenia") with materials originating in the realm of fantasy and imagination. It emerges as yet another form of autobiographical memoir, taking its structure this time from the extra-literary genres of the journal and the letter rather than from the reminiscences of childhood, the author's "handbook," or the satirical feuilleton. Its tone is predominantly contemplative rather than narrative; its style emphasizes the lyrical and imaginative rather than descriptive or objective mode of vision.

If *The Noise of Time* contains Mandelstam's first published literary definition of the origin and destiny of "philology," and offers his challenging and perverse esthetic of "literary savagery" or "philological nihilism," "Journey to Armenia" contains his last published literary statement on autobiographical truth, "oral instruction" and the physiology of reading. What is more, it establishes philological perversity in the more universal context of physiological, historical and philological continuity.

The autobiographical act—memory enhanced by the creative perception of that memory—helped to transform both the data of Mandelstam's journals and the contemplative musings of his lyrical fantasy or mythological perception of Armenia into a finished piece of literary prose. This work clearly expresses Mandelstam's continued fascination with the possibilities of literary prose in combining literary and extra-literary impulses. In addition, Mandelstam seems to recognize the opportunities offered by the autobiographical framework to address himself and his work simultaneously to the general reader and to a specific addressee or interlocutor. The interlocutor in this instance is Boris Sergeevich Kuzin, a biologist and close friend with whom Mandelstam shared many intellectual and esthetic discoveries in the early 1930s, and to whom he also dedicated several poems.

In "Journey to Armenia," Kuzin is essentially named to the role of the "ideal reader":

With these belated reflections, B.S., I hope to repay you, if only in part, for having disturbed your chess game in Erevan. (Part III)

I have received your eighteen-page letter, completely covered in a hand straight and tall as an avenue lined with poplars. Here is my answer (Part VII)

Mandelstam's "reflections" are often "philological" in nature:

The Armenian language cannot be worn down; its boots are of stone. Naturally, its word is thickwalled, its semi-vowels layered with air. But is that all there is to its charm? No! . . .

I experienced such joy in pronouncing sounds forbidden to Russian lips, mysterious sounds, outcast sounds, and perhaps, on some deeper level, even shameful sounds. . . .

As a result of my incorrect subjective orientation, I acquired the habit of looking upon every Armenian as a philologist. However, this is partly correct. These people jangle the keys of their language even when they are not using them to unlock any treasures.

Other "reflections" or "answers" are concerned with art, biological growth, space and speculation, while cryptic remarks harboring shared social and political values also abound, emphasizing the strong autobiographical impulse behind the text as well as its extra-literary intent. For instance, "How I longed to return to the place where people's skulls are equally beautiful in the grave and at work."

Thus, a good portion of this work is motivated by the perceptive "reflections" or "answers" offered by the author-narrator to his friend in distant Armenia. The vividness of the sections contrasting Moscow and Armenia, the strong flavor of nostalgia and yearning, as well as the esthetic control achieved through the remove of space and time are at least partially enhanced by the fact that "Journey to Armenia" was written in Moscow at least a year after Mandelstam's return.

The symbolic value of Armenia in Mandelstam's esthetic vision first emerged in the lyrical fantasy of "Fourth Prose." Indeed, the contemplative form of "Journey to Armenia" undoubtedly owes much to its origin in the realm of the imagination. However, in this work, the symbolic power of

34

Armenia is reinforced by the archaeological, ethnographical and philological imagery associated with the themes of physiological, philological and historical continuity. Whereas in "Fourth Prose," Armenia symbolized everything connected with life and the life-giving force, everything associated with freedom and the imagination in life's triumphant struggle against the forces of death and destruction, in "Journey to Armenia" the thematic emphasis is on the ideal of organic continuity perceived in the life cycle: birth, growth, decay, death and rebirth, and reinforced by the Christian symbolism so much a part of the Armenian landscape. Hence, in this work the Christian theme and Christian symbolism come to supercede the theme of the struggle between the forces of life and death or good and evil dominating "Fourth Prose."

In keeping with the dominant themes and imagery, the contemplative mood prevails in "Journey to Armenia" in direct contrast to the mood of perversity and challenge established in "Fourth Prose." Indeed, we can best describe "Journey to Armenia" as a contemplative journey, having as its spiritual quest the determination of a "better sense of the self in tradition."

The very first paragraph of "Journey to Armenia," in which Mandelstam describes the island of Sevan in terms of his response to its past and present, defines this mood: "I spent a month enjoying the lake waters . . . and teaching myself to contemplate the two or three dozen tombstones scattered so as to resemble a flowerbed among the monastery's recently renovated dormitories."

The imagery of the first few paragraphs is typical of the work as a whole. Mandelstam carefully juxtaposes images of death and decay (tombstones, graves, ruins, bones) with images of life and rebirth (growth, overgrowth, renovation, movement, change, freshwater winds, children, freedom), thus emphasizing the organic theme through his synthesizing esthetic vision: the theme of physiological, philological and historical continuity:

> The high steppe grasses growing on the lee hump of the island of Sevan were so strong, juicy and self-confident that you felt like carding them with an iron comb. The entire island is Homerically studded with yellow bones . . . .
>
> In addition, the island is literally paved with the fiery-red slabs of anonymous grave . . . .
>
> At the very beginning of my stay news came that some stonemasons digging a foundation pit for a lighthouse . . . stumbled across burial urns belonging to the ancient Urartu people.

Archaeological and etymological finds are as prevalent in this work as the tombstones marking their locations. Historical and philological revelations of the past in the present, and the discovery of the history and continuity of life, language and culture constantly pre-empt the contemplative subject

35

matter of the work.

What tense would you choose to live in?

I want to live in the imperative of the future passive participle—in the 'what ought to be.'

I like to breathe that way. That's what I like. It suggests a kind of mounted, bandit-like equestrian honor. That's why I like the glorious Latin "gerundive"—it's a verb on horseback.

Yes, the Latin genius, when it was young and greedy, created that form of imperative verbal tradition as the prototype of our entire culture, and not only "that which ought to be" but "that which ought to be praised"—*laudatura est*—that which pleases us . . . .

I carried on the above dialogue with myself as I rode horseback through the natural boundaries, the nomadic territories, and the vast pasturelands of Alagez.

What is more, the art of contemplation is given equal emphasis in discussions of works of art, in references to Armenian folklore, as well as in recollections of discussions about the naturalists from Lamarck to Darwin to Kuzin and the circle of Armenian scholars with whom Mandelstam associated during his sojourn in Armenia.

In his comments on an exhibition of French Impressionist painting which he viewed in Erevan, Mandelstam takes the opportunity to define his own esthetic vision. He even offers the reader rules for the esthetic contemplation of a painting. Concomitantly, he explains the role of art in expanding the mind and stimulating what he calls "creative cognition":

For all those recuperating from the benign plague of naive realism, I would advise the following method of observing paintings:

Don't go in, under any circumstances, as if entering a chapel . . . .

Cut through the large heat waves of oil painting space.

Calmly, not impetuously . . . dip your eye into the new material ambiance, however, always remember that the eye is a noble, but stubborn, animal . . . .

The eye, an organ which possesses its own acoustics, intensifying the value of the image, exaggerating its own accomplishments to the point of offending the sense over which it makes a great fuss, raises the picture to its own level, for painting is much more a phenomenon of internal secretion than of apperception, that is, of external perception . . . .

. . . The third and last stage of penetrating the picture begins—confronting the idea behind it.

Now the travelling eye presents its ambassadorial credentials to the consciousness. A cold treaty is drawn up between the viewer and the picture, something on the order of a state secret.

In his comments on the Impressionists, Mandelstam declares that a great artist, like Cezanne, "experiences the joy of ripening fruits," while someone less successful, like Matisse, "does not heal the vision, but offers it the strength of an ox so that your eyes become bloodshot." Commenting on his own vast resources of creative cognition, he states: "Then I stretched out my vision and dipped my eye into the sea's broad goblet."

Similarly, in his comments on the Naturalists, Mandelstam emphasizes that the precision of their descriptions is dependent on their love of life, on the way in which Lamarck, for instance, "fought for the honor of living nature." Mandelstam's interest in the Naturalists (see "On the Naturalists") coincided with his interest in the theory of organic growth and its relationship to the creative process. These subjects formed a major part of the poet's conversations with Kuzin while both were in Armenia.

> I gratefully recall one of our Erevan conversations which now, a year later, has already been aged by the confidence of personal experience and which now possesses that truth which helps us to form a better sense of ourselves in tradition.

> Without suspecting it, we are all carriers of an enormous embryological experiment: indeed, the very process of remembering, crowned with the victory of memory's efforts, is astonishingly similar to the phenomenon of growth . . . there is a sprout, an embryo, either some facial feature or some character trait, a half-sound, a name ending, something labial or palatal, some sweet pea on the tongue, which does not develop out of itself, but only responds to an invitation, only stretches forth, justifying your expectation.

In this way, Mandelstam's conversations, his memory of those conversations, as well as his perception of the act of memory as in itself a creative act, form the basis of his own creative autobiography. Mandelstam assures us that the act of memory is in itself a creative act, in that it is intimately connected with the "phenomenon of growth," with the life-giving force.

These two citations indicate the breadth and depth of Mandelstam's creative vision and its source in the autobiographical impulse. His exceptionally keen observations and highly imaginative insights are unified through the metaphorical vision of the poet and the autobiographical act. While the first quote expresses Mandelstam's universal quest to locate his perception of the self in relation to Time, the second compares the highly individual act of personal or creative memory with the universal phenomenon of growth.

Thus, for Mandelstam, the autobiographical impulse is fundamental to all his literary prose. In *The Noise of Time,* his first work of autobiographical prose, he claimed to be seeking "the germination of the seeds of time," a far cry from the egotistical self-analyses of the "decadent" novel, of Andrei

Bely's prose, or of the "psychological novelists" against whom he polemicized in "Literary Moscow: The Birth of Plot" or in "The End of the Novel." In "Journey to Armenia," Mandelstam perceives the autobiographical act as a vehicle for "creative cognition," through which he can establish an understanding of man's place in history "to form a better sense of ourselves in tradition." Mandelstam's ideal of creative cognition assures him an understanding of the "sense of life," for it includes: the art of contemplation, "confidence of personal experience," "the very process of remembering crowned with the victory of memory's efforts," "oral instruction, the lucid didacticism of intimate conversation," "the precision of description," and "the feeling for the fullness of life characteristic of the Armenian people." What is more, in "Journey to Armenia" the act of memory and its perception—the basic autobiographical act—itself becomes a subject of contemplation.

The contemplative act or Mandelstam's contemplative journey may be endless; however, a piece of literary prose must conclude somewhere. Hence, Mandelstam's meditations on life's conclusions and on literary conclusions. His reference to the conclusions of Armenian folktales which always recognize and reward the three modes of creative cognition is most revealing: the art of telling, the art of listening, and the art of understanding: "Three apples fell from the skies: the first for the one who told the tale, the second for the one who listened, and the third for the one who understood."

This citation may also be read as the basic paradigm of "Journey to Armenia," for Mandelstam's esthetic of contemplation recognizes these three modes of cognition as having equal value. Indeed, this folklore paradigm helps to illuminate the symbolic force invested in the rather cryptic legend of King Arshak, presented in Mandelstam's singularly laconic but bold outline, in the penultimate conclusion of "Journey to Armenia." This tale, for all its bitterness, nevertheless expresses the author's bold hope for some reprieve in this world for men of great spiritual powers, whether through the art of human kindness, the realm of the imagination, or through creative cognition. This idea of a reprieve represents Mandelstam's persistent, indeed insistent, sense of optimism or courage in the face of life's constant challenge, which is echoed in much of his poetry of this period:

> That courage might challenge future centuries,
> That the exalted tribe of men might triumph,
> I yielded my cup at the ancestral feast
> Along with my happiness and honor.
> (No. 227, March 1931)

Indeed, throughout Mandelstam's work, such refrains as the following persist: "Life is both terrifying and beautiful" ("The Egyptian Stamp"). "The Persian miniature regards you obliquely, with frightened, graceful almond eyes. Sinless and sensual, it convinces you that life is a precious, inalienable gift"

("Journey to Armenia").

Thus, "Journey to Armenia" may also have been experienced by Mandelstam as a kind of reprieve, or in Christian terms, as a second birth. It seems to function, like each of the poet's preceding works of literary prose, as a summation and conclusion of a particular phase in both his personal autobiography and in his creative consciousness.

However, like his other works of literary prose, it also appears as the beginning of a new phase, a new understanding and a new quest. The actual conclusion of "Journey to Armenia" offers sleep as the final reprieve for physical exhaustion. Mandelstam, however, can only conclude his temporary journey with sleep, not his life's journey. Hence, his "last thought" is not of sleep and rest, but of the continuation of life's journey: "Sleep is easy in nomad camps. The body, exhausted by space, grows warm, stretches itself out, and recalls the length of the journey . . . . Last thought: I must ride around some other ridge."

"Conversation about Dante" is a counterpart to "Journey to Armenia" thematically and structurally. While "Journey to Armenia" is concerned primarily with organic continuity, "Conversation about Dante" is concerned with the immortality of art. While the earlier work focuses on organic recurrence—physiological, philological and historical continuity, the life cycle, the relationship between the phenomenon of growth and the organic nature of memory—as a phenomenon of natural order, subtly enhanced by the Christian vision, the latter attempts to reveal the impulse behind the creative process itself, the instinct for form creation which underlies the immortality of art: the impulse to preserve the eternal verities through human creativity and the creative process as well as the phenomenon of the perpetuation of art through generations of readers. "Conversation about Dante" is Mandelstam's last extant attempt to identify the impulse behind the text both for himself as poet and reader, and for his interlocutor or ideal reader.

While Mandelstam first mentioned the significance of "oral instruction" and the "physiology of reading" in "Journey to Armenia," it is only in "Conversation about Dante" that he attempts to convey his own intimate reader's experience of an immortal poetic work. Indeed, while the structure of the earlier work depends to a large extent on dialogue, in the form of recollected "conversations" and "answers" to "letters" from Armenia, the latter emerges, as it were, as a practical example of the kind of oral instruction referred to in "Journey to Armenia": ". . . oral instruction, the lucid didacticism of intimate conversation [which] is far superior to the instruction and homiletic function of books."

What is more, while "Journey to Armenia" is a rather loosely structured work, based as it is on contemplation, or impressionistic responses to both old and new experiences, "Conversation about Dante" is much more tightly conceived, stemming as it does from Mandelstam's interest in the "seemingly forbidden themes" of the "physiology of reading," suggested in the earlier work but realized only in the latter.

Let us speak about the physiology of reading. It is a rich, inexhaustible, and seemingly forbidden theme. Of all the objects in the material world, of all the physical bodies, a book is the object which inspires man with the greatest degree of confidence. A book firmly established on a reader's desk is like a canvas stretched on its frame.

When we are completely immersed in the activity of reading, we admire above all our own generic attributes, we experience, as it were, the ecstasy of classifying ourselves in various ages and stages.

While Mandelstam's impressions of Dante and his experiences in reading Dante are highly original, spontaneous and often impressionistic, the format of the work emphasizes his erudition and even a quasi-scientific approach to literary interpretation. Indeed, while "Journey to Armenia" recognizes the art of telling, listening, and understanding as the three basic modes of creative cognition, "Conversation about Dante" applies them.

Nevertheless, the quasi-scientific aspect of Mandelstam's approach is balanced by his individual poetic vision which controls the work:

I am engaged in a struggle to make the work comprehensible as an entity, to graphically demonstrate that which is conceivable. Only through metaphor is it possible to find a concrete sign to represent the instinct for form creation by which Dante accumulated and poured forth his *terza rima*.

"Conversation about Dante" belongs to the essay genre in that it provides us with numerous definitions, yet each one is a metaphorical formulation, more in keeping with Pasternak's "definition" poems in his collection *My Sister, Life* (see "Definition of Poetry," "Definition of the Soul," "Definition of Creativity") than the traditional form of the essay, or even with Mandelstam's own essays of the 1910s and 1920s. A few examples should suffice:

Semantic adequacy is the equivalent of the feeling of having fulfilled a command.

Poetic discourse is a carpet fabric containing a multitude of textile warps differing from one another only in the partitura of the perpetually changing commands of the instrumental signalling system.

Ornament is stanzaic. Pattern is of the line.

The essay, whatever its stylistic merits, has conventionally been con-

40

ceived as a medium of instruction directed toward an audience of contemporaries. While Mandelstam's essay on Dante is "oral instruction," its major function is to convince the reader that he should allow his imagination to respond as freely and directly as possible to the dynamics of the poetic text.

Mandelstam's originality and the boldness of his approach is closely associated with his focus on the ideal reader. He is keenly interested in the effect of a great poet on himself as both a reader and as a poet. The essay is thus directed toward the active poetic perception of the impulses and inspirations of a poetic genius, the external model being Dante, the internal experience being his own creative cognition.

Thus, Mandelstam's essay is a demonstration of what it is that makes Dante "a master of the instruments of poetry"; it is Mandelstam's effort to convey just how the original creative impulse is transformed in the mind of the creative artist into living poetry.

As "Conversation about Dante" develops, we move from metaphorical definitions into Dante's text itself, focusing more deeply on the realm of the poetic consciousness as we enter the arena of the "performance."

Mandelstam first attempts to establish a new defintion of "poetic discourse" or poetry, to supercede the clichés of literary criticism, by identifying its uniqueness in "process," indeed, in its being a "hybrid process." For Mandelstam, "hybridization" was an organic phenomenon basic to the creative process, an essential element of literary form which made possible the proper unity of "memory" and "inventiveness." He perceived this ideal of "hybridization" much earlier, for example, in Blok's vision (see "Badger Hole"):

[Blok] sensed the life of language and literary forms not as a break, not as destruction, but as hybridization, as the conjoining of different species and strains, or the grafting of various fruits onto one tree.

Very significant in Mandelstam's attempts to avoid cultural and critical jargon is his appeal to the reader to consider poetry in a new way, to identify its essence and to establish the source of its quality. In the course of this essay, he attempts to convince the reader that the essence of poetry is in the performance, in the impulse behind the text. He emphasizes again and again that, "What is important in poetry is only the understanding which brings it about—not at all the passive, reproducing, or paraphrasing understanding."

"Meaning," he can explain only through metaphor, for it is inexplicable, unparaphrasable:

The quality of poetry is determined by the speed and decisiveness with which it embodies its schemes and commands in diction, the instru-

41

mentless, lexical, purely quantitative verbal matter. One must traverse the full width of a river crammed with Chinese junks moving simultaneously in various directions—thus the meaning of poetic speech is created. This meaning, the itinerary, cannot be reconstructed by interrogating the boatmen: they will not be able to tell how and why we were jumping from junk to junk.

Movement is as essential an element in poetry as durability, but both can only be expressed through metaphor:

[Poetic discourse] is an extremely durable carpet woven out of fluid: a carpet in which the currents of the Ganges, taken as a textile theme, do not mix with the samples of the Nile or Euphrates, but remain multicolored, in braids, figures, and ornaments, only not in patterns, for a pattern is the equivalent of paraphrase. Ornament is good precisely because it preserves traces of its origin like a piece of nature enacted.

Another major point in Mandelstam's definition of poetry is his assertion that it is neither a part of nature nor a reflection of nature. Rather poetry *acts out* nature. Poetry, and the instruments of poetic discourse, are always "acting" or performing:

. . .poetry estabishes itself with astonishing independence in a new extra-spatial field of action, not so much narrating as acting out nature by means of its arsenal of devices, commonly known as figures.
Ornament is good precisely because it preserves traces of its origin, like a piece of nature enacted. Whether the piece is animal, vegetable, steppe, Scythian or Egyptian, indigenous or barbarian, it is always speaking, seeing, acting.

A poet's greatness is measured in terms of his mastery of the instruments of poetry. Like Blok who "sensed the life of language and literary forms . . . as hybridization," so Dante is "a strategist of transmutation and hybridization." Indeed the earlier essay compares the Russian poet directly to Dante: "Poetic culture arises from the attempt to avert catastrophe, to make it dependent on the central sun of the system as a whole, be it love, of which Dante spoke, or music, at which Blok ultimately arrived."
On the other hand, "Conversation about Dante" differs from the typical critical essay of the 1920s-30s, for it contains numerous personal asides, or autobiographical digressions, in which Mandelstam focuses on his own emotional, often physiological "love of the word," his fascination with verbal texture, phonology, sound harmony, and the relationship of the poetic impulse to the text.

"When I began to study Italian and had barely familiarized myself with its phonology and prosody, I suddenly understood that the center of gravity of my speech efforts had been moved closer to my lips."

Digressions of this kind impress the reader as intimate revelations of the unique creative impulse informing Mandelstam's work. This should come as no surprise, however, when we recall the poet's previous efforts in literary prose, or remember the essay "On the Nature of the Word," in which he presents his first portrait of the ideal philologist. However, in "Conversation about Dante," that philologist has mellowed. The perverse element in Mandelstam's esthetic of philological nihilism is subordinated to the personal, intimate, indeed, physiological relationship between the poet and his poem.

The mouth works, the smile nudges the line of verse, cleverly and gaily the lips redden, the tongue trustingly presses itself against the palate.
The inner form of the verse is inseparable from the countless changes of expression flitting across the face of the narrator who speaks and feels emotion.

This physiological relationship is also emphasized in the essay on Dante as part of Mandelstam's unique philological approach to the reading of poetry, and as part of his attempt to re-educate the reader:

We must give some examples of Dante's rhythms. People are ignorant of this aspect of Dante. They must be shown. Whoever says, "Dante is sculptural," is influenced by the impoverished critical definitions of that great European. Dante's poetry partakes of all the forms of energy known to modern science . . . Above all, the reading of Dante is an endless labor . . . If the first reading brings on only shortness of breath and healthy fatigue, then equip yourself for subsequent readings with a pair of indestructible Swiss hobnailed boots. The question arises, in all seriousness: how many shoe soles, how many sandals, did Alighieri wear out during the course of his poetic work, wandering the goat paths of Italy?
Both the *Inferno* and, in particular, the *Purgatorio*, glorify the human gait, the measure and rhythm of walking, the footstep and its form. The step, bound up with breathing and saturated with thought, Dante understood as the beginning of prosody. He utilizes a quantity of varied and charming turns of phrase just to indicate walking . . . the metrical foot is the inhalation and exhalation of the step. Each step concludes, invigorates, syllogizes.

Here we also recall Mandelstam's fascination with the intimate accord of mind and movement, of abstract ideas and their physical articulation in

43

his acute perception of the actor, Mikhoels:

> All the power of Judaism, all the rhythm of abstract ideas in dance, all the pride of the dance whose single motive is, in the final analysis, compassion for the earth, —all this extends into the trembling of the hands, into the vibration of the thinking fingers which are animated like articulated speech.

This conversation or oral instruction differs radically from Mandelstam's own polemical diatribes against the uneducated reading public and the critics, translators and editors of the literary establishment who set literary standards in the 1920s: see "The Slump," "An Army of Poets," "Jacques was born and died," "Torrents of Hackwork," "On Translations," "The Duchess' Fan."

In addition to his incisive remarks on the poetics of rhythm and movement, Mandelstam discusses Dante's use of grammatical tenses in Canto X of the *Inferno* in an astonishingly original manner, bringing to mind his own careful juxtaposition of grammatical tenses in his literary prose. In this work he associates a "slip of the tongue" —introducing the main segment of the dialogue—with "a surprise explication of the situation." Furthermore, in "Conversation about Dante," he indicates just how a particular grammatical tense or any other element of poetic discourse acquires semantic significance, thus distinguishing poetic discourse from automatic everyday speech formulations. He attempts to demonstrate just how "any process involving the creation of form in poetry presupposes lines, periods or cycles of sound forms, as is the case with individually pronounced semantic units."

Thus, Mandelstam is responding to Dante as both a reader and a poet. He is hardly speaking only about Dante. Mandelstam's own instinct for form creation serves to illuminate his reading of Dante as well as his own work.

We have already mentioned Mandelstam's interest in the "physiology" of form, and in the physiological aspects of the relationship between the impulse and the text. See, in addition, his poems, "Notre Dame" (1912) or "Batyushkov" (1932). Another persistent motif in Mandelstam's own work is space or spatial form (see, for instance, "On the Nature of the Word" or the poetic cycle "The Octets"—*Vos'mistishiia*). Of Dante he says:

> Alighieri constructed in verbal space an infinitely powerful organ and was already delighting in all of its imaginable stops . . . .

> Dante's comparisons are never descriptive, that is, purely representational. They always pursue the concrete task of presenting the inner form of the poem's structure or its driving force.

> The inner illumination of Dantean space derived from structural ele-

ments alone was of absolutely no interest to anyone.

O poetry, envy crystallography, bite your nails in anger and impotence! For it is recognized that the mathematical formulas necessary for describing crystal formation are not derivable from three-dimensional space. You are denied even that element of respect which any piece of mineral crystal enjoys.

Mandelstam's quest for precision of perception, for clarity of understanding, for exact knowledge is also constantly reiterated in his perceptive comments on Dante:

There is not just one form in Dante, but a multitude of forms. One is squeezed out of another and only by convention can one be inserted into another.
Dante himself says:
"I would squeeze the juice out of my idea, out of my conception," that is, he considers form as the thing which is squeezed out, not as that which serves as a covering.
In this way, strange as it may seem, form is squeezed out of the content-conception which, as it were, envelops the form. Such is the precision of Dante's thought.

Dante himself was striving for clear and precise knowledge.

It is inconceivable that anyone could grasp with the eye alone or even visually imagine to himself this form of thirteen thousand facets, so monstrous in its exactitude.

And, of course, one of the major impulses informing Mandelstam's esthetic vision is the idea of recurrence and its expression through images of metamorphosis. See, for instance, the poem "Tristia," the essays "The Word and Culture," "Storm and Stress," "Mikhoels," or the "Journey to Armenia." Hence, Mandelstam's assertion that Dante was chosen as the theme of this conversation, "because he is the greatest, the unrivaled master of transformable and convertible poetic material."

And finally, Mandelstam's constantly reiterated critical judgment that the ideal reader must be an educated reader. He must be able to consider all perspectives, all structural levels of a given text to obtain a proper reading: poetic and extra-poetic, historical, theological, political, social, psychological, physiological as well as the specifically linguistic, technical and formal aspects. He has hope for the sciences if, and when, they become sufficiently refined to "think in images," but meanwhile he is concerned with refuting the all-pervasive clichés of literary scholarship:

> The purely historical approach to Dante is just as unsatisfactory as the political or theological approach. The future of Dante criticism belongs to the natural sciences when they will have achieved a sufficient degree of refinement and developed their capacity for thinking in images.

Mandelstam asserts that "instinct" must be accepted as "the guiding principle" behind the creative process, and that the traditional mode of critical analysis—"our habit of grammatical thinking," or "the syntactic mode of thinking"—cannot cope with "genuine poetry."

> The process of creating this poem's form transcends our conceptions of literary inventiveness and composition. It would be far more correct to recognize instinct as its guiding principle.

> Our criticism tells us: distance the phenomenon and I will deal with it and absorb it. "Holding something at a distance" (Lomonosov's expression) and cognoscibility are almost identical for our criticism.

> In its cold state, forcibly torn from its incandescence, Dante's *Commedia* is suitable only for analyses with mechanistic tweezers; it is unsuitable for reading, for performing.

The reader, according to Mandelstam, must immerse himself fully in the text, oblivious of his normal mode of thinking, feeling, and responding:

> When you read Dante with all your powers and with complete conviction, when you transplant yourself completely to the field of action of the poetic material, when you join in and coordinate your own intonations with the echoes of the orchestral and thematic groups continually arising on the pocked and undulating semantic surface, when you begin to catch through the smoky-crystalline rock the sound-forms of phenocryst inserted into it, that is, additional sounds and thoughts conferred on it no longer by a poetic but by a geological intelligence, then the purely vocal, intonational and rhythmic work is replaced by a more powerful coordinating force—by the conductor's function—and the hegemony of the conductor's baton comes into its own, cutting across orchestrated space and projecting from the voice like some more complex mathematical measure out of a three-dimensional state.

Thus, Mandelstam said, "I should hope that in the future Dante scholarship will study the coordination of the impulse and the text."

The same might be said of Mandelstam scholarship. Seen in this light,

Mandelstam's autobiographical impulse—the various direct and indirect auto-biographical comments and auto-reminiscences interspersed in the essay on Dante—takes on a deeper meaning, and firmly establishes this masterful piece of prose in Mandelstam's *oeuvre*.

Mandelstam's insights into Dante's poetics, as well as into the "psychological foundation" of Dante's creative process—the relationship between the poet and the man, the link between his psychological and creative impulses—reveal much that is fundamental to Mandelstam's own esthetic vision.

On one level then, "Conversation about Dante" presents the autobiographical experience of a poet or "philologist" reading the work of an immortal poet while discoursing on his own poetic experience, defining it, clarifying it. Hence, Mandelstam's reference to Dante as a fellow *raznochinets* begins to make sense. This harks back to the imagery of *The Noise of Time*, for Dante could be considered a *raznochinets* only in terms of Mandelstam's bold metaphor:

Dante is a poor man. Dante is an internal *raznochinets*. . . . Courtesy is not at all characteristic of him, rather something distinctly the opposite. . . . Dante does not know how to behave, does not know how to act, what to say, how to bow. I am not imagining this; I infer it from the numerous admissions of Alighieri himself.

The inner anxiety and painful, troubled gaucheries which accompany each step of the diffident man, as if his upbringing were somehow remiss; the man untutored in the ways of applying his inner experience or of objectifying it in etiquette, tormented and outcast, such are the qualities which both provide the poem with all its charm, with all its drama, and serve as its background, its psychological foundation.

Moreover, Mandelstam insists on linking Dante not only to his image of himself as a *raznochinets-pisatel'*, but to his Russian mentor, Pushkin:

[Dante expressed] an inner awkwardness surmounted by agony, a purely Pushkinian, *Kammerjunker* struggle for social dignity and a recognized social position for the poet. The shade which frightens children and old women took fright itself, and Alighieri suffered fever and chills: all the way from miraculous bouts of self-esteem to feelings of utter worthlessness.

Other autobiographical reminiscences are related to the motivating impulses behind the actual composition of "Conversation about Dante":

I permit myself a brief autobiographical confession. Black Sea pebbles tossed up on shore by the rising tide helped me immensely in the conception of this conversation. I openly consulted with chalcedony, cornelians, gypsum crystals, spar, quartz, and so on. In this way, I came to understand that mineral rock is something like a diary of the weather. . . . A stone is nothing more than weather itself, excluded from atmospheric space and banished to functional space. . . . In this sense, meteorology is more fundamental than minerology, for it embraces it, washes over it, ages it and gives it meaning.

I am engaged in a struggle to make the work comprehensible as an entity, to graphically demonstrate that which is conceivable. Only through metaphor is it possible to find a concrete sign to represent the instinct for form creation by which Dante accumulated and poured forth his *terza rima.*

At other times Mandelstam also refers back to certain themes and images in his earliest essays, in particular "Morning of Acmeism" (1913), to indicate the limitations of his early work and the fact of having superceded them both thematically and structurally. In contrast to the mature poetic consciousness reading Dante, the author of the manifesto "Morning of Acmeism" is a mere fledgling poet. Immature and egocentric, the twenty-two-year-old poet concentrated on the "rules" for poetry making, on the craft rather than the performance. The mature poet of the "Conversation" reflects on the impulses to creation, on the continuity and viability of the dynamics of the poetic process and on a text which has withstood the test of time. Where the young Acmeist is polemical, and metaphorically vague, the mature poet is contemplative, erudite, and metaphorically concrete. Where the younger poet is essentially unsure of his audience, the mature poet is authoritatively accommodating and boldly original. The essence of the "I" has undergone many changes associated with the maturity of the poet, but basically the seeker has become the "finder."

Whether or not "Conversation about Dante" actually succeeds as an artistic experience may be less important than the fact that Mandelstam was attempting such an experiment. To categorize this work as but one more essay on the order of those collected in *On Poetry* is to fail to understand its unique poetic structure or to recognize its place in the poet's *oeuvre* as both a summation and conclusion to his ideas and formulations concerning the relationship of the impulse and the text.

"Conversation about Dante," then, should be read as the poet's supreme effort to explicate the creative process and the impulse behind it, while simultaneously participating in that process. Mandelstam is in essence explaining the art and the act of reading while performing the act of reading and the art of interpretation. What is more, this is genuine poetry as Mandelstam understands it—poetry exists only "in performance." In this sense, then, "Conversation about Dante" is also "poetry": it is simultaneously a reflection on the impulse to poetic creation and a poetic revelation in itself. The impulse becomes the text as the text reveals the impulse.

48

What is important in poetry is only the process of comprehension—not the passive, reproducing or paraphrasing understanding. Semantic adequacy is the equivalent of the feeling of having fulfilled a command.

The mouth works, the smile nudges the line of verse, cleverly and gaily the lips redden, the tongue trustingly presses itself against the palate.

I should hope that in the future . . . scholarship will study the coordination of the impulse and the text.

THE CRITICAL PROSE

1. FRANÇOIS VILLON

Astronomers can predict the precise date of a comet's return over an extensive time interval. For those familiar with François Villon,[1] the appearance of Verlaine[2] represents the same kind of astronomical miracle. The vibrations of these two voices are strikingly similar. However, in addition to voice timbre and biography, an almost identical mission connects each of these poets to the literature of his age. Each poet was fated to emerge in an epoch of artificial, hothouse poetry; thus just as Verlaine destroyed the *serres chaudes*[3] of Symbolism, so Villon rejected the call of the reigning Rhetorical School which might be properly considered the Symbolism of the fifteenth century. The famous *Roman de la Rose*[4] raised for the first time an impenetrable wall within which the hothouse atmosphere required for the living and breathing allegories created by this poem continued to thicken. LOVE, DANGER, ENMITY, PERFIDY were hardly dead abstractions. They did not lack corporeality. Medieval poetry endowed these apparitions with astral bodies as it were, and tenderly watched over the artificial atmosphere required to support their delicate existence. The garden where these particular personages lived was surrounded by a high wall. The lover, as narrated in the beginning of the *Roman de la Rose*, long wandered around this enclosure, seeking its invisible entrance in vain.

In the fifteenth century poetry and life were two independent, inimical forces. It is difficult to believe that Maître Alain Chartier[5] was really persecuted and endured daily trials for having incensed contemporary public opinion with too severe a judgment of the *Belle Dame sans merci,* whom he drowned in a well of tears following a brilliant trial which observed all the proprieties of Medieval legal procedure. Poetry was autonomous in the fifteenth century: it occupied a position in contemporary culture like a state within a state. We may recall Charles VI's Court of Love: more than seven hundred official ranks engaged people in a variety of duties, from the most noble *seigneur* down to the petty *bourgeois* and the lowliest clerics. The exclusively literary character of this institution explains its defiance of class distinctions. Literary hypnosis was so strong that members of similar associations reveled in the streets wearing green crowns—the symbol of the lover

—hoping to extend the literary dream into real life.

François de Montcorbier (or François des Loges) was born in Paris in 1431, during the period of English rule. The indigence surrounding his cradle reflected the national poverty and, in particular, the poverty of the capital. One would expect that the literature of that age would be filled with feelings of patriotic enthusiasm and a desire to avenge the injured dignity of the nation. Nevertheless, neither in Villon's work nor in the writings of his contemporaries do we find such feelings expressed. Occupied by foreigners, France showed herself as a true woman. Like a woman in captivity, France paid attention primarily to the trivia of her cultural and customary toilette, regarding her conquerors with curiosity. High society, following its poets, continued to be carried away by their dreams into the fourth dimension of the Gardens of Love and the Gardens of Delight, and for the populace at large the lights of the taverns glowed in the evenings, while on holidays farces and mystery plays were performed.

This passive-feminine epoch left a deep impression on Villon's character and on his fate. Throughout his entire dissolute life he held the intransigent conviction that someone should be there to care for him, to manage his affairs and to come to his rescue in difficult situations. Even as a grown man, abandoned in the dungeon of Meung sur Loire by the Bishop of Orléans, he plaintively pleaded with his friends: "Le laisserez-vous là, le pauvre Villon?" The public career of François de Montcorbier began when he was taken in hand by Guillaume de Villon, venerable canon of the monastery church of Saint-Benoît-le-Bestourné. In his own words, the poet claimed the old canon was "more than a mother." In 1449 he received his baccalaureate, in 1452—his lycée certificate and his Master's degree.

> But in the days of my mad youth
> if only I had used my head
> and learnt to behave in truth,
> I'd have a house and a soft bed.
> But like a naughty boy instead
> I ran away from school. I make
> these lines and soon as they are said
> I feel my heart would almost break.[6]

Strange as it may seem, Maître François Villon at one time had several pupils whom he taught scholastic wisdom as best he could. But in his own honest estimation of himself he realized that he had no right to the title of Maître, thus in his ballads he preferred to call himself a "poor young scholar." Moreover, it was particularly difficult for Villon to study since, as luck would have it, his school years (1451-53) coincided with a period of student riots. In the Middle Ages people liked to refer to themselves as the children of such and such city, church or university... But only "the children of the university" exhibited a taste for pranks. Such pranks included organizing a heroic hunt for the most popular house signs of the Paris market, after which the Stag was supposed to unite the Goat and the Bear in marriage. The Parrot was to be presented to the newlyweds as a gift. On another occasion the students stole a stone boundary marker from the estate of Mademoiselle de Bruyères and carted it off to Mont Sainte Geneviève,[7] having dubbed it "La Vesse." They fastened it down with iron bands after forcefully repulsing the authorities. On top of this circular marker they placed another marker with an oblong shape— "Le Pet-au-deable,"[8]—and carried on nightly revels, bowing before the markers, strewing them with flowers, and dancing around them to the music of flutes and tambourines. The infuriated butchers of the Sainte Geneviève district and the insulted Madam went to the police. The Provost of Paris declared war on the students. Two jurisdictions[9] clashed; but the bold *sergents* were finally forced to their knees, with burning candles in their hands, to beg mercy of the Rector. Villon, undoubtedly at the very heart of these activities, inscribed them for posterity in his romance, "Le Rommant du Pet-au-Deable," which unfortunately has not been preserved.

Villon was a Parisian. He loved his city and its life of idle pursuits. He lacked any tender feelings toward nature, and even ridiculed it. Fifteenth-century Paris was already like a sea in which one could swim without ever experiencing boredom, oblivious of the rest of the universe. But how easy to run aground on one of those innumerable reefs of idle existence! Villon became a murderer. The passivity of his fate is remarkable. It was as if his fate were waiting to be fertilized by chance, indifferent to good or evil. In an absurd street fight on June 5, Villon killed the priest Philippe Chermoye with a heavy rock. Sentenced to death by hanging, he appealed and was mercifully pardoned. He went into self-imposed exile. His itinerant life finally shattered his morality and led him to join the criminal band known as La Coquille. Upon his return to Paris, he participated in the great robbery of the Collège de Navarre and then immediately fled to Angers, claiming it was because of an unhappy love affair. Actually, it allowed him to prepare for the robbery of his rich uncle. While in hiding from the Paris scene, Villon published his *Petit Testament*. This was followed by years of itinerant wandering, interspersed with sojourns in feudal courts and prisons. Amnestied by Louis XI on October 2, 1461, Villon experienced deep creative excitement, his thoughts and feelings emerged with extraordinary clarity, and he composed his *Grand Testament*, his monument to the ages. In November 1463, François Villon was witness to a quarrel and murder on the Rue Saint-Jacques. Here our information about his life ends, and his dark biography comes to an abrupt conclusion.

The fifteenth century was extremely harsh on individuals. It transformed many respectable and sober men into Jobs, grumbling at the lower depths of their stinking dungeons and accusing God of injustice. A particular genre of prison poetry developed, suffused with biblical bitterness and severity, insofar as it was even known to the courtly Romance soul. Villon's voice, however, was sharply distinguishable amidst the chorus of prisoners. His revolt had more in common with legal action than with mutiny. He managed to combine in one person both plaintiff and defendant. Villon's attitude toward himself never exceeded the familiar limitations of intimacy. He expressed no more tenderness, attentiveness or concern for himself than a good lawyer would show his client. Self-compassion is a parasitical emotion, corrupting both the soul and the organism. But the cold juridical compassion which Villon granted himself was his source of inspiration and confirmed his immutable certainty in the justice of his "case." His world was devoid of morality; he lived entirely in a legal world, as an extremely "amoral" person, a true heir of Rome. He could not recognize any attitude outside that jurisdiction and norm.

The lyric poet is a hermaphrodite by nature, capable of limitless fissions in the name of his inner dialogue. Nowhere is this "lyrical hermaphroditism" so clearly expressed as in Villon's work. What a varied selection of enchanting duets: the aggrieved and the comforter, the mother and child, the judge and the judged, the proprietor and the beggar...

Property enticed Villon all his life like a musical siren and made him a thief...and a poet. A pitiful vagabond, he attained for himself the unattainable aided only by his sharp irony.

Modern French Symbolists fell in love with things, like proprietors. Perhaps, the true "soul of things" is nothing other than proprietary feelings engendered and ennobled in the laboratory of successive generations. Villon was exceptionally conscious of the abyss between subject and object, but he understood it as the impossibility of ownership. The moon and other such neutral "objects" were completely excluded from his poetic usage. On the other hand, he livened up immediately whenever the discussion centered on roast duck or on eternal bliss, objects which he never quite lost the hope of acquiring.

Villon painted an enchanting *intérieur* in Flemish style, while peeping through a keyhole.

Villon's sympathy for the dregs of society, for everything suspicious and criminal, is far from demonism. The dark company with whom he so quickly and intimately made friends captivated his feminine nature with its excitable temperament and its powerful sense of the rhythm of life which he could not satisfy among other social strata. One need only listen attentively to Villon's depictions of the profession of *souteneur,* to which he was obviously no stranger, in his "Ballade à la grosse Margot": "When the clients come, I grab a pitcher/And run off after some wine." Neither anemic feudalism nor the newly rising bourgeoisie with its inclination toward Flemish gravity and grandiosity could have produced such a dynamic and major talent, amassed and concentrated by some miracle in this Parisian cleric. Dry and dark, eyebrowless, and thin as a chimera, with a head which he himself admitted resembled a shelled, roasted nut. With a sword tucked under his semi-feminine student garb, Villon lived in Paris, like a squirrel on a treadmill, never knowing a moment of rest. He loved the lean and cunning little animal in himself and took great pride in his own crumpled hide. Having been spared the gallows, he wrote to his prosecutor: "Isn't it true, Granier, that I did well by appealing. Not many animals would have managed to extricate themselves that way." If Villon had been in a position to express his poetic *credo*, he would undoubtedly have exclaimed, like Verlaine: *Du mouvement avant toute chose!*[10]

A dynamic visionary, Villon dreamed of his own hanging on

the eve of his own probable execution. But it is strange how, in his "Ballade des pendus," he combined incredible cruelty with rhythmical inspiration in depicting the wind swinging the bodies of the condemned back and forth, back and forth, at will... He also endowed death with dynamic qualities and, here too, managed to display his love for rhythm and movement... I think that Villon was captivated not by the demonic, but by the dynamics of criminal life. Might there not be some inverse ratio between the moral and the dynamic development of the soul? In any case, both of Villon's *Testaments,* the *Petit* and the *Grand*, are incurably amoral; they are celebrations of magnificent rhythms such as French poetry had not previously known. Twice the pitiful vagabond wrote his "Last Will and Testament," dividing up his imaginary possessions left and right, like a poet ironically affirming his mastery over all those things he would like to own. If, for all their originality, Villon's spiritual experiences are not distinguished by particular profundity, his human relationships, his intricate network of acquaintances, connections and reckonings, represent a composite of brilliant complexity. This man contrived to establish vital, fundamental relationships with enormous numbers of people of the most varied backgrounds, from every rung on the social ladder—thieves to bishops, barmaids to princes. With what pleasure he tells their most cherished secrets! How precise he was, how detailed! Villon's *Testaments* captivate the reader simply by the mass of precise information they communicate. The reader can imagine himself using the data, and can experience the life of the poet's contemporaries. The passing moment can thus endure the pressure of centuries and preserve itself intact, remaining forever the same "here and now." You need only know how to extract that "here and now" from the soil of Time without harming its roots, or it will wither and die. Villon knew how to extract it. The bell of the Sorbonne, having interrupted his work on the *Petit Testament*, rings forth to this day.

Like the Troubador princes, Villon "sang in his own tongue": once, as a student, he had heard about Alcibiades; subsequently, the stranger *Archipiade* joined the grand procession of the "Dames du temps jadis."[11]

The Middle Ages held on to its children tenaciously and did not give them up voluntarily to the Renaissance. The blood of the Middle Ages flowed in Villon's veins. He was obliged to the

Middle Ages for his integrity, his temperament, for the source of his spiritual values. Gothic physiology (and such it was; the Middle Ages was precisely a physiologically brilliant era) took the place of a world view for Villon and generously rewarded him for his lack of traditional bonds with the past. Furthermore, it assured him of an honorable place in the future since nineteenth-century French poetry derives its strength from that same national Gothic treasure chest. People ask: what do the magnificent rhythms of the *Testaments* (now quick juggling motions as of a bilboquet, now the slow crescendo as of a cantilena) have in common with the skillful craftsmanship of Gothic architects? But is not Gothic architecture the triumph of dynamics? Or another question is raised: which is more mobile, which is more fluid—a Gothic cathedral or the ocean surge? What, if not architectonics, explains the miraculous equilibirum of the stanzas in which Villon entrusted his soul to the Trinity through the Virgin Mary—*Chambre de la divinité*—the nine legions of heaven. This is no anemic flight on the waxen wings of immortality; it is an architecturally founded Ascension, corresponding to the tiers in the Gothic cathedral. He who first proclaimed in architecture the dynamic equilibrium of the masses or first constructed the groined arch brilliantly expressed the psychological essence of feudalism. In the Middle Ages a man considered himself just as indispensable and just as bound to the edifice of his world as a stone in a Gothic structure, bearing with dignity the pressures of his neighbors and entering the common play of forces as an inevitable stake. To serve meant not only to act for the common good. In the Middle Ages a man unconsciously recognized the plain fact of his own existence as service, as a kind of heroic act. Villon, last born child of the Middle Ages, epigone of the feudal disposition, proved unreceptive to its ethical aspect, to its mutual guarantee! Gothic stability and morality were completely alien to him. On the other hand, greatly attracted by its dynamics, he elevated the Gothic to the heights of amoralism. Twice Villon received *Lettres de rémission* from the Kings of France, from Charles VII and from Louis XI. He was firmly convinced that he would receive a similar letter from God, pardoning him all his sins. Perhaps, in the spirit of his dry and rational mysticism, he extended the ladder of feudal jurisdiction into eternity, and perhaps, somewhere in his soul there lurked an untamed but profoundly feudal sense of a God of Gods...

"How well I know that I am not the son of an angel crowned with a diadem of stars or galaxies," he said of himself, of that poor Parisian student, capable of anything for the sake of a good dinner.

Such disclaimers are the equivalent of positive convictions.

* * *

Addendum to "François Villon"[12]

By its very nature French verse like no other verse adapts it-self to the finest rhythmical nuances. It is impossible to talk of iambs or trochees in French verse just as it is useless to divide it into feet. Indeed, each line of French poetry lives its own inde-pendent life as a result of the fundamental principle of French poetics that both length and stress are variables.

If one says that the charm of Villon's *Testaments* lies in their unexpected transitions, in the alternation of moods, like waves washing over one another, then one must find it equally in their rhythmical variety. Villon's *Testaments* are truly a rhythmical kaleidoscope. It would seem that he chose the *huitain* only in order to smash it to pieces. In reading Villon, it is difficult to be-lieve that one is dealing with a strict eight-syllable *huitain*. The rhythm always corresponds strictly to the content. In the frivolous part of his work, he juggles words both adroitly and carelessly, like a true juggler, and even resorts to *enjambement*:

> *Beaulx enfans, vous perdez la plus*
> *Belle rose de vo chappeau.*

2. MORNING OF ACMEISM

1

Given the immense emotional excitement associated with works of art, it is desirable that discussions of art display the greatest restraint. A work of art attracts the great majority only insofar as it illuminates the artist's world view. The artist, however, considers his world view a tool and an instrument, like a hammer in the hands of a stonemason, and his only reality is the work of art itself.

To exist is the artist's greatest pride. He desires no other paradise than existence, and when people speak to him of reality he only smiles bitterly, for he knows the infinitely more convincing reality of art. The spectacle of a mathematician who, without seeming to think about it, produces the square of some ten-digit number, fills us with a certain astonishment. But too often we fail to see that the poet raises a phenomenon to its tenth power, and the modest exterior of a work of art often deceives us with regard to the monstrously condensed reality contained within. In poetry this reality is the word as such. Right now, for instance, in expressing my thoughts as precisely as possible, but certainly not in a poetic manner, I am essentially speaking with my consciousness, not with the word. Deaf mutes can understand each other perfectly, and railroad signals perform a very complex function without recourse to the word. Thus, if one takes the sense as the content, everything else in the word must be regarded as a simple mechanical appendage that merely impedes the swift transmission of the thought. "The word as such" was born very slowly. Gradually, one after another, all the elements of the word were drawn into the concept of form. To this day the conscious sense, the Logos, is still taken erroneously and arbitrarily for the content. The Logos gains nothing from such an unnecessary honor. The Logos demands nothing more than to be considered on an equal footing with the other elements of the word. The Futurists, unable to cope with the conscious sense as creative material, frivolously threw it overboard and essentially repeated the crude mistake of their predecessors.

For the Acmeists the conscious sense of the word, the Logos, is just as magnificent a form as music is for the Symbolists.

And if, for the Futurists, the word as such is still down on its knees creeping, in Acmeism it has for the first time assumed a dignified upright position and entered the Stone Age of its existence.

2

The sharp edge of Acmeism is neither the stiletto nor the sting of Decadence. Acmeism is for those who, inspired by the spirit of building, do not like cowards renounce their own gravity, but joyously accept it in order to arouse and exploit the powers architecturally sleeping within. The architect says: I build, that indicates I am right. The consciousness of our rightness is dearer to us than anything else in poetry, and, rejecting the games[1] of the Futurists, for whom there is no greater pleasure than catching a difficult word on the end of a crochet hook, we introduce the Gothic[2] element into the relationship of words, just as Sebastian Bach established it in music.

What madman would agree to build if he did not believe in the reality of his material, the resistance of which he knew he must overcome? A cobblestone in the hands of an architect is transformed into substance, but a man is not born to build if he does not hear metaphysical proof in the sound of a chisel splitting rock. Vladimir Soloviev[3] experienced a peculiar prophetic horror before gray Finnish boulders. The mute eloquence of the granite mass startled him like sorcery. But Tyutchev's stone, which "having rolled down the mountain, lay in the valley, torn loose itself, or loosened by a sentient hand," is the word. The voice of matter in this unexpected fall sounds like articulate speech. Only architecture can answer this challenge. Reverently the Acmeists raise this mysterious Tyutchevian stone and make it the foundation stone of their own building.[4]

It was as if the stone thirsted after another existence. It revealed its own dynamic potential hidden within itself, as if it were begging admittance into the "groined arch" in order to participate in the joyous cooperative action of its fellows.

3

The Symbolists were poor stay-at-homes; they loved to travel, yet they felt unwell, uncomfortable in the cage of their own organisms or in that universal cage which Kant constructed with the aid of his categories.

Genuine piety before the three dimensions of space is the first condition of successful building: to regard the world neither as a burden nor as an unfortunate accident, but as a God-given palace. Indeed, what can you say about an ungrateful guest who lives off his host, takes advantage of his hospitality, all the while despising him to the depths of his soul, thinking only of how to deceive him? Building is possible only in the name of the "three dimensions," for they are the conditions of all architecture. That is why the architect must be a good stay-at-home, and the Symbolists were poor architects. To build means to conquer emptiness, to hypnotize space. The handsome arrow of the Gothic belltower rages because its function is to stab the sky, to reproach it for its emptiness.

4

We perceive what is particular in a man, that which makes him an individual, and we incorporate it into the far more significant concept of the organism. Acmeists share their love for the organism and for organization with the physiologically brilliant Middle Ages.[5] In chasing after refinement the nineteenth century lost the secret of genuine complexity.[6] What in the thirteenth century appeared to be the logical development of the concept of the organism—the Gothic cathedral—now has the esthetic effect of something monstrous: Notre Dame is the triumph of physiology, its Dionysian orgy.[7] We do not want to distract ourselves with a stroll through the "forest of symbols,"[8] because we have a denser, more virgin forest—divine physiology, the infinite complexity of our own dark organism.

The Middle Ages, defining the specific gravity of man in its own way, sensed and acknowledged it for each individual regardless of his merits. The title of *maître* was given readily and without hesitation. The humblest artisan, the lowest ranking cleric possessed the secret knowledge of his own true worth, of the devout dignity so characteristic of that epoch. Yes, Europe has passed through the labyrinth of fine open-work culture, when abstract being, completely unadorned personal existence, was valued as a heroic feat. From this stems the aristocratic intimacy uniting all people, which is so alien in spirit to the "equality and fraternity" of the French Revolution. There is no equality, there is no competition, there is only the complicity of all who conspire against emptiness and non-existence.

Love the existence of the thing more than the thing itself and your own existence more than yourself: that is Acmeism's highest commandment.

5

A=A: what a magnificent theme for poetry! Symbolism languished and yearned for the law of identity. Acmeism made it its slogan and proposed its adoption instead of the ambiguous *a realibus ad realiora.*[9]

The capacity for astonishment is the poet's greatest virtue.[10] Yet how can we not be astonished by the law of identity, the most fruitful of all poetic laws? Whoever has experienced reverence and astonishment before this law is a true poet. Hence, having recognized the sovereignty of the law of identity, poetry receives, absolutely and unconditionally, lifelong feudal claims over all existence. Logic is the kingdom of the unexpected. To think logically is to be perpetually astonished. We have come to love the music of proof. Logical connection for us is not some popular song about a finch, but a choral symphony, so difficult and so inspired that the conductor must exert all his energy to keep the performers under his control.

How convincing the music of Bach! What power of proof! The artist must prove and prove endlessly. The artist worthy of his calling cannot accept anything on faith alone, that is too easy, too dull... We cannot fly, we can ascend only those towers which we build ourselves.

6

The Middle Ages are very close to us because they possessed to an extraordinary degree the sense of boundary and partition. They never confused different levels, and treated the beyond with utmost restraint. A noble mixture of rationality and mysticism as well as a feeling for the world as a living equilibrium makes us kin to this epoch and encourages us to derive strength from works which arose on Romance soil around the year 1200.[11] And we will prove our rightness in such a way that in answer to us the entire chain of cause and effect, from alpha to omega, will shudder. And we will learn to bear "more easily and freely the mobile fetters of existence."

3. ON THE ADDRESSEE

I would like to know what it is about a madman which creates that most terrifying impression of madness. His dilated pupils, because they are blank and stare at you so absently, focussing on nothing in particular. His mad speech, because, even while speaking to you, the madman never takes you into account, nor even recognizes your existence, as if wishing to ignore your existence, since he is absolutely uninterested in you. What we fear most in a madman is that absolute and terrifying indifference which he displays toward us. Nothing strikes terror in a man more than another man who shows no concern for him whatsoever. Cultural pretense, that politeness by which we constantly affirm our interest in one another, holds a profound meaning for us all.

Normally, when a man has something to say, he goes to people, he seeks out an audience. Yet a poet does the opposite: he runs "to the shores of desert waves, to broad and resonant oaks."[1] The abnormal response is obvious... Suspicion of madness descends upon the poet. And people are right when they call a man mad who addresses his speech to inanimate objects, to nature, but never to his living brothers. And they would be within their rights to stand back terrified of the poet, as of a madman, if, indeed, his word were not actually addressed to anyone. But this is not the case.

The view of the poet as "God's bird"[2] is very dangerous and fundamentally false. There is no reason to believe that Pushkin had the poet in mind when he composed his song about the bird. But even in so far as Pushkin's bird is concerned, the matter is not all that simple. Before he commences to sing, the bird "hearkens to the voice of God." Obviously, the one who orders the bird to sing, listens to its song. The bird "flapped its wings and sang," because it was bound by a natural contract with God, an honor even the greatest poetic genius does not dare to dream of... To whom then does the poet speak? To this day, the question still plagues us; it is still extremely pertinent, because the Symbolists always avoided it, and never formulated it succinctly. By ignoring the contractual relationship, as it were, the mutuality which attends the act of speaking (for example: I am speaking: this means people are listening to me and listening to me for a reason, not out of politeness, but because they are committed to hear me out), Symbolism turned its attention exclusively to acoustics. It relinquished sound to the architecture of the spirit, but with its characteristic egoism, followed its meanderings under the archways of an alien psyche. Symbolism calculated the increase in fidelity produced by fine acoustics, and called it magic. In this respect, Symbolism brings to mind the French medieval proverb about "Prestre Martin," who simultaneously performed and attended mass. The Symbolist poet is not only a musician, he is Stradivarius himself, the great violin-maker, fastidiously calculating the proportions of the "sound-box," the psyche of the audience. Depending on these proportions, the stroke of the bow may produce a sound truly splendid in its fullness or weak and unconvincing. But, my friends, a piece of music has its own independent existence regardless of the performer, the concert hall, or the violin! Why then should the poet be so prudent and solicitous? More significant, where is that supplier of poet's needs, the supplier of living violins—the audience whose psyche is equivalent to the "shell" of Stradivarius's products? We do not know, nor will we ever know, where this audience is... François Villon wrote for the Parisian rabble of the mid-15th century, yet the charm of his poetry lives on today...

Every man has his friends. Why shouldn't the poet turn to his friends, to those who are naturally close to him? At a critical moment, a seafarer tosses a sealed bottle into the ocean waves, containing his name and a message detailing his fate. Wandering along the dunes many years later, I happen upon it in the sand. I read the message, note the date, the last will and testament of one who has passed on. I have the right to do so. I have not opened someone else's mail. The message in the bottle was addressed to its finder. I found it. That means, I have become its secret addressee.

> My gift is poor, my voice is not loud,
> And yet I live—and on this earth
> My being has meaning for someone:
> My distant heir shall find it
> In my verses; how do I know? my soul
> And his shall find a common bond,
> As I have found a friend in my generation,
> I will find a reader in posterity.[3]

Reading this poem of Baratynsky, I experience the same feeling I would if such a bottle had come into my possession. The ocean in all its vastness has come to its aid, has helped it fulfill its destiny. And that feeling of providence overwhelms the finder. Two equally lucid facts emerge from the tossing of the seafarer's bottle to the waves and from the dispatching of Baratynsky's poem. The message, just like the poem, was addressed to no one in particular. And yet both have addresses: the message is addressed to the person who happened across the bottle in the sand; the poem is addressed to "the reader in posterity." What reader of Baratynsky's poem would not shiver with joy or feel that twinge of excitement experienced sometimes when you are unexpectedly hailed by name.

Balmont asserted:

> I know no wisdom suitable for others,
> Only moments do I encase in my verse.
> In each transient moment I see worlds
> Changing in their iridescent play.
>
> Don't curse me, wisemen, what am I to you?
> A mere cloud overflowing with flame,
> A mere cloud, see, I shall float on
> Hailing all dreamers. But you I shall not hail.[4]

What a contrast between the unpleasant obsequious tone of these lines and the profound and modest dignity of Baratynsky's verse! Balmont seeks to vindicate himself, offering an apology, as it were. Unforgivable! Intolerable for a poet! The only thing which cannot be forgiven. After all, isn't poetry the consciousness of being right? Balmont expresses no such consciousness here. He has clearly lost his bearings. His opening line kills the entire poem. From the very outset the poet definitively declares that we hold no interest for him: "I know no wisdom suitable for others."

He doesn't suspect that we may pay him back in kind: if we hold no interest for you, you hold no interest for us. What do I care about your cloud when so many are floating by... At least genuine clouds don't taunt people. Balmont's rejection of the "addressee" is like a red line drawn through all his poetry, severely depreciating its value. In his verse, Balmont is always slighting someone, treating him brusquely, contemptuously. This "someone" is the secret addressee. Neither understood nor recognized by Balmont, he cruelly avenges him. When we converse with someone, we search his face for sanctions, for a confirmation of our sense of rightness. Even more so the poet. Yet the poet's precious consciousness of being right is frequently missing from Balmont's poetry because he lacks a constant addressee. Hence, those two unpleasant extremes in Balmont's poetry: obsequiousness and insolence. Balmont's insolence is artificial, contrived. His need to vindicate himself is downright pathological. He cannot utter the word "I" softly. He screams "I":

> I am a sudden crack
> I am a thunderclap breaking.[5]

On the scales of Balmont's poetry, the pan containing the "I" dips decisively and unjustly below the "Not-I." The latter is far too light. Balmont's blatant individualism is very unpleasant. As opposed to the quiet solipsism of Sologub, which is inoffensive, Balmont's individualism emerges at the expense of someone else's "I." Note how Balmont enjoys stunning his readers by turning abruptly to the intimate form of address. In this he resembles a nasty, evil hypnotist. Balmont's intimate "thou" never reaches the addressee; it shoots past its mark like an arrow released from a bow pulled too taut.

> As I have found a friend in my generation
> I will find a reader in posterity...

Baratynsky's piercing eye darts beyond his generation (yet in his generation he has friends) only to pause in front of an as yet unknown, but definite "reader." And anyone who happens across Baratynsky's poems feels himself to be that "reader," the chosen one, the one who is hailed by name... Why then should there not be a concrete, living addressee, a "representative of the age," why not a "friend in this generation"? I answer: appealing to a concrete addressee dismembers poetry, plucks its wings, deprives it of air, of the freedom of flight. The fresh air of poetry is the element of surprise. In addressing someone known, we can speak only of what is already known. This is a powerful, authoritative psychological law. Its significance for poetry cannot be underestimated.

Fear of a concrete addressee, of an audience of our "age," of a "friend in this generation," has doggedly pursued poets of all ages. And the greater the poet's genius, the more acutely he has suffered from this fear. Hence, the notorious hostility between the artist and society. What may be meaningful to the prose writer or essayist, the poet finds absolutely meaningless. The difference between prose and poetry may be defined as follows. The prose writer always addresses himself to a concrete audience, to the dynamic representatives of his age. Even when making prophecies, he bears his future contemporaries in mind. His subject matter brims over into the present, in keeping with the physical law of unequal levels. Consequently, the prose writer is compelled to stand "higher" than, to be "superior" to, society. Since instruction is the central nerve of prose, the prose writer requires a pedestal. Poetry is another matter. The poet is bound only to his providential addressee. He is not compelled to tower over his age, to appear superior to his society. Indeed, François Villon stood far below the median moral and intellectual level of the culture of the fifteenth century.

Pushkin's quarrel with the rabble may be viewed as an example of that antagonism between the poet and his concrete audience which I am trying to elucidate. Pushkin, with incredible dispassion, appealed to the rabble to vindicate itself. And, as it turned out, the rabble was not so wild and unenlightened. But then how did this very considerate rabble, imbued with the best intentions, wrong the poet? In the process of vindicating itself, one tactless phrase slipped from its tongue, overflowed the poet's cup of patience and kindled his enmity:

And here we are, all ears. . .[6]

What a tactless phrase! The obtuse vulgarity of these seemingly innocent words is obvious. Not without reason did the poet indignantly interrupt the rabble at just this point... The sight of a hand begging for alms is repulsive, but the sight of ears ready to listen may inspire others—an orator, a politician, a prose writer, anyone, that is, except the poet... Concrete people, the "philistines of poetry," will permit anyone "to offer them bold lessons." They are generally prepared to listen to anyone, as long as the poet designates a proper address: "to such and such a rabble." So it is that children and simple people feel flattered when they can read their names on the envelope of a letter. And there have been entire epochs when the charm and essence of poetry were sacrificed to this far from inoffensive demand. Such verse included the pseudo-civic poetry and the tedious lyrics of the 1880s. The civic or tendentious voice may be fine in itself, for example:

> You do not have to be a poet,
> But you are obliged to be a citizen.[7]

These lines are remarkable, flying on powerful wings toward a providential addressee. But put that Russian philistine of a particular decade, thoroughly familiar to us all, at his proper address, and those lines will immediately bore you.

Yes, when I address someone, I do not know whom I am addressing; furthermore, I do not care to know, nor do I wish to know, him. Without dialogue, lyric poetry cannot exist. Yet there is only one thing that pushes us into the addressee's embrace: the desire to be astonished by our own words, to be captivated by their originality and unexpectedness.[8] Logic is merciless. If I know the person I am addressing, I know in advance how he will react to my words, to whatever I say, and consequently, I will not succeed in being astonished in his astonishment, in rejoicing in his joy, in loving in his love. The distance of separation erases the features of the loved one. Only from a distance do I feel the desire to tell him something important, something I could not utter directly seeing his face before me as a known quantity. Allow me to formulate this observation more succinctly: our sense of communication is inversely proportional to our real knowledge of the addressee and directly proportional to our felt need to interest him in ourselves. Acoustics can take care of itself: we need not be concerned about it. Distance is another matter. Whispering to a neighbor is boring. But it is downright maddening to bore one's own soul (Nadson).[9] On the other hand, exchanging signals with the planet Mars (not fantasizing, of course) is a task worthy of a lyric poet. Here we run into Fyodor Sologub. In many ways, Sologub is a most interesting antipode to Balmont. Several qualities missing in Balmont's work abound in Sologub's poetry: for instance, love and admiration of the addressee, and the poet's consciousness of being right. These two remarkable characteristics of Sologub's poetry are closely related to that "distance of enormous dimensions" which he presumes lies between himself and his ideal "friend"—addressee:

> My mysterious friend, my distant friend,
> Behold.
> I am the cold and mournful
> Light at dawn...
> And so cold and mournful
> In the morning,
> My mysterious friend, my distant friend,
> I shall die.[10]

That these lines may reach their destination, perhaps hundreds of years are necessary, as many as a planet needs to send its light to another planet. Consequently, Sologub's lines continue to live long after they were written, as events, not merely as tokens of an experience which has passed.[11]

And so, although individual poems, such as epistles or dedications, may be addressed to concrete persons, poetry as a whole is always directed toward a more or less distant, unknown addressee, in whose existence the poet does not doubt, not doubting in himself. Metaphysics has nothing to do with this. Only reality can bring to life a new reality. The poet is no homunculus, and there is absolutely no basis for ascribing to him characteristics of spontaneous generation.

The point is very simply this: if we had no friends, we would not write them letters, and we would not take pleasure in the psychological freshness and novelty peculiar to this occupation.

4. REMARKS ON CHENIER[1]

The eighteenth century is like a dried-up lake: it has neither depth nor moisture—everything that was underwater has come to the surface. The people themselves were terrified by the transparency and emptiness of its values. *La Verité, la Liberté, la Nature, la Déité*, and especially *la Vertu*, provoke an almost syncopal dizziness of thought, like empty, transparent ponds. That century, which was compelled to walk along the sea floor, as on parquetry, turned out to be predominantly a century of morals. People were amazed by the most trivial moral truths, as if they were rare seashells. Human thought suffocated from a plethora of false truths but could not find peace. It was necessary to repeat them indefatigably since, apparently, they all proved to insufficiently effective.

The great principles of the eighteenth century were constantly in motion, in a state of mechanical flurry, like a Buddhist prayer wheel. For example, antiquity conceived of the Good as bounty or well-being; the inner emptiness of hedonism did not yet exist. The concepts of the Good, well-being, and health were merged into a single concept like a solid, homogeneous golden sphere.[2] There was no vacuum within this concept. This absolute character of classical morality, which is by no means imperative or hedonistic, even gives occasion to doubt the moral nature of this consciousness: is it not simply hygiene, that is, a prophylaxis of spiritual health?

The eighteenth century lost its direct link with the moral consciousness of antiquity. The pure, golden sphere no longer produced sounds of its own. Sounds were extracted from it by refined, exploitative devices, by considerations about the usefulness of pleasure and the pleasure of usefulness. This bankrupt consciousness simply could not maintain the idea of duty, and the idea was made manifest in the image "la Vertu romaine," more appropriate for supporting the equilibrium of bad tragedies than for governing man's spiritual life. Yes, the link with true antiquity was lost for the eighteenth century, yet the link with petrified forms of scholastic casuistry grew much stronger, so that the Age of Reason appears as a direct descendent of scholasticism with its rationalism, allegorical thinking, and personification of ideas, entirely in accord with Old French poetics. The Middle Ages[3] had its

own soul and an authentic knowledge of antiquity; indeed, it left
the Enlightenment far behind not only with regard to literacy, but
in its loving recreation of the Classical world. The Muses were unhappy around Reason; they were bored with it, although they acknowledged it reluctantly. All that was alive and healthy was di-
verted into trifles because they demanded less supervision, while a
child with seven governesses (Tragedy) grew up into a luxuriant
sterile flower precisely because the "great principles" leaned over
its cradle and nursed it so anxiously. The minor forms of poetry,
which fortunately escaped this fatal tutelage, will outlive the elevated forms grown sickly in its hands.

Chénier's poetic course is a departure, almost a flight, from
the "great principles" to the living waters of poetry, not to antiquity, but to a completely modern *Weltanschauung.*

In Chénier's poetry there seems to be a religious and, perhaps, a childishly naive presentiment of the nineteenth century.[4]

* * *

The Alexandrine[5] can be traced back to antiphony, that is,
to the responsive, alternate singing of the two halves of the chorus,
each vying simultaneously in the same amount of allotted time to
express its own will. However, this equality is violated when one
voice yields part of its allotted time to the other voice. Time is the
pure and unadorned substance of the Alexandrine. The distribution of time along the grooves of verb, noun, and epithet comprises the autonomous inner life of the Alexandrine line, regulates
its breathing, its tension and its degree of saturation. As a result
a sort of "struggle for time" takes place among the elements of
the line and each one, like a sponge, tries to absorb into itself the
greatest possible quantity of time, while contending with the
claims of the others. The triad of noun, verb, and epithet in the
Alexandrine line is not a stable compound because one absorbs
the contents of the other: the verb may take on the meaning and
weight of the noun, the epithet may bear the meaning of action,
that is, of the verb, and so forth.

This instability of relationships between the separate parts of
speech, their susceptibility to fusion and chemical transformation
even when the syntax remains absolutely clear and transparent, is
extremely characteristic of Chénier's style. The strictest hierarchy

of epithet, verb, and noun on the monotonous canvas of Alexandrine versification delineates the image and imparts prominence to the alternation of paired lines.

Chénier belonged to the generation of French poets for whom syntax was a golden cage from which they would not dream of escaping. This golden cage[6] was definitively constructed by Racine and furnished like a splendid palace. The syntactic freedom of the poets of the Middle Ages—Villon, Rabelais, indeed the whole of Old French syntax—was left behind, while the romantic turbulence of Chateaubriand and Lamartine had not yet begun. The golden cage was guarded by an evil parrot—Boileau. Chénier was faced with the problem of creating absolute poetic freedom within the bounds of an extremely narrow canon, and he solved this problem. The sense of each individual line as a living, indivisible organism, and the sense of verbal hierarchy within the confines of this integral line are particularly characteristic of French poetry.[7]

Chénier loved and understood this flexible individual line: he admired the line of Bion's "Epithalamium,"[8] and he preserved its spirit.

* * *

It is in the nature of the new French poetry, founded by Clement Marot,[9] father of the Alexandrine, to weigh each word before it is uttered. But Romantic poetics presupposes an outburst, unexpectedness,[10] it seeks after effect, unanticipated acoustics, and it itself knows what the song may cost. From the powerful, harmonic wave of Lamartine's "Lake" to the ironic ditty of Verlaine, Romantic poetry affirms the poetics of the unexpected. The laws of poetry sleep in its larynx and all of Romantic poetry, like a necklace of dead nightingales, will not convey, will not betray its secrets, does not know its legacy. A dead nightingale cannot teach anyone how to sing. Chénier ingeniously found the middle road between the Classical and Romantic manner.

* * *

Pushkin's generation had already transcended Chénier because there was a Byron.[11] The same generation could not simultaneously conceive of "the sound of the new, marvelous lyre, the sound of Byron's lyre" and of the abstract, externally cold and rational poetry of Chénier, which was still filled with Classical frenzy.

* * *

That by which Chénier still spiritually burned—the *Encyclopedia*, Deism, the rights of man—was for Pushkin already the past, pure literature:

> ... Diderot sat on his rickety tripod,
> Flung off his wig, closed his eyes enraptured,
> And preached ...

Pushkin's formula—the union of mind and the furies—combines the two elements of Chénier's poetry. The age was such that no one could escape obsession. Only its direction changed, at times toward the power of the iambics of political exposé.[12]

* * *

The iambic spirit descends on Chénier like a Fury. Imperative. Dionysian. Obsessive.

* * *

Chénier would never have said: "You live life for life's sake." He was completely alien to the Epicureanism of the age, to the Olympianism of lords and nobles.

* * *

Pushkin is more objective and more dispassionate than Chénier in his appraisal of the French Revolution. Where Chénier feels only hatred and acute pain, Pushkin knows contemplation and historical perspective:

> ... Do you remember Trianon and the noisy
> merrymaking?

* * *

Allegorical poetics. Very broad, and by no means fleshless allegories, including "Liberty, Equality, Fraternity," are almost living persons and interlocutors for the poet and his age. He catches their features and feels their warm breath.

* * *

In "Jeu de paume"[13] you can observe a struggle between the journalistic theme and the iambic spirit. Nearly the entire poem is a captive of the newspaper. A typical example of journalistic style:

> . . . *Pères d'un peuple, architectes de lois!*
> *Vous qui savez fonder d'une main ferme et sûre*
> *Pour l'homme un code solennel . . .*

* * *

The Classical idealization of the contemporary scene: the crowd of class representatives heading into the hall accompanied by the people is compared with the pregnant Latona, just about to become a mother.

> . . . *Comme Latone enceinte, et déjà presque mère,*
> *Victime d'un jaloux pouvoir*
> *Dans asile flottait, courait la terre entière . . .*

* * *

The dissolution of the world into rationally acting forces. Only man is irrational. The entire poetics of civic poetry, the search for curbs—*frein*:

> . . . *l'oppresseur n'est jamais libre . . .*

* * *

What are Chénier's poetics? Perhaps he has not one but several in different periods or, rather, moments of poetic consciousness?

Two aspects of his poetry are clearly discernible: the pastoral

(Bucoliques: Idylles) and the grandiose construction of an almost "Scientific poetry."

Does not Chénier's stay in England confirm the influence on him of Montesquieu and English common law? Cannot something like the following line be found in his work, "Here a fiery on-slaught, and there a stern rebuff . . ."[14] or is his abstract mind alien to Pushkinian practicality?

* * *

Although completely oblivious to the Old French literary tradition, some of its devices continued to be recreated automatically, having entered the bloodstream.

* * *

After the Classical elegy with all its accessories—the earthenware jug, the reed, the stream, the beehive, the rosebush, the swallow, and the friends and interlocutors, and the witnesses and spies of the lovers—it is strange to find in Chénier the predilection for a completely mundane elegy in the spirit of the Romantics; almost Musset-like, as, for example, the third elegy "A Camille"—a mundane love letter, delicately unaffected and agitated, where the epistolary form is almost free from mythological conventions, and the living, conversational speech of the thinking and feeling man of the Romantic age flows freely.

> . . . *Et puis d'un ton charmant ta lettre me demande*
> *Ce que je veux de toi, ce que je te commande!*
> *Ce que je veux!? dis-tu. Je veux que ton retour*
> *Te paraisse bien lent; je veux que nuit et jour*
> *Tu m'aimes! (Nuit et jour hèlas! je me tourmente).*
> *Présente au milieu d'eux, sois seule, sois absente;*
> *Dors en pensant à moi! rêve-moi près de toi;*
> *Ne vois que moi sans cesse, et sois toute avec moi.*

In these lines one can hear Tatiana's letter to Onegin, that same domestic quality of the language, that same tender careless-ness, better than any solicitude: it is just as much at the heart of the French language, just as spontaneous in French as Tatiana's letter is in Russian. Through the crystal of Pushkin's lines, these lines sound almost Russian to us:

> . . . The pink wafer dries
> On the inflamed tongue.

Thus, in poetry the national boundary is destroyed and the elements of one language call to those of another through the voices of space and time, for all languages are bound in a fraternal union which is strengthened in the freedom and domesticity of each, and within this freedom they are fraternally related, and they greet each other as members of a single family.

* * *

Addendum[15] to "Remarks on Chénier"

"O Eta, mont ennobli . . ."[16] is from *Fragments d'Idylles.*

Throughout this brief poem an intense power struggle ensues between verb, noun and epithet for effective functional power, for control over time, over the tonic measure of the line, for hegemony over image and action.[17] If we note the number of epithets in each line in the order in which they appear, from first to last, we come up with the following picture: on the average, the standard Alexandrine line contains no more than two epithets; here, lines 3, 4, 6, 7, 9, 10 and 13 contain one epithet each; lines 8, 11 and 12 contain zero epithets, that is, in inverse proportion to increased action the epithet's function is reduced. But the culminating lines present a kind of hiatus for the epithet, for lines 12 and 13 are divided by a pause.

Line 11 is particularly noteworthy for its lack of epithets: "Attend sa récompense et l'heure d'être un Dieu." ...It is supported by the object which follows the conjunction *et* and is dependent on the verb *attend—l'heure d'être un Dieu.* The noun, *l'heure,* fulfills the role of verb, that is, the noun is saturated by pure action and its temperature shows it is already like a noun fused into a verb.[18]

Chénier's elegies contain great internal variety: the verbs

nouns, and epithets are constantly at battle with each other in their primal and natural meanings; they "exhibit hiatuses" or take over the function of another part of speech.

Let's take for example the first half of line 12:

Le vent souffle et mugit . . .

Here two verbs—*souffle* and *mugit*—definitely function as epithets, and the construction of the phrase is nothing more than a masked sentence of two epithets—*whistling* and *moaning*, in apposition to the wind.

Line 10: "Et l'oeil au ciel, la main sur la massue antique" is characterized by the activity of the noun—*massue*—*club*. The noun is taken in its active verbal meaning, more as potential for action and as intense preparedness of the hero's muscular power than as a thing.

In Line 9: "Etend du vieux lion la dépouille héroïque," a hiatus occurs between the noun and the epithet, *héroïque*, which carries the function of the verb and the noun. The epithet functions as a verb because the true, exposed meaning of the phrase is: Hercules "acts heroically" stretching out the skin.

Thus, the variety of stylistic ploys compensates for the lack of syntactic flexibility in the Alexandrine. A way out of the golden cage of the Alexandrine line is found and it is very much a French way out.

Lines very close to Pushkin's:

And here we are, all ears

in "The Poet and Mob," are expressed by Homer in "L'Aveugle"[19]:

Chante . . .
Amuse notre ennui; tu rendra grâce aux dieux . . .

. . . And we will obey thee.

5. PETER CHAADAEV

I

The imprint left by Chaadaev[1] on the consciousness of Russian society is so deep and indelible that inadvertently one asks whether it was not made by a diamond drawn across glass. It is all the more remarkable that Chaadaev was not a public figure, neither a professional writer nor a tribune. He was a "private" man, what is called a *"privatier"* in every sense of the term. Yet he seemed to realize that his personality belonged not to himself but to posterity, and thus he treated it with a certain humility: whatever he did, he seemed to be serving, "fulfilling a holy obligation."

All those qualities which were lacking in Russian life and which it did not even suspect existed happened to come together in Chaadaev's personality: enormous inner discipline, lofty intellectualism, moral architectonics, and the chill of a mask, a medal, with which a man encases himself when he realizes that he is no more than a form in Time and prepares in advance the mold of his immortality.

Still more unusual for Russia was Chaadaev's dualism, the sharp distinction he drew between matter and spirit. In a young country, a country of half-animated matter and half-dead spirit, the gray-haired antinomy of the inert clod and the organizing idea was almost unknown. In the eyes of Chaadaev, Russia still belonged entirely to the unorganized world. He considered himself flesh of the flesh of this Russia, and he looked upon himself as raw material. The results were astonishing. The Idea organized his personality, not only his intellect, and gave his personality a structure, an architecture, subordinated it entirely and, as a reward for absolute subordination, granted it absolute freedom.[2]

The profound harmony, the virtual fusion of the moral and intellectual element, gave Chaadaev's personality its particular stability. It is difficult to say where Chaadaev's intellectual personality ends and where his moral personality begins, they are so nearly fused. For him, the strongest demands of the intellect were simultaneously the greatest moral necessity.

I am speaking of the demands for unity that determine the

structure of select minds.

"What shall we talk about?" he asked Pushkin in one of his letters. "I have, as you know, only one idea, and if some other ideas should accidentally turn up in my brain, they would immediately stick to the one idea: does that suit you?"

What is the celebrated "mind" of Chaadaev, that "proud" intellect, respectfully glorified by Pushkin[3] and hissed at by the provocative Yazykov, if not the fusion of the moral and the intellectual principle, a fusion so characteristic of Chaadaev and along which lines his personality matured.

With this profound, ineradicable demand for unity, for higher historical synthesis, Chaadaev was born in Russia. A native of the plains, he wanted to breathe the air of Alpine summits and, as we see, he found it in his own breast.

II

In the West there is unity! Ever since these words flared up in Chaadaev's consciousness, he ceased to belong to himself and was torn away forever from "domestically oriented" individuals and concerns. He had enough courage to tell Russia to her face the terrible truth—that she was cut off from universal unity, excommunicated from history, from God's "teacher of the people."

The fact is that Chaadaev's conception of history excludes the possibility of any *access* to the historical path. In keeping with this conception, one could be on the historical path only prior to any beginning. History was Jacob's ladder, down which angels descended from heaven to earth. It must be called sacred due to the continuity of the spirit of grace that inhabits it. Therefore Chaadaev did not utter a word about "Moscow, the Third Rome." In this idea he could see only a sickly fantasy of Kievan monks. Neither the will alone nor good intentions are sufficient to "begin" history anew. Indeed, the idea is unthinkable: *to begin* it. There is not enough continuity, unity. Unity cannot be created, invented, or learned. In its absence one has, at best, not history but "progress"—the mechanical movement of a clock hand and not the sacred bond and succession of events.[4]

As if enchanted, Chaadaev kept staring at the one point where this unity had become flesh, carefully preserved, bequeathed from generation to generation. "But the Pope! The Pope! Well, what of it? Is he not simply an idea, a pure abstraction? Look at this old man being carried in his palanquin under a canopy, wearing his triple crown, today just as a thousand years ago, as if nothing in the world had changed: indeed, where is the man here? Is this not an omnipotent symbol of time—not of that time which passes, but of that which is immobile, through which everything else passes, but which itself stands imperturbable, and in which and by means of which everything is perfected?"

Such was the Catholicism of the snob of Zamoskvorechie.

III

And so, in August of 1825, in a little seaside village near Brighton, a foreigner appeared whose bearing combined the solemnity of a bishop with the correctness of a worldly mannequin.

That was Chaadaev, fleeing Russia on a chance ship, with the haste of someone whose life was threatened; unburdened by external constraints, and yet he firmly intended never to return home.

A sickly, nervous, somewhat odd patient of foreign doctors, who had never known human relationships other than those of a purely intellectual nature, hiding the terrible confusion of his spirit even from close friends, Chaadaev had come to see his West, the kingdom of history and majesty, the birthplace of the spirit embodied in the Church and in the architecture.

This strange journey, which took two years of Chaadaev's life, two years about which we know very little indeed, sooner resembles agony in the wilderness than a pilgrimage; and then Moscow, a wooden mansion, "The Apology of a Madman," and the long, measured years of preaching in the English Club.[5]

Had Chaadaev grown weary? Had his Gothic thought resigned itself and ceased to raise its lancet towers to the sky?[6] No, Chaadaev had not resigned himself, although time's blunt file had touched even his thoughts.[7]

Oh, legacy of a thinker! Precious scraps! Fragments that end precisely where continuity is most wanted, grandiose beginnings of what we do not know—what is this: the outline of a plan or its fulfillment? In vain the conscientious researcher sighs over what is lost, over missing links: they, too, never existed, they were never lost—the fragmentary form of the *Philosophical Letters* is internally substantiated, as is their essential character of an extended introduction.

To understand the form and spirit of the *Philosophical Letters*, it is necessary to imagine that Russia serves as their vast and awesome canvas. The gaping wasteland among the well-known, written fragments is the missing thought about Russia.

It is better not to mention "The Apology." It was not there, of course, that Chaadaev stated his thoughts about Russia.

And like a hopeless, flat plain, the final, unfinished sentence of "The Apology" unfolds, that dismal, alluring beginning that promises nothing after so much has already been said: "There is one fact that reigns imperiously over our historical progress, which runs through all of history like a red thread, which encompasses, in a way, all its philosophy, which manifests itself in all epochs of our social life and defines its character. . . . That is—the geographical fact. . . ."

One can learn from the *Philosophical Letters* only that Russia was the cause of Chaadaev's thought.[8] What he thought about Russia remains a mystery. In inscribing the beautiful words: "Truth is dearer than the Motherland," Chaadaev did not discover their prophetic meaning. Yet is not this "Truth" an awesome spectacle, surrounded on all sides by a strange and alien "Motherland," as by some sort of chaos?

Let us attempt to develop the *Philosophical Letters* as if they were a negative photographic plate. Perhaps precisely those places that remain light will prove to be about Russia.

IV

There is a great Slavic dream about the cessation of history in the Western sense of the word, as Chaadaev understood it. This is the dream of universal spiritual disarmament, which is to be followed by a certain condition called "peace." The dream of spiritual disarmament has so possessed our domestic horizon that the ordinary Russian intellectual cannot otherwise conceive of the ultimate goal of progress, except in light of this unhistorical "peace." Tolstoi himself quite recently addressed mankind with an appeal to cease the false and unnecessary comedy of history and begin "simply" to live. "Simplicity" is what makes the idea of "peace" so attractive:

> Pathetic man . . .
> What does he desire? . . . The sky is clear,
> There is space enough for everyone under the sky.

Because of their uselessness, secular and divine hierarchies are being eliminated forever. The Church, the State, and the Law are disappearing from our consciousness like the absurd chimeras with which man populated the "simple" world, "God's" world, through idleness and stupidity. And at last man and the universe are left alone together without tiresome intermediaries.

> Opposite the sky, on earth,
> An old man lived in a village . . .[9]

Chaadaev's thought is a strict perpendicular confronting traditional Russian thinking. Chaadaev fled this formless paradise like the plague.[10]

Some historians saw the dominant tendency of Russian history in colonization, in the attempt to settle in as much freedom as possible over as vast an expanse as possible.

A parallel to this external colonization can be seen in the great endeavor to populate the outer world with ideas, values, and images, an endeavor which, for centuries, has been the agony and the ecstasy of the West, which has plunged its peoples into the labyrinth of history where they wander to this day.

There, in the forest of the social church,[11] where Gothic pine needles admit no light other than the light of an idea, Chaadaev's primary thought, his mute thought about Russia, took shelter and ripened.

Chaadaev's West bore no resemblance to the weathered paths of civilization. In the fullest sense of the word, he discovered his own West. Indeed, the foot of man had not yet stepped into these impenetrable thickets of culture.

V

Chaadaev's thought is national in its sources, national even where it flows into Rome. Only a Russian could discover this West, which is far denser and more concrete than the historical West itself. By virtue of this right Chaadaev, a Russian, stepped onto the sacred soil of a tradition to which he was not bound by heritage.[12] There, where everything is necessity, where every stone slumbers covered by the patina of time and enveloped in the firmament, Chaadaev carried moral freedom, the gift of the Russian earth, its finest flower. This freedom is worth the majesty petrified in architectural forms, it is as valuable as everything the West has created in the realm of material culture, and I see that the Pope himself, "that old man, being carried in his palanquin under a canopy, wearing his triple crown," has arisen to greet this freedom.

Chaadaev's thought can best be characterized as national-synthetic. Synthetic nationality does not bow down before national self-consciousness, but rises above it as sovereign individuality, independent and therefore national.

Contemporaries were astonished by Chaadaev's pride, and he himself believed that he was one of the elect. An aura of sacred solemnity enveloped him, and even children sensed the significance of his presence, although he did not deviate in any way from the conventional. He felt himself to be elect, the vessel of true nationality, but the nation was no longer a proper judge!

What a striking contrast to "Nationalism," that poverty of the spirit with its persistent appeals to the tribunal of the rabble!

For Chaadaev, Russia had only one thing to offer: moral freedom, the freedom of choice. Never in the West had it been realized with such grandeur, in such purity and fullness. Chaadaev took it as his holy staff and set off for Rome.[13]

I think that the country and the people have already justified themselves if they have created even one completely free man who is able to make use of his freedom.

When Boris Godunov, anticipating Peter's idea, sent young Russians abroad, none of them returned. They did not return for the simple reason that there is no road back from being to non-being, that they would have suffocated in stuffy Moscow once having tasted the immortal spring of undying Rome.

But after all, the first doves did not return to the ark.

Chaadaev was the first Russian who had actually lived in the West ideologically, and found the road back. His contemporaries sensed this instinctively and greatly valued Chaadaev's presence among them.

They could point to him with superstitious respect, as they once pointed to Dante: "He was there, he saw—and he returned."

And how many of us have spiritually emigrated to the West! How many are there among us who are living unconsciously divided, who physically are here, but who spiritually remained there!

Chaadaev signifies a new, deepened understanding of nationality as the supreme flowering of national individuality, and of Russia as the source of absolute moral freedom.

Having endowed us with inner freedom, Russia offers us a choice, and those who make this choice are true Russians, no matter what they affiliate themselves with. But woe unto those who, after circling their parental nest, faintheartedly return.

6. PUSHKIN AND SCRIABIN (FRAGMENTS)

Pushkin[1] and Scriabin[2] are two transformations of the same sun, two transformations of the same heart.[3] Twice the death of an artist has united the Russian people and lighted a sun above them. They served as an example of a collective[4] Russian death, they died a *full* death, as some people live full lives, for in dying, their individuality expanded to the dimensions of a national symbol, and the sun-heart of the dying man remained forever at the zenith of suffering and glory.

I wish to speak of Scriabin's death as the supreme act of his creative activity.[5] It seems to me that the death of an artist should not be excluded from the chain of his creative achievements, but should be viewed as its final, closing link. Seen from this wholly Christian point of view, Scriabin's death astonishes us. It is not only remarkable as the fantastic posthumous growth of the artist in the eyes of the masses,[6] but also serves, as it were, as the source of his creative work, as its teleological cause. If one removes the shroud of death from around this creative life, that life will flow freely from its cause, from death, and it will surround death as it surrounds its own sun, and will consume its light.

Pushkin was buried at night. He was buried secretly. The marble cathedral of St. Isaac's, that splendid sarcophagus, never received the poet's sun-filled body. The sun was placed in its coffin at night and the sledrunners scraped the frozen January ground as they bore the poet's remains away for the funeral.

I recall this picture of Pushkin's funeral so as to arouse in your memory the image of the night sun, the image of Euripides's last Greek tragedy—the vision of ill-fated Phaedra.

In the fateful hours of purification and storm, we raised Scriabin above us, Scriabin whose sun-heart burns above us, but alas!—his is not the sun of redemption but the sun of guilt.[7] In declaring Scriabin her symbol in a time of World War, Phaedra—Russia...

...Time can go backward: witness the entire course of recent history which, with a frightening force, has turned away from Christianity toward Buddhism and theosophy...[8]

There is no unity! "There are many worlds, all of them

arranged in orbits, one god reigning over another." What is this: delirium or the end of Christianity?

There is no individuality![9] Your "I" is a transient condition, you have many souls and many lives! What is this: delirium or the end of Christianity?

There is no time! The Christian calendar is endangered, the fragile reckoning of the years of our era has been lost[10] —time is rushing backwards with a roaring splash like the dammed up waters of mountain falls—and the new Orpheus flings his lyre into the seething foam: there is no more art...

Scriabin is the next stage of Russian Hellenism after Pushkin, the most extreme revelation of the Hellenistic nature of the Russian spirit possible. Scriabin's great value for Russia and for Christianity derives from his being a *mad Hellene.* Scriabin provides the link between Hellas and those Russian sectarians who burned themselves in their coffins. In any case, he is much closer to them than to the Western Theosophists. Scriabin's chiliasm expresses a purely Russian passion for salvation; the madness with which he expressed this passion is his legacy from the Ancient world.[11]

· ·

...Christian art is always based on the great idea of redemption.[12] It is an "imitation of Christ" infinitely varied in all its manifestations, an eternal return to the single creative act that began our historical era. Christian art is free. It is "art for art's sake" in its fullest meaning. No necessity of any kind, not even the highest, darkens its bright inner freedom, for its prototype, that which it imitates, is the very redemption of the world by Christ. Thus, neither sacrifice, nor redemption in art, but rather the free and joyous imitation of Christ is the keystone of Christian esthetics. Art cannot be sacrifice, because a sacrifice has already been made; it cannot be redemption because the world, along with the artist, has already been redeemed. What remains? Joyous communion with God, like some game played by the Father and his children, some blind-man's bluff or hide-and-seek of the spirit! The divine illusion of redemption in Christian art is explained precisely by this game in which the Divinity plays with us, allowing us to wander the pathways of mystery so that we might happen upon salvation on our own, as it were, having experienced catharsis, redemption in art. Christian artists are like men free of the idea of redemption, neither its slaves nor preachers. Our entire two-thousand-year-old culture, thanks to the marvelous charity of Christianity, is *the world's release into freedom* for the sake of play, for spiritual joy, for the free "imitation of Christ."

Christianity adopted a completely free relationship to art which no human religion either before or since has been able to do.

In nourishing art, in surrendering to it its flesh, in offering it the supremely real fact of redemption as an unshakable meta-physical foundation, Christianity demanded nothing in return. Thus the danger of inner impoverishment poses no threat to Christian culture. It is inexhaustible, infinite, for in triumphing over time, it repeatedly condenses grace into magnificent clouds from which it pours forth in life-giving rain. There is no way to sufficiently emphasize the fact that European culture owes its eternal, unfading freshness to the mercy of Christianity with re-spect to art.

Research into the realm of Christian dynamics had not yet been undertaken,—that is, into the spirit's activity in art as the free self-affirmation of the elemental fact of redemption,—in par-ticular, music.

In the ancient world music was considered a destructive ele-ment. The Hellenes feared flutes and Phrygian harmony, believing music to be dangerous and seductive, and Terpander[13] had to sur-mount great difficulties fighting for each new string of his cithara. The distrust of music as some dark and suspicious element was so great that the state took music under its own supervision, making it a state monopoly. And musical harmony became synonymous with eunomy; it became both the means and model for maintain-ing support for the political order, for maintaining civic harmony. Nevertheless, even in that form the Hellenes did not allow music any independence: the word served them as the requisite anti-dote, the faithful sentinel, and the constant companion of music. *Pure* music was unknown to the Hellenes; it belongs completely to Christianity. The mountain lake of Christian music grew calm only after the profound transformation which turned Hellas into Europe.

Christianity did not fear music. The Christian world smiled as it spoke to Dionysus: "All right, try it, just order your Maenads to tear me to pieces: I am wholeness, I am individuality, I am indivisible unity!" This confidence in the final triumph of individuality, integral and unharmed, is so powerful in the new music that I would say confidence in individual salvation enters Christian music as an overtone, clothing the sonority of Beethoven with the white marble of Sinaitic glory.

The voice is individuality. The piano is a Siren. Scriabin's break with the voice, his great passion for the Siren of pianism, signals the loss of the Christian sense of individuality, of the musical "I am." The wordless, strangely mute chorus of Prometheus continues as that very same seductive Siren.[14]

Beethoven's Catholic joy, the synthesis of the Ninth Symphony, that "triumph of white glory," was unattainable to Scriabin. In this sense Scriabin broke with Christian music to follow his own path...

. . . .

The spirit of Greek tragedy awakened in music. Music completed its cycle and returned from whence it came: Phaedra once again calls out to her nurse; Antigone again demands a proper burial and a libation for her beloved brother's body.

Something has happened to music, some wind has swooped down to break the dry and resonant "musical reeds." Again we demand a chorus, the murmur of the "thinking reed"[15] bores us... We played with music for a long, long time, never suspecting its inherent dangers; and while (perhaps out of boredom) we invented a myth to beautify its existence, music left us a new myth—not invented, but born, born of the sea and the sky, of royal blood, the legitimate heir of the myths of antiquity—the myth of long forgotten Christianity.

. . . .

...the vineyards of old Dionysus: I imagine closed eyes and a slight, small but triumphant head, tilted barely upward. It is the muse of memory—the light-footed Mnemosyne, the eldest in the circle of dancers. The mask of oblivion slips from her slight, fragile face, her features come into view; memory triumphs even at the price of death! To die is to remember, to remember is to die... To remember at all costs! To conquer oblivion even at the price of death: that is Scriabin's motto, that is the heroic aspiration of his art![16] It is in this sense that I meant Scriabin's death is the supreme act of his creativity, for it illuminates him with a blinding and unexpected light.[17]

. . . .

...finished—the war was at its peak. Anyone who senses the Hellene in himself must be on his guard now, just as he was two thousand years ago.[18] You cannot Hellenize the world once and for all the way you can paint a house. The Christian world is an organism, a living body. The fabric of our world is renewed through death. We must struggle against the barbarism of our new life, for in the new life which is flourishing, death is unvanquished! As long as death exists in the world, Hellenism *will exist*, for Christianity *Hellenizes death...* Hellenism, impregnated with death,[19] is Christianity. The seed of death, having fallen on the soil of Hellas, miraculously flourished: our entire culture has grown from this seed;[20] we reckon our history from the moment when the soil of Hellas accepted that seed. Rome was infertile because the soil of Rome is rocky, Rome being Hellas devoid of grace.[21]

Scriabin's art is directly connected with the historical task of Christianity that I call the Hellenization of death, and through that task it acquires its profound meaning.

. . . .

...there is music which contains in itself the atoms of our being. Just as pure melody *(melos)* corresponds to the unique feeling of individuality as it was known in Hellas, so harmony characterizes the complex post-Christian sense of the "I." For the world not implicated in the Fall, harmony was a kind of forbidden fruit. The metaphysical essence of harmony was most closely linked with the Christian concept of time.[22] Harmony as eternity crystallized, harmony contained in a cross-section of time, in that cross-section of time which knows only Christianity...the mystics energetically reject the idea of eternity in time,[23] assuming that this cross-section is perceptible only to the righteous, affirming that eternity is the Kantian category cloven by the Seraph's sword. The center of gravity of Scriabin's music lies in harmony: harmonic architectonics...

. . . .

7. S. GORODETSKY.[1] *OLD NESTS: TALES AND STORIES (STARYE GNEZDA. POVESTI I RASSKAZY).*[2] PUBLISHED BY A.S. SUVORIN, ST. PETERSBURG, 1913.

Gorodetsky's most recent book of stories leaves a twofold impression. The poet's free flight of spiritual life, his mature and ardent love for Russia, is combined with a despondent submissiveness to the clichés of our country's fiction. The reader is quite familiar with its themes: the deterioration of gentry estates, the story of the prodigal son, discord and decay in a prosperous peasant family. This book is superior to others of its kind only because it contains a spark of keen observation, occasional wit and unexpected stylistic inspiration, and likewise because it is not blindly partial to one particular social class or estate. If the author does have a preference, it is for children: "dear, darling beasts, our bare-legged future."

In the story "Solitary Path"[3] which, incidentally, is the best in the book, a child's vague attraction to death is excellently depicted: the schoolboy Mitya slowly poisons himself with vinegar and confides his secret, under a terrible oath, to the little girls Zoya and Raya, who run out onto a mill dike, getting their light-colored slippers dirty, and throw their breakfast into the water as the first step toward non-being.

Gorodetsky does not create a coherent, artistic world in his prose. Russian reality, not having been refined in the crucible of artistic contemplation, has a somewhat nightmarish appearance in his stories.

It seems that with time the author realized that it is impossible for the narrator of prose to gaze directly into the innermost recesses of his characters, and he therefore left it up to his readers to make conjectures based on purposeful words, gestures, and situations fused together by the writer.

8. JACK LONDON.[1] *COLLECTED WORKS.* INTRODUCTION BY LEONID ANDREEV. TRANSLATED BY A.N. KUDRYATSEVA. ST. PETERSBURG: N.N. MIKHAILOV'S "PROMETHEUS" PUBLISHING HOUSE, 1912.

A favorable testimonial by Leonid Andreev[2] appears on the cover of Jack London's *Collected Works.* If the publisher had intended to solicit the opinion of some contemporary professor of "poor taste," he could not have made a wiser choice. Andreev calls London a "fresh" new talent, wielding epithets in his usual feeble way; such an epithet is far more applicable to butter than to a testimonial to a literary gift. Jack London's unrestrained and robust character is hardly suitable to the taste of the anemic Russian philistine: his heroes are distinguished by their enthusiasm for living above the Arctic Circle, by their iron constitutions, by their capacity for drinking whisky instead of water, and so on. However, the relationship between this type of fictional savage-hero and the newest, purely American advances in technology is undeniable. In the realm of technical progress, the human organism *cum* machine occupies a back seat, whereas the emphasis on sports in conjunction with various ideals of physical well-being go a long way to meet this technical deficiency of contemporary life head on. With his Yankee sagacity, Jack London patented the ideal of the new man long before his type was actually realized through natural selection and sports. The high speed Arctic runner who wagered a bet to run 2000 miles in 60 days at -90° C *(Son of the Sun),* or the planter, sick with dysentery, who by sheer force of will prevailed over the mob of cannibals on the Solomon Islands *(The Adventure)* are magnificent human specimens. We must indeed be fair to Jack London: the fantastic courage of his heroes is occasionally plausible and sometimes inspires respect. Jack London serves as a good example of what an artistically sterile and spiritually weak writer can achieve if he is in concord with the instincts and precepts of his race. The apparent absence of sentimentality in the Anglo-Saxon world outlook combined with his sense of rigorous efficiency with regard to life is most appealing to the soft Slavic soul. The genius of the Anglo-Saxon race, about which London loves to speak, protects him and creates for his readers an illusion of artistic talent. However, the artistic significance of

London's work must be measured not by the depth of thought expressed by the author, but by the involuntary spiritual exhalations creating the atmosphere of his literary work. The most ordinary spiritual void surrounds Jack London's adventures, recalling a similar void which envelops the journalistic feuilleton or Sir Arthur Conan Doyle's detective stories. Jack London, like other Anglo-American writer-speculators, artificially arouses sharp curiosity at the same time that he seeks to satisfy that curiosity completely and conscientiously. If the first page suggests a fascinating new story, the last page is merely the deadly boring liquidation of some cashed-in promissory note. Jack London never rises above the wisdom of cinematography[3] ; indeed, his novels have somehow managed to absorb such typical cinematographic clichés as melodrama and the happy ending projected against the background of the natural environment or of "the heroine's head pressed against the hero's shoulder." "Landscape" ranks among the best features of cinematography. Jack London unwinds endless reels of monotonous northern landscape footage, resembling panoramic visions, actual photography, hypnotizing the reader with mechanically produced clichés via unlimited quantities of film footage.

Jack London's basic "artistic" device is continuous action. Every page provides a new sensation, like American newspapers featuring continuous murders. Jack London knows so little about how to manipulate people, and—this is very gratifying—he is so alien to turning them into mannequins, that he prefers to kill them off as soon as they perform their sensational feats. Jack London's ideology[4] shocks us with its poverty of ideas and its old-fashioned quality (from a European perspective). It is very consistent and well-assimilated Darwinism, adorned, unfortunately, by a cheap and poorly comprehended Nietzscheanism. However, it poses as the wisdom of nature itself and as the permanent law of life.

Jack London, at one point in his work, uttered a significant slip: "that enormous, terrifying and alien thing called culture." This modest self-appraisal and naive expression of reverence before the alien and incomprehensible complexity of culture is, perhaps, the most valuable utterance in London's work. The malady of the New World, the mysterious disease of its monstrous cities— its cultural wildness—found an unexpectedly appealing spokesman in Jack London. In London's view, the cause of this historical "wildness" is not personal degeneration; rather, it emerges most vividly when juxtaposed against the background of impeccable physical and spiritual health. Contemporary man does not need to travel to the Klondike or to the Pacific Islands to experience the sensations of a wild animal: it is easy enough to lose oneself in the labyrinths of New York or San Francisco, in the elemental forest of the new civilization whose mighty vegetation is impenetrable to the life-giving rays of culture. The inoffensive entertainment value and spiritual clarity of London's work make him an indispensable writer for youth. One can only welcome London's naive attraction for adult readers, for it indicates just how superficial were earlier appeals to the mass reader, and how, if genuine art is successful, then what penetrated the mind must have been contraband concealed beneath the banner of extraneous ideas.

The translation, which has been greatly slandered in the press, is done in good feuilleton language: Jack London, totally indifferent to questions of literary style, does not deserve another translation.

9. J.K. HUYSMANS. *PARISIAN ARABESQUES (PARIZHSKIE ARABESKI)* MOSCOW: K.F. NEKRASOV PUBLISHING HOUSE. BY YU. SPASSKY.

Parisian Arabesques,[1] an early work of Huysmans,[2] returns us to the sources of his creativity. This book is almost intentionally physiological. Its primary theme is the clash between the defenseless but refined external organs of perception and insulted reality. Paris is hell. Balzac has already concurred with this axiom. Baudelaire and Huysmans subsequently drew the following conclusions from it. Both poets consider it a great honor to live in hell, while the king's lot is the greatest misfortune. Huysmans's boldness and innovation stem from the fact that he managed to remain a confirmed hedonist under the worst possible conditions. Thus he depicts the martyrdom of Folantin, a minor official and a man of precise organization, whose entire existence is a series of petty sufferings and loathings. Strangely enough, if we merely take away Des Esseintes's[3] capital and his treasures of erudition, he is transformed into a unique sort of decadent Akaky Akakievich! Monastic asceticism is not Huysmans's last word. The decadents did not like reality, but they did know reality, and that is what distinguishes them from the romantics. They needed it as a shore from which to cast off. Huysmans is highly regarded as a decadent since his "other shore," *La-Bas,*[4] is indisputably concrete. He found his great antidote to the present not in the imaginary Middle Ages, but in the real Middle Ages. Physiological sensitivity, that quality Huysmans developed with hatred and bitterness in *Parisian Arabesques*, is essential for comprehending the infinite complexity of the Middle Ages.[5]

Although not a Simeon Stylites[6] of style like Flaubert, Huysmans had an organic style. Spassky's translation of Huysmans's style is barely literate and he is often hypnotised by a French phrase. Still another fault of the translator is that he garnished his translations with words of purely Russian and Muscovite origin.

10. INNOKENTY ANNENSKY. *THAMYRIS THE CITHARA PLAYER. BACCHANALIAN DRAMA (FAMIRA-KIFARED. VAK-KHICHESKAIA DRAMA).* MOSCOW: PORTUGALOV PUBLISHING HOUSE, 1913.

Innokenty Annensky[1] approaches Sophocles's cruel tale[2] with the sickly caution of a modern man.

In Annensky's work the theme of a mother's love for her own son is transformed into the agonizing emotion of lyrical love. The celestial beings are so far removed from those souls which have been confused and poisoned by music that when the nymph Argiope resolves to kill the cithara player enchanted by the Muses, she cannot immediately find the words with which to address Zeus. And when Hermes descends to the earth to proclaim the will of the gods, he seems more like a puppet made by the sorcerer Leonardo for some prince of the Italian Renaissance than a living Olympian god.

While Thamyris was privy to music he was tossed about between women and the stars. But when the cithara suddenly refused to serve him and the music gleamed in the burning coals of his eyes, he grew strangely indifferent to his fate and at once became alien to it, like the bird that perched on his outstretched hand.

Only Thamyris's homily sounds exactly like the voice of an ancient Greek chorus:

> Blessed are the gods, who preserve
> our consciousness even in suffering.[3]

Thamyris the Cithara Player is above all a work of verbal creation. Annensky's faith in the power of the word is boundless. His ability to convey in words all the colors of the spectrum is especially remarkable. The theatricality of the play is doubtful, however. It was written by a poet who nourished an aversion to theatrical spectacles; what is more, his marvelous stage directions, in no way inferior to the text itself in expressiveness, should be regarded not as directions for the actors, but as part of the performance itself.

While reading Annensky's stage directions for the dances and choruses, you perceive them as though they were being realized before your eyes; thus the staging of this work can add nothing to the splendor of the text of *Thamyris the Cithara Player* itself.[4]

Why, indeed, should the timpani and flutes, once they have been transformed into words, be returned to the primitive condition of sound?

Only one hundred copies of the book were published.

11. PAVEL KOKORIN.[1] *THE MUSIC OF RHYMES: POESO-PIECES (MUZYKA RIFM: POEZOP'ESY).* ST. PETERSBURG, 1913.

The strained seriousness of thought and word create a strange disharmony with the naive, futuristic exterior. The author combines a capacity for lofty abstraction with an original sense of rhythm. Stingy and aloof in his mode of expression, the poet prefers short lines (not uncommonly there is only one word per line) which gives his verses an abrupt and jerky tempo reminiscent of Polezhaev:

> Glittered and burned the crystal.
> I sipped and sang my sorrow.

Kokorin's rhythm is organic: it is in complete harmony with his breathing, like a folk song.

Kokorin's book is very close to folk art, but without any red calico cloth; it is also refined, despite many crude blunders resulting from the author's naiveté and lack of skill.

12. IGOR SEVERYANIN.[1] *THE THUNDER-SEETHING GOBLET*[2] *(GROMOKIPIASHCHII KUBOK).* POEMS. INTRODUCTION BY FYODOR SOLOGUB.[3] MOSCOW: "GRIF" PUBLISHING HOUSE, 1913.

As a poet Igor Severyanin is defined chiefly by the short-comings of his poetry.[4] His use of monstrous neologisms and foreign words, which apparently hold an exotic fascination for the author, produces a sense of gaudiness. Insensitive to the laws of the Russian language and unable to hear how a word grows and matures, he prefers words that have fallen into disuse, or that were never part of the language, to living words. He often sees beauty in an image of "urbanity." Nevertheless, Igor Severyanin is a poet by virtue of his simple rapture and his dry *joie de vivre*. His verse resembles a grasshopper in its powerful musculature. Having hopelessly confused all cultures, the poet is sometimes able to give charming forms to the chaos that reigns in his imagination. It is impossible to write verses that are "just good." If Severyanin's "I" is difficult to grasp, that does not mean that it does not exist. He is able to be unique only in his superficial displays, from which we must draw our own conclusions about his profundity.

13. ON CONTEMPORARY POETRY: *ALMANAC OF THE MUSES* (ALMANAKH MUZ). PETROGRAD: FELANA, 1916. 192 P.

An almanac containing works by twenty-five contemporary poets has just been published. On this occasion it would be fitting to speak of the high level of technical competence in contemporary poetry, to point out how nowadays everyone is capable of writing poetry, and to bemoan the fact that today's poetry is artificial and dead. However, I shall do nothing of the kind: why do critics so love to indulge in melancholy lamentations every time they see a batch of poems? It takes very little to attain "a high level" in their eyes, yet in their sweeping condemnation of artificiality they avoid the task (often beyond their strength) of analyzing the complexities of art. It would be beneficial to explain what "progress"[1] in poetry is, so as to end, once and for all, these hypocritical complaints by indifferent outsiders about the seeming impoverishment of poetry, as if poetry were congealed in some concept of "Alexandrine perfection." There is no such thing as a "high level" of contemporary poetry in comparison to the poetry of the past. Most poems today are simply bad, as most poems have always been bad. Bad poems have their own hierarchy and, if you like, even perfect themselves rushing after good poems, reworking and distorting them in their own peculiar fashion. Nowadays people write bad poetry in a new way—that is the only difference! And, indeed, what kind of progress can there possibly be in poetry in the sense of *improvement*? How absurd—progress in art![2] Did Pushkin[3] really *perfect* Derzhavin,[4] that is, annul him in some way? No one writes odes in the style of Derzhavin or Lomonosov[5] today, despite all our "victories." In retrospect, it is possible to imagine that the course of poetry is an uninterrupted, irretrievable loss. The lost secrets are as numerous as the innovations. All talk of progress in art is rendered meaningless by these lost secrets: the proportions of the matchless Stradivarius or the formulas of the paints used by the ancient ikon painters.

Almanac of the Muses[6] contains some extremely diverse contributions—good and bad poems are represented. To speak of some average level of achievement is impossible since the contributors to this collection are as distant from each other as the stars in the sky. The older generation of poets is represented by Valery

Bryusov[7] and Vyacheslav Ivanov,[8] whose poems are already capable of arousing the noble lament that no one writes like that anymore. There is a kind of satiety in Ivanov's poems: we know beforehand all that they contain.[9] Obviously, the poet has attained such sublimity, when he is able to touch the cithara even as he drowses, barely fingering its strings.

> But to me the visible faces of Spring
> Are as sorrowful as forgotten dreams.[10]

Valery Bryusov is energetic by nature even in the weakest of his poems. Two of Bryusov's poems included in the *Almanac of the Muses* belong to his most unpleasant manner and revive that dreadful literary vanity which, fortunately, has receded into the past along with the epoch which engendered it. An immodest apotheosis of versification bursts through the rather pallid landscape[11]:

> His vision is eternally woven into stanzas . . .[12]

And in another:

> Birches in their splendid mantles
> Hastily lower their heads
> Before the prophetic Magus.[13]

We can no longer astonish anyone with the "prophetic Magus." The tawdry mantle of pseudo-Symbolism has completely faded, lost all its form, and justifiably evokes a merry smirk from the younger poets.[14]

Kuzmin's[15] classicism is captivating. How sweet it is to read a classical poet living in our midst, to experience a Goethean blend of "form" and "content," to be persuaded that the soul is not a substance made of metaphysical cotton, but rather the carefree, gentle Psyche. Kuzmin's poems not only lend themselves easily to memorization, but also to recall,[16] as it were (the impression of recollection after the very first reading), and they float up to the surface as if out of oblivion (Classicism):

> Surely, the seraphim are as cold
> To each other in paradise.

Kuzmin's clarism, however, has its dangerous aspect. It seems that such magnificent weather as that evoked in his poetry, especially in the later poems, does not exist at all.

Akhmatova's[17] combination of the subtlest psychologism (Annensky's school)[18] with song-like harmony astonishes our sense of hearing because we are accustomed to associating the song with a certain spiritual simplicity, if not spiritual poverty. The psychological design in Akhmatova's songs is as natural as the veins in a maple leaf:

> While in the Bible a red maple leaf
> Is left to mark the Song of Songs.[19]

However, the poems in the *Almanac* contain little that is characteristic of the "new" Akhmatova. They are still very pointed and epigrammatic, while the poet has already entered a new phase.[20]

Akhmatova's most recent poetry indicates a propensity for hieratic significance, religious simplicity and solemnity: I would say that the *wife* has taken the place of the woman. Remember: "meek, dressed as a beggar, but with the majestic bearing of a regal wife."[21] The voice of renunciation grows ever stronger in Akhmatova's verse, and at the present moment her poetry is close to becoming a major symbol of Russia's grandeur.

14. GOVERNMENT AND RHYTHM

While organizing society, while raising it from chaos to the harmonious order of organic existence,[1] we tend to forget that what must be organized first of all is the individual. The greatest enemy of society is the amorphous person, the unorganized individual. Our entire educational system, as it is understood by our young government led by the People's Commissariat of Education, consists essentially in the organization of the individual. Social education paves the way for the synthesis of man and society in the collective. The collective does not yet exist. It must still be born. Collectivism appeared before the collective, and if social education does not come to its aid we shall be in danger of collectivism without the collective.

At the present moment we see certain educators who, although still weak and isolated, offer the government an efficacious method bequeathed to them by harmonious centuries: rhythm as an instrument of social education. It seems profoundly instructive to me that these hands are now extended toward the government with hope. They are returning that which rightfully belongs to it. An unerring instinct tells them that rhythmic education must be controlled by the government. They obey the inner voice of their pedagogical conscience and have now almost reached their goal: it is within our power either to help them reach this goal or else to set them back considerably.

What does the government have in common with women and children performing rhythmical exercises? And what connection is there between the difficult obstacles that life puts in our way and the silk cord that is pulled taut during those graceful exercises? Victors are being trained—that is the connection. Children capable of jumping over the braided cord are not afraid of social obstacles. They are in control of their own energies. During a race they are capable of adjusting the tension of their muscles to accommodate the difficulty of the obstacle. The difficulty of a task may increase excessively, but the habits acquired through rhythmic education remain. They are ineradicable. They are present both during times of peace and during the storm of war; they are present wherever human effort triumphs over adversity, wherever victors are needed.

The new society is held together by solidarity and rhythm. Solidarity means concord of goals. Concord of action is also essential. Concord of action in itself is already rhythm. The revolution was victorious because of its rhythm. Rhythm descended onto its head like a fiery tongue. It must be secured forever. Solidarity and rhythm are the quantity and quality of social energy. The masses have solidarity. Only the collective can have rhythm. And is not that conception of the masses, that purely quantitative measurement of social energy, already obsolete? Is it not merely a vestige from the lost paradise of ballot counters?

History has witnessed two renaissances: the first Renaissance was in the name of the individual, the second—in the name of the collective. The tendency of our age toward humanism is revealed in its Renaissance character, but humanistic concerns came to our age as if illuminated by sea foam. They are the same ideas, only they are covered by a healthy suntan and steeped in the salt of revolution.

In observing and comparing educational reforms in the new Russia with the "Scholastic Reforms" of the first humanistic Renaissance, we are struck by the fact that philology has suffered a defeat.[2] During the first Renaissance, philology was victorious; it became the foundation of universal education for the coming generations. This time philological concerns have definitely suffered—no one would dispute that. We can expect a philological impoverishment of the schools in the near future which, to a large extent, is the fruit of conscious educational policy and the inevitable consequence of our reform, for it is carried out partly in this spirit. However, the anti-philological character of our age does not prevent us from regarding it as a humanistic age, since it restores man himself to us: man in space and time, rhythmical, expressive man. Thus, on the one hand, we have philological treachery, and, on the other hand, man's fascination with the system of Jacques-Dalcroze[3] and with new philosophy. We live under a barbaric sky, yet we are still Hellenes. Nevertheless, man's fascination with the Dalcroze system has nothing in common with esthetic idealization. In general, estheticism is completely alien to his system and is only an accidental veneer, the result of a fashion started at Hellerau[4] among the European and American bourgeoisie. The system is best characterized not by estheticism, but by the spirit of geometry and strict rationalism: man, space, time, and motion are its four basic elements. However, it is not really surprising that rhythm, which had been banished from the community for an entire century, returned rather more anemic and abstract than it actually was in Hellas. The system does not belong only to Dalcroze. The discovery of the system is one of those brilliant finds like the discovery of gunpowder or steam power. Once a force is revealed it must develop of its own accord. The discoverer's name may be forgotten for the sake of clarifying the principle, although his disciples do not want to reconcile themselves to this fact. If rhythmic education is to become nationally accepted, a miracle must occur that transforms the abstract system into the people's flesh. Where yesterday there was only a blueprint, tomorrow the dancers' costumes will flash colorfully and song will resound. School precedes life. School sculpts life in its own image and likeness. The rhythm of the academic year will be determined by accents that fall on the holidays of the school Olympic games; rhythm will be the instigator and organizer of those games. On such holidays we shall see a new, rhythmically educated generation freely proclaiming its will, its joys and sorrows. Harmonious, universal, rhythmical acts, animated by a common idea, are of infinite significance for the creation of future history. Until now history has been created unconsciously in the agony of coincidence and blind struggle. From now on Man's inalienable right shall be the conscious creation of history, its birth from the holiday as a proclamation of the people's creative will. Social games will take the place of social contradictions in the society of the future and will function as enzymes, as catalysts to insure the organic flowering of culture.

Thus, no matter how favorable rhythmic education may be for esthetic development, no matter how grateful all the Muses will be to us for introducing rhythmics into the school program, rhythmics is still not esthetics.[5] However, it is even more incorrect to regard it merely as hygiene or gymnastics. Rhythm demands a synthesis, a synthesis of the spirit and the body, a synthesis of work and play. It was born of syncretism, that is, the fusion of non-differentiated elements. Furthermore, until these aspects are reunited and until our young monistic culture is firmly established, do not align rhythm with one side or the other, do not marry it off either to physical education or to psychology or labor. Our body, our labor and our science are not yet ready to accept rhythm unreservedly.

We must still prepare for its acceptance. But at least let rhythm occupy that intermediate, independent position which is suitable for a social force that has just awakened from prolonged lethargy and that has not yet realized all its possibilities.

15. THE WORD AND CULTURE

Grass on the streets of Petersburg—the first sprouts of a virgin forest that will cover the site of modern cities. This bright, tender verdure, astonishing in its freshness, belongs to a new, inspired nature. Petersburg is truly the most advanced city in the world. Speed, the pace of the present, cannot be measured by subways or skyscrapers, but only by the cheerful grass thrusting itself forth from under city stones.

Our blood, our music, our State—all will be continued in the tender life of a new nature, a nature-Psyche. In this kingdom of the spirit without man every tree will be a dryad and every phenomenon will tell of its own metamorphosis.[1]

Stop? Why? Who stops the sun as it rushes along its sparrow harness to its paternal home, possessd by the thirst for return? Is it not better to celebrate it with dithyrambs than to entreat it for a pittance?

> He did not understand anything,
> He was weak and shy, as children are,
> Strangers caught game and fish
> For him in nets.[2]

I thank you, "strangers," for your touching concern, for your tender care of the old world,[3] which is no longer "of this world," which has given way to expectations and preparations for the coming metamorphosis:

> *Cum subit illius tristissima noctis imago,*
> *Quae mihi supremum tempus in urbe fuit,*
> *Cum repeto noctem, qua tot mihi cara reliquit,*
> *Labitur ex oculis nunc quoque gutta meis.*[4]

Yes, the old world is "not of this world," yet it is more alive than it ever was. Culture has become the Church. A separation of Church-Culture and the State has taken place. Secular life no longer concerns us. We no longer take a meal, but a sacrament, not a room, but a monastery cell, not clothes, but raiment. We have finally found inner freedom, true inner joy.[5] We drink water in clay jugs like wine, and the sun is happier in a monastic refectory than in a restaurant. Apples, bread, potatoes—from now on they will quench not only physical but spiritual hunger. The Christian— and now every cultured person is a Christian—does not know mere physical hunger, mere spiritual nourishment. For him, the word is also flesh, and simple bread is a joy and a mystery.

Social differences and class antagonisms pale before the new division of people into friends and enemies of the word: literally, sheep and goats. I sense an almost physically unclean goat-breath emanating from the enemies of the word. Here the argument which emerges last in any serious disagreement is fully appropriate: my adversary smells bad.

The separation of Culture and the State is the most signifi- cant event of our revolution.[6] The process of secularization of the State did not stop with the separation of Church and State as the French Revolution understood it. Our social upheaval has brought about a more profound secularization. Today the State has a unique relationship to culture that is best expressed by the term *tolerance*. But at the same time a new type of organic inter- relationship is beginning to appear, one which connects the State with Culture in a way not unlike that which once linked the ap- panage princes to the monasteries. The princes maintained monas- teries for *counsel*. This explains everything. The isolation of the State insofar as cultural values are concerned makes it fully de- pendent on culture. Cultural values ornament the State, endowing it with color, form, and, if you will, even gender. Inscriptions on State buildings, tombs, and gateways insure the State against the ravages of time.

Poetry is the plough that turns up time[7] in such a way that the abyssal strata of time, its black earth, appear on the surface. There are epochs, however, when mankind, not satisfied with the present, yearning like the ploughman for the abyssal strata of time, thirsts for the virgin soil of time. Revolution in art inevitably leads to Classicism, not because David reaped the harvest of Robespierre, but because that is what the earth desires.[8]

One often hears: that is good but it belongs to yesterday. But I say: yesterday has not yet been born. It has not yet really existed. I want Ovid, Pushkin, and Catullus to live once more, and I am not satisfied with the historical Ovid, Pushkin, and Catul- lus.

It is indeed astonishing that all are obsessed with poets and cannot tear themselves away from them. You would think that once they were read, that was that. Transcended, as they say now. Nothing could be farther from the truth. The silver trumpet of Catullus—*Ad claras Asiae volemus urbes*[9] —alarms and excites us more forcefully than any Futurist riddle. Such poetry does not exist in Russian. Yet it *must* exist in Russian. I chose a Latin line because it is clearly perceived by the Russian reader as a category of obligation: the imperative rings more vividly in it. Such an imperative characterizes all poetry that is Classical. Classical poetry is perceived as that which must be, not as that which has already been.

Thus, not a single poet has yet appeared. We are free from the burden of memories. On the other hand, we have so many rare presentiments: Pushkin, Ovid, Homer. When in the stillness of the night a lover gets tangled up in tender names and suddenly remembers that all this already was: the words and the hair and the rooster crowing outside his window, exactly as it had been in Ovid's *Tristia,* the profound joy of recurrence seizes him,[10] a dizzying joy:

> Like murky water, I drink the turbid air
> Time is upturned by the plough, the rose is as the earth.[11]

Thus, the poet has no fear of recurrence and is easily intoxicated on Classical wine.

What is true of the single poet is true of all. There is no need to create poetic schools. There is no need to invent your own poetics.[12]

The analytic method applied to the word, movement, and form is a completely legitimate and clever device. Recently, destruction has become a purely formal precondition of art. Disintegration, decay, decomposition—all this is still *decadence*. But the Decadents were Christian artists, the last Christian martyrs in their own way. The music of decay was for them the music of resurrection.[13] Baudelaire's "Charogne"[14] is a lofty example of Christian despair. Conscious destruction of form is an entirely different matter. Painless Suprematism.[15] The denial of the appearance of things. Calculated suicide for the sake of curiosity. It is possible to take things apart, it is also possible to put them together: it might seem that form is being tested, but actually the spirit is rotting and decomposing. (Incidentally, having named Baudelaire, I would like to mention his significance as a kind of ascetic hero in the original Christian meaning of the word, *martyre*.)[16]

The life of the word has entered a heroic era. The word is flesh and bread. It shares the fate of bread and flesh: suffering. People are hungry. The State is even hungrier. But there is something still hungrier: Time. Time wants to devour the State.[17] The threat that Derzhavin scratched on his slate resounds like a clarion call.[18] Whoever shall raise the word on high and confront time with it, as the priest displays the Eucharist, shall be a second Joshua of Nun. There is nothing hungrier than the contemporary State, and a hungry State is more terrifying than a hungry man. To show compassion for the State which denies the word shall be the contemporary poet's social obligation and heroic feat.

> Let's glorify the fateful yoke
> Which the leader of the people bears in tears,
> Let's glorify the twilight yoke of power,
> Its intolerable weight.
> Whoever has a heart must hear, O Time,
> How your ship sinks to the bottom...[19]

Do not demand from poetry any special substantiality, materiality, or concreteness. It is that very same revolutionary hunger. The doubt of Thomas. Why must you touch it with your fingers? But most important, why equate the word with the thing, with grass, with the object it designates?

Is the thing really the master of the word? The word is a Psyche. The living word does not designate an object, but freely chooses for its dwelling place, as it were, some objective significance, material thing, or beloved body. And the word wanders freely around the thing, like the soul around an abandoned, but not forgotten body.

What is said about materiality sounds slightly different when applied to imagery:

Prends l'éloquence et tords lui le cou![20]

Write imageless verses if you can, if you are able. A blind man recognizes a beloved face by barely touching it with seeing fingers, and tears of joy, the true joy of recognition, will fall from his eyes after a long separation. The poem lives through an inner image, that ringing mold of form which anticipates the written poem.[21] There is not yet a single word, but the poem can already be heard. This is the sound of the inner image, this is the poet's ear touching it.

Only the instant of recognition is sweet to us![22]

Today a kind of speaking in tongues is taking place. In sacred frenzy poets speak the language of all times, all cultures. Nothing is impossible. As the room of a dying man is open to everyone, so the door of the old world is flung wide open before the crowd. Suddenly everything becomes public property. Come and take your pick. Everything is accessible: all labyrinths, all secret recesses, all forbidden paths. The word has become not a seven-stop, but a thousand-stop flute, brought to life all at once by the breathing of the ages. The most striking thing about speaking in tongues is that the speaker does not know the language he is speaking. He talks in a completely unknown language. It seems to everyone, and to himself, that he speaking Greek or Chaldean. It is something like a complete reversal of erudition. Contemporary poetry, despite all its complexity and inner inventiveness, is naive:

Ecoutez la chanson grise . . .

The modern poet-synthesizer, it seems to me, is not a Verhaeren, but a kind of Verlaine[23] of culture. For him all the complexity of the old world is like that same Pushkinian flute. He sings of ideas, systems of knowledge, and State theories just as his predecessors sang of nightingales and roses. They say the cause of revolution is hunger in interplanetary space. Grain must be scattered through the ether.[24]

Classical poetry is the poetry of revolution.[25]

16. ON THE NATURE OF THE WORD

> We have forgotten that the word alone
> Shone radiant over the troubled earth,
> And that in the Gospel of St. John
> It is written that the word is God.
> But we have limited its range
> To the paltry boundaries of this world,
> And like the dead bees in an empty hive
> Dead words emit a foul odor.
>
> —*N. Gumilev*[1]

I would like to pose one question: is Russian literature a unified whole? Is contemporary Russian literature in fact the same as the literature of Nekrasov, Pushkin, Derzhavin, or Simeon Polotsky?[2] If continuity has been preserved, how far back does it go into the past? If Russian literature remains unchanged, what constitutes its unity, what is its essential principle (its so-called criterion for being)?

The question I have posed becomes particularly acute in view of the quickening tempo of the historical process. It is certainly an exaggeration to regard each year of contemporary history as a century, but something like a geometric progression, a regular and natural acceleration, is perceptible in the stormy realization of the already accumulated and still-increasing potential of historical energy. Due to the quantitative change in the content of events occurring over a given time interval, the concept of a unit of time has begun to falter, and it is no accident that contemporary mathematical science has advanced the principle of relativity.[3]

To preserve the principle of unity amidst the vortex of changes and the unceasing flood of phenomena, contemporary philosophy in the person of Bergson[4] (whose profoundly Judaic mind is obsesssed with the urgent need for practical monotheism) offers us a theory of the system of phenomena. Bergson does not consider phenomena according to the way they submit to the law of temporal succession, but rather according to their spatial extension. He is interested exclusively in the internal connection among phenomena. He liberates this connection from time and considers it independently. Phenomena thus connected to one another form, as it were, a kind of fan whose folds can be opened up in time; however, this fan may also be closed up in a way intelligible to the human mind.

To compare phenomena united in time to form such a fan emphasizes only their internal connection. Thus, instead of the problem of causality (which has for so long dominated the minds of European logicians), [Bergson] poses the problem of the connection alone, purged of any admixture of metaphysics, and therefore more fruitful for scientific discoveries and hypotheses.[5]

A science based on the principle of connection rather than causality saves us from the bad infinity of evolutionary theory, not to mention its vulgarized corollary—the theory of progress.[6]

The movement of an infinite chain of phenomena having neither beginning nor end is precisely that bad infinity which has nothing to offer the mind seeking unities and connections. Such a concept hypnotizes scientific thought with a simple and easily accessible evolutionism, which, to be sure, gives an appearance of scientific generalization, but only at the cost of renouncing all synthesis and inner structure.[7]

The diffuseness, the non-architectonic character of nineteenth-century European scientific thought at the beginning of the present century has completely demoralized scientific thought. The active mind, which is not just knowledge nor a collection of bits of knowledge, but is rather an instrument, a means of grasping knowledge, has abandoned science, seeing that it can exist independently and find nourishment wherever it likes. It would be futile to seek such a mind in the scientific life of old Europe. Man's liberated mind has now divorced itself from science. It has turned up everywhere but in science: in poetry, in mysticism, in politics, in theology. As for scientific evolutionism and the theory of progress (insofar as it has not wrung its own neck as modern European science did), it, continuing to operate in the same direction, has beached itself on the shores of theosophy, like an exhausted swimmer who has reached a joyless shore. Theosophy is the direct heir of the old European philosophy. And its path leads in the same direction: the same bad infinity, the same spinelessness in the doctrine of reincarnation (karma), the same coarse and naive materialism in its vulgar conception of the suprasensible world, the same lack of will, the same taste for the knowledge of activity, as well as a certain omnivorousness based on laziness, an enormous, heavy cud, enough for thousands of stomachs, an interest in everything which verges on apathy, an understanding of everything which verges on an understanding of nothing.[8]

The theory of evolution is particularly dangerous for literature, but the theory of progress is nothing short of suicidal. If one listens to literary historians who defend evolutionism,[9] it would appear that writers think only about how to clear the road for their successors, but never about how to accomplish their own tasks; or it would appear that they are all participants in an inventors' competition[10] for the improvement of some literary machine, although none of them knows the whereabouts of the judges or what purpose the machine serves.

The theory of progress in literature represents the crudest, most repugnant form of academic ignorance. Literary forms change, one set of forms yielding its place to another. However, each change, each gain, is accompanied by a loss, a forfeit. In literature nothing is ever "better," no progress can be made simply because there is no literary machine and no finish line toward which everyone must race as rapidly as possible. This meaningless theory of improvement is not even applicable to the style and form of individual writers, for here as well, each gain is accompanied by a loss or forfeit. Where in *Anna Karenina*, in which Tolstoi assimilated the care for structure and the psychological power of a Flaubertian novel, is the natural instinct and physiological intuition of *War and Peace*? Where in *War and Peace* is the limpid form, the "clarism" of *Childhood and Youth*? The author of *Boris Godunov*, even if he wanted to, could not have repeated his Lyceum verses, just as today no one can write an ode in the manner of Derzhavin. Individual preference is an entirely different matter. Just as there are two kinds of geometry, Euclidian and Lobachevskian,[11] there may be two kinds of literary history, written in different keys, one treating only the gains, the other only the losses; both, however, would be treating the same subject matter.

Returning to the question of whether Russian literature is a unified whole, and if so, wherein lies its unifying principle, we must immediately eliminate the theory of progress. We shall discuss only the inner connection of the phenomena involved, and most important, we shall attempt to ascertain the criteria of possible unity, the pivot which will allow us to unfold in time the diverse and scattered phenomena of literature.

Language alone can be acknowledged as the criterion of unity for the literature of a given people,[12] of its conditional unity, all other criteria being secondary, transitory and arbitrary.

Although a language constantly undergoing changes never freezes in a particular mold even for a moment, moving from one point to another, such points being dazzlingly clear to the mind of the philologist, still, within the confines of its own changes, any given language remains a fixed quantity, a "constant," which is internally unified. Every philologist understands the meaning of personal identity as applied to the self-consciousness of a language. When Latin, once it had spread throughout the Roman lands, blossomed anew and put forth the shoots of the future Romance languages, a new literature was born, infantile and feeble, perhaps, in comparison with Latin literature, but already a Romance literature.

When the lively and image-laden speech of *The Tale of Igor's Campaign (Slovo o polku Igoreve)*[13] resounded, each turn of phrase temporal, secular, and Russian through and through, Russian literature began. And when Velimir Khlebnikov,[14] the contemporary Russian writer, plunges us into the very thicket of Russian word roots, into an etymological night, dear to the mind and heart of the intelligent reader, that very same Russian literature, the literature of *The Tale of Igor's Campaign,* comes alive once again. The Russian language, just like the Russian national spirit, is formed through ceaseless hybridization, cross-breeding, grafting, and external influences. Yet it will always remain true to itself in one thing, until our kitchen Latin resounds for us and until pale young shoots of our life begin to sprout on the mighty body of our language, like the Old French song about Saint Eulalia.[15]

Russian is a Hellenistic language. As a result of a number of historical conditions, the vital forces of Hellenic culture, having ceded the West to Latin influences and having tarried for a while in childless Byzantium, rushed headlong into the bosom of Russian speech, imparting to it the self-assured mystery of the Hellenistic world view, the mystery of free incarnation. *That is why Russian became the resonant, speaking flesh it is today.*

If Western cultures and histories lock their language in from the outside, surround it with the walls of State and Church, and become completely permeated by it, so as to decay slowly and blossom again in good season when it disintegrates, Russian culture and history are ever awash on all sides, circumscribed only by the threatening and boundless element of the Russian language, which cannot be contained within any governmental or ecclesiastical form.

The life of the Russian language in Russian historical reality outweighs all other facts in the abundance of its properties, in the abundance of its being. Such abundance appears to all the other phenomena of Russian life as but an inaccessible outer limit. The Hellenistic nature of the Russian language can be identified with its ontological function. The work in its Hellenistic conception is active flesh consummated in the event. Therefore, the Russian language is historical by its very nature, since in its totality it is a turbulent sea of events, a continuous incarnation and activation of rational and breathing flesh. No language resists more strongly than Russian the tendency toward naming and utilitarian application. Russian nominalism, that is, the idea of the reality of the word as such, breathes life into the spirit of our language and connects it with Hellenic philological culture, not etymologically nor literally, but through the principle of inner freedom, which is equally inherent in both languages.

Utilitarianism in any form is a mortal sin against the Hellenistic nature of the Russian language, regardless of whether it is a tendency towards a telegraphic or stenographic code used for the sake of economy and simple expediency, or whether it is utilitarianism of a higher order, sacrificing language to mystical intuition, anthroposophy, or any kind of omnivorous thought which is ravenous for words.

Andrei Bely,[16] for example, is an unhealthy and negative phenomenon in the life of the Russian language simply because he unsparingly and unceremoniously hounds the word, forcing it to conform to the temperament of his own speculative thought. Choking in his refined prolixity, he cannot sacrifice even one nuance, nor tolerate the slightest break in his capricious thought, and he blows up bridges which he is too lazy to cross. Consequently, after a momentary display of fireworks, he leaves but a pile of broken stones, a dismal picture of destruction, instead of the abundance of life, a sense of organic wholeness, and an active equilibrium.[17] The fundamental sin of writers like Andrei Bely is disrespect for the Hellenistic nature of the word, an unsparing exploitation of the word for personal intuitive ends.

The old theme of doubting the capacity of the word to express feelings is reiterated in Russian poetry more than in any other poetry:

How can the heart fully express itself?
How can someone else ever know you?[18]

Our language thus preserves itself from unceremonious attacks.

One cannot measure the growth tempo of a language in terms of the development of life. Attempts to adapt language mechanically to the demands of life are doomed in advance. Futurism, a concept devised by illiterate critics, is devoid of all content or scope; it is not merely a curiosity of vulgar literary psychology. It assumes an exact meaning if one views it precisely as this forced, mechanical adaptation, this distrust of language, as something which is simultaneously the tortoise and the hare.

Khlebnikov busied himself with words like a mole digging down into the earth to make a path into the future for the entire century, while the representatives of the Moscow metaphorical school, who call themselves Imaginists,[19] exhausted themselves attempting to make language more contemporary. However, they remained far behind language, and it was their fate to be swept aside like so much waste paper.

Chaadaev,[20] in stating his opinion that Russia has no history, that is, that Russian belongs to the unorganized, unhistorical world of cultural phenomena, overlooked one factor—the Russian language. So highly organized, so organic a language is not merely a door into history, but is history itself.[21] For Russia, defection from history, excommunication from the kingdom of historical necessity and continuity, from freedom and teleology, would have been defection from its language. Reduction to a state of "dumbness" for two or three generations could have brought Russia to historical death. Excommunication from language is the equivalent for us to excommunication from history. For that reason, it is certainly true that Russian history travels along the brink, along a ledge, over an abyss, and is on the verge of falling into nihilism at any moment, that is, of being excommunicated from the word.

Of all contemporary Russian writers, Rozanov[22] felt this danger most acutely. He spent his entire life struggling to preserve the connection with the word, to preserve the philological culture which is so firmly grounded in the Hellenistic nature of Russian speech. An anarchic attitude toward absolutely everything, a total confusion in which anything becomes possible; there is only one thing I cannot do: I cannot live without language, I cannot survive excommunication from the word. Such, approximately, was Rozanov's spiritual state. The anarchistic, nihilistic spirit recognized only one authority: the magic of language, the power of the word, and this, mind you, expressed the attitude not of a poet, nor of a collector or stringer of words, nor was it related to any concern for style; it was but the sentiment of a chatterer or grumbler.

One of Rozanov's books bears the title *By the Cathedral Walls.* It seems to me that Rozanov spent his entire life rummaging about in a soft, yielding void, groping for the walls of Russian culture. Like certain other Russian thinkers, such as Chaadaev, Leontiev, Gershenzon, he could not live without walls, without an Acropolis. Everything around him was collapsing, crumbling, everything grew soft and pliable. But we all have the desire to live in history; and in each one of us there is an invincible need to find the solid kernel of a Kremlin, an Acropolis: it doesn't matter whether that nucleus is called "state" or "society". Rozanov's craving for the nut and for whatever wall might symbolize that nut completely determined his fate and conclusively exonerated him from all charges of being an unprincipled anarchist.

"It is extremely difficult for one man to be an entire generation—nothing remains but for him to die—it's time for me to perish, for you to flourish." And Rozanov did not live. He died an intelligent and thinking death, as generations die. And Rozanov's life was the death of philology, its withering, the drying up of *belles-lettres* and the desperate battle for life which is warmed by kind words and small talk, by those meanings of words found in parentheses and personal references, but always by philology, only philology.

Rozanov's attitude toward Russian literature was most unliterary. Literature is a social phenomenon, while philology is domestic, intimate. Literature is a lecture, the street; philology is a university seminar, the family. Yes, it is precisely that university seminar where five students, friends calling each other by name and patronymic, listen to their professor, while branches of familiar trees in the university garden reach out toward the window. Philology is the family because every family clings to its own intonations, its personal references, and to its own special meanings of words defined in parentheses. The most casual utterance within a family takes on nuances of its own. Moreover, such perpetual, distinctive, and purely philological nuancing defines the atmosphere of family life. Hence, I would derive Rozanov's propensity for the domestic quality of life, which so powerfully informed the whole tenor of his literary activity, from the philological nature of his soul, which, in its indefatigable search for the kernel, nibbled and cracked his every word, every utterance, leaving us only empty shells. It comes as no surprise that Rozanov turned out to be an unnecessary and uninfluential writer.

How dreadful that man (the eternal philologist) has found a word for this: "death". Is it really possible to name it? Does it warrant a name? A name is a definition, a "something we already know." So Rozanov defined the essence of his nominalism in a most personal manner: the eternal cognitive movement, the eternal cracking of the nut which comes to nothing because there is no way to gnaw through it. But what kind of literary critic was Rozanov? Just a nibbler, a casual reader, a lost sheep—neither one thing nor the other. . .

A critic must know how to devour volumes in search of the essential, and he must generalize. But Rozanov could get bogged down in one line of poetry from any Russian poet, just as he got bogged down in Nekrasov's famous line: "Whether I am driving through the dark street by night . . ."[23] Rozanov's commentary was the first thing that popped into his head as he was driving along one night in a cab: You can hardly expect to find another line like that in all of Russian poetry.

Rozanov loved the church for expressing the same philology as the family. Here is what he said: "The church pronounced such marvelous words over the deceased, words which we are incapable of uttering over our own dead father, son, wife, or mistress, that is, the church expressed the same intimacy toward, and came as 'near to the soul' of, the dying or dead, as only a mother may experience toward her own dead child. How can one not give up everything for this? . . . "

The anti-philological spirit against which Rozanov struggled erupted out of the very depths of history; in its own way it was just as inextinguishable a flame as the philological flame.

Such eternal flames exist on the earth, and are fed by oil; something may accidentally catch fire and will continue burning for decades. There is no formula to neutralize it, absolutely nothing can quench it. Luther was a rather poor philologist because instead of argument he let loose his inkwell. An anti-philological flame ulcerates the body of Europe ablaze with burning volcanoes on the soil of the West, forever laying waste the ground on which culture erupted. Nothing can neutralize such ravenous flames. They must be allowed to burn, while the accursed places where no one needs to go, where no one will hasten, must be avoided.

Europe devoid of philology is not even America; it is a civilized Sahara desert, cursed by God, an abomination of desolation. As in the past the European Kremlins and Acropolises, the Gothic cities, the cathedrals built like forests and the onion-domed basilicas will continue to stand, but people will look upon them without comprehension, and what is more likely, they will take flight, unable to understand what force may have erected them, or what blood may flow in the veins of those powerful architectural monuments surrounding them.

Indeed, what can one say! America is better than this Europe, which, for the moment is still intelligible. Having expended its philological reserves brought over from Europe, America began to act like someone now crazed, now thoughtful. Then all of a sudden, she initiated her own particular philology from which Whitman emerged; and he, like a new Adam, began giving things names, began behaving like Homer himself, offering a model for a primitive American poetry of nomenclature. Russia is not America; we have no philological imports; no wild poet like Edgar Allan Poe could sprout up among us like a tree from a palm nut which had crossed the ocean on some steamship. The only possible exception is Balmont, the most un-Russian of our poets, an alien translator of Eolian harps; his kind was never found in the West: a translator by calling, by birth, even in his most original works.

Balmont's position in Russia is that of a foreign emissary from a non-existent phonetic kingdom, the rare case of a typical translation without an original. Although Balmont is a Muscovite by birth, an ocean lies between him and Russia. He is a poet completely alien to Russian poetry; he leaves less of a trace on it than his translations of Shelley or Poe, even though his own verse forces one to believe in the existence of highly interesting originals.

We have no Acropolis. Even today our culture is still wandering and not finding its walls. Nevertheless, each word in Dal's dictionary[24] is a kernel of the Acropolis, a small Kremlin, a winged fortress of nominalism, rigged out in the Hellenic spirit for the relentless battle against the formless element, against non-existence, which threatens our history from every side.

In the same way that Rozanov represents the domestic Hellenism of God's fools and the poor in Russian literature, Annensky[25] represents heroic Hellenism, martial philology. Annensky's lyric poetry and his tragedies can be compared to the wooden fortifications, the walled towns far out in the steppes, which served to defend the appanage princes against the Pechenegs, against the night of the Khazars.

> No longer do I begrudge my dark fate:
> Even Ovid was once naked and impotent.

Annensky's inability to wield any influence, to serve either as a mediator or translator, is truly astonishing. In a most original manner, he grasped in his talons all that was foreign, and still soaring high in the sky arrogantly dropped his plunder, allowing it to fall as it would. And the eagle of his poetry which had seized as its prey Euripides, Mallarmé, Leconte de Lisle, brought us nothing but handfuls of dry grass:

> Listen, a madman knocks at your door,
> God knows where and with whom he spent the night,
> His eyes wander, his speech is wild,
> And his hand is full of pebbles.
> Take heed, he is emptying the other,
> Scattering dry leaves over you.

Gumilev called Annensky a great European poet. It seems to me that when Europeans recognize him (having meekly educated their children in the Russian language as in the past they educated them in the ancient languages and classical poetry), they will be frightened by the audacity of this regal bird of prey who abducted the dove Eurydice from them for the Russian snows, who tore the classical shawl from Phaedra's shoulders, and who, as befits a Russian poet, tenderly placed an animal's pelt over Ovid's still frozen body.[26] How astonishing is Annensky's fate! Having touched the treasures of the world, he preserved only a piteous handful for himself, or rather, he raised a handful of dust and tossed it back into the flaming treasure house of the West. When Annensky kept vigil, everyone was sleeping. The realists snored. *The Scales*[27] had not yet been founded. The young student Vyacheslav Ivanovich Ivanov[28] was studying with Mommsen and writing a monograph in Latin about Roman taxation. At the same time, the director of the Tsarskoe Selo Lyceum was struggling late into the night with Euripides, imbibing the snake poison of wise Hellenic speech, preparing an infusion of bitter, absinth-flavored verse of a kind no one before or after him would write. Moreover, for Annensky poetry was a domestic affair, as Euripides was a domestic writer, filled with personal references and words whose special meanings were found only in parentheses. Annensky perceived all of world poetry as a shaft of light sent forth by Hellas. He understood distance; he experienced both its ardor and its chill, and he never attempted superficial combinations of the Russian and Hellenic worlds. The lesson to be drawn from Annensky's creative work for Russian poetry is not concerned with Hellenization *per se*, but rather involves an inner Hellenism, domestic Hellenism as it were, that which is suitable to the spirit of the Russian language. Hellenism is an earthenware pot, oven tongs, a milk jug, kitchen utensils, dishes; it is anything which surrounds the body. Hellenism is the warmth of the hearth experienced as something sacred; it is anything which imparts some of the external world to man, just as the pelts placed over the old man's shoulders in the following lines express a similar sense of awe:

When the rapid river froze
And the winter winds raged,
With fluffy pelts they covered
The old man's saintly frame.[29]

Hellenism is the conscious surrounding of man with domestic utensils instead of impersonal objects; the transformation of impersonal objects into domestic utensils, and the humanizing and warming of the surrounding world with the most delicate teleological warmth. Hellenism is any kind of stove near which a man sits, treasuring its heat as something akin to his own internal body heat. And finally, Hellenism is the Egyptian funerary ship in which the dead are carried, into which everything required for the continuation of man's earthly wanderings is put, down·to perfume phials, mirrors, and combs. Hellenism is a system, in the Bergsonian sense of the term, which man unfolds around himself, like a fan of phenomena freed of their temporal dependence, phenomena subjected through the human "I" to an inner connection.

In the Hellenistic sense, symbols are domestic utensils, but then any object brought into man's sacred circle could become a utensil and consequently, a symbol. One may rightfully ask then if an exclusive, specially contrived symbolism is necessary for Russian poetry? Is not such contrived symbolism a sin against the Hellenistic nature of our language, which creates images like domestic utensils for man's use?

There is essentially no difference between a word and an image. An image is merely a word which has been sealed up, which cannot be touched. An image is inappropriate for everyday use, just as an ikon lamp would be inappropriate for lighting a cigarette.[30] But such sealed-up images are also very necessary. Man loves interdictions, and even an uncivilized man will put magic prohibitions, "taboos," on certain objects. Nevertheless, once removed from circulation, the sealed-up image is inimical to man, for in its own way it becomes a kind of scarecrow, or effigy.

Anything transient is but a likeness.[31] Let's take for example a rose and the sun, a dove and a girl. To the Symbolists, none of these images is interesting in itself: the rose is a likeness of the sun, the sun is a likeness of a rose, a dove—of a girl, and a girl—of a dove. Images are gutted like scarecrows and packed with foreign content. In place of the Symbolist forest,[32] we are left with a workshop producing scarecrows.

This is where professional Symbolism leads. Perception is demoralized. Nothing is real, genuine. Nothing is left but a terrifying quadrille of "correspondences," all nodding to one another. Eternal winking. Never a clear word, nothing but hints and reticent whispers. The rose nods to the girl, the girl to the rose. No one wants to be himself.

That remarkable epoch in the development of Russian poetry

known as Symbolism (defined by the group associated with the journal, *The Scales*) which, although standing on clay feet, developed in the course of two decades[33] into a colossal structure, is best defined as the epoch of pseudo-Symbolism. However, do not take this definition to refer to Classicism; such a reference would degrade its magnificent poetry and the fertile style of Racine. Pseudo-Classicism was a slogan adopted out of scholarly ignorance and applied to a great style. Russian pseudo-Symbolism is truly pseudo-Symbolism. Jourdain discovered in his old age that he had been speaking "prose" all his life. The Russian Symbolists discovered the same prose, the primordial, image-bearing nature of the word. They sealed up all words, all images, designating them exclusively for liturgical use. An extremely awkward situation resulted: no one could move, nor stand up, nor sit down. One could no longer eat at a table because it was no longer simply a table. One could no longer light a lamp because it might signify unhappiness later.

A man was no longer master in his own house. He had to live either in a church or in a sacred grove of the Druids; a man could not rest his eyes for there was no place for him to seek peace. The domestic utensils all rose in rebellion. The broom begged for the Sabbath; the kettle refused to boil and demanded an absolute significance for itself (as if boiling had no absolute significance). The master was chased out of his house and no longer dared to enter. What can be done when a word is fettered to its denotative meaning: doesn't this amount to serfdom? But a word is not a thing.[34] Its significance is not a translation of itself. Indeed, it has never happened that anyone has christened a thing, calling it by an invented name. The most appropriate and, in scientific terms, the most correct approach, is to regard a word as an image, that is, as a verbal representation. In this way, the question of form and content is avoided, phonetics being the form, all the rest—content.[35] Also avoided is the question of giving primary significance to the word as opposed to its phonetic nature. A verbal representation is a complex composite of phenomena, it is a connection, a "system."[36] The significance of the word may be viewed as a candle burning inside a paper lantern, and conversely, its phonetic value, the so-called phoneme, may be located inside the significance, just as that candle may be inside that lantern.

Old psychology knew only how to objectify the representation and, having overcome this naive solipsism, regarded representations as something external. According to that view, the decisive factor was that of givenness. The givenness of the products of our consciousness makes them like the objects of the external world, thus permitting us to regard representations as something objective. However, the extremely rapid humanization of science, including the theory of knowledge, forces us to move in another direction. We can consider representations not only as objective data of consciousness, but also as human organs, just like the liver or the heart.

In its application to the word, such an interpretation of verbal representations opens up broad new perspectives, allowing us to dream about the creation of an organic poetics, a poetics of a biological rather than legislative nature, a poetics which would destroy the canon in the name of the internal unity of the organism, a poetics which would exhibit all the traits of biological science.

The organic school of Russian poetry which developed as a result of the creative initiative of Gumilev and Gorodetsky early in 1912, and which Akhmatova, Narbut, Zenkevich and the author of these lines officially joined, took upon itself the task of constructing just such a poetics.[37] The modest literature on Acmeism plus the frugal attitude toward theory exhibited by its leaders makes its study difficult. Acmeism arose out of a sense of repulsion: "Down with Symbolism! Long live the living rose!"—such was its original slogan.

In his day Gorodetsky[38] attempted to inoculate Acmeism with his literary world view, "Adamism," a form of doctrine of a new earth and a new Adam. His efforts were unsuccessful. Acmeism was not concerned with world views,[39] but brought with it a host of new taste sensations, much more valuable than ideas; of these, the most significant was the taste for the integral verbal representation, the image, understood in a new organic way. Literary schools thrive on tastes rather than ideas. To express a number of new ideas while ignoring new tastes means to establish a new poetics, not a new school. On the other hand, a school can be founded on tastes alone, without any new ideas. Acmeist tastes rather than Acmeist ideas dealt Symbolism its fatal blow. For Acmeist ideas turned out, at least in part, to be borrowed from the Symbolists, and Vyacheslav Ivanov himself was a great help in the formulation of Acmeist theory. But see what a miracle occurred: new blood began to course through the veins of Russian poetry. It has been said that faith will move mountains, but I say, as regards poetry, taste will move mountains. Because a new taste arose in Russia at the beginning of the century, such massifs as Rabelais, Shakespeare, and Racine were moved from their bases and came to pay us a visit. The moving force of Acmeism in the sense of its active love of literature, with all its difficulties and burdens, is extraordinary; and the key to this active love was precisely a change in taste, the indomitable will to create a man-centered poetry and poetics, with man as master of his own home, not man flattened into a wafer by the horrors of pseudo-Symbolism; genuine Symbolism surrounded by symbols, that is, by domestic utensils having their own verbal representations, just as men have their own vital organs.

More than once in Russian society there have been periods when the moving spirit of Western literature was read with genius. Thus did Pushkin and his entire generation read Chénier.[40] Thus did the following generation,[41] the generation of Odoevsky, read Schelling, E.T.A. Hoffmann, and Novalis. Thus did the men of the 1860s read their Buckle[42]; and although nothing significant emerged, a more ideal reader could not be found. The wind of Acmeism turned the pages of the Classicists and the Romantics, opening them to just that page which most appealed to the age. Racine was opened to *Phèdre*, Hoffmann to *The Serapion Brothers*. Chénier's *Iambes* were discovered along with Homer's *Iliad*.

Furthermore, Acmeism is a social as well as a literary phenomenon in Russian history. With Acmeism a moral force was reborn in Russian poetry.[43] Bryusov said:

> I want my free boat to sail in every direction;
> And I shall praise the Lord and the Devil equally.[44]

This bankrupt "nihilism" will never be repeated in Russian poetry. Until now the social inspiration of Russian poetry has reached no further than the idea of "citizen," but there is a loftier principle than "citizen," there is the concept of "Man."

As opposed to the civic poetry of the past, modern Russian poetry must educate not merely citizens, but "Men." The ideal of perfect manliness is provided by the style and practical demands of our age. Everything has become heavier and more massive; thus man must become harder, for he must be the hardest thing on earth; he must be to the earth what the diamond is to glass. The hieratic, that is to say, the sacred character of poetry arises out of the conviction that man is harder than everything else in the world.[45]

The age will shout itself out, culture will fall asleep, and the people will be reborn, having given their utmost to the new social class; and this current will draw the fragile ship of the human word away with it, out into the open sea of the future where there is no sympathetic understanding, where cheerless commentary will replace the fresh wind of contemporary enmity and sympathy. How can one equip this ship for its distant voyage, without furnishing it with all the necessities for so foreign and cherished a reader?[46] Once more I shall liken a poem to an Egyptian funerary ship. In that ship everything is provided for life, nothing is forgotten. But[47] I can already see in this original formulation innumerable potential objections and the beginning of a reaction against Acmeism equal to the crisis of pseudo-Symbolism. Pure biology is inappropriate to the construction of a poetics. A biological analogy may be good and fruitful, but to apply it consistently would be to develop a biological canon, no less oppressive and intolerable than the canon of pseudo-Symbolism. "The rational abyss of the Gothic soul"[48] gapes forth from the physiological conception of art. Salieri deserves respect and fervent love. It was not his fault that he heard the music of algebra as vibrantly as living harmony.

Instead of the romantic, the idealist, or the aristocrat dreaming about the pure symbols, about the abstract esthetics of the word, instead of Symbolism, Futurism and Imaginism, there has arisen a living poetry of the object-word; its creator is not Mozart, the idealist dreamer, but Salieri, the stern and strict craftsman, extending a hand to the master craftsman of things and material values, to the builder and creator of the material world.[49]

17. BADGER HOLE

(A. Blok: August 7, 1921–August 7, 1922)

The first anniversary of Blok's death[1] must be a modest one: the seventh of August is only just beginning to come alive on the Russian calendar. Blok's posthumous existence, his new fate, his *Vita Nuova*, is in its infancy.

The miasma of Russian criticism, the heavy, poisonous fog of Ivanov-Razumnik,[2] Aikhenvald,[3] Zorgenfrey[4] and others, which has thickened in the last year, has not yet begun to disperse.

Lyricism about lyricism continues. The worst form of the lyrical mating call. Conjectures. Arbitrary premises. Metaphysical guessing.

Everything is shaky, unsteady: pure concoction.

Pity the reader who attempts to obtain some information about Blok from the literature of 1921-1922.

Works, the genuine "works" of Eikhenbaum[5] and Zhirmunsky,[6] are drowned in this litany, in the miasma of lyrical criticism.

We must learn to *know* Blok from the very first steps of his posthumous life, to struggle with the optical illusions of perception, with its inevitable coefficient of distortion. By gradually expanding the field of unquestionable and universally compulsory knowledge about the poet, we will clear the road for his posthumous fate.

Establishing the literary genesis of the poet, his literary sources, his *ancestry* and origin, brings us at once to solid ground. A critic does not have to answer the question: what did the poet want to say, but he is obliged to answer the question: where did the poet come from...[7]

In examining Blok's poetic activity as a whole, two tendencies can be distinguished, two distinct sources: the domestic, Russian, provincial, on the one hand, and the European, on the other. The eighties were Blok's cradle, and it is not by chance that at the end of his career, as an already mature poet, he returned to his life sources,[8] to the eighties, in his long poem "Retribution" ("Vozmezdie").

The domestic and the European are the two poles not only

of Blok's poetry, but of all Russian culture of the modern age. Beginning with Apollon Grigoriev,[9] a deep spiritual fissure became apparent in Russian society. Disassociation from the great European interests, defection from the unity of European culture, a breaking away from the great womb in a manner that some regarded as almost heretical, was already an accomplished fact, even though they were ashamed and afraid to acknowledge it to themselves. As if racing to correct someone's mistake, to smooth over the guilt of a tongue-tied generation whose memory was short and whose love was ardent but limited, Blok solemnly vows, for himself and for the people of the eighties, sixties, and forties:

> We love everything: the hell of Paris streets
> And the Venetian coolness,
> The distant fragrance of lemon groves
> And the smoky masses of Cologne Cathedral[10]

Moreover, Blok possessed historical love, historical objectivity toward that domestic period of Russian history which existed under the sign of the intelligentisa and populism. To him Nekrasov's[11] ponderous accentual verse with its three stresses *(Trekhdolnik)* was majestic, like Hesiod's *Works and Days*. To him the seven-stringed guitar, the mistress of Apollon Grigoriev, was no less sacred than the classical lyre. He took the gypsy ballad and made it the language of universal passion. In Blok's resplendent world, suffused with the knowledge of Russian reality, one can almost feel the marble chill of genuine immortality wafting from the high, mathematical brow of Sofya Perovskaya.[12]

Blok's historical sensitivity is astonishing. Even long before he implored us to listen to the music of the revolution, Blok heard the subterranean music of Russian history, where the most highly attuned ear caught only a syncopated pause. Kostomarov,[13] Soloviev,[14] and Klyuchevsky[15] gaze at us from every line of Blok's poetry about Russia. It is Klyuchevsky, the benevolent genius, the domestic spirit, the patron of Russian culture, under whose aegis no ordeals and no trials are terrifying.

Blok was a man of the nineteenth century and he knew that the days of his century were numbered. Greedily he extended and deepened his inner world in Time like a badger digging in the earth, building his home with two exits. The age is a badger's hole and a man of his age lives and moves about in a narrowly restricted space, frantically trying to expand his domain, valuing above all the exits from his subterranean hole. Blok, moved by this badger instinct, deepened his poetic knowledge of the nineteenth century. He had long been tormented by English and German Romanticism, by the blue flower of Novalis, the irony of Heine, by an almost Pushkinian thirst to touch his burning lips to the gushing springs of European national folklore: the English, French, and German springs, which quench by their purity and dissociation, flowing separately. Among Blok's creations there are those directly inspired by the Anglo-Saxon, Romanic, and Germanic genius, and this directness of inspiration once again brings to mind *The Feast during the Plague (Pir vo vremia chumy)* and the place where "night smells of lemon and laurel" and the song "I Drink to Mary's Health" ("P'iu za Zdravie Meri").[16] The entire poetic culture of the nineteenth century circumscribes the boundaries of Blok's poetic power, that is where he is king, that is what gives his voice strength when his movements become powerful and his intonations imperative. The freedom with which Blok treats the thematic material of this poetic culture suggests the idea that several subjects, individual and incidental until recently, have won in our eyes the magnitude of myths, for example, the themes of *Don Juan* and *Carmen.* Mérimée's[17] concise, perfectly wrought novella was most successful; Bizet's light, martial music, like a clarion call, brought tidings of eternal youth and the Romantic lust for life to all godforsaken places. Blok's poetry provides a refuge for the youngest member of the European family of legends and myths. But the summit of Blok's historical poetics, the celebration of European myth that moves freely in traditional forms, that is not afraid of anachronism or modernity, is his "Steps of the Knight Commander" *(Shagi Komandora).* Here the strata of time are placed contiguously in the newly ploughed poetic consciousness, and the seeds of the old theme have produced bountiful shoots (The automobile, quiet, black as an owl... From a blessed, unfamiliar, distant land/the cock's crow is heard).[18]

2

In literary matters, Blok was an enlightened conservative. In everything that concerned questions of style, rhythm, and imagery, he was surprisingly cautious: not a single overt break with the past. Imagining Blok as an innovator in literature, one is reminded of an English Lord tactfully introducing a new bill into Parliament. Blok's conservatism was more English than Russian. It was an irreproachably loyal literary revolution within the framework of tradition.[19] Beginning with a direct, almost a disciple's dependence on Vladimir Soloviev[20] and Fet,[21] to the very end Blok never broke a single obligation, never discarded a single piety, nor trampled on a single canon. He only made his poetic credo more complex by introducing newer pieties; thus, quite late he introduced Nekrasov's[22] canon into his poetry, and later still he experienced the direct, canonical influence of Pushkin,[23] quite a rare phenomenon in Russian poetry. Blok's literary reserve was by no means the result of a lack of character: he experienced style very keenly, as if it were a species; indeed, he sensed the life and language of a literary form not as a break, not as destruction, but as hybridization, as the conjoining of different species and strains, or the grafting of various fruits onto one tree.[24]

The most distinctive and unexpected of all Blok's works, *The Twelve (Dvenadtsat')*, is nothing other than the application of a previously existing literary canon which had come into existence independent of him, namely, the *chastushka*.[25] *The Twelve* is a monumental dramatic *chastushka*. Its center of gravity is in its composition, in the arrangement of its parts. Hence, the transitions from one *chastushka* construction to another acquire a particular expressiveness, and each junction of the poem is the source of a new surge of dramatic energy. However, the power of *The Twelve* resides not only in its composition, but in its very material drawn directly from folklore. Here popular, colloquial expressions are seized upon and incorporated into the poem, often such ephemeral expressions as: "she has *kerenkys* in her stocking."[26] Moreover, they are masterfully woven into the general texture of the poem. The folkloristic value of *The Twelve* is reminiscent of the conversations of the younger characters in *War and Peace*. Despite various idle interpretations, *The Twelve* is immortal, like folklore.

The poetry of the Russian Symbolists was extensive and rapacious: Balmont,[27] Bryusov,[28] and Andrei Bely[29] discovered new lands for themselves, ravaged them and, like the conquistadors, proceeded on.

Blok's poetry, from beginning to end, from his "Verses about the Beautiful Lady" ("Stikhi o prekrasnoi dame") to *The Twelve*, was intensive and culturally creative. The thematic development of Blok's poetry proceeded from cult to cult. From "The Stranger" ("Neznakomka") and "The Beautiful Lady" ("Prekrasnaia Dama") through *The Puppet Show (Balaganchik)* and *The Snow Mask (Snezhnaia maska)* to Russia and Russian culture, and onward to the Revolution as the highest form of musical tension and the catastrophic essence of culture. The poet's spiritual temperament inclined to catastrophe. Cult and culture offered a hidden, protected source of energy, a uniform and expedient motion: "the love which moves the sun and all the luminaries."[30] Poetic culture arises from the attempt to avert catastrophe, to make it dependent on the central sun of the system as a whole, be it love, of which Dante spoke, or music, at which Blok ultimately arrived.

We can say of Blok that he is the poet of "The Stranger" and of Russian culture, but it is obviously absurd to suggest that "The Stranger" and "The Beautiful Lady" are symbols of Russian culture. What is significant is that the same need for cult, that is, for an expedient discharge of poetic energy, guided his thematic creativity and found its highest fulfillment in the service of Russian culture and the Revolution.

18. THE NINETEENTH CENTURY

Baudelaire's words about the albatross aptly apply to the nineteenth century: "He is affixed to the earth by his tent of giant wings."[1]

The beginning of the century still sought to struggle against the earth's pull with convulsive leaps and awkward, laborious half-flights; the end of the century already rested motionless, covered with the great tent of outsized wings. The rest of despair. Wings pressed downward, contrary to their natural function.

The giant wings of the nineteenth century are its cognitive powers. Its capacity for cognition did not correspond in any way to its will, its character, or its moral stature. Like an immense Cyclopean eye, the cognitive capacity of the nineteenth century was directed toward both the past and the future. Being nothing but vision, empty and rapacious, it greedily and impartially devoured any object, any epoch.

On the threshold of the nineteenth century, Derzhavin scratched several lines on his slate which could serve as the *leit-motif* for the entire coming century:

> The river of time in its onrush
> Bears along the affairs of men,
> And drowns in the abyss of oblivion
> All peoples and realms and kings.
> But if something should happen to remain
> Borne on high by lyre or trumpet,
> It too shall be consumed by Eternity's maws,
> It alone shall not escape the common fate.[2]

Here, in the rusty language of the doddering age, with all its power and perspicacity, the latent thought of the future is expressed—its loftiest lesson abstracted, its keynote sounded. This lesson is relativism, relativity: "But if something should happen to remain..."

The essence of nineteenth century cognitive activity is projection. The bygone age did not like to refer to itself in the first person, rather it enjoyed projecting itself onto the screen of some distant epoch; in that flowed its life, its dynamism. It used its restless mind like a huge careening projector to scatter histories through the black sky; with its gigantic illuminated feelers it probed the void of time; it would pluck something out of the darkness, burn it up with the blinding glitter of its historical laws, and then apathetically allow it to plunge back into nothingness, as if nothing at all had happened.

And it was not merely one projector that groped along that terrible sky: all the sciences were transformed into their own abstract and monstrous methodologies (the only exception being mathematics). The triumph of naked method over genuine cognition was complete and total—each of the sciences referred to its own method more openly, more eagerly, more spiritedly than to its proper activity. Method defined science: there were as many methodologies as sciences. Philosophy was most typical: throughout the entire century it preferred to limit itself to "Introductions to Philosophy"; it was perpetually introducing its subject matter, leading you on only to abandon you. And all the sciences together groped through the starless sky (and the sky of the century was astonishingly starless) with their methodological feelers, never encountering any opposition in the soft, abstract void.

I am constantly drawn to citations from the naive and wise eighteenth century; here I am reminded of the lines from Lomonosov's famous "Epistle on Glass":

> They think improperly about things, Shuvalov,
> Who value Glass less than Minerals.[3]

Whence this pathos, the elevated pathos of utilitarianism, whence this inner warmth which stimulates poetic meditation on the fate of the industrial crafts? What a striking contrast to the brilliant, cold indifference of nineteenth century scientific thought!...

The eighteenth century[4] was an age of secularization, that is, it recognized human thought and activity as worldly ventures. Hatred for the priesthood, the hieratic cult, and the liturgy was deep in its blood. Although not an age devoted predominantly to social struggle, it was a period when society was painfully aware of caste. The determinism inherited from the Middle Ages hung menacingly over philosophy and enlightenment, and over its political experiments right down to the *tiers état*. The caste of priests, the caste of warriors, the caste of landowners—those were the concepts through which "enlightened minds" operated. These castes should not be confused with classes: the above-mentioned elements were all considered necessary to the sacred architectonics of any society.[5] The immense, accumulated energy of social conflict sought an outlet. All the aggressive demands of the age, all the strength of its principled indignation, fell upon the caste of priests. It seemed as if the entire anvil of Great Principles served only to forge the hammer with which to destroy the hated priests. There was never an age more sensitive to anything smelling of the priesthood—incense vapors and smoke from any source burned its nostrils and stiffened the backbone of the beast of prey.[6]

> The bow twanged, the arrow shuddered,
> And in a cloud of smoke Python expired...[7]

The liturgy was a thorn in the side of the eighteenth century. It saw nothing around it that was not in some way connected with the liturgy, that did not issue from it. Architecture, music, painting—everything radiated from a single center, and this center was slated for destruction. One question conditions the dynamics and balance of color in the composition of a painting: whence the source of light? The eighteenth century, having repudiated the source of light of its historical legacy, had to resolve this question once again. It resolved it in an original manner, having opened a window onto an imaginary paganism, onto pseudo-Classicism, in no way inspired by authenticity or philology, but based rather on auxiliary, utilitarian principles, created for the express purpose of satisfying immediate historical demands.

The rationalistic elements of mythology fit the demands of the century perfectly, allowing it to populate the empty sky with human images, pliant and obedient to the capricious egotism of the epoch. As for Deism, it tolerated anything; it was prepared to endure anything, if only the modest significance of the underpainting it preserved, if only the canvas would not remain empty.

With the approach of the great French Revolution, the pseudo-Classical theatricalization of life and politics[8] made ever greater strides, and on the eve of the Revolution itself, the real actors were already moving and struggling amidst the dense crowd of personifications and allegories, within the narrow space of the real theatre wings, on the boards of a staged Classical drama. When the real furies of Classical vengeance gathered within this pitiful cardboard theatre, penetrating the pompous blather of civic holidays and municipal choruses, it was at first difficult to believe, and only the poetry of Chénier,[9] poetry inspired by genuine Classical vengeance, clearly proved that a union of the mind and the furies existed, and that the Classical iambic spirit which once inspired Archilochus to write the first Iambs, was yet alive in the rebellious European soul.

The spirit of Classical vengeance made its appearance with festal splendor and dark majesty at the time of the French Revolution. Isn't this what cast the Gironde at the Mountain and the Mountain at the Gironde? Isn't this what blazed up in the flaming tongues of the Phrygian cap and in the unprecedented lust for mutual extermination that tore open the womb of the Convention? Liberty, equality and fraternity—this triad left no room for the authentic furies of Antiquity. The queen of the Ancient furies was not invited to the feast, she came of her own volition, unsummoned; she appeared uninvited, and was spoken to in the language of reason, but little by little her fiercest opponents were converted into her disciples.

The French Revolution ended when the spirit of Classical vengeance abandoned it. The Revolution had reduced the priesthood to ashes, destroyed social determinism, and brought the secularization of Europe to its ultimate conclusion. It was then washed up on the shore of the nineteenth century as an already unfathomable thing, not as a Gorgon's head, but as a fascicle of seaweed. Out of the union of mind and the furies[10] a mongrel was born, equally alien to the high rationalism of the *Encyclopedia* and to the Classical raging of the revolutionary storm—Romanticism.

Nevertheless, as it developed, the nineteenth century moved much further away from its predecessor than Romanticism.

The nineteenth century was the conduit of Buddhist influence in European culture. It was the carrier of an alien principle, inimical and powerful, against which our entire history has been doing battle—an active, practical, thoroughly dialectical and vital conflict of forces which had brought each other to fruition. It was the cradle of Nirvana which does not permit even a single ray of active cognition.

In an empty cave
I am the rocking of the cradle
Under another's hand,
Silence, silence...[11]

Latent Buddhism, an inward tendency, a worm-hole. The century did not preach Buddhism, but harbored it within itself, like inner night, like blindness of the blood, like furtive fears and vertigo. Buddhism in science[12] under the subtle guise of priggish positivisim; Buddhism in art, in the analytical novels of the brothers Goncourt[13] and Flaubert[14] ; Buddhism in religion, staring out of every chink in the theory of progress, preparing the triumph of the newest theosophy, which is nothing more than the bourgeois religion of progress, the religion of the apothecary, Monsieur Hommais, being readied for further sailing, rigged out with metaphysical masts.

It seems no accident to me that the Goncourts and their ilk, the first French impressionists, should express an inclination for Japanese art, for Hokusai engravings, for the *tanka*[15] in all its aspects, that is, for the perfect, self-enclosed and static composition. *Madame Bovary* is written entirely according to the system of *tanka*. Flaubert wrote it so slowly and painstakingly, because he had to begin it anew after every fifth word.

The *tanka* is the favorite form of molecular art. It is not a miniature, and it would be a gross mistake to confuse it with a miniature because of its brevity. It has no dimensions because it contains no action. It is in no way related to the world because it is a world in itself; it is the constant inward vortical movement of molecules.

The cherry branch and the conical form of the beloved snow-capped mountain, the patrons of Japanese engravers, are reflected in the glittering lacquer of each phrase of the polished Flaubertian novel. Everything is covered with the lacquer of pure contemplation and, like the surface of rosewood, the style of the novel is capable of reflecting any object. If like works did not frighten their contemporaries, we must attribute this to their insensitivity and lack of esthetic perspicacity. Perhaps the most penetrating of all Flaubert's critics was the royal prosecutor who sensed a certain danger in the novel. But, alas, he did not seek it where it was hidden.

At its most extreme, the nineteenth century had to arrive at the form of the *tanka*, at the poetry of nonbeing, and Buddhism in art. Japan and China are fundamentally not the East, but rather the extreme West: they are more Western than London or Paris. The past century plunged ever deeper into the West, not into the East, but in its search for outer limits, it encountered the East-West boundary.

In examining the analytic French novel as the summit of nineteenth century Western Buddhism, we are convinced of its total literary sterility. It had no progeny, nor could it have had any. It had only naive epigones who even now still exist in large numbers. Tolstoi's novels are pure epic, a perfectly sound European art form. Romain Rolland's synthetic novel broke sharply with the tradition of the French analytic novel and moved closer to the tradition of the eighteenth century synthetic novel, namely Goethe's *Wilhelm Meister*, by means of its basic artistic techniques.[16]

There exists a peculiar form of synthetic blindness to individual phenomena. Goethe and Romain Rolland paint psychological landscapes, depicting both characters and spiritual conditions, but the Japanese-Flaubertian analytical *tanka* is a form alien to them. Alien blood flows in the veins of every century, but the stronger the age, the more historically intensive it is, the more heavily this alien blood weighs.[17]

On the heels of the eighteenth century, which understood nothing, which possessed not even the vaguest inkling of the comparative historical method and which was left, like a blind kitten in a basket on the doorstep of unfathomable worlds, came the century of total understanding—the age of relativism with its monstrous capacity for reincarnation—the nineteenth century. Nevertheless, a taste for historical reincarnation and total understanding is not constant; it is a transient taste. And our century has begun under the sign of great intolerance, exclusiveness, and conscious noncomprehension of other worlds. The heavy blood of extremely distant, monumental cultures, perhaps of Egypt and Assyria, flows in the veins of our century:

> The wind brought us consolation,
> And we sensed through the azure
> The Assyrian wings of dragonflies,
> Vibrations of the jointed darkness.[18]

We appear as colonizers to this new age, so vast and so cruelly determined. To Europeanize and humanize the twentieth century, to provide it with theological warmth—this is the task of those emigrants who survived the shipwreck of the nineteenth century and were cast by the will of fate upon the shores of a new historical continent.

In fulfilling this task, it is easier to find support in the historical models not of yesterday, but of the day before yesterday. The elementary formulas, the general conceptions of the eighteenth century, may once again prove useful. "The skeptical reckoning of the *Encyclopedia*," the juridical spirit of the social contract, the naive materialism mocked so arrogantly in the nineteenth century, the schematic intellect, the spirit of expediency, may yet serve mankind. Now is not the time to fear rationalism. The irrational root of the oncoming epoch, the gigantic, inextractable root of two, casts a shadow over us like the stone temple of an alien god. In times such as these, the intellect of the Encyclopedists is the sacred fire of Prometheus.

19. LITERARY MOSCOW

I

Moscow—Peking: here is the triumph of the continent, the spirit of the Middle Kingdom; here the heavy tracks of railway lines have been spliced into a tight knot; here the Eurasian continent celebrates its eternal nameday.

Whoever has not grown weary in the Middle Kingdom is a welcome guest in Moscow. Some prefer the smell of the sea, others —the smell of the world.

Here cabbies drink tea in the taverns like Greek Philosophers; here an American detective story is screened nightly on the flat roof of a modest skyscraper; here on the boulevard a proper young man, without attracting anyone's attention, whistles a complex aria from *Tannhaüser* to earn his daily bread, while on a park bench an artist of the old school will do your portrait on a silver medal in half an hour; here cigarette boys travel in packs, like the dogs in Constantinople, immune to competition; inhabitants of Yaroslavl sell pastries while Caucasians settle down in the cool shade of a grocery store. Here not a single person who is not a member of the all-Russian Union of Writers will attend a literary debate in the summertime, and Dolidze[1] travels, in spirit at least, to Azurketa for the summer months, where he has been planning to go for the past twelve years.

When Mayakovsky purged the poets in alphabetical order at the Polytechnic Museum, there were young people in the audience who volunteered, when their turn came, to read their own poetry, so that Mayakovsky's task was made easier. This is only possible in Moscow, for nowhere else in the world are there people who, like the Shiites, are ready to prostrate themselves so that the chariot of that stentorian voice might drive over them.

In Moscow, Khlebnikov[2] could hide from human eyes like a beast of the forest and, completely unnoticed, exchange his wretched Moscow overnight lodgings for a green Novgorod grave. On the other hand, it was also in Moscow, in the most modest of modest literary anthologies, that I.A. Aksenov[3] placed a splendid wreath of analytical criticism on the grave of the great departed archaist poet, having illuminated Khlebnikov's archaicism with

Einstein's theory of relativity and revealed the connection between his creative work and the ancient Russian moral ideals of
the sixteenth and seventeenth centuries. Meanwhile, in Petersburg,
the enlightened *Literary Herald (Vestnik literatury)* was barely
able to respond with an insipid arrogant news item about the great
loss. Objectively speaking, something is wrong with Petersburg if
it has forgotten how to speak the language of time and wild
honey.

For Moscow the saddest portent is Marina Tsvetaeva's[4] Ma-
donna-like needlework, her response to the dubious solemnity of
the Petersburg poetess, Anna Radlova.[5] Women's poetry is the
worst aspect of literary Moscow. Recent experience has shown
that the only woman eligible to join the poets' circle with the
rights of a new muse is the Russian science of poetics, summoned
to life by Potebnya and Andrei Bely, and grown mature in the
formalist school of Eikhenbaum, Zhirmunsky and Shklovsky.[6]
The vast realm of parody, in the most serious and formal meaning
of the word, has fallen to the lot of women in poetry. Feminine
poetry emerges as an unconscious parody of both poetic inventiveness and reminiscence. The majority of Moscow poetesses have
been injured by metaphor. These are the poor Isises, doomed to
the eternal quest after the second half of a poetic simile which
was lost somewhere, and which is obliged to return its primal
unity to the poetic image, to Osiris.

Adalis[7] and Marina Tsvetaeva are prophets, as is Sofia Parnok.[8] Their prophecy is a kind of domestic needlework. While
the elevated tone and intolerable bombastic rhetoric of men's
poetry has subsided, yielding to a more normal use of the vocal
apparatus, feminine poetry continues to vibrate at the highest
pitch, offending the ear, offending the historical, poetical sense.
The tastelessness and historical inaccuracy of Marina Tsvetaeva's
poetry about Russia—pseudo-populist and pseudo-Muscovite—is
much inferior to the poetry of Adalis, whose voice at times
achieves masculine force and truth.[9]

Inventiveness and memory[10] go hand in hand in poetry: to
remember also means to invent, and the one who remembers is
also the inventor. The radical illness of Moscow's literary taste
is its indifference to this dual truth. Moscow has specialized in
inventiveness at any cost.

Poetry breathes through both the mouth and the nose, both

memory and inventiveness. Only a fakir could reject one of these modes of breathing. The passion for poetic breathing through memory was revealed in the great interest with which Moscow greeted the arrival of Khodasevich[11] who, thank God, had already been writing poetry for twenty-five years but suddenly found himself in the position of a young poet just beginning.

Literary Moscow spread boundlessly from MAF[12] to the Lyrical Circle[13] as if from the Taganka to Plyushchikha. It seemed as though inventiveness were at one end and memory at the other: at one end, Mayakovsky,[14] Kruchenykh,[15] and Aseev,[16] and at the other, owing to the toal absence of local talent, Moscow had to resort to guest artists from Petersburg to define the counter position. Consequently, it is not even worth discussing the Lyrical Circle as a Moscow phenomenon.

Exactly what happens in the realm of pure inventiveness? If we disregard Kruchenykh, who is inconsequential and unintelligible, and not because he is leftist and extreme, but because pure rubbish does exist on this earth (Kruchenykh's pathos and intensity concerning poetry notwithstanding, which makes him interesting as a personality), we find that in the realm of pure inventiveness, Mayakovsky solves the great and fundamental problem of "poetry for everyone, and not just for the elite." Of course, the extensive broadening of poetry's base comes at the cost of intensity, pithiness, and poetic culture. Highly knowledgeable about the richness and complexity of world poetry, Mayakovsky, in establishing his "poetry for everyone," had to send everything incomprehensible to the devil, that is, everything that presupposed even the tiniest bit of poetic education in the audience. To read poems to an audience that is completely uneducated in poetry is just as thankless a task as trying to sit on a spiked fence. The absolutely uneducated person will understand absolutely nothing. Or else, poetry liberated from all culture will cease to be poetry, and then, by some strange peculiarity of human nature, will become accessible to an unlimited audience. And yet Mayakovsky writes poetry, and very cultivated poetry: his refined *raeshnik,*[17] whose stanza is broken by heavy antithesis, is saturated with hyperbolic metaphors and sustained in the short, monotonous *pauznik.*[18] Thus, Mayakovsky impoverishes his poetry in vain. He is in danger of becoming a poetess, something which has already partially happened.

If Mayakovsky's poetry expresses a striving to achieve universal accessibility, then Aseev's poetry reflects the organizational pathos of our era. The brilliant, rational imagery of his language creates an impression of something freshly mobilized. There is essentially no difference between the snuffbox poetry of the eighteenth century and the mechanical poetry of the twentieth century Aseev. Sentimental rationalism and organizational rationalism. Purely rationalistic, electro-mechanical, radioactive, and, generally speaking, technological poetry is impossible for one reason, understandable to poet and mechanic alike: rationalistic, mechanistic poetry does not accumulate energy, does not augment it, as does natural, irrational poetry, but rather wastes it, squanders it. The discharge is equal to the original charge. Something will unwind only to the extent that it is wound up. A mainspring cannot release more energy than was put into it originally. That is why the rationalistic poetry of Aseev is not rational, but sterile and asexual. A machine may live a profound and inspired life, but does not issue any seed.

Today the inventive fever of poetic Moscow is already subsiding, the patents are already filed, there have been no new patents for a long time. The dual truth of inventiveness and memory is as necessary as bread. That is why there is not a single poetic school in Moscow, not one single lively poetic circle, for all the factions adhere either to one side or the other of the divided truth.

Inventiveness and memory are the two elements which set Pasternak's[19] poetry in motion. Let us hope that his poetry will be studied as briefly as possible and that it will not be subjected to as many lyrical absurdities as has been the lot of every Russian poet since Blok.[20]

Cosmopolitan cities such as Paris, Moscow, and London are surprisingly tactful with regard to literature. They allow it to hide in a crack, to vanish without a trace, to live without a visa under a false name, to live without an address. It is as ridiculous to speak of Moscow literature as it is of world literature. The first exists only in the imagination of the reviewer, just as the second exists only in the name of a respected Petersburg publishing house.[21] To a person that has not been forewarned, it might seem that there is no literature at all in Moscow. If by chance he should encounter a poet, the latter will wave his arms, pretending to be in a terrible hurry, and disappear through the green gates of the boulevard, seen off by the blessings of cigarette boys, who are more capable than anyone of judging a man and of discerning in him the most recondite possibilities.

20. LITERARY MOSCOW: THE BIRTH OF PLOT

1

At one time monks would eat more or less lenten fare in their chilly Gothic refectories, while listening to excerpts from the *Book of Monthly Readings (Chet'i Minei),*[1] rather good prose for its day. The readings were provided not only for their edification, but because reading aloud was an adjunct to the refectory, like dinner music, and the seasonings offered by the reader helped maintain the harmony and order at the common table by refreshing the diners' minds.

But just imagine some enlightened and modern social group today that would like to resurrect the custom of reading at meals, and imagine that it invites a reader. In his desire to please everyone, the reader picks up Andrei Bely's *St. Petersburg.*[2] But as he begins to read, something incredible happens: someone gets a piece of food lodged in his throat; someone else starts eating his fish with a knife; a third person burns his tongue on the mustard.

It is impossible to imagine what kind of proceedings, what kind of work, what kind of group occasion could warrant the accompaniment of Andrei Bely's prose. His prose periods can only be intended for an age of Methuselahs, they are unsuitable for any human activity. Even the tales of Scheherazade are intended for three hundred and sixty-six days, one for each night of a Leap Year; and the *Decameron* is also amenable to the calendar, obedient to the succession of days and nights. But what of the *Decameron*! Dostoevsky is excellent for reading at meals; if not just now, then in the very near future when, instead of weeping over him and being moved by him, as chambermaids are affected by Balzac and by popular dime novels, he will be accepted for his literary merit; then he will be read and understood for the first time.

To extract a pyramid from the depths of your own soul is like having a cannula inserted into your stomach—an odious and antisocial activity. It is not work, but a surgical operation. Ever since the ulcer of psychological experimentation penetrated the modern literary consciousness the prose writer has become a surgeon and prose—a clinical catastrophe not at all to our taste. I would forego a thousand times over the psychological *belles-lettres* of Andreev,[3] Gorky,[4] Shmelev,[5] Sergeev-Tsensky,[6] and Zamyatin[7] for the sake of the magnificent Bret Harte in a translation by some unknown student of the nineties: "Without a word, with a single motion of hand and foot, he threw him down the stairs, then, completely calm, he turned to the unknown woman."

Where is this student now? I am afraid that he is unduly ashamed of his literary past and spends his leisure hours offering himself to the vivisectionists—the psychological authors—not the crude bumblers from the clinic of the *Anthologies of Knowledge (Sborniki znaniia),*[8] where the most minor operation, the removal of an intellectual's tooth, threatened blood poisoning; rather to the skilled surgeons from Andrei Bely's clinic,[9] equipped with the latest methods of Impressionistic antisepsis.

2

Mérimée's *Carmen* ends with a philological discourse on the place of the gypsy dialect[10] in the family of languages. The highest tension of passion and plot is unexpectedly resolved in a philological tract which bears resemblance to the epode of a tragic chorus: "And everywhere are fateful passions, and there is no defense against the Fates." This preceded Pushkin.

Why should we be so surprised if Pilnyak[11] or the Serapions[12] introduce notebooks, construction estimates, Soviet circulars, newspaper announcements, manuscript fragments and God knows what else into their narratives? Prose belongs to nobody. It is essentially anonymous. It is the organized movement of the verbal mass cemented together by anything you please. The primary element of prose is accumulation. Prose is entirely fabric, morphology.

Today's prose writers are often called eclectic, that is, collectors. I think that no offense is meant by this, that this is a good thing. Every true prose writer is precisely an eclectic, a collector.[13] Leave personality out of it. Make way for anonymous prose. This is why the names of the great prose writers, those contractors of grandiose literary plans, anonymous in essence and collective in their execution, like Rabelais's *Gargantua et Pantagruel* or *War and Peace,* are transformed into legend and myth.

The rage for anonymous, "eclectic" prose coincided with our Revolution. Poetry itself demanded prose. It had lost all perspective because there was no prose. It reached an unhealthy flowering and was unable to satisfy its readers' demands to align itself with the pure movement of verbal masses, bypassing the author's personality, bypassing everything incidental, personal, and catastrophic (the domain of the lyric).

Why precisely did the Revolution prove to be so favorable to the rebirth of Russian prose? Because it promoted the anonymous prose writer, the eclectic, the collector, who does not create verbal pyramids from the depths of his own soul, but is the Pharaoh's humble overseer assuring the slow but true construction of real pyramids.

3

Russian prose will advance when the first prose writer that is independent of Andrei Bely appears. Andrei Bely is the summit of Russian psychological prose—he soared upward with astonishing power, but merely perfected the groundwork of his predecessors, the so-called belletrists, with his varied and high-flown devices.

Are his disciples, the Serapion Brothers and Pilnyak, actually returning to the bosom of *belles-lettres*, thereby coming full circle? Are we really on the verge of new *Anthologies of Knowledge*, where psychology and "daily life" will resurrect the old novel, the novel of the convict and his wheelbarrow?

As soon as plot disappeared, "daily life" replaced it. Before Jourdain, no one guessed that people speak in prose, no one knew that there was such a thing as "daily life."

"Daily life" is a dead plot, a decaying plot, a convict's wheelbarrow that drags psychology along behind it because it needs something to lean on; a dead plot will do if there is no living one. "Daily life" is always a foreignism, a false exoticism; it does not exist for its own native, domestic eye: a native notices only what is necessary and to the point. A foreign tourist (that is, a belletrist) tries to take in everything with his indiscriminate gaze and talk of everything with his pointless, inappropriate chatter.

Today's Russian prose writers, such as the Serapions and Pilnyak, are psychologists just as much as their pre-revolutionary predecessors and Andrei Bely. They forego plot. They are unsuitable for reading at meals. However, their psychology is riveted to another convict's wheelbarrow—not to "daily life," but to folklore. I would like to discuss this distinction in more detail, for it is a very significant one. They are not at all the same. Folklore is superior, qualitatively better.

"Daily life" is a kind of night-blindness to things. Folklore is a conscious consolidation and accumulation of linguistic and ethnographic material. "Daily life" is the deadening of plot; folklore is the birth of plot. Listen closely to folklore and you will hear thematic life stirring in it, the plot breathing, and, in every folklore transcription, the rudiments of a plot are present—this is where interest begins, where everything is fraught with plot. It sets everything in motion, it intrigues, it threatens. The brood hen sits on a heap of straw, cackling and clucking; likewise a folklorist-prose writer cackles and clucks about something, and anyone who so desires may sit and listen to him. In actual fact, however, he is occupied with something more important—he is hatching a plot.

The Serapions and Pilnyak (their elder brother who does not need to be treated separately) are not suited for the serious reader. Their anecdotes are suggestive, that is, they threaten us with plot. Their work contains no trace of a plot, that is, of a larger narrative breath, but the anecdote twitches its whiskers from every nook and cranny, just as in Khlebnikov[14] :

> Winging his golden flourish of most delicate veins,
> The grasshopper laid his belly in a basket
> Of myriad herbs and faiths

Pilnyak, Nikitin, Fedin, Kozyrev and others, and Lidin (another Serapion, who for some reason did not join the brotherhood) and Zamyatin and Prishvin are all "of myriad herbs and faiths." The beloved anecdote, the first free and joyous fluttering of plot, is the liberation of the spirit from the gloomy, funereal cowl of psychology.

4

Meanwhile, we shall dig in. Folklore is descending upon us like a voracious caterpillar. A swarm of locusts is advancing toward us: a plague of observations, commentaries, notes, sayings, quotation marks, small talk. The crops are threatened by a great invasion of gypsy moths. Thus, the alternation of plot and folklore is canonized in literature,[15] and folklore gives birth to plot just as a voracious caterpillar gives birth to a delicate moth. If we did not notice this alternation previously, it was because folklore made no attempt to consolidate its strength and vanished without a trace. But as a period of accumulation, of voracious invasion, it preceded the flowering of any plot. And since it did not aspire to literature, not being acknowledged as such, it remained only within personal letters, in legends of native storytellers, in partly published diaries and memoirs, in petitions and office reports, in court protocols and on signboards. I do not know—perhaps some people like Pilnyak's discourses, so similar to those with which Leskov endowed his first railroad conversationalists, those who were breaking the monotony of the long haul. But to me the most endearing thing in all Pilnyak is the epic conversation in the bathhouse between the deacon and a certain Draube on the meaning of the universe: it does not contain a single "something," nor a single lyrical simile, so intolerable in prose, but it does consist of the elementary game of a plot being born, as in Gogol, where, if you recall, as you approach Plyushkin's, you cannot immediately discern "whether it is a man or a woman, no, a woman, no, a man."

To this day prose continues to vacillate between "daily life" and folklore. The Serapions, Pilnyak, Zamyatin, Prishvin, Kozyrev, and Nikitin should be forgiven all their differences because of the use of folklore which gives their work unity and serves as proof of their vitality. All of them, like the legitimate children of folklore, have a predilection for the anecdote. Vsevolod Ivanov does not have any predilection for the anecdote, and what was stated above regarding daily life applies to him.

If you listen carefully to prose during a period when folklore is flourishing, you will hear something like an intense ringing of grasshoppers coupling in the air—such is the universal sound of contemporary Russian prose. You do not want to dismantle this ringing sound, for it was not a watchmaker's invention, but was assembled from countless multitudes of winged herbs and faiths. During the period that inevitably follows, during the period when multitudes of plots flourish, the chirring of grasshoppers is transformed into the sonorous song of the skylark—of the plot, and then the skylark's high, ringing voice is heard, of which the poet said:

> Lithe, frolicsome, sonorous, clear—
> He has shaken me to the depths of my soul.[16]

21. A LETTER ABOUT RUSSIAN POETRY

During that splendid era of international exhibitions in Paris, Brussels, Nizhegorod, and other centers of world reknown, it was accepted practice to erect architectural monuments in the grand style. However, the grandeur of those pavilions housing the arts, domestic industry, agriculture, and so on, was of an ephemeral nature: when the exhibition closed, the wooden planks were carted away.

The grandiose creations of Russian Symbolism remind me of those exhibition pavilions. I sometimes think that Balmont, Bryusov, and Andrei Bely were especially created for some international exhibition soon to be dismantled. Actually, they have already been dismantled. Balmont,[1] with his burning buildings and cosmic themes, his superhuman audacity and demonic narcissism, has left very few good, unpretentious poems. Bryusov[2] still stands; he has survived the "exhibition," yet we all know what he is. All that remains of Vyacheslav Ivanov's[3] cosmic poetry is a small Byzantine chapel in which the scant splendor of numerous burned out temples has been collected. And finally, Bely[4] ... Here I must abandon my architectural analogy: Bely, quite unexpectedly, turned out to be a *grand dame*, sparkling in the blinding brilliance of universal charlatanism: Theosophy.

"Who are you, O contemporary poets, compared with your elders?" sigh the dilettantes of the grand style, educated at exhibition pavilions. "Now, they were genuine poets! What themes, what breadth, what erudition!..."

It never occurred to the dilettantes of Russian Symbolism that this might be the great poisonous mushroom of the swamps of the 1890s, elegantly attired in multiple chasubles.

At the close of the last century, Russian poetry departed the provincial circle of indigenous melodies sung by Fet[5] and Golenishchev-Kutuzov[6] to enter the international realm of European thought, demanding universal recognition. The young writers at *The Scales (Vesy)*[7] —Bryusov, Ellis,[8] Zinaida Gippius[9] —perceived everything in a new light. To this day, in leafing through old issues of *The Scales*, I am elated by the joyous astonishment and feverish excitement of discovery which possessed that entire epoch. Universal thought which had never died even in the poetry of the

Russian landed gentry (although after Pushkin it assumed a latent form in the obscure creations of Tyutchev and Vladimir Soloviev), washed away the domestic debris of Russian poetic thought in a roaring flood, and once again discovered the West. The West appeared new and seductive; it was immediately welcomed in its totality as the sole religion, whereas in reality it was nothing more than a composite of conflicting ideas and contradictions. Russian Symbolism is no more than a belated form of naive Westernization transferred into the realm of esthetic perception and poetic technique. Instead of serene possession of the repositories of Western thought:

> We remember everything—the hell of Paris streets
> And the Venetian coolness,
> The distant fragrance of lemon groves
> And the smoky masses of Cologne Cathedral...[10]

we find youthful passion, infatuation, but most important, the inevitable companion of infatuation—the regeneration of intense individualism and hypertrophy of the creative "I" which confused its boundaries with the newly discovered boundaries of the world of passion. The creative "I" lost its distinctive features and its own self-awareness. It was infected by the morbid dropsy of cosmic themes. Under such circumstances, the most interesting process in poetry—the growth of the poetic persona—destroyed itself. Poets immediately adopted the highest, most intense pitch and deafened themselves; they failed to recognize the organic quality of their own voices.

* * *

It is convenient to gauge our poetry against Blok's poetic thermometer. His is a living thermometer, measuring both heat and cold, yet it is always hot there. Blok developed normally: from a youth immersing himself in the works of Soloviev and Fet, he grew into a Russian Romantic educated by his English and German brothers and, finally, he became a full-fledged Russian poet who realized Pushkin's cherished dream—to stand as an equal with his age in expressing its culture.

Just as a land-surveyor can chart vast expanses on his graph based on measurements taken from a single calculation, so we can measure the past with reference to Blok. We see Pushkin, Goethe, Baratynsky, and Novalis through Blok, but we see them in a new way, for they all appear as tributaries of Russian poetry rushing toward the future, united and enriched through poetry's eternal movement.[11]

Where did Blok come from...? Always an intriguing and puzzling question. He emerged from the labyrinth of German *Natürphilosophie*, from Apollon Grigoriev's[12] student quarters, and—how strange!—he somehow returns us to Nekrasov's[13] seventies, to that time when anniversaries were celebrated in the taverns, when Garcia was singing at the theatre.

Kuzmin[14] brought dissident songs from the Volga shores, an Italian comedy from his own native Rome, and the entire history of European culture insofar as it had become music—from Giorgione's "Concert"[15] at the Pitti Palace to the most recent tone poems of Debussy.

Klyuev[16] came from the majestic Olonetsk region where Russian life and Russian peasant speech repose in Hellenic dignity and simplicity. Klyuev is a national poet because the iambic spirit of Baratynsky lives harmoniously in his verse along with the prophetic melody of the illiterate Olonetsk teller of tales.

Akhmatova[17] introduced all the enormous complexity and wealth of the nineteenth century novel into the Russian lyric. If not for Tolstoi's *Anna Karenina*, Turgenev's *Nest of Gentlefolk (Dvorianskoe gnezdo)*, all of Dostoevsky and even some Leskov, there would be no Akhmatova. Akhmatova's genesis lies entirely in the realm of Russian prose, not in poetry. She developed her poignant and unique poetic form with a backward glance at psychological prose.

Her poetic form derives entirely from the asymmetrical parallelism of the folksong, and the narrow wasp stinger is capable of transferring psychological pollen from one flower to the next.

Thus, none of our poets is without a legacy; each one has come a long distance and will travel still further.

During the fluorescence of tawdry Russian Symbolism, and even prior to its emergence, Innokenty Annensky[18] showed us what an organic poet should be: a ship could be built entirely from foreign planks, but it must have its own form. Annensky never belonged to the epic heroes on clay feet of Russian Symbolism; he endured his lot of resignation and renunciation with dignity. The spirit of resignation which sustains Annensky's poetry is nourished in turn by his consciousness of the impossibility of tragedy in modern Russian art owing to the indisputable and total absence of integrated national consciousness, the necessary pre-requisite for tragedy. Hence, the poet born to be the Russian Euripides casts a doll onto the waters instead of launching the ship of universal tragedy, for "our heart feels an insult to a doll is more piteous than an insult to oneself."[19]

22. A WORD OR TWO ABOUT GEORGIAN ART

There is a Georgian tradition in Russian poetry. When our poets of the past century touch on Georgia their voices take on a peculiarly feminine softness, while each line seems to sink into a soft, moist atmosphere:

> Nocturnal gloom settled over the hills of Georgia...

In all Georgian poetry no two lines, perhaps, are as Georgian in their intoxicating and heady effects as Lermontov's

> A drowsy Georgian pours
> The foam of sweet wines

Russian poetry, I would say, has its own Georgian myth, first proclaimed by Pushkin:

> Don't sing to me, my beauty,
> Songs of melancholy Georgia—

and later developed by Lermontov into a full-fledged myth centered around the legendary heroine, Tamara.[1]

It is a curious fact that Georgia, rather than Armenia,[2] became the mythological Promised Land of Russian poetry. Georgia seduced our Russian poets with its distinctive eroticism, its unique love so appropriate to the Georgian national character, with its light, chaste spirit of intoxication, and with that melancholy and festive drunkenness in which the national soul is immersed. Russian poets were seduced by the Georgian Eros. Exotic love has always been dearer and closer to us than our own, and Georgia knew how to love. Ancient Georgian art, the craftsmanship of Georgian architects, painters and poets, is permeated with exquisite love and heroic tenderness.

Yes, the very culture intoxicates us. Georgians keep wine in long, narrow jugs buried beneath the earth. Therein lies the prototype of Georgian culture—the earth has preserved the narrow but noble forms of its esthetic tradition, and has sealed the vessels full of fermentation and fragrance.

It is precisely this spirit of intoxication, this product of a mysterious internal fermentation (the long, narrow amphora of wine buried under the earth) that is impossible to deduce from the rational data of a culture, from an inventory of its accumulated riches.

Russian culture has never imposed its values on Georgia. Russification of the region never exceeded administrative formalities. Although Russian administrators, led by Vorontsov-Dashkov, mutilated the region's economic life and suppressed its communal organizations, they never managed to encroach upon its life-style, treating it with reluctant respect. Cultural Russification of Georgia was never even mentioned. Therefore Georgia's national and political self-determination, which falls into two sharply distinct periods—before and after Sovietization—must have been a test of faith for Georgian art and culture; and cultural Russia, which had admiringly watched over Georgia for an entire century, now looks anxiously at that country as one prepared to betray its cultural calling. The essence of Georgian culture always lay in its Eastern orientation, despite the fact that Georgia had never merged with the East, maintaining its independence. I would include Georgia among the world's ornamental cultures: in bordering on vast, fully developed foreign territories, such cultures may assimilate certain patterns of their powerful neighbors, while simultaneously offering fierce resistance to their innately hostile essence.

Today Georgia's motto: "Get out of the East, turn to the West! We are not Asiatics, we are Europeans, Parisians!" sounds like a moan. How naive the Georgian artistic intelligentsia! The tendency to "get out of the East" has always existed in Georgian art, but it was expressed in lofty esthetic forms and devices, not in crude sloganizing.

Enter the National Museum of Georgian Art in Tiflis and you will see before you a long line of portraits, predominantly women, which both by virtue of their technique and their profound static calm remind you of German painting. At the same time, however, flattened form and linear composition (the rhythm of the lines) breathes with the devices of the Persian miniature. Moreover, you frequently see a gold background and rich gold ornamentation. These anonymous masterpieces exemplify the genuine triumph of Georgian art over the East. How paltry in comparison the dancing fragments of a violin, smashed some time ago by Picasso, which have now captivated modern French painting... The same thing has now happened with this violin as happened long ago with the fraudulent relics of the monks—there was only one violin, it was smashed only once, but today there is not a single city which does not exhibit its splinters—here are a few tidbits of Picasso!

The life of a language is revealed to everyone—everyone speaks and participates in the movement of language and every spoken word leaves a living furrow in the language. Signboards offer us a marvelous opportunity to observe the development of the language of painting, especially the signboards of Tiflis which grow into the powerful art of Pirosmanishvili before our very eyes.

Niko Pirosmanishvili[3] was a simple and illiterate sign painter. He painted on oilcloth with three colors: ochre, earth green and black bone. His customers, the Tiflis innkeepers, demanded interesting subjects, and he worked to meet their demands. On one of his pictures I read his handwritten inscription:

Shamil ad hiss own guard

(I preserve the spelling). We cannot help but bow down before the splendor of his "illiterate" (not anatomically correct) lions, his splendid camels standing alongside oddly proportioned human figures, and his tents which overcome the one-dimensional flatness of his medium through the power of color alone. If the French had known of Pirosmanishvili, they would have come to Georgia to study painting. Incidentally, they shall soon come to know him, for due to an oversight, nearly all his things have been taken abroad.

Another phenomenon of modern Georgian art representing European values is the poet Vazha Pshavela.[4] His work is being republished by the National Ministry of Education (Narkompros), while Georgian youths have developed something of a cult of Vazha Pshavela. But, my God, how limited is his immediate influence on contemporary Georgian poetry!... A veritable hurricane of the word swept through Georgia, uprooting trees:

Your encounters are people of peace,
So unlike the man of war—

> The dark curly-haired enemy eats iron
> And uproots trees...

His imagery, almost medieval in its epic majesty, contains an elemental force. It seethes with the concrete, the tangible, with everyday reality. Every utterance inadvertently becomes an image, and yet the word does not suffice—he must rip each word to pieces, as it were, with his teeth, making the most of the passionate temperament of Georgian poetry.

Wine ages—therein lies its future; culture ferments—therein lies its youth. Preserve your own art: those narrow clay jugs buried beneath the earth.[5]

23. FROM AN INTERVIEW: COMMENTS ON THE LYRIC AND THE EPIC

O. Mandelstam: I agree with Trenev. We must write about the past.[1] Right now people are saying that we have enough lyric poetry, give us an epic. I was also reminded of an Old French epic.[2] A fine epic. I even snatched something from it, yes indeed, without a beginning or an end. You may recall that a well-known critic once said of Goethe that in his best lyrics there is always something left unsaid. It's time for us to introduce this sense of the unfinished statement into the epic.

24. SOME NOTES ON POETRY

Modern Russian poetry did not just fall from the skies; it was foreshadowed by our nation's entire poetic past.[1] After all, didn't Yazykov's[2] trilling and clicking anticipate Pasternak? And isn't this example enough to show how batteries of poetry converse with one another in connecting salvos, not embarrassed in the least by the indifference of Time which seeks to divide them? In poetry, war is always being waged. It is only in periods of social imbecility that there is peace or a peace treaty is concluded. Like generals, the bearers of word roots take up arms against each other. Word roots battle in the darkness, depleting each other's food supplies and the juices of the earth. The battle of the Russian language,[3] that is, of unwritten secular speech, derived from domestic word roots, from the secular tongue of the peasantry, rages on even today against the written language of the monks, against their hostile, Church Slavonic, Byzantine literacy.

The first intelligentsia in Russia were the Byzantine monks. They foisted an alien spirit and an alien form on the language. In Russia, the black cassocks—the intelligentsia—have always spoken a different language than the laity. The widespread introduction of the Slavonic dialect by Cyril and Methodius[4] was for their age what the widespread introduction of *Volapük*[5] would be for ours. Colloquial speech craves adaptation. It fuses contradictory elements. Colloquial speech always finds the convenient middle path. In its relationship to the history of language, it is conciliatory, and it is defined by a vague sense of benevolence, that is, by a sense of opportunism. Poetic speech, however, can never be sufficiently "pacified," and after many centuries old discords are revealed within; poetic speech may be compared to a piece of amber in which a fly still buzzes, having long ago been buried under layers of resin, the living foreign body continuing to live even when fossilized. Everything in Russian poetry which works to perpetuate an alien monasticizing literature, any body of literature produced by the intelligentsia, in a word, by "Byzantium," is reactionary; that means evil bearing evil. On the other hand, everything which works toward the secularization of poetic speech, toward the expulsion of the monasticizing intelligentsia, of Byzantium, brings only good or longevity to the language, and helps it, as one might help a righteous man, to accomplish the feat of independent existence within the family of dialects. The reverse would be possible if, say, a nation governed by native theocracy, such as Tibet, were to liberate itself from foreign secular invaders, such as the Manchurians. Only those who were directly involved in the great secularization of the Russian language, in making it the language of the laity, helped to accomplish the task of primary significance in the development of Russian poetry. These include Trediakovsky,[6] Lomonosov,[7] Batyushkov,[8] Yazykov, and most recently, Khlebnikov[9] and Pasternak.[10]

At the risk of sounding too elementary or of over-simplifying my subject, I would like to describe the positive and negative poles of the poetic language as the turbulent morphological flowering on the one hand, and the petrifaction of the morphological lava under the semantic crust, on the other hand. A roaming root of multiple meanings animates poetic speech.

The multiplier of the root, the index of its vitality, is the consonant (the classical example being Khlebnikov's "Laughter" poem).[11] A word multiplies its meaning through consonants, not through vowels. The consonants thus act both as the seed and as the pledge of the posterity of the language.

A decline in linguistic consciousness is the equivalent of an atrophied consonantal sense.

Russian verse is saturated with consonants: it clicks, crackles, and whistles with them. This is genuine secular speech. Monastic speech is a litany of vowels.

Because the war with the "Byzantine" monasticizing intelligentsia on the battlefield of poetry abated after Yazykov, and because a new hero did not emerge on that glorious field for a long time, one after another Russia's poets began to grow deaf to the noise of language, to become hard of hearing and to miss the surf of sound waves, and only through an ear-trumpet did they finally discover their own meager vocabulary amidst the noise of the dictionary. For example, everyone shouts to the deaf old man in Griboedov's *Woe from Wit:* "Prince, Prince, come back!" (Sologub).[12] A small vocabulary is neither a sin nor yet a vicious circle. It may even enclose the speaker in a circle of fire, but it is a sign that the speaker does not trust his native soil nor feel free to step anywhere he pleases. The Russian Symbolists were true pillars of style. Just think, among them they have no more than five hundred words—the vocabulary of a Polynesian. But at least they were

simple ascetics, anchorites. They stood on unhewn logs. Akhmatova,[13] however, stands on a parquet floor; this is already parquet pillardom. And Kuzmin[14] scatters grass over the parquetry,
to make it resemble a meadow (see his "Otherworldly Evenings").

Pushkin had two expressions for poet-innovators. The first:
"Only to fly away again, having bestirred in us, children of dust,
that wingless desire"; the second: "When the great Glück appeared
and revealed to us new mysteries."[15] Any poet who would lead his
native poetry astray with sounds and forms of foreign speech
would be an innovator of the first sort, that is, a seducer. For it is
not true that Latin sleeps in Russian speech, nor that Hellas sleeps
in it. If so, we could conjure up in the music of the Russian language African drumbeats and the monosyllabic utterances of the
Kaffirs. Russian speech and only Russian speech sleeps in itself.
To say a Russian poet's verses sound like Latin is a direct insult,
not praise. But what of Glück? Profound, captivating mysteries?
For Russia's poetic fate, the profound, captivating mysteries of
Glück are not to be found in Sanskrit or Hellenisms, but in the
consistent secularization of poetic speech. Give us the Vulgate,
we don't want a Latin Bible.

Whenever I read Pasternak's *My Sister Life,*[16] I experience
the sheer joy of the vernacular, of secular speech free from all
foreign influences, the common everyday tongue of Luther, after
the strained and, although intelligible (of course, intelligible),
unnecessary Latin, that which had once been a trans-sense language, but which to the great chagrin of the monks had long
since lost its trans-sense quality. That is just how the Germans in
their tile houses rejoiced when, for the first time, they opened
their new Gothic Bibles still smelling of printer's ink. And reading
Khlebnikov can be compared to a still more magnificent and instructive event, to a situation in which our language, like a righteous man, could have and should have developed, unburdened and
undesecrated by historical necessity and adversity. Khlebnikov's
language is so completely the language of the laity, so completely
secular, that it seems as if neither the monks, nor Byzantium, nor
the literature of the intelligentsia had ever existed. His speech is
the absolutely secular and mundane Russian language, resounding
for the first time in the history of Russian letters. If we accept
this view, there is no need to regard Khlebnikov as a sorcerer or
a shaman. He projected different paths of development for the

language, transitional and intermediate paths, but the historically unprecedented path of Russia's oral destiny was realized only in Khlebnikov's work. It took hold there in his trans-sense language, which meant no more than those transitional forms which succeeded in not being covered by the semantic crust created by the properly and correctly developing language.

When a ship moves out to the open sea after cruising along the shore, those who cannot endure the inevitable rolling return to shore. After Khlebnikov and Pasternak, Russian poetry is once again moving out to the open sea, and many of its passengers are finding it necessary to debark. I see them already, suitcases in hand, standing near the gangway dropped onto the shore. But how welcome is each new passenger stepping onto the deck precisely at this moment!

When Fet[17] first made his appearance, he stirred Russian poetry with "the silver and the swaying of a sleepy stream." When he departed, he said: "And with the burning salt of undying words." In Pasternak's poetry this "burning salt" of certain words, this whistling, crackling, rustling, sparkling, splashing, this fullness of life, this fullness of sound, this flood of images and feelings leaps out at us with unprecedented force. Once again the momentous patriarchal phenomenon which Fet presented to Russian poetry stands before us.

Pasternak's magnificent, domestic Russian poetry is already old-fashioned. It is tasteless because it is immortal; it is styleless because it chokes over banalities with the classical ecstasy of a nightingale trilling his song. Yes, Pasternak's poetry is truly a mating call (the wood-grouse in its nest, a nightingale in the spring), the direct result of the anatomical structure of the throat, just as much a mark of genus as a bird's plumage or crest.

> It's a steeply suffused whistle,
> It's a crackling of compressed icicles,
> It is night frosting leaves,
> It is two nightingales in a duel...[18]

To read Pasternak's verse is to clear your throat, to fortify your breathing, to fill your lungs; surely such poetry could provide a cure for tuberculosis. No poetry is more healthful at the present moment! It is *koumiss* after evaporated milk.

To me Pasternak's book, *My Sister Life*, is a collection of marvelous breathing exercises: each time the voice is arranged anew, each time the powerful breathing apparatus is adjusted differently.

Pasternak uses the syntax of a passionate person speaking with conviction, heatedly and excitedly proving something; but what is he proving?

> Isn't it true the Arum's
> Begging alms of the swamp?
> Nights inhale in vain
> The putrescent tropics.[19]

So, waving its arms and muttering under its breath, poetry moves off, staggering, its head swimming, blissfully crazy, and yet it is the only sober one, the only one completely awake in the whole world.

Of course, when Herzen and Ogarev[20] stood as boys on Sparrow Hills, they experienced physiologically the sacred ecstasy of space and bird's flight. Pasternak's poetry tells us of such moments; it is a shining *Nike,* carried off from the Acropolis to Sparrow Hills.

25. STORM AND STRESS

From now on Russian poetry of the first quarter of the twentieth century shall be read simply as Russian poetry, and need not be perceived as "Modernism" with all the ambiguity and contempt associated with that term. This shift is the result of what may be called the knitting together of the spines of two poetic systems, two poetic epochs.[1]

The Russian reader, having experienced not one, but several poetic revolutions over the last quarter of a century, has grown accustomed to grasping almost immediately what is objectively valuable from among the various types of poetic creation available to him. Each new literary school—be it Romanticism, Symbolism, or Futurism—emerges at first in an artificially inflated condition, exaggerating its unique qualities, ignoring its external historical limitations. It inevitably passes through a period of "Storm and Stress." Only later, when the main representatives of the school have lost their freshness of vision and capacity for work, is their rightful place in literature established and their objective values clarified. Moreover, after the flood tides of "Storm and Stress," the literary current must recede to its natural channel, and it is precisely these incomparably more modest boundaries and outlines which posterity shall remember.

Russian poetry experienced two sharply definable periods of "Storm and Stress" during the first quarter of this century, the first being Symbolism, the second—Futurism. Both major tendencies revealed a desire to remain at the crest of their respective waves, and both failed in this desire, for history was already preparing the crests of new waves, and at the appropriate moment, imperiously ordered them to recede, to return to the maternal bosom of literature, to the common elements of language and poetry. However, while Symbolism and Futurism complemented each other historically, they were completely different in their poetic development.

The "Storm and Stress" of Symbolism must be seen as a stormy and passionate process of introducing European and world poetry into the mainstream of Russian literature. Hence, this stormy phenomenon had an essentially external cultural significance. Early Russian Symbolism blew in like a powerful draft from the West. Russian Futurism, on the other hand, is much closer to Romanticism. It contains all the features of a national poetic revival, in particular, its reworking of the national treasury of language and its conscious concern over poetic heritage—both indicative of its ties to Romanticism. As opposed to this, Russian Symbolism was an alien force, a *Kulturträger*, a bearer of poetic culture from one land to another. Here we see the fundamental distinction between Symbolism and Futurism: the former presents a model of external aspirations, the second—of internal aspirations. The focal point of Symbolism was its passion for grand themes, themes of a cosmic and metaphysical nature. Early Russian Symbolism is a kingdom of grand themes and ideas "with a capital letter," direct borrowings from Baudelaire, Edgar Allan Poe, Mallarmé, Swinburne, Shelley and others. Futurism lived primarily on poetic method, focussing on the poetic device rather than the theme, that is, creating something internal, corresponding to the nature of the Russian language. For the Symbolists the theme stood in the foreground like a shield, concealing the device. The themes of early Bryusov, Balmont, and the others were extraordinarily intelligible. In the work of the Futurists, however, it is difficult to distinguish the theme from the device, and the inexperienced eye, for instance in Khlebnikov's compositions, will see only the pure device of the naked language of trans-sense.[2]

It is easier to sum up Symbolism than Futurism, for the latter never developed so distinctly, nor was it terminated quite so abruptly as Symbolism, which was extinguished by hostile influences. The Futurists repudiated the extremes of their "Storm and Stress" almost unnoticed and proceeded to concentrate on what seemed to represent objective values in the spirit of the general history of language and poetry. Hence, it is comparatively easy to sum up Symbolism. Almost nothing remains of early Symbolism, swollen as it was from the dropsy of great themes. Balmont's grandiose cosmic hymns turned out to be immature and inept in poetic practice. The glorified urbanism of young Bryusov, who entered poetry as the singer of the universal city, was obscured by history, since the poet's sounds and images turned out to be far from compatible with his favorite theme. Andrei Bely's transcendental poetry proved incapable of keeping his metaphysics from becoming shabby and outmoded. Vyacheslav Ivanov and his complex Byzantine-Hellenic world fared somewhat better. Actually as much of a pioneer and colonizer as his fellow Symbolists, he did not treat Byzantium and Hellas as foreign lands destined for conquests, but rightly perceived in them the cultural springs of Russian poetry. However, because he lacked a sense of proportion (a peculiarity of the Symbolists in general), Ivanov overburdened his poetry with an incredible quantity of Byzantine-Hellenic images and myths which depreciated its value.

As for Sologub and Annensky, they deserve to be treated separately since they never participated in the "Storm and Stress" of Symbolism. Blok should also be treated separately since his poetic fate was so closely bound up with the fate of nineteenth-century Russian poetry. Here, however, we should discuss the work of the younger Symbolists, or Acmeists,[3] who preferred not to repeat the mistakes of early Symbolism, so swollen with the dropsy of great themes. The Acmeists, in soberly assessing their strengths and weaknesses, repudiated the mania for the grandiose characterizing early Symbolism, some exchanging it for the monumentality of the device, some for the clarity of expression, with far from equal success.

No poetic heritage grew so shabby and antiquated in such a short period as Symbolism. Russian Symbolism should be known more properly as pseudo-Symbolism, to emphasize its abuse of great themes and abstract concepts so poorly represented in its language. The whole of pseudo-Symbolism, that is, an enormous chunk of what the Symbolists wrote, is of little interest except as literary history. What has objective value is concealed under heaps of window-dressing, of pseudo-Symbolist rubbish. A most noble and industrious generation of Russian poets paid a heavy tribute to the era and its cultural work.

Let's begin with the father of Russian Symbolism, Balmont.[4] Astonishingly little of Balmont's work has survived, no more than a dozen poems. However, what did survive is truly superb; both in its phonetic brilliance and in its profound feeling for word roots and sounds, it bears comparison with the best of trans-sense verse. It is not Balmont's fault that undemanding readers encouraged him to develop the worst aspects of his poetry. In his best poems, such as "O Night, Stay with Me" ("O noch', pobud' so mnoi") and "The Old House" ("Staryi dom"), he extracted new sounds from Russian poetry, never-to-be-repeated sounds having a kind of foreign, seraphic phonetics. This quality may be explained by

Balmont's phonetic eccentricity, by his exotic perception of consonantal sounds. It is here, and not in the vulgar musicality of his verse, that we must seek the source of his poetic power.

Bryusov's[5] best (non-urban) poems contain one feature which will never become obsolete, that feature which makes him the most consistent and skillful of the Russian Symbolists. This is his courageous approach to the theme, his perfect mastery over it, his capacity to exhaust the theme completely, to extract from it everything it can and must give, and then to find for it the most appropriate and capacious stanzaic vessel possible. His best poems are models of absolute control over his theme: "Orpheus and Eurydice," "Theseus and Ariadne," "Demon of Suicide" ("Demon samoubiistva"). It was Bryusov who taught Russian poets to respect the theme as such. We can also learn something from his latest books, from *Distances (Dali)* and *Last Dreams (Poslednie mechty)*, where he offers models of the capaciousness of his verse and of the astonishing arrangement of a semantically rich and varied lexicon within a frugally measured space.

Andrei Bely's[6] *Urn (Urna)* enriched the Russian lyric with its sharp prosaicisms from the lexicon of German metaphysics, revealing the ironic sounds of philosophical terminology. In his book, *Ashes (Pepel')*, Bely skillfully introduced polyphony, or the element of many voices, into the poetry of Nekrasov, whose themes he subjected to a very original orchestration. Bely's musical populism became a gesture of beggarly plasticity to accompany his grand musical theme.

Vyacheslav Ivanov[7] is more of a genuine populist and in the future shall be more accessible than all the other Russian Symbolists. Much of our fascination with his majestic poetry stems from our philological ignorance. In the work of no other Symbolist poet does the noise of his lexicon, the mighty clamor of the bell of popular speech rushing up and waiting its turn, echo as clearly as in the voice of Vyacheslav Ivanov, for instance, in his "Deaf Night, Dumb Night" ("Noch' nemaia, noch' glukhaia") or "The Maenad" ("Maenada"), et cetera. His sense of the past as the future makes him akin to Khlebnikov. Ivanov's archaicism derives not from his choice of themes, but from his incapacity to deal with relative thought, that is, to compare different periods of time. His Hellenic poetry seems not to be written after Greek poetry, nor at the same time, but to precede it, for he never once forgets himself, speaking his own native barbarian idiom.

Such are the founders of Russian Symbolism. Their work did not go for naught. We can learn something from each one today as well as in the future. Let's now turn to the work of their contemporaries, Sologub and Annensky, whose fate from the very beginning was the bitter satisfaction of not sharing the historical mistakes of the others, but also of not enjoying the invigorating storms of the first Symbolist feasts.

Sologub[8] and Annensky[9] began their activity as complete unknowns as far back as the 1890s. The extraordinary force of Annensky's influence is revealed in the subsequent development of Russian poetry. As the first teacher of psychological perspicacity in the modern Russian lyric, he bequeathed to Futurism the art of psychological composition. Sologub's influence, although almost as potent as Annensky's, found expression in a purely negative manner: by subjecting the devices of the older Russian lyric of the decline (including Nadson, Apukhtin, and Golenishchev-Kutuzov)[10] to lofty rationalism, he took them to the limits of simplicity and perfection, and having purged these devices of their trashy emotional adulteration while daubing them with the colors of an original erotic myth, he made any attempt to return to the past impossible, and, it would seem, any attempt to imitate him equally impossible. By nature sympathetic to banality and tenderly indulgent toward the moribund word, Sologub created a cult of moribund and obsolete poetic formulas, infusing them with a miraculous last gasp of life. Thus, Sologub's early poetry and his collection, *The Flaming Circle (Plamennyi krug)*, a cynical and cruel assault on the poetic cliché, serve not as tempting examples but rather as ominous warnings to any bold fool who might dare to attempt such verse in the future.

Annensky, with the same perseverance as Bryusov, introduced the historically objective theme into poetry and psychological contructivism into the lyric. But burning with a desire to learn from the West, he could not find a proper teacher, and was forced to pretend to be an imitator. Annensky's psychologism was not a whim, nor the ephemeral glimmer of a refined sensibility; it was a genuine, firm construction. Indeed, one can draw a straight line from Annensky's "Steel Cicada" ("Stal'naia tsikada") to Aseev's "Steel Nightingale" ("Stal'noi solovei"). Annensky taught us how to use psychological analysis as a working instrument in the lyric.

He was the forerunner of psychological contructivism in Russian Futurism, so brilliantly practiced by Pasternak. But even today Annensky has still not reached the Russian reader; he is known only through Akhmatova's vulgarizations of his methods. He was one of the most genuinely original Russian poets. Every poem in his *Quiet Songs (Tikhie pesni)* and *Cypress Chest (Kiparisovyi larets)* demands to be anthologized.

If Russian Symbolism had its own Virgils and Ovids, it also had its own Catulluses, not so much with respect to age as to type of creation. Here we must mention Kuzmin[11] and Khodasevich. Both are typical minor poets with all the purity and charm of sound characteristic of minor poets. Kuzmin has acted as if the more traditional line of world literature never existed. Completely biased against it, he has become fully involved in canonizing the minor line, on a level not much higher than the comedies of Goldoni or the love songs of Sumarokov. He has very successfully cutivated in his verse an illusion of conscious neglect and awkward speech, sprinkled with Gallicisms and Polonisms. Fired up by the minor poetry of the West, for example de Musset's "New Rolla" ("Novyi Rolla"), he presents the reader with an illusion of a completely artificial and premature senility in Russian poetic speech. Kuzmin's poetry is the prematurely senile smile of the Russian lyric.

Khodasevich[12] has cultivated Baratynsky's[13] theme, "My gift is poor, my voice is not loud" ("Moi dar ubog i golos moi negromok") and has produced every possible variation on the theme of the child prematurely born. His minor line follows the poetic traditions of the second-rank poets of the Pushkin and post-Pushkin periods, of such domestic amateurs as Countess Rastopchina, Prince Vyazemsky, and so on. However, in developing during the best period of Russian poetic dilettantism, the era of home albums, of epistles to friends, of epigrams on everyday themes, Khodasevich has managed to carry into the twentieth century the intricacy and tender crudities of the unrefined Moscow idiom used by the gentry in the literary salons of the last century. His poetry is very folksy, very literary, and very elegant.

An intense interest in the entire body of Russian poetry, from the powerful but clumsy Derzhavin[14] to Tyutchev,[15] the Aeschylus of Russian iambics, preceded the rise of Futurism. At about that time, just before the World War, all the older poets were suddenly perceived anew. A fever of reappraisal and hasty correction of historical injustice and short memory overtook everyone. What happened essentially was that all of Russian poetry appeared to the new curiosity and renewed ear of the reader as trans-sense. A revolutionary reappraisal of the past preceded the creative revolution. Affirmation and justification of the real values of the past is just as revolutionary an act as the creation of new values.[16] Unfortunately, however, memory and action quickly parted company and ceased to go hand in hand. The proponents of the future and the proponents of the past soon found themselves in hostile camps. The proponents of the future indiscriminately rejected the past, although their negativism was merely dietetic. They denied themselves the reading of the older poets for reasons of hygiene, or they read them surreptitiously, not admitting it in public. The proponents of the past prescribed precisely the same type of diet for themselves. I would even venture to say that until recently, when forced into it, many respected men of letters refused to read the works of their contemporaries. Never before, it seems, has the history of literature known such irreconcilable enmity and lack of understanding. The enmity of the Classicists and Romantics was child's play compared to the monumental gulf that opened up in Russia. But criteria soon developed to facilitate our understanding of this impassioned literary debate between two generations: whoever fails to comprehend the new has no sense of the old, while whoever understands the old is bound to understand the new. Nevertheless, it is our great misfortune when, instead of the real past with its deep roots, we understand the past merely as "yesterday." "Yesterday" is easily assimilated poetry, a fenced-in chicken coop, a cosy little retreat where domestic fowl cackle and peck about the yard. This is not labor devoted to the word; it is respite from the word. The boundaries separating the world of comfortable repose from the world of active poetry are now defined approximately by the poets Akhmatova and Blok. However, this is not because Akhmatova or Blok, after certain deletions have been made from their work, are bad in themselves, for, surely, Akhmatova and Blok were never intended for people with a moribund consciousness of language. If the linguistic consciousness of the epoch was dying in them, it was dying a glorious death. What did set Akhmatova and Blok off from the proponents of the future was "what in rational being we call the heightened diffidence of suffering;"[17] however, this must never be confused with that ingrained stupidity, bordering on malicious ignorance, of their sworn critics and disciples.

Akhmatova,[18] using the purest literary language of her day, introduced into her poetry with extraordinary steadfastness the traditional devices of the folk song, and not only the Russian folk song, but the folk song in general. We find in her verse not psychological affectation, but rather the typical parallelism of the folk song with its sharp asymmetry of two contiguous theses, such as: "My elderberry is in the garden, but my Uncle is in Kiev." Hence, her two-part stanza with its unexpected thrust at the end. Her poems approach the folk song not only in structure but in essence, for they emerge always, invariably, as laments. If we are attentive to her purely literary lexicon, filtered as it were through clenched teeth, it is possible to divine an old peasant woman within this Russian literary lady of the twentieth century—a quality which makes her poetry especially interesting.

Blok,[19] the most complex phenomenon of literary eclecticism, was a collector of Russian poetry, of all that was scattered and lost by the historically shattered nineteenth century. Blok's valuable work of collecting Russian poetry is still not evident to his contemporaries; they only sense it instinctively as a kind of melodic power. Blok's acquisitive nature, his striving to centralize poetry and language, brings to mind the political instinct of the historical leaders of Muscovy. His is a powerful, stern hand with regard to provincialisms: everything for the historically formed poetry of the traditional language of the rulers of the State. Futurism is all in its provincialisms: in the stormy struggles of the appanage principalities, in folkloric and ethnographic dissonance. Try finding that in Blok! Poetically, his work was at odds with history, and serves as proof of the fact that the sovereign state of language lives its own special life.[20]

Futurism should have essentially directed the edge of its attacks against Blok, the living and truly dangerous poet, not against the paper fortress of Symbolism. If it did not, it was only due to its innate sense of piety and literary decorum.

Futurism confronted Blok with Khlebnikov. What could they possibly say to each other? Their battle continues even now, although neither one is still alive. Like Blok, Khlebnikov viewed language as a kind of sovereign state, but not in the geographical, spatial sense, in time only. Blok is contempora ɟ to the marrow of his bones; and although his age will perish and be forgotten, he will remain a contemporary of his time in the consciousness of future generations. Khlebnikov does not know the meaning of the word "contemporary." He is a citizen of all history,[21] of the entire system of language and poetry. Some kind of idiotic Einstein incapable of distinguishing which is closer—a railroad bridge or "The Lay of the Host of Igor" ("Slovo o polku Igoreve"). Khlebnikov's poetry is "idiotic" in the original Greek, non-pejorative meaning of the word. His contemporaries could not and still cannot forgive him for omitting in his work any allusion to his epoch's temporary insanity. How terrifying it must have been when this man, completely oblivious of his audience, drawing no distinction between his own time and other ages, turned out to be unusually convivial and to possess to an extraordinary degree the purely Pushkinian gift of poetic small talk. Khlebnikov made jokes, and no one laughed. Khlebnikov uttered light, elegant allusions, and no one grasped them. A large part of what Khlebnikov wrote was no more than poetic small talk, as he understood it, comparable to the lyrical digressions in Pushkin's *Eugene Onegin*, or to such lines as "Order yourself some macaroni with Parmesan in Tver', and make an omelet" ("Zakazhi sebe v Tveri s parmazonom makaroni, da iaishnitsu svari"). He wrote comic dramas, such as *The World Hind Part Foremost (Mir s kontsa)*, and tragic buffonades, such as *Miss Death (Baryshnia Smert')*. He gave us examples of marvelous prose, as virginal and obscure as children's stories, the result of an incessant stream of images and ideas squeezing each other out of the reader's consciousness. Every line he wrote is the beginning of a new long poem. And every tenth line is an aphorism seeking a stone or bronze plaque on which to rest. Khlebnikov wrote neither lyric poetry nor epics, but rather one enormous all-Russian book of prayers and ikons from which, for centuries and centuries to come, everyone who may will find something to draw on.

It is almost as if some mocking genius of fate gave us Mayakovsky and his poetry of common sense as an intentional contrast to Khlebnikov.[22] There is common sense in all poetry. But professional common sense is nothing more than a pedagogical tool. Pedagogy, instilling known truths in children's heads, makes use of visual aids, that is, of poetic tools. The pathos of common sense is a part of school pedagogy. Mayakovsky's[23] merit is to be found in the poetic perfection of pedagogy for schools, in the application of the powerful techniques of visual education for the enlightenment of the masses. Like a schoolmarm, Mayakovsky walks about holding a globe of the world or some other emblem of the audio-visual method. He substituted the simple, wholesome school for the repulsive newspaper of our day which no one could understand. A great reformer of the newspaper, he has left a profound imprint on poetic language, simplifying syntax to its outermost limits, elevating the noun to the position of honored priority in the sentence. The aptness and the force of his language link Mayakovsky with the traditional itinerant showman. As both Khlebnikov and Mayakovsky were so national in their orientation, it would seem that populism, that is, folklore with a crude sugar coating, would find no place alongside them. However, populism continues to exist in the poetry of Esenin and, to a certain extent, in the poetry of Klyuev.[24] The significance of these poets must be sought in their rich provincialisms which join them to one of the basic tendencies of the epoch.

Aseev[25] stands completely to Mayakovsky's side. He created the vocabulary of a skilled technician. He was a poet-engineer, a specialist, a labor organizer. In the West such people as engineers, radio technicians, inventors of machines are poetically mute or they read the works of François Coppée. It is characteristic of Aseev that the machine as an efficient mechanical device stands at the foundation of his poetry, although his poetry never speaks of the machine at all. The turning on and off of the lyrical current gives the impression of a rapid fusing and a powerful emotional discharge. Aseev is extraordinarily lyrical and sober in his relation to the word. He never poeticizes, but simply installs the lyrical current, like a good electrician, using the appropriate materials.

At the present moment, the dikes artificially holding back the development of our poetic language have burst, and all foppish or uniformed innovation appears unnecessary, even reactionary.

What is strictly creative in poetry is not the age of invention, but rather the age of imitation.[26] When the prayerbooks have been written, then it is time for the Service. The most recent Russian Poetic Prayer Book issued for general prayers and everyday use is Pasternak's *My Sister Life*.[27] So new and so mature a harmony has not sounded in Russian poetry since the days of Batyushkov.[28]

Pasternak is neither a fabricator nor a magician, but the founder of a new mode, a new system of Russian poetry which fully corresponds to the maturity and manhood achieved by the language. One can express whatever one wishes with this new harmony; everyone will use it, whether he wishes to or not, because from now on it is the common property of all Russian poets. Up to now the logical structure of the sentence ended only with the poem itself, in other words, logical structure was the most concise means of expressing the poetic thought. However, due to its frequent use in poetry, customary logical movement has been worn down and has become imperceptible as such. Syntax, that is, the circulatory system of poetry, has been stricken with sclerosis. But a new poet has arrived to resurrect the virginal power of logical structure in the sentence. It was just this aspect of Batyushkov's poetry which so astonished Pushkin; now Pasternak awaits his Pushkin.

26. HUMANISM AND THE PRESENT

There are epochs which maintain that man is insignificant, that man is to be used like bricks or mortar, that man should be used for building things, not vice-versa—that things be built for man. Social architecture is measured against the scale of man. Sometimes it may turn against man to enhance its own grandeur by feeding on his humiliation and insignificance.

Assyrian prisoners swarm like baby chicks under the feet of an enormous king; warriors personifying the power of the state inimical to man kill bound pigmies with long spears while Egyptians and Egyptian builders treat the human mass as building material in abundant supply, easily obtainable in any quantity.

Nevertheless, there is also another form of social architecture whose scale and measure is man. It does not use man to build, it builds for man. Its grandeur is constructed not on the insignificance of individuality but on the highest form of expediency, in accord with its needs.[1]

Everyone senses the monumentality of the forms of social architecture now approaching. The mountain is not yet visible, but it is already casting its shadow over us, and we who have grown unaccustomed to the monumental forms of social life, who have been trained in the governmental-juridical flatness of the nineteenth century, move in this shadow fearful and bewildered, uncertain whether this is the wing of approaching night or the shadow of our native city which we must enter.

Simple mechanical enormity and naked quantity are inimical to man, and it is not a new social pyramid which tempts us, but social Gothic: the free play of weights and forces, a human society conceived as a complex and dense architectural forest wherein everything is efficient and individual, and where every detail answers to the conception of the whole.

The instinct for social architecture, that is, for structuring life in grandiose monumental forms far exceeding man's immediate needs, as it were, has deep roots in human societies and is not dictated by idle whim.

Repudiate social structure and the simplest, the most necessary and universally accepted structure will collapse: man's home, the human dwelling place will fall.

In countries threatened by earthquakes people build flat houses and, beginning with the French Revolution, the tendency toward flatness, the repudiation of architecture, dominated the entire juridical life of the nineteenth century, which was spent entirely in the intense anticipation of some subterranean tremor, some social shock.

But the earthquake did not spare even the flat houses. The chaotic world burst in—into the English "home" as well as into the German *Gemüt*; chaos sings in our Russian stoves, banging our dampers and oven doors.[2]

How can we guard our human dwellings against such menacing shocks, how can we ensure their walls against history's subterranean tremors? Who dares to say that the human dwelling, the free house of man, should not stand upon the earth as its finest ornament, as the most stable element in existence?[3]

The juridical creations of recent generations have proven powerless to defend that for which they were created, over which they struggled and fruitlessly philosophized.

No laws concerning the rights of man, no principles of property and inviolability any longer protect the human dwelling, no laws preserve the house from catastrophe, provide it with any assurance or security.

The English, more than any other people, are hypocritically concerned over the legal guarantees of individual freedom, but they forget that the concept of "home" arose many centuries ago in their own country as a revolutionary concept, as the natural justification of the first social revolution in Europe, a kind of revolution more deeply rooted and akin to our age than the French.

The monumentality of the approaching social architecture is conditioned by its calling to organize the world's economy according to the principle of universal home economy to meet man's greater demands, broadening the scope of his domestic freedom to universal proportions, fanning the flame of his individual hearth to the dimensions of a universal flame.

The future appears cold and terrifying to those who do not understand this, but the internal warmth of the future—the warmth of efficiency, home economy and teleology—is just as tangible to the contemporary humanist as the heat of the incandescent stove of the present.[4]

If the social architecture of the future does not have as its foundation a genuinely humanistic justification, it will crush man as Assyria and Babylon did in the past.

The fact that the values of humanism have now become rare, as if taken out of circulation and hidden underground, is not a bad sign in itself. Humanistic values have merely withdrawn, concealed themselves like gold currency, but like the gold reserves, they secure contemporary Europe's entire circulation of ideas, and control them the more competently for being underground.

The transition to gold currency is the business of the future, and in the province of culture what lies before us is the replacement of temporary ideas—of paper banknotes—with the gold coinage of the European humanistic tradition; the magnificent florins of humanism will ring once again, not against the archaeologist's spade,[5] but when the moment comes, they will recognize their own day and resound like the jingling coins of common currency passing from hand to hand.

27. HENRI-AUGUSTE BARBIER[1]

The July revolution of 1830 was a classically unsuccessful revolution.[2] The name of the people had seemingly never been so cynically abused. Actually, the revolution was but a footbridge between two monarchies: the Bourbon monarchy of Charles X and the Orléans monarchy of Louis Philippe. It was a footbridge leading from the semi-feudal restoration to the genuine bourgeois monarchy of Louis Philippe. The former was pious, sanctimonious, and untalented in economic matters, unable to understand either the spirit or the needs of the age. It was supported by the lions surviving the former emigration and by the wealthy landowners. Louis Philippe, on the other hand, was the king of financiers and stockbrokers, the patron of factory owners to whom the bourgeoisie gladly yielded after having seen the likes of themselves on the throne. The wave of European revolutions between 1830 and 1848 coincided with the beginning of the railroad era, with the real emergence of the steam engine. Everywhere the urban proletariat shuddered, as if it had felt the new, unprecedented force of steam gurgling through its breast. But this was only the initial jolt. The movement was yet to come.

Meanwhile the picturesque, theatrical aspect of the 1830 Paris revolution was magnificent and in no way corresponded to its practical achievements. Once again Paris copied, as it were, the brilliant production of '93.[3] Three days—the twenty-seventh, twenty-eighth, and twenty-ninth of July—profoundly impressed the Parisians. The mighty alarm that shook the air during those days is especially engraved in their memory because the Cathedral of the Parisian Virgin[4] was seized by the insurgents. It seemed as if a hurricane were sweeping through the city: trees were felled, streetlights uprooted, cabs overturned, and barricades were fashioned from odds and ends, like a bird's nest, by the ancient art of the revolutionary hive: that is what the three-day July storm left in its wake.

Those three days deserved and received a poet of their own. Henri-Auguste Barbier was not a revolutionary. He was born in 1805, the son of a lawyer. Until the revolution he worked as a clerk for the notary Delavigne (the brother of the famous Romantic writer). This notary's office served as the meeting place for a sizable group of romantically inclined young writers, theatre fanatics enchanted by Hugo, and admirers of the picturesque Middle Ages. Barbier shared their tastes and, had it not been 1830, he would have remained a pale, insipid romantic forever.

It is interesting that Barbier was not in Paris during the July days. He had departed the city and returned only when fresh traces of the struggle remained in the streets and the division of power had already occurred. Barbier was not an eyewitness to the "three days." His poetry was born from a sense of contrast between the grandeur of the passing hurricane and the squalor of its results.[5] A few days before his famous poem "La Curée"[6] appeared in the *Revue de Paris*, the journalist Girardin wrote to Barbier: "The days of popular revolt, those minutes of bravery and enthusiasm were two weeks ago. Now the revolt is of an entirely different order; it is an uprising of all those trying to find jobs. People rush ardently into antechambers just as they threw themselves into battle. Beginning at seven o'clock in the morning, batallions dressed in tailcoats rush to all corners of the capital. Their numbers grow with every street: on foot, in cabs, in cabriolets, sweaty and panting, with cockades in their hats and tricolored ribbons in their buttonholes. You see this great crowd descending on ministerial palaces, rushing into antechambers, laying siege to the office door, and so on..."

After the publication of "La Curée," Barbier's literary enemies accused him of borrowing, almost of paraphrasing that newspaper article. I believe, however, that the ability to utilize the daily news as a source of inspiration does not detract from a poet's merits in any way, to the contrary, it can only augment them.

"La Curée" was printed in the *Journal des Débats*. The printer's ink had not yet dried before the poet's name was on everyone's lips. Fame was his with one stroke, with one poem, then it faded away. By what methods and means of artistic expression did Barbier produce such a stunning impression on his contemporaries?

In the first place, like his predecessor Chénier,[7] he used the masculine iambic line, a line restrained by its meter, with energetic stresses suitable for powerful, oratorical speech, for the expression of civic enmity and passion.

In the second place, he was not confined by the decorum of literary language but knew how to use vulgar, scathing, and cynical words. This was entirely in the spirit of French Romanticism which had been fighting for a renewed, refreshed poetic lexicon.

In the third place, Barbier proved to be a master of grand poetic similes seemingly predestined for the orator's tribune. Barbier learned the power of poetic imagery directly from Dante whom he read zealously; indeed, we must never forget that *The Divine Comedy* was the greatest political lampoon of its day.[8]

Barbier's *Iambes*, born of the outburst of 1830, succeeded each other like a volley: "La Curée," "Le Lion" ("J'ai vu pendant trois jours, j'ai vu plein de colère/Bondir et rebondir le lion populaire/Sur le pavé sonnant de la grand cité"), "Quatre-Vingt-Treize," "L'Emeute," and especially the last two poems directed against the cult of Napoleon: "La Popularité" and "L'Idole."[9] Barbier's hatred of Napoleon distinguishes him from all the other Romantics.[10] He reserves his most shattering, Dantesque images for Napoleon. For him Napoleon was still alive. He regarded the poison of the Napoleonic cult, which demoralized the democracy of the age and was prepared in the laboratories of the best poets and artists, as the most dangerous toxin.

Following his volley of *Iambes*, the breath of the grand style left Barbier. He was to live on for many years, until 1882; he traveled in Italy and England, sang the praises of azure grottos and the cemeteries of antiquity, and left a series of sentimental poems in the spirit of justice and humanity.

Barbier reached Russia very early, despite the censorship prohibition under Nicholas. Lermontov became engrossed in reading him in the guardhouse and was greatly influenced by him. The members of the Petrashevsky Circle were familiar with Barbier and translated him. The generation of the sixties, while unable to properly evaluate Barbier's poetic strength, admired him as a satirist. Characteristically, the editor of *The Herald of Europe*, Stasyulevich, shocked by Barbier's use of "holy bastard" in the original, asked his translator to soften it or replace it with another expression. Nekrasov transposed Barbier's poem "The Prophet" ("Do not say he forgot caution").[11] Contemporary revolutionary poetry, taking very different directions, has not experienced Barbier's Classical influence. We hear echoes of his voice in Lermontov and even in Tyutchev when he speaks of Napoleon. Nevertheless, it is not merely the passion in Barbier's poetry that captivates us, but a certain almost Pushkinian trait: the ability to define the essence of an important historical phenomenon in a single line, in a single apt expression.[12]

28. THE MOSCOW ART THEATER AND THE WORD

The Moscow Art Theater[1] is the child of the Russian intelligentsia, the flesh of its flesh and the bone of its bone.

The theater of the Russian intelligentsia! That is a contradiction in terms! Such a theater cannot exist! But it did exist! And what is more—it exists even now. Since the days of my childhood I remember the fragrant atmosphere that surrounded this theater.[2]

For the intelligentsia to go to the Moscow Art Theater was almost equal to taking communion or going to church.

Here the Russian intelligentsia held its highest and most essential form of worship by clothing it in the garb of a theatrical performance. A society, which by its very nature was hostile to theater of any kind, constructed its own theater from everything dear to it; but if you gather together all that you love, even the most beloved things, and put it all in a single place, you still do not end up with theater, and the Russian intelligentsia's love was not transformed into theater.

Literature, not theater, characterized that entire generation. It was a typically literary generation, even a generation of "literati."[3] They understood theater exclusively as an interpretation of literature. They saw the theater as an *interpreter of literature* which translated it, as it were, into another, more comprehensible and completely natural language.

This theater originated out of their unique attempt to *touch* literature as if it were a living body, to feel it and put their fingers into it.[4]

The pathos of the generation and of the Moscow Art Theater was the pathos of Doubting Thomas. They had Chekhov, but Thomas the intellectual did not trust him. He wanted to touch Chekhov, to feel him, to be convinced of his reality. It was essentially a distrust in the reality of even the most beloved authors, a distrust in the very existence of Russian literature.[5]

When the actors took *The Cherry Orchard* to a certain large, provincial Russian town, the news that the troupe had not brought the "pot-bellied commode" with them spread through the town. The inhabitants related this detail to each other with sincere grief. After all, it's just not the same without the commode. It will no longer be possible for Thomas to touch it with his fingers.

What are the famous "pauses" used in *The Seagull* and other productions of Chekhov's plays?

They are nothing other than a holiday of pure tactile sensation. Everything grows quiet, and only a silent tactile sensation remains.[6]

The path to theater went through literature, but they did not believe in literature as a reality: they did not touch or hear the *words*.

An *interpreter*, a translator was needed for literature. They forced this role upon the theater.

All the work of the Moscow Art Theater went under the banner of *distrust* in the word and a craving to physically touch literature.

The line from *Fyodor Ioannovich*[7] to *Lysistrata* is *unbroken*. It led to a curious state of affairs: Elizabethan Shakespeare done in a Classical mode.

In real life people revolted, wept, sang, and shot themselves. But I remember their production of *The Lower Depths*. It was no more than a masquerade of cheap calico and slums. A tidy little lair. A sleek slum. Among other things, they did not succeed in *touching* the stench and the filth. In reality they touched only themselves.

I speak of the Moscow Art Theater respectfully, without any hostility: the theater could not be any different. It was retribution for the literary muteness of an entire generation, for its hostile inarticulateness, for its distrust of the word. Instead of *reading* the word,[8] people searched for whatever might shine through it (the theory of transparent action). Would it not have been simpler to replace the text of *Woe from Wit* with their own psychological stage directions and conjectures?

They never read the text of a work, but always relied on their own conjectures. The true and righteous path to theatrical tangibility lies through the word; the director is hidden in the word. The highest form of expressiveness is found in the structure of speech, verse, or prose.[9]

They did not know this. They tried to correct and assist the word. While reading Pushkin's poems they made mistakes, faltered, and became confused, helplessly waving their crutches of declamation: expressive reading.

Several times they did a version of *An Actor's Handbook*,[10] but they still enacted the actors' code rather than the truth.

The Moscow Art Theater is a theater of everyday life and has always been conventional, an interpreter-theater that translates the text into *An Actors' Handbook*.

I remember their production of *A Month in the Country*. One would think that the play should be merely a trifle, a lightweight trinket. But the voices of Verochka and the others sounded pert and unnatural, since their speech was drawn out and filled with hysterical laughter.

In *Lysistrata* all the women read in the old way, according to *An Actor's Handbook*.

Nearly all the men have liberated themselves from *An Actor's Handbook*, and it is no coincidence that all the women's movements are awkward, as if they had stepped out of a Semiradsky painting,[11] while the men's movements are superb.

In the theater one must speak in order to move because theater is entirely contained in the word.

29. AN ARMY OF POETS

1

And they are hundreds of thousands strong

In the French gymnasium-lycée, versification—the art of writing poetry—is a subject of study. Young French boys practice writing twelve-syllable Alexandrine verses according to an old, tried and true formula.

In the French gymnasium there is hardly any poetry other than official poetry. Young people receive laurels and awards for "academic" verse, externally literate but in actual fact seriously flawed and false.

It is obvious that school studies destroy any fondness for writing poetry and the young generation, average bourgeois youth, upon leaving the gymnasium, shake themselves free of poetic dust along with their textbooks.

In Russia the writing of poetry by young people is so widespread that it should be treated as a major social phenomenon and should be studied like any mass-scale operation which, although useless, has profound cultural and physiological causes.

Being acquainted, if only superficially, with the circle of those who write poetry, draws one into a sick, pathological world, a world of eccentrics, of people whose central nerve of both will and brain is diseased, of outright failures who are incapable of adapting in the struggle for existence and who frequently suffer not only from intellectual, but also physical cachexia.

About ten years ago, during the epoch of Stray Dog[1] snobbery, young people's poetry had a totally different character. Because of idleness and material security, young people who were in no hurry to choose a profession, lazy functionaries of privileged institutions, mama's boys, eagerly disguised themselves as poets, with all the paraphernalia of this profession: tobacco smoke, red wine, returning home late, and a dissipated life.

This generation has now degenerated, their toys and paraphernalia are broken, and among the masses of poets one rarely encounters idle and secure poet-snobs.

In the exceptionally difficult struggle for existence, tens of thousands of Russian youths manage to take time off from their studies and daily work to write poetry which they cannot sell and which wins approval, at best, from only a few acquaintances.

This, of course, is a disease and the disease is not accidental. It is not surprising that it attacks the age group of approximately seventeen to twenty-five. In this ugly and reclusive form, the awakening and formation of the personality occur, although that is no more than abortive sexual maturation, the attempt to win public approval, that pitiful but normal manifestation of a fundamental need to attach oneself to society, to become part of its living game.

A basic character trait of such people, useless but persistent in their activity, is disdain for any profession; any serious professional education, any inclination for a definite trade is nearly always lacking. The idea that poetry begins where every other trade ends is, of course, false, since the combination of poetic activity with professional activity (mathematical, philosophical, engineering, or military) can produce only brilliant results. A government official, philosopher, or engineer often shines through in a poet. A poet is not a person without a profession who is unfit for anything else, but rather a person who transcends his profession and subordinates it to poetry.[2]

An adjunct to this disdain for a profession, and on this point I am most insistent, is the absence of any physical enjoyment of life; there is only physiological apathy, an ignorance and dislike of sports and movement, and chronic anemia, the absence of genuine health.

After our difficult transitional years, the quantity of poets greatly increased. Because of widespread malnutrition there was an increase in the number of people whose intellectual awakening had a sickly character and had no outlet in any healthy activity.

The concurrence of the famine years, rations, and physical deprivations with the highest peak of mass poetry writing is not a coincidence. During those years when cafes such as the Domino, the Coffeehouse of Poets, and the various Stables[3] thrived, the younger generation, especially in the capital cities, was by necessity alienated from normal work and professional knowledge since only a professional education offers an antidote to the disease of poetry, a real and serious disease because it deforms the personality, deprives a youth of a solid foundation, makes him the butt of jokes and poorly concealed disgust, and deprives him of the social respect given others of his own age.

A person with "poetry disease" is infected with total disorientation not only toward his own art and literary schools, but also toward issues of general concern to society, history, and culture.

Try to change the subject of conversation from so-called poetry to another topic and you will hear pathetic and helpless answers or else simply: "I'm not interested in that." What is more, a person suffering from "poetry disease" is not even interested in poetry itself. He usually reads only two or three contemporary authors whom he tries to imitate. He is unfamiliar with the development of Russian poetry through the ages.

In the majority of cases, writers of poetry are very poor and inattentive readers of poetry. To them, writing is supposed to be only grief. Extremely inconsistent in their tastes, lacking any training, born non-readers, they are invariably offended by advice to learn to read before they begin to write.

It never occurs to them that to read poetry is a most sublime and difficult art, and that the vocation of reader is no less respectable than the vocation of poet. They are dissatisfied with the humble vocation of reader and, I repeat, are born non-readers.

Naturally, everything I am saying here concerns a widespread phenomenon. Later I will attempt to treat it in more detail, to classify it and give a few typical examples.

I only wish to say that the wave of poetry disease must inevitably subside with the general recuperation of the country. The most recent vintage of youth is producing fewer poets, but more readers and healthy people.

You might ask why we do not introduce courses in poetry writing and versification in our elementary schools, following the example of the French bourgeois schools, to demonstrate its difficulty and teach respect for it.

To this I answer: the study of versification in French schools is absurd because it has meaning only where a commonly accepted poetic method exists, one which has not changed for centuries, for example, the system of prosody in ancient Greece.

Both Russian and European poetry is now undergoing a fundamental change because the schools, lacking a traditional and canonical model, are at a loss for what to teach, and produce at best only epigones and minor poets.

It is one thing for young people to learn to write in an accepted and popular manner, that is, to acquire simple literacy. Literacy can be taught.

It is another thing to imitate individual authors. That is a matter of the imitator's taste and conscience.

Who are they, these people who cannot look you straight in the eye, who have lost their love of life and their will to live, who vainly attempt to be *interesting* while they themselves *are not interested in anything*? I will discuss them next, in all seriousness, as sick people.

2

Who are They?

My first example concerns an encounter in the editorial office of a ponderous, antediluvian monthly magazine that no longer exists. A nice young man comes in, well-dressed, with an unnaturally loud laugh and the completely misplaced mannerisms of a man of the world. After he has filled the room with tobacco smoke and is on the verge of leaving, he apparently remembers something and casually addresses the bearded director, a man stupefied by ideology and integrity: "Tell me, could you use some French translations of Yazykov's poetry?" Everyone stared—it was like a delirium. He had come to offer French poetry and, moreover, translations of Yazykov. When they mumbled to him politely that they could not use his translations, he went away cheerfully and unperturbed. The insane image of this youth remained in my memory for a long time. It set a record for uselessness. Everything was useless: Yazykov to him, and he to the magazine, and French translations of Yazykov to Russia. I do not know if it is easy for him to approach people with such a product, but he is an outcast, he is a fop and proud of it.

Once upon entering my room I found a gloomy, adult man standing there, decisively, somberly, and glaring at me full of hatred. He was wearing a hat and holding a thick briefcase. Neither a hint of politeness, nor a smile, nor even the usual entreaty was expressed in his face; his face was hostile and his eyes full of hatred. With intense hostility he announced that many "of your crowd," as he expressed it with a shade of disgust, had listened to him or given him approval; suddenly he sat down and pulled five oilcloth notebooks out of his briefcase: "I have here dramas, tragedies, poems, and lyrical pieces. Which shall I read to you?" It had to be read aloud, it had to be read slowly. Demands plus the same implacable hatred. "I don't know what you prefer, what kind of thing you need. Your crowd likes it. I have something for every taste." After he was politely sent packing, I was left with the impression that a madman had just been in my room. But I was mistaken: he was a rational, grown man, a family man, a technician by trade, but unsuccessful. He had given up engineering and was working somewhere, feeding a family. But sometimes he is "overcome" with a gloomy, animal hatred, even for his own leather notebooks. Then he bursts into other people's houses and insists that some "crowd" praise him, that someone help him and acknowledge him. It is impossible to converse with him. He insults you and slams the door. A conversation with him would finish somewhere in a tavern with a stormy confession and tears.

One more case: he has blue eyes, a wholesome look, a German civility, the tidiness of a sales clerk, and a Schubertesque light-blue haze in his eyes. His arrival is not abnormal: there is nothing in it that is forced or that disfigures human relations. Simply, casually excusing himself, he leaves behind a manuscript written in a child's hand. And what, exactly, does it contain? The noble spirit of German romanticism, the themes of Novalis, strange coincidences, effete creations of a genuinely lofty spirit lie there in wretched tongue-tied melodies. He is a sales clerk in a music store, a former piano tuner, half German. "Look, just read Novalis, Tieck, Brentano. Here is a whole world to which you, it seems, are akin." But he has not read them, he has no inkling of all that—he prefers to write. He will either recover completely from this lofty disease or become a real person.

During the famine a young man went to a classical poet and read him Assyrian poetry. In order to force the poet to listen he brought him some sugar. Convinced that in general everything was absurd and that anything could be counterfeited, he brought sugar and Assyrian mythology as an offering to the poet. He was ashamed of poverty and any kind of squalor—he maintained self-respect with his strange sacrificial offerings. Fate lifted him very high: now he runs an international office for philatelists. He has retained only his scepticism, disrespect for his Assyrian teacher, and the conviction that anything can be counterfeited.

Siberia, Tashkent, even Bukhara and Khorezm send poets to Moscow and Petersburg. All these people think that it is impossible to go to Moscow empty-handed, so they equip themselves with whatever they can: poetry. They bring poetry instead of money, instead of underwear, instead of references, as a means of establishing relationships with people, as a means of conquering life. An infant cries because it breathes and lives. Later it stops crying and starts to babble, but the inner cry does not subside, and a grown man cries with the same ancient cry of a newborn baby muffled within. Social decorum drowns out this cry—it is a pure abyss. The poetry of young people and adults is often this very cry, the atavistic, ceaseless cry of an infant.

Words are of no consequence: this cry is eternal: I live, I want, I am sick.

He arrived from Irkutsk, a worker with enormous self-love, not afraid of the truth when they tell him that "it's bad"; he has brought not poetry but an unadulterated cry. He thinks it resembles something of a cross between Mayakovsky and the Imagists. It resembles nothing. Short lines, two or three words, it splinters, gnaws, chokes, suffocates, rages, subsides, then again clambers up somewhere, roars, words are of no consequence, words are disobedient, everything comes out not the way he wants, but as an ancient roar: I live, I want, I am sick, and perhaps, still more from a grown and conscious man: help! There are tens of thousands such as these. Most important, they must be given help so that they will stop shouting. When they are done with poetry, with this atavistic howling, they will begin to babble, they will begin to speak, they will begin to live.

I wonder how they hear themselves, for this is very important. The trouble is they drown themselves out and are stupefied by the sound of their own voices. Some simply shout, disregarding syntax, feeling, and logic; others sing along through their noses; still others mumble, rocking back and forth Arab-style. Someone has invented a recitative refrain and begins to sing in a muted melody. If you look at the paper it is written on, you will think: "After all, the person who wrote this was not stupid—how can he find anything in it?" But then listen to how he reads it: it is so solemn and so nasal that it no longer resembles the Russian language. You might mistake it for a liturgy and the speaker for a prophet. Those few remaining esthetes emphasize the adjectival endings—*annyi, onnyi*; admirers of vulgar poetry read in an innovative way, as if they were cursing, attacking their listeners with oaths and threats. Of course the voice, being a worker's tool, is inconceivable without recitatives, like a geometrical plane. Poets work with the voice, the voice. Correct. But these people's voices are their own enemies. Nothing will harmonize with such a voice.

Another characteristic feature is their desire to see themselves published, regardless of where or how. They are convinced that as soon as they are published a new life will begin. Nothing will begin. Printing is not a great event. Even good poetry does not stir the literary heights. Young girls and young ladies, the seamstresses of poetry, you who like to call yourselves Maya and remember with reverence the condescending caresses of a great poet. Your case is simpler: you write poetry in order to be loved. To combat this tendency we shall form a conspiracy of Russian youth: we shall not look at young ladies who write poetry.

Who will write poetry? But does this question have to be answered? Indeed, we all wear shoes, but very few people make shoes. Are there many people who can read poetry? And yet almost everybody writes it.

The novel[1] may be distinguished from the novella, the chronicle, memoirs, or any other prose genre by the fact that it is a closed compositional narrative, extensive but complete in itself, having to do with the fate of one person or a group of persons. *Saints' Lives,* despite their concern with plot development, could not be considered novels because they lacked a secular interest in the fate of their protagonists; they concentrated instead on illustrating a common ideal. The Greek novella, *Daphnis and Chloe*, is regarded as the first European novel because this secular interest appears there for the first time as an independent motivating force. The novel was perfected and strengthened over an extremely long period of time as the art form to interest the reader in the fate of the individual. Moreover, this art form was perfected in two distinct directions: compositional technique transformed biography into plot,[2] that is, into a dialectically meaningful narrative, while psychological motivation,[3] another aspect of the novel essentially auxiliary to the plot, developed simultaneously. Storytellers of the Quatrocento and *Cents nouvelles nouvelles* limited motivation to the juxtaposition of external situations which gave their stories an exceptional dryness, a subtle elegance, and put the accent on diversion. Novelist-psychologists, on the other hand, such as Flaubert and the brothers Goncourt, focussed all their attention on psychological verisimilitude at the expense of plot. They handled this task brilliantly, transforming an auxiliary device into an autonomous art form.

Until quite recently the novel has been not only a major, organized form, but a central, vital necessity of European art. *Manon Lescaut, Werther, Anna Karenina, David Copperfield, Le rouge et le noir, La peau de chagrin,* and *Madame Bovary* were as much social, as artistic, events. Two interesting phenomena concurred: the massive self-knowledge of contemporaries who gazed into the mirror of the novel, and the widespread imitation or adaptation by contemporaries of typical images of the novel. The novel educated entire generations; it was an epidemic, a social mode, a school, and a religion. During the Napoleonic era, an entire vortex of lesser, imitative biographies developed around the biography of Napoleon. They reproduced the fate of the central historical figure with variations in different modes, without, of course, carrying it to its historical end. In *Le rouge et le noir*, Stendhal told one of these vortical, imitative biographies.

If characters in the novel were at first extraordinary, gifted people, then the reverse phenomenon may be observed as the European novel declined: the ordinary man became the hero of the novel and social motivation became the center of gravity, that is, society began to participate as an actual character in the novel, as in the work of Balzac or Zola.

All this suggests a connection between the fate of the novel and the status at a given time of the problem of the individual's fate in history. It is less important here to discuss the actual fluctuations of the individual's role in history than to consider the popular resolution of this problem at a given moment, insofar as it educated and formed the minds of contemporaries.

The flourishing of the novel in the nineteenth century must be viewed as directly dependent on the Napoleonic epos, which caused the stock value of the individual in history to rise in an extraordinary manner, and, through Balzac and Stendhal, enriched the soil for the subsequent development of the French and European novel. The typical biography of Bonaparte, the aggressive man of destiny, was scattered throughout Balzac's work in dozens of so-called "novels of success' *(roman de réussite)*, where the primary motivation was no longer love, but the career, that is, the striving to break out of the lower and middle social orders and into the upper-class milieu.

It is clear that when we entered the epoch of powerful social movements and organized mass actions, both the stock value of the individual in history and the power and influence of the novel declined, for the generally accepted role of the individual in history serves as a kind of monometer indicating the pressure of the social atmosphere. The measure of a novel is human biography or a system of biographies.[4] Very early on, the new novelist sensed that individual fate did not exist, and he attempted to uproot the social vegetation he needed, its entire root system, radicles and all. Thus the novel always suggests to us a system of phenomena controlled by a biographical connection and measured by a biographical measure; moreover, the novel holds together compositionally only as long as the centrifugal force of our solar system remains alive within, as long as the centripetal force, the force from the center to periphery, has not completely overwhelmed the centrifugal force.[5]

We may consider Romain Rolland's *Jean Christophe*, that swan song of European biography, with its majestic fluency and noble mastery of synthetic devices reminiscent of Goethe's *Wilhelm Meister*, the last example of the centrifugal .biographical European novel. *Jean Christophe* closes the circle of the novel. Despite its modernity, it is an old-fashioned work. The ancient centrifugal honey of the German and Latin races is gathered within. To create the last novel required two races combined in the personality of Romain Rolland, and even this was not enough. *Jean Christophe* is set in motion by the same powerful jolt of the Napoleonic revolution that inspired the European novel—the Beethovenian biography of Christophe, contact with the powerful figure of the musical myth born of the same Napoleonic flood in history.

The future development of the novel will be no less than the history of the atomization of biography as a form of personal existence; what is more, we shall witness the catastrophic collapse of biography.[6]

The sense of time that man possesses in order to act, to conquer, to perish, to love—this sense of time gave the European novel its basic tonality, for, I repeat again: the compositional measure of the novel is human biography. A human life is not in itself biography, nor does it provide a backbone for the novel. A man functioning in the time system of the old European novel serves as a pivot for the entire system of phenomena that cluster around him.

Today Europeans are plucked out of their own biographies, like balls out of the pockets of billiard tables, and the same principle that governs the collision of billiard balls governs the laws of their actions: the angle of incidence is equal to the angle of reflection. A man devoid of biography cannot be the thematic pivot of the novel, while the novel is meaningless if it lacks interest in an individual, human fate, in a plot and all its auxiliary motifs. What is more, the interest in psychological motivation (by which the declining novel so skillfully sought to escape, already sensing its impending doom) is being radically undermined and discredited by the growing impotence of psychological motives in the confrontation with the forces of reality, forces whose reprisals against psychological motivation become more cruel by the hour.

The modern novel was thus simultaneously deprived of both plot, that is, of the individual acting in accord with his sense of time, and psychology, since it could no longer support action of any sort.[7]

31. THE SLUMP

In poetry there must be Classicism. In poetry there must be Hellenism, there must be an elevated sense of imagery, the rhythm of the machine, urban collectivism, peasant folklore... Poor poetry shies away from the countless revolver muzzles of unconditional demands aimed at it. What should poetry be? Perhaps it is not obliged to be anything, perhaps it is not obliged to anyone, perhaps its creditors are all fraudulent! Yes, nothing is easier than to talk about requirements, about what is obligatory in art:[1] in the first place, such talk is always arbitrary and not incumbent upon anything; in the second place, it is an inexhaustible theme for philosophizing; in the third place, it avoids a very unpleasant matter that hardly anyone is capable of, namely, gratitude for what is, the most ordinary gratitude for what poetry is at a given time.

Oh, monstrous ingratitude: to Kuzmin, Mayakovsky, Khlebnikov, Aseev, Vyacheslav Ivanov, Sologub, Akhmatova, Pasternak, Gumilev, Khodasevich—how different these poets are, made from various clays! These are all Russian poets not merely for yesterday or today, but for all time. With such poets has God endowed us. A nation does not choose its poets, just as a child does not choose its parents. A nation that cannot honor its poets deserves... No, it does not deserve anything. Irrelevant, you say, but what a difference between the pure ignorance of a people and the incomplete knowledge of an ignorant fop. Hottentots test their old men by forcing them to climb a tree and shake it: if the old man is so decrepit that he falls, he must be killed. The snob imitates the Hottentots. His favorite method is reminiscent of what has just been described. This practice should be regarded with disdain. Some prefer poetry, some—the Hottentot game.

Nothing facilitates the growth of snobbery amidst a generation of readers as much as rapid changes in poetic schools. The reader having grown accustomed to thinking of himself as the audience in the orchestra pit frowns, grimaces, and grows fastidious as successive schools file past him. Finally, he develops a completely unfounded sense of superiority, for he sees himself as the only constant in the face of perpetual change, immobile in the face of motion. The rapid succession of poetic schools in Russia, from the

Symbolists down to the present day, has come crashing down on the same reader.

The reading public of the 1890s was in a slump; it proved insubstantial and completely incompetent as far as poetry was concerned. The Symbolists therefore were forced to wait a long time for their readership, and by strength of circumstances, by dint of their intellect, education, and maturity, they appeared much older than the raw youth they were addressing. With regard to the decline in public taste, the first decade of the twentieth century fared marginally better than the nineties, for *The Scales*, the militant citadel of the new school, existed alongside the illiterate tradition of the *Sweetbriars*,[2] that vulgar almanac literature full of ignorant pretensions.

When individually perfected poetic phenomena emerged from the womb of Symbolism, when the tribe disintegrated and the reign of individuality, of the poetic personality dawned, the reader raised on the tribal poetry of Symbolism (the source of all modern Russian poetry), became confused in the world of blossoming variety, where everything was no longer covered by the tribal banner and where every individual stood separately, with his head bared. After the tribal epoch that infused new blood into Russian poetry and proclaimed a canon of extraordinary capaciousness, after the rich medley crowned by the dense gospel of Vyacheslav Ivanov, the age of personality, of individuality dawned. Nevertheless, all modern Russian poetry emerged from the tribal Symbolist womb. The reader has a short memory—he does not want to acknowledge that. Oh acorns, acorns, who needs an oak when we have acorns.

2

Someone once succeeded in photographing the eye of a fish. The picture contained a railroad bridge and a few details of the landscape, but the optical law of fish vision showed all this in an unbelievably distorted way. If you could photograph the poetic eye of Academician Ovsianiko-Kulikovsky[3] or of an average Russian intellectual, to capture his unique vision of Pushkin, for instance, a picture would result that was just as surprising as a fish-eye view of the world.

The distortion of a poetic work in the reader's perception is an inevitable social phenomenon. It is difficult and useless to fight it: it is easier to spread electrification throughout Russia than to teach all literate readers to read Pushkin as he is written, rather than as their spiritual needs require or their intellectual capacities allow.

In poetic notation, for instance, in contrast to musical notation, there is a large gap, a glaring absence of the multitude of implicit signs, markers, and indicators that alone make the text comprehensible and standard. However, all these signs are no less exact than musical notes or the hieroglyphics of dance. The poetically literate reader supplies them himself, as if extracting them from the text.[4]

Poetic literacy in no way coincides either with ordinary literacy, that is, with reading, or even with literary erudition. If the percentage of the ordinary kind of illiteracy and literary illiteracy is extremely high in Russia, then poetic illiteracy is simply monstrous and, worst of all, it is confused with the ordinary kind; thus anyone who can read considers himself poetically literate. This is particularly true of the semi-educated intellectual masses, who, infected with snobbery, have lost their innate feeling for language. They are already essentially languageless, amorphous with regard to language. They tickle their long numbed language nerves with cheap and easy stimuli, with dubious lyricism and neologisms, often alien and hostile to the principles of the Russian language.

Current Russian poetry *must* satisfy the demands of this linguistically déclassé public.

The word, born deep in the womb of speech consciousness, serves the deaf and dumb, the inarticulate, the cretins and degenerates of the word.

The great merits of Symbolism, that is, its proper stance vis-à-vis the Russian reading public, lay in its teaching, in its innate authority, in its partiarchal preponderance and in the legislative gravity through which it educated the reader.

The reader must be put in his place; and so must the criticism he has nourished. Criticism should not exist as arbitrary interpretation of poetry.[5] It must give way to objective, scholarly research, to the science of poetry.

Perhaps the most comforting thing about the general state

of Russian poetry is the people's sheer ignorance of their own poetry.

The masses, that is, those classes in which the morphology of language grows, strengthens, and develops, have retained a wholesome philological sense, and have not yet encountered individualist Russian poetry. Poetry has still not reached its readers. Perhaps it will reach them only after the extinction of those poetic luminaries which have sent their rays to that distant and as yet unattainable destination.

32. FOR THE ANNIVERSARY OF F.K. SOLOGUB

Today Leningrad and all literary Russia are celebrating the fortieth anniversary of Fyodor Kuzmich Sologub's (Teternikov's) literary career. While the sources of Sologub's poetry connect it with the remote past—the eighties and the nineties—its fundamental nature connects it to the remotest future.

Of all the poems published by the young Sologub and his contemporaries, Sologub's poems were immediately singled out for their particular strength, their confident harmony, and their lofty, humanistic clarity.[1]

For the first time after a lengthy interlude in Russian poetry, it was as if a volitional nature suddenly resounded—a will to life, a will to being.

A whole person, thirsting after the fullness of existence, trembling with the consciousness of his bonds with this world, emerged from among the demi-lives, from among the mongrels of life and literature.

During those sorrowful years, nothing was even called by its proper name: prose was called *belles-lettres* and pathetic poeticizing was called "poetry." There was no shortage of writers of a journalistic persuasion; lyrical whimpering abounded. Under such conditions there seemed to be no room for the majestic or even the significant. But Sologub took an enormous task upon himself. With the collective strength of the human spirit he endowed his age with the significance of an epoch, and with that collective strength he elevated the feeble babbling of his contemporaries to an expression of eternal, classical formulas.

His legacy from the past consisted of a mere handful of words, a meager vocabulary, and a few images. And yet, like a child playing marbles, he taught us to play with even these meager gifts of time with unabashed freedom and inspiration.

For the people of my generation, Sologub was a legend twenty years ago. We asked ourselves: who is this man whose aged voice rings with such immortal force? How old is he? Where does he get his freedom, his fearlessness, his tenderness and soothing sweetness, his spiritual clarity even in the depths of despair?

At first, because of our immaturity, we perceived Sologub merely as a bearer of solace, muttering somniferous words, as a skillful singer of lullabies teaching oblivion,[2] but in time we came to understand Sologub's poetry as a science of action, a science of will, a science of courage and love.

Sologub's poetry flowed from Tyutchev's Alpine summits like limpid mountain streams. These streams babbled so close to our domicile, to our home. And yet somewhere in the rosy Alpine chill the eternal snows of Tyutchev are melting. Sologub's poems presupposed the existence and melting of eternal ice. There, on the summit, in Tyutchev's Alps, is their cause, their origin. This is a descent into the valley to the level of life and habitation. It is a descent of the snowy, ethereally cold deposits of Russian poetry (perhaps too immobile and egoistical in their icy indifference and accessible only to the courageous reader). Tyutchev's snows are melting, melting over half a century; Tyutchev is descending to our houses: it is the second act, as indispensable as exhaling after inhaling, as a vowel following a consonant in a syllable; it is not an echo, not even a continuation, but the cycle of matter, the great cycle of *Nature* in Russian poetry with its Alps and plains:

> I do not understand why
> A miraculous power recreates
> In barren, dying nature,
> The triumph of the One Life.

There is the voice of epochs requiring interpretation, and there are inarticulate times devoid of voices. From inarticulateness the most limpid voice is born. From limpid despair it is but one step to joy. And all of Sologub's poetry is addressed to the future. He was born in timelessness and was slowly saturated with time; he learned how to breathe and came to teach us how to love.

Our grandchildren and great-grandchildren will understand Sologub and will understand him in their own way, and for them *The Flaming Circle* will be a book that burns up melancholy, that transforms our sluggish nature into pure, light ash.

Fyodor Kuzmich Sologub loves, as few do, all that is genuinely new in Russian poetry. It is not to refrains and hackneyed forms that he beckons us. The best lesson to be learned from his poetry is this: if you can, if you are able, do something new; if you cannot, then bid farewell to the past, but bid farewell in such a way that you will burn up the past with your farewell.[5]

33. A REVOLUTIONARY IN THE THEATER

Ernst Toller's *Masse-Mensch (Mass Man),*[1] which has not yet been staged in Russia, is undoubtedly a play with a future, regardless of its artistic and theatrical merits. It must be classified along with such dramatic works as Leonid Andreev's *Life of a Man.* The crude yet brilliant symbolism of its staging, and its lucid, schematic action are both forceful and rudimentary, making it a play comprehensible to everyone.

Ernst Toller, a courageous German Sparticist revolutionary, is one of the founders of the young German dramaturgical society known as the "Dramatic Freedom" society. However, upon closer examination, at least insofar as it is possible to judge from Toller's own work, the dramatic freedom associated with his group actually lies outside the realm of theater: it is not theatrical freedom. The powerful and noble social instinct, the courageous revolutionary freedom of the German proletariat which animates Toller's ideas, splashes across his theater, cleansing it. This social instinct creates nothing for the theater as such, but rather acts through it, using it only as a vehicle for another end. Thus, despite his pathos, energy, and tension, Ernst Toller cannot be considered a revolutionary in dramaturgy. Nevertheless, he is a revolutionary in the theater; he adroitly adapts the theater to his own militant goals by using traditional means, in this instance, the techniques of German Symbolist drama. To our Russian audience, these techniques are extremely reminiscent of Leonid Andreev, of Andreev's "school"[2]; they recall the recent past so painful to remember (God forbid it should be resurrected), when *He, She, It,* and other *dramatis personae* wreaked havoc among the impressionable Russian intelligentsia. But what a difference we find (in Toller's favor) when we compare his experiments with their kindred Russian prerevolutionary works. Instead of pallid, intellectual impotence, we see vitality, genuine pathos, and an iron revolutionary will in Toller's works:

> We, from eternity imprisoned
> In the abyss of towering towns;
> We, laid up on the altar of mechanical
> And mocking systems. We,

> Whose face is blotted in the night of tears,
> Who from eternity are motherless—
> From the abysses of factories we cry:
> When shall we live in love?
> When shall we work at will?
> When is deliverance?

There is something Promethean and primordially Germanic in Toller's mass choruses. He was able to compose a genuine hymn based on variations of the Internationale:

> Arise from universal slumber
> Slaves and workers all,
> The thunder peals tidings of your rights,
> Your day is coming, your star is shining.

Toller's pathos is majestic, the pathos of high tragedy:

> The factories.belong to workers
> And not to my lord Capital.
> The time is past when our bowed backs
> Perched him up greedily to scan for distant treasures,
> Plot wars to enslave foreign folk...[3]

Thus, it is all the more annoying that as a playwright Toller is entirely the captive of Munich modernist Symbolism, and that all his tragic pathos hangs helplessly on Symbolist mannequins.

A completely true-to-life situation underlies the plot of *Masse-Mensch*: a woman from a good bourgeois family, the wife of some bureaucrat, public prosecutor, or eminent lawyer, has joined the workers' movement and, as a leader and instigator, volunteers to accept full responsibility for the merciless acts of the masses. However, at the last minute her resolution abandons her, humanistic prejudices ("anything you please, but not violence") get the upper hand, and she comes to nothing. No one wants to listen to her; she is not fit to be a leader, and is replaced by a truly merciless leader. This woman, obviously a dilettante in the workers' movement, is simply called *the Woman* with a capital "W" in Toller's play. Except for a husband, she is devoid of any realistic attributes. The husband, despite his capital letter, is realistic almost to the point of being a comical everyday figure, and his manner of speaking corresponds to the level of his education and his position, which destroys the general pathetic tone of the action. The protagonist of the drama, known as the *Nameless One*, is the *Masse-Mensch* or the mass man.

Completely abstract, the mass man is devoid of even the slightest trace of individualization. Pathos in a mannequin. We will be told that it is absurd to demand individualization in representatives of the collective will and collective action, and that Toller has deliberately rounded all the edges in his characterization of the *Nameless One*. I would answer that the mass man must also be perceived as a man, and that every mass man is a unique mass man. The dramatization of the mass man, just like the dramatization of the individualist Faust, demands dramatic characterization. Otherwise the result is not dramatic force, but some cliché moving about in space. The whole play flows out of, and consists entirely in, the polemic between the Woman and the Nameless One: it is a political rally through and through. The rally alternates with scenes of delirium: a scene of bankers in which the stock market is shown at a cinematographic tempo; a prison yard scene, a fantasy from the near future in which the shadows of the executed prisoners dance a symbolic dance. We recognize the prisoners as bankers. Naturally, it is naive to interpret the mass action as a rally. It is precisely the rally which is the action; it is not the rally-like character of the social revolution nurtured by mass causes and maturation of the masses, but the revolution originating in the businessman's environment which makes even Toller's most powerful scenes unrealistic and unconvincing. Important events that determine the course of a revolution are never born at a rally. It is also possible to depict mass action by connecting any three people at their respective homes by telephone. Due to their naive confusion of mass action and rallies, nearly all European revolutionary plays are strikingly similar. Even the scenario deals with the same workers' cafe, meeting hall, or something of the sort. However, because he created the great pathos of a genuine, though artistically defective tragedy, Toller is forgiven everything, absolutely everything, including the confusion of mass action with a rally and the bankers' shadows dancing a symbolic dance of death à la Leonid Andreev to the pipe of the Nameless One.

Toller juxtaposed two principles with unusual force: humanism, the best of the old world, and the new collective imperative, which subordinated humanism for the sake of action.[4] It is not without reason that the word *action, Tat*, resounds in his play like an organ, drowning out all other sounds. He puts the strongest, most ardent words the old world could muster in defense of humanism into the mouth of his heroine, who perishes as a result of her own divided sentiments. The woman's tragedy is Toller's own tragedy. He overcame and outgrew his humanism in the name of action, and that is why his collectivist rapture is so valuable. Ernst Toller's play *Masse-Mensch* is one of the most noble monuments of the German revolutionary spirit.

34. ANDREI BELY. *DIARY OF AN ECCENTRIC.* BERLIN: GELIKON. 1922. 475 P.

Russian Symbolism is still alive. Russian Symbolism has not died. The python is coiling. Andrei Bely[1] is continuing the glorious traditions of the literary epoch when a waiter reflected in the double mirrors of the restaurant in the Hotel Prague was regarded as a mystical phenomenon, as a double, and when a decent man of letters was ashamed to retire without having accumulated his five or six "horrors" for the day.

In his afterword to the *Diary of an Eccentric,*[2] Bely makes a slip, admitting that he has deliberately written a bad book. Such a confession from the author's lips is nearly always insincere and, indeed, it is followed here by the statement, "but on the other hand my book is unusually truthful." The problem of the sincerity of Bely's work lies outside the scope of literature and outside anything of universal importance. A bad book, however, is always a literary and social crime, always a lie. The devices used in writing *Diary of an Eccentric* are not new by any means and offer no revelations: they make this book both a caricature of, and the logical consequence of, the worst elements of Andrei Bely's early prose, of the crude, unpleasant-sounding musicality of poetry in prose (virtually the entire book is written in hexameter), of the pompous, apocalyptic tone, the bombastic declamation overloaded with astrological terminology that alternates with the beautiful aspects of the poetic language of the nineties which have already been driven into the ground.

The book's plot can be uncovered only by raking up heaps of verbal trash: a Russian tourist, stranded in Switzerland by the war, builds St. John's Cathedral in honor of theosophic wisdom. The Swiss, after observing the suspicious foreigner, banish him. Then, pursued by an espionage mania, he returns safely to Russia through England and Norway. The plot of this book is so meager, however, that it would not be worth mentioning, except that one pauses greedily on anything concrete, be it a description of the clean-shaven detective or the ship's *table d'hôte,* or simply a human word faithfully recorded. The book endeavors to relate some grandiose spiritual events but is not concerned with the spiritual journey. Consequently, we get something like the following:

while crossing a street a man bumped into a lamppost and wrote a whole book about the sparks falling from his eyes. Bely's book is written in complete accord with German textbooks of theosophy, and its rebelliousness reeks of barley coffee and wholesome vegetarianism. Theosophy is merely a cover for degenerating religion. Even from a great distance it reeks of the spirit of pseudoscientific charlatanism.[3] Respected professional mystics and the representatives of science both reject this feminine nonsense with equal disdain.

What an absurd, tasteless idea to build a "cathedral of universal wisdom" in such an inappropriate place. Surrounded by the Swiss, their hostels and hotels, the inhabitants live there cutting coupons and recuperating from illnesses. It is the most prosperous place in the world, a clean, neutral little piece of territory, and yet, at the same time, it is the most unclean corner of Europe because of its sated international prosperity. It is in this very place, among family hostels and sanitoriums, that some new Sophia is being built. Was it necessary to lose all sense of significance, all tact, and all sense of history in order to think up such an absurdity? The absence of measure, tact, and taste is a lie, the first sign of a lie. A single spiritual event was sufficient for Dante's whole life. If a person undergoes major spiritual catastrophes three times a day we cease to believe him. We have a right not to believe him, for he appears ridiculous. Thus, it is a sin not to want to laugh at Bely, the author of *St. Petersburg,*[4] in which he expressed prerevolutionary anxiety and utter confusion more forcefully than any other Russian writer. But if he has turned his thought, his anxiety, and his humanistic and literary style into an absurd and tasteless dance, so much the worse for him. The dancing prose of *Diary of an Eccentric* is the ultimate in literary narcissism: to tell of oneself, to turn oneself inside out, to show oneself in the fourth, fifth, and sixth dimension. The other Symbolists were more cautious, but in general Russian Symbolism shouted so much and so loudly about the "ineffable" that this "ineffable" was passed from hand to hand like paper money. Bely shows unusual freedom and levity of thought when he tries to describe literally what his spleen is thinking or when he states "an event of indescribable importance consisted in convincing myself that this infant was myself" (the infant, naturally, was totally allegorical and abstract). The central nerve of Bely's prose is his original striving for elegance, for the dance, the pirouette, his striving to embrace the unembraceable while dancing. Nevertheless, the absence of any stylistic considerations in his new prose makes it extremely elementary, governed only by two or three laws. Prose is asymmetrical, its movement is the movement of the verbal mass, the movement of the herd, complex and rhythmical in its incorrectness; true prose is discord, disorder, polyphony, and counterpoint; but *Diary of an Eccentric* is reminiscent of a schoolboy's diary written in hemistichs.

While in Russia people are racking their brains in an attempt to revive independent prose discourse, free from its lyrical fetters, in Berlin in 1922 Gelikon goes and publishes some stunted prose piece, a return to the *Symphonies. Diary of an Eccentric* testifies to the cultural backwardness and desolation of the province of Berlin and to the low level of esthetic culture of even its best representatives.[5]

35. GERHART HAUPTMANN.[1] *THE HERETIC OF SOANA.* PETERSBURG: ATENEI, 1923. 105 pp.

The Heretic of Soana is a typical modernistic German novella. German modernism, while fluctuating between light reading matter and so-called "symbolist and mystic quests," has developed its own peculiar variety of narration, which is garnished with psychology and bombastic symbolism but is not devoid of a superficial entertainment factor. On the one hand, it is saturated with dubious profundities, on the other hand, it cannot ignore the frivolous taste of the average reader. The result is an entire pantheon of cheap symbolism in which the "depths of the spirit" are brilliantly adapted for light reading on the train. *The Heretic of Soana*, however, a tale about a priest turned goatherd (Italian-Swiss landscape, Dionysian goats, priapic cult, mountain girl temptress, and so forth), is not even fit for reading on the train. It is a modernistic German novella grown decisively heavier, bloated with fat. It is completely devoid of plot, characterization, and narrative unity. It is monstrous lyricism in prose, for example: "the mysteries of dark embraces in the green grass, mother-of-pearl passion, ecstacy, and intoxication, the secrets of the golden grains of maize and of all fruits, all colors." The time of action is not designated (from the fifteenth to the twentieth century!)— and the story itself, which deals with the temptation of a young priest, develops at a snail's pace, while the boring, ecstatic tone of the narrative suffocates even the rudimentary action. It is astonishing to what extent *The Heretic of Soana* is a traditional and stereotypical work. The belated cult of the Renaissance and the absolutely innocent "pagan-pantheistic" hostility towards Christianity has long been a familiar mark of German modernism. It is an assistant professor vacationing in a sanitorium, sporting sandals and a goatskin coat over a chasseur's sweater, an assistant professor who prefers to vacation on a lake in the Italian part of Switzerland, at Lugano or some similarly blessed spot abounding in hostels and hotels, because such a location is conducive to an elevated mythological and philological mood. Hauptmann, the author of *The Heretic of Soana*, seems to be precisely such a sanitorium professor in a goatskin coat. Hauptmann's connection with the awful literary taste of the average philistine reader has caused his work to be stricken from the list of the active ranks of contemporary German literature. Weighty, ecstatic stories about priests tempted by girls and goats—a throwback to popular literature extraordinarily widespread in Germany about the Renaissance with its apotheosis of paganism (a mystic pantheism is attributed to the Renaissance which in fact is completely alien to its spirit) —and the inclusive triangle of the university, a Munich cafe, and a Swiss sanitorium, are all typical of German novellas; it is enough to drive one to despair. No amount of respect for the author of *The Weavers* should keep us from renouncing such literary mongrels as *The Heretic of Soana*.

36. AN. SVENTITSKY. *A BOOK OF TALES ABOUT KING ARTHUR AND THE KNIGHTS OF THE ROUND TABLE.* MOSCOW: MIR, 1923. 120 P., 2,000 COPIES.

An. Sventitsky adapted part of the vast Celtic cycle about King Arthur for this book. The Arthurian cycle has many variants, but more important than that, the original version is lost; it no longer exists. The famous romances in verse by Chrétien de Troyes[1] (entertaining literature of the adventure story genre) provide the major source of the Arthurian legend for European poetry.

Chrétien de Troyes is a thirteenth-century Frenchman. He is an excellent teller of adventure stories and a master of verse narration.

However, neither the Tristan and Isolde nor the Merlin variant adapted by Sventitsky come from Chrétien. The Latin *Historia regum Britanniae* by the monk Gaufrei de Monmouth is regarded as the original source of the Merlin legend. It is difficult to say which late French or Italian version Sventitsky used as his standard. The chivalric romance of the Russian marketplace and popular literature is incomparably better. Sventitsky's version is no more than a prose rendition of Shchepkin-Kupernik's[2] verses: "the bright helmet," "witchcraft," and "shining armor," where the phrases are rounded off as in bureaucratic protocol. Where in Sventitsky's work is the aptness and variety of Chrétien's epithets, where is the refreshing stream of the adventure story?

The book is a total misinterpretation. At first glance it seems to be a "romantic" stylization of the "Middle Ages." It contains no reference to sources, no commentary, and gives no indication of whether it is a translation, an adaptation, or a stylization. The text is naked prose: Sventitsky's name and nothing more.

It contains no trace of the true Middle Ages and their philological spirit.[3] It is a product of the prevailing taste for mass-produced French tapestries with "knights," "sorcerers," and "tournaments." Nevertheless, the book does have sources and does have its own ideology. The poeticization of stories from the Arthurian cycle, the empty incorporation of verbiage, the adaptation of those stories for the most banal modern understanding— the "work" is singularly useless both to the philologist and the general reader. It is yet another bit of slander against the Middle

Ages and its healthy, refined, artistic organism, against its amazingly agile canon of forms. It is astonishing how the marvelous fabric of a medieval plot can be so cheapened, made to appear so colorless, and be transformed beyond recognition in the hands of a "poetic" amateur. We can only blame love for the "poetic," for the "French tapestry," combined with the complete absence of a philological education.

It is obvious that Sventitsky was tempted by the laurels of Bédier,[4] the leading expert on the modern romance. Bédier reconstructed the lost plot of *Tristan and Isolde* on the basis of Chrétien and other sources. Bédier's *Tristan and Isolde* is a true miracle of reconstruction, virtually the original. There is no doubt that it should be translated into Russian.

37. THE RETURN

In August of 1919 a delapidated barge accustomed only to the Azov Sea, managed to drag us all the way from Theodosia to Batum. Some wily colonel furnished us with visas and released us to the cheerful Georgians firmly convinced that he would retrieve us, for as we later found out, there were very rigid regulations concerning emigration and travel. The special maritime counter-intelligence blessed our departure. We sat on deck among merchants and suspicious-looking Daghestanis in felt *burkas*.[1] The steamer had already rounded the Theodosian coast when it had to turn back: it had forgotten its provisions. Never before had I encountered a boat that forgot things like some scatterbrain.

For five days and nights our Azov craft plied the warm salt waters of the Hellespont. For five days and nights we crawled on all fours across the deck to obtain boiled water, for five days and nights fierce Daghestanis cast suspicious glances our way: "Why are you travelling?" "I have relatives in Tiflis!..."[2] "But why are they in Tiflis?" "They own a house there..." "Well, O.K., go ahead then... Every man is entitled to his own house," and a glass of St.-John's-wort brew would be extended, so potent it elicited lightning and spasms which lacerated our stomachs.

On the evening of the fifth day we arrived in Batum and anchored in the roadstead. The city glowed like a fused mass of electric lights, like a gigantic casino pulsating with electric arcs, a glittering honeycomb in which a strange but festive people lived out their lives. This impression was all the stronger following the semi-darkness of chipped and peeling Theodosia, with its Italian Street, formerly the haunt of southern scandalmongers, with its inn which boasted colonnades dating from the time of Alexander I, and where by night the apothecary shops and the undertakers' establishments alone were illuminated. In the morning the spell of the casino had vanished only to be replaced by a magnificent shoreline graced by a vista of delicately etched hills reminiscent of a Japanese coiffure—its pure lines undulating through its limpid details, through miniature trees floating across the transparent air, gesticulating vividly, and climbing ever upward from pass to pass. There she is—Georgia!... Now they'll let us ashore...

We were not kept from going ashore, but at the gangway some students, rather of the same ilk as the organizers of a charity ball (for some reason they are always Georgians) took our passports, saying: "You can always get them back, and it's more convenient for us." Being passportless in Batum was not so bad: who needs a passport in a free country?

Nowhere in the world can a man find himself completely homeless. We had helped two venerable old ladies along the way, and now in port as we unloaded their cumbersome mass of baggage, we suddenly found ourselves in the midst of a cozy Batumian family whose guiding spirit was someone known as "Uncle." This "Uncle" actually lived in London and was on his way to Constantinople. Rotund and kind-hearted, it was as if the exchange rate itself had taken on the image of a man and come down to earth to sow joy and good will. After dinner this delightful family sent us off to the city.

Nothing is comparable to the joyful sensation when, after a lengthy sea voyage, the earth still swims beneath your feet but you know it is the earth, and you can laugh at the deception of your senses and rejoice by stamping on the ground. As foreigners, of course, we made fools of ourselves: we asked passersby where to find the cafe *Mazzoni*, only to find out later that in Batum soured milk is called *mazzoni* in Greek, something that should have been obvious from the signs on all the cafes and coffeebars in town.

We finally found our *mazzoni* with mushroom-umbrellas over the tables and crowned our day with cups of steaming hot Turkish coffee and glasses of liquid sun—hot Martel. There we also had a strange encounter: some lanky fellow, quite intoxicated and shackled in a fantastic silver bracelet, leaned over to welcome us. However, no sooner did he learn we were headed for Moscow than he sobered up and vanished.

The next day we set out after our passports to make sure everything was in order. On the most spotless street in town where everything emitted an odor of order, where tropical holly appeared to be ashamed to grow in pots, we were met by an extremely obliging Commissar and questioned about our future intentions. I was under the impression that we charmed each other by our mutual sincerity and goodwill. He went over everything with us, and got terribly upset that I might lose myself in a foreign country without my friends. I tried to calm him down and mentioned Sergei X. He was overjoyed: what do you know, what do you know, yes, we know him, we deported him a week ago... I mentioned another name, I believe it was Riurik Ivnev[3] —again he rejoiced, again it turned out that he knew him, and had deported him... Now only one little formality remained—to obtain a visa from the governor-general. His office was quite close by, we would be shown the way...

As we walked to the governor's we noticed that our guide's pocket was turned out. Someone immediately attempted to evaluate this detail. That pocket, as it were, represented the incubation period preceding our deprivation of freedom. Nevertheless, we continued on to our meeting with pure and sincere hearts. We were ushered in to see the governor-general immediately. A bad sign indeed! Tall and thin, he resembled an Italian general in stature; he wore a uniform with an upright collar, trimmed in gold braid. He was surrounded by people with nasty expressions who immediately began poking about, clucking and slamming doors. Amidst that bird-like din, one word was repeated incessantly, accompanied by emphatic gestures and goggling eyes: "Bolshevik..." "Bolshevik..."

The governor declared: "You will have to go back!" "Why?" "Not enough bread..." "But we aren't planning to stay here, we are going to Moscow." "No, it's impossible. We have our orders: since you have come from the Crimea, you will have to go back to the Crimea..."

Further discussion was useless. Our audience was terminated. The decision pertained to an entire group, people who had never laid eyes on each other before. We were obviously not trusted to go back to the Crimea on our own, so we were turned over to the police. The police considered us a group of conspirators and, when one member of the group disappeared, they held knives to our throats demanding to know where our friend was hiding.

At the very heart of the port of Batum, near the Customs House, where the grubby Turkish coffeebars put out small stools, hookahs, and cups of steaming coffee in the street, where the offices of the Lloyd-Triestino Line are located, where feluccas rock gently and Turkish flags burn like poppies in the sun, where carriers with faces of evangelical bandits haul monstrous bales of goods and enormous flour sacks on their backs, where young merchants sniff the air, there the port police is domiciled in the premises of some former mercantile enterprise—a single room, inside the arcade, is set aside for all those waiting to be deported "back to where they came from."

Oh, prisons, prisons! O ancient prisons with your oaken doors and creaking locks, where prisoners fed and trained spiders and clambered up the embrasures of windows to drink in a bit of light and air through the tiny sturdy apertures, romantic prisons of Silvio Pelliko, favorites of anthologies, with disguises, swords baked into loaves of bread, prison wardens' daughters, or how about the enchanting feudal prisons of François Villon, my friend and favorite—oh, prisons, prisons, you all surged up before me when, suddenly, the noisy door banged shut and the following sight met my eyes: inside the filthy, empty room a young Turk was crawling around the stone floor concentratedly cleansing the crevices with a toothbrush. Our arrival displeased him immensely for it interfered with his work. He attempted to throw us out, but that proved absolutely impossible...

Here it was that we were to wait for the steamer to take us back to the Crimea. The windows afforded a view of the delicate Japanese hills and of an entire forest of motor launches and sailboats...

· ·

Accompanied by an armed guard, I paid a visit to the Russian newspaper which, sad to say, turned out to be a Wrangel operation. There I was asked: "If you aren't guilty of anything, why shouldn't you want to return to the Crimea?"

After a lengthy ordeal, we found a second, more sympathetic newspaper. The editor recognized me immediately, threw up his hands, and telephoned some Veniamin Solomonovich. This Veniamin Solomonovich proved to be the present Civilian Governor Chikvishvili. I had apparently fallen into the paws of his military deputy, Mdivani. Chikvishvili, a man with a look of intelligence, the severe countenance and long patriarchal beard of an ikon, sat me down in an armchair and sent away my guard with a laconic "beat it!" He immediately handed me someone's notebook and began questioning me: "For God's sake, what do you think of this work? This man is literally compromising us..." The notebook was an album of poems by Mazurkevich[4] dedicated to the Georgian rulers. Each poem began approximately: "Oh great Chikvishvili, you..." "Oh you, Zhordania, hope of the world..."

"Tell me," said Chikvishvili, "is he really considered a good poet in your country?... Why, he was even awarded the Surikovsky prize..."

38. MENSHEVIKS IN GEORGIA

1

A greenhouse. A hummingbird city. A city of palm trees in tubs. A city of malaria and gentle Japanese hills. A city that resembles a European district in any colonial country, that rings with mosquitoes in the summer and offers fresh mandarin oranges in December. Batum,[1] August, 1920. The shops and offices are closed. A festive quiet reigns. Red flags are hoisted over little white, colonial houses. In the port a dozen idlers are held back by the administration and police. The giant Lloyd Triestino from Constantinople rocks in the roadstead. Women-patronesses with bouquets of red roses and several imposing gentlemen board a motor launch and cast off for the three-story palace.

Today the shopkeepers and the Sunday bourgeois took it into their heads to catch a glimpse of Kautsky[2] himself. Now the launch hurries back: on the wooden bridge the smiling leaders of "true European socialism." Top hats. Charming, fashionable dresses—and many, many moist and trembling roses.

Each guest is carefully seated in an automobile as if in a velvet-lined box and seen off with hurrahs. The uninformed crowd on the shore takes one of the delegates for Kautsky, but the mistake is realized and there is great disappointment: Kautsky is very sorry, he sends his regards, he cannot come. Meanwhile another version is circulating: the indiscreet flirting of the Georgian rulers with the Entente offended Kautsky's German sensibilities. All the same, Germany was licking its fresh wounds... Vandervelde[3] came instead. They were already standing on the balcony of the trade union "Palace of Labor." Vandervelde was speaking. I will never forget that speech. It was a model of official, bombastic, empty, and fundamentally comic eloquence. I recalled Flaubert, Madame Bovary, and the Yonville Agricultural exhibition, the classical eloquence of the prefecture which Flaubert engraved forever in the provincial speeches with their high-pitched sentiments, their theatrical intonations, now raising, now lowering the voice; and the bourgeois, enamored, completely enamored of his own declamation (and, indeed, everyone, to a man, felt that before them stood a true bourgeois), stated: "I am honored to set foot in the land of a true socialist republic.[4] I am touched (broad gesture) by these flags, these closed shops, this extraordinary ceremony to welcome our socialist delegation.

"You have civilized this little corner of Asia," (as the superficial ignorance of the French bourgeois and their disdain for an age-old culture was usually expressed here). "You have transformed it into an island of the future. The eyes of the whole world are watching your socialist experiment, the only one in the world."

2

A week before Vandervelde's arrival in Batum another steamer had docked. A small, flat-bottomed Azov Sea barge, unsafe for travel on the Black Sea, carrying deck passengers who had been in transit for seven days, not from Constantinople, but from Theodosia.

Crimean refugees had arrived on this steamer. Iphigenia's motherland had collapsed under the soldier's heel. And I had to gaze on the beloved, dry, wormwood hills of Theodosia, on the Cimmerian hills, from a prison window[5] and stroll about a parched little courtyard where frightened Jews huddled, where starched officers searched for lice in their field shirts, listening to the roar of soldiers down by the seashore hailing their commander.

In those days Georgia was the Crimea's only air vent, the only road into Russia. Visas to enter Georgia were given out fairly easily to the counterintelligence. Communications between the Mensheviks' and Wrangel's counterintelligence were firmly mended. People were shuttled there and back again. They were allowed into Georgia to see *where and how* they would run—and then they were raked up—and sent back.[6]

The taut, dark-blue canvas of the waves had been turbulent for seven days. People crawled on all fours to get boiling water. Daghestanis in felt *burkas*[7] treated them to a brew of St.-John's-wort. It is nice to get out of prison and step right onto a ship, into a collapsible chamber of space with a moist, carpeted floor.

On the gangway stands a student invested with authority. I recalled the masters of ceremonies directing Caucasian balls at the Assembly of the Nobility. "Your passport—and yours—and yours! You will receive it in three days." An empty formality. Why not everybody? A formality. Daghestanis in felt *burkas* look askance.

In the city people are warned: do not go to the Soviet mission—they will shadow you and seize you. We do not go. We will go to Tiflis, the capital, all the same. The city lives on the blissful memory of Englishmen. Seven-year-old children know the exchange value of the *lira*. All professions and occupations have long since lost their importance. Commerce, or rather, the extracting of value in the hot California malarian air, is considered man's singular achievement. Menshevik Batum was a wretched Georgian city.[8]

Tall Adzhars in women's kerchiefs, native inhabitants, made up the lowest caste of petty commerce at the bazaars. The dense rabble of many tribes coalesced in a friendly, commercial nation. All of them, Georgians, Armenians, Greeks, Persians, Englishmen and Italians, spoke Russian. A savage *Volapük*, a Black Sea Russian Esperanto filled the air.

3

Three days after my arrival I unwittingly became acquainted with the military governor of Batum. We had the following conversation[9] :

"Where have you come from?" "From the Crimea." "It is forbidden to come here." "Why?" "We do not have enough bread." He unexpectedly explains:

"Our country is so prosperous that if we allowed it, everyone would come here." This astoundingly naive, classical phrase was deeply imprinted on my memory. A small, "independent" state which had grown up on foreign blood wanted to be bloodless. It hoped to go down in history as pure and prosperous and, surrounded by threatening powers, to become something like a new Switzerland,[10] a neutral patch of land, "innocent" since birth.

"You will have to go back."

"But I don't want to stay here, I'm going to Moscow."

"It makes no difference. That's the way it is in our country. Everyone goes back to where he came from."

The audience was over. During the conversation suspicious-looking people poked about the room, greedily and triumphantly pointing at me, trying to convince the governor of something. Only one word stood out clearly in the whole torrent of words: *Bolshevik.*

People are lying on the floor. It is as crowded as a chicken coop. An Austrian prisoner of war, a sailor from Kerch, a man who had carelessly blundered into the Russian mission, a bourgeois from Constantinople, a mad young Turk scratching the floor with a toothbrush, a white officer who had fled from Gandzha. The French mission was standing bail for the officer. The Turk is being kicked out to freedom. The rest are to be sent to the Crimea. There are many of us. We are fed nothing, as in an Eastern prison. A few people have money. The guard good-naturedly fetches bread and grapes. They open the door and let in a ruddy, strapping tavern-keeper with a tray of Persian tea. I read the scribbled inscription; one has remained in my memory: "We do not fear the tortures of bandits, we cleverly counterfeit banknotes of Zhordania..."[11] One was released. Out of stupidity, he again wandered into the Soviet mission, and the next day he is back. It is like a farce, like some operetta. With jokes and quips people are sent to their death, because to the Crimean counterintelligence deportation from Georgia is incriminating evidence, a certainty. I went into the city for bread with a convoy escort. His name was Chigua. I remembered his name because he saved my life. He said: "We have two hours, we can fool around, go wherever you want." And he added mysteriously: "I love the Bolsheviks. Perhaps you are a Bolshevik?"

The two of us, I, with the ragged look of hard labor and a torn trouser leg, and my guard, with his rifle, walked together along toy streets, past coffee houses with orchestras, past Italian offices. It smelled of strong Turkish coffee, it reeked of wine cellars. Spreading panic in our wake, we stopped in at editorial offices and trade union headquarters, we knocked on the doors of peaceful homes with fantastic addresses. We were invariably chased away. But Chigua knew where he was leading me; some man in a printing house threw up his hands and made a telephone call. He spoke to the civilian governor general. My orders: report immediately to the convoy. The old Social Democrat was embarrassed. He apologized. Military power acts independently of civilian power. Nothing can be done about it. I am freed. I can smoke

English tobacco and go to Moscow.

The Batum-Tiflis line. Little girls and boys with baskets are selling black Isabella grapes—fleshy and healthy like a cluster of night itself. People are drinking cognac in the railroad car. The flushed atmosphere of a picnic and the pursuit of happiness. Vandervelde and his comrades are already in Tiflis. Red banners decorate palaces and automobiles. Tiflis, like a circus clown, is dangled on a thread from Constantinople. It was converted into a branch of the Constantinople stock market. Russian newspapers are full of good will and mild tolerance; it is all redolent of the *Russian Word*,[12] of 1912, as if nothing had happened, as if there had not only been no revolution, but not even a World War.

39. BATUM

I

Batum in its entirety resembles an object easily fitting into the palm of your hand. You never experience its boundaries or distances. You can move around in it as you would inside a room, and what is more, the air in Batum is always as steamy as it is inside a room. The mechanism controlling this tiny toy-like town, raised by the conditions of our times to the status of a Russian-style California gold-rush city, is extraordinarily simple. It rests on one mainspring—the Turkish *lira*. The exchange rate of the *lira* alters by night, as it were, when the town is fast asleep, for in the morning the inhabitants wake up to a new exchange rate, no one knowing quite how it all happened. The *lira* pulses in the blood of every Batumian, indeed, it is the bakers who announce the morning rate with the morning bread.

The bakers are very calm, courteous, and pleasant Turks who sell traditional *lavash*[1] made from very clean, bland American wheat. First thing in the morning bread costs ten *lira*, in the afternoon it reaches fourteen, by evening—eighteen, but by the next morning it has fallen to twelve again for some reason.

A Batumian has no set occupation. Trade is considered man's natural condition. Against the background of the native population Soviet workers stand out sharply for two reasons: their lack of *lira* and their close association with black bread to which no true Batumian has ever even consciously paid attention

The hierarchy of speculative enterprise in Batum is also very straightforward and simple. It is organized around a dozen foreign firms familiar to every child and surrounded by an aura of divine reverence—Valazzi, Lloyd Triestino, Saga, Sala, Vitali, Kamka, and so on... But such reverence has never prevented the enthusiastic foreigner, however corpulent and suntanned, from keeping pace with the rest of the population rushing along Greek Street from office to office, from store to store practicing witchcraft over sacred foreign currency.

There is no winter in Batum. Mandarin orange peddlers and grubby street urchins hawk *baklava* and *guzinaki* at every turning. The delicate blue of the sun-warmed sea caressingly laps against the S.S. Prince Ferdinand (just in from Constantinople), a multistory ocean-going hotel where "the expensive *table d'hôte* glitters like crystal."

Young merchants from Constantinople sporting bright yellow boots and fingering amber beads fly along the embankment. Glorious in their own bright plumage, they also remind you somehow of Africans decked out in European finery, or even of the exotic performers who recently appeared on the music hall stage.

The doors of all the embankment shops are wide open. In the cosy twilight corpulent, apathetic Persians discuss important questions nearly crushed under the weight of their own wares— cloth, sugar, soap, shoes. Woe to anyone who considers entering merely to ask for a price: he is sure suddenly to find himself the mistaken owner of merchandise costing two billion *lira*—here everything is wholesale.

The reigning language in Batum is Russian: even the most inveterate foreigners begin speaking Russian by their third day in the city. This is all the more amusing since there are hardly any Russians in Batum, and for that matter, very few Georgians. It is a city devoid of nationality—its nationality was lost in the chase after speculative profits.

Here is a fine example of Batum's profound isolation—in the largest local cinema an Italian film about Russian life is playing; its title alone, *Wanda Warenina*, is worth the price of admission! Russian women walk through this incredible scenario like Turks, their heads covered with black veils which they remove only after they are safely indoors. Russian "Princes" prance about in costumes straight from the opera, *A Life for the Tsar*,[2] and travel across broad expanses in troikas equipped with English harnesses, while their sleighs exhibit the intricate designs of Scandinavian Viking ships.

I attended a showing of this film. No one in the overcrowded auditorium expressed surprise or even laughed—they all obviously found it quite natural. It was only when the Italian film portrayed a Russian wedding scene with the young couple being led into church adorned with some enormous crowns that a few Red Army men could no longer restrain themselves and began to grumble.

Emigration from the Crimea to Batum is a very common occurrence now. The Crimea is so impoverished that it is extremely difficult to manage there, thus the *Pestel* carries a new cargo of refugees to Batum from Theodosia, Yalta and Sevastopol on every voyage. At first they wander uncertainly down Greek Street, but given a few days they don their feathers and become full-fledged citizens of the free city.

II

Rain, rain, rain—in such torrents, it seems you can't go out. More rain can be expected tomorrow and the day after tomorrow. Winter rain in Batum resembles a warm showerbath lasting several weeks. No one is put off by it, and if business demands it, any Batumian will go anywhere, even into a flood such as Noah himself would have feared to meet head on. There goes a Consumer Society worker rushing off to his job at *Tsentrosoiuz* (the Central Union of Consumer Cooperatives) in his hunting boots—the cooperative's latest issue of footgear. Boldly he fords the most dangerous crossings and intentionally chooses the deepest spots.

Tsentrosoiuz appears to be flourishing. Work is in full swing from morning till night in a small, clean private residence situated right down on the shore boulevard lined with silver firs, oleanders and palms, in the very house where, according to recent legend, the English conducted their military tribunal. Very early in the morning the indefatigable members of *Tsentrosoiuz*, sporting rain-capes and mackintoshes, equip their automobiles for inspection trips to the Chakvin tea plantations and fruit orchards. Since early morning foreign buyers, driven like lambs to the slaughter, push and shove in the anterooms along with the local merchants (it is always possible to distinguish between those who are led and those who lead), and not without due sycophancy on their part they finally penetrate the Director's office only to encounter the keen and shrewd court of the Biblical King Solomon or the Cadi of *A Thousand and One Nights.*

"We are the buyers for the Consumer Cooperatives," the Batumian *Tsentrosoiuz* members proudly announce.

"We're neither for nor against the *Tsentrosoiuz*," asserts one local inhabitant. Nevertheless, he demands "a bird in hand," he requires something tangible now. On the other hand, if not for *Tsentrosoiuz* (closely associated with *Vneshtorg*, the Ministry of Foreign Trade), there would be no control, no restraints against foreign exploiters who now, at least, face rebuffs to their greed in addition to a strong authority before whom they are forced to yield.

But rain does not fall forever. As if by magic the cleansed streets dry up. Batum's flood is the reign of running water, after which the city is purified, refreshed. On the boulevards the winter promenade begins. In January the beaches are packed with people sitting on sun-warmed pebbles right down at the water's edge. The only thing people don't do is dive in. It is also during this season that the holiday begins for the port's Turkish coffee bars which form the hub of the entire city, providing its small clubs and exchanges. The coffee bars are dark and smoky. The steam of strong aromatic coffee permeates the air. Deep inside never extinguished braziers, golden coals smolder while above in special copper pots the coffee bar owners prepare the divine brew themselves. Waiters wear themselves out carrying tiny coffee cups back and forth accompanied by glasses of cold water.

The newsboy drops in with a supply of papers in every tongue. Everyone takes his own.

A venerable old Turk purchases a Turkish paper, *Communist,* and slowly reads it aloud to his compatriots. What can he, merchant and patriarch, grasp from these new doctrines? He wrinkles his brow but does not smile. Like most of his people, he is well-trained and accustomed to respecting the opinions of others.

The finest establishments in commercial Batum are the houses of commerce themselves. There is a quality of beauty and culture about them which is severely lacking in the hastily constructed Italian and other European business enterprises where confusion and an evil predatory spirit prevail. There is one point in which European commerce can never match its Oriental counterpart: Oriental commerce is far more than an apparatus of distribution, it is a social phenomenon. Indeed, in the very customs of Oriental commerce you come to recognize its inherent respect for man: no man exists simply to be robbed and eaten with *kasha.*

Twilight falls, but Batum does not wish to go to bed. Late into the night a solid avalanche of festive people promenade up and down Marinskaya Street. You have the distinct feeling that every person in the crowd has just "closed a deal" and is now reaping the fruits of his commercial finesse. The brightly illuminated stalls and gateways are piled high with fruits and the delight

of the southern winter—mandarin oranges. Some grubby enterprising street urchins begin to dance the *lezghinka*, only to throw
themselves under the feet of passersby who, suddenly terrified,
find they can extricate themselves for a small fee. The crowd is
so lively its loud and joyous rumbling reaches the fourth story and
lulls your first sleep.

Furthermore, at that hour entire city blocks are as barren as
a desert. Those are the special blocks of shops along the water-
front. Entire streets, their lights extinguished, in darkness, their
shutters tightly locked with heavy iron padlocks. Watchmen alone
wander those streets with their ever vigilant cudgels guarding the
sleeping billions. There are certain places, however, where light
filters through the iron shutters, for people also live in many of
the shops. The fact is that there are no apartments in Batum.
There is not even a "housing crisis." It was eliminated very simply
—the dearth of rooms is so absolute that no one even takes it into
his head to look for one. A newcomer to Batum is not asked
where he is living, but rather, how he is spending the night. Anxiety over the homeless newcomer is so great you can't even leave
your belongings temporarily in a cafe for the owners are certain
that you will return to spend the night, a possibility they fear
like the plague. Petty tradesmen take shelter in stalls and booths
which are no larger than dog kennels. Just how the important
foreign merchants are housed remains a complete mystery. Obviously, the *lira* conquers the laws of space.

In the spirited bustle of its international commerce, Batum
resembles some colonial port city or the European quarter of
distant Shanghai. Novorossiisk seems so impoverished after Batum, even with its magnificent, enormous, well-equipped port,
with its grain elevators which hoist incredibly long storage bins
resembling bathhouses high above the port on narrow chicken
legs. In Batum everything sleeps in the expectation of being
aroused, for you sense in that city a special kind of seriousness:
it is as if the city were preparing for the fulfillment of an im-
minent commercial venture on the grandest scale. Meanwhile, in
the cold and deserted stores where here and there bits of coarse
calico lie demonstratively flung down on countertops, intrepid
commercial travellers accustomed to various types of thievery
feverishly cram suitcases full of Batumian goods and drag their suspicious hundred-pood weights off down some dark and dangerous

alley, constantly on the lookout for the shores of their own Arcadia.

III

The foreigner whose trip to Soviet Russia is limited to a visit to Batum must gain a very strange impression, although for us our sojourn completely sufficed to judge of the charms of Constantinople.

In Batum no one ever complains of hard times, and only one detail reminds you of the existence of poverty—the small placards which inevitably add to the decor of every shop, of every small inn: "No credit" or even "Credit forbidden," in the most varied orthographies. But genuine trade cannot exist without credit, thus it is actually enough to obtain a box of cigarettes somewhere one day to receive credit for a second box on the following day.

All this serves only the belly and the *lira*; nevertheless, loftier demands also exist in Batum—something to serve the soul. There is the ODI circle (the Society of Workers in the Arts) on Marinskaya Street where absurd exhibitions of paintings representing the latest craze are organized. Such paintings are snatched up immediately by visiting Greeks, while the local esthetes and snobs pace up and down under colorful oleographs imagining themselves in some gallery somewhere showing the genuine article. There are also poets living in Batum, but it is difficult to imagine a more recherché group. The city is constantly being subjected to the onslaughts of visiting charlatans, so-called professors and lecturers. One of them organized a public trial of Judas Iscariot. He even voluntarily announced on a public poster the participation of a local revolutionary tribunal to which he made himself answerable.

Every Saturday the city reverberates with the strains of military music coming from the public festivities: an all-night feast, a weekly philanthropic affair is held for the benefit of the starving—with lotto, an American auction, and other amusements of the same order. People drop *lira* there by the billions.   .

If it is a Georgian affair, the hypnotic music of the Sazandari[3] never ceases; the musicians move about from table to table until one of the feasters arises menacingly and begins to dance the *lezghinka* to the accompaniment of the heart-rending *tari*.

How can modern Batum be described? As a free trade center, a California of the gold rush era, a filthy cauldron of exploitation and treachery, as a dubious window on Europe for the Soviet nation... As an enchanting, semi-Oriental Mediterranean port with Turkish coffee bars, courteous merchants and Russian trader-sailors who trample its rapacious soil as carelessly as their predecessors trampled the soil of Shanghai and San Francisco.

We will always remember how the air of present-day Batum, sunny, damp and unhealthy, is impregnated with disrespect for the future of Proletarian Russia, its government, its moral image, and its suffering.

Yes, and how meagre are Batum's commercial profits and how vastly inflated. If you examine the mountains of goods piled up in Batumian warehouses, you will see the scandalously cheap goods which in former times were destined for colonial markets and the savages.

Our new slogan should be: let's free ourselves as swiftly as possible from the hegemony of Batum so that the salty sea breezes may refresh our house of labor and blow through the windows of our healthy ports—Odessa, Novorossiisk, Sevastopol and Petersburg—where, with good luck, the inner window frames[4] are now visible.

40. THE BLOODY MYSTERY-PLAY OF JANUARY NINTH

When the producer of a play undertakes an epic production, he assembles an enormous cast of characters, points out their places to them, instills motion in them by means of a powerful electric current, and they come alive under his fingers; they make noise, cry, and are dashed about like reeds under the pressure of the wind. Historical events do not have producers. Without any direction or prior agreement the participants, driven out of their cozy dwellings by a vague anxiety, make their entrance onto the streets and public squares. A mysterious force casts them onto the city squares, leaving them to the mercy of the unknown.

It is good if there is a tribune in their midst whose voice can create a structure, an order out of elemental human forces; it is good if there is a mighty goal—a fortress to be seized or a Bastille to be razed. Then the ant-hill, loosened by a stick, is transformed into an orderly system of vessels rushing toward the center where everything will inevitably be resolved and where an event will inevitably occur.[1]

On the tragic day of January ninth[2] that majestic epic production had to manage without a center, without an event; the human throngs did not make it to the Winter Palace.

The Petersburg workers were not fated to meet the Tsar, and the people's movement, conceived according to a strictly defined plan, was beheaded by the will of history, and not one of the actors of that great day carried out the directions of the producer, not one of them made it to the horseshoe-shaped square, as huge as a lake, with the marble pillar-angel at its center.

How many times was the procession of Petersburg workers dispersed after it had made its way to the last tollgate, how many times was the mystery-play of January ninth repeated? The procession developed simultaneously in all parts of the great city, behind both the Moscow tollgates and the Narva tollgates, on the Okha, on Vasilevsky Island, and at the Vyborg tollgates... There were several small theaters with equal rights instead of a single grandiose theater. And each one coped independently with its task: to undermine faith in the Tsar and to inscribe an apotheosis of regicide with blood in the snow.

Every child's cap or mitten, every woman's kerchief that was pitifully tossed onto the Petersburg snow that day remained as a manifesto that the Tsar must die, that the Tsar would die.

In the entire chronicle of the Russian Revolution there is, perhaps, no other day as saturated with substance as the ninth of January. At the time people's consciousness of that day's significance outweighed the obvious meaning of the day; this consciousness weighed upon them like something ominous, burdensome, and unaccountable.

The lesson learned from the ninth of January—regicide—is the genuine lesson of tragedy: it is impossible to live unless the Tsar is killed. The ninth of January was a tragedy performed only by the chorus: it had no hero, no spiritual leader. Father Gapon[3] remained in the background. As soon as the action began he was already nothing, he was already nowhere to be found... How many were killed, how many were wounded—and not a single famous person among them... (Only Professor Tarle[4] was wounded on the head with a sabre—he was the only celebrity...) The chorus was forgotten on the stage, abandoned and left to its own devices... Anyone familiar with the laws governing Greek tragedy[5] will understand that there can be no sight more pathetic, heart-rending, or crushing. It was precisely then that the tragic depth of the people's consciousness was ignited. When the bullets began to whistle, people rushed helter-skelter, falling to the earth and forgetting each other in their animal fear.

It is characteristic that no one heard the signal before the shooting began. According to all hearsay accounts, the massacre apparently began without any warning. No one heard the last clarion call of Imperial Russia—its death agony, its dying groan—resound in the frosty January air. Imperial Russia died like a wild beast—no one heard its final wheeze.

The ninth of January is a Petersburg tragedy; it could have happened only in Petersburg. The design of the city, the arrangement of its streets, and the spirit of its architecture left an ineradicable trace on the very nature of that historical event. The ninth of January would not have succeeded in Moscow. The centripetal force of that day, the regular movement along the radii from the circumference toward the center, so to speak, the whole dynamics of January ninth was conditioned by the architectural-historical design of Petersburg. The architectural idea of Petersburg inevitably led to the concept of a powerful central unity. Petersburg, with all its chipped, yellow, and gray-green streets, flows naturally into the mighty granite reservoir of the Winter Palace square, toward the red buildings in horseshoe formation divided only by the forged bronze arch with its team of four jousting horses rearing on their hind legs.

The people did not go to the Bronze Horseman on Senate Square because only the whole of Russia would be equal to do battle with him; the tournament with him was yet to come.

The people went to the Winter Palace square as bricklayers to lay the last brick, thus crowning their revolutionary construction. The workers built the Winter Palace: they then set out to put the Tsar to the test.

That failed. The Tsar had already been destroyed. The palace had become a coffin and a wasteland, the palace square—a gaping abyss, the most structured city in the world—an absurd conglomeration of buildings.

What then? Only the huge yellow Obukhovskaya Hospital with its palisades, courtyards, and mortuaries did not lose its head: it knew what had to be done. Like an old aunt who visits the family when there is a death or a birth, this old yellow midwife took in the thousands accidentally killed—each fowl shot down with an inconspicuous wound or a lead pellet embedded in its body.

On that yellow wintry day no one knew that she was admitting the newborn, red Russia, that each of those deaths was a birth.

Even the clever peasant in distant Siberia did not yet know whom he was destined to save, nor was he equipped for the long journey.

Beheaded Petersburg stood shrouded in gloom; bonfires were smoking in the streets; outmoded and superfluous patrols were freezing on the street corners. And yet, a city without a soul is unthinkable: the new, liberated soul of Petersburg was already wandering through the snow like the tender, melancholy Psyche.[6] The first workers' procession had failed. It had set forth from the brick and wooden gates for the granite chalice of the Neva, for the pure architectural mass, as a sanctuary, with its Admiralty shrine and the sarcophagus of St. Isaac's Cathedral. But that procession formed again: all Petersburg, from all its dirty, yellow, box-like houses, from its shacks, factories, and wastelands, rose up and once more, twelve years later, approached the Winter Palace square from all sides to complete the edifice it had started long ago and, with the last freely laid brick, to justify the mighty and splendid stronghold of workers' labor erected on the workers' bones.

41. COLD SUMMER

The team of four horses above the entrance of the Bolshoi Theater... Thick doric columns... The opera square—an asphalt lake illuminated by the straw-colored flashes of streetcars—is awakened as early as three a.m. by the clattering of humble city horses...

I know you, Bolshoi Opera Square: you are the umbilical cord of European cities, but in Moscow you are no better and no worse than your sisters.

When I emerge onto the square, still blinded and gulping down light, from the dusty anomaly of the Metropole—an international hotel—where I have been wandering under the glass-covered arcade through corridors of streets in an interior city, stopping occasionally before an ambush of mirrors or resting on a tranquil grassy knoll fenced off by bamboo furniture, my eyes are struck by the majestic reality of the Revolution, and a grand aria for a robust voice drowns out the honking of automobile horns.

Petite perfume vendors stand on the Petrovka across from the Miur-Meriliz department store,[1] flattening themselves against the wall, elbow to elbow, like a bevy of quails. This small detachment of saleswomen is only a flock, a sparrowish, snub-nosed army of Moscow girls: pretty secretaries, flower sellers, and bare-legged girls who subsist on crumbs and who blossom in the summer...

During a downpour, they remove their shoes to run through the golden streams, along the reddish clay of eroded boulevards, pressing their precious slipper-boats to their breasts. Without these girls there is an abyss: a cold summer. It is as if a bag filled with ice that cannot melt is concealed in the thick greenery of the Neskuchny Gardens,[2] and from there a chill crawls over all web-footed Moscow...

I recall Barbier's *Iambe*[3]: "When the heavy, sultry heat burned through huge rocks." In the days when freedom was being born ("that vulgar wench, the Bastille swallow"), Paris was delirious from the heat, but we must live in Moscow, gray-eyed and snub-nosed, with its sparrowish chill in July...

How I love to run outside in the morning, to run along the clean, light street, through the orchard where summer snow—

featherbeds of downy dandelions—has formed drifts overnight, and head straight to the kiosk for a copy of *Pravda*.

I love to go, tapping an empty tin can like a small boy, in search of kerosene, not to a shop, but to a slum. This slum is worth telling about: first you see a gateway, then to the left a crude, almost monastic staircase and two open stone terraces. Resonant footsteps, a sunken ceiling, upturned slabs. The doors are covered with thick felt and twine is stretched across them. Cunning, emaciated children in long dresses rush about underfoot: it is a real Italian courtyard. From behind a heap of trash a Greek woman of indescribable beauty stares out one of the windows. She is one of those people for whom Gogol[4] did not spare any of his bombastic, magnificent similes.

He does not love the city who does not value its rags and tatters, its modest and pathetic districts, who has not gasped for breath on its back stairways, becoming entangled in scraps of tin to the din of cats, who has not contemplated, from the prison yard of Vkhutemas,[5] a splinter in the azure, the living, the animal charm of an airplane...

He does not love the city who does not know its petty habits: for example, the inevitable trail of beggars and flower-sellers when your cart clambers up Kamergersky hill and your horse is forced to a walk...[6]

At a major streetcar stop on the Arbat beggars throw themselves at the motionless car to collect their tribute. If the car is empty, however, they do not stir from their places; they bask in the sun like animals under the awnings of the streetcar bathrooms, and there I saw blind men playing with their guides.

And I saw flower-sellers, stepping off to the side, spit on their roses.

In the evening, the din and revelry begins on the thick, green Tverskoi Boulevard—from Pushkin Street to Timiriazevsky's vacant lot. But how unexpectedly these green gates of Moscow fade away!

I pass by lottery tables which have been covered from time immemorial with the same bottles, then I pass three blind men singing "Talisman" in unison, and I come upon a dark mass of people crowding under a tree...

A man is sitting in the tree: with one hand he is holding out a straw bag on a long sieve, and with the other hand he is shaking the tree desperately. Something is hovering around his head. Bees! An entire hive and its queen have flown down from somewhere and settled in the tree. The stubborn hive hangs from the branch like a brown sponge, but the strange beekeeper from Tverskoi Boulevard keeps on shaking his tree and offering his bag to the bees.

During a storm it is pleasant to speed through the green belt of Moscow on the "A" car, chasing the storm cloud. At the Church of the Savior[7] the city broadens out into layers of chalky terraces; chalky hills burst into the town along with the fluvial expanses. Here the heart of the city pumps the bellows, and farther on Moscow writes with chalk.[8] The white bone of houses can be seen more and more frequently. Against the lead-colored backdrop of the storm the white starlings of the Kremlin first appear and, finally, you glimpse the mad stone of the Foundling Home, that orgy of plaster and windows, laid out like a game of solitaire, symmetrical as a honeycomb, an accumulation of measurements devoid of all majesty.

Moscow's deathly boredom first paraded itself as enlightenment, then as a smallpox vaccination; and as soon as it begins to take shape it will no longer be able to stop but will rise like leavened dough.

But I do not seek traces of antiquity in this shaken and combustible city: surely no wedding procession will pass by in four cabs—the bridegroom resembling a gloomy nameday boy and the bride a white cockle; surely no choirmaster, robust as a deacon, will walk out into the middle of a tavern where Trekhgorny beer is served with a little plate of soaked peas and a salted crust, and commence singing with his choir the devil knows what kind of mass.

Now it is summer and expensive fur coats lie in the pawnshop: a racoon as red as fire and a fresh, brand new marten are lying side by side on the table, like big fish killed by harpoons...

I love banks, those menageries of moneychangers, where clerks sit behind bars like dangerous beasts...

I am less happy with the sturdy footgear of the townspeople and the fact that men wear gray English shirts and that the Red Army man's raspberry-colored ribs shine through his translucent chest like an X-ray.

42. SUKHAREVKA

Sukharevka[1] does not begin abruptly. The approaches to it are wide and smooth, and it gradually sucks a stormy trade into its fierce funnel. The highway becomes rougher, the road seethes with hillocks and potholes. Apparently, Sukharevka is impatient: it has already laid out its belongings—right on the main highway: pamphlets used as fans, toys, wooden spoons—the lighter the better. Trifles, paltry wares...

On the outskirts of the market barbers sit on barrels, giving vigorous, clean shaves to tenacious martyrs. The barber stools are like red-hot coals, but you can't jump off them, you can't run away.

Under the Sukharevka tower itself, under the tower-baroness built of tender, rosy bricks, under the tower-hen, as portly as a forty-five-year-old empress, a Kholmogori[2] cow stands tethered to a sickly little tree. When the tower was built, the market-garden seventeenth century came to an end. Peter built it because he was frightened by a bad dream, and overjoyed at seeing everything turn out well, he had that fantastic feat of civil engineering erected on the garden land: neither warehouse nor watchtower, it was something landbound to the core, a place where seafaring was studied.

Sukharevka is market-garden land despite its cover of rock: the miserly, malicious Moscow loam can be felt beneath it, and trade gushes out from the earth as if generated by the very soil.

The market in the middle of the city is a savage spectacle: here a man can be torn to bits for a stolen pastry and bounced about like a rubber doll; here people are dough, and like it or not, someone's sinewy hands are sure to knead you.

Sukharevka leans against you like a broad peasant woman—it is not by chance that Moscow is famous for the matronly breadth of its markets. Shallow-water haggling laps against the yellow-green tavernly shores; to the left the empty Sheremetev courtyard, like a horseshoe, has taken a running leap; the building is light and winged like a young maiden's white foot. The market is like a field planted in rows: first rows of rye, then oats, then buckwheat. It is furrowed, segmented by parallel lines, and crisscrossed by paths; and if you close your eyes you can guess by the mere smell, by the fumes, you might say, what kind of garden beds you are passing. First the musky, healthy smell of a fresh slaughter overwhelms you—the smell of animal corpses is innocuous because we do not want to understand its meaning; then the cubic smell of tanned leather, a smell of labor and the yoke, and then the same smell, but subtler and more cunning, of the boot trade; then your nose is tickled by the innocent smells from rows of greens, like a snowstorm of parsley and celery, or by the round, damp smell of the dairy rows.

I have seen the marketplaces of Tiflis and the black bazaars of Baku. The faces of Georgian, Armenian, and Turkish merchants are angry and cunning, but always human[3] in their dynamic and impassioned expressiveness—but I have never seen anything like the pettiness and monotony of the Sukharevka tradespeople. They are some kind of cross between a polecat and a human being, a real "wretched Slavism." It is just as if their cunning eyes, little ears, wolfish foreheads, and the cheap rouge on their cheeks had been parceled out in equal portions.

They say that from many years of living together, a husband will begin to resemble his wife. If you look closely, the merchant also resembles his wares. The grain merchants are the most content and the most handsome: everything else may fluctuate—bread alone remains a staple product.

The butchers' faces express the ingenuity of a primitive surgeon—they are more complex, more dynamic, and more kind-hearted; the game of muscles inevitably goes along with their work: skinning the carcass, chopping the meat from the shoulder, and estimating by sight has left its mark on them.

Women textile workers who trade in trifles like pins and needles have sharpened faces and pursed lips.

And then your eyes casually fall on the swarthy, candid faces of some Caucasian devils puttering with shoe polish and laughing blissfully.

Sukharevka sways slowly, flies into a rage, and grows intoxicated on the vendors' cries, on the flagellant ritual of buy-and-sell. It is already tossing a man from side to side who had just managed to break away from one market stall, pursued by some questionable two-legged booths, when he was carried off by one of the swift, garrulous streams and hammered against a dead end; and now, drowned out by record players, he continued on amidst the hot primus stoves, hardware scattered on the ground, and books.

Books. What books. What titles: *Pretty Dark Eyes, The Talmud and the Jew,* and unsuccessful poetry anthologies whose birth pangs sounded fifteen years ago.

Over here you see a corner reminiscent of the aftermath of a fire—the furniture seems to have been thrown from a burning house onto the highway: oaken tables with a checkerboard design, walnut buffets recalling women in caps and headdresses, the bilious green of Turkish sofas, ottomans intended for camels, and bourgeois chairs with straight, rickety backs.

The astonished man was swept back once more. He almost stepped on the white foam of lace flounces, whipped like cream, and without knowing how, found himself in the midst of a circle of accordianists who seemed to be vamping for someone's wedding, making havoc of the harmonies with a polite, apologetic motion that left the accordians' wail hanging in the air.

There is something savage in the spectacle of the bazaar: those tens of thousands of people pressing their wares to their breast as if holding a child rescued from a fire. Bazaars always smell of a fire, of unhappiness, or of great misfortune. It is not for nothing that bazaars are herded into a place and fenced off like an area quarantined against the plague. If you give a bazaar free rein it will spread to the city and the city will grow fur; but meanwhile it makes itself felt through literature emerging out of drab and unexpected wrappings, from bags and sacks that turn out to be a Saint's Life or an anthology of wild anecdotes or the directives of some long-dead business.

But the fierce throngs make Russian bazaars such as Sukharevka especially cruel and sad. A Russian is attracted to bazaars not only to buy and sell, but also to wallow in the crowds, to let his elbows, which have been reluctantly at rest in the city, have a workout, and to put his back under the besom of oaths, curses, and obscenities; he loves the market cockfight and the strong word sent in pursuit. In the city people talk idly. Here the din of living speech is a means of defense and attack; it is as if a tame polecat were poking about the market stalls; the speech of the bazaar bares its small teeth like a predatory beast.

Bazaars such as Sukharevka are possible only on the mainland, on the very driest land, like Peking or Moscow.[4] The fierce, burgeoning trade, which covers the very earth like a man, is possible only on dry, middle earth that is accustomed to being trampled underfoot.

A few piercing whistles—and everything disappears, is packed up and dragged off, and the square grows empty at the same hysterical speed with which timbered bridges were emptied when the barbed broom of fear swept them clean.

43. THE FIRST INTERNATIONAL PEASANTS' CONFERENCE

A Draft

The staircase leading to Andreev hall swells up like a mountain and leads to a popular painting: Alexander III receiving his district officers. The canvas is enormous: the Tsar, looking very jaunty, is surrounded by courtiers in longwaisted coats and badges, and by coronation Buryats.

If you go past this museum treasure you come to a hall with an extremely high ceiling, with ballroom illumination, where courageous multilingual friends, gathered together as guests of our country for an important conversation, have taken shelter.

The first impression was precisely that of a conversation, and not a "conference." Many had risen from their seats and were clinging to the interpreter. The latter, with the accent of a German Volga settler, is translating a foreign speech. Two or three people are listening to him in a peasant manner, leaning forward and stretching out their heads.

Nearby the same speech is being babbled in English paraphrase for the American farmers, Hindus, and Japanese silently listening, without rising from their seats.

A Finnish orator is speaking. A baggy jacket rests on his broad shoulders, clumsily, Sunday-like. He is speaking, breathing deeply and sublimely, holding his large head high, just as if he were standing in his own country before a Finnish auditorium.

A Pole is speaking, groping for Russian expressions. He is at a loss for words and friendly prompting flies from the peasants' table.

I glance at the Chinese delegates. I can vividly picture the vast, vital path of these little people, these emaciated students with skinny matchstick bodies and pale lusterless faces. European clothes seem empty on them. They have so little flesh and everything has been converted into restless thought, into enormous, active tension.

I immediately recognize the French Southerners, natives of Gascony and Provence: winegrowers with imperials and luxuriant, artistic hairstyles.

The Indian delegates are characterized by that inherent

elegance and nobility of movement attributed to the ancient Hindu people.

Nearby, at the last table, the Russian delegates are seated, middle-aged women in black scarves with stern, maternal faces. The delegates—Russian peasants—reach out for the leaflets of theses being distributed. It is apparent that they want to move closer to the foreigners. They pull their chairs up next to them and gaze at them with affectionate curiosity.

Faces can be glimpsed in the French delegation that seem to have emerged from a gallery of the Paris commune. These are bearded men with large heads, with the stubborn foreheads of thinkers, philosophers of action, passing inconspicuously from the study to the barricades.

The center of focus for everyone is his work at home. And each delegate is anxious about the effect on his country of what is said here. The Southerner, the Frenchman, the Finn, the Pole, the Norwegian, each one speaks with a view to his own domestic situation and bears a note of shame in his voice for his brothers if they are apathetic or have become grovelers.

The composition of the conference is very motley. There are people who have just recently emerged from the masses and are still warm from contact with them. There are important people, organizers on the European scale, nevertheless, a bit of peasant stirs within each one and everyone wants to lift the same enormous burden.

Suddenly, after a conversation with a man of the land, it is as if one were transported to a lecture hall in a German univeristy to hear a highly structured, polished, and methodical speech.

Those who do not understand go out to the lobby and come back in a throng to hear the interpreter. Geography is not observed. Places are interchanged. The honored guest of the conference, Klara Zetkin,[1] like a sweet old grandmother, is surrounded by respectful attention. These people have something to tell each other. Now the Chinese lays his hand on the young Mexican's shoulder. Both are surprised and happy.

In the lobby a small relic is trembling: the new, August bulletin of the Proletarian Association of the Arts, banished from Bavaria by the fascists, which has now migrated to the city of Jena.

44. NGUYEN AI QUOC (HO CHI MINH): A VISIT WITH A COMINTERN MEMBER

"How has Gandhi's movement affected you in Indochina? Have you experienced any vibrations, any echoes?" I asked Nguyen Ai Quoc.[1]

"No," answered my companion. "The Annamese people, the peasants, live buried in the profoundest night. They have no newspapers, no idea of what's going on in the outside world. It is night, truly night."

Nguyen Ai Quoc is the only Annamese in Moscow. He represents an ancient Malaysian race. At heart he is but a boy, thin and lithe, sporting a knitted wool jacket. He speaks French, the language of his oppressors, but his French words sound flat and faint, like the muffled bell of his native tongue.

Nguyen Ai Quoc pronounces the word "civilization" with disgust. He has travelled throughout most of the colonial world, he has been in northern and central Africa, and he has seen enough. He often uses the word "brothers" in conversation. By "brothers" he means Negroes, Hindus, Syrians, Chinese. He wrote a letter to René Maran,[2] the French-educated Negro author of the thick and exotic *Batouala*, and asked him directly: Did he, Maran, wish to contribute to the liberation of his colonial brothers? René Maran, crowned by the French Academy, answered reticently and evasively.

"I come from a privileged Annamese family. In my country such families do nothing. Young men study Confucianism. Did you know that Confucianism is not a religion, but rather the study of morality and behavior? At its very source it presupposes a 'social world.' As a boy of thirteen I first heard the French words, "liberty, equality and fraternity"; well, for us every white man is a Frenchman. I wanted to find out about French civilization, to explore what actually lay hidden behind those words. In our native schools, however, the French train only parrots. They hide books and newspapers from us, they forbid us to read not merely contemporary writers, but Rousseau and Montesquieu as well. What could I do? I decided to leave. The Annamese are serfs. We are not only forbidden to travel, but even to move about in our own land. The railroads were built for 'strategic' purposes; the

French regard us as too immature to use them. I made my way to the coast and...well, I just left. I was nineteen at the time. France was in the midst of elections. The bourgeoisie were slinging mud at each other." A spasm of almost physical revulsion crosses over Nguyen Ai Quoc's face. His face, normally pale and soft, takes on a sudden glow. He squints his large watery eyes and stares at me with the piercing vision of a blind man.

"When the French came, all the fine old families scattered. Bastards who know how to worm their way into favor grabbed up the abandoned houses and estates. Now they are rich; they are the new bourgeoisie; and they are the ones who raise their children in the French way. If a boy in my country attends a Catholic missionary school, it means he is already trash, scum. They pay cash for that. So all the morons go there; there's no difference between going to those schools or serving in the police or militia. A fifth of our entire country is owned by the Catholic missionaries. The concessionaires alone can compete with them.

"What is a French colonizer? Oh, what a narrow, untalented lot. His first priority is getting his relatives fixed up. Then he grabs and steals as much and as quickly as he can, his ultimate goal being a little house, "his own little house" in France.

"The French are poisoning my people. They introduced the obligatory use of alcohol into our country. We make an excellent drink from a small amount of good quality rice—to serve when friends come to visit or at some family celebration of ancestors. The French took the poor quality, cheap rice and distilled liquor by the barrelful. No one wanted to buy their liquor. There was a surplus. The governors were then ordered to make an obligatory per capita liquor apportionment and they forced the people to buy liquor which nobody wanted."

I could vividly picture in my mind how this gentle people with their love of tact and moderation and their hatred for excess had been forced to drink. Nguyen Ai Quoc's temperament radiated nothing but innate tact and delicacy. European civilization operates with bayonets and liquor, concealing them beneath the Catholic missionary's *soutane*. Nguyen Ai Quoc breathes culture, not European culture, but perhaps the culture of the future.

"Right now in Paris there is a group of comrades from the French colonies—five or six men from Cochin China, the Sudan, Madagascar, Haiti—publishing a little magazine called *The Pariah,* dedicated to the struggle against French colonial policy. It's a very small magazine. Instead of receiving honoraria, the staff members pay for the publication of each issue out of their own pockets.

"A bamboo cane with an appeal scratched on it was circulated surreptitiously among the villages. It was replanted in each village and a secret compact was made. It cost the Annamese dearly—there were executions, hundreds of heads fell.

"The Annamese have no clergy and no religion in the European sense of the term. The cult of ancestors is a purely social phenomenon. There are no priests. The oldest member of the family or the village elder performs the memorial rites. We are unfamiliar with the authority of the priest or clergy.

"Yes, it is interesting how the French authorities taught our peasants the words, 'Bolshevik' and 'Lenin.' They began to hunt down so-called Communists among the Annamese at a time when no Communists existed or were even thought of. That's the way they spread the propaganda."

The Annamese are a simple and courteous people. In the nobility of his manner and in the soft, even voice of Nguyen Ai Quoc one can hear the voice of tomorrow, the oceanic silence of universal brotherhood.

A manuscript lies on the table. A calm, businesslike report. The telegraphic style of a correspondent. He lets his imagination run freely: a Congress of the International in 1947. He sees and hears the agenda, he is present, he is taking minutes.

As we were about to say goodbye, Nguyen Ai Quoc suddenly remembered something: "Yes, we had one other 'rebellion.' It was begun by a minor Annamese prince named Zjuntan. It was against the deportation of our peasants to the French slaughter. Zjuntan escaped. Now he is in exile. Please say something about him as well."

45. KIEV

I

The oldest, most indomitable city in the Ukraine.[1] Chestnut trees clothed in shining candles, comfits draped with pink and yellow plumes. Young ladies in contraband silk jackets. The down of the lindens, reminders of pogroms in the neurotic May air. Wide-eyed, large-mouthed children. An itinerant cobbler at work under the lindens, rhythmically exuding the joy of life... Old-fashioned "milkbars" where recent refugees from the North took their meals of *prostokvasha* (soured milk) and pancakes to the roar of Petlyura's[2] cannons still positioned everywhere. People still recall the last Kievan dandy who sauntered along the Kreshcha-tik[3] during the days of panic in patent-leather pumps and a checked cape, chirping the politest bird language. They also recall Grishka Rabinovich, billiard boy from Petersburg's Café Reuter, who for a brief instant suddenly found himself chief of the criminal police and the militia.

In the very center of Kiev, enormous mansions still stand, giant arks capacious enough to house the population of an ocean liner, but on their broad front verandas severe warnings are posted for those delinquent in their payments for water, for other trifling adjustments and shares.

I hear some muttering just underfoot. Can it be a *cheder*[4]? No... It's a basement synagogue. A hundred venerable old men in striped *talesim*[5] are seated like schoolchildren behind narrow yellow desks. No one pays any attention to them. If only Chagall[6] were here!

Yes, a Kievan mansion is a storm-tossed ark, creaking but enamoured of life. Nowhere is the grandeur of the house manager as palpable as in Kiev, nowhere is the struggle for living space as romantic. Supersititious fear induces people to whisper: "That seamstress controls apartment politics—Botvinnik[7] himself is seeking her hand!"

Every Kievan apartment house is a tight little world of its own, torn by hatred, jealousy, and tortuous romantic intrigue. The entryways are occupied by demobilized Red Army men, the majority of whom are completely destitute, possessing no linens, no belongings whatsoever. The terrorized inhabitants cook for them on their primus stoves and buy them handkerchiefs.

A Kievan house is an ark of panic and scandalmongering. Drach, a tiny man with a rat's visage, goes out for a stroll under the chestnut trees.

"Have you heard of him? He's a specialist in arbitration. He acts as an attorney, *sub rosa*. People come to him from as far away as Vinnitsa."[8]

And it is true, court is permanently in session behind Drach's door. His jurisdiction is vast and bounteous—he settles complicated disputes over leases, quarrels between petty business associates, accounts of every variety; he even handles the liquidation of pre-revolutionary debts. People come from remote villages just to consult him. He prosecuted a former contractor who owed a hundred thousand Tsarist rubles and ordered him to pay his creditor thirty rubles a month—and he paid it.

The club of the Department of Municipal Services and Nutrition. A poster announcing Nikolai Erdman's *Mandate*[9] covers the billboard. To be followed by a fancy dress ball. By night the street is filled with a savage roar, truly terrifying if one is unaccustomed to it. The Kreshchatik and Marat street bear the imprint of some illustrious Warsaw confectionery. The Hotel Continental—onetime citadel of responsible workers—has restored all its decorative incrustation. At each window there is a Negro jazz musician. The crowd stares up at the second-story balcony. What is going on? Durov is currycombing one of his pupils...

The Kievan people are proud: the whole world has descended on their city simultaneously: a genuine Negro jazz band, the Moscow Jewish Chamber Theater,[10] Meyerhold[11] and Durov,[12] to mention but a few.

Durov's lame dwarf takes his celebrated mathematician-dog out for a stroll—what an event! A Negro circulates among the populace with his saxophone—what an event! Jewish dandies, actors from the Chamber Theater, are stopped at the streetcorner —once again, what an event!

A roulette wheel operates on the Kreshchatik in broad daylight. The silence of a funeral parlor. Heavy kettles give off electrical discharges. The hustle and bustle of two or three paltry customers creates an aura of meek eagerness. By day a sinister air hangs over this poor roulette wheel.

Kievan events take on legendary dimensions. For instance, I had been told, at least a dozen times, the anecdote about some homeless waif who, having bitten a lady holding a small handbag, had infected her with some frightful disease.

Homeless waifs dressed in elegant rags (through which their Italian olive-colored nakedness was visible) acted as if they were on guard duty near the cafe. Never before have I encountered such a select company of crafty and colorful waifs.

This splendid city rising up in terraces along the banks of the Dniepr river has surmounted adversity.

The "Passage," a building an entire block in length, seasoned with the sulphur of war communism... The famous ruins... Opposite the former Duma—the Provincial Council—stands a monument to Marx. Or is it Marx, no, it must be someone else! Some outstanding house manager or an accountant of great genius? No, it is Marx.

The Kiev of the College of Pavel Galagan,[13] of Governor Funduklei, the Kiev of Leskov's anecdotes and of tea taken under the lindens in the public gardens still abounds, scattered in and about the capital city of the Soviet district. Sloping, labyrinthine courtyard thoroughfares are still to be found, or vacant lots with narrow paths leading out among the rocks. And in the evening, the attentive passerby may glimpse through an open window the frugal supper of some Jewish family—a loaf of challah,[14] some herring and a pot of tea.

II

The tram descends rapidly on its way to the Podol.[15] The Slobodka and Turukhanov Island are even below sea level. A lacustrine and petty bourgeois Venice, the Podol has always paid for the splendor of the upper city. The Podol has burned. The Podol has been flooded. The Podol has been ravaged by pogroms. The Podol is kept in a harshly shabby style. An entire street deals only in ready-made clothing. Signboards direct us: "To the Louvre," "To the Zmichka."

At "Contract" Square—the site of the Kievan marketplace— a wooden mockery of a watchtower stands guard over the provincial arcade and the onion domes of monastic hostelries.

Contempt for the Podol is rampant in the bourgeois city: "She shrieks as if she were in the Podol," "Some hat, fresh from the Podol," "What can you expect from him? A dealer in the Podol."

I walked toward the Dniepr along the flat streets of the Podol to see old Roziner, whose partnership in a private sawmill had turned into misfortune. This wise old patriarch and former senior partner in a private lumber business was sitting on a rough-hewn, sun-warmed board. A pile of sawdust lay at his feet, delicate as swansdown. He sniffed a pinch of wood dust and said: "This beam is sick—tuberculosis... Can healthy wood possibly smell like this?"

Staring up at me with his yellowed sheep's eyes, he began to weep, as a tree weeps, tears of resin. "You have no idea what private capital means! Private capital is a martyr!" The old man raised his arms heavenward, miming his helplessness and the martyrdom of private capital.

The martyrs of private capital revere the memory of the famous entrepreneur Ginzburg, the fabulously wealthy landlord who died a pauper (Kievans love passionate expressions) in a Soviet hospital. But after all is said and done, life is still possible: as long as there is strong raisin wine any ordinary day may be transformed into Passover, and thick, transparent plum brandy, the mere taste of which is a miracle in itself, and cherry jam with a slightly salty aftertaste.

On this trip to Kiev I encountered no rumors nor tales more fanciful than the firm conviction that snow was still falling in Leningrad.

Only one thing now is truly terrifying in Kiev: the fear of losing one's job, fear of unemployment. "I had a goal in life. How much does a man need, really? Just a humble job!"

A man may lose his job because of cutbacks (for measures of economy) or because of Ukrainianization (for ignorance of the national language), but it is impossible to find another one. Dismissed personnel cannot even fight back, they simply suffer the death of a scalded fly or a beetle turned on its back. Terminal cancer cases are not killed, they are merely shunned.

Aggrieved Kievan housewives take revenge on their husbands not by resorting to sulphuric acid, but by securing their dismissal. I was privileged to hear such tales told in the sinister-romantic

Kievan manner. Listen attentively to the speech of the Kievan crowd: what unexpected and extraordinary turns of phrase! The South Russian dialect is flourishing—no one can deny its expressiveness!

"Don't drive the carriage into the shadows, drive it along the sun!"

And how many charming formulas there are for health enunciated in a singsong mode, such as: "She's blossoming like a rose," "He's healthy as an ox," indeed no form of the verb "to regain one's health" is forgotten.

In Kiev there is an enormous emphasis on health. Booths with physicians' scales and even an "electric medical vending machine," which allegedly provides relief for all and sundry illnesses, are to be found at the very entrance to the luxurious gardens spanning the Dniepr embankment. Crowds eagerly formed lines for both the scales and the "medical machine."

I saw some pilgrims on Proreznaya Street. A hundred barefoot women walking Indian file behind a monk-Cicerone. The women walked straight ahead, never turning their heads to either side, blind to everything around them, hostile and devoid of all curiosity, as if passing through a Turkish village.

Present-day Kiev leaves a strange and bitter impression. As in the past the love of life expressed by the young people is extraordinary, but their helplessness is also deeply rooted. The city has a splendid and indomitable soul. This Ukrainian-Jewish-Russian city breathes a deep triple breath.

A few things still recall the years of its epic struggle. On the Kreshchatik the frame of a seven-story colossus resembling some Coliseum still protrudes, yawning through its grand but draughty windows, while directly opposite, facing it from across the street, stands another colossus, evidently a bank in former times.

The Dniepr reenters its banks. Space bursts into the city everywhere, and the broad thoroughfare of Bibikov Boulevard is open once again—but this time not to enemy hordes, rather to the warm winds of May.

I saw only the farewell performance of the *Berezil* Theater Company[1] —a festive spectacle resembling a mosaic composed of fragments. Although that was far too little to allow me to form an opinion of the theater, it was more than adequate to get a sense of its style.

The small Solovtsovsky Theater was electrified with excitement. Each fragment, which was concluded by announcing the name of the director, met with great applause. I arrived near the end of the feast, it was therefore difficult to fully apprehend the ecstacy and intoxication of the *Berezil* audience.

Each fragment conveyed a single message that this is a profoundly democratic theater, the theater of a country where neither snobbery nor dandyism is possible, where any esthete is doomed to become a laughing-stock.

I would like to discuss briefly the techniques used by the *Berezil* Theater Company. According to those closely connected with the theater, the *Berezil*'s most expensive production cost merely one thousand five hundred rubles (!). Considering the achievements of the *Berezil*, that is virtually a miracle.

The production of Mérimée's *La jacquerie*[2] creates an impression of operatic elegance with its gothic construction and luxurious costuming. The play itself is beyond recognition: the actors perform as our actors would perform *Tsar Maximilian*.[3] This is deliberate, naturally, just as everything done at *Berezil* is conscious and deliberate.

The major emphasis of the theater is on collective, mass action. All the autocracy and unlimited despotism of the contemporary director was revealed in *Jimmy Higgins*.[4] The ordinary actor is oppressed and transformed into a somnambulist. Somnambulists dressed in work clothes speak in sing-song voices, extend their arms, dash here and there, rush about, and clamber up ladders and onto boxes depicting America: everything proceeds according to a highly structured, preconceived plan.

The Ukrainian actors gasp for breath like poisoned mice in those Tolleresque and Kaiseresque cages as well as in the Sinclair play which is garnished à la Toller.[5] No stools or staircases can help here, for this is not a united vision, but rather several conflicting directions. An honorable and benevolent ruin awaits *Berezil*: the basic forms of the Ukrainian theater of the future will emerge from it and, following their own directions, will continue the cause of the *Berezil*.

The moment of the theater's conception was extremely significant. It was born in the age of transient productions which burned up like gunpowder in the front line arena, surrounded by the amateur theatricals of night clubs and armies: it was born in an age of forced theatricality, of militant revolutionary theatrical conscription, when rations did the directing—and, it must be admitted, sometimes did extraordinarily well.

The *Berezil* did not look down at those small theatrical forms produced by the Revolution; rather, it assimilated their partisan mobility, the ease of their curtailment and deployment, their capacity for exchanging winks with the audience, for recruiting the audience into its own ranks and returning it only a month later in an altered form.

There is a tendency in the work of the *Berezil* which issues directly from the amateur theater of the clubs; this tendency is strongly felt in *Commune of the Steppe*[6] and *Jimmy Higgins*. In these productions the *Berezil* reveals itself as the elder brother of the club productions.

The "living tableau," the most primitive achievement of the revolutionary theater, can be sensed in even the most festive and luxurious productions of *Berezil*. The *Haidamaks*[7] contains "living tableaux" as splendid as old Ukrainian chapbooks. Moreover, this production belongs to the same theater which revealed in *The Rabble*[8] how theatrical mobility can transform raw "Chaplinism"[9] into a triumphant new form of comedy.

The Moscow Theater was another powerful influence in helping to shape the *Berezil*. Aspects of Meyerhold's theater and the *Chamber Theater* also vie with each other within the *Berezil*; remote echoes can be heard of all the various "old" theaters that flourished before the war and crossed the Revolution in the form of Chamber Theaters or Theater Studios.

The graphic simplicity of pure construction and the rich splendor of oil painting express the two poles of the *Berezil*'s productions. Like colorfully decked out chessmen, the cast of characters is in constant motion within this construction; living figures rush about an abstract cage...

The Rabble was crowned with public recognition. The result was a comedy in the grand style. The *Berezil* had embarked upon a new and fascinating course.

However, this young and profoundly rational theater, cautiously enchanted by biomechanics, cannot seem to liberate itself from the monkey claws of expressionism and theatrical pseudo-symbolism, from Tollerism, in other words.

I witnessed one stunt which appeared malicious in its very rationality: the actor Buchma[10] (who played Jimmy) swung on a rope out of an American torture chamber and into a crowd depicting the collective. Swinging across the crowd on his rope, Jimmy derives solace from the collective and returns to the torture chamber. It is insanely precise, and therefore insanely boring.

The Ukrainian actor is too much a natural-born actor to ever lose his individuality. He is disgusted by the director's despotism. The blood flowing in his veins is rational yet sunny like Molière's. He would prefer to write plays himself, hiring a messenger woman or a Bessarabian greengrocer as his advisor.

There is no need for horror tales, no need for a Ukrainian footstool vision of America, no need for mysticism, even though it may be social mysticism, and there is no need for symbolic groupings or for plunging into the collective on a rope.

The Ukrainian theater seeks rationality and transparency so that the ruddy sun of Molière may illuminate it.

Our Soviet comedy, namely, *The Mandate*[11] and *The Meringue*[12] is gravitating away from Ostrovsky and toward Gogol. Ukrainian comedy is revolving around Molière's sun. Tragedy and lofty genres are as yet concealed in the clouds.

47. MIKHOELS

I

The long-skirted figure of a stranger completely oblivious to his surroundings made his way along the plank sidewalks of an unprepossessing little Belorussian town—a large village with its brick factory, tavern, public gardens and cranes. From the train window, I watched how this extraordinary pedestrian crept along like a black bug, his telling hands widespread, how he made his way among the small houses and through the squelching mud, and how the skirts of his tailcoat were flecked with golden red. Although his gestures expressed aloofness from his environment, his concentrated sense of purpose made it seem as if he were conditioned, like some robot, to run perpetually "back and forth" across the landscape.

That's nothing, you think, a long-skirted Jew[1] walking down a village street! And yet, the image of that hastily moving *rebbe* stuck firmly in my mind; without him the modest landscape appeared devoid of meaning. The chance glimpse of that insane, charmingly absurd, eternally elegant, porcelain-like pedestrian helped me to evaluate my impressions of the Jewish State Theater[2] which I recently encountered for the first time.

Yes, not long before that incident, I would have readily approached such a venerable bearded gentleman on a Kievan street, inquiring: "Did Altman make your costume?" I would have done so without any sign of mockery, most sincerely. However, my plans were foiled. I had thought Granovsky[3] had it made! Just find two or three synagogue members and a cantor, call in a matchmaker—grab some middle-aged broker off the street—and there's your production, ready-made; even Altman was fundamentally unnecessary.

Could it really be so simple? Absolutely not. The Jewish State Theater both professes and justifies the conviction that no Jew, wherever he may be, will ever cease to resemble fragile china, will ever cast off his most elegant and vital *lapserdak*.[4]

This paradoxical theater, in the opinion of certain well-intentioned and serious critics, having declared war on Jewish philistinism and having come into existence solely in order to eradicate prejudices and supersititions, became intoxicated like a woman at the mere sight of a Jew and immediately began to lure him into its workshop—into the porcelain factory, to be baked and hardened into a remarkable piece of biscuit, a painted statuette of a green matchmaker-grasshopper, a group of brown glazed musicians and Radlov's Jewish wedding, or a group of bankers with close-shaven, protruding occipitals who danced like modest young maidens clasping hands around a ring.

Both the plasticity and power of Judaism come from its having managed to develop and perpetuate down through the ages a feeling for form and movement which governs all aspects of style, making it permanent, millennial... I am speaking here not of the cut of a man's coat, something which is always changing and which it is pointless to evaluate; nor have I taken it into my head to justify on esthetic grounds the ghetto or the village life style. Rather, I am speaking about the inner plasticity of the ghetto, about that immense artistic power which is surviving the ghetto's destruction and which shall emerge completely only after the ghetto is destroyed.

Violins are playing the wedding march. Mikhoels[5] approaches the footlights, and with the cautious movements of a fawn, goes up to listen to the minor chords. This is a fawn who has blundered into a Jewish wedding: a moment of indecision. Although not yet intoxicated, he is already aroused by the caterwauling of the Jewish minuet. This moment of indecision is, perhaps, more effective than all the dancing that follows. Standing stock still for a fraction of a second, he suddenly becomes intoxicated—but it is that light-headed intoxication that comes from two or three sips of sweet raisin wine, quite enough to make a Jew's head spin: the Jewish Dionysus is not demanding, and immediately offers him the gift of gaiety.

Mikhoels's face takes on the expression of world-weariness and mournful ecstasy in the course of his dance as if the mask of the Jewish people were drawing nearer to the mask of Classical antiquity, becoming virtually indistinguishable from it.

The dancing Jew now resembles the leader of the ancient Greek chorus. All the power of Judaism, all the rhythm of abstract ideas in dance, all the pride of the dance whose single motive is, in the final analysis, compassion for the earth—all this extends into the trembling of the hands, into the vibration of the thinking fingers which are animated like articulated speech.[6]

Mikhoels attains the summit of ethnic Jewish dandyism: the dancer Mikhoels, the tailor Soroker,[7] the forty-year-old child, the blissful failure, the wise and gentle tailor...

On the same stage yesterday there also appeared svelte girl dancers in *lapserdaks* resembling English jockey coats, and patriarchs who drank tea in the clouds like the old men on the balcony in Homel...[8]

II[9]

...and some little man all puffed up and the whole thing is utter nonsense: an overdue business trip and five lumps of sugar. What's the source of his demonic despotism, of his passionate conviction? Shindel hypnotizes us, compels us to want him to take both the sugar and an actual business trip.

The temperature range of Mikhoels's performance is as true to life as physical heat and cold. And yet he communicates the fever of a historical day just as realistically, and the words, "Narkompros! Narkompros!"[10] on Shindel's lips resound like the deep sighs of an aeolian harp.

When Shindel steps off the platform portraying his room, and then out into the street, the figure of the devil with his rations shrivels up completely; the audience can virtually hear the snow crunching under the felt boots issued to him by the Education Commission. Such an actor must be kept off the realistic stage—things will just melt away under his touch. He creates his own props—a needle and thread, a glass of pepper vodka, a mirror, any object from daily life that he needs—whenever he takes it into his head to do so. Do not interfere—this is his right; do not divest him of the joy of creation. Sometimes, worn out from his capers, exhausted by his own clever deviltry on a stage completely devoid of props, Mikhoels will sit down on the floor and cry out: "Enough! Let's end the performance!..." He resembles a watchmaker examining tiny cogwheels under his magnifying glass. He may be a Jew contemplating his own inner world. He is quite alone, with merely a candle burning in his hands, and the expression of a martyr's ecstasy, as in *The Sorceress*.

Epileptic extremes are dear to Mikhoels's heart: he is often on the verge of a fit *(A Night in the Village of Ra)*, only to be verily saved...

. . . .

Mikhoels once said: "I implore my fellow artists to preserve my countenance for me."[11] Indeed, the entire repertory of the Jewish State Theater revolves around the revelation of Mikhoels's masks. In each play he accomplishes the extremely difficult and glorious journey from Jewish meditation to dithyrambic ecstasy, to freedom and the unfettering of the dance of wisdom.

. . . .

Just a few days ago in Kiev I came across two remarkable theaters—the Ukrainian *Berezil* and the Moscow Jewish Chamber Theater. On seeing the *Berezil* theater off to Kharkov, the great Jewish actor, Mikhoels, turned to the Ukrainian director, Les Kurbas, and said: "You and I are truly blood brothers..." Enigmatic words containing so much more than slogans about peaceful coexistence and international cooperation.

Moreover, these two theaters are very dissimilar, even antipodal. The Jewish Chamber Theater, now in Kiev for a six-week tour, has touched down on its native soil: it is completely at home here and is extremely successful when Jewish crowds seethe around it, when Jewish voices resound, when Jewish taste, fashions, and gestures reign supreme...

The *Berezil* could have arisen only in the Ukraine. Its youthful rationality, the sobriety of its theatrical ideas, its farcical vitality which has attained an apotheosis in the Ukrainian...

48. JACQUES WAS BORN AND DIED

In Russian a sentence expressing direct speech is set off from its explanation by a dash and quotes: —"What a glorious day"— he said, smirking into his beard. That's the way it appears in all books, even though no one ever talks or tells stories that way. I do not know why this device is almost imperceptible in ordinary books, that is, in books written in the original language, whereas in translations[1] it buzzes like a monotonous spindle.

I also do not know why I have been persecuted of late by a nonsensical, monumentally syntactic construction, a synthesis, as it were, of a cardboard pyramid of this verbal world of papier-mâché: "Jacques was born and, having lived his life, died..."

Who is he, this Jacques? Was he born in Champagne, Touraine, or Alsace? Was he put through the meatgrinder of the war by the author of a novel in a yellow cover or did some dashing supporting role named Benois chase him to Tunis, to the Arabs? Did he reject his fiancée? Did he come into an inheritance? Was he a benefactor to the workers in some model quarry?

Does it make any difference?!... Translations resemble Ecclesiastes, o vanity of vanities. That terrifying cardboard pyramid will stand for a long, long time:

"Jacques was born and, having lived his life, died..."

There is an evil, murderous ambiguity in the very word "translation," similar to the ambiguity present in the forms of the same verb: "to court" and "to do someone in..."[2]

The translation of foreign authors which flooded and ravaged an entire epoch in the history of Russian publishing, which descended on the fields of thought and the word like a thick cloud of locusts, was, naturally, "translation," that is, a waste of an unheard-of amount of labor, energy, time, persistence, and vital human blood. Godunov, when there was a plague in Moscow, ordered the Sukhareva tower[3] to be built, while the Tsarist rations and the copper *grivna*[4] probably came in handy for the unemployed of the seventeenth century. Oh, *World Literature,*[5] the Sukhareva tower of the famished intelligentsia of 1919, I don't know if I should praise or curse you. Only authors whose names are found in the world Pantheon were slated for translation and were printed, practically on vellum paper, with the grandiose luxury of jubilee editions. Grain was scarce in the granaries of *World Literature*: it was pecked away while stacks of unprinted manuscripts rose up to the ceiling.

The course of least resistance leads to handouts! Pens chirred in pink, gouty fingers. Two thousand new, more flexible clichés were added to the devices of Irinarkh Vvedensky.[6] No one asked himself whether he would want to translate Stendhal or whether anyone would want to read his translation. Buddhist prayer wheels were turning. The bookkeeping department counted the pages.

There was a time when the translation of a foreign book into Russian was an event, an honor for the foreign author and a special occasion for the reader. There was a time when equals translated equals, contending only for the glory of the language, when a translation resembled a graft of foreign fruit and a wholesome gymnastic exercise for the spiritual muscles. Both Pushkin and Zhukovksy, the good genius of Russian translators, took translations seriously.

The decline began approximately in the 1860s, when the completely false conception of mental dirty work arose, of intellectual day labor, when the corrosive disease of Russian culture began, when the brain began to be valued cheaply. Labor may be heavy and tedious, but "dirty" it does not dare to be, whether it is the labor of a stevedore or of a translator. When a schoolgirl could go to Moscow to get work or a translating job, when the spiders in bookstores realized that cheap brain power could be a profitable business, then the production of dirty, low-level reading matter began. People like Stasiulevich,[7] afraid of printing Leskov in their *Heralds* and obtusely complaining about the scarcity of literature, stuffed the thick journals full of "Jacques," while plump ladies busied themselves disfiguring Edgar Allan Poe, whose stories were translated in their time with the horrors expurgated because they seemed too terrifying to their female translators.

In a typical cheap novel of the seventies the author, in describing a novelty of his day—the horse car—relates an overheard conversation: a certain poor Nastenka, deceived by the merchants of Apraksin Dvor[8] for whom she sewed shirts, tells how she had to go to the "store" where she was "given" a book to translate for five rubles a page and two rubles in advance. At least then it was all out in the open and, although it was hard on Nastenka, the "store" was like any other store.

The translator's greatest reward is to see the assimilation of the book he has translated into the annals of Russian literature. Can we name many such instances since Balmont, Bryusov, and the Russian version of *Enamels and Cameos* by Théophile Gautier?

The translated literature of recent years, despite its universality, is over-refined, excessively accurate and academic. Produced by an advanced guard of translators, it is forced, accidental, and, in the final analysis, unnecessary. Even the most careful translation of a foreign work, if it is not provoked by an inner necessity, is not a living echo of a national culture, but leaves extremely harmful traces in the subconscious workshop of language, obstructing its path, corrupting its conscience, making it compliant, evasive, and impersonally conciliatory.

Cheap brain power is being carted away by the pood along the course of least resistance to the grain scales of the stores.

As a result of a very complicated and not exactly accidental confluence of circumstances, we stand face to face with a bitter, humiliating disease: in our country a book has ceased to be an event. Yes, in its own way every issue of a newspaper is an event, a pulsebeat, the vital blood which we respect, while a book is but half a pound of something—isn't it all the same—half a pound of Vsevolod Ivanov, Pilnyak, or "Jacques." A book will not survive demoralization, its illnesses are contagious. We must not allow hundreds of thousands of unesteemed, unrespected, or semi-respected books to flood the market, although they may be marketable or in circulation.

All books, both good and bad, are sisters, and the Russian book, "Jacques's" sister, suffers from its proximity to "Jacques." If a particle of a country's precious brainpower burns in the voracious ovens of the translation kitchen, if even a part of the precious gold reserves are consciously and persistently melted down into foreign currency, there must be serious reasons and justifications. I see as many reasons as you please, but there are no justifications and there will never be any.

Some loathsome Chichikovian[9] mug shines through "Jacques." Someone makes an obscene gesture and asks in a foul falsetto: "Well, brother, isn't it boring to live in Russia?..."

49. YAKHONTOV

Yakhontov[1] is a young actor who has studied with Meyerhold, Stanislavsky and Vakhtangov, but who has never fit in anywhere. He is an "ugly duckling," he is unique.

Yakhontov's performances resemble those of a conjurer: he is a one-man theater. His theater is the theater of one actor.

His props are so few they can be transported in a cab: a coat hanger, two or three umbrellas, an old checkered laprobe, an intriguing pair of tailor's shears, and a top hat as suitable for playing Eugene Onegin as a Jewish linkman.

And yet there is another object which always accompanies Yakhontov, and which is inseparable from him: space.[2] A sense of space is indispensable to any actor: Yakhontov always carries his sense of space with him, tied up in the tailor Petrovich's handkerchief, as it were, or ready to be pulled out of a top hat like some magician's egg.

It comes as no surprise that Yakhontov and his producer Vladimirsky[3] have selected Gogol and Dostoevsky for their repertory, that is, they have chosen writers with a taste for the event, a taste for the momentous occasion.

Yakhontov's acting, which under Vladimirsky's tutelage has attained graphic perfection, is thoroughly permeated with his anxiety and anticipation of space, with his foreboding and fear of the impending event.

Our classical repertory resembles a powder keg on the verge of exploding. It is no accident that mad Eugene[4] was resurrected in Yakhontov; once again, in our own epoch, he lost consciousness, regained it, and then lost his senses again.

Yakhontov presents us with a rare spectacle: he is an actor who, having rejected declamation and despaired of finding the play best suited to his personality, began the study of universally recognized literary models, of the great masters of structured speech, in order to present to the masses a graphically precise and spare picture, a pattern of movement and a design of the word.

There is nothing extraneous about Yakhontov's acting—it involves only the barest essentials. In the intensity and purity of his performance, Yakhontov recalls a trapeze artist working without a net. He has nowhere to fall.

The tailor Petrovich,[5] somewhat of a crank, shears the air so that you actually see scraps of fabric falling; some minor official in a threadbare overcoat minces along the sidewalk so that you virtually hear the cold crackling beneath his feet; coachmen warm themselves by the fire when suddenly a policeman from the days of Nicholas falls upon them, halberd in hand, like a bear; and Mashenka in her calico dress and parasol, straight out of *White Nights*, suddenly looms in the distance, walking along the granite parapet of the Fontanka Canal.

All this can be conveyed by one man, all this can flow continuously and organically without resorting to cinematic techniques, because it is welded together by the word and revolves about the word. The word is Yakhontov's second space.[6]

In seeking literary sources for their productions, Yakhontov and Vladimirsky were compelled to resort to literary montage, that is, to an artistically ordered union of heterogeneous materials. In certain works, such as *Lenin*, this emerges as a montage of the epoch. There the impression of grandiosity is achieved through the juxtaposition of political speeches, fragments from the Communist manifesto, newspaper chronicles and so on. In other pieces, Yakhontov's montage emerges as a harmonious literary whole, precisely reproducing the internal world of the reader in which a variety of literary works coexist side by side, often colliding with each other or pushing one another into the background. A typical example is *Petersburg*,[7] Yakhontov's finest work, spliced from fragments of Gogol's *Overcoat*, Dostoevsky's *White Nights*, and Pushkin's *Bronze Horseman*.

The basic theme of *Petersburg* is "the little man's" anxiety before the great and hostile city. The anxiety of space is constantly experienced in the actor's movements as is his striving to conceal himself from the impending void.

Yakhontov performs on a large stage, wearing a simple jacket, and using his above-mentioned props (a laprobe, a hanger, etc.).

In his portrayal of the tailor Petrovich dressing Akaky Akakievich in his new overcoat, Yakhontov recites Pushkin's "I covered her glittering shoulders with black sable," thereby emphasizing the poverty of this lyric moment. In the text, while the gallery applauds, Yakhontov is already portraying footmen with fur coats or coachmen freezing outside in the cold, thus expanding his picture to encompass the *entire* theater, from the tailor's room to the frozen night. At each given moment, he conveys an image of a broadly expanding perspective. It is the rare theatrical company that can ever fill up and populate an empty stage so thoroughly.

Yakhontov, with his extraordinary sensitivity to the visual pattern of a line of prose, handles his role of reader-interpreter with complete independence, while his producer, Vladimirsky, vigilantly traces his actions with props, which so precisely suggest Yakhontov's picture and emphasize it with such mathematical severity, that the picture seems to have been outlined in charcoal, as it were.

Yakhontov is unique among contemporary Russian actors in that he is able to move about both in the word and in space. He enacts "the reader."

But Yakhontov is not a professional reader, he is not an interpreter of the text. He is a living reader; he stands on an equal footing with the author, arguing with him, disagreeing with him, fighting with him.[8]

In the work of Yakhontov and Vladimirsky there is something obligatory for the Russian theater as a whole. This is the return to the word, the revival of its integral power and flexibility. A revolution was required to liberate the word in the theater. Nevertheless very little came of it... Yakhontov is one of the actors of the future and his work must be seen by the broad public.

50. JULES ROMAINS: FOREWORD TO A VOLUME OF TRANS-LATIONS

Jules Romains[1] is not an isolated figure in contemporary French literature, rather he is the central figure of a literary school called Unanimism.[2] After deciphering the French logic of naming schools, we arrive at the following: Unanimism is the poetry of collective breathing, the poetry of the collective soul. Jules Romains, René Arcos, Duhamel, and Vildrac are all writers of a single work, bearing a single yoke.

It is rare to find a harmonious literary group. The Unanimists are literary brothers and are not afraid of concurrence and similarity. They work with the same material, striving, as it were, to resemble each other: their voices, demeanor, and the nature of their efforts are very similar.

The poetry and prose of Jules Romains and his colleagues repeatedly and insistently express the desire to speak in simple words about simple, rudimentary, and ordinary things, about the average common man, about the average man's love and work. It would not be a mistake to say that the average man is the material of their poetry.

Flaubert and the Goncourts were also drawn toward the mundane human being in his unadorned and unembellished form. But the great novelists of the nineteenth century performed their fascinating work somewhat arrogantly, like anatomical surgeons: they combined artistic fastidiousness with curiosity.

This is not true of Jules Romains and his group. Their work is the heroic epic of the common man. It is filled with respect for his fate, for his individuality, for his joys and sorrows.

The "hero" of one of Jules Romains's latest works, *Mort de quelqu'un*, is a Parisian railroad engineer. Jules Romains leads us into the world of this man's vital interests with a kind of stern reverence and genuine deference.

It is appropriate to note than in Unanimist poetry and prose the phrase "one of many, somebody" is frequently encountered, like a leitmotif (cf. Duhamel: "Ode to a Few").[3]

In Jules Romains's play, *L'Armée dans la ville*, which preceded *Cromedeyre-le-Vieil*, and which was written before the war, not one of the *dramatis personae* is called by name, social traits and social groups alone are identified: the mayor, the mayor's wife, the first bourgeois, the second bourgeois, the first customer in the cafe, the second customer in the cafe, and so forth. And yet Romains is never inconsistent in his characterization of these "numbers": both the third bourgeois and the fourth customer, carefully drawn with exact, miserly strokes, are "condensed, prefabricated people."

Where did this society of young French writers acquire such affectionate respect, such heroic fondness for the common man when, on the threshold of the European war, human flesh was being prepared for the slaughter?

It seems to me that this unique artistic tendency could best be defined as racial democracy. Eternally alien to nationalism and chauvinism, Jules Romains and his friends are writers not only of French blood, but also, more profoundly, of Romanic and Latin blood. They bring a unique racial esthetic, a thirst for health, strength and equilibrium to French literature. They demand the rebirth of the Romanic race and of its brother, the Germanic race. They demand to hear "the stratified noise of a thousand breaths" growing in the din. They are ready to give their blessing to both cities and villages that are heated by the joyous human warmth of a robust race.

We cannot deny that this is a dangerous and slippery path. How easy it would be to latch on to the groundless romance of race and sentimental twaddle. And where can one find, ultimately, the nucleus of this robust race in contemporary France?

Jules Romains, however, escaped this danger. His artistic sense prompted him to find the right path, the robust race of labor. The spirit of Whitman was reborn in his clear and concise Latin formulas. "Somebody" and "one of many" became a measure of things, the golden measure of the age, a source of rhythm and strength.

Poets as cart-horses, poets as dray horses drew the heavy chariot of Latin genius once again.

Contemporary France has no room for populist illusions. The historical character of the French peasantry is sufficiently well-defined and does not lend itself to any idealization: it is more capable of serving as a scarecrow for the socialistically oriented city-dweller. The hide of the French peasant has been tanned by an entire century of petty management, and to treat it with poetic populism is just as difficult as treating a rock with kid gloves.

Jules Romains, however, gave us *Cromedeyre-le-Vieil*. By encountering the peasantry directly, without sentimentality, without "populism," and by employing his usual devices of characterization—laconicism and typicality—to create a monumental vision of the Cromedeyre peasant society without digressing from ethnographic truth, he has, perhaps, revealed certain subconscious possibilities of the traditional French peasant psychology.

Jules Romains very tactfully avoids the time and place of the action of *Cromedeyre-le-Vieil*. He has invented for it an entire legendary ethnography, precise and convincing, but as fantastic as Shakespeare's ethnography of Poland or Muscovy. The endings of certain names, the landscape and the architecture tempt one to place Cromedeyre in the Pyrenées and to regard the inhabitants of Cromedeyre as some sort of Basques. However, the thickset inhabitants of the mountain village ("like compressed rye sourdough") and the inhabitants of the Laussonne valley speak the same language: thus the antagonism between Cromedeyre and the valley (and the entire drama revolves about this) cannot be explained in crude ethnographic terms. We must take Jules Romains's fantastic ethnography and convincing topography on faith.

It is difficult to name a play in the world repertory in which the topography and landscape are as well fused with the action as they are in *Cromedeyre-le-Vieil*. The raising and lowering of the voice, the ascent and the descent, the breath of human speech, the peculiar gait,[4] and even the slightest movement are intimately connected with the very composition of the soil and are governed by the necessity of adapting to its rough and uneven surfaces, to its geographical architecture.

In this manner Romains achieves a verisimilitude of plasticity, an extraordinary authenticity of all the gestures and intonations comprising the picture of *Cromedeyre*.

The simplicity of Jules Romains's dramatic ideas is reminiscent of the Classics and even smells of Classical borrowings. *L'Armée dans la ville* achieves the monumentality of Aeschylus.[5] A Romanic town is occupied by an army of the Germanic type. The inhabitants organize a mock celebration of reconciliation with the conquerors and lure them to their various homes. An attempt at slaughter follows, the insidious combat of antiquity. *Cromedeyre* is constructed around the abduction of young girls from the Laussonne valley, allegedly an ancient, ritualistic tradition in Cromedeyre.

Jules Romains emphasizes the archaic character of Cromedeyre society which guards its law and its primitive "Communism" in every possible way. Cromedeyre has no intention of descending into the valley to preach its "Communism." It has the laws of primogeniture behind it. The kidnapped girls can still be converted to their tribe, but it is obviously impossible to raise the valley up to their own level—one must be born a citizen of this staunch village. Contradictions between the two levels of peasant psychology are displayed in perfect Classical nakedness.

Jules Romains's intuition allows us to glimpse not only the subconscious collectivism of the French peasant, but it also casts light on the very obscure, religious recesses of his psyche. Perhaps secularization of the French peasant psyche has gone further than most people think. Although he may be infinitely remote from the cheerful domestic paganism of Cromedeyre, he is just as far removed from Rome and is silently waging war with it.

What kind of literary work is *Cromedeyre*? (For aside from its social and even revolutionary insights, it is a literary work to the marrow.)

Cromedeyre-le-Vieil is a rare variety of pastoral drama or a heroic pastoral in dramatic form. Echoes of Old French folk poetry and music soften the austere simplicity of the action which ripens slowly but steadily, comprising only a single incident—the abduction that casts a shadow over all five acts. The play fluctuates between a pastoral and a dramatic aria (a monologue for a strong voice), since the naive, precious details only set off the monumentality of the bold strokes. The artificially isolated world of Cromedeyre lives according to ancient and well-wrought laws, but the very isolation of Cromedeyre, its tendency toward reduction, is indicative of the poet's weariness with the complex relationships of modern society.

51. FROM THE AUTHOR[1]

The essays included in the present volume were written at various times between 1910 and 1923, and share a commonality of thought.

None of these pieces aims at literary definitiveness; literary themes and patterns serve only as concrete examples.

Incidental essays falling outside the scope of this common bond have not been included in this volume.

52. A POET ABOUT HIMSELF

Response to the questionnaire: "The Soviet Writer and October"

The October Revolution could not but influence my work since it took away my "biography,"[1] my sense of individual significance. I am grateful to it, however, for once and for all putting an end to my spiritual security and to a cultural life supported by unearned cultural income... I feel indebted to the Revolution, but I offer it gifts for which it still has no need.[2]

The question about what a writer should be is completely incomprehensible to me: to answer it would be tantamount to inventing a writer, that is, to writing his works for him.

What is more, I am deeply convinced that, in spite of all the limitations and dependence of the writer on social forces, modern science does not possess any means of causing this or that desirable writer to come into existence. Rudimentary eugenics alerts us to the fact that any kind of cultural interbreeding or grafting may produce the most unexpected results. The State procurement of readers is a more likely possibility: for this there exists a direct means: school.

53. A STATEMENT ABOUT "THE BASSOONIST"

The basis for narrative action is the "family chronicle." The starting-point is Kiev at the time of Stolypin's murder.[1] A barrister handling the affairs of powerful contractors, and his clients, small fry, shady characters, are presented as puppets. The action of the epoch—the peculiar atmosphere of the second decade of the twentieth century—unfolds on a very small stage with an extremely colorful social complement of heroes.

The main protagonist is an orchestra member of the Kiev Opera, "the Bassoonist." To a certain extent the device of "The Egyptian Stamp"[2] is repeated: a "bird's eye" portrayal of the epoch. The difference between "The Bassoonist" and "The Egyptian Stamp" resides in the former's strong documentary aspect, right down to the use of barratrous business archives. The second part of "The Bassonist"—the search for a lost, unknown Schubert song—will allow for the presentation of the musical theme (Germany) on the historical plane.

54. THE DOLL WITH MILLIONS[1]

Ladies and gentlemen, citizens, how dreary to live in a republic of labor! Life is insipid. Purposeless. What drabness, what squalor! Look at the names of the stores alone! On my right—The Communard, on my left—The Workers' Coop. Only the barbershop George has a European ring to it. And what a fellow this George is! A loathsome travesty of a human being: he grabs his client by the nose, smokes and shaves, shaves and smokes right in his customer's face, and shoves a copy of *The Flame*[2] at him—dusty, greasy, and oily from the multitude of hands that have touched it—a product of the Americans from the Petrovka: Koltsov and Zozulya. How dreary to live in a certain country, ladies and gentlemen, and you can guess just what kind of country it is. Some low-class Bulgarians or Czechorumanians sew suits on commission for the tailor, while we squeeze our frames into ready-made, standardized clothes without having our measurements taken, as if we were hangers: the shoulders are puckered and the armholes are too tight.

There is another world, however, into which one isn't even allowed to set foot, wearing a trade-union Tolstoian shirt. In that world you don radio headphones to listen to the strains of a Hawaiian guitar or buy a translated novel at a railroad newsstand. A hot item from Paris! *Daily Telegraph*—Joan of Arc minus the mysticism with truffles. There you find a world of shining advertisements... "From a blissfully exotic foreign land come the sounds of a rooster crowing..." It is a temperamental film-rooster, the rooster of Pathé and Co.[3], that firm of vociferous chicken fanciers...

However, my friends, we cannot get visas to go there, so couldn't we somehow adapt the Petrovka to French styles? No, don't argue, Moscow has certain essentials, even some cute-looking little Komsomol members... Don't laugh at physical education. Right this way, grunting citizens in Tolstoian shirts, come to the state movie theater, where film rations adapted from pornography are given out like bread... Today is the premiere. A harmless, minor operation is about to be performed on Moscow—it is very risqué and completely patriotic. Moscow will be shown from a room in the Savoy Hotel occupied by a certain very wealthy person who has just arrived on the international train, purpose unspecified.

Don't worry, citizens, nothing criminal will happen. When are we to live, citizens? Just once in your life you should sigh wholeheartedly... Sergei Komarov is the film producer, Oleg Leonidov is the scriptwriter, K. Kuznetsov is the cameraman, Rodchenko is the artistic director, and the actors Ilinsky and Fogel "burn Moscow."

The Doll with Millions is a new film released by the International Workers' Relief Fund (Mezhrabpom)[4]: it is a war cry, a smash hit, a lighthearted Soviet comedy. It is the second part of another remarkable picture, based on a script by Fyodor Mikhailovich Dostoevsky, performed in a certain Petersburg cemetery by fresh corpses, by very young people, by no means Komsomol members, who are in cahoots with a privy counsellor and a young maiden. The other film was called *Bobok*. Do you recall, reader, the little meaningless word *bobok* which signified graveyard gaiety?

This is the real thing: people sat and cried on the shores of trade union rivers... Who would have guessed that on the Petrovka, right under the Central Institute of Labor where Gastev[5] teaches how to board things up with nails à la Taylor, that it's possible to set up a *bobok*-movie house, to undress, as if it were spring, Soviet Moscow—a "Komsomol girl"—never mind, she's so young!

An old millionairess lies dying in Paris. In a Cardinal's quadruple bed a monkey is grieving: the symbol of the world growing senile. The source of the film is foreign, from the age of Max Linder.[6] The first yet extremely promising steps of the Great Silent film. Ilinsky is visiting Max Linder.

"Well, brother Linder, we have something to talk about... You, brother Linder, will soon be obscured by Chaplin, while in our country, brother Linder, Glupyshkin[7] is still mincing his steps..."

"I, a French millionairess, bequeath three million to my licentious nephew who is beaten by a mannish ballerina, and to my great-niece, a little Russian girl whose scatterbrained mother dropped her in a Soviet train station. The documents are sewn into a doll..."

The relatives weep and then depart. Her nephews rush straight to Moscow from Paris (Leonidov omits any mention of how they got visas).

However, I am probably mistaken. *The Doll with Millions* must have been conceived as a very subtle ideological grotesque. Rodchenko, having defected from LEF, will erect a pavilion in the Pathé Frères Louis XIV style. The producer will sweat long and hard to beat all the nonsense out of Ilinsky; all the more ridiculous, effete, and pathetic so that the viewer will be touched and shed tears of compassion for the great tenth anniversary of Glupyshkin—a pre-war, pre-foxtrot Charlie.

And Moscow is transformed into a most despicable piece of exoticism.

Two Frenchman are in Moscow searching for a Komsomol girl with a birthmark on her shoulder so that, after being united with her in marriage at the Palace of Weddings and again in the Polish Roman Catholic Church, they can obtain their aunt's millions. At the Alexandrovsky railroad station one of the Frenchmen pounces upon a handicraft stall like a beast and begins to disembowel Russian dolls. Amusing, Oleg Leonidov!... In the corridor of the Savoy Hotel the other Frenchman lines up Russian girls answering an announcement (for sixteen-year-olds) to be examined for the above-mentioned birthmark. Not very amusing, Oleg Leonidov. A Moscow schoolboy, a rather lighthearted gamin who visits the public bulletin board daily to savor the pasted-up ads for models, smudges the number sixteen so it looks like sixty-six, thus frightfully old women report to the Frenchman. Ah, that wasn't necessary... What a horror... Hideous... "Tell me, are you sixteen years old yet?" The old women are kicked out. Amusing, Oleg Leonidov...

Meanwhile, the other Frenchman has brought dolls from all over Moscow to his hotel room and is hacking, cutting and disemboweling them, his sleeves rolled up like a butcher's. There are many scenes in *The Doll with Millions* that are physically nauseating, but that particular scene which, despite the authors' intention, takes on a crudely sadistic tone, is one of the most loathsome. However, instead of four dozen girls drilled in the military manner, instead of those platoons of herons from a high-class theatrical review, the authors of *The Doll with Millions* show us athletic boys and girls waving their arms and legs to the health of Semashka and Podvoisky and to the delight of the "Frenchmen from Bordeaux."

Citizen-authors of *The Doll with Millions,* film-making is an awesome, honest, and vindictive art. Everything is motivated by pure profit. Your Frenchmen have stepped off the screen and onto the real streets of Moscow. The shadow has escaped, catch it. But your Komsomol members...

We are shown Komsomol members from *The Doll with Millions.* They are the blood brothers of their bereaved French relatives. They are like rams chewing rubber in splendid Empire style dormitories and butting the granite walls of science with invisible crutches. These "Komsomol members" are far worse than the frivolous Parisians. They are fops, apaches, pimps turned inside-out. "Instead of a skirt—the third volume of Bukharin's works..." Instead of cocaine—a bulletin board announcing the blasphemous distribution of millions: 500,000 francs to MOPR (International Organization to Aid the Heroes of the Revolution) and the remainder to Aviakhim, Avtodor, and other Soviet saints. Instead of a kiss in the diaphragm, we have a college scholarship in memory of Mister Svidrigailov, whose blue-gray brain is the only place this whole delirium could have been conceived.

No, Glupyshkin has nothing to do with it. Glupyshkin is no lackey. He is the forefather of fruitful film madness, the town dervish, drunk without wine, an absurd Zarathustra of asphalt squares.

Zoshchenko's forty thousand heroes holding their suspenders in one hand and, in the other, a pastry with a bite taken out of it, hail *The Doll with Millions.*

Incidentally, the Parisian editor has all the characteristics of a Moscow bully from a bar in the Herzen House.[8] Is it possible to become so calloused that even a real beard seems fake?

Nonetheless, this film is interesting for its bestial atavism, its mousy scurrying, its infantile sense of film tempo not as speed but as haste, very memorable from the days when celluloid rain fell in the cinemas and the maid climbed up the wall with her broom.

55. CHILDREN'S LITERATURE

It is a difficult task to write children's literature. On the one hand, the anthropomorphization[1] of animals and inanimate objects is forbidden; on the other hand, a child must play, but that little rascal spoils everything as soon as be begins to play by immediately anthropomorphizing everything. Children's literature must be strictly supervised. This requires a scientific approach and well-trained, experienced middle-aged women. A certain scientifically trained older woman of my acquaintance had mastered the ideology to such an extent that she was literally torn to pieces. Now she works as a consultant and attends conferences sponsored by the State Academic Council.[2] She was not immediately promoted, although she had first class credentials: she had once been a child herself, and she had an exceptionally lively mind for her age. Outwardly, this old woman appeared quite ordinary, rather tidy, carefully dressed. She supported herself, and since the age of sixty,[3] she had earned her livelihood through literary work.

Nevertheless, even she did not hit the target immediately, and was forced to beat around the bush for some time. First, she thought she would give the old way a try, so she submitted a fairy-tale that was completely inappropriate and even harmful. Literally every insect and animal in her story had something to say; grass-hoppers sporting frockcoats served some prince, and a rabbit played the drums. Whoever read the story would grow dizzy, as if he had taken an overdose of camomile. Frankly speaking, the devil alone knows what it was all about.

It was the rabbit who saved the old woman. She ought to erect a monument to his memory.

"Your rabbit will do," said the exhausted secretary. "Drumming, after all, is a form of labor..."

The old woman returned home and quickly re-educated herself. In the next story she submitted, the sheep and the rams were embarrassed to say "baa" and "maa." As the tale was told, the sheep silently grew wool for a useful purpose. In recognition of the story's transformation, the editor himself came out to greet the old woman and express his views, however vaguely: "It fits the production plan, even though it's a bit boring..."

That night the old woman had a dream. She saw a rabbit-drummer shear a sheep, gather the wool on his drum and then carry it to some board meeting, where the board members talked incessantly, sniffed at the wool, and then broke up quite late in the evening...

56. TORRENTS OF HACKWORK

Speaking bluntly, the Russian translations of foreign *belles-lettres* that are currently flooding the marketplace are no more than torrents of hackwork. The name "Sinclair," "Pirandello," or "Maupassant" appearing on a book jacket does not make that book actually belong to the specified foreign author. The average reader, who knows only his native language, is systematically deluded by the publisher. The individual consumer and the libraries are both drawn into disadvantageous transactions. The "open secret" is something that takes courage to reveal frankly and directly: in our publishing houses the translation of a foreign book is not viewed as literature at all; it is merely *a large edition for which royalties need not be paid.* Even the most inattentive reader will notice that virtually all foreign writers—from Anatole France to the latest dime novelist—speak the same clumsy language in Russian translation. The flabbiness, pettiness, and confusion of the social environment from which translators in our country (déclassé, unemployed intellectuals who know foreign languages) are often recruited, puts a mark of indelible mediocrity on all their handiwork. They reveal not only the authors, but themselves as well. From their hands we receive the riches of foreign nations in a debased and tendentiously degraded form.

In our country a foreign book is royalty-free for all practical purposes. Royalty payments received by the translator and editor for such a book in comparison with an original work are so insignificant they are hardly worth mentioning.

Although indifferent to the quality of the translated product, publishing houses are nonetheless fervidly interested in its circulation. A contemporary Russian book, in contrast to a book translated into Russian, is virtually unreadable. Foreign *belles-lettres* literally overwhelm contemporary Russian *belles-lettres*.

It is extremely profitable and convenient for publishing houses to deal with a book whose author is deceased. In the first place, they do not need his permission to publish; in the second place, they do not have to go through the exhausting and risky business of haggling with him; and in the third place, he will not protest, regardless of the form the published product takes.

However, besides this pathetic economic reason, there is yet another reason for foreign books to become gravely and chronically ill in our country. This reason is cultural.

The quality of translations in any country is a direct indicator of its cultural level. It is just as indicative as the statistics on soap consumption or the percentage of literacy. In our country the quality of translations is literally in desperate straits.

What is more, the administrators and business managers of publishing houses retrieve their losses on translators. The State Publishing House, the keeper of culture, that same GIZ[1] we have entrusted with the progressive sector of the cultural front, not only failed to raise its paltry rates for translations at the last conference for reviewing its standard contract with our translators, but even lowered them.

Does the public know how much publishing houses pay translators? Does the public know where translators are recruited? Does it know what positions are given to the handful of masters and specialists who have managed to survive on this inauspicious front?

A publishing house pays our translators from thirty to sixty rubles per printed page (per forty thousand letters). And how it pays! In truly sadistic installments! Upon receipt of the manuscript, the first half is paid, and only after publication is the second installment paid. Long months pass between the receipt of the manuscript and publication of the book. But that is not all. The translator incurs heavy expenses: a typist (from four to six rubles per printed page), copying the book, etc.

The translation itself is treated as if one were pouring grain from one sack into another. To prevent the translator from concealing or stealing any grain while he is transferring it, he is paid for the Russian text, and not for the original, as a means of grain control. Thus, for this seemingly insignificant reason, books swell from year to year and fall ill with dropsy. Translators add to the number of pages in order to make ends meet somehow.

Translation is one of the most difficult and responsible aspects of literary work. It is essentially the creation of an independent speech system on the basis of foreign material. Switching this system over to the Russian system requires tremendous effort, attention, will power, a wealth of inventiveness, intellectual freshness, philological sensibility, a huge lexical keyboard, and the ability to listen carefully to rhythm, to grasp the picture of a phrase and to convey it; and what is more, this must all be accompanied by the strictest self-control. Otherwise the translation is merely interpolation. The very process of translation requires an enormous expenditure of nervous energy. This work exhausts and dessicates the brain more than many other kinds of creative work. A good translator, if he is not provided for, soon wears out. Proper working conditions are required. We must study the professional disease to which translators are prone and take preventive measures. We must insure our translators and assure them periodical rest. Have any preventive measures been taken in the State Publishing House, in Land and Factory,[2] or in Young Guard?[3]

If we want to make good foreign literature available we must destroy the very *roots* of this senseless system of hackwork, which is actually worsening every year.

A novel by Flaubert and a dime novel cost almost the same. The beginner, the dilettante, and the mature master craftsman of literary translation all receive nearly identical royalties. At the same time the scale of per-page remuneration for original prose vacillates between one hundred fifty and five hundred rubles. No wonder publishing houses, with their work "system," have frightened away from translation not only men of letters, but even people of ordinary literacy.

The State Publishing House has recently undertaken the task of translating the complete works of Goethe in eighteen volumes. One is surprised at the boldness, or rather the impudence, of the State Publishing House, which is making an attempt on Goethe's life's work while totally ignoring the entire business of translation.

Consequently, its enormous cultural function is most often fulfilled by untalented, second-rate salary-seekers.

People are taken to court for pouring poison into wells, for damaging and polluting canals and waterways, for the pots and pans in communal kitchens being in poor condition. But to this day no one has taken responsibility for the hideous condition of the workshops (so outrageous that you refuse to believe it) in which world literature is prepared for our readers or for the damage done to the conveyor belts which unite the brain of the average Soviet reader with the creative life of East and West, of Europe and America, of all mankind past and present—this unprecedented sabotage escapes unnoticed although it is a daily occurrence. It must be blared through megaphones at every crossroads! Let our public organizations actively support the campaign we are just beginning. We need a fundamental restructuring of this entire business: it must undergo all the stages of purge, revision, and reconstruction and end as a victory for legislative order. Let all these stages be made public, with extensive information in the press, under supervision of authoritative public organizations.

There are staff editors sitting in the various departments of every publishing house who, to earn their monthly wages, are obliged to let dozens of printed manuscript pages pass through their retorts. In most cases these editors are literate and literarily competent people. They "caught on" to their work very quickly. A manuscript becomes unrecognizable in their hands. Do you think that they collate the translation with the original, approximate the text to it? Nothing of the kind! An editor basically does not edit but rather disinfects the translation. He clips it down to elementary literacy, rounds off phrases, removes absurdities, and annihilates thousands of words like "which" and "that." During this process he only glances at the original when he stumbles across some obvious absurdity. A step-by-step collation would too often lead to the logical necessity of crumpling up the manuscript and throwing it into the wastebasket, but this is impossible because the manuscript has already been ordered and paid for, and the translator himself, good or bad, is nonetheless a client of the publishing house.

Some fairly decent translators could be found among the editors. But editors do not go in for that line of work.

Incidentally, not all editors are in the job for which they are best suited, and what was said about translators is also, at least in part, applicable to editors.

Are we ever given the translators' names? No. The press is also to blame for this. Reviewers are infected with the general disrespect for craftsmanship, for art, and for the translator's skills. Foreign literature is often reviewed by people who are indifferent to literary form.

No one will believe how books are selected for translation in our country. In the Leningrad State Publishing House, subscribing to books from abroad was a very common practice. They were conscientiously screened in several ways. First, official purveyors abroad would provide the necessary rough information. Then experienced reviewers would read through dozens, hundreds of books, since reviews of books which had never even been published were quite often more literate, more literary, and more substantial than those printed in the thick journals. Out of forty or fifty books selected in this manner, three or four would be marked as candidates for translation.[4] And only then, by agreement with the ideological leadership, would one or two books finally be submitted for translation. At present, the publishing houses have virtually ceased subscribing to books from abroad, giving financial exigency as the reason. The translators themselves have become brokers; they have their own agents. Some relatives in Paris or New York decide what the Soviet reader should read: "Give me some work." "Well, suggest one, and if it is interesting then we..." That is a typical conversation now in publishing houses. Like a merchant's eligible daughters, publishing houses cross their hands over their bellies and wait for an offer. Translators begin corresponding with naive foreign authors. I am well aware of cases when the rights to an authorized translation were obtained by such semi-literate, but energetic methods.

We must not plead the absence of foreign currency credits for publishing books. The initiative must be forcibly removed from the enterprising translator. It seems to me that in the matter of book selection, along with qualified reviewers, the unions of proletarian writers in Europe and America could render a greater service than someone's relatives in Paris or London. It is essential, finally, to establish an Inter-Publishing House "Information Bureau" for the selection and recommendation of books.

The fate of a book is decided by a reviewer who works for a publishing house writing reviews for "internal use." He can kill a book or push it through. Every review should be written so that it is not embarrasing to read in print and so that its author takes full responsibility for it. However, these reviews are too often reduced to heartless bureaucratic form letters, so petty, disgraceful, and insipid that it is impossible to publish them. Our reviewers, no less than our translators, are regarded as second-rate clients.

A reviewer produces "an opinion plus," while the editorial board, in total ignorance of the book's contents, decides whether or not to publish it on the basis of such bureaucratic reports.

The status of revision[5] is just as catastrophic, if not more so, as that of translation, reviewing, and editing. Publishing house "scholars" love revision and even prefer it to translation because it is cheaper and quicker to "manufacture." Moreover, revision is restricted and standardized. We do not share their hypocritical piety toward the text. We value scholarly editions, but the writer of another age and culture is not a fetish for us. Our epoch has the right not only to read in its own way, but also to sculpture, re-work, creatively modify, and emphasize whatever seems impor-tant. It is not just that the average reader has made progress to-ward Cervantes, Walter Scott, and Swift, but they also have come closer to those writers. Our readers can be introduced to entire historical worlds only through revision which removes the tedious passages and gives the book a rhythm accessible to them. Revision of the original is more difficult and involves more responsibility than translation, but the person who does the revision must be given time. He must not be hurried and his work must be properly paid for. None of this is currently practiced in our publishing houses.

We must convene an urgent all-Union conference on the problems of publishing foreign literature. Let the Federation of Writers and the most important publishing houses take the initia-tive to call such a conference. The conference program and parti-cipants should be limited and careful advance planning must be made so that it does not degenerate into chaotic chatter. Besides writers delegated by various organizations and responsible heads of publishing houses, experts on foreign literature and acknowledged masters of translation must also participate. The conference will propose how to create healthy working conditions, how to elicit and utilize existing strengths and talents, and how to rationally organize the production of translated literature. The conference will formulate a mature plan for the creation of an Institute of Foreign Literature with a permanent Department of the Theory and Practice of Translation, offering a series of seminars on transla-tion from European and Eastern languages, as well as on transla-tion from Ukrainian and other languages of the Soviet Union. The Institute must be headed by an efficient and ideologically mature administration. *The Herald of Foreign Literature*[6] must be trans-ferred to its jurisdiction and be completely reorganized. The Institute must participate directly in the work of publishing houses.

This authoritative Institute must work steadfastly to raise

the cultural level of foreign literature in translation and to provide us with the necessary personnel. The Federation of Writers, the Communist Academy, the State Academy of the Arts, as well as the State Publishing House, Land and Factory, Young Guard, and the Institute of Journalism must be directly and organically involved in the creation of this Institute.

57. ON TRANSLATIONS

Translation first became a social phenomenon in our country during the forties of the last century or thereabouts, coinciding with the emergence of the class of non-gentry intellectuals and impoverished young students unable to feed themselves in any other way.

From the time of Pisarev[1] to the present nothing has changed in the social nature of translating: it was and still is the *regulator of unemployment of intellectual labor*, a crutch which supports everything weak and shaky, a form of pittance that a class sets aside for its underdeveloped members. For the older, established publishing houses, translators were suppliers of cheap brainpower. The main consumers of translated literature were the philistines who did not know any foreign languages.

Translators of modern literature catered to the upper crust of the reading public by providing it with Ibsen, Hamsun, and Maeterlinck in small and expensive editions. All other literature, like a water bug, took the course of appendices to the journals *The Field* and *The Herald of Foreign Literature.*[2] Hungry students and failures produced it for a miserable pittance. Sablin,[3] for example, was squeezed in between Soikin and Sytin and the kitchen pulp-literature of "appendices." His inclusion brings to mind the average installment in a translated book from the State Publishing House. After the revolution, the intelligentsia immediately grabbed its habitual translating crutch. World Literature,[4] the child of Gorky and the great-aunt of TsEKUBU[5] was established. The result was a new type of hungry, yet "skilled" academic translation. A catalogue of the classics of world literature was printed on vellum paper and their names were gradually covered by Russian score-counters. A highly original game of lotto! Incidentally, even now there are a few people who dream about the Renaissance of the "magnificent volumes" of World Literature.

In our country the three basic orientations of prerevolutionary translation continue to live and struggle in a disguised form: the collective tendency that came from the "appendices," the tendency aimed at the literate peasant that stems from the so-called "cultural" editions, and, finally, the modernist tendency which can be traced from the Symbolists and World Literature to the Academia Publishing House[6] and the classics printed by the State Publishing House. At present the phenomenon of popular foreign *belles-lettres* is also closely related to filmmaking. As a rule the popular books are short-lived, not preserved and easily forgotten. Russian translations of foreign *belles-lettres* form a special world that lies outside of literature, subject to its own fate and its own laws of development.

As the circulation of translated literature increases, we can observe the growth of interest in language study among the Komsomol masses, among the working youth, and in the colleges. Just how young people undertake the study of foreign languages is of interest: they approach language learning with the triumphant spirit of a conqueror invading previously forbidden territory. Knowledge of languages is a mighty weapon in the hands of the ruling class. With the aid of this weapon the composition of the entire cultural present is counterfeited and world literature is falsified until it reaches the condition demanded by people of position.

Besides academic collations with the original (it is better not to mention how that is done in our country), one other kind of collation is important to us: collation with the author's inner, historical truth which will be realized by the working intelligentsia when it masters foreign languages. This re-evaluation is unavoidable. I have already written about the flabbiness of the second-rate staff of translators, who are for the most part déclassé outsiders.[7] The translator is a powerful interpreter of the author: he is fundamentally uncontrolled. His unwitting commentary seeps into the book through a thousand cracks. While revising some old translations of Walter Scott, I noticed that they had been done in the police jargon common to passports, and no amount of effort can erase that caddish brand. Publishing houses do not consider that at all, and old translations are merely "adapted." We must work not for the traditional, passive "easy mark," but to reach the reader who is buying up the stock of German lessons in *Komsomol Truth*.[8] We must bridge the gap between the translated book and the study of languages, making the book a stimulus and teaching aid for language study. What has the State Publishing House provided along these lines? So far, nothing. Its monumental series of classics, that *work for the bookshelf*, is essentially meaningless. It is a pyramid erected to the glory of a misunderstood culture. The only feasible consumer of editions such as the eighteen-volume Goethe, included in the five year plan of the State Publishing House, is some chimerical, fairytale creature. I would like to see such a subscriber with my own eyes! It will ornament the bookshelf of an intellectual fluent in German, and will stand next to the original Goethe. The translation of the complete works of Goethe (I am using Goethe as an example because it is with this most significant and "exemplary" edition that the State Publishing House began its series of classics) provides enough work for an entire generation. Due to the collective nature of translation, looseness and flabbiness are inevitable. Only a minute portion of it will sound genuinely Russian, be tightly composed and worthy of the original. The priestly academic caste, which controls the editions of classics, wields an enormous influence on modern literature in translation; it fully affirms the scholastic approach to translation, is completely insensitive to language, to its strength, truth, or expression, and lacks any feeling for the living reader. Assistant professors of literature are the bearers of masticated papier-mâché that is collated with the original. For example, they lavish praise upon Bryusov's translation of *Faust*, a toothless, pseudo-scholarly mumbling which, with all due respect to Bryusov, is as far removed from Goethe's might as it is from the stars in the sky. There are only two choices: gilt-edged bindings or living, socially effective books. We must break through the caste partition that divides the translators' kitchen from the Soviet literary community.

The work of the State Publishing House must be brought under control! Literary organizations must start reviewing the five year plan; *it must be reviewed!* We should not be producing classics to decorate oak bookcases, but for the working intelligentsia and (this cannot be emphasized enough) for schools. We will create a new type of Soviet edition of the classics: strictly utilitarian, intended to assuage cultural hunger, neither for collector's bookshelves nor the satiated. Who does not remember, for example, Manshtein's edition of Ovid? The old school possessed the knowledge and ability to campaign for the ancient languages because it was important politically. Let us try to do the same with all models of world literature for the broad reading public. I propose that we put our best literary talents to work on a *series of selected classics for schools* and provide the series with a first-rate scholarly commentary. The series must be durable; it must serve an entire generation, it must be issued in huge first editions and second editions. Wring the neck of the myopic commercial approach! Every book should be an incentive to studying the language. Every book should provide at least some contact with the original, for example, a parallel text and a glossary. At present we are struggling to take the translation business away from the caste leader, for whom the mass reader is a fiction, an "easy mark" ignorant of foreign languages.

Both the State Publishing House and Land and Factory responded to my article in *News*[9] with proposals for some reforms, but everything is proceeding in a strictly bureaucratic fashion. Public organizations were represented as that part of the Federation which supports the caste approach. Every significant literary group has a mandate to participate in this venture. Let all the mandates be declared. Our writers are accustomed to shunning the translators' kitchen, but they are responsible for what happens in it. Besides Aseev's two or three very sensible performances, I do not know of a single case in which a writer interfered with offers of advice and instruction.

Now I shall discuss the Young Guard publishing house.[10] It has a monopoly on youth. It has a very unique understanding of youth: young people gobble up everything. Adaptations are good enough for them! Instead of utilizing the most qualified and talented people for this work, Young Guard turns out pulp literature year after year, continuing the tradition of Soikin and Sytin, even profiting from their legacy. Young Guard is our most reckless and most commercial publishing house. It is Young Guard that provides the majority of anonymous texts "edited by." It is Young Guard that cultivates an impudent expertise and adaptibility. Is it becoming to Young Guard to mumble in the jargon of bureaucrats and passports? How could it fence itself off from even those barely professional translations made available by the State Publishing House and Land and Factory, and cultivate instead such completely infantile, third- and fourth-rate translations? We will not permit our youth to be catered to by housewives, ladies with quill pens, or by dignified men of indeterminate occupation... The other day at an exhibit of Japanese children's books we saw to what extent the Japanese militaristic bourgeoisie is bringing "virtuosity," in appearance at least, to their books for young people. Japanese publishers have developed an exceptional talent in this direction: they have energetically "adapted" all of world literature from Dante to Tolstoi to serve their iron class pedagogy. You can imagine what they did to the content of those books! Our task is to shorten the path from reader to writer, a path that is not paid for with rent, inherited leisure, or satiety. It is sometimes a mockery to publish an author's complete works. On the other hand, wherever it is possible to replace a translation with the original, it should be replaced, and this applies first of all to books for young people. We need our own juvenile adventure series with ethnographic and similar padding. Today Mayne Reid[11] has meaning only in retrospect, as wholesome romance. Mayne Reid's vitality can be explained by the fact that he took young people's great thirst for knowledge of the vast geographical world into consideration. He is a brilliant pedagogue who combined, in his educational journeys, the scientific knowledge of his own day with an unsophisicated plot. Here's to the creation of a "Soviet Mayne Reid!" We must set our best prose writers to this task, and a whole scientific apparatus (ethnography, physical geography, and so on), must be created for their disposal. After all, no one skimps on the creation of an entire institution, on a full-time staff and apparatus to work for the *Large* and *Small Encyclopedias*. Isn't a series of juvenile novels dealing with knowledge of the world truly deserving of like honors? It is just as fundamental, it provides reserves of fodder for an entire generation. Many years are necessary for its realization, and we must begin work on it immediately.

Selection of new foreign books is not within the powers of our publishing houses. An Inter-Publishing House Bureau to deal with the subscription and recommendation of books is being planned. However, it is to be granted only moral authority, and it is unlikely that representatives of literary organizations will participate in it. Such a bureau will degenerate into the likes of the honorable Commission on Children's Literature.[12] We need authoritative "Councils on Foreign Literature" in the publishing houses. Public-spirited writers to the Bureau! Power and control must be given to editorial supra-publishing councils!

The pursuit of an ideologically consistent book often leads to the repetition of clichés: the class struggle is frequently presented in a sentimental or even Quaker fashion. Having been rebuffed in the war, many Western writers have been swept to the left. Now they are steadily retreating to new positions. The circle of these fellow-travellers is narrowing. We are threatened by a "reviewer's famine." The same old trustworthy but mediocre names are appearing. Duhamel[13] is the ideal golden mean, but you can't feed everybody on Barbusse! It seems to me that the excessive cowardice and constraint shown in our selection of books is conditioned by our inability to provide them. If a book deviates so many degrees from one hundred percent "ideological purity," it is rendered harmless by a foreword, that is, a bureaucratic addendum that no one reads. Having wrung the neck of pulp literature once and for all, we must now preserve as much as possible for the reader all the "events of foreign literature." No one prevents us from doing battle with the book's author, however, as is done with filmmakers. The annotator gnaws into the text, becomes a participant in the action, polemicizes, taunts, exposes the author at the turning points, discredits bigots and hypocrites, dethrones the imaginary hero, underscores what is truly of value, and wedges himself into the silences. Where does such timidity come from, comrades? As soon as we have the book in our hands, we can twist it however we wish. Thus the crisis in the selection of foreign *belles-lettres* is lessened for the sake of the reader's horizons and prospects for enlightenment.

The distribution of work among translators, however, is done with no less divine blindness than the distribution of rolls of paper tickets from Mosselprom's[14] lottery wheel. Incidentally, this blindness is not ultimate: masters of the word do translate that writer-snob Marcel Proust or Henri de Régnier, but only hacks translate the "simpleton" Kléber, even though he may be issued in an edition of tens of thousands (Kléber, of course, is taken as a generic term). I do not want to say that it should be the other way around. But isn't it possible to achieve at least some degree of balance? The best translators, concentrated in Leningrad, are now being exploited by Academia, which Land and Factory has adopted for its strictly esthetic undertakings. Why can't we shake things up, why can't these good translators be utilized in collective undertakings? After all, the worker-reader, like a young animal, is getting second-rate fodder. The opposition shown by the publishing apparatus and the priestly caste of foreign literature (the academic pride of the publishing houses) to the projected reorganization of the whole venture is enormous and will grow even larger. Is it easy to refuse an "escheated" field, a "regulator of unemployment," social security? The most to which the State Publishing House has agreed is the selection of the best translators and a small increase in royalties, but this is not enough. As long as this policy of secrecy, this caste seclusion, and this unconscious repetition of the past remains part of such an important endeavor, it will decay. The translating business is being drawn gently back into some department, where it will be abused as before.

In conclusion I will say a few words about the training of a new generation of translators. The wave of grass-roots interest in studying foreign languages will not, needless to say, produce this new generation. Meanwhile, running counter to this wave, the knowledge of languages among intellectuals is decreasing catastrophically. Some "aunty," who has read Maupassant in French, is the extent of their interest. Professional translators, veterans of their craft, no longer understand the new authors. The rich flourishing of the entire postwar lexicon has bypassed them. For them it is just vocabulary, requiring the use of a dictionary. My suggestion is to create a workshop to train the new generation of translators which would be affiliated with the Library of Foreign Literature and under the jurisdiction of the Central Scientific Administration. Such a workshop has already begun. The best young people, head and shoulders above the professional translators, study there without any hope of someday obtaining practical work. Let us pour fresh teaching strength into this modest seminary and raise it to the level of an all-Union technical school for the art and craft of translation. Literary colleges will send their promising young people to this institute and eventually we will acquire a strong new generation of translators. We may even offer foreign assignments for promoted workers. The reviewing of foreign books in our press should be discussed separately.[15] It serves as an example of how reviews should not and must not be written. I will say only that the publication of a Biannual of Foreign Literature devoted to surveys, to the evaluation of current foreign literature, as well as to the theory and practice of translation, would by no means be a luxury for the State Publishing House.

58. THE DUCHESS' FAN

Marcel Proust tells the story of how a certain duchess listened to music. The duchess was very proud; she was a descendent of some incredibly blue-blooded family—the Bourbons, the Brabantines or an even more aristocratic family. She once chanced to drop in at a reception for a poor relative, a shabby viscountess whose coat of arms was somehow flawed. The concert, however, was good. The ladies listened to Chopin, swaying their heads and fans in time with the music. The duchess was confronted with a problem: should she keep time with her fan as the women around her were doing, or not? Would not such unbridled approval on her part be too much for the musician? But then that blue-blooded personage found a way out of her difficulty: she began waving her tortoise-shell fan, not in time with the music being performed, but out of time—for the sake of independence.

Our criticism—alas!—is in many ways reminiscent of Proust's duchess : it is arrogant, condescending, and patronizing. The critic, to be sure, is not a schoolteacher. It is not his business to give grades, distribute marks of excellence, confer awards, or write on the blackboard. A genuine critic is first of all an informant, an informant of public opinion. He is obliged to describe a book as a botanist describes a new floral species, to classify it and locate it among other books. This should inevitably raise questions about the scope of the book, about the significance of its appearance, about the spiritual values of the author, about everything that gives him the right to converse with the reader. I can see no real difference between a major piece of criticism expanded into an article and criticism on a smaller scale, a review. However, the methodological mediocrity is more apparent on a small scale, in a review.

I choose a random example from the *Leningrad Red Evening News* of January 12th. The review is of Aleksei Lipetsky's[1] novel *In Defiance.*

The heroine of the novel, a young peasant girl named Masha, has grown up among the kulaks. She cannot endure her father's despotism and rises "in defiance" of her fate. She leaves home, works as a village librarian and then, after marrying one of the party activists from her village, becomes an activist herself, devoting all her energy to the struggle against the sluggish masses of the village. That is a brief summary of the novel's plot.

Such a plot, if I may say so, can be thought up while sitting in a streetcar or lacing up one's boots. Nonetheless, the reviewer presents the book seriously: it came to him with a "good recommendation." However, the author's real strengths or weaknesses are not even mentioned. The duchess' fan was mechanically set in motion.

We know nothing about how Lipetsky writes and we learn absolutely nothing about our glorious Masha. No court reporter could allow such a vapid retelling of circumstances revealed in the courtroom. We have no guarantee that this same Masha, "under the yoke of her despotic father," will not tomorrow get a divorce from the conscientious village librarian and submerge herself once again in the kulak way of life.

"Lipetsky's novel is interesting as an attempt to construct a new literary hero..." "Now it's beginning," muses the naive reader. "I'll learn something about Lipetsky and about Masha." It doesn't matter that the plot is simplistic. Flaubert, Henri de Régnier, and Bunin embroidered on an even more primitive warp. A word to the reviewer... Why is a new type constructed?

It turns out that "Masha's geneology, the progressive woman who seeks and finds satisfaction for herself in socially useful work, can undoubtedly trace its literary heritage back to Turgenev's activist heroines: Elena in *On the Eve* and Marianna in *Virgin Soil*."

Now wait a minute... The reader grabs the reviewer by his sleeve... Something is wrong here. Stop, fan!... Either I'm sleeping or he's raving... After all, it's exactly the opposite... After all, that's an old literary type... What a strange slip of the tongue!

The reviewer still has twenty lines left at his disposal. It's still not too late to correct himself...

"It must be admitted that, although daily life occupies a less prominent position in the structure of the novel than the heroes, it is nonetheless rendered more succesfully than the heroes..."

Worst of all, this is not simple nonsense, it is ritual nonsense. It is a kind of shamanism written in savage, bombastic jargon. "Daily life proved to be more successful than the heroes..." I shall translate this rubbish for you: daily life is depicted better than the characters. These are not only empty words, but nonsense, for the characters themselves are part of daily life.

The review continues saying that the author failed particularly with the undernourished party member, stuffed with political ABC's, and with the equally lifeless village schoolteacher.

Where, then, was the author successful? Where is the book? What was the reviewer writing about? The secret is simple—the "recommendation" let him down. He should have said that Lipetsky wrote a worthless, completely inappropriate book (I am surmising, of course, on the basis of timid hints made by the reviewer, like Cuvier constructing his ichthyosaurus bone by bone). After having presented examples demonstrating why Lipetsky's book is so bad, he should have shown how it is a typical phenomenon produced by the artificial demand for books of this type. He should have compared it to its sisters in misfortune and then drawn a literary and social conclusion, for what is written about bad books is neither here nor there.

The same issue of the journal contains, along with the review of Lipetsky's book, a review of the interesting and, in many respects, remarkable book by Kaverin[2]: *The Brawler, or Evenings on Vasilevsky Island*. This is how the review begins: "Zinaida Gippius wrote a novel about the Symbolists—*The Devil's Doll*. Venyamin Kaverin wrote about the Formalists and others. Every literary school leaves behind its excrement in a libelous novel..."

From the very first words of the review, this book by a serious prose writer, a master of the word and the author of such great achievements as *The End of the Gang*, is impudently called the "literary excrement of an epoch," and for some reason an arrogant, scornful tone predominates. The first thing the reviewer does is purse his lips, and, without even noticing it, makes a face. Although this reviewer (N. Berkovsky[3]) says some very flattering things about Kaverin, primarily his insistence that the book is interesting, his semi-disdainful tone is maintained throughout. Instead of an attentive and absorbing analysis of a book which unquestionably belongs to the realm of genuine literature both by virtue of the entertainment value of the genre and because of its craftsmanship, we are presented with a pat on the back, and needless irony. The reader is left with the impression that Kaverin got himself into some serious trouble.

* * *

Instances of critics and reviewers lagging behind the reader are fairly common in our country. They sometimes assume an extremely pitiful character and lead to great misunderstandings. I need only mention the case of the scandalous underestimation of Kataev's[4] novel *The Embezzlers*, published in 1926. The novel is ambiguous. It has been picked up abroad and is being made into an instrument of anti-Soviet libel. However, there is something to seize hold of in that novel. There is no reason to fear it. As with any major work of art it lends itself to various interpretations. We cannot refute the maliciously eulogistic articles about *The Embezzlers* in the foreign press with our own interpretation because in our country the book was underestimated. It was treated on the same level as most new books and "awarded" faint praise and empty, arrogant pats on the back. Instead of an analysis of Kataev's book, kangaroo courts, of no use to anyone, were set up to judge the embezzlers themselves—his heroes. A keenly interesting book was totally overlooked.

In conclusion I must cite an inordinately disgraceful and farcical example of "ignoring" a significant book. Vast segments of our society are now literally choking with laughter over a book by the young authors Ilf and Petrov,[5] called *The Twelve Chairs*. The only opinion made public so far about this satirical book, gushing with merriment and youthfulness, was Bukharin's comment at a trade union conference. Bukharin needed Ilf and Petrov's book for something, but so far the reviewers have found no need for it. They will eventually get around to it, of course, and rebuke it properly.

Let me recall the duchess' fan once again. It moves not in time with the music, but with suspicious independence. We have no need of the duchess' fan, even though thrice-tried ideological blood may flow in her veins.

59. I WRITE A SCENARIO

Shklovsky[1] advised me to write a scenario and vanished, flashing his cucumber head. I did not see him again, but I cursed Shklovsky through seven generations, for this is what happened.

I decided to try to write a scenario about the life of a fire brigade. A magnificent frame in the style of Eisenstein[2] immediately came to mind: a firehouse, doors flung wide open, and fire engines, like gigantic lizards, racing toward the viewer.

Then, I thought, what about a frame depicting the alarm: bells ringing, someone on telephone duty, firemen leaping up from their cots...

On the other hand, what if we began with a peaceful scene: firemen sitting on their cots reading the newspaper. Or we might intensify the social element: let's say the firemen call some kind of meeting for the election of delegates or for a struggle against something. A game of chess is in progress... Suddenly, someone's wife enters, the wife of one of the firemen, and the conflict begins...

Yes, the conflict, it's easy enough to say: conflict! But, why did she enter? What did she want?

No, it's better to approach the subject indirectly. Somewhere in Zamoskvorechie a bookkeeper and his family sit down to tea, completely oblivious to the impending danger: in but half an hour their life's possessions, including the walnut buffet, will go up in flames. In the kitchen, meanwhile, the primus stove[3] is ablaze, the baby playing beside it.

The essence of film is in the composition of its frames and in the montage. Things must act. The stove must be of monumental proportions.

The primus stove, for example, must be presented in a close-up. Forget the baby. It all begins with the bent primus needle (the fine detail). The needle must also appear in a close-up. The terrified eyes of the woman.

Or maybe it would be better to begin with the Chinese peddler of primus stove needles, near the monument of the First Printer. This will be the frame. A film without a hero—that's fine, but there must be a Fire Chief. Let him still be fondly attached to his home village. On the one hand, he loves the agricultural inventory, on the other—he is drawn to the firefighting equipment. Here's a conflict: the fireman might, unbeknownst to anyone, steal into the firehouse at night and invent something.

No, that's no good: I feel some ideal looming up before me. I need a conflict, a conflict! They pay good money for a conflict. A conflict is not a pound of smoke.

How about the following:

Many years ago, before the war, the Fire Chief had worked in a factory owned by a private capitalist. In 1917, before fleeing abroad, the capitalist had bricked up his valuables in a safe...

But we have to have a clash between the fireman and the bookkeeper. What did they have in common? Here's the climax of the whole film. Having answered this question, we must move speedily away from a dead end.

One fireman is not enough; since nothing appears to show his development, we must contrast him with... But what do we know of his life? Nothing, except that he is still very attached to his home village, but this does not jibe with the fact that he worked for a private capitalist.

All right: let one have worked for a private capitalist, and the other still be attached to his village. But then what do these two have in common?

Let things play out their own roles, and let the firemen act out completely separate roles. Things reflect the pathos of events, but people reflect the social ammunition. Equipment, that is, the firehoses and ladders, educate the firemen. The woman has no role here: she has no place in this conflict.

Film is not literature. One must think in frames.

Let the Fire Chief be on duty in the theater, while his friend treats his wife to pastries.

No, this is absurd.

My theme burned up in the creative process. My mind is blank. I've got to catch that Shklovsky.

In terms of genre, Jean-Richard Bloch's[1] book[2] borders on "light and entertaining" philosophy. It is brilliant, often virtuoso small talk on significant cultural-historical and political themes, a feuilleton with pretensions to prophecy. In terms of content, it belongs to that cumbersome family of books on the "decline of Europe," but in sharp contrast to Spengler's dogmatism and mathematics, Bloch presents himself as a free-thinker: he is above political parties and above social classes. As an intellectual radical profoundly shaken by the war, he is seeking a new world view, while simultaneously struggling with the world's paradoxes.

Everything is shattered, is the book's leitmotif. Democracy has been desecrated. World revolution has been bankrupted. The police, alas! have become insolent and think nothing of bursting into private homes. That noble generation, educated on Tolstoi, Romain Rolland and Gandhi, refuses to follow the commercial traveller of politics, Monsieur Viviani. Jean-Richard Bloch devotes innumerable sardonic pages to the collapse of European socialist parties, but never doubts their sincerity: he has great respect for any expression of pathos.

War and revolution for Jean-Richard Bloch are by no means normal phenomena; rather they represent an elemental catastrophic order. There is no allusion whatsoever throughout the entire book to any possible preparations for such changes in the past. So-called "humankind" passes on ideas from hand to hand; the passive East contemplates itself in the soul of the rebellious, active West. Communism is nothing more than the foreshadowing of a new religion. The European is the highest species of man, the master of the world. He will put a bridle on himself, he will find new words—clear magical formulas, and civilization will be saved.

As an example of Jean-Richard Bloch's meditations, I cite the episode on the bench at Chartres Cathedral. For whom is the organ music intended, for whom the fiery colors of stained-glass windows? For the small group of shopkeeper-parishioners with wooden faces... Does this mean that the people are not receptive to more great art? Thus shall we learn high style from the Middle Ages; we shall paraphrase it into a new, as yet unknown harmony.

Masses of demobilized proletarians and bourgeoisie wavered

between Wilson and Lenin. For Bloch, America is a bugbear, an automated monster, but Wilson is a noble failure and a Biblical prophet. The people followed Wilson because he promised immediate peace, while Lenin called them to civil war.

The Revolution realized is no longer revolution: its spirit leaves it. There is a kind page on Trotsky: he is the keeper of the eternal light. And, generally speaking, according to Jean-Richard Bloch, revolution as such is dead. The USSR betrayed it in its preoccupation with economic construction. On the other hand, in sport the paganism of classical antiquity was resurrected and the Greek religion was revived in the cult of great men and state symbols. Napoleon and Beethoven are European myths. So is Lenin. Bolshevism is but Napoleonism turned inside out.[3] All his fine distinctions are invoked to create a colossal distance between East and West, and to prove that the proletarian revolution will triumph somewhere in the next world.

A mass of citations, names, scientific and pseudo-scientific quotations are collected in this book: Maurice Barrès, Stravinsky, Diaghilev, Marx, Fustel de Coulanges, Ferrero, Unamuno, Gladkov, and even a conversation between Gorky and Bloch in the Summer Garden. It all resembles a magpie's nest crammed full of glittering objects.

In sum, I must conclude that Bloch's book, with all its superficial pretensions to Leftist thought, is profoundly reactionary. It is an enormous step backward from the spirit of Romain Rolland. It is no more than the dismantling of pacifism. The war of the future, says Bloch, will be won without armies because ideas alone will suffice for the struggle.

61. GEORGES DUHAMEL: *GEOGRAPHIE CORDIALE DE L'EUROPE*

Duhamel[1] refuses to be either a "citizen" or a "politician," a publicist or a voter—he prefers to be a tourist even in his own country. The choice of Holland, Greece and Finland—hardly three "serious" countries—already provides strong evidence: down with politics, long live Dutch tulips and Finnish skis.[2]

The poet of social sympathy and homilies full of respect for the little man has shown himself to be a friend of law and order. The book is remarkable. Duhamel assumes victory, he calls it "our bitter victory." In Greece, he rushes along the French-built highway, his heart fluttering with pride beneath his flannel shirt. Chauvinism, however, serves no purpose, even though the old, somewhat sullied France with its tardy trains, chestnut trees, prefectures and provincial comforts, remains beautiful, and one always yearns to return. Europe is alive because it is a conglomerate of nations which survived the war and even flourished as a result of its mercy.

The author dedicates a lengthy introduction to America in which he apologizes to France for he does not like savior-nations. His clumsy French suitcase was exchanged for the standard American variety, and Duhamel lost his temper at the railway station.

America is the nidus of infection corrupting organic European culture. We live among things made by machines, but the elect of the spirit must despise machine technology. The limits of Duhamel's thought lie in this obvious conflict.

To get himself going, Duhamel alludes to ancient poetic legends and invents new ones: for Finland a bit of the *Kalevala*—about Väinämöinen, the ancient bard; for Holland the anecdote of the Lord of Sabaoth and his archangels; for Greece a bit of archaeology. Greece gives him cause for contemplating the idea that Frenchmen are the true heirs of the Hellenic spirit; he weeps upon seeing the bindings of French books in the library of a modern Greek poet: wherever you go, you find Racine and Molière!

If one ignores his saccharine quest after poetry and local color, much good, sensitive material remains in Duhamel's book: the Dutch flood control system and porcelain, both of which rest upon a solid foundation of swine-breeding, he elevates to a pearl of creation. If only the Dutch hadn't ceased wearing their fourteen national skirts! In his depictions the Dutch emerge as fine housekeepers and tidy animals; indeed, at night the homeowner, without so much as stepping from his bed, can survey his electrically illuminated pigsty through some novel optical device. Duhamel believes that contemporary Finland is alien to all forms of hypocrisy: that small country takes pleasure in its independence and originality, in love, labor and the songs of the *Kalevala*.

The entire book is a pitiful spectacle of social obesity, written by an undisputed, although minor, literary artist. The book possesses a sharp political timbre: genuine civilization unifies antitheses and eradicates social contradictions. Holland is a classic example of national individualism: it has, thank God, 146 parties, and in Amsterdam just as many bus companies. A bürgermeister's wife iceskates with her servant, while the director of a Netherlands bank chats simply with his lowest-paid clerk.

As a writer, Duhamel has always held sway among the first-rate creators and legislators of French literature. He has constantly reduced Anatole France, Romain Rolland, and even Jules Romains to the golden mean. Our critics have never noticed this and have been too myopic and indulgent toward Duhamel. In his latest book, Duhamel kicks his own teachers with the well-shod heel of a tourist.

62. LOUIS PERGAUD: STORIES FROM THE LIVES OF ANIMALS

Stories from the lives of animals? Are such stories possible? In the end the real heroes will either turn out to be humans, or human characteristics will be ascribed to the animals!

Louis Pergaud,[1] however, has proven that proper dramatic penetration into the inner world of animals is possible; he has discovered a bridge between the human psyche and the unknown world of animal existence. Modern science has made this bridge available to Louis Pergaud through its study of conditioned reflexes. Pergaud has taken on each of his stories as he would confront a move in a chess game: animals are not substituted for men; rather, men are placed in animal roles, burdened by the same conditional reflexes, and required to make the same choices, simultaneously noting their own behavioral responses to the given situations.

Almost all of Pergaud's stories are constructed around the theme of adaptation. Each story's dramatic action derives from the fact that Pergaud compels the animals torn from their habitual environment to accomplish the most impressive feats (an entrapped weasel, a magpie gone crazy, intoxicated on vodka). "Needs," states Pergaud, "are the rulers of our feelings and actions." And Pergaud's animals are justified because their behavior is defined by blind necessity.

Pergaud is miles away from artificial babytalk. He does not liken animals to children. He is not afraid of complex linkages. He is rigorous and simple at the same time. In moments of danger and suffering a man is closer to an animal, but an animal at such moments is also closer and more comprehensible to man. Pergaud has thus turned the innocent old fairytale about the ugly duckling into a socio-biological study. In his stories people not only do not push the animals into the background, but they are shown in a new light themselves, often with astonishing force and surprise.

Pergaud's stories, although they preserve a superficial link with the traditional fable, have moved far beyond that genre's naive moralizing. They are far more comparable to the healthy art of primitive man, best expressed, for example, in the charm of Negro art.

The social attitudes of an author writing about animals always emerge with exceptional clarity. Kipling's stories are imperialistic, his mongoose belongs to the white man, it is the Englishman's servant. Only a European with a highly developed sense of his own responsibility toward life, with a cautious and aroused conscience, could write animal stories in the style of Pergaud. The weasel, the crow, and the magpie are his heroes. They serve no one, instead they introduce us to the basic terrors and joys of existence.

63. ABEL ARMAND: *THE SCEPTRE*[1]

"What is this, an operetta or Shakespeare?" Archduke Paul repeatedly asks himself in his most pathetic moments. The Archduke is quite receptive to humor and well read in *belles-lettres*. "An operetta?" he asks suspiciously, but not completely convinced, decides, "No, Shakespeare."

Abel Armand's book is a witty, often contagiously merry satirical lampoon on the decline of the bourgeois-democratic world. It mocks the remnants of feudalism, the ermine purchased on credit, the most august "international" of the "ruling" families of Europe, the pact between the King and the Bishop, whose hands are joined by a police agent serving as a guide in a first-class hotel: the clever youth is a new Figaro,[2] who merrily writes manifestoes for his future sovereign.

The Sceptre was written in 1896 when the political map of Europe was colored almost entirely in the variegated tones of the reigning monarchies, when the political structure of capitalism was still carefully faced with a fine feudal veneer.

The book's *succès de scandale* was extinguished immediately by the loyal Republican censorship. After twenty years of lying concealed, Abel Armand's book not only has not lost interest, but has even won the day as a grotesque portrait of a bygone age.

The 1890s was an era of political scandals in constitutional Europe: the Dreyfus affair, the escapades of crowned heads, the Panama affair, the notoriously fraudulent bloodbaths in Budapest and Vienna, and the modest Tyrolean hat of Leopold of Belgium, found crumpled up in Parisian bars and circus dressing rooms, the hat of a king who adored high living, courtesans, and restaurant flunkeys.

For the contemporary reader, the political piquancy of this lampoon is underscored by a sense of distance: the automobile is still unknown, the highest officials travel about in a landau; the bicycle has just become a fashionable novelty... The aroma of the epoch is everywhere.

Innocent bourgeois satire directed against the human foibles of VIPs was a common phenomenon in the nineties. The princes of Monaco, Luxembourg, Albania, Montenegro, and the minor German principalities were often cast in the roles of benign targets in operettas and popular literature, but Abel Armand's political spice is much sharper. It is more than cheap mockery.

When the political philosophy of the Monarchy is communicated through a single colorful exclamation, and when the future Monarch, in signing a manifesto slipped to him by his clever blackmailer, reads: "We will continue to serve as a firm bulwark of the European world, but we are obliged to crush the enemy's heirs," we understand that we are no longer witnessing an operetta, but, if you will, Shakespeare. When we see that this good-hearted Monarch, the humble victim of blackmail, asks his mentor how he should interpret this clause, and who, in particular, must be crushed, he receives the answer, "But this is an accepted formula for manifestoes."

Archduke Paul is not interested in the least in becoming King. He is one who abdicates. He commits sabotage. His character is a blend of Leopold of Belgium, who remained too long among the heirs, and the Prince of Wales, who was a confirmed bachelor. But he who does not work, does not eat! Isn't it strange how this severe maxim can turn up and be applicable in this context! Paul had a childishly simple plan, like the Tatar in the old joke, who, when asked the question, "What would you do, if you were Tsar?" answered: "I'd steal 100 rubles and run away with it." It turns out that *incognito*, the modest disguise of Monsieur Leroi does not keep him from misdeeds, does not secure him in his pleasure, does not save him from bankruptcy or criminal responsibility. The comedy unfolds with the ease of Italian *commedia dell'arte*. Slowly but surely the heir-saboteur falls into the clutches of his blackmailer.

He is never alone. Even when traveling *incognito*, he is accompanied by a small entourage: the thick-headed and devoted Field Marshal Lutzberg, the court nurse Eshbach, forever reminding his Highness, both appropriately and inappropriately, that it was she who once bathed and diapered him, and, finally, the Bishop Levek, faithful friend and companion of his journeys, who, having fled his church for the worldly pleasures of bourgeois existence, was identified at a lotto game and associated with the small party.

A bitter fate befell poor Paul in his bourgeois disguise. The assembly of royal familes at the spa, Paul and his party, simply out of habit, wormed their way into the august group posing for a photographer. The photographer roars: "Out of the way, please, you're blocking my vision." Even a prince treats him as a "Nothing," while some Dutch princesses whose ball accidentally hits him in the face, comfort themselves, saying, "Don't worry, his are not the eyes of a blue-blood."

The secret police agent—the guide of the Hotel Continental—Figaro—the blackmailer Alfred, controls the destiny of Europe. His method for clearing up the Archduke's financial difficulties involves a proposal that his Highness make a stage appearance at the Alhambra Theater to sing his country's national hymn. Of course, only his initials appear on the poster. The next day the embassy sends him 500,000—to prevent a scandal. The money is divided up among the Archduke's creditors, the theater and the clever guide. The performance is thereby cancelled... The alternatives are reduced to: the throne, or a trial by jury, the throne or a legal scandal...

64. FOURTH PROSE

I

Benjamin Fyodorovich Kagan[1] approached this matter with the sage meticulousness of a Magus and an Odessa-born Newtonian mathematician. All Benjamin Fyodorovich's conspiratorial activity rested upon a foundation of infinitesimal calculus. Benjamin Fyodorovich perceived the law of salvation in slow motion, in proceeding at a snail's pace. He allowed himself to be shaken out of his professorial cubicle, he answered the telephone at any hour, he never renounced anything nor did he deny anyone anything; but most of all, he worked to retard the dangerous course of the disease.

The involvement of a professor, even more so of the great mathematician, in the improbable case of the salvation of five lives by means of those cognoscible, utterly imponderable integral moves known as "pulling strings," promoted general satisfaction.

Isaiah Benedictovich[2] behaved from the very first as if the disease was contagious, something catching like scarlet fever, so that he too, Isaiah Benedictovich, might be shot, for the common good. Isaiah Benedictovich bustled about to no apparent purpose. It was as if he were dashing from doctor to doctor begging for an instantaneous remedy.

If Isaiah Benedictovich had had his way he would have hired a taxi and rushed around Moscow at random, destinationless, imagining that such was the ritual.

Isaiah Benedictovich was perpetually repeating, and reminding everyone, that he had a wife who had remained behind in Petersburg. He even found himself a companion to serve as a kind of secretary, a small, stern and sensible relative who had already begun to look after him, Isaiah Benedictovich, like a nanny. To make a long story short, by appealing to various people at various times, Isaiah Benedictovich seemed to have inoculated himself against the firing squad.

All Isaiah Benedictovich's relatives had died in their Jewish beds of carved walnut. Just as the Turk travels to the black stone of Kaaba, so these Petersburg bourgeois—descended from rabbis of patrician blood and acquainted with the works of Anatole

France through the translator, Isaiah—made pilgrimages to whatever spas bore the imprint of Lermontov and Turgenev, preparing themselves by taking the cure for passage into the next world.

In Petersburg Isaiah Benedictovich had been living the life of a pious Frenchman, eating *potage*, choosing friends as innocuous as the croutons in his bouillon, and visiting, in accord with his profession, two dealers in trashy translations.

Isaiah Benedictovich was good only at the very beginning of his campaign to pull strings, when mobilization began and the alarm, so to speak, was sounded. From then on, however, he faded, withered, stuck out his tongue, and his own relatives pooled their money to send him back to Petersburg.

I have always been interested in the question of just how the bourgeoisie acquired its fastidiousness and so-called decency. Decency is that quality which links the bourgeoisie to animals. Many Party members can relax in bourgeois company for the very same reason that many adults seek the companionship of rosy-cheeked children.

The bourgeois, of course, is more innocent than the proletarian, being closer to the womb, to the infant, the kitten, the angel and cherubim. There are very few of these innocent bourgeois in Russia, and this has had a bad effect on the digestion of true revolutionaries. We must preserve the bourgeoisie in its innocent aspect, entertain it with amateur theatricals, and lull it to sleep on Pullman car springs, tucking it into envelopes of snow-white railroad dreams.

II

A boy clad in goatskin boots and long-waisted velveteen Russian coat, his hair carefully combed back over his temples, stands surrounded by mamas, grandmamas, and nanas, while next to him stands a cook's brat or coachman's kid, some ragamuffin from the servants' quarters. And this whole pack of lisping, hooting, sniveling archangels is urging the lord's young son on:

"Get 'im, Vasenka, give it to 'im!"

Now Vasenka gets in a lick, and the old biddies, the vile old toads, nudge each other and restrain the grubby little coachman's kid:

"Get 'im, Vasenka, give it to 'im, while we grab his curly locks, while we dance him 'round..."

What is all this? Some genre painting in the style of Venetsianov? A scene by some serf-artist?

No, this is the training offered some shaggy Komsomol brat under the tutelage of his agit-mamas, grandmamas and nanas so that Vasenka can get 'im, Vasenka can stomp on 'im, while we hold the brute back, while we dance around...

"Get 'im, Vasenka, give it to 'im!"

III

A crippled girl comes up to us from the street, a street as long as a night without streetcars. Setting her crutch to one side, she hastens to sit down so as to appear like the rest of us. Who is this husbandless cripple? The light cavalry...[3]

We mooch cigarettes off each other and polish up our Chinese gibberish, encoding into crude, cowardly formulas the exalted, powerful and taboo concept of class. Crude animal fear hammers on the typewriters, crude animal fear proofreads the Chinese gibberish on sheets of toilet paper, scribbles denunciations, strikes those that are down, demands the death penalty for prisoners. Just like small boys drowning a kitten in the Moscow River before a host of onlookers, our grown-up boys playfully apply pressure; during recess they put the squeeze on:

"Hey, come on, push, till you can't see it anymore..." Such is the sacred rite of mob rule.

A shopkeeper on the Ordynka gave a woman short weight: kill him!

A cashier came out five cents short: kill her!

A director signed some rubbish by mistake: kill him!

A peasant hid some rye in his barn: kill him!

A girl approaches us, dragging along on her crutch. One leg is shorter than the other, and her crude artificial limb brings to mind a wooden hoof.[4]

Who are we? We are schoolboys who do not study. We are Komsomol freebooters. We are hoodlums with a dispensation from the saints.

Filipp Filippich has a toothache. Filipp Filippich has not and will not come to class. Our notion of studying has as much to do with scholarship as a hoof has with a foot, but this does not embarrass us.

I have come to you, my artiodactylic friends, to stomp my wooden limb in the yellow, socialist arcade created by the frantic fantasy of that reckless entrepreneur Giber, from elements of the chic hotel on Tverskoi Boulevard, from the night telegraph and telephone exchange, from a dream of eternal bliss realized in a permanent foyer with a buffet, from an office with saluting clerks operating round the clock, from the arid air of the postal-telegraph agency that tickles one's throat.[5]

Here it is continually a bookkeeper's night illuminated by the yellow flame of second class railway lamps. Here, as in Pushkin's tale, a Jew is married to a frog, that is, a continuous marriage ceremony is taking place between a goat-footed fop spawning theatrical eggs and his double bathed in the same filth, the Moscow editor-coffin maker, who turns out silk brocade coffins on Monday, Tuesday, Wednesday, and Thursday. He rustles his paper shroud. He opens the veins of the months of the Christian calendar which still preserve their pastoral Greek names; January, February and March... He is the terrifying and illiterate horse-doctor of occasions, of deaths and events, and is pleased as punch when the black horseblood of the age spurts forth like a fountain.

IV

I came to work on the newspaper *Moscow Komsomol*[6] straight from the caravansarai of TsEKUBU.[7] There were twelve pairs of earphones there, nearly all of them broken, and a reading room without books made over from a chapel, where people slept like snails on small curved couches.

The staff at TsEKUBU despised me for my straw basket and for not being a professor.

Afternoons I liked to go and observe high tide, and I firmly believed that the obscene waters of the Moscow River would flood the erudite Kropotkin Embankment forcing the TsEKUBU authorities to telephone for a boat.

Mornings I liked to stand in the street drinking sterilized milk straight from the bottle.

In the evening I would borrow someone else's soap from the professors' shelves and wash myself, and I was never caught even once.

People passed through there from Kharkov and Voronezh, on their way to Alma-Ata. I was accepted as one of them and consulted as to which republic would be the most advantageous.

At night TsEKUBU was locked up like a fortress, and I would bang my stick against the window.

Every decent man received telephone calls at TsEKUBU, and each evening a servant would hand him his messages as if he were handing a funerary list to a priest. The writer Alexander Grin, whose clothes the servants cleaned with a brush, lived there. I lived there. I lived at TsEKUBU like everyone else, and no one bothered me until I moved out for reasons of my own in the middle of the summer.

When I moved to another apartment, my fur coat lay draped across the cab as it does when someone has just been discharged from a hospital after a long stay or has just been released from prison.

V

It's now reached the point where the only thing I value in the literary trade is the raw flesh, the insane excrescence:

> And the entire gorge was wounded
> To the bone by the falcon's cry—[8]

That is what I need.

I divide all of world literature into authorized and unauthorized works. The former are all trash; the latter—stolen air. I want to spit in the face of every writer who first obtains permission and then writes. I want to beat such writers over the head with a stick and sit them all down at a table in the Herzen House,[9] placing a glass of police tea before each one and handing each one an analysis of Gornfeld's[10] urine.

I would prohibit such writers from marrying and having children. How can they have children? Our children must carry on for us, must finish our most important work, seeing as their fathers have sold themselves to the pockmarked devil for three generations to come.

Now there's a literary page.

VI

I have no manuscripts, no notebooks, no archives. I have no handwriting, for I never write. I alone in Russia work with my voice, while all around me consummate swine are writing. What the hell kind of writer am I? Get out, you idiots!

Nevertheless, I have many pencils, of various colors and all of them stolen. They can be sharpened with a Gillette razor blade.

The Gillette razor blade with its sharp, barely serrated edge has always seemed to me one of the noblest products of the steel industry. A good Gillette blade cuts like sedgegrass, bends but does not break on one's hand. It is like a Martian's calling card or a memo from some dapper devil with a hole pierced through its middle.

The Gillette razor blade is the product of the Death Trust whose shareholders include packs of American and Swedish wolves.

VII

I am a Chinaman, no one understands me. Higgledy-Piggledy! Let's go to Alma-Ata where the inhabitants have raisin eyes, where the Persian has eyes like fried eggs, where the Sart has the eyes of a sheep.

Higgledy-Piggledy! Let's go to Azerbaijan!

I had a patron once, Mravian-Muravian, the Peoples' Commissar of the Armenian nation, younger sister of the Jewish nation. He sent me a telegram.

My patron died, the Peoples' Commissar, Mravian-Muravian. The black ant-Commissar is gone from the Erevan anthill.[11] No longer will he travel to Moscow in the international railway car, naive and curious as a priest from a small Turkish village.

Higgledy-Piggledy! Let's go to Azerbaijan!

I had a letter for the Peoples' Commissar Mravian. I handed it to the secretaries at the Armenian residence on the cleanest, most ambassadorial street in Moscow. I was just about to depart for Erevan under the auspices of the ancient Peoples' Commissariat for Education to conduct a terrifying seminar for the round-headed youths in their wretched monastery-university.

Had I traveled to Erevan, I would have spent three days and three nights eating black caviar sandwiches at the huge railway station buffets.

Higgledy-Piggledy!

On the way, I would have read Zoshchenko's best book and exulted like a Tatar running off with a hundred stolen rubles.

Higgledy-Piggledy! Let's go to Azerbaijan!

I would have taken courage with me in my yellow straw basket piled high with fresh, clean-smelling linen, and my fur coat would have danced on a golden hook. And I would have descended at the Erevan station, bearing my winter coat in one hand, and my walking stick—my Jewish crozier[12] —in the other.

VIII

There is a splendid line of Russian poetry which I can never tire of reciting on bitchy cold Moscow nights, a line whose magical power, as it were, scatters evil spirits to the winds. Try to guess the line, my friends. It inscribes itself in the snow like sleigh runners, it scrapes in the lock like a key, it darts into the room like a sharp frost:

> . . . I did not shoot the wretched in the dungeons . . .[13]

Herein lies the symbol of faith, the true canon of the genuine writer, the mortal enemy of Literature.

Living in the Herzen House is a milksop vegetarian, a philologist with a Chinese noggin, the kind who tiptoes about our bloodied Soviet land muttering *hao-hao, shango-shango,* while heads continue to fall, a certain Mitka Blagoi,[14] a Lyceum swine, authorized by the Bolsheviks to guard Seryozha Esenin's suicide rope in a special museum for the advancement of science.

But I say: To the Chinese with Blagoi! Send him back to Shanghai, to the Chinks where he belongs! Think how beautiful

Mother Philology once was, and how she looks today... How pure-blooded, how uncompromising she was then, but how mongrelized and tame she is today...

IX

To the ranks of murderers or would-be murderers of Russian poets must be added the tarnished name of Gornfeld.[15] This paralytic D'Antès, this Uncle Monya from Basseiny Street, preaching morality and State power, carried out the orders of a regime completely alien to himself, accepting them as he would a mild case of indigestion.

To die at the hands of Gornfeld is as stupid as being run over by a bicycle or being bitten by a parrot. But even a parrot can be a literary murderer. For instance, I was almost killed by a parrot named for his Majesty King Albert and Vladimir Galaktionovich Korolenko. I am very glad that my murderer is alive and has, in a certain sense, survived me. I feed him sugar and listen with the utmost satisfaction as he recites from *Till Eulenspiegel*: "The ashes are striking my heart," a line which he alternates with another, less beautiful one: "There is no greater torment in this world than the torment of the word." A man capable of entitling his book *Torments of the Word* must have been born with the mark of Cain (as the sign of the literary murderer) on his brow.

I met Gornfeld only once, in the dingy editorial office of some unprincipled, third-rate magazine, where, as in the buffet of Kvisisan, a throng of spectral figures hovered around. In those days there was still no ideology, and no one to lodge a complaint with if you were insulted. When I recall that time of deprivation —how were we able to live!—enormous tears well up in my eyes... Someone introduced me to the biped critic, and I shook his hand.

Uncle Gornfeld, why did you have to lodge a complaint in *The Stock Exchange News*, or rather *Red Evening News*[16], in the Year of Our Soviet 1929? You would have fared far better crying into Mr. Propper's pure literary Jewish waistcoat. You would have fared far better bearing your woes to your banker with his sciatica, potato kugel and *talesim*...

X

Nikolai Ivanovich's[17] secretary, if the truth must be told, is an honest-to-goodness squirrel, a little rodent. She gnaws a nut with each visitor and darts to the telephone like a new and inexperienced mother to her sick baby.

Some scoundrel once told me that in Greek "truth" is *Mria*.

So this gentle little squirrel is genuine Truth with a capital letter in Greek. But simultaneously she is that other truth, that uncompromising Party virgin—Party Truth...

Our little secretary, frightened and compassionate as a hospital nurse, does not work but rather lives in the anteroom of the office, in the telephone dressing room. Poor *Mria* of the anteroom with her telephone and classical newspaper!

This little secretary[18] is quite different from the rest in that she sits like a nurse at the threshold of power, guarding its bearer as if he were mortally ill.

XI

No, allow me to be tried! Permit me to enter myself as evidence!... Give me a chance, so to speak, to put myself on file. Do not, I beg of you, deprive me of my own trial... The legal proceedings have not yet ended and, I dare you to bear witness, shall never end. So far we have heard only the overture. Bosio[19] herself shall sing at my trial. Bearded students in checked plaids, mingling with capeswinging police, and directed by a goat-like precentor, ecstatically singing a syncopated version of Eternal Memory,[20] will carry a police coffin with the remains of my case out of the smoke-filled halls of the district court.

> Papa, papa, papochka,
> Where, O where is mamochka?
> The Federation of Writers
> Sent the Plague to try us.
> Your mama's lost an eye,
> Your case is sewn up tight[21] ...

Alexander Ivanovich Herzen!... Allow me to introduce myself... It seems that in your home... As host, you should be answerable in some way...

So you chose to go abroad?... Meanwhile, something unpleasant has happened here... Alexander Ivanovich! Dear Master! What can I do? There's absolutely no one to turn to!

XII

In a certain year of my life grown men from that tribe which I despise with all my heart and to which I do not want to, nor ever will, belong, conceived the idea of collectively introducing me to a hideous and repugnant ritual. The name of this ritual is literary pruning and dishonoring, and it is performed in accordance with tradition and the calendar needs of the writers' tribe, the sacrificial victim being selected by the Elders.

I insist that the writer's profession as it has developed in Europe and, in particular, in Russia, is incompatible with the honorable title of Jew, in which I take great pride. My blood, burdened with the heritage of sheep breeders, patriarchs and kings, rebels against the shifty Gypsy character of the writers' tribe.[22] When I was still a child a raucous camp of unwashed Gypsies kidnapped me and for many, many years, dawdling along their obscene routes, ardently prevailed upon me to learn their one craft, their one art: thievery.

The race of professional writers emits a repugnant odor from its hide and exhibits the filthiest habits of food preparation. It is a race that camps and sleeps in its own vomit, is expelled from cities and persecuted in villages; yet it is forever close to the authorities, who find its members shelter in the red light districts, as prostitutes. For literature is forever fulfilling a single assignment: it helps the rulers keep their soldiers in line and it helps the judges arbitrarily dispose of the condemned.

A writer is a mixed breed of parrot and priest. He is a parrot in the loftiest sense of the word. He speaks French if his master is French, but sold in Persia he will speak Persian: "Polly's a fool" or "Polly wants a cracker." A parrot knows no age, nor can he tell day from night. If he begins to bore his master, he is covered over with a black cloth, and that, for literature, is the surrogate of night.

XIII

There were two brothers Chénier.[23] The contemptible younger brother who belongs entirely to literature; the executed older brother who executed literature himself.

Jailers love to read novels, and more than any other men express a need for literature.

In a certain year of my life grown men wearing beards and peaked fur caps brandished a flint knife over me with the aim of castrating me. Judging by the evidence, these were the priests of the tribe: they smelled of onion, novels, and goat flesh.

And it was all as terrifying as a child's nightmare. *Nel mezzo del'cammin di nostra vita*[24] —midway along life's path—I was stopped in the dense Soviet forest by bandits who called themselves my judges. They were the elders: veins protruded from scrawny necks topped by tiny goose-heads unfit to bear the burden of years.

It was the first and only time in my life that Literature had need of me, and it crushed, pawed, and squeezed me, and it was all as terrifying as a child's nightmare.

XIV

I bear moral responsibility for the fact that the ZIF[25] Publishing House did not sign a contract with the translators Gornfeld and Kariakin. I, a dealer in precious furs, nearly suffocating under the weight of literary pelts, bear moral responsibility for the fact that I inspired a Petersburg rogue with the desire to refer in some libelous anecdote to the warm Gogolian fur coat torn at night from the oldest of Komsomol Members, Akaky Akakievich. I tear off my own literary fur coat and trample it underfoot. I shall run three times around the boulevard rings of Moscow in nothing but my jacket in a thirty-degree frost. I shall run away from the yellow hospital of the Komsomol arcade straight toward mortal pneumonia, if only not to see those twelve illuminated Judas holes in that obscene building on Tverskoi Boulevard,[26] if only not to hear the ringing of pieces of silver and the counting of printer's sheets.

XV

My dear Gypsies of Tverskoi Boulevard, we have written a novel together of which you have not even dreamed. I love to come across my name among official papers, in court-ordered subpoenas and other serious documents. There my name takes on a completely objective ring: a rather new sound to my ear, and I must say, a rather interesting one. I am often curious myself to find out what I have been doing wrong. What sort of bird is this Mandelstam, who, for so many years was supposed to have done such-and-such, but has always managed, the rogue, to evade it? How much longer can he go on evading his duty? That's precisely why the years have not reaped profits for me. Others gain respect with each passing day, but for me the reverse is true: time is flowing backwards.

I am guilty. No two ways about it. I can't squirm out of this guilt. I'm constantly in debt. I keep myself secure, however, through evasion. How much longer can I go on this way?

When a tin subpoena arrives or a reminder comes from some social organization, so Greek in its simplicity; when they demand that I betray my accomplices, cease my thievery, admit my source of counterfeit money, and sign a warrant limiting my right to travel beyond certain specified zones, I agree on the spot, but immediately afterwards, as if nothing had happened, I begin my evasions again. And so it goes.

In the first place, I ran away from somewhere, and they are convinced that I must be returned, extradited, investigated and settled. In the second place, I have been mistaken for someone else. I haven't the strength to prove my identity. My pockets are filled with trash: cryptic notes at least a year old, telephone numbers of dead relatives and addresses of unknown persons. In the third place, I signed with Beelzebub or the State Publishing House, a grandiose unfulfillable contract on Whatman paper, rubbed with mustard and sprinkled with emery-powder pepper, a contract which obliged me to return everything I had acquired twice over, to belch back four times the quantity of items I had misappropriated, and to accomplish sixteen times in succession that impossible, unimaginable, unique task which might, at least partially, bring about my acquittal.

With each passing year I become more crafty. It's as if I have been punched full of holes with a conductor's steel punch and stamped with my own surname. Whenever someone calls me by my first name and patronymic, I tremble (I simply can't get used to it), what an honor! If only once in my life someone would call me Ivan Moiseich!...[27] "Hey, Ivan, go scratch the dogs! Mandelstam, go scratch the dogs!" A Frenchman may be called *cher maître*, dear teacher, but me? Never. It's always: "Mandelstam, go scratch the dogs!" To each his own.

I'm a man who is growing old, and with the stump of my heart I scratch the master's dogs... But for them it's not enough, it's never enough... Russian writers stare at me with canine tenderness in their eyes, imploring me: drop dead! Where does such obsequious malice, such slavish contempt for my name originate? Even the gypsy owned a horse, but I am gypsy and horse all rolled into one...

Little tin subpoenas beneath my pillow... A forty-sixth contract in lieu of a burial wreath, and a hundred thousand lighted cigarettes in place of candles...

XVI

No matter how hard I work, whether I carry a horse slung across my shoulders, whether I turn millstones, no matter what I do, I shall never become a worker. My work, regardless of the form, is considered mischief, lawlessness, mere accident. But I like it that way, and I agree to my calling. I'll even sign my name with both hands.

There are different ways to approach a subject. For me a doughnut's value resides in the hole.[28] But what about the dough of the doughnut? You can gobble up the doughnut, but the hole remains.

Making Brussels lace involves real work, but its major components, those supporting the design, are air, perforations, and truancy.

As for me, brothers, work has reaped no profits. It hasn't even gone on my record.

We have a Bible of work, but we fail to appreciate it. I mean Zoshchenko's[29] stories. The one writer who has shown us the life of the working man has been trampled in the mud. But I demand monuments to Zoshchenko in every city and village of the Soviet Union, or at least a monument in the Summer Garden, like the one dedicated to Grandfather Krylov.

Now there's a man whose work breathes truancy, in whose work Brussels lace lives on!

At night along the Ilinka, when the department stores and trusts are at rest and conversing in their native Chinese, at night along the Ilinka jokes and jests run rampant. Lenin and Trotsky embrace as if nothing ever came between them. One carries in his hand a pail and a fishing rod from Constantinople. Two Jews walk hand in hand, an inseparable pair; one—the inquirer, the other—the respondent; one is forever asking, asking, the other—forever evading, evading, and there is no way to interrupt their dialogue.

A German organ-grinder passes with a barrel organ playing Schubert, such a failure, such a parasite... *Ich bin arm*. I am poor.

Sleep, my darling...M.S.P.O...[30]

Viy is reading the telephone directory on Red Square. "Lift up my eyelids..."[31] "Give me the Central Committee..."

Armenians from the city of Erevan walk past with green-painted herrings. *Ich bin arm*. I am poor.

But in Armavir the motto inscribed on the city's heraldic arms reads: the dog barks, the wind carries it.[32]

ADDENDA TO "FOURTH PROSE"

64a. LETTER TO THE EDITORIAL STAFF OF *EVENING MOSCOW*,[1] PUBLISHED IN *EVENING MOSCOW*, NO. 288, 1928

> If, while wandering through a flea market, I recognize my coat, which only yesterday was hanging in my anteroom, even though it may have changed in appearance, then I have the right to say: "that coat was stolen."
>
> —*A. Gornfeld*

I am forced to make a public appearance in a role very unusual for me, namely, as a defendant charged with plagiarizing someone else's material. This statement pertains to the letter from the critic Gornfeld in No. 338 of *Red Evening News*, questioning my revision of old translations of *Till Eulenspiegel*, which I was commissioned to do by the Land and Factory Publishing House.

My conflict with Gornfeld has resulted from the improper practices of publishing houses which print dozens of edited and revised translations anonymously, and without prior permission, since an agreement between the publisher and the translator is invariably obtained by antedating.

In spite of this state of affairs, and because I consider myself morally responsible before my fellow translators, I was the first to inform the unsuspecting Gornfeld of the situation upon publication of the book. Furthermore, I stated that I would answer for his royalties with the entire sum of my literary earnings.

For some reason Gornfeld does not mention this.

His answer was a letter to the editorial staff of *Red Evening News*.

I shall answer the respected critic and reviewer Gornfeld bluntly, leaving his conscience to answer for the tone and insinuations of his letter which attempted to depict the matter in a criminal light with its references to "flea markets" and "fur coats."

I will permit myself to address Gornfeld in technical language which he might not expect: my tenure as a translator—more than thirty volumes in ten years—gives me this right. Our country greatly underestimates the metamorphosis of those momentous cultural treasures that we must push through to the reading masses. Only great artists of the word are capable of translating foreign classics. Publishing houses are not yet capable of mobilizing these artists. Although compelled to work on a primitive lathe, we nevertheless publish texts which are better than previous ones. Pedantic collation with the original text was a lesser priority than the incomparably more important cultural task of making each phrase sound Russian and agree with the spirit of the original. For us the important thing is that young people do not confuse *Till Eulenspiegel* with *William Tell*, but for the bibliophile-pharisees the important thing is a "flawless book" on the shelf and an empty place in the readers' minds and hearts. Therefore I am not embarrassed if, in enumerating the pieces of a typical costume, caps which are not in the least offensive to de Coster, and which are properly worn on a Flemish woman's head, sneak into the text instead of socks and skirts.

"And King Philip resided in unremitting grief and rage. In impotent ambition he prayed to the Lord . . ." (Gornfeld's translation). Is that really how de Coster talks? I don't believe it: the bureaucratic "resided in unremitting grief," the Old Slavonic "Lord," a double prepositional object with a numbing parallelism of adjectives. Listen to how this sounds: ". . . meanwhile King Philip grieved and raged. The ambitious imbecile prayed to God. . ." Here we have two divergent verbs ("grieves" and "rages"), a single apt epithet ("ambitious"), plus a characterization of Philip casually dropped in passing ("imbecile"). The structure of the phrase defines the system of thought (my example). My corrections, or, to be more precise, my reworking of Kariakin, which gave rise to an oppressive mass of text (18 sheets), did not consist in mechanical maneuvering between his text and Gornfeld's text, but rather in consciously enlivening nearly every phrase.

I have struggled long and hard with the conventional language of translation. It is terrifying, hair-splitting, disfiguring work, and it always obscures the author. In our country neither porridge-like syntax, the absence of prose rhythm, nor rubbery language is regarded as a translator's intrusion into the text so long as Makarov's dictionary is not abused. "Furry feet with cloven hooves" (about the devil) is not permissible, but "cloven feet" is. I was even corrected on this point by Gornfeld, who stands a whole head higher than the majority of translators, but whose version of *Till Eulenspiegel* is an overly cumbersome text.

However, the issue is not whether I did a good or a bad job in correcting old translations or whether I created a new text based on them. Does Gornfeld really not care at all about the peace of mind and moral fortitude of the writer who traveled two thousand versts to him for explanations in an attempt to smooth out absurd and annoying mistakes (his own and the publisher's)? Does he really want us to behave like shopkeepers seizing each other by the hair, to the philistines' great delight? How is it possible to separate a writer's "rough" everyday work from his life's mission, to make an ugly "literary scandal" out of accidental negligence in the spirit of the petty tabloids of the good old days?

Did Gornfeld really need me as an example of the literary predator?

Now that my apologies are made and I have abandoned all sentimentality, I, a Russian poet and man of letters, having erected over twenty years a mountain of independent labor, ask the literary critic Gornfeld how he could have stooped so low as to permit himself the phrase about the "fur coat." My mistake and Gornfeld's transgression are incommensurable. I should have insisted that the publishing house reach an agreement with the translator in good time, but in his letter Gornfeld publicly distorted my entire image as a writer. The path he has chosen is inexpedient and petty. Gornfeld has shown so much indifference to his younger contemporary, a man of letters, so much disdain for this man's work, and so much apathy toward the social and comradely bond that preserves literature, that both man and writer are horrified.

We should wring the necks of bad habits and practices, but that does not mean that writers should wring their fellow writers' necks.

O. Mandelstam

64b. LETTER TO THE EDITORIAL STAFF OF *THE LITERARY GAZETTE*,[2] PUBLISHED IN *LITERARY GAZETTE,* MAY 13, 1929

Esteemed Comrade Editor!

Do not refuse to include the following in the next issue of *The Literary Gazette*:

The appropriation of authorship is called plagiarism.

The appropriation of material goods is called theft.

The publication of intentionally false, incomplete, inaccurate, or garbled information, and likewise the publication of any derogatory, unfounded statements in the press is called slander.

Citizen Zaslavsky's[3] treatment of me must be called by name (see his article "The Modest Plagiarist and Ostentatious Hackwork" in No. 3 of *The Literary Gazette*).

Sincerely,

O. Mandelstam
May 10, 1929

65. ON THE NATURALISTS

1.

The natural scientist is not free to select his own writing style, nor does he find it ready-made. Every scientific mode requires its own unique method of organizing scientific material. Its formal aspect always supports a particular ideology and its attendant goals. The problem of a scientific literary form is especially evident in the natural sciences which have always served as an ideological battleground during times of crisis. Only after we have thoroughly studied the history of people's attitudes toward nature will we understand the laws governing the changes in the literary style of natural science.[1]

Darwin never claimed to be a natural philosopher. He never imposed any teleological attributes on nature. Furthermore, he consistently rejected the idea of a benign nature, and the idea of will or rational motivation in nature was even more alien to him. The formal aspect of his scientific writings, in other words, the totality of his logical and stylistic devices, arises from a purely biological point of view.

Darwin's work appeared at a time when dilettantism in the natural sciences had grown to unprecedented proportions. Amateur nature study was flourishing both in England and on the Continent. Educated burghers and gentlemen studied plants, collected specimens, and kept notebooks of their observations and descriptions. They were ridiculed by both German Romantics and British satirists. Charles Dickens's *Pickwick Papers* is, in fact, a scathing satire on such amateur activity. As we know, Mister Pickwick and his cohorts at the club are naturalists. However, they have absolutely nothing to do. They manage to keep themselves occupied with the devil only knows what pastimes, and their antics are a source of great amusement for young girls and street urchins. Venerable gentlemen such as these, equipped with butterfly nets and botanical backpacks, had no universal purpose to guide them. Their frenzied observations and descriptions began to resemble caricatures. However, along with the purely domestic variety of amateur activity taken up by squires and ministers, there was simultaneously a great surge of interest in world geography. Around-the-world voyages became pedagogically fashionable. Not only the aristocracy of the financial world, but the entire middle class now sought to provide their children with the opportunity to travel around the world by securing positions for them on merchant ships or military vessels.

This new variety of curiosity about nature differed radically from Linnaeus's thirst for knowledge or Lamarck's intellectual inquisitiveness. The era beginning with Darwin's voyage on the *Beagle* and ending with the famous artist Claude Monet's around-the-world journey on the *Brigitte* was a period of colossal apprenticeship in analytic observation, a time when people strove to augment their experience of the world with a firm foundation of practical activity and personal initiative.

Darwin's scientific descriptions are amazingly true to life. He utilizes sunlight, air, and shadows, as well as carefully calculated distances to produce the greatest possible effect in his writing. The result is an intriguing picture of some animal or insect caught unawares, as if on camera, in its most characteristic posture:

> The elater, when placed on its back in preparation to spring, moved its head and thorax backward, so that the pectoral spine was drawn out and rested on the edge of its sheath. In continuing the same backward movement, the spine, by the full action of the muscles, was bent like a spring; and the insect at this moment rested on the extremity of its head and wing cases.[2]

It is difficult for the modern reader to fully appreciate the entirely unprecedented freshness of this description, which today sounds exactly as if it were taken from a documentary film. In order to comprehend the full extent of Darwin's revolutionary literary-scientific style, let us compare this utterly functional sketch of a beetle with a description by Pallas,[3] a disciple of Linnaeus and the author of *A Geological Journey through Various Provinces of the Russian Empire*. Pallas's description of "The Asian Gnat" reads as follows:

> In height, the size of a beetle of the family Salticidae, but in appearance roundish with a spherical thorax. The abdomen and legs are greenish, while the thorax is darker and the head is a copper color. The elytra are smooth and glossy, black with a tinge of violet. The antennae are of equal length and the front legs are slightly longer. The specimen was caught in the vicinity of Lake Inderskoe.

Pallas arrays the insect in a costume and stage makeup, as if it were about to perform in the Chinese Royal Theater or the Imperial Ballet. It is presented as if it were a precious gem or a portrait in a locket. Linnaeus's[4] system of classification relied on such descriptions: nature has a sagacious plan which can be directly comprehended through classification, for rapture is in the act of recognition, they are one and the same. Linnaeus wrote: "The elegant structure of the heart, with all the veins that lead into it, is the sole cause of the circulation of the blood."

During the interval of nearly a century separating Linnaeus and Darwin, the evolutionists Cuvier,[5] Buffon,[6] and Lamarck,[7] dominated the field of natural science. During this time the description of structural and anatomical traits triumphed over that of purely esthetic features in works on natural history. The imperial feudal art of miniature painting began to decline. Essentially, however, very little had changed.

The conception of nature as a fixed, immobile system was supplanted by the idea of a living chain of organic beings, a perpetual mobile ever striving toward perfection. The Deist Lamarck did not perceive of God as a master architect, but rather as a constititutional monarch who does not interfere with nature's internal affairs. Lamarck's system of classification was somewhat artificial, encompassing the most diverse phenomena like a net cast over everything in sight. What else could the naturalist do subsequently but experience rapture as before? Nevertheless, the rapture was no longer caused by isolated, individual natural phenomena, but by categories or groups arranged in order of gradual development.

The French Revolution also exerted a major influence on the naturalist's style. Buffon used his own scientific treatises as a platform for revolutionary demagoguery. He extolled the natural state of horses living wild in herds and exhorted us to follow their example, eulogizing the steed's spirit of civic valor.

Lamarck, whose best works were written at the height of the National Convention, repeatedly lapsed into a legislative tone of voice. He did not describe, but decreed the laws of nature.

The remarkable prosaic quality[8] of Darwin's works was preconditioned, to a large extent, by history. Darwin purged the scientific language, eradicating every trace of bombast, rhetoric, and teleological pathos. He possessed the courage to be prosaic precisely because he had so much to say and did not feel obligated to express rapture or gratitude to anyone.

2

On the Origin of Species comprises fifteen chapters, each of which is divided into ten or fifteen subsections no longer than a feuilleton in the Sunday *Times*. The book is arranged in this manner so that the reader can survey the whole of the work from any given point. No matter what Darwin discussed, no matter where the meanderings of scientific thought led him, he always presented a given problem in its totality. The reader encounters facts at every turn, not only accidentally, as isolated examples. Facts are unfurled before him like a mass of troops being deployed. The ebb and flow of scientific truth, like the rhythm of a fairytale, animates each chapter and subsection. Darwin's scientific examples acquire significance only in the light of universal experience.

When *On the Origin of Species* first appeared, it stunned the reading public with its revolutionary content and innovative ideas. Darwin's equally innovative and forceful style, however, went unnoticed, although it was largely responsible for allowing such vast segments of the population to comprehend his theory.

The old scientific style employed by the naturalists of the Linnaean era consisted of two elements only: bombastic clichés and metaphysical or theological homilies on the one hand, and passive, contemplative description on the other hand. Buffon and Lamarck introduced into scientific style a civic, revolutionary, and publicistic rhetoric.

Darwin's attitude toward nature resembles that of a war correspondent, an interviewer, or a daring reporter furtively pursuing a news story at the scene of the event. Darwin never described anything, he only characterized it. In this sense Darwin, the writer, incorporated the popular tastes of the English reading public into natural history. We must not forget that Dickens and Darwin were contemporaries and that both were popular with the reading public for the same reason.[9]

Darwin never described the features of a plant or animal in the kind of copious detail common to official documents. He used nature as one would use an enormous, highly systematized card catalogue. He relegated taxonomy to its proper place: it had ceased to be an end in itself. Consequently, he attained a greater degree of freedom in ordering scientific material. He also acquired a great variety of deductive arguments and an increased capacity for exposition.

As a result of his extreme loathing for dogma, Darwin always confined himself to a simple recounting of how his convictions were formed. Thus, in relating how terrestrial predators can become amphibious, and in explaining this transformation, a slip of the tongue inadvertently gave him away:

> If a different case had been taken, and I had been asked how an insectivorous quadruped could possibly have been converted into a flying bat, the question would have been far more difficult, and I could have given no answer. Yet I think such difficulties have very little weight.[10]

The journal Darwin kept during his voyage on the H.M.S. Beagle introduced that new standard of vigilance into the natural sciences which is continued in *On the Origin of Species*. In the latter, however, Darwin extended the scope of his reporting to countless addressees around the world engaged in similar work. His laboratory was vast. It included stud farms, poultry yards, apiaries, and greenhouses belonging both to specialists and amateurs. Moreover, all these voluntary assistants proved to be vitally important to Darwin's work. The author of *On the Origin of Species* kept up a regular correspondence with them in his book,[11] constantly referring to them and expressing his gratitude to them.

Darwin's solidarity with the international elite of the world of natural science imparts a secure self-confidence to his style and lends his argumentation additional strength, the strength of a comradely handshake. The naturalist is at home anywhere in the world. The flag of Great Britain's merchant marine flutters over every page of Darwin's book.

We should also mention Darwin's predilection for the average reader, his desire to share his thoughts with an average gentleman, some Sir Eliot, let us say, who once sent him a couple of pigeons as a gift. Darwin wrote as a person who is counting on support from the vast majority of his readers.

To ignore the formal side of scientific writing is just as incorrect as ignoring the content of literary works, for the elements of art are present in both. Zoological terminology, brilliantly refined after centuries of endeavor, has acquired an exceptionally forceful capacity for images. The apt names for plants and animals that we encounter in Darwin's works sound as though they were coined only recently.

The same public read both Darwin and Dickens. Darwin's scientific success was also to a certain extent comparable to a literary success. The average reader detested the didactic, sentimental, bittersweet literature that Dicken's predecessors had stuffed down his throat. That reader would prefer characterizations (photographic pictures of nature, social contrasts) to anything else on earth.

Charles Darwin's prose style could not have emerged at a more appropriate time. His scientific prose, with its geographical aridity and atmospheric perspective, with its multitudinous examples exploding like cartridges, was received as a literary, autobiographical document.[12] Perhaps the reader was ultimately won over by the fact that Darwin never went into literary, teleological raptures over the laws and tendencies of nature which he affirmed with such brilliant clarity.

The naturalist's power of perception is as much an instrument of his thought as is his literary style. Invigorating clarity, like a beautiful day during the temperate English summer, and a certain quality in the author which could be called good scientific weather, that is, a moderately elevated mood, work together in Darwin's writings to infect the reader with the same mood and to help him comprehend Darwin's theory.

No one can popularize Darwin's theory better than Darwin himself. It is essential that we study his scientific style, although it is futile to imitate it, for the historical milieu of which he was a part will never be repeated.

ADDENDA TO "ON THE NATURALISTS"

65a. DARWIN'S LITERARY STYLE

I had been accustomed since my childhood to regard Darwin as no more than a mediocre mind.[1] His theory struck me as suspiciously condensed: natural selection. I wondered if it was worth troubling nature for the sake of such a laconic and obscure conclusion. But, now that I am more familiar with the works of the famous naturalist, I have sharply altered my immature evaluation.

That is what I must record right now: it was Darwin who eradicated every trace of oratory, rhetoric, and pomposity from the natural scientist's literary style.

[The gold coin of facts supports the "balance" of his scientific enterprises, just as the million in sterling in British bank vaults secures the circulation of the national currency.]

The organization of scientific material is the naturalist's style.

There is a popular-serial character to Darwin's scientific experiments.

For the Linnaean naturalist attention is focussed on but a single phenomenon. Description. The Picturesque. "The miniatures" of Buffon and Pallas. Theology. Gratitude. Emotion. The celebration of nature.

There is oratory in the work of Linnaeus, Buffon, and Lamarck.[2]

Darwin's work is prosaic. Popular. It is aimed at the average reader. Its tone is conversational.

Darwin's method is the serial development of signs. Bunches of examples. The selection of heterogeneous series. Putting functional examples at the center of his argument.

The ebb and flow of authentification like the rhythm of a musical exposition. (The origin of species.) An *autobiographical quality*. Elements of geographer's prose. School by means of around-the-world voyages (H.M.S. Beagle).[3]

The role of vision. The power of perception functions as an instrument of thought.

From his preacher's pulpit Linnaeus extolled the elegant and expedient structure of living creatures. [His system served his mass.] [He demonstrated—for the glory and proof of the wisdom of the Creator—every little thing, the curiosities, rarities and beauties of organic nature.] Buffon constructed his own brilliant treatises...

The Creator of nature equipped man with five organs, known as the senses; all perfectly constructed.

The elegant structure of the heart, with all the veins that lead into it, is the sole cause of the circulation of the blood.

One never ceases to wonder at Divine Providence, of course, seeing how the heart, lungs and other internal organs are protected by a bony structure.

The skin covering our body is composed of the most splendid fibers, interwoven and everywhere strewn with blood vessels and nerve endings in the most remarkable way. It can be stretched miraculously and then tightened again.

Linnaeus. *Systema naturae.*

On the Origin of Species stunned Darwin's contemporaries. People were enticed by the book. Its success rivaled that of Goethe's *Sorrows of Young Werther.* It was clearly acclaimed as a literary *event*; and the novelty of its form was recognized as both major and serious.

[As opposed to other books] this one was calculated to appeal to the broadest reading public. [It was the direct successor of the newspaper, socio-political journalism, and the political feuilleton.] And it was taken as popular scientific *journalism.*

Darwin always addressed himself to professional naturalists or to broad circles of amateurs. He had a tendency to create his own "public," meaning the upper crust of the educated bourgeoisie.

Darwin's work in the natural sciences taken as a literary *whole*, as a mass of thought and style, is nothing less than a perpetually pulsating *newspaper* of nature, seething with life and facts.

Darwin organized his material like an editor of a large and influential—let's be even more blunt—political organ.

He was not alone. He had numerous contributors—correspondents scattered throughout every country, colony and dominion of the United Kingdom, throughout every country around the globe.

"I have obtained," he said, "every species (of pigeon) that one can purchase or get a hold of in some way with the help of friends in various countries. I am especially obliged to Sir Eliot..."

[The merchant flag] of the British merchant marine flutters over the pages of his work.

The common sense of a businessman, the knowledge of when to take the initiative, the feeling of solidarity and courage in the face of competition, self-confidence and a somewhat reserved geniality—those are the levers moving Darwin's scientific imagination.

What is more, these factors are no less influential on his style and manner, on the functional forms of his exposition; they saturate his writings and determine the literary structure of his *life work*.

Of course, a *naturalist's style* is one of the keys to understanding his *world view*, just as his *powers of perception,* his *manner of seeing,* are the key to his *methodology.*

It was when I was struck by these truths and the desire to communicate them to my students, that I first understood the necessity of establishing *general principles applicable to all animals*, of indicating the whole before going into details and specifics.

(The Philosophy of Zoology)

Compare modest Darwin with the theologians, orators, and legislators in the natural sciences, Darwin up to his ears in facts, carefully leafing through the book of nature—not as a Bible—what Bible—but as a businessman's handbook, as a stockbroker's guide, as an index of prices, signs, and functions.[4]

His system of notecards, that enormous and ongoing card catalogue which Darwin mentions in his autobiography, left a decisive mark on his scientific style.

Darwin avoids copying out the entire lengthy "police" record of each animal or plant. He enters into a relationship with nature like some war correspondent, or interviewer, or some desperate reporter who has finally achieved the status of an eyewitness. He never describes, he only characterizes, and in this sense...

Taxonomy, the pride and glory of Linnaean natural science, favored the art of description. It engendered the remarkable mastery of detailed and self-contained contemplative characterization. Among ungifted scribblers it gave birth to an accumulation of police notations, among the artistically gifted naturalists it blossomed into designs, miniatures, lace...

The independent mastery and highly original art of passive-contemplative nature descriptions reached its peak in the latter half of the 18th century. One of the most brilliant examples of this genre, *A Geological Journey through the Various Provinces of the Russian Empire,* was compiled by Academician Pallas in 1767...

In the work of Pallas the noble subtlety and sensitivity of the eye, the attention to detail, and the sheer virtuosity of description attained their utmost limits, reached the heights of miniature painting. [The *Chrisomela asiatica* described by Pallas is costumed as if it were about to perform in the Chinese Royal Theater or the Imperial Ballet. The naturalist pursues the magical pictorial effect.]

> The Asian gnat *(Chrisomela asiatica).* In height the size of a beetle in the Salticidae family, but in appearance roundish with a spherical thorax. The abdomen and legs are greenish, while the thorax is darker and the head is a copper color. The elytra are smooth and glossy, black tinged with violet. The antennae are of equal length, the forelegs are slightly longer. The specimen was caught in the vicinity of Lake Inderskoe.

... The naturalist pursues the magical pictorial effect. [He fails to mention the anatomical structure of the insect.]

About the time of Darwin's emergence on the scene, the art of the miniaturist, of the aristocracy of the natural sciences, was experiencing the final stages of collapse. The principles of Linnaean taxonomy were shattered by Lamarck.

The bourgeoisie no longer needed a natural scientific ideology glorifying the rational foundations of reality.

Dickens performed the very same role in debunking contemporary English society. In England with its young textile industry and feudal judicial machinery...

Instead of scribbling and compiling catalogues, Darwin offered a new principle: the principle of natural scientific patrol duty. *On the Origin of Species* is as much a travel diary as *The Zoology of the Voyage of the H.M.S. Beagle*. [The naturalist carries out his patrol duty from the captain's bridge.]

... The new bourgeoisie voluntarily sent its children on around-the-world cruises. An around-the-world cruise on a frigate was incorporated into the educational plans of every young man with a serious future. Innumerable artists, scholars, and poets participated in this arould-the-world pedagogy. That is why in Darwin's scientific writings we come across elements of geographer's prose, rudiments of a colonial tale, or a seafarer's adventure story. [He skillfully alternates the evidence of eyewitness accounts with scholarly citations.]

Darwin's dislike of direct quotes is characteristic. He very rarely cites a text word for word.[5] He usually quotes another opinion in the most lapidary form, rephrasing it in a concise, energetic and absolutely objective formulation.

If we want to define the tone of Darwin's scientific speech, it is best to call it *scientific conversation*.[6] It partakes neither of the ordinary professional lecture nor of an academic course. Imagine a scholar-gardener leading guests around his estate, stopping among his flowerbeds to offer explanations; or an amateur zoologist welcoming his good friends in a zoological garden.

Darwin's extraordinary geniality with respect to the majority of the educated representatives of his class, his confidence in their support, his exceptional frankness, the affability of his scientific thinking, of his very mode of expression, is the result of class solidarity and the desire for widespread cooperation with the international scientific forces of the bourgeoisie.

We should also mention Darwin's appeal to the average reader, his great desire to be understood by the bourgeoisie with a secondary school education, by the average gentleman as he considered himself. It was no accident that the most erudite man of his age spoke directly to the broad reading public over the heads of the scholarly caste. It was important to him to relate directly to this public. And the public did understand Darwin far better than the scholar-pedants. He brought his readers something actual, strikingly in tune with their sense of well-being; he answered a social demand.[7]

Hence, Darwin's geniality, his avoidance of scientific terminology in the extended panorama which he gradually unfolds before the reader.

As a literary genre, *On the Origin of Species* represents a form of natural-scientific thinking on a grand scale. Compared with a musical composition, it resembles neither a sonata nor a symphony with their crescendos and their slow and stormy movements, but is rather closer to the suite. It contains small independent chapters...

The energy of the argument is discharged in "quanta,"[8] in batches. Accumulation and release, inhalation and exhalation, ebb and flow.

Darwin adhered strictly to the tenets of his argument. In variously seeking a starting point, he created truly heterogeneous series, that is, he grouped together dissimilar, contrasting, and variously colored animals.

Here the demands of science happily correspond to one of the most fundamental esthetic laws. I have in mind the law of heterogeneity which encourages the artist to seek to unite in one form the greatest number of different sounds, concepts of various origins, and even antithetical images.

In Darwin's field of vision the entire organic world always

appeared as a unified whole. He dealt with the most varied kinds of living creatures with astonishing freedom and ease.[9]

The eye of the naturalist, like the eye of a predatory bird, acquired the capacity for accommodation.[10] It might be turned into military binoculars equipped for the most distant vision, or, just as quickly, into a jeweler's magnifying glass.

In *On the Origin of Species* animals and plants are not described merely for the sake of description. The book seethes with natural phenomena, but they are turned upside down only when absolutely necessary; they play an active role in the argument and then yield their place to their successors. Above all, Darwin prefers to use a *serial unfolding of signs* and the collision of intersecting series. His gradual accumulation of essential signs gives rise to his crescendoing scale.

Darwin constructed his scientific arguments volumetrically. He extended the coordinates of his examples in length, width, and depth, using his original selection of materials to obtain his effects:

> I will cite only three cases of instinct: the cuckoo laying her eggs in other birds' nests, the slave instinct among ants, and the bees' instinctive construction of beehives.

Only his genius for conceptualization combined with the natural scientist's powerful instinct to experiment allowed Darwin to achieve such results. Here I have in mind the genuine capacity for choice, for collecting and selecting data which support the scientific argument and provide auspicious conditions for generalization.[11]

The ebb and flow of testimony enlivens each small chapter of *On the Origin of Species.*

But what is most astonishing and instructive for any writer is Darwin's concern that the reader not get bogged down in facts, in "naturalia" [that there be layers of light and air...]. Here we see Darwin, the writer, and his meticulous concern with obtaining the most efficient physical illumination of each detail.[12]

The healthy disposition of the natural scientist's experimental spirit is revealed in the free disposition of scientific material. Darwin shows marvelous taste in disposing of facts. He allows them to breathe. He scatters them in sculpted constellations, he groups them in shiny masses.

Stimulating atmospheric *clarity*, like some fine English summer day, is what I would like to call "fine scientific weather"; nothing less than *fine*, insofar as the elevated mood of the author infects his reader and helps him to assimilate Darwin's theories.

66. JOURNEY TO ARMENIA

1. Sevan

On the island of Sevan,[1] which is distinguished by two of the most valuable architectural monuments of the VIIth century as well as by the mud huts of some recently deceased, lice-ridden hermits, densely overgrown with nettles and thistles but no more frightening than the neglected cellars of summer cottages, I spent a month enjoying the lake waters standing at a height of four thousand feet above sea level and teaching myself to contemplate the two or three dozen tombs scattered so as to resemble a flower-bed among the monastery's recently renovated dormitories.

Each afternoon at exactly five o'clock, the lake, which was teeming with trout, would foam up as if someone had cast an enormous pinch of soda into it. This was no less than a mesmeric seance caused by a change in the weather; it was as if some medium had cast a spell over the hitherto peaceful lime-water, at first invoking some playful little ripples, then some seething twitter, and, finally, a tempestuous Lake Ladogan frenzy. At that point it was simply impossible to deny myself the pleasure of measuring off three hundred paces along the narrow beach path just opposite the somber Gunei shore.

Here Lake Gokcha[2] forms a strait five times broader than the Neva. The magnificent freshwater wind rushes into the lungs with a whistle. The velocity of the clouds increases by the minute and the incunabular surf races to publish by hand in half an hour the plump Gutenberg Bible under the humorless, frowning heavens.

Children constituted no less than seventy per cent of the island's population. Like little wild animals they would clamber over the tombs of the monks, bombard some tree roots peacefully snagged on the lake bottom, taking their icy spasms for the writhing of a sea serpent; or they would drag forth from their damp holes some bourgeois toads and garter snakes with jewel-like feminine heads, or give chase to some panic-stricken ram who could in no way figure out whom he might have disturbed with his poor body, and who would just stand there shaking his tail grown fat in freedom.

The high steppe grasses growing on the lee hump of the island of Sevan were so strong, juicy and self-confident that you felt like carding them with an iron comb. The entire island is Homerically studded with yellow bones, leavings from the pious picnics of the local populace.

In addition, the island is literally paved with the fiery-red slabs of anonymous graves, some sticking up, others knocked over or crumbling away.

At the very beginning of my stay news came that some stone-masons digging a foundation pit for a lighthouse on the long and melancholy spit of land known as Tsamakaberda had stumbled across burial urns belonging to the ancient Urartu[3] people. Previously, I had seen in the Erevan museum a skeleton crouched in a sitting position jammed into a large clay amphora, with a tiny hole drilled in its skull for the evil spirit.

I was roused early in the morning by the chirring of an automobile engine. The sound seemed to be marking time. Two mechanics were warming up the tiny heart of an epileptic engine, pouring fuel oil into it. But just as it seemed ready to go, its tongue-twister—something like "still thirsty, won't go, still thirsty, won't go"—would lose its power and dissipate over the water.

Professor Khachaturian,[4] over whose face an eagleskin was so tightly stretched that his muscles and ligaments stuck out, all numbered and labelled with their Latin names, was already taking his morning constitutional along the wharf, wearing his long black frockcoat fashioned in an Ottoman cut. A teacher as well as an archaeologist by calling, he had spent the major part of his career as the director of a secondary school, the Armenian *gymnasium*, in Kars. Invited to join the Department of Archaeology at the University in Soviet Erevan, he brought along with him his devotion to the Indo-European theory of languages, his blind hatred for Marr's[5] Japhetic fabrications, as well as his shocking ignorance of the Russian language and of Russia, where he had never been.

Having somehow struck up a conversation in German, we joined Comrade Karinian, former chairman of the Armenian Central Executive Committee, in a motor-launch.

This proud and full-blooded man, doomed to waste his time in idleness, cigarette smoking and the somber reading of Onguardist literature, obviously found it difficult to give up the routine of his official duties, and boredom had imprinted plump kisses on his ruddy cheeks.

The automobile engine continued muttering "still thirsty, won't go," as if reporting to Comrade Karinian, and the little island raced off swiftly behind us, straightening up its bear-like back with the octahedrons of monasteries. The launch was accompanied by a swarm of midges, through which we sailed as if through muslin hung over the morning lake of blancmange.

We actually uncovered some clay shards and human bones at the excavation site, and, in addition, we found a knife handle with the trademark "N.N." of ancient Russian make.

And, I respectfully wrapped up in my handkerchief the porous calcified little cavity of someone's cranium.

Life on any island, be it Malta, St. Helena or Madeira,[6] flows on in noble anticipation. This has its charm as well as its inconvenience. In any case, everyone is perpetually busy, suffers from a slight loss of voice, and is a little more attentive to others' needs than on the mainland with its wide scorching roads and negative freedom.

The helix of the ear is more delicately formed and takes on new whorls.[7]

To my good fortune an entire gallery of wise and distinguished old men had gathered on the island of Sevan: the highly esteemed expert on regional lore and history, Ivan Yakovlevich Sagatelian, the above-mentioned archaeologist, Khachaturian, and finally the effervescent chemist, Gambarian.[8]

I preferred their peaceful company and the quality of strong coffee permeating their talk to the flat conversations of the young people which, as everywhere else in the world, revolved around examinations and physical culture.

The chemist Gambarian speaks Armenian with a Moscow accent. He has happily and voluntarily Russified himself. He is young in heart and has a dry, wiry body. Physically, he is an extremely pleasant man and a splendid partner in games.

He was anointed with some kind of military unction, as if he had just returned from the regimental chapel, which proves nothing, although it often happens with superb Soviet people.

He is a chivalrous Mazeppa[9] with women, caressing Maria with his lips alone. In male company he is the enemy of sarcasm and vanity, but let him get involved in a quarrel, and he flares up like a Frankish fencer.

The mountain air had rejuvenated him; he would roll up his sleeves and fling himself at the volleyball court fishnet, drily working the small palms of his hands.

What can be said for the climate on Sevan?

"Gold currency of cognac in the secret cupboard of the mountain sun."

The glass tube of the summer cottage thermometer was cautiously passed from hand to hand.[10] Doctor Herzberg was frankly bored on that island of Armenian mothers. He seemed to me like a pale shadow of an Ibsen problem or like some actor from the Moscow Art Theater on vacation.[11]

Children would often stick out their narrow tongues at him, extending them for a moment like lumps of bear meat...

Toward the end of my stay we were visited by hoof-and-mouth disease, imported in milk cans from the remote island of Zeynal, where some former Khlysts[12] who lived in gloomy Russian peasant huts and had long ago ceased to rejoice in anything, held their peace.

What is more, to atone for the sins of the adults, the hoof-and-mouth disease struck only the shameless children of Sevan.

One after another those pugnacious, wiry-haired children, overtaken by high fever, succumbed on the women's laps or fell back onto their pillows.

Once, in competition with Kh., a young Komsomol member, Gambarian undertook to swim around the entire island of Sevan. His sixty-year-old heart could not hold out, and Kh., himself exhausted, was forced to abandon his comrade, return to the starting point, and throw himself out half alive on the pebbly beach. The only witnesses to the accident were the volcanic walls of the island fortress, which precluded any thought of mooring...

Then what a hullabaloo! There turned out to be no life raft on Sevan, even though one had been requisitioned long ago.

People rushed about the island, taking pride in their knowledge of the irremediable accident. Unread newspapers clattered in their hands like tin. The island felt nauseated, like a pregnant woman.

We had neither telephones nor carrier pigeons to communicate with the mainland. The motor launch had left for Elenovka about two hours earlier, and no matter how you strained your ears, not the least chirring sound could be heard across the water.

When the expedition headed by Comrade Karinian, equipped with a blanket, a bottle of cognac and so on, returned with Gambarian, whom they had picked up on a rock, stiff with cold but smiling, he was met with enormous applause. That was the most beautiful applause I have ever heard in my life: a man was being congratulated for not yet being a corpse.

At the fishing wharf in Noraduz, where we were taken on an excursion which, fortunately, managed to avoid choral singing, I was astonished by the hull of a newly completed barge hoisted up in its raw state in the drydock. In size it resembled a good Trojan horse, but its fresh musical proportions recalled a bandore box.

All around lay curly shavings. The salt was corroding the earth, and fish scales glimmered like little discs of quartz.

In the cooperative cafeteria, built of logs in the Mynheer-Peter-the-Great style like everything in Noraduz, we sat side by side to eat the thick artel cabbage soup cooked with mutton.

The workers, noting that we were without wine, filled our glasses as befits proper hosts.

In my heart I drank to the health of young Armenia with its houses of orange stone, to its pearly-toothed commissars, to its horse sweat and the stamping of people standing in lines, and to its mighty language which we are unworthy of speaking, but can only avoid in our feebleness. In Armenian "water" is *dzhur*; "village" is *g'iur*.

I will never forget Arnoldi. Although he was somewhat lame and walked with the aid of crutches, he moved so courageously that everyone envied his gait.

The island's academic authorities lived along the main road in Molokan[13] Elenovka, where the gendarme-like mugs of the giant trout preserved in formaldehyde showed blue in the semi-darkness of the academic Executive Committee.

And what guests they were!

An American yacht cutting through the water like a lancet, as speedily as a telegram, ferried them to Sevan. And Arnoldi stepped on shore like some terror of science, like some genial Tamerlane.

I had the distinct impression that a certain blacksmith lived on the island of Sevan who was constantly busy keeping him in shoes, and it was, in fact, to consult with him that he visited the island.

There is nothing more instructive or more satisfying than to immerse yourself in the society of people of a completely different race, whom you respect, with whom you sympathize, and of whom you are, however distant, proud.

The feeling for the fullness of life characteristic of the Armenian people, their coarse tenderness, their noble love of labor, their inexplicable aversion to anything metaphysical and their magnificent familiarity with the world of real things—all this kept repeating to me: now stay awake, don't fear your own age, don't be sly.

Wasn't this because I found myself among a people, renowned for their zealous labor, who nevertheless know who to live not according to the clock in some railway station or institution, but according to the sundial like the one I glimpsed among the ruins of Zvartnots in the form of an astronomer's wheel or of a rose inscribed in stone?

2. Ashot Ovanesian

The Institute of Oriental Peoples is located on the Bersenev Embankment right next door to the pyramidal structure of the Government House. Somewhat farther on a ferryman earned his keep collecting three kopeks a trip, even while allowing his overloaded boat to sink right up to its oarlocks.

The air on the Moscow River Embankment is viscid and gritty.

A bored young Armenian came out to greet me. Among the Japhetic books with their prickly script, I could also see, like a Russian cabbage butterfly in a library of cactuses, a blonde young lady. The arrival of an amateur brought no one any pleasure, and my request for help in learning the ancient Armenian language did not touch the heart of these people. Moreover, the young woman did not even possess this key of knowledge herself.[14]

As a result of my incorrect subjective orientation, I acquired the habit of looking upon every Armenian as a philologist... However, this is partly correct, for these people jangle the keys of their language even when they are not unlocking any treasures.

My conversation with the young graduate student from Tiflis did not go very well and ended on a note of diplomatic reserve.

The names of the most highly esteemed Armenian writers were brought up, Academician Marr was mentioned, as he had just dashed through Moscow on his way from the Udmurt or Vogul District to Leningrad, and the spirit of Japhetic thinking which penetrates the deep structure of every language was duly praised...

I was already getting bored and kept glancing at the bit of overgrown garden outside the window, when an elderly man with the manners of a despot and the bearing of an aristocrat walked into the library.

His Promethean head radiated a smoky ash-blue light like the most powerful quartz lamp... The blue-black locks of his wiry hair, fluffed out with a certain amount of self-satisfaction, contained something of the root strength of an enchanted feather.

The broad mouth of this sorcerer did not smile, firmly re-minding everyone that speech is work. Comrade Ovanesian's head had the capacity for distancing itself from his interlocutor, like a mountaintop that only accidentally resembled the shape of a head. But the blue quartz radiating from his eyes was worth anyone's smile.

"Head" in Armenian is *glukh'e* with a soft *l* and a short as-piration after the *kh*. It contains the same root as the Russian word for "head" *[golova, glava]*... But would you like a Japhetic novella? If you please: "To see," "to hear," "to understand"—all these meanings coalesced at once into a single semantic bundle. At the very deepest levels of language there were no concepts, just directions, fears and longings, needs and apprehensions. The con-cept of "head" was sculpted over a dozen millenia out of a bundle of foggy meanings, and its symbol became "deafness" *[glu-khota]*.[15]

But never mind, dear reader, you will confuse it all anyway, and it's not for me to teach you.

3. Zamoskvorechie[16]

Not long before that, as I was rummaging about under the staircase of the dusty rose house on the Yakimanka, I discovered a tattered book by Signac[17] defending Impressionism. The author explained the "law of optical blending," glorified the method of "pointillism," and suggested how meaningful using only the pure colors of the spectrum could be.

Signac based his arguments on citations from his idol, Eugène Delacroix.[18] Time and again he referred to his *Journey to Morocco*, as if leafing through a codex of visual training intended as obligatory reading for every thinking European.

Signac was trumpeting on his chivalric horn the last, ripe gathering of the Impressionists. He summoned all the Zouaves, the burnooses, and the red Algerian skirts into their bright camps.

At the very first sounds of this triumphant theory, my nerves grew taut. I felt a shiver of novelty, as if someone had summoned me by name...

I seemed to have exchanged my heavy, dust-laden urban footgear for a pair of light Moslem slippers.

I have been as blind as a silkworm all my life.

What is more, a certain lightness has invaded my life,[19] my normally arid and disorderly life, which I imagine to myself as a kind of ticklish anticipation of some never-fail lottery, out of which I might draw whatever I wish: a bar of strawberry soap, a chance to sit in the archives of the Firstprinter's Chambers,[20] or my long-desired journey to Armenia, of which I never cease dreaming...[21]

It must appear extremely impertinent to speak about the present with the reader in that tone of absolute courtesy which we have, for some reason, conceded to the memoirists.[22]

It seems to come from the impatience with which I live and change my skin.

A salamander does not even suspect the black and yellow spots on his back. The thought never dawned on it that these spots may form two chains or may fuse into a single continuous thread, depending on the dampness of the sand, or on whether the terrarium is papered in a cheerful or mournful pattern.

As for that thinking salamander—Man—capable of divining tomorrow's weather, if only he could determine his own coloration!

Some grim families of philistines lived next door to me.[23] God had denied them the least shred of affability, which, no matter how you look at it, provides life with some adornment. Sullenly, they had formed a kind of passionate consumer association, and they kept ripping off the days due them in their ration booklets, smiling, as if they had just pronounced the word "cheese."

Inside, their rooms were done up like craft shops, with various symbols of kinship, longevity, and domestic fidelity. White elephants predominated, of both the large and small variety, china renditions of dogs and seashells. These were no strangers to the cult of the dead, and even indicated a certain respect for those who were no longer among the living.[24] It seemed that these people with their fresh, cruel Slavic faces ate and slept in a photographer's chapel.

And I thanked my lucky stars that I was but an accidental guest in Zamoskvorechie and that I would not spend my best years there. Nowhere, never have I experienced so strongly the watermelon emptiness of Russia; the brick-colored sunsets over the Moscow River, the tile-colored tea, brought to mind the red dust of the blast-furnace on Mount Ararat.

How I longed to return to the place where people's skulls are equally beautiful, whether at work or in the grave.

We were surrounded by, heaven help us, such cheery little houses with such mean little souls and cowardly windows. Indeed, only about seventy years ago serf girls used to be sold here, docile young girls, quick to catch on, who had been taught to sew and to mend.

Two barren linden trees,[25] deaf with age, raised their brown forked trunks in the courtyard. Frightening in the rather bureaucratic corpulence of their girth, they heard and understood nothing. Time fed them with flashes of lightning and watered them with downpours; thunder, blunder, it was all the same to them.

Once a committee of adult males living in the house resolved to fell the oldest linden tree and chop it up for firewood.

They dug a deep trench around the tree. The axe began to attack the indifferent roots. Woodcutting demands certain skills. There were too many volunteers. They bustled about like the incompetent executors of some vile lynch mob.

I called to my wife: "Look, it's about to fall."

Meanwhile, however, the tree appeared to be putting up a kind of reasoned resistance: it seemed to have regained full consciousness. How it despised its assailants and the pike's teeth[26] of the saw.

Finally, they threw a noose of thin clothesline around the dry fork, around the very place from which flowed the tree's age, its lethargy, and its verdant beauty. Then they began to rock it gently back and forth. It became loose like a tooth in its gum, but all that time continued to reign in its false sense of security. One moment more, and the children ran up to the fallen idol.

That year the *Tsentrosoiuz*[27] administration appealed to Moscow University to recommend a man who could be sent to Erevan. They needed someone to supervise the production of cochineal, an insect of whom most people have never heard. A superb carmine dye is made from the cochineal once it is dried and pulverized.

The university appointed B.S.K.,[28] a well-educated young zoologist. B.S. lived with his aged mother on Bolshaia Yakimanka Street and belonged to the trade union. Out of a sense of pride he would snap to attention before anyone and everyone, and he singled out for special attention from the entire academic staff, old Sergeev, who had himself built and installed all the tall red cabinets in the zoology library and who, with his eyes closed, just by running his palm over a piece of finished wood, could unerringly tell whether it was oak, ash, or pine.

B.S. was hardly a bookworm. He studied science as the opportunity presented itself. He had somehow been involved with the salamanders of the famous Viennese professor (and suicide) Kammerer; and more than anything else on earth he loved the music of Bach, especially one invention for wind instruments which seemed to soar upwards like some Gothic fireworks.

B.S. was also very well-travelled in the USSR. In both Bukhara and Tashkent his field shirt had been sighted, and his infectious military laugh had resounded. He sowed friends everywhere. Not so long ago a certain mullah, a holy man, now buried on a mountaintop, sent him a formal death announcement in pure Farsi. In the mullah's opinion, that fine, erudite young man, after he had used up his supply of health and engendered a sufficient quantity of children—but not before!—should come and join him.

Hurrah for the living! All forms of work are estimable!

B.S. prepared rather reluctantly for his journey to Armenia.

He was perpetually running after buckets and sacks to collect the cochineal and complaining about the craftiness of bureaucrats who hindered his packing efforts.

Parting is the younger sister of death.[29] For those who respect the rationale of fate, there is a kind of malicious nuptial animation connected with the ritual of seeing someone off.

The front door was constantly banging as guests of both sexes kept arriving up the mousy Yakimanka staircase: students from Soviet schools of aviation, carefree skaters on air; colleagues from remote biological research stations; specialists in mountain lakes; people who had been in the Pamirs[30] and in Western China; as well as some ordinary young people.

The filling of wineglasses with Moscow wines began, accompanied by the sweet refusals of the women and girls, and tomato juice was splashed about like the generally aimless sounds of the voices: there was talk about flying, about performing loops in the air, when you fail to notice that you are upside down and the earth, like some huge brown ceiling, comes rushing at your head, about the high cost of living in Tashkent, about Uncle Sasha and his flu, about everything...

Someone told about the invalid with Addison's disease who lay sprawled below on the Yakimanka, who actually lived right there, drinking vodka, reading newspapers, playing dice, and who, at night, removed his wooden leg so he could use it for a pillow.

Someone else compared this Diogenes of the Yakimanka to a medieval Japanese woman, a third shouted out that Japan was a country of spies and cyclists.

The subject of the conversation kept merrily sliding about like a ring passed around the back, and the knight's move, always to the side, reigned over the table talk...

I don't know how it is with others, but for me a woman's charm increases if she is a youthful traveler, capable of spending five days on a scientific trip sleeping on the hard bench of the Tashkent train, is well versed in Linnaean Latin, knows which side she is on in the dispute between the Lamarckians and the epigeneticists, and is not indifferent to soy, cotton, or chicory.[31]

And there on the table lies an elegant syntax of confused, grammatically incorrect field flowers, their names printed in a variety of alphabets, as though all the pre-school forms of vegetative being were merging in a pliophonic anthology poem.

Stupid vanity and a sense of false pride held me back from berry-picking as a child, nor did I ever stoop over to pick mushrooms. I preferred the Gothic pine cones and hypocritical acorns in their Monk's caps to mushrooms. I would stroke the pine cones. They would bristle. They were beautiful. They were attempting to persuade me to do something. In the tenderness of their shells, in their geometric giddiness, I sensed the rudiments of architecture whose demon has accompanied me all my life.

And as for summer houses on the outskirts of Moscow, I hardly ever spent any time there. You can't count the automobile trips to Uzkoe along the Smolensk highway, past corpulent log huts, where the piles of cabbages waiting to be trucked to market resembled cannonballs with green fuses. Those pale green cabbage bombs, heaped up in shameless abundance, dimly reminded me of the pyramid of skulls in Vereshchagin's[32] dreary painting.

Things are different now, but the change may have come too late.

Just last year on the island of Sevan in Armenia, as I wandered through the tall, waist-high grasses, I was captivated by the shameless burning of the poppies. Bright to the point of surgical pain, like some kind of artificial cotillion badges, huge, too huge for our planet, fireproof, ravenous moths, they grew on disgusting hairy stalks.

I envied the children... They hunted zealously after poppy wings in the grass. I bent down once, twice... And there was fire in my hands, as if a blacksmith had lent me some coals.

Once in Abkhazia[33] I happened upon vast beds of northern wild strawberries.

At a height of several hundred feet above sea level, young forests clothed the entire hillside. Peasants were hoeing the sweet ruddy earth preparing beds for the hothouse-grown transplants.

How I rejoiced at the coral-red coins of the northern summer! Ripe ferruginous berries were hanging in triads and pentads, singing in chorus and in tune.

So, B.S., you'll be leaving first. Circumstances do not yet permit me to follow. I hope they'll change.

You'll be staying at 92 Spandarian Street, with those extremely kind people, the Ter-Oganians. Do you remember how nice it was? I'd come running "down Spandarian Street" to see you, swallowing the caustic construction dust for which new Erevan[34] is famous. I still found the ruggedness, roughness and solemnity of the Ararat valley pleasurable and novel, although it had been repaired right down to its wrinkles; and the city which appeared to have been upended by divinely inspired plumbers; and the broad-mouthed people with eyes drilled straight into their skulls—the Armenians.

Past the dry pump houses, past the conservatory, from whence you could hear a quartet being rehearsed in the basement and the angry voice of the professor shouting: "Lower, lower!", that is, play *decrescendo* in the *adagio*—all the way to your gateway.

But it wasn't a gate at all, it was a long cool tunnel cut into your grandfather's house, and at the end of it, as into a spy-glass, a little door covered with greenery glimmered, greenery so unseasonably dull it seemed to have been burnt with sulphuric acid.

Wherever you look, the eyes seem not to have enough leavening. You grasp forms and colors, and it's all *lavash*. Such is Armenia.

On the little balcony you showed me a Persian pen-holder covered with a lacquer painting, the color of blood baked with gold. It was offensively empty. I wanted to smell its venerable musty panels which had served Sardar justice and the invoking of instantaneous sentences to put out men's eyes.

Then you disappeared momentarily into the walnut dusk of the Ter-Oranian's apartment and returned with a test tube to show me the cochineal. Reddish-brown peas settled on a small piece of cotton.

You had taken that sample from the Tatar village of Sarvanlar, about twenty versts from Erevan. From there Father Ararat[35] is clearly visible, and in the arid frontier atmosphere you can't help feeling like a smuggler. Laughing, you told me about the extraordinary girl glutton, a member of a friendly Tatar family in Sarvanlar... Her cunning little face was always smeared with sour milk, and her fingers greasy with mutton fat... During dinner you, who are not at all fastidious, nevertheless quietly secreted for yourself a piece of *lavash*, because that little glutton was in the habit of resting her feet on the bread as on a footstool.

I liked to watch the accordion of Infidel wrinkles on your forehead as they came together and drew apart; it is undoubtedly the most inspired part of your physical appearance. Those wrinkles, seemingly polished by your lambskin hat, reacted to every significant phrase, and they roamed over your forehead, shaking, staggering and swaggering about. There was something about you of Boris Godunov, of the Tatar, my friend.

I used to compose similes for your character reference and plunged more deeply into your anti-Darwinian essence; I studied the living language of your long ungainly arms, created for a handshake in some moment of danger, and for heated protestations, as we went walking, against natural selection.

One of the minor characters in Goethe's[36] *Wilhelm Meister* is named Jarno; he is a skeptic and a naturalist. He hides for weeks on end in the *latifundium* of his model world, sleeping in tower rooms on cold sheets, and emerges from the castle depths only at dinnertime.

This Jarno was a member of a unique order, founded by the powerful landowner, Lothario, for the purpose of educating his contemporaries in the spirit of *Faust*, Part II. This secret society had an enormous network of secret agents extending all the way to America. Its network was organized along Jesuit lines. Secret records were maintained, its tentacles extended everywhere, people were forever being caught.

Jarno himself was sent to watch Wilhelm Meister.

Wilhelm was travelling with his little boy Felix, the son of the unfortunate Marianna. A paragraph in the organization's code pertaining to novitiates forbade living in the same place for more than three days. Rosy-cheeked Felix, a playful and pedantic child, would gather strange plants, break off bits of mineral rock, and strike up one-day acquaintanceships, all the while shouting *"Sag mir, Vater,"* hounding his father with questions.

Children in Goethe's books are generally very tiresome and well-behaved. If we trust Goethe's description, children are but little Cupids of curiosity, armed with quivers of well-aimed questions slung over their shoulders...

It was there in the mountains that Meister met up with Jarno.

Jarno literally snatched Meister's three-day itinerary and tickets out of his hands. Behind them and ahead of them lay years of separation. So much the better! All the more resonant the echo of the geologist's lecture in the forest university!

And that's why the warm light of oral instruction, the lucid didacticism of intimate conversation, is far superior to the instructive and homiletic function of books.

I gratefully recall one of our Erevan conversations which now, a year later, has already been aged by the confidence of personal experience and which now possesses that truth which helps us to form a better sense of ourselves in tradition.

We were discussing the "theory of the embryonic field," proposed by Professor Gurvich.[37]

The embryonic leaf of the nasturtium has the form of a halberd or of an elongated, bifurcated purse which grows into a little tongue. It also resembles some Paleolithic arrowhead. But the tension in the field of force ranging around the leaf at first transforms it into a segmented figure with five parts. The lines of the cave arrowhead take on the shape of an extended arc.

Take any point and join it with a bundle of coordinates to a straight line. Then extend these coordinates, intersecting the line at various angles, to a section of identical length, then join them together again, and there you have convexity!

But later the field of force sharply changes its function and drives the form to its geometrical limit, creating the polygon.

A plant is a sound extracted by the wand of a termenvox, which pulsates in a sphere oversaturated with wave processes. It is the envoy of a living storm permanently raging in the universe, akin in equal measure to stone and lightning! A plant in the world is an event, a happening, an arrow, hardly some boring, bearded "development"![38]

Not long ago, B.S., a certain writer[39] publicly repented for having been an ornamentalist, or for having endeavored with all his sinful strength to be one.

It seems to me that a place awaits him in the seventh ring of Dante's Hell, where the bleeding thornbush grew. When some day a tourist out of curiosity breaks a branch off that suicide, he shall implore him in a human voice, like Pier delle Vigne: "Don't touch! You're hurting me! Or have you no pity in your heart? We were once men, who are now trees..."

And a drop of black blood will fall...[40]

What Bach, what Mozart does variations on the theme of the nasturtium leaf? Finally, a phrase exploded: "the world's record speed for the bursting of a nasturtium pod."

Who has not envied chess players? A peculiar field of alienation can be sensed in the room which emits a chill inimical to non-participants.

However, these little Persian horses of fine ivory are immersed in a solution of power. The same thing happens to them as happens with the nasturtium of the Moscow biologist E.S. Smirnov and the embryonic field of Professor Gurvich.

The threat of displacement hangs over each chessman throughout the game, throughout the entire stormy course of the tournament. The chessboard puffs up from the attention concentrated on it. The chess figures grow like coral cap mushrooms in Indian summer when they fall under the ray of focus of particular maneuvers.

The problem is solved not on paper nor in the *camera-obscura* of causality, but in a vital Impressionistic milieu, in the temple of air, light, and glory established by Edouard Manet and Claude Monet.

Is it true that our blood radiates mitogenetic rays, which the Germans have captured on a phonograph record, rays which, as I was informed, help to intensify tissue cell division?

Without suspecting it, we are all carriers of an enormous embryological experiment: indeed, the very process of remembering, crowned with the victory of memory's effort, is astonishingly similar to the phenomenon of growth. In both instances, there is a sprout, an embryo, either some facial feature or character trait, a half-sound, a name ending, something labial or palatal, some sweet pea on the tongue, which does not develop out of itself, but only responds to an invitation, only stretches forth, justifying our expectation.[41]

With these belated reflections, B.S., I hope, at least in part, to repay you for having interrupted your chess game in Erevan.

4. Sukhum

I arrived in Sukhum[42] early in April. It is a city of mourning, tobacco, and aromatic vegetable oils. This is where one ought to begin studying the alphabets of the Caucasus, for here every word begins with "a."

The language of the Abkhazians is powerful and pleophonic, but it abounds in upper and lower guttural compound sounds which make pronunciation extremely difficult; you might say that this language was torn out of a larynx overgrown with hair.[43]

I am afraid that the good bear Baloo has not yet been born to teach me, as he taught the boy Mowgli in Rudyard Kipling's *Jungle Book*, the magnificent language of the jungle, although I predict that in the distant future there will be academies for the study of the Caucasian languages scattered about the globe. The phonetic ore of Europe and America is drying up. Its deposits are limited. Young people are already reading Pushkin in Esperanto. To each his own.

But what a sinister warning!

Sukhum is clearly visible from Mt. Cherniavsky, as it is known, from Ordzhonikidze Square. It is completely linear and flat; what is more, it sucks into itself, to the tune of Chopin's funeral march, a huge crescent of the sea, inhaling it through its colonialist health resort chest.

Sukhum is situated below like a compass in a case of draftsmen's instruments, which having just described the bay, sketched the eyebrow arcs of the hills, now lies, closed up, ensconced in the velvet.[44]

Although in the public life of Abkhazia there is much naive crudeness and many abuses, you cannot help being enchanted by the administrative and economic elegance of this small maritime republic, proud of its rich soil, its boxtree forests, its State Farm olive grove at New Athos, and the exceptional quality of its Tkvarchel coal.[45]

Rose thorns pierced your kerchief, the tame bear cub with the gray snout of some ancient Russian, of some Ivan-the-Fool in a dunce cap, squealed, and his squeal shattered the glass. Brand new automobiles kept rolling right up from the sea, their tires ripping across the eternally green mountain... The gray bast used for theatrical wigs was extracted from beneath the bark of the palm, while in the park the flowering agave plants, like candles weighing six poods, shot up almost two inches a day.

Ley uttered impassioned sermons about the dangers of smoking and reproved the gardener in a fatherly fashion. Once he asked me a profoundly astonishing question:

"What was the mood of the petty bourgeoisie in Kiev in 1919?"

I think his dream was to quote Karl Marx's *Kapital* in the cabin of Paul and Virginie.

On my twenty-verst[46] walks in the company of taciturn Latvians, I developed a feel for the local landscape.

Theme: a race to the sea of the gently sloping volcanic hills, united by a mountain chain—for the pedestrian.

Variation: the little green altitude key is passed from mountain peak to mountain peak, and each new slope locks up the hollow below.

We made our way down to the Germans, to the *dorf*, into the hollow where we were completely surrounded by barking sheepdogs.

I was a guest of Beria,[47] the president of the Society of the Friends of Caucasian Letters, and I all but brought him greetings from Tartarin de Tarascon and the gunsmith Costecalde.[48]

What a marvelous Provençal figure!

He complained of the difficulties connected with creating the Abkhazian alphabet, spoke with respect of the Petersburg theater director Evreinov[49] who was seduced by the Abkhazian goat cult, and lamented the inaccessibility of serious scientific research because of the remoteness of Tiflis.

The hard thud of billiard balls is as pleasant to men as the clicking of ivory knitting needles is to women. As the brigand-cue destroyed the pyramid, four epic heroes from Blücher's army, as alike as peas in a pod, on duty, but clearly with the seeds of laughter in their chest, exclaimed delightedly over the charm of the game.

And the older Party men did not lag behind them.

Looking down from the balcony with army binoculars, both the race track and the judge's stand on the swampy billiard-green parade ground were clearly visible. Once a year there are great horse races open to anyone who wishes to test his endurance.

A cavalcade of Biblical elders would accompany the boy victor.

Relatives scattered over miles of the ellipse extended wet cloths on long poles to the flushed horsemen as they galloped past.

In the distant swampy meadow a lighthouse rotated its beam like the Tate diamond.

And somehow I saw the dance of death, the nuptial dance of the phosphorescent insects. It seemed at first as if the tips of some barely perceptible roving cigarettes were puffing out little bits of light, but their flourishes were too venturesome, free and bold.

The Devil only knows where the wind carried them!

Upon closer inspection, I noticed some insane electrified ephemera winking, twitching, making fine tracings, and then devouring the black hackwork of the present moment.

Our heavy fleshly body decays in precisely the same way, and our activity will be transformed into the similarly alarming pandemonium if we do not leave behind us substantial proof of our existence.

It is frightening to live in a world consisting only of exclamations and interjections!

Bezymensky,[50] the strong man who lifts cardboard weights, a roundheaded, kindly and inkstained blacksmith, no, not a blacksmith but a bird vendor, no, not even a vendor of birds, but of the balloons of RAPP—Bezymensky was forever stooping, humming and butting people with his blue eyes.

An inexhaustible operatic repertory gurgled in his throat. His open-air-concert, mineral-water cheeriness never left him. A loafer with a mandolin in his soul, he lived on the string of a ballad, and his heart of hearts sung under the needle of a phonograph.[51]

5. Frenchmen

Then I stretched out my vision and dipped my eye into the sea's broad goblet, so that every mote and tear would rise to the surface.

I stretched my vision like a kid glove, stretched it on a board, out across the blue neighborhood of the sea...

Swiftly and rapaciously, and with feudal fury, I surveyed the domain of my purview.

That is how you dip the eye into a goblet brimful so that a mote will come out.

Only then did I begin to understand the obligatory force of color—the ecstasy of bright blue and orange sport shirts—and to realize that color is no more than the sense of the start of a race,[52] tinged by distance and circumscribed in its space.

Time circulated in the museum in keeping with the hourglass. The brick dust ran down as the goblet emptied itself, and then the same stream of golden simoom from the upper part of the bottle would now be on the bottom.

Hello, Cézanne![53] Dear old grandfather! A master worker. The best acorn of the French forests.

His painting was certified by the village notary on an oaken table. Cézanne is as permanent as a testament left by a man of sound mind and firm memory.

I was enchanted by the old man's still-life. Roses which must have been cut in the morning—firm and tightly rolled, extraordinary young tea roses. Exactly like little scoops of rich vanilla ice cream.

On the other hand, I took a dislike to Matisse,[54] the artist of the wealthy. The red paint of his canvasses fizzes like soda water. He has not experienced the joy of ripening fruits. His mighty brush does not heal the vision, but offers it the strength of an ox, so that your eyes become bloodshot.

I've had enough of his carpet chess and odalisques!

Persian whimsies of a Parisian *Maître*!

Van Gogh's[55] cheap vegetable pigments were purchased by accident for only twenty sous.

Van Gogh spits blood like a suicide in furnished rooms. The floorboards in the night cafe slope downwards and stream like

a gutter in their electric madness. The narrow trough of the billiard table resembles the trough of a coffin.

Never have I seen such barking colors!

And his railroad conductor's vegetable-garden landscapes!
The soot of suburban trains has just been wiped off with a wet rag.

Van Gogh's canvases, smeared with the omelette of catastrophe, are as clear as visual aids, as the charts in a Berlitz school.

Visitors move about taking tiny steps as though in church.[56]

Each room has its own climate. River air hovers over the
Claude Monet[57] room. Gazing at Renoir's[58] water you feel blisters
on your palm as if you had been rowing.

Signac[59] invented the corn sun.

A woman guide leads a group of cultural workers around the
pictures.

To look at them you might say a magnet was attracting a
duck.

Ozenfant[60] worked out something truly astonishing with the
use of red chalk and gray slate squirrels against a background of
black slate, and by modulating the forms of glass-blowing and
fragile laboratory equipment.

Moreover, Picasso's[61] dark-blue Jew bowed to you as did
Pisarro's[62] raspberry-gray boulevards, flowing like the wheels of an
enormous lottery with their little boxes of hansom cabs, fishing-
pole-whips over their shoulders, and the shreds of splashed brain
on kiosks and chestnut trees.

But isn't that enough?

Generalization stands in the doorway, already bored.

For all those recuperating from the benign plague of naive
realism, I would advise the following method of observing pictures[63] :

Don't go in, under any circumstances, as if entering a chapel.
Don't let yourself be overwhelmed, don't freeze, don't get glued
to the canvas...

Walk straight on, with the strides of a stroller along the
boulevard!

Cut through the large heat waves of oil painting space.

Calmly, not impetuously—the way Tatar children bathe their
horses in Alushta—dip your eye into the new material ambience,
however, always remember that the eye is a noble, but stubborn,

animal.

Standing before a picture to which the body heat of your vision has not yet adjusted, for which the crystalline lens has not yet found its proper accommodation, is like serenading in a fur coat behind storm windows.

Only when you have achieved the proper equilibrium, and only then, begin the second stage of restoring the picture, its cleaning, the removal of older coats of varnish, of the external and most recent barbaric layer. This is the stage which unites the picture with a sunny, solid reality.

With its extremely subtle acid reactions, the eye, an organ which possesses its own acoustics, intensifying the value of the image, exaggerating its own accomplishments to the point of offending the senses over which it makes a great fuss, raises the picture to its own level, for painting is much more a phenomenon of internal secretion than of apperception, that is, of external perception.

The material of painting is organized so that nobody loses anything, hence its distinction from nature. But the probability of a lottery is in inverse proportion to its feasibility.

And it is only now that the third and last stage of penetrating the picture begins—confronting the idea behind it.

Now the traveling eye presents its ambassadorial credentials to the consciousness. A cold treaty is then established between the viewer and the picture, something on the order of a state secret.

I left the embassy of painting and went out into the street.

Immediately after the Frenchmen, the sunlight appeared like a phase of some waning eclipse, while the sun itself seemed to be wrapped up in silver foil.

Near the entryway of the cooperative stood a mother with her son. The boy was tabetic and obedient. Both were in mourning. The woman was sticking a bunch of radishes into her reticule.

The end of the street, as if crushed by binoculars, bunched up in a squinting lump; and all of this, distant and distorted, was stuffed into a string bag.

6. On the Naturalists[64]

Lamarck[65] fought sword in hand for the honor of living nature. Do you think he was as easily reconciled to evolution as the scientific savages of the nineteenth century[66]? I think Lamarck was embarrassed for nature, and his sense of shame burnt his swarthy cheeks. He could not forgive nature for a trifle called the variability of species.

Forward! *Aux armes!* Let us cleanse ourselves of the dishonor of evolution.[67]

Reading the taxonomists (Linnaeus, Buffon, Pallas) has a marvelous effect on your disposition; it straightens out the eye and communicates to the soul a mineral quartz calm.[68]

Look at Russia as it is described by the remarkable naturalist Pallas[69]: peasant women distill the dye "mariona" from a mixture of birch leaves and alum[70]; the bark of linden peels off by itself to form bast, ready to be woven into slippers and baskets. The peasants use some thick oil for medicinal purposes. Chuvash girls[71] jingle trinkets in their long braids.

Whoever does not admire Haydn, Glück, and Mozart will never understand Pallas[72]!

Let us speak about the physiology of reading. It is a rich, inexhaustible, and seemingly forbidden theme. Of all the objects in the material world, of all the physical bodies, a book is the object which inspires man with the greatest degree of confidence. A book firmly established on a reader's desk is like a canvas stretched on its frame.[73]

When we are completely immersed in the activity of reading, we admire above all our generic attributes, above all we experience, as it were, the ecstasy of classifying ourselves in various ages and stages.[74]

But if Linnaeus, Buffon, and Pallas have colored my mature years, then I am indebted to a whale for having awakened in me my childish awe of science.[75]

In the zoological museum[76] you hear, "drip...drip...drip..," nothing to speak of in the way of empirical experience.

Oh, turn off that faucet!

Enough!

I have signed a truce with Darwin and placed him next to Dickens on my imaginary bookshelf. If they should dine together, the third member of their party would be Mister Pickwick.[77] You cannot help but be charmed by Darwin's geniality. He is an unintentional humorist. Situational humor comes naturally to him, it follows him everywhere.

But is geniality a method of creative cognition, a suitable means of gaining a sense of life[78]?

In Lamarck's reversed, descending movement down the ladder of living creatures resides the greatness of Dante.[79] The lower forms of organic existence are humanity's Inferno.

The long gray antennae of this butterfly had an aristate structure and resembled perfectly the little branches on a French academician's collar or the silver palm fronds on a coffin. Its powerful thorax is shaped like a small boat. Its unprepossessing head, like that of a kitten.

Its wings with enormous eyes were made of the exquisite silk of an Admiral who had been both at Cesme and at Trafalgar.

And suddenly I caught myself madly wishing to have a look at nature through the painted eyes of that monster.

Lamarck feels the rifts between classes. He hears the pauses and syncopes in the evolutionary line.[80]

Lamarck cried his eyes out over his magnifying glass.[81] He is the only Shakespearean figure in the natural sciences.

See how this blushing, semi-respectable old man races down the staircase of living creatures, like a young man just favored by a government minister or made happy by his mistress.

No one, not even an inveterate mechanist, views the growth of an organism as resulting from the variability of the external environment. That would be far too presumptuous a conclusion.[82] The environment merely invites the organism to grow. Its functions are expressed in a certain benevolence which is gradually and continually cancelled by the severity binding the living body together and rewarding it finally with death.

Thus, for the environment, the organism is probability, desire, and expectation, while for the organism, the environment is a force which invites: not so much a covering as a challenge.

When the conductor draws a theme out of the orchestra with

his baton, he is hardly the physical cause of that sound.[83] The sound is already present in the symphonic score, in the spontaneous collusion of the performers, in the throngs filling the auditorium, and in the structure of the musical intruments.

The beasts of the fables appear in Lamarck's work. They adapt themselves to the conditions of life. In the manner of La Fontaine. The legs of the heron, the neck of the duck[84] and the swan, the tongue of the anteater, the asymmetrical or symmetrical structure of the eyes in certain fish.

La Fontaine, if you will, prepared the way for Lamarck's teachings. His rational beasts, forever philosophizing and moralizing, provided magnificent living material for evolution. They had already apportioned its mandates among themselves.

Mammalian artiodactylic reason clothes the mammal's fingers with rounded horn.

The kangaroo moves forward in logical jumps.

This marsupial, according to Lamarck's description, consists of weak forelimbs (i.e., legs which have been reconciled to their own uselessness), of strongly developed hind legs (i.e., legs convinced of their significance), and of a powerful thesis known as the tail.

Children have already settled down to play at the pedestal of the evolutionary theory of Grandfather Krylov, that is to say, of Lamarck-La Fontaine. Having found refuge in the Luxembourg Gardens, Lamarck's theory became overgrown with balls and shuttlecocks.

How I love it when Lamarck allows himself to be angry, and smashes all his Swiss pedagogical boredom to smithereens. And the *Marseillaise* bursts into the concept of "nature"!

Male ruminants butt foreheads. They have not yet acquired horns.

But inner feelings, born of anger, direct "fluids" to the forehead, aiding the formation of the substance of horn and bone.

I tip my hat and let the teacher walk ahead of me. May the youthful thunder of his eloquence never be silent!

"Still" and "already" are the two shining points of Lamarckian thought, the spermatozoa of evolutionary glory and photogravure, the signalmen and pioneers of morphology.

He came from a breed of oldtime piano-tuners who strum

with their bony fingers on pianos in other peoples' mansions. He was permitted only the chromatic scale and juvenile arpeggios.

Napoleon allowed him to tune nature because he considered it the Emperor's property.

The influence of the county fair menagerie, and Linnaeus's dependence on it, is obvious in his zoological descriptions. The proprietor of the itinerant showbooth or the hired barker strove to show his merchandise at its best. In drumming up business, these showmen never dreamed that they would play a role in creating the style of classical natural science. They lied through their teeth—whatever came to mind on an empty stomach—yet at the same time they were captivated by their own art. Someone would intervene to save them, but they were also saved by their professional experience and the enduring tradition of their craft.

As a youngster in the small town of Uppsala, Linnaeus could not have failed to visit the fair and listen to the explanations of the itinerant menagerie.[85] Like boys everywhere, he swooned and melted under the power of the big fellow sporting jackboots and brandishing a whip, that doctor of fabulous zoology who sang paeans to the puma while waving his huge ruddy fists.

In associating the significant accomplishments of the Swedish naturalist with the garrulous eloquence of the sideshow, I have no intention of belittling Linnaeus. I only want to remind you that the naturalist is also a professional storyteller,[86] a public demonstrator of a new and interesting species.

The colorful portraits of the animals in Linnaeus's *Systema Naturae*[87] could easily hang next to pictures of the Seven Years' War or an oleograph of the Prodigal Son.

Linnaeus painted his monkeys in the tenderest colonial colors. Dipping his brush in Chinese lacquers, he would paint with brown and red pepper, with saffron, olive oil and cherry juice. He even managed his task deftly and gaily, like a barber shaving some bürgermeister, or a Dutch housewife grinding coffee on her lap in a big-bellied mill.

The Christopher Columbus brilliance of Linnaeus's monkey-house is simply delightful.

It is Adam handing out certificates of merit to the mammals, having invoked the aid of a wizard from Baghdad and a Chinese monk.

The Persian miniature regards you obliquely, with frightened, graceful almond eyes. Sinless and sensual, it convinces you that life is a precious inalienable gift.[88]

I love Moslem enamels and cameos!

Continuing my simile, I would say: a beautiful woman's impassioned, equine eyes fall obliquely but graciously on the reader. The charred cabbage stumps of manuscripts crunch like Sukhum tobacco.

How much blood has been spilled over these untouchables! How their conquerors have enjoyed them!

Leopards have the cunning ears of punished schoolboys.

The weeping willow, having curled itself into a ball, floats on.

Adam and Eve confer, dressed in the latest fashions of paradise.

The horizon is abolished. There is no perspective. Charming slow-wittedness prevails. The vixen's noble ascent up the staircase and the feeling that the gardener is inclined toward the landscape and the architecture.

Yesterday I was reading Firdusi[89] and I felt as if a bumblebee were sitting on the book sucking it.

In Persian poetry ambassadorial winds carry gifts out of China.

Persian poetry scoops up longevity with a silver ladle, endowing whoever wants it with millennia by threes and fives. That explains why the rulers of Djemdjid dynasty are long-lived, like parrots.

After having been good for an immeasurably long time, Firdusi's favorites suddenly, for no apparent reason, become wicked, simply out of obedience to their master's luxurious and arbitrary literary whimsy.

The earth and the sky in the book of *Shah-nama* are afflicted with goiter; they are delightfully goggle-eyed.

I got Firdusi from the State Librarian of Armenia, Mamikon Artemevich Gevorkian. I was given a whole pile of little blue volumes, eight, I think, in number. The words of the noble prose translation (the French edition of Von Mohl) gave off a fragrance of attar of roses.

Mamikon, chewing his drooping gubernatorial lip, sang me a few lines in Persian in his unpleasant, camel-like voice.

Gevorkian is eloquent, clever and courteous, but his erudition is far too sensational and insistent, while his speech reminds you of some fat lawyer.

Readers are forced to satisfy their curiosity right there in the director's office, under his personal supervision, and books which are placed on that satrap's table take on the taste of pink pheasant meat, bitter quails, musky venison and knavish hare.

7. Ashtarak[90]

I was lucky enough to observe the clouds performing their devotions to Ararat.

It was the ascending and descending motion of cream poured into a glass of ruddy tea, dispersing in various directions like curly-headed tubers.

The sky over the land of Ararat, however, brings little joy to the Lord of Sabaoth: it was invented by the blue titmouse in the spirit of the most ancient atheism.

Coachman's Mountain glittering in the snow, a small field sown with stone teeth, as if its intended purpose were mockery, the numbered barracks of construction sites, and a tin can brimming over with passengers—there you have the environs of Erevan.

And suddenly a violin, divided up into gardens and houses, and subdivided terraces, into a system of terraces with crossbars, partitions, poles and bridges, much like stone shelves.

The village of Ashtarak hung on the babbling of the waters as on a wire frame. The stone baskets which were its gardens would make the most magnificent gift for a coloratura at a benefit performance.

Lodgings for the night were found in a spacious four-bedroom house which had once belonged to some dispossessed kulaks. The administration of the local collective farm had let the furnishings be appropriated at will and had transformed the building into the village hotel. On a terrace capacious enough to have lodged all the seed of Abraham, a milkstand turned washstand stood grieving.

The orchard was a dancing class for trees. The schoolgirl timidity of the apple trees, the crimson talent of the cherries...

Just look at their quadrilles, their ritornellos and rondos.

I listened to the babbling of collective farm calculations. In the mountains there was a downpour, and the muddy streams in the gutters ran more swiftly than usual.

The waters resonated and welled up on all the floors and all the stone shelves of Ashtarak; it was wet enough for a camel to slip through a needle's eye.

I have received your eighteen-page letter, completely covered in your straight and tall hand, straight and tall as an avenue lined with poplars. Here is my answer:

My first sensual encounter with an ancient Armenian church.

The eye seeks form, an idea, and anticipates it, but it stumbles instead upon the moldy bread of nature or upon a stone pie.

The teeth of vision crumble and break up when you encounter Armenian churches for the first time.

The Armenian language cannot be worn down; its boots are of stone. Naturally, its word is thickwalled, its semivowels layered with air. But is that all there is to its charm? No! Then, whence its attraction? How can you explain it? Understand it?

I experienced such joy in pronouncing sounds forbidden to Russian lips, mysterious sounds, outcast sounds, and perhaps, on some deep level, even shameful sounds.[91]

There was some magnificent boiling water in a pewter teapot, and suddenly a pinch of marvelous black tea was tossed into it.

That's how I felt about the Armenian language.

I have cultivated a sixth sense[92] in myself, an "Ararat" sense; I can feel the mountain's gravitational pull.

Now, no matter where fate may lead me, it already has a speculative existence, and will accompany me forever.[93]

The little church in Ashtarak is of the most ordinary kind and, for Armenia, is rather meek. It is one of those little churches in a six-sided headdress with a rope ornament along its roof ledges and similar stringy eyebrows above the narrow lips of its chink-like windows.

Its door is quiet as a dormouse. I stood on my tiptoes and peered inside; I saw a cupola in there, a cupola[94]!

A real one! Like the one in Rome, in St. Peter's, under which thousands thronged, along with the palms, and a sea of candles, and the Pope's sedan chair.

There the recessed spheres of the apses sing like seashells.

There are the four bakers, north, south, east and west, who, with their eyes plucked out, stumble about in funnel-shaped niches, fumbling about the hearths and spaces between, incapable of finding themselves a place.

Whose idea was it to imprison space in this wretched cellar, this nasty dungeon, so as to render homage to it worthy of the psalmist David?

The miller, whenever he can't get to sleep, goes out bare-headed to inspect his millstones. Sometimes when I wake up at night, I review the conjugations in Marr's[95] grammar.

The teacher Ashot is immured in his flat-walled house, like one of *les misérables* in Victor Hugo's novel.

Tapping his finger on the case of his captain's barometer, he would go out into the courtyard and over to the well. Then on some graph paper, he would plot the curve of precipitation.

Since he cultivated a small garden, a tenth of a hectare, a tiny orchard baked in the stone-grape pie of Ashtarak, he was excluded from the collective farm as an extra mouth to feed.[96]

In a hollow recess in his bureau, he stored a university diploma, his high school certificate, and a limp paper case of watercolor sketches—innocent mark of his character and talent.

The imperfective past rumbled within him.

A toiler in a black shirt, theatrically open at the neck, with a heavy fire in his eyes, he retreated into the perspective of historical painting, back to the Scots martyrs, to the time of the Stuarts.

The tragic tale of the semi-educated has yet to be written. I think the biography of this rural schoolteacher may yet become the handbook for our day as *The Sorrows of Young Werther* once was.[97]

Ashtarak is a rich and comfortably nestled settlement, far older than many European cities. It was famous for its harvest festivals and for the songs of the Ashugs. People raised near vineyards are fond of women, sociable, and skeptical, with a tendency toward touchiness and idleness. The people of Ashtarak are no exception.

Three apples fell from the skies: the first for the one who told the tale, the second for the one who listened, and the third for the one who understood. Such is the ending of most Armenian fairytales. Many of them were written down in Ashtarak. This region is the granary of Armenian folklore.

8. Alagez[98]

What tense would you choose to live in?

"I want to live in the imperative of the future passive participle—in the 'what ought to be.'"

I like to breathe that way. That's what I like. It suggests a kind of mounted, bandit-like, equestrian honor. That's why I like the glorious Latin "Gerundive"—it's a verb on horseback.[99]

Yes, the Latin genius, when it was young and greedy, created that form of the imperative verbal traction as the prototype of our entire culture,[100] and not only "that which ought to be" but "that which ought to be praised"—*laudatura est*—that which pleases us...

I carried on the above dialogue with myself as I rode horseback through the natural boundaries, the nomadic territories, and the vast pasturelands of Alagez.

In Erevan, Alagez stuck up before my eyes like "hello" or "goodbye." I saw how its snow-covered crown melted from day to day and how, especially in good weather, in the mornings, its tinted slopes crunched like dry toast.

And I was drawn towards it, over the mulberry trees and the earthen roofs of the houses.

A piece of Alagez lived right there with me in the hotel. On my windowsill, for some reason, lay a heavy specimen of the black volcanic glass-like rock known as "obsidian." A ponderous calling card left behind by some geological expedition.

The approaches to Alagez are not fatiguing, and it is no trouble at all to reach the top on horseback, despite its 14,000 feet. The lava is contained in earthen blisters, along which you can easily ride.

From the fifth floor window of my Erevan hotel room, I formed a totally mistaken picture of Alagez. I saw it as some monolithic ridge. In actual fact, it is a folded system which gradually opens up, proportionately to the rise, the accordion of diorite rock untwists itself like an Alpine waltz.

And what a capacious day fell to my lot!

Even now, when I think back on it, my heart throbs. I got tangled up in it as in a long robe pulled out of one of the trunks of my ancestor Jacob.

The village of Biurakan is famous for its baby chick hunt. Like little yellow balls, they rolled about the floor, doomed victims of our cannibal appetites.

We were joined in the school by an itinerant carpenter, skilled and worldly-wise. Having downed a few cognacs, he told us he had no use for either artels or trade unions. Wherever he went, he said, his golden hands were recognized, he was offered work and greatly respected. Customers were never a problem, even without a labor exchange—he could sniff them out, he always knew where he was needed.

He turned out to be a Czech by birth and looked the spit and image of the Pied Piper of Hamlin.

In Biurakan I purchased a large clay salt-cellar which was to give me inordinate trouble later on.

Try to imagine a coarse Easter cake mold made to resemble a woman in a farthingale or *robe ronde*, and, peering up out of the very middle of her gown a feline head with a large rounded mouth into which an open hand, its five fingers outspread, could easily reach.

My lucky find was merely part of a rich collection of such objects. But the symbolic force invested in it by some primitive imagination did not escape even the casual attention of the towns-folk.

Everywhere we saw peasant women with tearful faces, shuffling feet, reddened eyelids and chapped lips. Their movements were as graceless as if they had the dropsy or sprained ankles. Like hills of tired rags, they stirred up the dust with their hems.[101]

Gathering in clusters in the corners of their eyes, flies eat the children.

The smile of an elderly Armenian peasant woman is inexplicably beautiful—it contains so much nobility, exhausted dignity, and a kind of solemn, married charm.

Horses walk along divans, stepping on pillows and trampling bolsters. You ride along feeling as if you have an invitation from Tamerlane in your pocket.[102]

I saw the tomb of a giant Kurd of fabulous dimensions and accepted it as quite normal.

The lead horse minted rubles with her hooves, and her generosity knew no bounds.

An unplucked chicken killed that morning in Biurakan dangled from the pommel of my saddle.

From time to time my horse would bend down to munch the grass, and its neck expressed its allegiance to the Stubborns, a people older than the Romans.

A milky calm ensued. The whey of silence curdled. The little curd bells and the cranberry bells of various calibers muttered and clanged. Around each watering place you could hear sounds of a karakul meeting. It seemed as if dozens of small circus owners had pitched their tents and show booths on the lice-ridden heights and, unprepared for a full house, taken completely unawares, they now swarmed about in their camps, rattling their milk bowls, cramming lambs into their sheds, and racing to lock up for the night in their ox-realm, each to his own allotted stall in bark-town, all the tired, steamy and damp herds of cattle.

Armenian and Kurdish camps do not differ in their layout. They are settlements of cattle-breeders established on the terraces of Alagez, nomadic camps laid out in well-selected spots.

Stone markers indicate the floor plan of the tent and the small adjoining yard with its wall molded out of dung. Abandoned or unoccupied camps resemble burned-out sites.

Our guides from Biurakan were glad to spend the night at Kamarlu for they had relatives there.

A childless old couple welcomed us for the night into the bosom of their tent.

The old woman moved about and worked with lachrymose, retiring and blessing motions as she prepared a smoky supper and the felt bedding:

"Here, take this felt! Here, take a blanket...and tell us something about Moscow."

Our hosts prepared for bed. An oil wick lit up the tent, giving it the height of a railroad station. The wife took out a coarse army nightshirt and dressed her husband in it.

I felt as shy as if I were in a palace.

1. The body of King Arshak[103] is unwashed and his beard is wild.

2. The King's fingernails are broken, and wood lice crawl over his face.

3. His ears have grown deaf from the silence, but they once appreciated Greek music.

4. His tongue is covered with scabs from the jailers' food, but once there was a time when it would press grapes against his palate and was as adroit as the tip of a flutist's tongue.

5. The seed of Arshak withered away in his scrotum and his voice grew as feeble as the bleating of a lamb...

6. King Shapukh, so thinks Arshak, took advantage of me and, what is more, usurped the very air that I breathed for himself.

7. The Assyrian grips my heart.

8. He controls my hair and my fingernails. He grows my beard and swallows my saliva, so accustomed is he to the thought that I am here in the fortress of Anyush.

9. The Kushan people rose up in revolt against Shapukh.

10. They burst the frontier at some undefended place, like a silk thread.

11. The Kushan attack stung King Shapukh and caused him pain, like an eyelash in his eye.

12. Both sides (enemies) squinted so as not to see each other.

13. A certain Darmastat, the kindest and most educated of the King's eunuchs, finding himself in the very center of Shapukh's army, encouraged the Cavalry commander, wormed his way into his master's favor, and led him like a chessman to safety, all the while keeping himself in the public eye.

14. He had been governor of the province of Andekh in the days when Arshak gave velvet-throated orders.

15. A King yesterday, a fallen man today, he has adopted a crouched fetal position; he now warms himself with lice, and finds his greatest pleasure in scratching.

16. When it came time to claim his reward, Darmastat plied

the Assyrian's sharp ears with a request as ticklish as a feather:

17. Give me a pass to the fortress of Anyush. I would like Arshak to spend one more day in full possession of his senses— hearing, tasting, and smelling—as he was once, when he found his greatest pleasure in hunting and planting trees.

Sleep is easy in nomad camps. The body, exhausted by space, grows warm, stretches itself out, and recalls the length of the journey. The paths of mountain ridges run like shivers along the spine. Velvet meadows burden and tickle the eyelids. Bedsores of the ravines hollow out the sides. Sleep immures you, walls you in. Last thought: I must ride around some other ridge.

1. Sevan

Life on any island, be it Malta, St. Helena or Madeira, flows on in noble anticipation...[1] The helix of the ear is more delicately formed and takes on new whorls [in conversations we discover greater leniency and tolerance toward other opinions, everyone being devoted to the Maltese Order of tedium, scrutinizing each other with that inane politeness typical of the opening night of an exhibition.

Even books are passed from hand to hand more cautiously than a glass thermometer at a summer cottage...]

[Notwithstanding, the terrain is laid bare]

But in the evening you can see how automobile headlights devouring the highway paved with Roman fortitude dance in zigzag patterns with the lights of St. Elm.

A. Kh., a local schoolteacher on the island of Sevan, volunteered to teach me the Armenian language. Her seven-year-old daughter cut out a paper doll of the underfed lioness: tough-looking arms and legs were added to the dress used as the doll's base and after a moment's hesitation, a rigid head was also affixed.

A. was animated by her hatred of White Guards, her suspicion of Dashnaks,[2] and by pure Soviet rage. Bold and quick as a Red Army soldier, she had left her Komsomol husband, a rather poor comrade. Alone, she had raised two bandit-sons, Ragin and Khagin, who were forever raising their fists against her.

He was the Armenian model of *Les Misérables*. An already middle-aged man who, having obtained a military education in the medical corps in St. Petersburg, grew intimidated at the sounds of his wife's hoarse voice...the voice of his homeland. Deafened by the sounds of her guttural coughing, of her most holy cities, he was perpetually frightened by the sight of pregnancy, by large feminine eyes, and by the leonine pressure of lines of women waiting for bread, for grapes, or at the water-supply.

Who was he? A born widower whose wife was still among the living, whose strong and powerful hand had long ago stripped him of his collar and tie.

Something in his character recalled a man taken unawares by the visit of his boss or some relative, just as he was about to wash his socks under a cold water spigot...

It always seemed as if his wife were saying: "You're no husband, you're a widower..." So did he exemplify pure-blooded masculine perplexity. His own neck tormented him. Where others wore collars and ties, he had an empty space for shame. He was a man burdened by the consciousness of his own guilt before his wife and children...

He exhausted everyone he met with his desperate, thoroughly ingratiating frankness, a frankness which we Russians express only on night trains.

Choral singing—the scourge of Soviet rest homes is completely absent from Sevan. The ancient Armenian people are sickened by secular singing whose pseudo-epic sweep is bottled and labeled by the state.

2. Moscow

No one sent me to Armenia, as, let's say, Count Paskevich sent Griboedov's German and Shopen,[3] the most enlightened of bureaucrats (see his *Camera Description of Armenia*, a work which won the praise of Goethe himself).

Having wangled some official papers, which in good conscience I could not regard as anything but forged documents, I set off for Erevan in May of 1930, my straw basket under my arm,[4] [set off for a foreign country prepared to visually probe its cities and graves, to collect the sounds of its speech, and to inhale its most noble and intransigent historical spirit].

I encountered the firm will and hand of the Bolshevik party absolutely everywhere I went. Socialist construction was becoming something of a second nature to Armenia.

But my eye [used to falling for anything out of the ordinary, for anything fleeting or ephemeral] picked up in my journey only the shimmering tremor of [chance], the cultivated ornament of [reality]...

Can I really compare myself to some spoiled child turning a pocket mirror in his hands to guide the sunbeams, urging them to follow wherever he goes?

But readers cannot be fed on mere trifles! They eventually grow angry and send you to the devil! And yet you can satisfy them to a certain extent with the wooden balls of our best quality skittles.

In my opinion even the silkworm's empty cocoon is superior to wooden balls... [Let's try to feel how objects are more than mere skittles!] Draw your own conclusions.

I received my first Armenian lesson from a girl named Margot Vartanian. Her father was an important foreign Armenian...and, as it also turned out, a consul for foreign sympathizers of the Soviet government expressing the nationalistic sympathies of their bourgeois circles. He was made a Commissar in Echmiadzin in the early days of Sovietization. According to Margot, the last Catholicos[5] lived solely on chickens. Margot discussed the priesthood, wealth, and the government with the naive horror of a pensioner.

In the Vartanians' model apartment, rose petal sherbet and the electric teakettle were closely associated with Komsomol studies. Even poor Margot's tuberculosis, uncured in Switzerland, was [cultivated in Armenia like a precious hothouse plant] restrained by the dust of Erevan's streets: "You must not die at home!"

Margot was a Pioneer leader, and she had mastered the argot of street fights and grub [studied after she had mastered Italian].

Frequenting the Vartanian home, I invariably ran into a friend of Margot's father, the proud owner of such a markedly Hapsburgian profile that I wanted to ask him how the Holy Inquisition was going.

Generally speaking, I learned nothing from my ancient Komsomol queen. Margot not only lacked proper pedagogical skills, but quite obviously had no feel for the mysterious and sacred charm [beauty] of her native language.

The lessons, agreed to hastily out of politeness, lasted no longer than half an hour. The heat exhausted us. The hotel staff rushed through the corridors roaring like orangutans. I remember one sentence we were composing: "A man and his wife came to the hotel."

Feminine lips, beautiful in gossip and idle chatter, cannot formulate a genuine concept.

This was the peak of my Armenian studies. And now, back in Moscow, in the spring,[6] a year after my return from Erevan—[a sorrowful], mute period in my life—I must record my impressions, through the prism of that year.

Moscow has grown kinder: the city is full of marvels, details, divisions, with multiple and complex vision, like the structure of [the eye of a house fly] a fly's eye.

What do we see? In the morning—a piece of strawberry soap, in the afternoon...

In January my fortieth birthday struck. I have entered the age of the rib and the devil.[7] The perpetual quest after shelter and the insatiable hunger for thought.

A.N., having looked me over with the mournful, fleshy face of an embassy clerk tormented by his orders, having mustered all his unctuous innocence and all the overseas persuasiveness of the Muscovite   intonation—a Muscovite living in India—having donned his raven-black beard...

I am living poorly now. I am living without perfecting myself; rather, I am squeezing out of myself some last bits of residue, some remnants.

This fortuitous sentence just burst out of me one evening after a dreadfully incoherent day in lieu of my so-called "creative work."

For Nadya.[8]

What is more, a certain lightness has invaded my life, my normally arid and disorderly life, which I imagine to myself as a kind of ticklish anticipation of some never-fail lottery, out of which I might draw whatever I wish: a bar of strawberry soap, a chance to sit in the archive of the Firstprinter's chambers, or my long-desired journey to Armenia, of which I never cease dreaming.[9]

The proprietor of my temporary apartment, a young lawyer with curly blond hair, would burst in of an evening, grab his rubber raincoat off the hanger, and that same night fly off on a "Junker" sometimes to Kharkov, sometimes to Rostov.

His unstamped correspondence would pile up for weeks on the unwashed windowsills and tables.

The bed of this perpetually absent man was covered with a Ukrainian rug held up with pins.

When he returned he would merely shake his blond curly head; he would never say anything about his flight.

[My neighbors in our communal apartment were working people, by nature rather hardened. The men washed at the spigot in their net undershirts. The women tightly primed the primus stove, and all of them checked on each other's strict observation of the code of communal living.] God had denied these people the least shred of affability which, no matter how you look at it, provides life with some adornment...

These people could hardly have been worthy repositories of labor, of that energy which is the salvation of our country...

...They were not strangers to the cult of the dead, and even indicated a certain respect for those who were in absentia. [We are reminded of both.] Porcupines, hair parted down the middle, high temples, cabbage hairdos and beards...

Chickens hung upended over the courtyard like question marks. Flowers stood exchanging lights like old acquaintances. Between the flowerbeds lay the inviolable air, the sacred possession of a small housing cooperative. Our courtyard was a thoroughfare. A favorite of postmen and garbagemen. I was constantly plagued by the mysteries of the stables and sheds, and by two aged and barren linden trees, subsisting for so long on brown pensions, their crowns having long since ceased to rustle.

Old age had struck them with lightning like an executioner.

The day of departure was approaching. K[uzin][10] purchased a devilishly expensive suitcase and ordered a reserved seat via pistachio green Tiflis...

I will never forget the scene of that family feast at K's: the gifts of Moscow's gourmet counters on tables drawn together for the occasion, salmon of a pale rose hue, like the face of a frightened young bride (one of the guests compared its jeweled fat to the fat of a seagull), caviar grains as black as the oil used by the printer's devil—if such exists.

Parting is the younger sister of death. For those who respect the rationale of fate, there is a kind of malicious nuptial animation connected with the ritual of seeing someone off. And, one might include birthday parties... I approached old Madame K[uzin]'s apartment as silently as a moth, and uttered a few flattering words about her son. The happiness and youth of her guests almost frightened her... Everyone tried very hard not to upset her.

Brown-tiled Moscow night... Lindens fragrant with the scent of cheap perfume.

The calico-colored luxury of field flowers stared out of washbasins and pitchers. The heart rejoiced in their genuine democratic charm... How many times people had bent over them with happy expressions on their faces, how much time had they passed in those pitchers—bluebells, pinks, snapdragons.

Flowers are a great nation and thoroughly literate. Their [excited] language consists only of proper names and dialects.

3. Sukhum

The six weeks allotted for my visit to Sukhum I viewed as a portal through which I must pass, indeed, as a kind of quarantine preceding my summons into Armenia. The Commandant of the city, who went by the name of Sabua, was a gracefully built Abkhazian with the legs of a dancer and the ruddy complexion of a painted tin soldier; he assigned me a sunny attic room in the Ordzhonikidze House [which stands like a mountain upon a mountain born aloft as if on a silver salver of sliced mountain; and so it floats on the sea along with its salver].

Swiftly and greedily, with the ferocity of a feudal lord, I surveyed my domain as far as the eye could see: and in addition to the sea, I could make out every quarter of Sukhum from the show booth at the circus, and the barracks...

Isn't it because my recollection of places where we have been is so distinct that...

It was in Sukhum in April, that I received the news of Mayakovsky's death, which overwhelmed me like a great ocean. My spine spurts blood like a mountain waterfall, inhibiting my breathing and leaving a salt taste in my mouth.

For three weeks I sat at a table opposite B[ezymensky] and [never guessed what we could talk about].

Then suddenly, running into me one day on the stairs, he informed me of Mayakovsky's death. Man is built like a lightning rod. We must ground ourselves in order to bear such news. And the news, having rolled down upon me in the form of B[ezymensky], then rolled away somewhere below the steps.

B[ezymensky] invented an interesting means of communicating with people with the aid of a detachable phonograph record adapted to his mood.

Pouring himself a glass of Borzhomi mineral water, he would purr something from *Traviata*. Then suddenly an aria from *Rigoletto*. Then Chaliapin's "flea" would burst forth laughing...

What is more, "Growth" is a predator, not a reformer. It is a folklore fool, weeping at weddings and laughing at funerals—you can lead a horse to water, but you cannot make him drink. It is not for nothing that we are most tactless at the age when our voices are cracking.

Critics of Mayakovsky express the same attitude toward him as the old woman who cured the Hellenes of inguinal hernias, expressed toward Hercules...

In his *best* poems you can hear how cranial joints are sewn together, how the mouth gains power [and sensual bitterness] and [how the frontal sinuses take in air, how the aortas wear out] and how blood comes to reign over the salt of the sea.

The society which gathered in Sukhum accepted the news of our unique poet's death with disgraceful equanimity. [After all, he was no Chaliapin nor even Kachalov!] The very same evening they danced Cossack dances and crowded around the piano, singing rowdy student songs.

As is always the case on a journey [en route], a man caught my attention, he simply caught my fancy, or whatever...

I am referring to the collector of Abkhazian folk songs, M. Kovach. A Jew by birth and an unlikely mountain dweller, or a Caucasian, he whittled down his waist, sharpened himself like a pencil, to somehow resemble a Caucasian cutthroat.

His eyes mesmerized you in their nakedness, with their furious glitter, they were somewhat colored, yellowish...

His approach alone caused sharp kitchen knives to be transformed into hunting knives.

[For him the world was divided into two halves: Abkhazians and women. Everything else was immaterial and of no consequence. He was given short-legged peasant horses... What an important person... If only he had a saddle. Look: he's already attached to the horse, he's embraced it by the haunches—what a man he was...]

It is astonishing how Abkhazian songs convey a sense of being in the saddle.[11] Here the mountain peak is well worn by horses' hooves; a choral note resounds, endless like the road winding into the mountain and down under the mountain, turning and straightening itself out—that long drawn-out wordless "a-a-a" of a tuning fork! And having sat down on this flat, repeatedly hoof-worn sound, much like dropping into the saddle, the mountain peak set the tune, now drawing forth some naughty ditty, now some doleful soldier's melody...

The songs which Kovach published have extraordinarily simple arrangements. I remember one of them: a musical jest or mockery. Like all the others, it was composed on a particular occasion. An old man in Ochemchirakh began to annoy the assembled group: he kept talking and talking and found he could not stop.

Kovach himself, that ethnographer and mountain-dweller, played it for me on the piano with his [extraordinary] insolent fingers.

[In Sukhum I was transfixed by the ancient rite of the

funeral lament. In the evening I took a walk...]

The Georgian Anatoly Kakavadze produced quite a different impression on me. He was the curator of the Tiflis National Museum and was staying at the same blissful rose-covered summer cottage as I. His lips were sewn closed with silk thread, and after each word he uttered, he seemed to sew them up again...

By the way, never explain to a man the symbolic essence of his physical appearance. Even your best friend will never forgive such tactlessness.

Kakavadze and I—he was the most outstanding radio expert in his native land—went to the Club of Subtropical Agriculture to catch [the Mediterranean] Milan wave on his six-tubed receiver.

He drove some reckless amateur away from the apparatus, one of those who swarm about in the homespun linen of the airwaves: he donned some earphones with a monkish hoop, and immediately probed about to find something to his taste.

[But his taste was as bitter as bitter almonds. Once he even admitted: "Beethoven is too sweet for me," and then stopped short...]

The fate of our contemporaries is astonishing! —The fate of your sons and your stepsons, oh, U.S.S.R.

Man is being exploited like a theme and variations, he is being caught on the wavelengths.

Thus, Engineer Kakavadze originally took the oath of electrical engineering: somewhat later on he worked at unraveling a network of lies in RKI[12]; and today he stands guard over a Georgian fresco with its, may God preserve me, enormous malarial eyes.

Afterwards, significantly later, I [got to know] guessed Kakavadze's spiritual formula.

It seemed that [somewhere and at some time] he had had an entire lemon grove squeezed out of him. Jaundice and malaria dragged after him. Even in his dreams he calculated his own personal fatigue. He struggled against it, however, and his health returned [as soon as people asked him about something interesting]. His fatigue was but a secret form of energy.

He had the sleepy expression of a mathematician who produced from memory, without a blackboard, multinomial...

Eyelids with styes...

In the reception room of the Council of People's Commissars[13] I saw peasants come to lodge complaints. These old men were tobacco growers wearing black homespun woolens just like those worn by French peasants, grape-growers.

Nestor Lakoba,[14] the head of the government, had the movements of a hunter shooting his bow and arrow... It was he who [brought a bearcub in an automobile] received a bearcub as a gift from a peasant orator at a meeting in Tkvarchel. Deaf Lakoba's eartrumpet was taken as a symbol of authority.

[He kills boars and brings their magnificent...]

The Abkhazians came to Marxism [bypassing the Christianity of Smyrna, bypassing Islam] not via Smyrna, nor having sharpened their sabres, but directly from paganism. They have no historical perspective, thus for them Lenin comes first, before Adam. They constitute but a handful in all—a mere 200,000 people.

Glory be to the cunning linguistic freshness and rustling huntsman's language—glory be!

4. Frenchmen

An artist is by nature a doctor, a healer.[15] But if he does not cure anybody, who needs him?

Such a determinate quality of light, such delicious boldness of colors are found only at the races [in which you[16] personally have shown such a deep interest...]

Each little courtyard twitching in the rays of the chiaroscuro was being sold on the sly.

Visitors move about taking tiny steps as in church.

[A Moscow beauty with deep brown eyes, wearing a short dress the color of indigo, sits in the corner on a divan looking at a Monet.] Each room has its own climate. [Each one differs so much from the others that the eye, crossing from Gauguin to Cézanne, can catch cold. Yet who knows what may blow in from the painter's drafts.]

River air hovers over the Claude Monet [and Renoir] rooms. [You enter into the picture along the narrow underwater steps of a bathhouse. The temperature is 16° Réaumur... Don't look back, or amber blisters will arise on the palms of your hands, like on the hands of a pampered oarsman who takes his boat against the current, a boat full of laughter and muslin.]

Move back! The eye demands a bath. It is keen on it. It is a swimmer. Let the fresh colors of the Île de France once more bring it joy...

The Venetians laughed when Marco Polo told them that in China people used paper money. For such money you can purchase whatever you wish in your dreams. Gold will not adhere to silken paper.

Something hissed in the shadows, but no one heard it. The lindens were standing with finely chopped ruble foliage.

...As a rule this broad street saturated with aristocratic labor was always giving off the same impulse [pellet waves of the faintly blue canvases outstripped by chintz shadows;] idle pediments shivered like canvas, and streamed with light.

Claude Monet continued on, there was no escaping him.

...Luxurious thick lilacs of the Île-de-France, their tiny stars flattened into a porous, lime-like sponge, formed a menacing mass of petals; wondrous bee lilacs which exclude [all feelings from universal citizenship] everything on earth except the bumblebee of slumbering perceptions, burned on the wall like the burning bush[17] [and were more sensual, more crafty and more dangerous than impassioned women], more complicated and sensual than women.

5. On the Naturalists[18]

Since that time when my friends—no, that's too strong, I should say, "acquaintances,"—lured me into their circle of natural scientists,[19] a broad green glade arose before my eyes. A new door opened before me into a bright and active field.

We approached the mysteries of organic life. Indeed, the most difficult thing for an adult is making the transition from inorganic thinking (the mode in which we have been trained during the most active period of our lives, when thought is but an adjunct to action) to organic thinking.

That task is resolved in iridescent carefree space in an Impressionistic milieu [where artists at the mercy of the air layered one color on top of another].

The most peaceful monument I have ever seen stands at the Nikita Gates,[20] swaddled in granular granite. The figure of a thinker condemned to life.

Lamarck feels the *rifts* between classes. [These are the gaps in the evolutionary line. Empty spaces gape up at us.] He hears the pauses and syncopes in the evolutionary line. He foretells the truth, and chokes on the absence of supporting evidence. (Hence, the legend about his fear of the concrete.) [Lamarck] was above all a legislator. He speaks like the French National Convention. He combines in himself both Saint-Just and Robespierre. He does not so much prove what nature is, as decree it.
[In Lamarck's reverse, descending movement down the ladder of living creatures resides the greatness of Dante. The lower forms of organic existence are humanity's Inferno.]

Lamarck cried his eyes out over his magnifying glass. His blindness is equal to Beethoven's deafness.
The [wise] beasts of the fables recur in Lamarck's work. They adapt themselves to the conditions of life depicted by La Fontaine. The legs of the heron, the neck of the duck and the swan—[these are all examples of the kind, rational resourcefulness of the obliging and sober fable.]
There is not and cannot be any semantic orientation in embryology. At the most it is capable of an epigram.

As a child in the small medieval town of Uppsala, Linnaeus could not but delight in the explanations of the itinerant menagerie...

The audience understood animals very simply: each one was exhibited as a *freak* merely because of its natural characteristics, because of its essential features [merely by the fact of its existence]. The animals were sharply divided into two categories: the less interesting domestic breeds and the "overseas" variety. And as forefathers of the "overseas," imported kinds, truly fabulous beasts were imagined, for whom there was neither admission nor passage, for it would have been most embarrassing to have to locate them on any map.

6. [Pallas] [21]

No one has succeeded like Pallas in lifting the gray shroud of coachman's ennui covering the Russian landscape. In its [imaginary] monotony, which has driven some of our poets to despair, others into a state of melancholic ecstasy, Pallas found [an incredible variety of granular fragments, materials, and strata] the rich contents of life. Pallas is a talented soil scientist. Streaked feldspar and blue clay touch him to the heart... ...

He experiences genuine pride in discovering the deep sea origins of the yellowish-white Simbirsk mountains and rejoices in their geological nobility.

While reading Pallas I grow short of breath and cannot hurry. Slowly I leaf through the water-colored versts. I sit in my postchaise with an intelligent and affectionate traveler. I feel the coils and springs and the pillows. I inhale the scent of sun-warmed resin and leather. I roll from side to side as we jolt over the rutted road. Pallas stares out the window at the Volga's steep slopes. Then I change my position, squeezed in by the trunks. The stream rushes on, twisting along the white marl. [Flint clay... Streaming class... But inside the chaise...

Let's imagine that Pallas's companion is none other than N.V. Gogol. Everything would be different for him. How they would quarrel and wrangle along the way. The chaise keeps trying to turn on the plowed earth.]

[The picture of Russia's enormity is shaped by Pallas out of infinitesimal magnitudes.[22] You will say: those were not Gogolian horses hitched to his post-chaise, but rather cockchafers. Some species of ants dragged it in tandem from highway to highway, from cart-track to cart-track, from the Chuvash countryside to the distillery, from the distillery to a sulphurous stream, from the stream to the river of milk and honey, the breeding ground of otters.]

Pallas knows and likes only the *proximate*. He ties proximity to proximity with his ornate ligatured script. He extends his horizon through tiny hooks and hinges.[23] He moves facilely and unnoticed from neighborhood to neighborhood in his ant-drawn post-chaise.

Pallas whistles tunes from Mozart. He hums Glück. Whoever does not admire Handel, Glück, and Mozart cannot possibly grasp the essence of Pallas. He is truly a writer for the sensitive ear. He brings to the Russian plains a feeling for the corporeal roundness and civility characteristic of German music. [He does not use subtle or superficial vegetable colors. He paints and tans and distills nature out of red sandalwood. He makes extractions out of steep slopes and pine forests. The plowed fields and birch groves of Simbirsk, the Khirghiz steppes bubble up in his cauldron of Arzamas manufacture. He distills dyes out of a mixture of birch leaves and alum for the Nankeen cloth used by Nizhegorod peasant women and for the blueprints of the heavens.]

[Mores, customs, rituals, wedding and funeral rites, women's headdresses, local handicrafts and industries], everything that a traveler sees are but colors and designs, printed on the earth's canvases, on its hand towels.[24]

Pallas was an extraordinary German. It seems that he managed to travel the length and breadth of Russia, from Moscow to the Caspian Sea, with a large spoiled Siberian tomcat on his lap. [He saw enormous amounts][He made accurate observations; keen descriptions; he was a geographer, a pharmacist, a dyer, a tanner, and a currier; he was a botanist, zoologist, ethnographer; he wrote a useful and charming book, fragrant from its freshly painted canvas and mushrooms, and never once did he shake his cat from his lap; rather, he scratched its deaf, gray-haired ear, and thus never disturbed it throughout the journey.] The cat was undoubtedly deaf, with a gray streak behind its ears.

But, if his honor had taken it into his head to go out again for a ride he might have fallen into the hands of Pugachev.[25] He might even have written him manifestoes in Latin or orders in German. Indeed, Pugachev favored educated people. He would not have wanted to be hung while Pallas was still alive. In Peter Fyodorovich's Chancellery there was another German, a Lieutenant Shwanych or Swanwich. He scribbled off some nothing... He eventually finished off his life in the baths.

Pallas's radiant and voluminous book was printed on astonishingly dry Chinese paper. Its pages were wide and granular. Reading this naturalist has a marvelous effect on your disposition; it straightens out the eye and communicates to the soul a mineral quartz calm.

The physiology of reading[26] still remains to be studied. Moreover, this subject differs radically from bibliography, and must be related to the organic phenomena of nature.

A book in use, a book established on a reader's desk, is like a canvas stretched on its frame.

While not yet a product of the reader's energy, a book is already a crack in the reader's biography; while not yet a find, it is already an extraction. A piece of streaked feldspar...

Our memory, our experience including its gaps, the tropes and metaphors of our sense perceptions and associations, all fall into the book's rapacious and uncontrolled possession.[27]

And the wiles of its proprietary powers are as varied as military subterfuges.

The reading demon breaks loose from the depths of *cultural wastes*. The ancients did not know that. They did not seek illusion in the reading process. Aristotle read without passion. The best of the ancient writers were geographers. Whoever was not bold enough to travel, did not dare to write.

Modern literature presented the reader with high demands [unfortunately, poorly observed and often profaned], which gave many writers headaches: never dare to describe anything in which the inner workings of your soul cannot be expressed in some way.

[Thus the author's schema intrudes on your past experience.]

We read books in order to refresh our memory, but therein lies the problem, for you can read a book only during the process of remembering.

When we are *completely* immersed in the activity of reading, we admire above all our own *generic* attributes. We experience, as it were, the ecstasy of classifying ourselves in various ages and stages.

[In the dark vestibule of the Zoological Museum on Nikitskaia Street, a whale's jaw lies in a display case untended, calling to mind an enormous plough. Whenever I visit my scientific friends there, I admire this extraordinary exhibit.]

But if Lamarck, Buffon and Linnaeus have colored my mature years, then I must thank the [Nikitskaia Street] whale for having awakened in me my childish awe of science.

Reality has the character of a continuum.

Prose which corresponds to reality, no matter how expressly and minutely, no matter how efficiently and faithfully, is always a broken series.

Only that prose is truly beautiful which is incorporated into the continuum as an entire system, although there is no power or method to prove it.

Thus, a prose tale[28] is nothing more than a broken sign of the unbroken continuum.

The continuous filling up of reality has always been the sole theme of prose. However, to imitate this continuous process would lead the prose reality into a dead end because [it has to do with intervals only] the unbroken continuum demands newer and newer impulses and determinants all the time. [We need signs of the unbroken continuum, by no means self-engendered matter.]

A characteristic[29] lacking intervals is impossible.

A permanent precise description of matter rests on its lighting effect: the so-called Tyndall[30] effect (the oblique indicator of the molecule in the ultra-microscope)...but then everything must be done from scratch; describe the light, etc.

The ideal description would be reduced to one single all-encompassing phrase in which all objective reality would be expressed.[31]

[But the speech of a prose writer never forms, never takes shape, no matter how it is assembled...]

For prose *content* and *place* are important, but form is not content.[32]

Prose form is synthesis.

Semantically significant lexical particles which scatter to their proper places.

The inconclusive quality of the place to which they scatter. The freedom of arrangement. In prose it is always "St. George's Day."[33]

7. Ashtarak

I want to get to know my bones, my lava, the very depths of my grave [how life below begins to play with magnesium and phosphorus, how life below will smile at me: arthropodal, reproachful, and droning life.] I want to go out toward Ararat to its croaking, cracking, expectorating borders. With all the fibers of my being I want to exert pressure against the impossibility of choice, against the total absence of freedom. I want to repudiate voluntarily the clear absurdity of will and reason.[34] [If I accept total immersion in sound, steadfastness, and vigor as time-honored and just, my visit to Armenia has not been in vain.]

If I accept as time-honored both the shadow of the oak tree and the shadow of the grave, and, indeed, the steadfastness of speech articulation, how shall I ever appreciate the present age?[35]

[What is that to me? But a bundle of exclamations and interjections! And for that I am living...]

That is precisely why I turned to the study of the ancient Armenian language...

8. Alagez

We did not dare feel tired. The sun of the Pechenegs and the Kasogs stood above us.

I had only one book with me, Goethe's *Italienische Reise* in an expensive leather binding, as worn from use as a Baedeker.

[Instead of a Kodak camera, Goethe took Knipp, the rosy-cheeked artist, with him to Italy. In accord with Goethe's[36] instructions, Knipp sketched the remarkable landscapes with photographic accuracy.

[The enormous distance covered by Tamerlane's conquests obliterates any normal conceptions of near and far. The horizon emerges in the form of a Latin Gerundive.][37] As you travel along, you can feel Tamerlane's invitation in your pocket.

66b. [From a Letter: 1931-1932][38]

My notebooks tell how the eye is an instrument of contemplation, how light is power and how ornament is thought. In my notebooks there is talk of friendship, of science, of intellectual passion, but not of "things."

Travel is absolutely essential and not only travel to Armenia or Tadzhikistan. The artist's greatest reward is to explore and exploit the worlds of thinking and feeling people other than himself.

67. CONVERSATION ABOUT DANTE

Cosi gridai cola faccia levata . . .[1] (*Inferno*, XVI, 76)

I

Poetic discourse is a hybrid process, one which crosses two sound modes: the first of these is the modulation we hear and sense in the prosodic instruments of poetic discourse in its spontaneous flow; the second is the discourse itself, i.e. the intonational and phonological performance of these instruments.

Understood in this way, poetry is not a part of nature, not even its best or choicest part, let alone a reflection of it—this would make a mockery of the axioms of identity; rather, poetry establishes itself with astonishing independence in a new extraspatial field of action, not so much narrating as acting out in nature by means of its arsenal of devices, commonly known as tropes.[2]

It is only with the severest qualifications that poetic discourse or thought may be referred to as "sounding"; for we hear in it only the crossing of two lines, one of which, taken by itself, is completely mute, while the other, abstracted from its prosodic transmutation, is totally devoid of significance and interest, and is susceptible of paraphrasing, which, to my mind, is surely a sign of non-poetry. For where there is amenability to paraphrase, there the sheets have never been rumpled, there poetry, so to speak, has never spent the night.[3]

Dante is a master of the instruments of poetry; he is not a manufacturer of tropes. He is a strategist of transmutation and hybridization; he is least of all a poet in the "general European" sense or in the usage of cultural jargon.[4]

Wrestlers tying themselves into a knot in the arena may be viewed as an instance of the mutation of instruments into harmony:

> These naked, glistening wrestlers who walk
> Back and forth, strutting about
> And showing off their physical
> Prowess before grappling in the decisive
> Fight . . .

(*Inferno*. XVI, 22-24)

whereas the modern film, metamorph of the tapeworm, turns into the wickedest parody of the use of prosodic instruments in poetic discourse, for its frames simply move forward without conflict, merely replacing one another.[5]

Imagine something intelligible, grasped, wrested from obscurity, in a language voluntarily and willingly forgotten immediately after the act of intellection and realization is completed...

What is important in poetry is only the understanding which brings it about—not at all the passive, reproducing, or paraphrasing understanding.[6] Semantic adequacy is equivalent to the feeling of having fulfilled a command.[7]

The signal waves of meaning vanish, having completed their work; the more potent they are, the more yielding, and the less inclined to linger.[8]

Otherwise stereotypes are inevitable, the hammering in of those manufactured nails known as images of cultural history.

Superficial explanatory imagery is incompatible with suitability as an instrument of poetic discourse.

The quality of poetry is determined by the speed and decisiveness with which it embodies its schemes and commands in diction, the instrumentless, lexical, purely quantitative verbal matter.[9] One must traverse the full width of a river crammed with Chinese junks moving simultaneously in various directions—this is how the meaning of poetic discourse is created. The meaning, its itinerary, cannot be reconstructed by interrogating the boatmen: they will not be able to tell how and why we were skipping from junk to junk.

Poetic discourse is a carpet fabric containing a plethora of textile warps differing from one another only in the process of coloration, only in the partitura of the perpetually changing commands of the instrumental signaling system.

It is an extremely durable carpet, woven out of fluid: a carpet in which the currents of the Ganges, taken as a fabric theme, do not mix with the samples of the Nile or the Euphrates, but remain multicolored, in braids, figures, and ornaments—not in patterns, though, for a pattern is the equivalent of paraphrase.[10] Ornament is good precisely because it preserves traces of its origin like a piece of nature enacted. Whether the piece is animal, vegetable, steppe, Scythian or Egyptian, indigenous or barbarian, it is always speaking, seeing, acting.

Ornament is stanzaic. Pattern is of the line.

The poetic hunger of the old Italians is magnificent,[11] their youthful, animal appetite for harmony, their sensual lust after rhyme—*il disio*!

The mouth works,[12] the smile nudges the line of verse, cleverly and gaily the lips redden, the tongue trustingly presses itself against the palate.

The inner form of the verse is inseparable from the countless changes of expression flitting across the face of the narrator who speaks and feels emotion.

The art of speech distorts our face in precisely this way; it disrupts its calm, destroys its mask...

When I began to study Italian and had barely familiarized myself with its phonetics and prosody, I suddenly understood that the center of gravity of my speech efforts had been moved closer to my lips, to the outer parts of my mouth. The tip of the tongue suddenly turned out to have the seat of honor. The sound rushed toward the locking of the teeth. And something else that struck me was the infantile aspect of Italian phonetics, its beautiful child-like quality, its closeness to infant babbling,[13] to some kind of eternal dadaism.[14]

> *E consolando, usava l'idioma*
> *Che prima i padri e le madri trastulla;*
> *... Favoleggiava con la sua famiglia*
> *De' Troiani, de Fiesole, e di Roma.*
>
> *(Paradiso, XV, 122-126)*

Would you like to become acquainted with the dictionary of Italian rhymes? Take the entire Italian dictionary and leaf through it as you will... Here every word rhymes. Every word begs to enter into *concordanza*.

The abundance of marriageable endings is fantastic. The Italian verb increases in strength toward its end and only comes to life in the ending. Each word rushes to burst forth, to fly from the lips, to run away, to clear a place for the others.

When it became necessary to trace the circumference of a time for which a millennium is less than a wink of an eyelash,[15] Dante introduced infantile"trans-sense"language[16] into his astronomical, concordant, profoundly public, homiletic lexicon.[17]

Dante's creation is above all the entrance of the Italian language of his day onto the world stage, its entrance as a totality, as a system.

The most dadaist of the Romance languages moves forward to take the first place among nations.

II

We must give some examples of Dante's rhythms. People know nothing about this, but they must be shown. Whoever says, "Dante is sculptural,"[18] is influenced by the impoverished definitions of that great European. Dante's poetry partakes of all the forms of energy known to modern science. Unity of light, sound and matter form its inner nature.[19] Above all, the reading of Dante is an endless labor, for the more we succeed, the further we are from our goal. If the first reading brings on only shortness of breath and healthy fatigue, then equip yourself for subsequent readings with a pair of indestructible Swiss hobnailed boots. In all seriousness the question arises: how many shoe soles, how many oxhide soles, how many sandals did Alighieri wear out during the course of his poetic work, wandering the goat paths of Italy.

Both the *Inferno* and, in particular, the *Purgatorio* glorify the human gait, the measure and rhythm of walking, the footstep and its form. The step, linked with breathing and saturated with thought, Dante understood as the beginning of prosody.[20] To indicate walking he utilizes a multitude of varied and charming turns of phrase.

In Dante philosophy and poetry are constantly on the go, perpetually on their feet. Even a stop is but a variety of accumulated movement: a platform for conversations is created by Alpine conditions. The metrical foot is the inhalation and exhalation of the step. Each step draws a conclusion, invigorates, syllogizes.

Education is schooling in the swiftest possible associations.[21] You grasp them on the wing, you are sensitive to allusions—therein lies Dante's favorite form of praise.

The way Dante understands it, the teacher is younger than the pupil, for he "runs faster."[22]

> When he turned aside he appeared to me
> like one of those runners who chase each other
> over the green meadows around Verona,
> and his physique was such that
> he struck me as belonging to the host of winners, not to
> the losers . . .

The metaphor's rejuvenating power brings the educated old man, Brunetto Latini, back to us in the guise of a youthful victor at a Veronese track meet.[23]

What is Dantean erudition?

Aristotle, like a double-winged butterfly, is edged with the Arabian border of Averroes.

> *Averrois, che il gran comento feo*
> *(*Inferno, *IV, 144)*

Here the Arab Averroes accompanies the Greek Aristotle. They are both components of the same drawing. They can both find room on the membrane of a single wing.

The conclusion of Canto IV of the *Inferno* is truly an orgy of quotations. I find here a pure and unalloyed demonstration of Dante's keyboard of references.

A keyboard stroll around the entire horizon of Antiquity. Some Chopin polonaise in which an armed Caesar with a gryphon's eyes dances alongside Democritus, who had just finished splitting matter into atoms.[24]

A quotation is not an excerpt. A quotation is a cicada. Its natural state is that of unceasing sound. Having once seized hold of the air, it will not let it go. Erudition is far from being equivalent to a keyboard of references for the latter comprises the very essence of education.

By this I mean that a composition is formed not as a result of accumulated particulars, but due to the fact that one detail after another is torn away from the object, leaves it, darts out, or is chipped away from the system to go out into a new functional space or dimension, but each time at a strictly regulated moment and under circumstances which are sufficiently ripe and unique.[25]

We do not know things themselves; on the other hand, we are

highly sensitive to the facts of their existence. Thus, in reading Dante's cantos we receive communiques, as it were, from the battlefield and from that data make superb guesses as to how the sounds of the symphony of war are struggling with each other, although each bulletin taken by itself merely indicates some slight shift of the flags for strategic purposes or some minor changes in the timbre of the cannonade.

Hence, the thing emerges as an integral whole as a result of the simple differentiating impulse which transfixed it. Not for one instant does it retain any identity with itself. If a physicist, having once broken down an atomic nucleus, should desire to put it back together again, he would resemble the partisans of descriptive and explanatory poetry for whom Dante represents an eternal plague and a threat.

If we could learn to hear Dante, we would hear the ripening of the clarinet and the trombone, we would hear the transformation of the viola into a violin and the lengthening of the valve on the French horn. And we would be able to hear the formation around the lute and the theorbo of the nebulous nucleus of the future homophonic three-part orchestra.[26]

Furthermore, if we could hear Dante, we would be unexpectedly plunged into a power flow, known now in its totality as a "composition," now in its particularity as a "metaphor," now in its indirectness as a "simile," that power flow which gives birth to attributes so that they may return to it, enriching it with their own melting and, having barely achieved the first joy of becoming, they immediately lose their primogeniture in merging with the matter which is rushing in among the thoughts and washing against them.

The beginning of Canto X of the *Inferno*. Dante urges us into the inner blindness of the compositional clot:

> We now climbed up the narrow
> path between the craggy
> wall and the martyrs—my teacher
> and I right at his back . . .

All our efforts are directed toward the struggle against the density and darkness of the place. Illuminated shapes cut through it like teeth. Here strength of character is as essential as a torch in a cave.

Dante never enters into single combat with his material without having first prepared an organ to seize it, without having armed himself with some instrument for measuring concrete time as it drips or melts. In poetry, where everything is measure and everything derives from measure, revolves about it and for its sake, instruments of measure are tools of a special kind, performing an especially active function. Here the trembling hand of the compass not only indulges the magnetic storm, but makes it itself.

And thus we can see that the dialogue of Canto X of the *Inferno* is magnetized by the forms of verb tenses: the perfective and imperfective past, the subjunctive past, even the present and the future are all categorically and authoritatively presented in the tenth canto.

The entire canto is constructed on several verbal thrusts which leap boldly out of the text. Here the table of conjugations opens like a fencing tournament, and we literally hear how the verbs mark time.

First thrust:

> *La gente che per li sepolcri giace*
> *Potrebbesi veder?* . . .

"May I be permitted to see those people laid in open graves?"
Second thrust:

> . . . *Volgiti: che fai?*

The horror of the present tense is given here, some kind of *terror praesentis*. Here the unalloyed present is taken as a sign introduced to ward off evil. The present tense, completely isolated from both the future and the past, is conjugated like pure fear, like danger.

Three nuances of the past tense (which has absolved itself of any responsibility for what has already occurred) are given in the following tercet:

> I fixed my eyes on him,
> And he drew himself up to his full height,
> As if his great disdain could disparage Hell.

And then, like a mighty tuba, the past tense explodes in Farinata's question:

> *. . . Chi fur li maggior tui?—*

"Who were your forefathers?"

How that auxiliary verb is stretched out here, that little truncated *fur* instead of *furon*! Wasn't it through the lengthening of a valve that the French horn was formed?

Next comes a slip of the tongue in the form of the past perfect. This slip felled the elder Cavalcanti: from Alighieri, a comrade and contemporary of his son, the poet Guido Cavalcanti, still thriving at the time he heard something—it little matters what —about his son using the fatal past perfect: *ebbe*.

And how astonishing that precisely this slip of the tongue opens the way for the main stream of the dialogue: Cavalcanti fades away like an oboe or clarinet, having played its part, while Farinata, like a deliberate chess player, continues his interrupted move, and renews the attack:

> *"E se," continuando al primo detto,*
> *"S'egli han quell'arte," disse, "male appresa,*
> *Cio mi tormenta piu che questo letto."*

The dialogue in the tenth canto of the *Inferno* is an unanticipated explicator of the situation. It flows out all by itself from the interstices of the rivers.

All useful information of an encyclopedic nature turns out to have been already communicated in the opening lines of the canto. Slowly but surely the amplitude of the conversation broadens; mass scenes and crowd images are obliquely introduced.[27]

When Farinata rises up contemptuous of Hell, like a great nobleman who somehow landed in jail, the pendulum of the conversation is already swinging across the full diameter of the gloomy plain now invaded by flames.

The scandal in literature is a concept going much further back than Dostoevsky,[28] however, in the thirteenth century and in Dante's writings it was much more powerful. Dante collides with Farinata in this undesirable and dangerous encounter just as Dostoevsky's rogues run into their tormentors in the most inopportune places. A voice floats forward; it remains unclear to whom it belongs. It becomes more and more difficult for the reader to conduct the expanding canto. This voice—the first theme of Farinata—is the minor Dantean *arioso* of the suppliant type—extremely typical of the *Inferno*:

> O Tuscan, who travels alive through
> this fiery city and speaks so
> eloquently! Do not refuse to
> stop for a moment. . . Through
> your speech I recognized you
> as a citizen of that noble
> region to which I, alas! was
> too much of a burden. . .

Dante is a poor man. Dante is an internal *raznochinets*,[29] the descendant of an ancient Roman family. Courtesy is not at all characteristic of him, rather something distinctly the opposite. One would have to be a blind mole not to notice that throughout the *Divina Commedia* Dante does not know how to behave, does not know how to act, what to say, how to bow. I am not imagining this; I take it from the numerous admissions of Alighieri himself, scattered throughout the *Divina Commedia*.

The inner anxiety and painful, troubled gaucheries which accompany each step of the diffident man, as if his upbringing were somehow insufficient, the man untutored in the ways of applying his inner experience or of objectifying it in etiquette, the tormented and downtrodden man—such are the qualities which both provide the poem with all its charm, with all its drama, and serve as its background source, its psychological foundation.

If Dante had been sent forth alone, without his *dolce padre*, without Virgil, scandal would have inevitably erupted at the very start, and we would have had the most grotesque buffoonery rather than a journey amongst the torments and sights of the underworld!

The gaucheries averted by Virgil serve to systematically amend and redirect the course of the poem. The *Divina Commedia* takes us into the inner laboratory of Dante's spiritual qualities. What for us appears as an irreproachable Capuchin and a so-called aquiline profile was, from within, an awkwardness surmounted by agony, a purely Pushkinian, *Kammerjunker* struggle for social dignity and a recognized social position for the poet. The shade which frightens children and old women took fright itself, and Alighieri suffered fever and chills: all the way from miraculous bouts of self-esteem to feelings of utter worthlessness.

Dante's fame has up to now been the greatest obstacle to understanding him and to a profound study of his work, and this situation shall continue for a long time to come. His lapidary quality is no more than a product of the enormous inner imbalance which expressed itself in dream executions, in imagined encounters, in elegant retorts prepared in advance and fostered on bile, aimed at destroying his enemy once and for all and invoking the final triumph.

How often did the kindest of fathers, the preceptor, reasonable man, and guardian snub the internal *raznochinets* of the XIV century who found it such agony to be a part of the social hierarchy, while Boccaccio, practically his contemporary, delighted in the same social system, plunged into it, gamboled about in it?

"Che fai?" (What are you doing?) sounds literally like a teacher's cry: you've lost your mind!... Then the sounds of the organ come to the rescue, drowning out the shame and concealing the embarrassment.

It is absolutely false to perceive Dante's poem as some extended single-line narrative or even as having but a single voice.[30] Long before Bach and at a time when large monumental organs were not yet being built and only the modest embryonic prototypes of the future wonders existed, when the leading instrument for voice accompaniment was still the zither, Alighieri constructed in verbal space an infinitely powerful organ and already delighted in all its conceivable stops, inflated its bellows, and roared and cooed through all its pipes.

> *Come avesse lo inferno in gran dispitto*
>
> *(Inferno, X, 36)*

is the line which gave birth to the entire European tradition of demonism and Byronism. Meanwhile, instead of raising his sculpture on a pedestal as Hugo, for instance, might have done, Dante envelops it in a sordine, wraps it round with gray twilight, and conceals it at the very bottom of a sack of mute sounds.

It is presented in the diminuendo stop, it falls to the ground out of the window of the hearing.

In other words, its phonetic light is turned off. The gray shadows have blended.[31]

The *Divina Commedia* does not so much take up the reader's time as augment it, as if it were a musical piece being performed.

As it becomes longer, the poem moves further away from its end, and the very end itself approaches unexpectedly and sounds like the beginning.

The structure of the Dantean monologue, built like the stop mechanism of an organ,[32] can be well understood by making use of an analogy with rock strata whose purity has been destroyed by the intrusion of foreign bodies.

Granular admixtures and veins of lava indicate a single fault or catastrophe as the common source of the formation.[33]

Dante's poetry is formed and colored in precisely this geological manner.[34] Its material structure is infinitely more significant than its celebrated sculptural quality. Imagine a monument of granite or marble whose symbolic function is intended not to represent a horse or a rider, but to reveal the inner structure of the marble or granite itself.[35] In other words, imagine a granite monument erected in honor of granite, as if to reveal its very idea. Having grasped this, you will then be able to understand quite clearly just how form and content are related in Dante's work.[36]

Any unit of poetic speech, be it a line, a stanza or an entire lyrical composition, must be regarded as a single word. For instance, when we enunciate the word "sun," we do not toss out an already prepared meaning—this would be tantamount to semantic abortion—rather we are experiencing a peculiar cycle.

Any given word is a bundle, and meaning sticks out of it in various directions,[37] not aspiring toward any single official point. In pronouncing the word "sun," we are, as it were, undertaking an enormous journey to which we are so accustomed that we travel in our sleep. What distinguishes poetry from automatic speech is that it rouses us and shakes us into wakefulness in the middle of a word.[38] Then it turns out that the word is much longer than we thought, and we remember that to speak means to be forever on the road.

The semantic cycles of Dantean cantos are constructed in

such a way that what begins, for example, as "honey" *(med)*, ends up as bronze *(med')*, what begins as "a dog's bark" *(lai)*, ends up as "ice" *(led).*[39]

Dante, when he feels the need, calls eyelids "the lips of the eye." This is when ice crystals of frozen tears hang from the lashes and form a shield which prevents weeping.

> *Gli occhi lor, ch'eran pria pur deutro molli,*
> *Gocciar su per le labbra . . .*
> > *(*Inferno, *XXXII, 46-47)*

Thus, suffering crosses the sense organs, producing hybrids, and bringing about the labial eye.

There is not just one form in Dante, but a multitude of forms.[40] One is squeezed out of another and only by convention can one be inserted into another.

He himself says:

> *Io premerei di mio concetto il suco—*
> > *(*Inferno, *XXXII, 4)*

"I would squeeze the juice out of my idea, out of my conception"—that is, he considers form as the thing which is squeezed out, not as that which serves as a covering.

In this way, strange as it may seem, form is squeezed out of the content-conception which, as it were, envelops the form. Such is Dante's precise thought.

But whatever it may be, we cannot squeeze something out of anything except a wet sponge or rag. Try as we may to twist the conception even into a plait, we will never squeeze any form out of it unless it is already a form itself. In other words, any process involving the creation of form in poetry presupposes lines, periods, or cycles of sound forms, as is the case with individually pronounced semantic units.[41]

A scientific description of Dante's *Commedia*, taken as a flow, as a current, would inevitably assume the look of a treatise on metamorphoses, and would aspire to penetrate the multitudinous states of poetic matter, just as a doctor in making his diagnosis listens to the multitudinous unity of the organism. Literary criticism would then approach the method of living medicine.[42]

III

Examining the structure of the *Divina Commedia* as best I can, I come to the conclusion that the entire poem is but one single unified and indivisible stanza. Rather, it is not a stanza, but a crystallographic figure, that is, a body. Some incessant craving for the creation of form penetrates the entire poem. It is strictly a stereometric body, one continuous development of the crystallographic theme. It is inconceivable that anyone could grasp with the eye alone or even visually imagine to oneself this form of thirteen thousand facets,[43] so monstrous in its exactitude.[44] My lack of even the most obvious information about crystallography, an ignorance in this field as in many others common in my circle, deprives me of the pleasure of grasping the true structure of the *Divina Commedia*, but such is the marvelously stimulating power of Dante that he has awakened in me a concrete interest in crystallography, and as a grateful reader—*lettore*—I shall try to satisfy him.

The process of creating this poem's form transcends our conceptions of literary invention and composition. It would be much more correct to recognize instinct as its guiding principle.[45] The exemplary definitions proposed here are hardly intended to show off my own metaphorical capacity. Rather, I am engaged in a struggle to make the work comprehensible as an entity, to graphically demonstrate that which is conceivable. Only through metaphor is it possible to find a concrete sign to represent the instinct for form creation by which Dante accumulated and poured forth his *terza rima*.

We must try to imagine, therefore, how bees might have worked at the creation of this thirteen-thousand-faceted form, bees endowed with the brilliant stereometric instinct, who attracted bees in greater and greater numbers as they were required. The work of these bees, constantly keeping their eye on the whole, is of varying difficulty at different stages of the process. Their cooperation expands and grows more complicated as they participate in the process of forming the combs, by means of which space virtually emerges out of itself.

The bee analogy[46] is suggested, by the way, by Dante himself.

Here are three lines, the opening of Canto XVI of the *Inferno*:

> *Già era in loco ove s'udia il rimbombo*
> *Dell' acqua che cadea nell' altro giro,*
> *Simile a quel che l'arnie fanno rombo . . .*

Dante's comparisons are never descriptive, that is, purely representational. They always pursue the concrete task of presenting the inner form of the poem's structure or driving force.[47] Let us take the very large group of "bird" similes—all of them extensive caravans now of cranes, now of grackles, now of swallows in classical military phalanxes, now the anarchically disorderly crows so unsuited to the Latin military formation—this entire group of extended similes always corresponds to the instinct for the pilgrimage, the journey, colonization, migration. Or, for example, let us take the equally large group of river similes, portraying the rise in the Apennines of the river Arno which irrigates the valley of Tuscany, or the descent of the Alpine wet nurse, the river Po, into the valley of Lombardy. This group of similes is distinguished by its extraordinary breadth and its graduated descent from tercet to tercet, always leading to a complex of culture, homeland and settled civilization, to a political and national complex, so conditioned by the watersheds and, in addition, by the power and the direction of the rivers.

The force of a Dantean simile, strange as it may seem, operates in direct proportion to our ability to do without it. It is never dictated by some beggarly logical necessity. Tell me, if you can, what necessitated Dante's comparing the poem as it was being concluded with part of a *donna*'s attire (what we call a "skirt" nowadays, but in old Italian would, at best, have been called a "cloak" or in general, a "dress"), or comparing himself with a tailor who had, excuse the expression, exhausted his material?

IV

In succeeding generations, as Dante moved further and further beyond the reach of the public and even of the artists themselves, he became shrouded in ever greater mystery. Dante himself was striving for clear and precise knowledge. He was difficult for contemporaries, exhausting, but he rewarded their efforts with knowledge. Later everything became much worse. An ignorant cult of Dantean mysticism[48] was elaborately developed, devoid, like the very concept of mysticism, of any concrete substance. There also appeared the "mysterious" Dante of the French engravings,[49] consisting of a monk's hood, an aquiline nose, and his procuring of something among the mountain crags.

Among us in Russia none other than Alexander Blok fell victim to this voluptuous ignorance on the part of the ecstatic adepts of Dante who never read him:

> Dante's shade with his aquiline profile
> Sings to me of the New Life . . .[50]

The inner illumination of Dantean space derived from structural elements[51] alone was of absolutely no interest to anyone.

I will now show how little concern Dante's early readers indicated for his so-called mysticism. I have in front of me a photograph of a miniature[52] from one of the very earliest copies of Dante, dating from the middle of the 14th century (from the collection of the Perugia library). Beatrice is showing Dante the Trinity. There is a bright background with peacock designs, like a gay calico hanging. The Trinity in a willow frame is ruddy, rose-cheeked, and round as merchants. Dante Alighieri is depicted as a dashing young man, and Beatrice as a vivacious, buxom young girl. Two absolutely ordinary figures, a scholar brimming over with health courts a no less flourishing city maiden.

Spengler,[53] who dedicated some superb pages to Dante, nevertheless viewed him from his loge at the German State Opera Theater, and when he says "Dante," we must nearly always understand "Wagner" on the Munich stage.

The purely historical approach to Dante is just as unsatisfactory as the political or theological approach. The future of Dante criticism belongs to the natural sciences when they will have achieved a sufficient degree of refinement and developed their capacity for thinking in images.

With all my might I would like to refute that loathesome legend which depicts Dante's coloring as either indisputably dull [54] or of an infamous Spenglerian brownish hue.[55] First of all, I will cite the testimony of a contemporary, an illuminator.

This miniature is from the same collection of the museum in Perugia. It belongs to Canto I: "I saw a beast and turned back."

Here is a description of the coloring of that remarkable miniature, of a higher quality than the preceding one, and fully in accord with the text:

"Dante's clothing is *bright blue (adzhura chiara)*. Virgil's beard is long and his hair is gray. His toga is also gray; his cloak is *rose colored*; the denuded mountains are gray."

In other words, we see here bright azure and rosy flecks against smoky-gray nature.

In Canto XVII of the *Inferno* there is a monster of conveyances by the name of Geryon, something on the order of a super tank equipped with wings.

He offers his services to Dante and Virgil, having obtained from the ruling hierarchy proper orders for transporting the two passengers to the lower, eighth circle.

> *Due branche avea pilose infin l'ascelle;*
> *Lo dosso e il petto ed ambedue le coste*
> *Dipiute avea di nodi e di rotelle.*
> *Con più color, sommesse e soprapposte,*
> *Non fer mai drappo Tartari nè Turchi,*
> *Nè fur tai tele per Aragne imposte.*
>
> *(*Inferno, *XVII, 13-18)*

Here the subject is the color of Geryon's skin. His back, chest and sides are variously colored, ornamented with small knots and shields. Dante explains that neither the Turkish nor Tatar weavers ever used brighter colors for their carpets...

The textile brilliance[56] of this comparison is blinding, but the commercial perspectives of textiles revealed in it are completely unexpected.

With respect to its theme, Canto XVII of the *Inferno*, devoted to usury, is very close to both the commercial inventory and to the turnover of the banking system. Usury, which made up for a deficiency in the banking system where a constant demand was already being experienced, was a crying evil of that age; however, it was also a necessity which eased the flow of goods in the Mediterranean region. Usurers were condemned both in the church and in literature; nevertheless, people still ran to them. Even the noble families practiced usury, peculiar bankers with major land-holdings and an agrarian base—this especially peeved Dante.

Scorching hot sands make up the landscape of Canto XVII, that is, something reminiscent of the Arabian caravan routes.[57] The most exalted usurers are sitting on the sand: the Gianfigliacci and the Ubbriachi from Florence, the Scrovegni from Padua. Each one wears a small sack around his neck or an amulet or little purse embroidered with the family coat-of-arms outlined against a colored background: one wears an azure lion on a gold ground; another wears a goose, whiter than freshly churned butter, against a blood-red background; the third bears a blue swine on a white background.

Before plunging into the abyss, gliding down on Geryon's back, Dante examines this strange exhibit of family crests. I call your attention to the fact that the usurers' sacks are presented as emblems of color. The energy of the color epithets and the way in which they are placed in the verse line muffles the heraldry. The colors are listed with a kind of professional harshness. In other words, the colors are presented at that stage when they are still found on the artist's palette, in his studio. And what is so astonishing about that? Dante felt right at home in the world of painting; he was a friend of Giotto, and attentively followed the struggle between the various schools of painting and the fashionable trends.

> *Credette Cimabue nella pittura . . .*
>
> *(*Purgatorio, *XI, 94)*

Having observed the usurers long enough, they embarked on Geryon. Virgil threw his arms around Dante's neck and cried out to the official dragon: "Descend in broad, flowing circles: remember your new burden . . ."

The craving to fly tormented and exhausted the men of Dante's era no less than alchemy. A hunger after cloven space. All sense of direction vanished. Nothing was visible. Only the Tatar's back lay before them, that terrifying silk dressing gown of Geryon's skin. Speed and direction can be judged only by the air whipping across the face. The flying machine was not yet invented, Leonardo's plans did not yet exist, but the problem of gliding to a safe landing was already resolved.

Then at last, falconry bursts in with an explanation. Geryon's maneuvers in slowing down his descent resemble the return of a falcon from an unsuccessful flight, who having flown up in vain, slowly returns at the call of the falconer and having landed, flies away offended, assuming a perch somewhere off in the distance.

Now let's try to grasp all of Canto XVII as a whole, but from the point of view of the organic chemistry of Dantean imagery, which has nothing in common with allegory. Instead of merely retelling the so-called content, we will look at this link in Dante's work as a continuous transformation of the substratum of poetic material, which preserves its unity and aspires to pierce its own internal self.

Dante's thinking in images, as is the case in all genuine poetry, exists with the aid of a peculiarity of poetic material which I propose to call its convertibility or transmutability.[58] Only in accord with convention is the development of an image called its development. And indeed, just imagine an airplane (ignoring the technical impossibility) which in full flight constructs and launches another machine. Furthermore, in the same way, this flying machine, while fully absorbed in its own flight, still manages to assemble and launch yet a third machine. To make my proposed comparison more precise and helpful, I will add that the production and launching of these technically unthinkable new machines which are tossed off in mid-flight are not secondary or extraneous functions of the plane which is in motion, but rather comprise a most essential attribute and part of the flight itself, while assuring its feasibility and safety to no less a degree than its properly operating rudder or the regular functioning of its engine.

Of course, only by stretching the point can one apply the term "development" to this series of projectiles constructed in flight, which fly away, one after the other, in order to maintain the integrity of movement itself.

Canto XVII of the *Inferno* is a brilliant confirmation of the transmutability of poetic material in the above-mentioned sense of the term. The figures of this transmutability may be drawn approximately as follows: the little flourishes and shields on Geryon's mottled Tatar skin—silken carpets woven with ornaments, spread out on Mediterranean counters—a perspective of maritime commerce, of banking and piracy—usury and the return to Florence via the heraldic sacks with specimens of fresh colors that had never been used—the craving for flight underscored by Eastern ornament, which turns the material of the canto toward the Arabic fairytale with its technique of the flying carpet—and, finally, the second return to Florence with the aid of the falcon, irreplaceable precisely because he is unnecessary.

Not being satisfied with this truly miraculous demonstration of the transmutability of poetic material, which leaves all the associative gambits of modern European poetry far behind, Dante, as if to mock his slow-witted reader, after everything has been unloaded, played out, given away, brings Geryon down to earth and graciously equips him for a new journey, like the tuft of an arrow released from a bowstring.

V

Dante's drafts, of course, have not come down to us. There is no opportunity for us to work on the history of his text. But it does not follow, of course, that there were no inkstained manuscripts or that the text hatched out full grown like Leda out of the egg or Pallas Athena out of the head of Zeus. But the unfortunate interval of six centuries plus the quite excusable fact of the absence of rough drafts have played a dirty trick on us. For how many centuries have people been talking and writing about Dante as if he had expressed his thoughts directly on official paper?

Dante's laboratory? That does not concern us! What can ignorant piety have to do with that? Dante is discussed as if he had the completed whole before his eyes even before he had begun work and as if he had utilized the technique of moulage, first casting in plaster, then in bronze. At best, he is handed a chisel and allowed to carve or, as they love to call it, "to sculpt." However, one small detail is forgotten: the chisel only removes the excess, and a sculptor's draft leaves no material traces (something the public admires). The stages of a sculptor's work correspond to the writer's series of drafts.

Rough drafts are never destroyed.

There are no ready-made things in poetry, in the plastic arts or in art in general.

Our habit of grammatical thinking[59] hinders us here—putting the concept of art in the nominative case. We subordinate the very process of creation to the purposeful prepositional case, and we reason like some robot with a lead heart, who having swung about as required in a variety of directions, and having endured various jolts as he answered the questionnaire—about what? about whom? by whom and by what?—finally established himself in the Buddhist,[60] schoolboy calm of the nominative case. Meanwhile, a finished thing is just as subject to the oblique cases as to the nominative case. Moreover, our entire study of syntax is the most powerful survival of scholasticism and, by being in philosophy, in epistemology, it is put in its proper subordinate position, and completely overwhelmed by mathematics which has its own independent, original syntax.[61] In the study of art this scholasticism of syntax still reigns supreme, causing colossal damage by the hour.

Precisely those who are furthest from Dante's method in European poetry and, bluntly speaking, in polar opposition to him, go by the name Parnassians: Hérédia, Leconte de Lisle. Baudelaire is much closer. Verlaine is still closer, but the closest of all the French poets is Arthur Rimbaud. Dante is by his very nature one who shakes up meaning and destroys the integrity of the image.[62] The composition of his cantos resembles an airline schedule or the indefatigable flights of carrier pigeons.

Thus the safety of the rough draft[63] is the statute assuring preservation of the power behind the literary work. In order to arrive on target one has to accept and take into account winds blowing in a somewhat different direction. Exactly the same law applies in tacking a sailboat.

Let us remember that Dante Alighieri lived during the heyday of sailing ships and that sailing was a highly developed art. Let us not reject out of hand the fact that he contemplated models of tacking and the maneuvering of sailing vessels. He was a student of this most evasive and plastic sport known to man since his earliest days.[64]

Here I would like to point out one of the remarkable peculiarities of Dante's psyche: he was terrified of the direct answer, perhaps conditioned by the political situation in that extremely dangerous, enigmatic and criminal century.

While as a whole the *Divina Commedia* (as we have already

stated) is a questionnaire with answers,[65] each of Dante's direct responses is literally hatched out, now with the aid of his mid-wife, Virgil, now with the help of his nurse, Beatrice, and so on.

The *Inferno*, Canto XVI. The conversation is conducted with that intense passion reserved for the prison visit: the need to utilize, at whatever cost, the tiny snatches of a meeting. Three eminent Florentines conduct an inquiry. About what? About Florence, of course. Their knees tremble with impatience, and they are terrified of hearing the truth. The answer, lapidary and cruel, is received in the form of a cry. At this, even Dante's chin quivers, although he made a desperate effort to control himself, and he tosses back his head, and all this is presented in no more nor less than the author's stage direction:

> *Cosi gridai colla faccia levata*[66]
> *(*Inferno, *XVI, 76)*

Sometimes Dante is able to describe a phenomenon so that not the slightest trace of it remains. To do this he uses a device which I would like to call the Heraclitean metaphor; it so strongly emphasizes the fluidity of the phenomenon and cancels it out with such a flourish, that direct contemplation, after the metaphor has completed its work, is essentially left with nothing to sustain it. I have already taken the opportunity several times to state that Dante's metaphorical devices exceed our conception of composition inasmuch as our critical studies, fettered by the syntactic mode of thinking, are powerless before them.

> When the peasant, climbing up the hill
> During that season when the being who illuminates
> >> the world,
> Is least reticent to show his face to us,
> And the water midges yield their place to
> >> the mosquitoes,
> Sees the dancing fireflies in the hollow,
> In the same spot, perhaps, where he
> >> labored as a reaper or plowman—
> So with little tongues of flame the
> >> eighth circle gleamed,
> Completely visible from the heights where
> >> I had climbed;

And as the one who took his
                     revenge with the aid of bears,
Upon seeing the departing Chariot of Elijah,
When the team of horses tore away into the heavens,
Stared as best he could but could
                     make out nothing
Except one single flame
Wasting away, like a small cloud
                     rising in the sky—
So the tongue-like flame filled
                     the chinks in the tombs,
Appropriating the wealth of the graves
                     as their profit,
While enveloped in each flame
                     a sinner was concealed.

(Inferno, XXVI, 25-42)

If your head is not spinning from this miraculous ascent, worthy of Sebastian Bach's organ music, then try to indicate where the first and second members of the comparison are to be found, what is compared with what, and where the primary and secondary explanatory elements are located.[67]

An impressionistic preparatory introduction awaits the reader in a whole series of Dante's cantos. Its purpose is to present in the form of a scattered alphabet, in the form of a leaping, sparkling, well-splashed alphabet the very elements which, in accord with the laws of the transformability of poetic material, will be united into formulas of meaning.

Thus, in this introduction, we see the extraordinarily light, glittering Heraclitean dance of the summer midges which prepares us to apprehend the serious and tragic speech of Odysseus.[68]

Canto XXVI of the *Inferno* is the most oriented toward sailing of all Dante's compositions, the most given to tacking, and by far the best at maneuvering. It has no equals in versatility, evasiveness, Florentine diplomacy and Greek cunning.

Two basic parts are clearly distinguishable in this canto: the luminous, impressionistic preparatory introduction and the well-balanced, dramatic tale, which Odysseus tells about his last voyage, about his journey out into the deeps of the Atlantic and his terrible death under the stars of an alien hemisphere.

In the free flow of its thought this canto comes very close

to improvisation. But if you listen more attentively, you will see that the poet is improvising inwardly in his beloved, secret Greek, using only the phonetics and the fabric of his native Italian idiom to carry out his purpose.

If you give a child a thousand rubles and then suggest that he make a choice of keeping either the coins or the banknotes, he will of course choose the coins, and in this way you can retrieve the entire sum by giving him some small change. Exactly the same experience has befallen European literary criticism which nailed Dante to the landscape of Hell familiar from the engravings. No one has yet approached Dante with a geologist's hammer to ascertain the crystalline structure of his rock, to study its phenocryst, its smokiness, or its patterning, or to judge it as rock crystal subject to the most varied of nature's accidents.

Our criticism tells us: distance the phenomenon and I will deal with it and absorb it. "Holding something at a distance" (Lomonosov's expression) and cognoscibility are almost identical for our criticism.[69]

Dante has images of parting and farewell. It is most difficult to descend through the valleys of his verses of parting.[70]

We have still not succeeded in tearing ourselves away from that Tuscan peasant admiring the phosphorescent dance of the fireflies, nor in closing our eyes to the impressionistic dazzle of Elijah's chariot as it fades away into the clouds before the pyre of Eteocles has been cited, Penelope named, the Trojan horse flashed by, Demosthenes lent Odysseus his republican eloquence, and the ship of old age fitted out.

Old age, in Dante's conception of the term, means, above all, breadth of vision, heightened capacity, and universal interests. In Odysseus's canto the earth is already round.

It is a canto concerned with the composition of human blood which contains in itself the salt of the ocean. The beginning of the voyage is located in the system of blood vessels.[71] The blood is planetary, solar and salty...

With all the convolutions of his brain Dante's Odysseus despises sclerosis just as Farinata despised Hell.

> Is it possible that
> we are born merely to enjoy
> animal comforts and

that we will not devote
the remaining portion of our
vanishing senses to an act
of boldness—to Westward
sailing, beyond the Gates of
Hercules, where the world
unpopulated, continues on?

The metabolism of the planet itself takes place in the blood, and the Atlantic sucks in Odysseus, swallowing up his wooden ship.[72]

It is inconceivable to read Dante's cantos without directing them toward contemporaneity. They were created for that purpose. They are missiles for capturing the future. They demand commentary in the *futurum*.

For Dante time is the content of history understood as a simple synchronic act; and vice-versa: the contents of history are the joint containing of time by its associates, competitors, and co-discoverers.[73]

Dante is an antimodernist. His contemporaneity is continuous, incalculable and inexhaustible.[74]

That is why Odysseus's speech, as convex as the lens of a magnifying glass, may be turned toward the war of the Greeks and Persians as well as toward Columbus's discovery of America, the bold experiments of Paracelsus, and the world empire of Charles V.

Canto XXVI, dedicated to Odysseus and Diomed, is a marvelous introduction to the anatomy of Dante's eye, so perfectly adjusted alone for the revelation of the structure of future time. Dante had the visual accommodation of predatory birds, but it was unadjusted to focussing in a narrow radius: his hunting grounds were too large.

The words of the proud Farinata may be applied to Dante himself:

> *Noi veggiam, come quei ch'ha mala luce.*
>
> *(Inferno, X, 100)*

That is, we, the souls of sinners, are capable of seeing and distinguishing only the distant future, but for this we have a special gift. We become absolutely blind as soon as the doors to the future slam shut before us. And in this respect we resemble those who struggle with the twilight, and, in discerning distant objects, fail to make out what is close by.

In Canto XXVI dance is strongly expressed as the origin of the rhythms of the *terza rima*. Here one is struck by the extraordinary light-heartedness of the rhythm. The meter is organized according to waltz time:

> *E se già fosse, non saria per tempo.*
> *Così foss' ei, da che pure esser dee;*
> *Chè più mi graverà com' piu m'attempo.*
> *(*Inferno, *XXVI, 10-12)*

It is difficult for us as foreigners to penetrate the ultimate secret of foreign poetry. We cannot be judges, we cannot have the last word. But it seems to me that it is precisely here that we find the enchanting pliability of the Italian language which only the ear of a native Italian can perceive completely.

Here I am quoting Marina Tsvetaeva, who once mentioned the "pliability of the Russian language . . ."[75]

If you attentively watch the mouth of an accomplished poetry reader, it will seem as if he were giving a lesson to deaf-mutes, that is, he works with the aim of being understood even without sounds, articulating each vowel with pedagogical clarity. And thus it is enough to see how Canto XXVI sounds in order to hear it. I would say that in this canto the vowels are anxious and twitching.

The waltz is primarily a dance of undulation. Nothing even remotely resembling it was possible in Hellenic or Egyptian culture. (I am indebted to Spengler for this juxtaposition.) The very foundation of the waltz is the purely European passion for periodic undulating movements, the very same close listening to sound and light waves found in all our theory of sound and light, in all our scientific study of matter, in all our poetry and music.

VI

O Poetry, envy crystallography, bite your nails in anger and impotence! For it is recognized that the mathematical formulas necessary for describing crystal formation are not derivable from three-dimensional space. You are denied even that element of respect which any piece of mineral crystal enjoys.

Dante and his contemporaries did not know geological time. Paleontological clocks were unknown to them: the clock of coal, the clock of infusorial limestone, the clocks of sand, shale and schist. They circled round in the calendar, dividing up days into quarters. However, the Middle Ages did not fit into the Ptolemaic system: they found shelter in it.

Aristotle's physics were added to Biblical genetics.[76] These two poorly matched things did not want to merge. The enormous explosive power of the Book of Genesis (the idea of spontaneous generation) fell upon the tiny island of the Sorbonne from all sides, and we will not be mistaken if we say that the men of Dante's age lived in an antiquity which was completely awash in modernity, like the globe embraced by Tyutchev's ocean. It is already very difficult for us to imagine how things which were familiar to absolutely everyone—school trots, which became a part of the obligatory elementary school program—how the entire Biblical cosmogony with its Christian appendages could have been accepted by the educated people of that time so literally, as if it were a special edition of the daily newspaper.

And if we approach Dante from this point of view, it will appear that he saw in Biblical tradition not so much its sacred, dazzling aspects as subject matter which, with the help of zealous reporting and passionate experimentation, could be turned to his advantage.[77]

In Canto XXVI of the *Paradiso*, Dante goes so far as to have a private conversation with Adam, to conduct a real interview. St. John the Divine, the author of the Apocalypse, acts as his assistant.

I maintain that every element of the modern experimental method may be found in Dante's approach to Biblical tradition. These include the creation of specially contrived conditions for the experiment, the use of instruments of such precision that there is no reason to doubt their validity, and clear verification of the results.

The situation in Canto XXVI of the *Paradiso* can be defined as a solemn examination performed on optical instruments in concert hall surroundings. Music and optics create the basis of the situation.

The major antinomy of Dante's experience[78] is to be found in his rushing back and forth between the example and the experiment. Examples are extracted from the patriarchal bag of ancient consciousness with the understanding that they be returned as soon as they are no longer needed. Experiments, the drawing of certain required facts out of the total sum of experience, no longer return them in accord with some promissory note, but rather launch them into orbit.

The Evangelical parables and the little examples of the scholastics are but cereal grains to be consumed and destroyed. Experimental science, on the other hand, drawing facts out of coherent reality, forms a kind of seed-fund out of them, an inviolable preserve, which comprises, as it were, the property of a time as yet unborn but already indebted.

The position of the experimenter with respect to factology, insofar as he aspires toward a trusting union with it, is by nature unstable, agitated and off balance. It brings to mind the above-mentioned figure of the waltz, because after each half-turn on the toes, in coming together the dancer's heels always meet on a new square of the parquetry and in a qualitatively different way. The dizzying Mephisto Waltz of experimentation originated in the Trecento, or perhaps even long before that; furthermore, it originated in the process of poetic formation, in the undulations of formulating procedure, in the transformability of poetic matter, the most precise, prophetic and indomitable of all matter.

Because of theological terminology, scholastic grammar, and our ignorance of allegory, we have overlooked the experimental dances in Dante's *Commedia*. In keeping with the formulas of outmoded scholarship, we made Dante look better, and at the same time used his theology as a vessel for the dynamics of his poetry.

To the sensitive palm placed on the neck of a warm pitcher, the pitcher gains form precisely because of its warmth. Warmth in this case is felt before form, thus it fulfills the sculptural function. In its cold state, forcibly torn from its incandescence, Dante's *Commedia* is suitable only for analyses by mechanistic tweezers; it is unsuitable for reading, for performing.

> *Come quando dall'acqua o dallo specchio*
> *Salta lo raggio all' opposita parte,*
> *Salendo su per lo modo parecchio*
> *A quel che scende, e tauto si diparte*
> *Dal cader della pietra in egual tratta,*
> *Sì come mostra esperienza ed arte . . .*
>
> *(*Purgatorio, *XV, 16-21)*

"Just as a ray of sunlight striking the surface of water or a mirror is reflected back at an angle corresponding to the angle of incidence, which differentiates it from a falling stone bouncing up at a perpendicular from the earth—a fact attested by both science and art . . ."

When the need for empirical verification of Biblical tradition first dawned on Dante, when he first indicated a taste for what I propose to call a "sacred induction," the conception of the *Divina Commedia* had already taken shape, and its success was virtually assured.

The poem, when most densely covered with foliage, is directed toward authority; its sound is fullest; it is most concert-like at that point when it is caressed by dogma, by canon, by the firm eloquent word. But therein lies the problem: in authority, or to be more exact, in authoritativeness, we can see only insurance against error and we are not at all equipped to understand that grandiose music of trustfulness, of trust, to make out those nuances of probability and conviction as delicate as an Alpine rainbow, which Dante has under his control.

> *Col quale il fantolin corre alla mamma—*
> *(*Purgatorio, *XXX, 44)*

So Dante fawns upon authority.

A number of the cantos of the *Paradiso* are enclosed in the hard capsule of an examination. In certain passages one can clearly make out the examiner's basso and the candidate's shy tinkling response.[79] The insertion of the grotesque and the genre picture ("the examination of a candidate for the Baccalaureate")[80] comprises a necessary attribute of the elevated and concert-like composition of the third part. However, the first example of it is presented as early as the second canto of the *Paradiso* (Beatrice's argument about the origin of spots on the moon).

In order to grasp the very nature of Dante's intercourse with the authorities, that is, the forms and methods of his cognition,[81] it is necessary to take into account both the concert-like circumstances of the scholastic cantos of the *Commedia* and the very preparation of the organs of perception. Here I am not even speaking about that most remarkably staged experiment with the candle and three mirrors,[82] where it is proven that the reverse path of light has as its source the refraction of the ray, but I must not fail to mention the preparation of the eye for the apperception of new things.

This preparation is developed into an actual dissection: Dante divines the layered structure of the retina: *di gonna in gonna...*[83]

Music here is not merely a guest invited to step indoors, but a full participant in the argument; or to be more precise, it promotes the exchange of opinions, coordinates it, and encourages syllogistic digestion, stretches premises and compresses conclusions. Its role is both absorptive and resorptive: it is a purely chemical role.

When you read Dante with all your powers and with complete conviction, when you transplant yourself completely to the field of action of the poetic material, when you join in and coordinate your own intonations with the echoes of the orchestral and thematic groups continually arising on the pocked and undulating semantic surface, when you begin to catch through the smoky-crystalline rock the sound-forms of phenocryst inserted into it, that is, additional sounds and thoughts conferred on it no longer by a poetic but by a geological intelligence, then the purely vocal, intonational and rhythmical work is replaced by a more powerful coordinating force—by the conductor's function— and the hegemony of the conductor's baton comes into its own, cutting across orchestrated space and projecting from the voice like some more complex mathematical measure out of a three-dimensional state.[84]

Which comes first, listening or conducting? If conducting is no more than the nudging along of music which rolls forth of its own accord, then of what use is it when the orchestra is good in itself, when it performs impeccably by itself? An orchestra without a conductor, as a long-cherished hope, belongs to the same order of vulgar pan-European "ideals" as the international language Esperanto, symbolizing the linguistic teamwork of all mankind.

Let us investigate how the conductor's baton first appeared and we will see that it arrived neither sooner nor later than when it was needed; what is more, it arrived as a new and original form of activity, creating in the air its own new domain.

Let us listen to how the conductor's baton was born, or better, how it was hatched out of the orchestra.

1732: Time (tempo or beat)—formerly tapped out with the foot, now usually with the hand. Conductor—*conducteur, der Anführer* (Walther. *Musical Dictionary*).

1753: Baron Grimm calls the conductor of the Paris Opera a woodcutter due to his habit of beating time aloud, a habit which since the time of Lully has reigned at the Paris Opera (Shunemann, *Geschichte des Dirigierens*, 1913).

1810: At the Frankenhausen musical festival Spohr conducted with a baton made of rolled-up paper, "without the least noise and without any grimaces"(Spohr, *Autobiography*).[85]

The conductor's baton[86] was badly overdue when it was born: the chemically radioactive orchestra anticipated it. The usefulness of the conductor's baton is far from being its only justification. The chemical nature of orchestral sounds finds its expression in the dance of the conductor who stands with his back to the audience. And this baton is far from being an external, administrative accessory or a distinctive symphonic police which could be done away within an ideal state. It is no less than a dancing chemical formula which integrates reactions perceptible to the ear. I beg of you not to regard it merely as a supplementary mute instrument, invented for greater visibility and to provide additional pleasure. In a certain sense this invulnerable baton qualitatively contains in itself all the elements in the orchestra. But how does it contain them? It gives off no smell of them, nor can it. It does not smell of chlorine, as the formula of ammonium chloride or ammonia does not smell of ammonium chloride or of ammonia.

Dante was chosen as the theme of this conversation not because I wanted to focus attention on him as a means to studying the classics and to seat him alongside of Shakespeare and Lev Tolstoi, as some kind of Kirpotin style *table d'hôte*,[87] but because he is the greatest, the unrivaled master of transmutable and convertible poetic material,[88] the earliest and simultaneously the most powerful chemical conductor of the poetic composition existing only in the swells and waves of the ocean, only in the raising of the sails and in the tacking.

VII

Dante's cantos are scores for a particular chemical orchestra in which the external ear can easily distinguish comparisons identical with the impulses and solo parts, that is, the arias and ariosos, peculiar self-avowals, self-flagellations or autobiographies, sometimes brief and capable of fitting into the palm of the hand, sometimes lapidary, like a tombstone inscription, sometimes unrolled like a certificate awarded by some medieval university, sometimes well-developed, articulated, and capable of achieving a dramatic, operatic fullness, as for instance, Francesca's famous cantilena.

Canto XXXIII of the *Inferno*, containing Ugolino's tale about how he and his three sons died of starvation in the prison tower of Archbishop Ruggieri of Pisa, is enveloped in the dense and heavy timbre of a cello like rancid, poisoned honey.

The density of the cello timbre is best for communicating expectation and agonizing impatience. There is no power on earth which can hasten the movement of honey pouring out of a tilted jar. Hence, the cello could only take shape and be given form when the European analysis of time had made sufficient progress, when sundials were superseded and the ancient observer of the shadow stick moving around Roman numerals drawn in the sand had been transformed into an impassioned participant of differential torture, into a martyr to the infinitesimal. A cello retards sound, no matter how it hurries.[89] Ask Brahms—he knew it. Ask Dante—he heard it.

Ugolino's tale is one of the most remarkable of Dante's arias, one of those events when a man, who has been offered some singular never-to-be-repeated opportunity to audition, is completely transformed right in front of his audience; he plays on his unhappiness like a virtuoso, and draws out of his misfortune a timbre completely unheard of before and unknown even to himself.

We must remember that timbre is a structural principle much like the alkalinity or acidity of some chemical compound. However, the chemical retort is not the space in which the chemical reaction takes place. That would be far too simple.

Ugolino's cello-like voice, overgrown with a prison beard, starving and locked up with his three fledgling sons, one of whom bears the sharp, violin-like name of Anselmuccio, flows out of a narrow crack:

Breve pertugio dentro dalla muda

It matures in the box of the prison resonator, and thus, in this instance, the cello fraternizes in all seriousness with the prison.

Il carcere—the prison—supplements and acoustically conditions the vocal work of the autobiographical cello.[90]

In the subconscious of the Italian people prison played a prominent role. Nightmares of prison life were imbibed with the mother's milk. The Trecento tossed men into prison with astonishing unconcern. Ordinary prisons were open for viewing, like our churches and museums. The interest in prisons was exploited by the prison wardens as well as by the fear-inspiring machinery of the small states. There was a lively intercourse between the prisons and the free world outside resembling diffusion, mutual infiltration.

And thus Ugolino's story is one of those migratory anecdotes, one of those horror stories which mothers used to frighten their children, one of those entertaining horror tales which are mumbled with great satisfaction as a remedy for insomnia while tossing and turning in bed. It is well known as a ballad, like Bürger's *Lenore,* the *Lorelei*, or the *Erlkönig.*

It thus corresponds to a glass retort; it is so accessible and comprehensible, irrespective of the quality of the chemical process taking place within it.

However, the largo for cello presented by Dante in Ugolino's name has its own space, its own structure as revealed in the timbre. The ballad-retort with its familiar motif is smashed to smithereens. Chemistry with its architectonic drama takes over.

I 'non so chi tu sei, nè per che modo
Venuto se' quaggiù; ma Fiorentino
Mi sembri veramente quand' io t'odo.
Tu dei saper ch'io fui Conte Ugolino . . .

*(*Inferno, *XXXIII, 10-13)*

. . . I know not who thou art, or how thou camest
here, but by your speech it seems thou must be a true
Florentine. Thou must know that I was Count Ugolino . . .

"Thou must know"—*tu dei saper*—the first note on the cello,
the first thrust of the theme.

The second note on the cello: "if thou dost not weep now, I
know not what can wring tears from thine eyes." Here are revealed the truly boundless horizons of compassion. Moreover,
the compassionate one is invited to enter as a new partner, and we
already hear his quavering voice from the distant future.[91]

Nevertheless, I did not make mention of the ballad accidentally. Ugolino's story is a ballad precisely because of its chemical
properties, despite its being incarcerated in the prison retort. The
following elements of the ballad are to be found: the conversation between the father and his sons (remember the *Erlkönig*);
the chase after time which is slipping away, that is, continuing
the parallel with the *Erlkönig*—in that case, the father's mad
dash with his trembling son in his arms, in the other, the prison
situation, that is, counting the dripping of the water as a measure
of time which brings the father and his three sons closer to the
mathematically conceivable threshold of death by starvation, no
matter how impossible it may seem to the father's consciousness. The same rhythm of the mad dash emerges here in disguise,
in the mute wailing of the cello, which strives with all its might
to break out of the situation and gives a sound picture of a still
more terrifying, slow chase, breaking speed down into the most
delicate fibers.

Finally, just as the cello is wildly conversing with itself and
squeezing out of itself questions and answers, Ugolino's story
is interpolated with the touching and helpless rejoinder of his
sons:

.... *ed Anselmuccio mio*
Disse: "Tu guardi sì, padre! Che hai?"
> *(*Inferno, *XXXIII, 50-51)*

...And my Anselmuccio said: "Father,
where art thou looking? What is
the matter?"

That is, the dramatic structure of the story flows out of the timbre itself, for the timbre is in no way sought after and stretched over the story as over the last of a shoe.

VIII

It seems to me that Dante made a careful study of all speech defects, listening closely to stutterers and lispers, to nasal twangs and inarticulate pronunciation, and that he learned much from them.

I would very much like to speak about the auditory coloration[92] of Canto XXXII of the *Inferno*.

A peculiar labial music: "abbo"—"gabbo"—"babbo"—"Tebe"—"plebe"—"zebe"—"converrebbe." It's as if a nurse had participated in the creation of phonetics. Now the lips protrude in a childish manner, now they extend into a proboscis.

The labials form some kind of "numbered bass"—*basso continuo*, namely, the chordal basis of harmonization. They are joined by smacking, sucking and whistling sounds, and also by dental "zz" and "dz" sounds.

I pulled out a single thread at random: *cagnazzi—riprezzo—guazzi—mezzo—gravezza.*

The tweaking, smacking and labial explosives do not cease for a single second.

The canto is interlarded with a vocabulary which can best be termed an assortment of seminary student insults and cruel schoolboy taunts: *coticagna* (nape); *dischiomi* (to pull out hair, locks); *sonar con le mascelle* (to bawl, to bark); *pigliare a gabbo* (to brag, to loaf about). With the aid of this blatantly shameless, intentionally infantile orchestration, Dante grows the crystals for his auditory landscapes of Giudecca (the circle of Judas) and

Caina (the circle of Cain).

> *Non fece al corso suo sì grosso velo*
> *D'inverno la Danoia in Osteric,*
> *Nè Tanaï la sotto il freddo cielo,*
> *Com'era quivi; chè, se Tambernic*
> *Vi fosse su caduto, o Pietrapana,*
> *Non avria pur dall'orlo fatto cric.*

Suddenly, for no apparent reason, a Slavic duck begins quacking: *Osteric, Tambernic, cric* (the onomatopoeic word for crackling).

The ice explodes phonetically and is scattered across the names of the Danube and the Don. The cold-generating tendency of Canto XXXII arises from the intrusion of physics into a moral idea—betrayal, a frozen conscience, the ataraxia of shame, absolute zero.

Canto XXXII is written in the tempo of a modern scherzo. But what is that? An anatomical scherzo which is studying the degeneration of speech based on onomatopoeic infantilisms.

A new link is revealed here between food and speech. Shameful pronunciation is turned back to where it came from; it is turned back to champing, biting, gurgling and chewing.

The articulation of food and speech almost coincide. A strange locust-like phonetics is created:

> *Mettendo i denti in nota di cicogna—*

"Working with their teeth like grasshopper's jaws."[93]

Finally, we must note that Canto XXXII is overflowing with anatomical lust.

"That same famous blow which simultaneously destroyed the wholesomeness of the body and injured its shade . . ." There is also purely surgical satisfaction: "The one whose gorget was sawed by Florence . . ."—

> *Di cui segò Fiorenza la gorgiera . . .*

And further: "Just as a hungry man greedily falls upon bread, so one of them fell on the other, sinking his teeth into the very place where the nape becomes the neck . . ."—

Là 've il cervel s'aggiunge con la nuca . . .

All this danced about like a Dürer skeleton on hinges and leads you off to German anatomy.

After all, isn't a murderer something of an anatomist?

Didn't an executioner in the Middle Ages slightly resemble a scientific worker?

The art of war and the art of execution remind you a bit of the threshold of a dissecting room.

IX

The *Inferno* is a pawnshop in which all the countries and cities known to Dante were left unredeemed. This extremely powerful construct of the infernal circles has a framework. It cannot be conveyed in the form of a crater. It cannot be portrayed on a relief map. Hell hangs suspended on the wire of urban egoism.

It is incorrect to think of the *Inferno* as something with three dimensions, as some combination of enormous circuses, of deserts with scorching sands, of stinking swamps, of Babylonian capitals with mosques burning red-hot. Hell contains nothing inside itself and has no dimensions; like an epidemic, an infectious disease or the plague, it spreads like a contagion, even though it is not spatial.

Love of the city, passion for the city, hatred for the city[94] — these serve as the materials of the *Inferno*. The rings of Hell are no more than Saturn's circles of emigration. To the exile his sole, forbidden and irretrievably lost city is scattered everywhere—he is surrounded by it. I would like to say that the *Inferno* is surrounded by Florence. Dante's Italian cities—Pisa, Florence, Lucca, Verona—these precious civic planets, are drawn out into monstrous rings, stretched into belts, restored to a nebulous, gasiform state.

The anti-landscape nature of the *Inferno* forms, as it were, the conditions of its graphic character.

Imagine Foucault's grandiose experiment carried out not

with one pendulum, but with a multitude of pendulums all swinging past one another. Here space exists only insofar as it is a receptacle for amplitudes. To make Dante's images more precise is as unthinkable as listing the names of all the individuals who participated in the migration of peoples.

> Just as the Flemish between
> Wissant and Bruges, protecting
> themselves from the sea's floodtide,
> erect dikes to push the sea back;
> and just as the Paduans construct
> embankments along the shores of
> the Brenta to assure the safety of
> their cities and castles in
> the expectation of spring with its
> melting snows on the Chiarentana
> [part of the snowy Alps] —so these
> dams were built, though not so
> monumental, almost despite the engineer . . .
>
> (*Inferno*, XV, 4-12)

Here the moons of the polynomial pendulum swing from Bruges to Padua, teaching a course in European geography, lecturing on the art of engineering, on the techniques of urban safety, on the organization of public works, and on the significance of the Alpine watershed for the Italian state.

What have we, who crawl on our knees before a line of verse, preserved from these riches? Where are its godfathers, where are its enthusiasts? What will become of our poetry which lags so disgracefully behind science?

It is terrifying to think that the blinding explosions of contemporary physics and kinetics were used 600 years before their thunder sounded. Indeed, words do not suffice to brand the shameful, barbarous indifference shown toward them by the pitiful compositors of clichéd thought.

Poetic speech creates its own instruments on the move and cancels them out without halting.

Of all our arts painting alone, and in particular modern French painting, has not yet ceased to hear Dante. This is the painting which elongates the bodies of horses as they approach the finish line at the hippodrome.

Whenever a metaphor raises the vegetable colors of existence to an articulate impulse, I gratefully remember Dante.

We describe the very thing that cannot be described. That is, nature's text comes to a standstill, but we have unlearned how to describe the single thing which, by its structure, yields to poetic representation, that is, the impulses, intentions and amplitudes of fluctuation.[95]

Ptolemy has returned via the back door. Giordano Bruno was burned in vain!...

While still in the womb our creations become known to everyone, but Dante's multinomial, multi-sailed and kinetically kindled comparisons preserve to this day the charm of the as-yet-unsaid.[96]

His "reflexology of speech" is astonishing—a science, still not completely established, of the spontaneous psycho-physiological influence of the word on those who are conversing, on the audience surrounding them, and on the speaker himself, as well as on the means by which he communicates his urge to speak, that is, by which he signals with a light his sudden desire to express himself.

Here he comes closest to approaching the wave theory of sound and light, determining their relationship.

> Just as an animal covered
> with a cloth grows nervous and
> irritable, only the moving
> folds of the material indicating
> his displeasure, so the first
> created soul (Adam's) expressed
> to me through the covering
> (light) the extent of its
> pleasure and sense of joy in
> answering my question . . .
>
> (*Paradiso*, XXVI, 97-102)

In the third part of the *Commedia* (the *Paradiso*), I see a genuine kinetic ballet. Here we see every possible kind of luminous figure and dance, down to the tapping of heels at a wedding celebration.

> Four torches glowed before me,
> and the nearest one suddenly came
> to life and grew as rosy as if Jupiter
> and Mars were suddenly
> transformed into birds and were
> exchanging feathers.
>
> (Paradiso, XXVII, 10-15)

Isn't it strange that a man who is preparing to speak should arm himself with a tautly strung bow, a full supply of feathered arrows, prepare mirrors and convex lenses, and squint at the stars like a tailor threading a needle?...

I devised this composite quotation, merging various passages from the *Commedia*, in order to best exhibit the characteristics of the speech-preparatory moves of Dante's poetry.

Speech preparation is even more within his sphere than articulation, that is, than speech itself.

Remember Virgil's marvelous supplication to the wiliest of the Greeks.

It is completely suffused with the softness of Italian diphthongs.

These are the writhing, ingratiating and sputtering tongues of small unprotected oil lamps, muttering about the greasy wick...

> *O voi, che siete due dentro ad un foco,*
> *S'io meritai di voi, mentre ch'io vissi,*
> *S'io meritai di voi assai o poco . . .*
>
> (Inferno, XXVI, 79-81)

Dante ascertains the origin, fate and character of a man according to his voice, just as the medicine of his day diagnosed a man's health according to the color of his urine.

X

He is filled with a sense of the ineffable gratitude toward the copious riches[97] falling into his hands. For he has no small task: space must be prepared for the influx, the cataract must be removed from the rigid vision, care must be taken that the bounty of poetic material pouring out of the cornucopia does not flow through the fingers, does not flow away through an empty sieve.

> *Tutti dicean:* "Benedictus qui venis!"
> *E, fior gittando di sopra e d'intorno:*
> "Manibus o date lilia plenis!"
>
> *(*Purgatorio, *XXX, 19-21)*

The secret of Dante's capacity resides in the fact that he introduces not a single word of his own fabrication. Everything sets him going except fabrication, except invention.[98] Indeed, Dante and fantasy are incompatible!... You should be ashamed of yourselves, O French Romantics, you unfortunate *incroyables* in red vests,[99] for slandering Alighieri! What fantasy can you find in him?[100] He writes to dictation, he is a copyist, he is a translator... He is completely bent over in the posture of a scribe casting a frightened sidelong glance at the illuminated original he borrowed from the prior's library.[101]

It seems that I have forgotten to say that preceding the *Commedia* there was some presage, some kind of hypnotic seance, as it were. But this, I suppose, is too implausible. If one considers this astonishing work from the angle of written language, from the viewpoint of the independent art of writing which in the year 1300 was on an equal footing with painting and music, and was regarded as among the most venerated professions, then we may add yet one more analogy to all the analogies proposed above— taking dictation, copying, transcribing.

Sometimes, but very rarely, Dante shows us his writing tools. His pen is termed *penna*, that is, it participates in a bird's flight; his inks are called *inchiostro*,[102] that is, monastery accessories; his verse lines are also called *inchiostri*, although sometimes they are designated as Latin school *versi*, or even more modestly, *carte*, which is an astonishing substitution, "pages" instead of "verse lines."

But even when written down and ready, this is still not the end of the process, for then the written object must be taken somewhere, must be shown to someone to be checked and "praised."

It is not enough to say "copying," for what we are involved with here is calligraphy in response to dictation by the most terrifying and impatient dictators. The dictator-overseer is far more important than the so-called poet.[103]

> . . . Now I must labor a little longer,
> and then I must show my
> notebook, bathed in the tears of
> a bearded schoolboy, to my most
> severe Beatrice, who radiates not
> only beauty but literacy.

Long before Arthur Rimbaud's alphabet of colors,[104] Dante linked color with the pleophany of articulate speech. But he is a dyer, a textile-maker.[105] His ABC is the alphabet of fluttering fabrics dyed with chemical powders and vegetable dyes:

> *Sopra condido vel cinta d'oliva*
> *Donna m'apparve, sotto verde manto,*
> *Vestita di color di fiamma viva.*
> *(*Purgatorio, *XXX, 31-33)*

His impulses toward color may sooner be called textile than alphabet impulses. Color is for him only in the fabric. For Dante the greatest intensity of material nature as a substance defined by color is found in textiles. And weaving is the occupation closest to qualitativeness, to quality.[106]

Now I will attempt to describe one of the innumerable conductorial flights of Dante's baton. We shall take this flight as if immersed in the actual setting of precious and instantaneous labor.

Let us begin with the writing. The pen draws calligraphic letters, tracing out both proper and common nouns. The quill pen is a small bit of bird's flesh. Dante, who never forgets the origin of things, remembers this, of course. His technique of writing with broad strokes and curves is transmuted into the figured flight of a flock of birds.

> *E come augelli surti di rivera*
> *Quasi congratulando a lor pasture,*
> *Fanno di sè or tonda or altra schiera*
> *Sì dentro ai lumi sante crëature*
> *Volitando cantavano, e faciensi*
> *Or D, or I, or L, in sue figure.*
> *(*Paradiso, *XVIII, 73-78)*

Just as the letters emanating from the hand of a scribe who is obedient to the dictation and who stands outside literature as a finished product, chase after the bait of meaning, as after sweet fodder, so precisely do birds, magnetized by green grass—sometimes separately, sometimes together—peck at what befalls them, sometimes coming together in a circle, sometimes stretching out into a line...

Writing and speech are incommensurate. Letters correspond to intervals. The grammar of Old Italian exactly like our new Russian grammar partakes of the same fluttering flock of birds, the same motley Tuscan *schiera*, that is, the Florentine mob which changes laws like gloves, and forgets by evening those laws promulgated the same morning for the general welfare.

There is no syntax—merely a magnetized impulse: a yearning for the stern of a ship, a yearning for worm's fodder, a yearning for an unpromulgated law, a yearning for Florence.[107]

XI

Let us return once more to the question of Dante's colors.

The interior of mineral rock, the Aladdin-like space concealed within, the lantern-like, lamp-like, chandelier-like suspension of piscine rooms deposited within, is the best key to understanding the coloration of the *Commedia*.

The most beautiful organic commentary to Dante is provided by a minerological collection.

I permit myself a small autobiographical confession. Black Sea pebbles tossed up on shore by the rising tide helped me immensely when the conception of this conversation was taking shape. I openly consulted with chalcedony, cornelians, gypsum crystals, spar, quartz and so on. It was thus that I came to understand that mineral rock is something like a diary of the weather, like a meteorological blood clot. Rock is nothing more than weather itself, excluded from atmospheric space and banished to functional space. In order to understand this you must imagine that all geological changes and displacements can be completely decomposed into elements of weather. In this sense, meteorology is more fundamental than mineralogy, for it embraces it, washes over it, ages it and gives it meaning.[108]

The fascinating pages which Novalis devotes to miners and mining make concrete the interconnection between mineral rock and culture. This interconnection is illuminated out of rock—weather in both the formation of culture and in the formation of mineral rock.[109]

Mineral rock is an impressionistic diary of weather accumulated by millions of natural disasters[110]; however, it is not only of the past, it is of the future: it contains periodicity. It is an Aladdin's lamp penetrating the geological twilight of future ages.

Having combined the uncombinable,[111] Dante altered the structure of time or, perhaps, to the contrary, he was forced to a glossolalia of facts,[112] to a synchronism of events, names and traditions severed by centuries, precisely because he had heard the overtones of time.

Dante's method is anachronistic—and Homer, who emerges with his sword at his side in the company of Virgil, Horace and Lucian from the dim shadows of the Orphic choirs, where the four of them while away a tearless eternity together in literary discussion, is its best expression...

Indices of the standing still of time in Dante's work are not only the round astronomical bodies, but positively all things and all personalities.[113] Everything mechanical is alien to him. He is disgusted by the idea of causality[114]: such prophecies are suited only for bedding down swine.

> *Faccian le bestie Fiesolane strame*
> *Di lor medesme, e non tocchin la pianta,*
> *S'alcuna surge ancor nel lor le tame...*
>
> *(Inferno, XV, 73-75)*

I would answer the direct question, "What is a Dantean metaphor?" saying, "I don't know," because a metaphor can be defined only metaphorically,[115] and this can be substantiated scientifically. But it seems to me that Dante's metaphor designates the standing-still of time. Its roots are not to be found in the little word "how," but in the word "when." His *quando* sounds like *come*. Ovid's rumbling was far more congenial to him than Virgil's French elegance.

Again and again I find myself turning to the reader and

begging him to "imagine" something; that is, I must invoke analogy, having in mind but a single goal: to fill in the deficiency of our system of definition.[116]

Hence, just try to imagine that Patriarch Abraham and King David, the entire tribe of Israel including Isaac, Jacob and all their kin, as well as Rachel, for whom Jacob endured so much, have entered a singing and roaring organ, as if it were a house with its door left ajar, and have concealed themselves within.

And, imagine that even earlier, our forefather Adam with his son Abel, old Noah, and Moses, the lawgiver and the law-abiding, had also entered...

> *Trasseci l'ombra del primo parente,*
>   *D'Abel suo figlio, e quella di Noè,*
>   *Di Moisé legista e ubbidente;*
> *Abraam patriarca, e David re,*
>   *Israel con lo padre e co' suoi nati,*
>   *E con Rachele, per cui tanto fe'...*
>
>   *(Inferno, IV, 55-60)*

Following this, the organ acquires the capacity to move— all its pipes and bellows become extraordinarily agitated, when suddenly, in a frenzied rage, it begins to move backwards.

If the halls of the Hermitage were suddenly to go mad, if the paintings of all the schools and great masters were suddenly to break loose from their nails, and merge with one another, intermingle and fill the air of the rooms with a Futurist roar and an agitated frenzy of color, we would then have something resembling Dante's *Commedia*.

To wrest Dante from the grip of schoolroom rhetoric[117] would be to render a major service to the history of European culture. I hope that centuries of labor will not be required for this, but only joint international endeavors which will succeed in creating an original anti-commentary to the work of generations of scholastics, creeping philologists and pseudo-biographers. Insufficient respect for the poetic material which can be grasped only through performance,[118] only through the flight of the conductor's baton—this was the reason for the universal blindness to Dante, to the greatest master and manager of this material, to the greatest conductor of European art, who forestalled for many centuries ago the formation of an orchestra adequate (to what?)—to the integral of the conductor's baton...

The calligraphic composition realized through means of improvisation—such, approximately, is the formula of a Dantean impulse, taken simultaneously as flight and as something finished. His similes are articulated impulses.[119]

The most complex structural passages of the poem are performed on the fife, like a bird's mating call. The fife is nearly always sent forth to scout ahead.[120]

Here I have in mind Dante's introductions, released by him as if at random, as if they were trial balloons.

> *Quando si parte il giuoco della zara,*
> *   Colui che perde si riman dolente,*
> *   Ripetendo le volte, e tristo impara;*
> *Con l'altro se ne va tutta la gente:*
> *   Qual vi dinanzi, e qual di retro il prende,*
> *   E qual da lato gli si reca a mente.*
> *Ei non s'arresta, e questo e quello intende;*
> *   A cui porge la man più non fa pressa;*
> *   E così dalla calca si difende.*
>
> *(*Purgatorio, *VI, 1-9)*

When the dice game is ended, the loser in cheerless solitude replays the game, despondently throwing the dice. The whole group tags along after the lucky gambler; one runs up ahead, one pulls at him from behind, one curries favor at his side, reminding him of himself. But fortune's favorite walks right on, listening to all alike, and with a handshake for each, he frees himself from his importunate followers . . .

And there goes the "street" song of the *Purgatorio*[121] (with its throngs of importunate Florentine souls demanding above all, gossip, secondly, protection, and thirdly, gossip again), enticed by the call of the genre, resounding on the typical Flemish fife which, only three hundred years hence, would become wall paintings.

Another curious consideration arises. The commentary (explanatory) is integral to the very structure of the *Commedia*. The miracle-ship left the shipyard with barnacles adhering to its hull. The commentary derives from street talk, from rumor, from Florentine slander passing from mouth to mouth. The commentary is inevitable like the halcyon circling about Batyushkov's ship.[122]

> ... There now, look: it's old Marzzuco ...
> How well he held up at his son's
> funeral! A remarkably staunch old man ...
> But have you heard, Pietro de la
> Borgia's head was cut off for no
> reason whatsoever—he was as clean
> as a piece of glass ...
> Some woman's evil hand was
> involved here ... O yes, by the way,
> there he goes himself—let's go
> up and ask him ...

Poetic material does not have a voice. It does not paint with bright colors, nor does it explain itself in words. It is devoid of form just as it is devoid of content for the simple reason that it exists only in performance. The finished poem is no more than a calligraphic product, the inevitable result of the impulse to perform. If a pen is dipped in an inkwell, then the resultant thing is no more than a set of letters fully commensurate with the inkwell.

In talking about Dante it is more appropriate to bear in mind the creation of impulses than the creation of forms[123]: impulses pertaining to textiles, sailing, scholasticism, meteorology, engineering, municipal concerns, handicrafts and industry, as well as other things; the list could be extended to infinity.

In other words, syntax confuses us. All nominative cases must be replaced by the case indicating direction, by the dative. This is the law of transmutable and convertible poetic material existing only in the impulse to perform.[124]

...Here everything is turned inside out: the noun appears as the predicate and not the subject of the sentence. I should hope that in the future Dante scholarship will study the coordination of the impulse and the text.[125]

67a. ADDENDA TO "CONVERSATION ABOUT DANTE"

That Russian readers are unacquainted with the Italian poets (I have in mind Dante, Ariosto and Tasso) is all the more striking, since no less a poet than Pushkin clearly grasped the explosiveness and unexpectedness of Italian harmony.

According to Pushkin's interpretation, loosely inherited from the great Italians, poetry is a luxury, but such a vital, essential luxury that it is sometimes bitter like bread.

> *Da oggi a noi la cotidiana manna . . .*
> (Purgatorio, *XI, 13)*

The poetic hunger of the old Italians is magnificent, their youthful, animal appetite for harmony, their sensual lust after rhyme—*il disio*!

Pushkin's splendid white teeth are the masculine pearls of Russian poetry!

What links Pushkin to the Italians? His lips work, his smile nudges the line of verse, cleverly and gaily the lips redden, the tongue trustingly presses itself against the palate.

Pushkin's stanza or Tasso's octave restores our youth once more and rewards the efforts of the reader a hundredfold.

The inner form of the verse is inseparable from the countless changes of expression flashing across the face of the narrator who speaks and feels emotion.

The art of speech distorts our face in precisely this way, it disrupts its calm, destroys its mask...

Pushkin alone stood on the threshold of an original, mature interpretation of Dante.

Indeed, the entire body of modern European poetry is no more than Alighieri's emancipated serf woman. Didn't she rise up like the frolicsome little brats of the national literatures on the foundations of the international Dante, still undisclosed and but partially read?[1]

Although never directly admitting the influence of Italian poetry on his own work, Pushkin was nevertheless attracted to the harmonious and sensual sphere of Ariosto and Tasso. It seems to me that he could never get enough of the unique physiological charm of Tasso's verse, that he feared to be enslaved by it and thus bring on himself Tasso's tragic fate, his morbid fame and legendary disgrace.[2]

For the genteel mob of that age the Italian language, heard only from the seats at the opera, sounded like some poetic chirping. Both then and now, no one in Russia studied Italian poetry seriously, considering it merely a property of the voice or an adjunct to music.

Thus, Russian poetry developed as if Dante had never existed. We still have not acknowledged our misfortune. Batyushkov —the notebook of the unborn Pushkin[3] —perished because he took a sip from Tasso's goblet, not yet having been inoculated against Dante. [From First Version of Essay, *IRLI*, fund 630, p. 125]

In Blok's work we find:

> Dante's shade with his aquiline profile
> Sings to me of the New Life . . .

He saw absolutely nothing beyond the Gogolian nose!!

Dante's scarecrow inherited from the nineteenth century! In order to say this of Dante's pointed nose, he would have been obliged not to have read Dante!

What is an image? An instrument in the metamorphosis of hybridized poetic discourse.

We can comprehend this concept with Dante's help. However, Dante does not teach us about instruments: he has already turned and vanished. He is the actual instrument in the metamorphosis of *literary time*, in the withholding and unfolding of literary time which we have ceased to *hear* but which we are taught, both here and in the West, is the narration of so-called "cultural structures."

This is a good place to talk a bit about the concept of so-called culture and to inquire whether it is really an incontrovertible fact that poetic discourse is completely tied into the context of culture, culture being no more than the correlative proper behavior of historical structures suspended in their development and concentrated in a passive conception.[4]

Proponents of the concept of culture are drawn willy-nilly into the circle, so to speak, of "improper proper behavior." It is precisely this context of culture worship which overwhelmed the schools and universities of Europe during the nineteenth century, which poisoned the blood of the authentic builders of normally recurring historical structures, and, most offensive of all, nearly always imparted a cast of consummate ignorance over what might have been alive, concrete, brilliant and knowledge-bearing in both the past and the future.

To squeeze poetic discourse into "culture" or into the narration of historical structures is unfounded, for by such an act its essentially raw nature is completely ignored. Contrary to our accepted way of thinking, poetic discourse is infinitely more raw, infinitely more unfinished than so-called "conversational" speech. Being raw material is precisely what brings it into contact with performing culture. I will give evidence of this using Dante as an example and, to preface my remarks, I will note that there is not one element in all of Dante's *Commedia* which would not support the idea of the autonomous raw nature of poetic discourse either directly or indirectly.

The usurpers of the Papal Throne could not but fear the sounds which Dante rained down on them, although they could be indifferent to the torture by instruments through which he betrayed them in heeding the laws of poetic metamorphosis. However, the breach in the Papacy as a historical structure is envisaged here and acted out insofar as the infinite raw material of poetic sound—which is inappropriately offered to culture as proper, which is ever distrustful and offensive to culture because of its suspiciousness, and which spits culture out like water used for gargling—is revealed and brought to light. [Rough Draft]

There exists an intermediary activity between the act of listening and the act of speech delivery. This activity comes closest of all to performance and constitutes its heart, as it were. The unfilled interval between the act of listening and the act of speech delivery is absurd to its very core. Material is not matter. [Rough Notes]

To Dante a child is an infant, "il fanciullo." Infancy resembles a philosophical concept with extraordinarily constructive powers of endurance.[5]

How fine it would be to copy out all those passages in the *Divina Commedia* in which children are mentioned.

And how many times does he knock up against Virgil's hem—*"il dolce padre!"* Or, suddenly, in the midst of the strictest school examination on the seventh story of heaven, an image of a mother appears, dressed only in her nightgown, rescuing her child from a fire. [Excluded from Final Version of Essay by Author]

The reason they were offended by the seminarist's nick-name for the "classics" lies precisely in the fact that one has to run with them somewhere along the ellipse of dynamic immortal-ity, that there are no limits to understanding, and that it is actual-ly this which forces one to evade one's labors, to wink, to seek out new meanings in old wisdom, not in books but in squinting eyes... [Rough Draft]

Dante can be understood only with the help of quantum theory. [Excluded from Final Version of Essay by the Author]

...Dante's question is itself already bursting forth in Virgil's answer. With his peculiar pedagogical and professional perspicac-ity, he responds to the impulse behind the question, carefully extracting it from Dante's formulation. They will all be covered, says Virgil, their tombs will be sealed shut, when the resurrected flesh of these personages, driven off through the valley of Jeho-saphat to the Last Judgement by the archangel's trumpet, will return; and no longer in real graves, they shall come hither with their flesh and bones to lie down in the shade. Such pleasures await Epicurus and his disciples. [Rough Draft]

What was previously said about the plurality of forms is equally applicable to lexicon. I see in Dante's work a great quan-tity of lexical thrusts. There is the barbarian thrust toward Ger-man hushing sounds and Slavic cacophony; there is the Latin thrust, at times toward *Dies irae* and *Benedictus qui venit*, at other times toward kitchen Latin. There is the great impulse toward the speech of his native province—the Tuscan thrust. [Rough Notes]

Here is an example. Canto XXXII of the *Inferno* is suddenly taken ill with a barbarian Slavicitis, absolutely insufferable, even indecent to the Italian ear.

...The fact is that the *Inferno*, taken as a series of problems, is given up to solid state physics. Here in various guises—some-times in the historical drama, sometimes in the mechanics of landscape dreams—we find analyzed gravity, weight, density, the acceleration of falling bodies, the rotary inertia of the gyroscope, leverage, the mother of the windlass, and finally, the human gait or step, as the most complex form of movement regulated by consciousness.[6]

The closer we come to the center of the Earth, that is, to Giudecca, the more powerful the music of gravity resounds, the more developed the scale of density, and the more rapid the internal molecular movement which forms the mass. [Rough Draft]

Dante never regarded human speech as an island of isolated rationality. Dante's lexical groupings were thoroughly barbarianized. To assure the health of his poetic discourse he always supplemented it with a barbarian touch. A surplus of phonological energy[7] distinguished it from other Italian poets and poets of world renown, making it seem as if he is not only speaking, but eating and drinking, at times imitating domesticated animals, at times the chirping and chirring of insects, at times the bleating of the old man's lament, at times the cry of the tortured on the rack, at times the voice of a woman keening at a funeral, at times the babble of a two-year-old infant.

For Dante the phonology of common speech was only a dotted line and a conventional sign. [Rough Notes]

The questions and answers of "the journey with conversations," otherwise known as the *Divina Commedia*, yield to classification. A significant part of the questions fall under the rubric we might designate: "How did you get here?" Another group of encounter questions sound much like: "What's new in Florence?"

The first set of questions and answers usually erupts between Dante and Virgil. Dante's own curiosity, his impulse to inquiry, is always well-founded in some concrete occasion, in some detail. He asks questions only after being bitten by something. He loves to define his own curiosity as a sting or a bite, etc. He very often uses the term, "il morso," that is, a taste. [Excluded from Final Version of the Essay by the Author]

The power of culture lies in our incomprehension of death. This is one of the essential qualities of Homeric poetry. That is why the Middle Ages had a weakness for Homer and a fear of Ovid. [Rough Draft]

It is imperative that we create a new commentary for Dante, directed toward the future and revelatory of its bonds with modern European poetry.

Falterona (*Convivio*, IV, 78; *Purgatorio*, IV, 17). Every so often we come across a personal intonation. My sources are obscure. I am still a stranger here. I will show myself eventually. The Arno River in its downward course becomes overburdened with muck and brutalized.

Convivio, IV is an apology for the possible significance of a poor observer's views of industrial economics. The views of a non-participant. A challenge to consumption and accumulation in all its forms (compare this with Savonarola).

Dante is most favorable to the merchants. He is sympathetic to honest, reasonable trade: *quando per arte o per mercantazia o per serviglio meritato...* We imagine *rewards* as the only proper source of revenue: *per serviglio meritato.* He is deaf to the system of economics and commodity circulation of his day. Everything is judged indiscriminately. He imagines first the Florentine, then the ordinary Italian, and finally, the *universal* system of the distribution of rewards. Dante does not favor any particular active social group in his economic views, but behind the backs of the producers he extends a hand to the distributors. He seeks the removal of all the middlemen standing between labor (service) and value (reward). Hence, the tragic element in his conception of the economics of his age.

Here and there in the *Convivio* living kernels of Dante's personal conversational style are interspersed; here is one example:

> *Veramente io vídi lo luogo, ne le coste*
> *d'un monte che si chiama Falterona*
> *in Toscana, dové lo più vile villano*
> *di tutta la contrada, zappando,*
> *più d'uno staio di santolene d'argento*
> *finissimo vi trovò, che forse più*
> *di dumilia anni l'aveano aspettato.*

(IV, 11, 76-91)

He has no love for agriculture. He always refers to it with disdain and even irritation:

> *... gizi Fortuna la sua rota*
> *Come le piace, e il villan la sua mazza.*

(Inferno, XV, 15, 95-96)

It would seem that he found the techniques of agriculture insufficiently interesting. He becomes excited only about wine-making. And he is affectionate and considerate toward sheep-herding (*pecozelle... mandrian...* There are numerous pastorals in the *Purgatorio*).

Meanwhile, nearly all his patrons, noble or otherwise, were *landowners*. Dante was a poor judge of how they actually lived...

> *né la diritta torre*
> *fa piegar rivo che da lungi corre.*
> (Canzone *III, 54-55*)

> A river current does not make an
> upright tower lean

Here (*Convivio*, IV) the concept of "nobleness" *(le nobilta)* is clarified in a very prolix manner, with reference to its social and economic privileges. The river as inherited "wealth." The tower as nobleness itself.

The commonest school comparison containing both the positive and negative parts of a proof, carries an additional burden: comparison struggles against determinism in its application to poetry and, it may be, in its application to science as well. Christian-feudal virtue is analyzed as one might analyze the composition of a painting.

In Canto V, 14-15, of the *Purgatorio*:

> *Sta come torre ferma, che non crolla*
> *Giammai la cima per soffiar de'vente.*

The river and the tower assure the Tuscan landscape permanent harmony. Painters utilize the tower to emphasize the sinuous course of the river; it even appears to guide the river as it were.

Dante is disturbed because the tower and the river are not causally connected. He would definitely like the tower to be guiding the river, divining its course.

It is common knowledge that Dante "had the greatest regard" for weather, and indeed, he served as no less than a model Alpine meteorological station with the finest equipment and splendid observers. No less remarkable are the lighting effects derived from weather conditions which he utilized in the *Inferno* and the *Purgatorio*—cloud conditions, humidity, indirect illumination, artificial sunlight, and so forth.

The superbly inventive pyrotechnics of the *Paradiso* are wholly directed toward the public celebrations and fireworks of the Renaissance.

The vitally active role now played by light in the modern European theater—be it in drama, opera or ballet—was foreshadowed, of course, by Dante.

To what lofty heights concert-like feelings, feelings of virtuosity, were developed in Dante's work! In Canto XVIII of the *Paradiso*, Charlemagne, Roland, Godfrey of Bouillon and Robert Guiscard, illuminated in the Cross of Mars, could not restrain themselves from answering Beatrice as she announced their names through light signals: they exchange bows and offer an encore... And the good soul of the Florentine elder, Dante's great-grandfather, Guido Cacciaguida, fishes for compliments from his great-grandson now in his presence: "My grandfather," Dante says, "gave me the impression that he is far from being the worst singer amidst the assembled throng of choral performers."

It is pleasant to think of Dante as a clockmaker, as a builder of a planetarium with an extra-spatial center, an empyrean which spews forth power and quality across seven other floating spheres through an intermediate circle with immovable stars. Even more important, Dante's planetarium is far removed from the conception of the mechanical clock, for the prime mover of this great crystal set works not on transmissions or cogwheels, but is indefatigably occupied with the translation of power into quality, not to mention... The prime mover himself is no longer the first principle, being merely a radio station, a communicator, a transmitter... The next heaven, to which the immovable stars are fixed (although inserted in the sphere, they are yet distinguishable from it), discharges an electrical current through those stars, the electrical current of existence which is received directly from the prime mover, that is, from the distributor. The seven other moveable spheres already contain within themselves qualitatively differentiated existence which acts as a stimulus for the varied provenance of concrete reality. And just as a single vitalistic flow creates organs for itself (ears, eyes, a heart) and makes their spheres concrete, so hothouses of qualities are inserted into matter.

Have you ever noticed that in Dante's *Commedia* it is quite impossible for the author to function, that he is doomed only to move about, to gather information, and to ask and answer questions?

But the compositional roots of the tenth Canto [of all the Cantos] of the *Inferno* lie in the gathering of the storm which matures like a meteorological phenomenon, and all the questions and answers rotate about a single issue—did it thunder or not?

To be more exact, this is the gathering of a storm which is bypassing us, taking a roundabout route.

Urban curiosity was a powerful force among the Italians of Dante's day. Florentine slander flitted from house to house like a sunbeam, sometimes even crossing the hills and slopes, moving from town to town. Each and every upstanding citizen —the baker, the merchants, the young cavalier...

The true privy councillors of the Catholic hierarchy were the apostles themselves, and the schoolboy facing them was not one who became flustered easily or began to shout out of immature pride or anticipated adulation, rather he emerged as a solemn bearded fledgling of the kind Dante himself would recommend—of necessity bearded—just to spite Giotto and the whole of European tradition. [From First Version of Essay, *IRLI*, fund 630, p. 125]

"I compare, therefore I am," so Dante might have put it. He was the Descartes of metaphor. Because matter is revealed to our consciousness (and how could we experience someone else's?) through metaphor alone, because there is no existence outside of comparison, because existence itself is comparison. [Rough Notes]

Allow me to give an obvious example involving nearly the entire *Commedia* taken as a whole.

The *Inferno* is the outer limit of medieval man's dream of urban life. It is, in the fullest meaning of the word, a universal city. What is tiny Florence, with its *bella cittadinanza* turned upside down by the new lifestyle so hateful to Dante, before this universal city! We might substitute Rome for the *Inferno* and hardly recognize the difference. Indeed, perhaps the comparative relationship—"Rome to Florence"—served as the impulse to form-creation which resulted in the *Inferno*. [Rough Draft]

68. GOETHE'S YOUTH: RADIODRAMA

I

The senate had a monopoly on deer hunting rights. The senators were served roast venison annually at a solemn state dinner. However, the nobles shot all the deer in the area, infringing on the senators' rights, so a new herd had to be reared. As the deer park was located within the municipal boundaries, the senators were served roast venison daily. Eventually the deer park was abolished and a house constructed on the site. Goethe[1] was born in this house.

There was no room for a garden near the house. Instead of a garden, flowers were planted in the window of the nursery known as the "garden room." The windows faced the neighbors' gardens. In the environs of the Horse Market, burgher home-owners marked off their gardens for games of skittles. Balls rolled noisily, knocking down the skittles.

"Whose gardens are those?"

"The neighbors'."

"May I go there?"

"No. You may only look out the window."

* * * * * *

The fairgrounds, on the other hand, are open to everyone. You go past the town hall, called "The Römer," with its huge vaulted halls (if you ask the guard nicely for permission, you can walk through and see the frescoes, the judges' bench, the honorable burghers' bench, the craftsmen's bench, and the reporter's desk), then you go past the medieval Nürenburg inn enclosed in a fortress wall, past a factory, past a dye-works, past a bleaching works—and on to the fairgrounds!

* * * * * *

Many dishes were purchased at the fair, and the little boy got some toy crockery.

"And what if I were to throw a dish out the window? No

one is home!..." What a splendid clanging sound the crockery made as it crashed to the ground!... The boy clapped his hands, laughed and shouted. The Ochsenstein brothers, his neighbors, heard the clatter of a broken dish and shouted:

"Come on, do it again!"

And a pot came flying after the dish.

"Come on, do it again!" the neighbors shouted. He had to run into the kitchen to fetch more dishes: more and more plates came flying out the window! Still more plates on the shelves: more and more plates kept flying out the window!

"Come on, do it again!" the neighbors shouted. Once again he went into the kitchen. And once again—more dishes came flying out the window. A whole heap of crockery lay under the windows. A heap of broken dishes.

The demolitionist was Johann Wolfgang von Goethe, three and a half years old; he had broken every dish in the house.

* * * * * *

Twice a year the Nile overflowed,
flooding all of Egypt in the deluge . . .
The Ganges is a mighty river road
Where pilgrims seek eternal refuge . . .

His entire German grammar and his Latin grammar as well were written in rhyme.

* * * * * *

A mahogany music stand in the shape of a tiered, truncated pyramid stood in the boy's room—very convenient for playing quartets. A mineral collection was beautifully displayed on its tiered shelves: transparent mica, fragile limestone, pink spar, veined marble, and crystalline crystal, and right next to them were soil samples—from black earth to red clays—and other gifts of nature: ears of grain, dried twigs, seeds, and pine cones.

"What a lovely mineral collection," people would say as they entered the room. The little boy would remain silent—no one knew that this was his altar of nature. Every morning when the sun, rising behind the walls of neighboring houses, finally burst over the rooftops, he would pick up his magnifying glass and aim its beams at the smoking candle that stood in a china cup at the top of the pyramid.

The music stand was his altar of nature, omnipotent nature. The little boy was the priest of nature and the candle was a sacrifice. It did not burn, but smoldered. Each morning the fragrant flame of the sacrifice was lit on the altar. No one knew about that.

* * * * * *

His sister is having a music lesson. The teacher taps out the rhythm:

> Strike the pinky, the pinky—faster!—one, two!
> *Mi-mi* with the pinky and *fa* with the pointer...
> Strike the middle finger—*sol*, like the sun.
> Now hit the black key...more lightly, more quickly...

Each key had its own name, each finger its own nickname.

* * * * * *

Do not malign the puppet theater. Remember how much joy it gave you. All his life Goethe remembered the gestures and leaps of those Moors, shepherds, and dwarfs, and the heavy tread of Doctor Faustus who sold his soul to the devil.

One evening the boy recited one of his favorite soliloquies from the puppet comedy *David* to his mother who, wishing to boast of her son's unexpected talent, related this incident to the head puppeteer. From then on Goethe became a permanent assistant to the puppeteer, who initiated him into all the mysteries of the art of puppetry. The little boy operated the puppet strings himself. Once during a show for the neighborhood children, he inadvertently dropped his giant; he immediately leaned out and set the giant on its legs, destroying the illusion entirely, while the audience laughed loudly.

Soon, however, he grew tired of the familiar plays. He decided to renovate the repertoire and began rehearsing his own fantasia, composing all kinds of dramatic passages, cutting out

new sets from cardboard and painting them. Once he even enticed his friends into putting on a real performance. He used gray
paper to make a costume for his hero—a stern and generous
knight—and gold and silver paper for the costumes of the enemies.
In all the bustle of preparation, however, he completely forgot
that his actors must know when to speak and what to say. The
audience had already assembled and his confused actors were
asking each other what they were supposed to do. Having changed
his clothes and feeling like Tancred, he walked on stage and read
a few bombastic verses. None of the actors came on stage. No one
answered him. The audience laughed.

Finally, forgetting about knightly passions and jousts, he
turned his attention to the Biblical story of the frail King David
and the giant Goliath who challenged him to a fight. The children
were glad to see a familiar play, and they ran out to join him. The
show was saved.

II

A young citizen of a large city is wandering through the
streets. Every so often some event upsets the tranquil flow of
life: a fire destroys someone's home or a crime is committed, and
the city spends several weeks pursuing and punishing the criminal.

Why has a throng of people gathered in the streets? A bonfire is reflected in the windows of the neighboring houses...

...The court has ordered all copies of a frivolous French novel
burned for its affront on religion and morality. Iron pitchforks
turn a heap of burning paper.

Suddenly a wind came up and hundreds of burning pages—
burning paper butterflies with crackling red wings—soared through
the air. The crowd rushed about trying to catch them.

But Goethe, taking advantage of the commotion, pulled a
copy of the forbidden book, still untouched by flames, out of
the bonfire.

Every bird has its own bait.

* * * * * *

A large, dark room in someone's unfamiliar house. Johann Wolfgang von Goethe, a burgher's son, is in the company of merry, convivial young people. By the window at the spinning wheel sits a young girl—Gretchen, Margaret...

"Margaret, go to the store and get some more wine."

Goethe: "How can you send a helpless girl out on such a dark night all alone without an escort..."

First Youth: "Don't worry, she's used to it. The wine shop is just across the street. She'll be back shortly."

Second Youth: "Do you know how that rich man Leerman got started? He sold matches, and now he's one of the wealthiest people in Frankfurt."

First Youth: "A clever man can never fail."

Second Youth: "What did you do today?"

First Youth: "I ran errands for the textile manufacturer. He's grown so lazy that he's willing to share his profits with the broker."

Second Youth: "Goethe, we got another order for you to write wedding poems. The ones you wrote—the funeral poems, remember—have already been spent on drink. Get to work on some poems. We'll be back in an hour."

A large slate is on the desk. Goethe jots down verses in his minute handwriting, erases them with a sponge, and begins again.

Margaret: "Why do you have to do that? Give up this business. You must leave before you get into trouble. Take my advice and go away..."

Goethe: "Gretchen, if a man who loves you, respects you, treasures you..."

Margaret: "Just don't kiss me... After all, we're only friends..."

The band of young people which had duped the police with its many mischievous pranks was discovered by the town hall bloodhounds. Counsellor Schneider was conducting the interrogation, bowing and smiling sweetly, in the home of Goethe's father.

"Where did you first become acquainted?"

"Out walking."

"Where was your meeting place? Who met there? Name the street..."

Johann Wolfgang took to his bed with neurasthenia.

It is difficult to find anything in common between the Gretchen of Frankfurt and the Gretchen in *Faust*. What became of her, this first Gretchen? Goethe never found out. He had to escape Frankfurt as quickly as possible.

III

Strasbourg.[2] Goethe is finishing his studies at the university. The lofty towers of the Strasbourg Cathedral are visible from all points in the city. This is the first magnificent example of Gothic architecture that Goethe has seen. The arrow-shaped masses of Gothic cathedrals towered above the large river roads, trade centers, and fairgrounds. From a distance they resembled stone forests crowned with towers. At close range they astonished the eye with their abundance of plant tendrils, their fantastic sculptures of animal faces, their leaves and flowers. Mighty ribs branched out from the main point of each vault. The architectural law canonized equilibrium and flight.[3]

Life is one in all its manifestations. You must experience everything, be capable of everything, and rejoice in everything.

Strasbourg is the border of France.

What is it that so excites this group of young people who call each other geniuses even among their own circle of friends, even face to face? Are they, perhaps, possessed by the French ideas of liberation? France is already stirring in anticipation of the great bourgeois revolution. These young people are naturally familiar with the philosophers of tomorrow's revolution, especially Voltaire. However, the lives of these youths are guided entirely by internal spiritual storms. They think that the contemptible feudal princelings must be made to tremble before their inspiration. The fury of spiritual passions, free poetry that derives its strength from folk art, will triumph over German inertia and will destroy the squalid social structure that has outlived itself.

How will this come to pass?

* * * * * *

A youth with a receding forehead, a sharp, inquisitive nose, and brown, inquiring eyes, his hair pulled tightly back into a braid, was strolling through rooms with waxed floors in the solemn silence of an art gallery. Close at his heels the museum guide—an inveterate interpreter of pictures—minced his steps. The young man, while observing the rules of politeness, tried in every way possible to escape his guide; the latter regarded the young man as his lawful prey and showered the names of schools of painting and names of artists upon him like peas... The youth was clearly annoyed by the eulogistic exclamations: divine, charming, inexplicable, airy, matchless...

Escaping his companion at last, he walked with a firm step through the rooms of Italian paintings, where shepherds with their flocks, and women with elongated faces holding flowers in their outstretched hands or bending over cradles with plump little boys, were portrayed against backgrounds of bright blue sky, pointed cliffs, and trees with slender branches.

This is all wonderful, but not now, later... He wants to go as quickly as possible to see the Dutch painters, the immortal Northern masters...apples, fish, kegs; peasants dancing under an oak who appear like adult dwarfs under the huge tree, the skirts of their caftans fluttering. Women wearing heavy velvet dresses and broad-faced children clinging to their skirts; shaggy tinsmiths and coopers completely absorbed in their work. And, finally, a shoemaker's family: a bedroom, a living room that is really a workshop, brown dusk, a piece of bread stuck with a knife on the table, a hammer striking a shoe on the last, a cradle resembling a wooden boat with a sailcloth, an open cupboard with glittering dishes, and fantastically engraved scraps of leather scattered on the floor.

For this is the workshop of the shoemaker Fritz the jester! Art and life have merged.[4]

Before his departure the shoemaker presented Goethe with a pair of sturdy but ugly boots.

* * * * * *

Events...joys...passions...suffering...

Events? What can happen in a feudal German town? The duchess' favorite dog died. The Secretary of State's wife gave birth to twins. The choir director fired the flutist because he blew his nose loudly during the court concert.

New liveries are being sewn for the court lackeys. The weavers' guild and the tailors' guild are jubilant.

A fashionable architect has come to town and is building a house with stairs on the outside, not inside. The house is intended to serve several families. Just imagine: three families will live under one roof!

The country is impoverished. Industry slumbers. The burghers have no room to turn around. Middle-class youth does not know what to do with its strength. However, you cannot quench the aspiration for growth.

The misty Vosges mountain range extends southward, receding into the distance. Below lies the Saar River Valley. The towers of the Strasbourg Cathedral are left behind.

The old guide is wearing a slipper on one foot and a shoe on the other. He constantly adjusts his socks, which keep slipping down. His son is employed as a smelter.

What stream is that? Whenever you find yourself in a new place, observe in which direction the rivers, and even the streams, flow. This will enable you to recognize the relief, the geological structure of the environment.

What does bread cost here? The country has inexhaustible natural resources—coal, iron, alum, sulphur—yet it is on the verge of famine. Yesterday a shopkeeper in Falzburg refused to sell them bread.

Whence that smell of sulphur, of burning and smoke arising out of fissures in the earth?

A subterranean fire envelops the depleted adit... It has been burning for ten years.

Here is a two-story house with white curtains in the window. The chemist Stauf, the philosopher of the coal mines, lives in this mountainous mining region. Goethe, in his travels along the Saar River, paid him a visit to discuss the country's economy and the utilization of natural resources.

"On the other hand, the wire industry intrigued me. That sight's enough to delight anyone: heavy manual labor has been replaced by the machine. The machine works like a rational creature."

IV

Goethe placed his miner's hammer on the table.

"Have you heard, the writer Gottsched got married. His bride is nineteen years old and he's sixty... Shouldn't we pay Gottsched a visit?"

Gottsched[5] lived very decorously on the first floor of a hotel called "The Golden Bear." A grateful editor had given him the apartment.

The guests were led into a large room. Gottsched himself entered the room: an enormous fat man, wearing a green silk robe lined with red taffeta. Not a single hair sat on his bald head. A servant ran after him holding a huge wig trailing ringlets down to the elbows. Timorously, he handed this luxuriant headpiece to his master. Gottsched calmly weighed out a full slap for his servant, put on his wig, sank into an armchair, and began to converse with the young students about lofty matters.

* * * * * *

"Who knows how to sharpen crow feathers?"

"But you write with goose feathers."

"You don't understand a thing..."

Behrisch[6] is an eccentric and a wit, a joker and a loafer. He has a long nose and sharp facial features. Hat under his arm and a sword at his side, he resembles an elderly Frenchman whose shirts are always gray but of a most complex range of gray hues. Everyone scoffed at him. The thirty-year-old Behrisch, a tutor who had been thrown out of the count's home because of his friendship with the student Goethe and his predilection for literary treatises, was a master of verbal caricature.

"I prefer fresh pastries from our dear baker Handel—note that the sign over his shop soothes the ear recalling the splendidly sonorous and tranquil music of his namesake—to Professor Gottsched's stale dinner rolls of rotten historical flour spiced with foreignisms... Old man Klopstock[7] is called a divine poet. I agree. He's good if only because he didn't swallow the ancient Greek columns. But his famous *Messias,* his epic retelling of the Gospels, is so long you'd have to hire a porter to drag it along with you on your walks. The speeches of his pious characters lull you to

sleep like church sermons, but suddenly the author grows lively
and acquires strength, fire, color, sonority. Poor Klopstock! He
is able to divine the language of passions, the language of living
nature—but to listen to organ music and wring tears out of oneself for forty-eight hours on end!... No thank you..."

Behrisch ridicules burghers and lovers of martial exploits
that sing the praises of Friedrich the Second, who waged a devastating war for seven consecutive years and was still unable to
end it. Behrisch laughs at pedantic professors:

"How are your lectures? The property relations of Roman
Quirites and the study of pandects from the standpoint of possession, ownership, seizure, capture and...utter confusion. A
professor 'from four to five,' it makes no difference what his
name is..."

* * * * * *

Thursday, November 10, 1767. 7:00 p.m.
"Ah, Behrisch, Behrisch! What a horrible moment! Oh God,
oh God! If only I could calm down a little... Behrisch, may love be
damned... If you could see me you would moan from pity.

"My blood has quieted down. I'm calmer and able to talk
now. Is it reasonable? Can a madman be rational? If my hands
were in chains at least I would have something to bite into...

"I sharpened my pen to give myself a break. Be quiet, be
quiet... I'll tell you everything in order..."

He is sitting at a small desk by a high, curtainless window.
The fretted chair with its extremely high back moved slightly
to the side. It is the room of a student, a young artist. An easel
standing in the room holds an unfinished painting: a gnarled tree
drawn in the Dutch style. Next to it is a pot-bellied flask containing some kind of beverage and a glass covered by a saucer. Goethe
is wearing a short smock. His face is malicious and tense. His hair
is disheveled, his braid is coming undone. He has the firm chin of
a stubborn schoolboy. His handwriting is a combination of harmony and wild motion. The letters resemble slanting fish-hooks, as
if a whole flock of swallows were soaring, smoothly yet powerfully, diagonally across the page.

"All this has wounded me so painfully that I actually fell
ill with a fever. I suffered hot and cold spells all night. I stayed at

home all day. In the evening for some reason I sent the servant girl out—and what happened? The girl returned and said that Katchen[8] and her mother are—where do you think—at the theater! She's at the theater while her beloved is ill..."

A new theater had just been built in the town. A throng of students was visiting the set designer in his garret. A freshly painted curtain was spread out on the floor. The muses no longer soared in the heavens but were standing on the earth. A man walked towards the portico. Everyone was glad to see that he was not wearing a Greek tunic, but ordinary clothes. It was Shakespeare. The painter's idea was clear: Shakespeare alone had paved a road for himself to the pantheon of the arts. People are engrossed in Shakespeare, enraptured by Shakespeare. He is valued for the boldness of his thought, the profundity of his spiritual sensibility, his miraculous transitions from rage to tenderness, the scope of his portrayal of human nature, and above all for the bitterness and shame he feels for his epoch, recognizable in Shakespeare's works in any guise.

The students watched the stage from their balcony seats, but it appeared too small for a Shakespearean work. They all hoped that *Götz von Berlichingen*,[9] Goethe's youthful tragedy, would be worthy of Shakespeare.

* * * * * *

Basedow[10] planned his model school. He would have to extort money from rich patrons. Basedow begins his entreaties and inadvertently insults the man he is addressing. Is it any wonder that he is refused?

The mordant Merck[11] is the prototype for Mephistopheles. Goethe compares him to a snail that shows people his horns only now and then.

Goethe's estimation of Lavater is quite remarkable: "Who can this great observer of detail be that he has no goal? Who can name each wrinkle on a man's brow, yet does not know what it may indicate or how it should be."

As we know, photography did not yet exist.

There is another man with such a gentle expression on his face, such a plump mouth, and with eyebrows that arch like a composer's, whose every feature bears the mark of sickliness and strength. This is the folksong collector, the poet and thinker—Herder.[12] Goethe learned from him that poetry is never a private, individual matter. Poetry is serious work. Herder smiles and says: thought and word, feeling and expression, are inseparable from one another, unseverable like twins.

* * * * * *

In order to understand the decisive turning points in Goethe's life and work, we must also remember that his friendships with women, for all their emotional depth and passion, were strong bridges which he crossed to get from one period of his life to another.

Friederike Brion[13] has long braids and wears a short-sleeved peasant dress. She tosses her scarf-covered head like a lamb at the sound of a bell. She is a pastor's daughter. She comes from an active village family.

Lotte,[14] another man's bride, forever bustling about and friendly to everyone, is the prototype of the older sister in *The Sorrows of Young Werther*, with little brothers and sisters clinging to her skirt. Theirs is a limited and quite moderate burgher household.

Lili Schönemann,[15] or simply Lili, has a laughing, lively profile, but imprint her profile on a coin, and those same thin lips and her Grecian coiffure would take on an imperious air; a banker's daughter, she plays the clavichord and is stubbornly capricious.

At this point one is prompted to ask why Goethe, the sociable, loving and popular author, depicted the theme of solitude more profoundly than all the poets of his day.

> The man who pines for solitude
> His wish may soon obtain;
> For friends will pass in various moods,
> And leave him to his pain.
> Then leave me to my woes!
> And when no friend is near,
> I shall have naught to fear,
> Nor solitude shall know.

The lover soft with footstep light,
Alone would meet his dear.
And thus to me, by day and night,
Grief comes when none are near—
Grief comes when I'm alone,

But soon I shall cease to moan,
  And in my silent grave
  Rest I shall gladly crave,
Then I shall be alone.[16]

The answer to this question can be found in *The Sorrows of Young Werther,* the young Goethe's book of despair. That book which caused an epidemic of suicides among the prosperous burgher milieu. Sensitive youth understood it as a guide to suicide, although the author wrote it with the opposite intention, just as a convalescent tells about his illness. Werther's light blue frockcoat served as a symbol of victorious withdrawal from reality, whereas in actual fact, despite the death of a few dozen ill-fated imitators of Werther, this literary model, the model of a sensitive young bourgeois who towered above his environment, served only to strengthen the vitality of his class; hence, it was not without reason that Napoleon read *The Sorrows of Young Werther* seven times, even taking it along on his campaigns.[17]

... The moral of this fable is obvious: a man does not have the courage to be humiliated. The five senses, according to the chronicler, are merely vassals in the feudal service of the "I": rational, thinking, and conscious of its own worth.

It would seem that such things are created because people jump out of bed in the middle of the night frightened that they have accomplished nothing, but have blasphemously experienced so much. Creative insomnia, a person awakened by despair sitting on his bed at night in tears, is just as Goethe portrayed it in *Wilhelm Meister*[18]...

The art of nations moves like a cavalry of insomniacs, and wherever it has trampled there is sure to be either poetry or war.

V

Tra-ta-ta-ta! Tra-ta-ta-ta! Sound your trumpet, postman on your high coach-box. Burn the tops of the red maples! Farewell to unwieldy but dear Germany...

The highway is not completely smooth, but that is no misfortune.

You want to talk to everyone as if they were good friends.

You want to say a kind word to every beggar.

The raucous vagabond barrel-organ is better than concert music. The mooing of fattened Tyrolean cows seems full of meaning and life, as if the earth itself had found a voice and were telling us how well the autumnal downpours nourished her.

The coach slackens its pace. Two figures are standing in the middle of the road. A girl about eleven years old waves the edge of her red coat in desperation. Beside her stands a black-bearded man with a huge, triangular case resting on his shoulders.

The shy little girl with the harp is Mignon. She is a Southern girl, but not an Italian, who has lost her homeland; she is the embodiment of longing for the flourishing South. The old man glances proudly and humbly from behind his scowling brows:

"The girl is tired. Mister traveler, don't refuse her a ride."

In the speeding coach Goethe jokes with the timid little animal, the proud little harpist. He teases her, quizzes her. She cannot tell the difference between a maple and an elm. The girl can hold her own, however. In between she explains how the harp is an excellent barometer: whenever the treble string is slightly sharp, there's sure to be good weather.

Beyond Brenner, at the edge of the Alpine pass, he saw his first larch, and beyond Schönberg—his first Siberian maple. Here, too, the young harpist undoubtedly asked him all kinds of questions.

* * * * *

"I want this journey to sate my soul once and for all in its aspirations toward the sublime. May the images of the sublime arts be imprinted upon my consciousness so that I may preserve them for quiet, intense enjoyment. Later, when I return, I will take up a profession once again, I will study mechanics and chemistry. The age of the sublime is passing. Our age is governed only by usefulness and strict necessity."

It is hard to believe that those words were written in Italy at the very crest of a powerful, animated, spiritual surge. Cannot this entry be explained by the great spiritual agitation that possessed Goethe during his travels through Italy?

* * * * * *

He ran away from home to plunge himself into antiquity, into the ancient Classical world, because for him understanding was seeing and empirically confirming.[19] His first encounter with the monuments of Classical antiquity was with a model of living antiquity, as vital as a natural phenomenon—the Veronese amphitheater, one of the circuses built by the Roman Emperors for entertaining the masses.

He walked around the circus along the top tier of benches, and it made a strange impression on him: one should never look at an amphitheater when it is empty, only when it is thronged with people. When people see themselves assembled, they must be astonished—so many voices, so loud and excited—they must suddenly see themselves united in one noble whole, merged into a single mass, a single body, as it were. Each head in the audience serves as a measure of the enormity of the entire building.

A wind is blowing from the graves of the ancients, sweeping across rose-covered hills, and saturated with their fragrance. The monuments are expressive, moving, and lifelike. Like that man gazing at his wife from a niche, as from a window... And over there, a mother and father with their son between them, gaze at each other fondly with ineffable tenderness.

A few days later a rather ridiculous play was performed at a small Venetian theater: in the course of the action nearly all the actors stabbed themselves with daggers. The violence-loving Venetian audience called the actors forth with howls of "Bravo, corpses!"

What was it that brought Goethe such incessant, lavish, and dazzling happiness in Italy?

The popularity and infectiousness of art, the proximity of the artists to the masses, the vivacity of the public's response, its talent and receptivity. What disgusted him most of all was the insulation of art from life.

Listen closely to the foreigner's footsteps along the deserted, sun-warmed stone embankment of the Great Venetian Canal. He does not resemble a man waiting for a rendezvous. The area he covers in his stroll is too large and he turns too decisively and abruptly after having measured off 200 or 300 paces.

In the resilient night air you inevitably hear ahead of you as well as behind you, the sound of men's voices exchanging melodies. They sing on and on, seemingly unable to bring their quivering story in verse to an end.

Each time Goethe encounters a new, fresh melody, he turns back to the singer who has just grown silent and, pursued by the melody, retreats from it toward the new, anticipated wave of its continuation.

Boatmen sing of the ancient poet Torquato Tasso,[20] exchanging verses with one another. All Italy knows Torquato Tasso. The insane Tasso who spent seven years chained up in the duke's dungeon in Ferrara is the same Tasso who was to have been crowned with roses in the Roman capitol... However, he died before the ceremony was to have taken place. The singer of Mediterranean expanses, Tasso tells how a tree was felled in an enchanted grove and a tower on wheels built for the siege of Moslem cities.

The magnanimous poet did not distinguish between Turkish, Arabic, and European crusaders; he ranked sorcerers and devils even slightly higher than the Christian God; he went out of his mind from fear that both the Church and State would declare him a heretic.

An old boatman approaches Goethe:

"It's astonishing how deeply this singing touches the soul, especially when it is skillful and heartfelt."

On October 14, 1876, Goethe left Venice for Rome. On July 18 he returned to Weimar.

69. NOTES, JOTTINGS AND FRAGMENTS

1. For 1931:
   A. On Nekrasov.[1]
   May 2, 1931. On reading Nekrasov. "Vlas" and "The Poor Knight."[2]
   Nekrasov:

> His delirium, they say,
> Was always haunted by the same vision:
> He saw this world passing away,
> He saw all the sinners in Hell.

Pushkin:

> He had but one vision,
> Inaccessible to the mind,
> Its impression was deeply
> Engraved on his heart.

"From that day forth"—and a second mysterious voice seems to follow:

> *Lumen coelum, Sancta Rosa . . .*

The very same poetic image, the very same theme of memory and exploit.

It is here that we find the common link between East and West. In the portrait of Hell. A cheap woodcut of Dante from an old Russian cookshop:

> The six-winged black tiger . . .
> Vlas recognized the outer darkness . . .

* * * * * * * * * * * *

B. [On Pasternak[3]]

1. He drank until he drank his fill of the universe and kept mum. He kept mum forever and ever. Downright terrifying.

> Having swallowed up the sea,
> May he sprinkle the universe with it.

2. Whom is he addressing?

People who never complete anything...

Like Tirtius before a battle—but what of his reader?—He will listen and run off...to some concert...

* * * * * * * * * * * *

C. On the verb

In our contemporary practice verbs have vanished from literature. They have but an oblique relationship to poetry. Their role is purely auxiliary: for an accepted fee they convey you from place to place. Only in government decrees, in military orders, in judicial verdicts, in notarial acts and in such documents as the Last Will and Testament does the verb live a full life. Nevertheless, the verb is, in its primary function, the act, the decree, the order.

2. For 1932: On Apollon Grigoriev

Our memory, our experience including its gaps, the tropes and metaphors of our sense perceptions and associations, all become part of the book's rapacious and uncontrolled possessions.

In this way, "the purpose of catharsis and the purpose of self-creation" is achieved, as our Apollon Grigoriev put it, having grown hoarse from venting his wrath against paraphrasers and... ...describers.

In poetry, the word "conclusion" *(vyvod)* must be understood literally as a "departure" *(vykhod)*[4] beyond the bounds of everything previously told, a departure naturally in keeping with the force of its own gravity and fortuitously in keeping with its own structure.

3. For 1935-1936

If a writer imposes upon himself, by whatever means, the duty of "informing us about the tragic aspect of life," when his palette fails to contain deep contrasting colors, and, more significant, when he does not exhibit any sensitivity to the law, according to which the tragic (regardless of how minute its sphere) inevitably emerges as a *universal representation of the world*, he merely offers us "prepared raw materials" of horror or stagnation, raw materials which evoke in us feelings of disgust, yet are best known in positive critical parlance by the euphemism *byt* (everyday life).[5]

Vigilance is the courage of the lyric poet; confusion and dissipation—the subterfuges of lyric indolence.

4. Undated Notes

...the storm in nature serves as the prototype of the historical event. The movement of the hour hand around the clockface may be considered the prototype of the non-event. It was five minutes to six; twenty minutes were left... Here you have the appearance of change according to a grand plan, when in reality nothing happened. Just as history may be said to have been born, so it may also die; and what, really, is progress, that creation of the twentieth century, if not the denial of history's death in which the spirit of the event disappears? Progress is the movement of the hour hand, and what with its peculiar emptiness, this commonplace represents an enormous danger to the very existence of history.[6] Let us intently heed Tyutchev, that connoisseur of life, in the birth of the storm. This natural phenomenon never occurs in Tyutchev's poetry except where...

5. An Unidentified Fragment

I maintain that a large number of our young poets have spent much more time studying the verse in the popular magazines *Small Flame, Red Fields,* and *Searchlight* than the so-called classics or masters.[7] We have students of irresponsible werewolves,

professional muddleheads and purveyors of ugly, vague, and con-
formist piecework.

No one as yet has expressed the majority of new emotions.
Some beginning poet may acknowledge the historical rights of
his generation. But what is he to do with these rights? Must he
always agree to everything and shout "true, true"? Of course not!
It gives me great pleasure to see that there are poets who express
their own approach to the world—rudiments of individual lyric
themes...

THE LETTERS

No. 1. To V.V. Gippius, Paris, April 19-27, 1908

My esteemed Vladimir Vasilievich[1]!

If you recall, I promised to write you "when I got settled."

But I did not get settled, that is, I have not been aware until very recently that I was doing what was "necessary," and therefore I have not broken my promise.

I have always felt a need to talk with you but have never succeeded in telling you what I consider important.

The history of our relationship or, perhaps, of my relationship to you, seems to me to be...generally quite remarkable.

Lately I have felt a special attraction to you and at the same time I have sensed a special kind of distance separating me from you.

Any kind of intimacy between us was impossible, but I felt a special satisfaction and a sense of triumph at certain of your malicious tirades: "but all the same..." You will forgive my boldness if I say that for me you were what some people call a "friendly enemy."

It cost me a great deal of time and trouble to recognize this feeling for what it was...

But I always regarded you as the representative of some dear yet hostile principle, and the charm of that principle lay in its duality.[2]

It is clear to me now that that principle is nothing other than religious culture, whether or not it is Christian I do not know, but in any case it is religious.

Having been raised in a milieu where there was no religion (family and school), I have long been striving hopelessly and platonically, but ever more consciously, toward religion. My first religious experiences go back to the period of my childish passion for Marxist dogma and are inseparable from that passion.

But for me the bond between religion and society was severed when I was still a child.

At the age of fifteen I passed through the purging fire of Ibsen, and although I did not hold out on the "religion of will," in the end I stood firmly on the soil of religious individualism and opposed society.

I accepted Tolstoi and Hauptmann, the two greatest apostles of love for the people, ardently yet abstractly, just as I accepted the "philosophy of the norm."

My religious consciousness never rose above Knut Hamsun and his worship of "Pan," that is, of an unacknowledged God, and to this day that remains my "religion."[3] (Oh, don't be alarmed. This is not "Maeonism" and in general I have nothing in common with Minsky.)[4]

In Paris I have read Rozanov and love him very much, but I do not like that concrete cultural content to which he is devoted with his pure, Biblical devotion.

I have no definite feelings toward society, God, or man, but for this reason I love life, faith, and love all the more.

All this should help you to understand my passion for the music of life which I have found in a few French poets and, among Russian poets, in Bryusov's school. The latter captivated me by their ingenious boldness of negation, pure negation.

I live quite alone here and am occupied with almost nothing except poetry and music.

Besides Verlaine, I have also written about Rodenbach and Sologub and am planning to write about Hamsun. After that, some prose and poetry. I plan to spend the summer in Italy and, after I return, to enroll in the university[5] and to make a systematic study of literature and philosophy. Forgive me, but I have absolutely nothing to write about except myself. Otherwise the letter would turn into a "correspondence from Paris."

If you answer my letter, perhaps you will tell me something that may be of interest to me.

Your Pupil,
Osip Mandelstam
My address: rue de la Sorbonne, 12

No. 2. To V.I. Ivanov [A postcard. Postmark: Pavlovsk, St. Petersburg, June 20, 1909]

My dear and greatly esteemed Vyacheslav Ivanovich[1]!

Wherever my letter finds you, I beg one thing of you. Let me know your address, and also if and when you will be in Switzerland.

Until our departure abroad I am living with my family at Tsarskoe Selo without ever going out. Your seeds have been implanted deep in my soul, and I am frightened looking at their enormous sprouts.

I rejoice in the hope of meeting you somewhere this summer.

From the almost ruine'd by you but repaired,
Osip Mandelstam

[in the corner, written at a slant: St. Petersburg, Kolomenskaia 5]

No. 3. To V.I. Ivanov [August 13/26, 1909]

Kurhaus de Territet et Sanitorium
l'Abri
Montreux-Territet

Dear Vyacheslav Ivanovich!

First allow me a few reflections on your book.[1] It seems impossible to dispute—it is captivating and destined to win hearts.

When a person steps under the vaults of Notre Dame does he really ponder the truth of Catholicism, and does he not become a Catholic merely by virtue of being under those vaults?

Your book is magnificent in the beauty of its great architectural creations and astronomical systems. Every true poet would write just as you did if he could write books on the basis of the precise and immutable laws of his work.

You are the most incomprehensible and, in the everyday sense of the word, the obscurest poet of our time, precisely because you are, as is no one else, faithful to your nature, having consciously entrusted yourself to it. However, it seems to me that your book is too—how shall I say it?—too circular, without any angles. No matter which direction one approaches it from, it is impossible to cause injury to it or to oneself, since it has no sharp edges.

Even the tragedy in it is not an angle because you give it your consent.

Even the ecstasy is not dangerous because you foresee its outcome. And your book is fanned only by the breathing of the Cosmos, which imparts to it a charm it shares with *Zarathustra* and which compensates for the astronomical circularity of your system, which you yourself flaunt in the best parts of the book, and even flaunt persistently. Your book has something else in common with *Zarathustra*: each word in it fulfills its destiny with ardent hatred and each sincerely hates its place and its neighbors.

Excuse me for this outpouring...

I spent two weeks in Beatenburg² but then decided to spend a few weeks in a sanitorium and went to Montreux.

Here I observe a strange contrast: the sacred quiet of the sanitorium, interrupted by the dinner gong, and the call to evening roulette in the casino: *faites vos jeux messieurs!—remarques messieurs! rien ne va plus!*—the shouts of the croupiers, full of symbolic horror. I have a strange taste: I love the patches of electric light on Lake Leman, the deferential lackeys, the noiseless flight of the elevator, the marble vestibule of the hotel, and the Englishwomen who play Mozart in a half-darkened salon for an audience of two or three official listeners.

I love bourgeois, European comfort and am attached to it not only physically, but also emotionally.

Perhaps my poor health is to blame for this? But I never ask myself whether it is good or bad.

I would also like to tell you the following:

There is one place in your book where two great perspectives open up, as if from the rational solution of the postulate about the two parallel geometries—Euclid's and Lobachevsky's. This is the amazingly penetrating image where the man who refused to dance covers his face with his hands and leaves the circle of dancers.

Have our friends already gathered in St. Petersburg³?

What is *Apollon*⁴ doing? And *Island*⁵?

How I long to see one of our poet friends, or even one of our poets with whom I am not acquainted. Do you know what, V.I.? Write to me (I know you will answer me, but what if you suddenly don't?) when someone goes abroad. Perhaps somehow I will see someone, and to see you I am ready to travel a very great distance if necessary. One more request. If you have an extra copy, a completely extra copy of *Guiding Stars*, could it not somehow find its way into my careful hands?...

Tell me also, V.I., what kind of lyric poets there are in Germany these days. Besides Dehmel,[6] I do not know of a single one. The Germans likewise do not know—but all the same there must be lyric poets.

I kiss you affectionately, V.I., and am grateful to you, I myself do not know for what, which is the best kind of gratitude.

Osip Mandelstam

P.S. I am sending some poems.[7] Do whatever you want with them —whatever I want—whatever you can.

No. 4. To V.I. Ivanov [Postcard. Heidelberg, October 13/26, 1909]

Dear Vyacheslav Ivanovich!

If you want to write me and are not answering me for some extraneous reason, write me all the same.

There are many things I want to tell you, but I can't. I'm not up to it.

Love,
Osip Mandelstam

No. 5. To V.I. Ivanov [Postcard. Heidelberg, October 22/November 4, 1909]

Dear, as before, Vyacheslav Ivanovich!

I cannot help sending you my lyrical quests and achievements. Just as I am obliged to you for the former, so the latter also belong to you by right although you, perhaps, are not even aware of it.

Yours,
Osip Mandelstam

No. 6. To V.I. Ivanov [On train: Frankfurt—Karlsruhe—Basel, November 11/24, 1909]

Dear Vyacheslav Ivanovich!
　　Here are some more poems.[1]

With unfailing love,
Osip Mandelstam

No. 7. To V.I. Ivanov [Heidelberg, December 13/26, 1909]

Dear Vyacheslav Ivanovich!
　　Perhaps you will read through these poems[1]?

With profound respect,
O. Mandelstam

P.S. Please excuse all the awful things you have received from me.

No. 8. To V.I. Ivanov [Heidelberg, December 17/30, 1909]

Dear Vyacheslav Ivanovich!
　　This poem was supposed to be a "romance sans paroles"[1] *(Dans l'interminable ennui...)*. "Paroles," that is, intimate-lyrical, personal: I tried to restrain, to bridle it with the bridle of rhythm.
　　I am curious to know whether this poem is bridled securely enough.
　　I can't help remembering your remarks on the anti-lyrical nature of iambics. Could you have meant, perhaps, an anti-intimate nature? The iambus is a rein on mood.

With profound respect,
O. Mandelstam

No. 9. To V.I. Ivanov [Postcard. Postmark: Hyvinge Sanitorium, Hyvinkaa, March 2/15, 1911]

Dear Vyacheslav Ivanovich!

I have gone to Finland for several weeks due to my poor health. Accept my deep regards and be very strict if you read me at the "Academy of Verse."[1]

With sincere respect,
Osip Mandelstam

No. 10. To V.I. Ivanov [Vyborg, August 21/September 3, 1911]

Dear Vyacheslav Ivanovich!

I hasten to inform you of the joyous news that some new poems by Tyutchev may have been discovered. Namely: Senator A.F. Koni told me that his archives contain a series of letters from Tyutchev to Pletneva. The content of this series is of a very intimate nature. Koni obtained the letters directly from Pletneva herself. They contain individual lines of verse (some of them from known poems), as well as poems in their entirety which illuminate the text.

There is one poem, incidentally, with the following content: the poet would like to walk in the intense heat, along a thorny path, so that through physical exhaustion he might alleviate his suffering from love. Some time ago Koni reported to the Academy about these treasures, but was met with profound indifference! Within a few days the precious papers will be at my disposal and then we shall know what kind of holiday awaits us...

Hoping to see you soon,
With profound respect,
Iosif Mandelstam

No. 11. To Fyodor Sologub, April 27, 1915

Greatly esteemed Fyodor Kuzmich[1]!

I read your letter with great astonishment. In it you speak of your intention to keep your distance from the Futurists, Acmeists, and those affiliated with them. Although I do not presume to judge your relations with the Futurists and their "affiliates," as an Acmeist I consider it my duty to remind you of the following: the initiative for your estrangement from the Acmeists belonged entirely to the latter. You were not recruited as a member of the Guild of Poets, whatever your wishes may have been, nor were you invited to contribute to the magazine *Hyperboreus*[2] or to print your books with the publishing houses Guild of Poets, Hyperboreus, and Akme.[3] The same applies to the public appearances of the Acmeists as such. As for my suggestion that you participate in the Tenishev School Benefit for one of the military hospitals, in that instance I was acting as a former pupil of the school and not as the representative of any particular literary group. It is true that several Acmeists, including myself, visited your home in response to an invitation from you and A.N. Chebotarevskaia,[4] but after your letter I have every reason to conclude that that was a mistake on their part.[5]

With sincere respect,
Osip Mandelstam

No. 12. To S.K. Makovsky, May 8, 1915

Greatly esteemed Sergei Konstantinovich[1]!

In November of last year I submitted an article on Chaadaev[2] to *Apollon* which was accepted for publication. This article has still not been printed although half a year has passed. I do not know what reasons prevented the article, each month, from being included in the following issue. However, since I do not wish to wait until these reasons are inoperative, I consider my article free and ask you to return me a copy of it, since at the present time I do not remember where the original manuscript of the article is located.

Respectfully yours,
Osip Mandelstam
Monetnaia Boulevard,
Bldg. 15, apt. 38

No. 13. To his mother, July 20, 1915 [Theodosia]

Dear Mama!
I received a telegram just yesterday about Shura's[1] arrival, which must have crossed with mine. I am expecting Shura tomorrow and I strongly approve of his coming here. August and September are wonderful here. He will live in Voloshin's summer house.[2]

I kiss Papa, Zhenya,[3] and Grandmother
Your Osia

No. 14. To his mother, July 20, 1916

Dear Mama[1]!
Everything has turned out well for us. Shura has recovered and gotten into the rut of a peaceful life. He is no longer bored and he looks completely different. The day before yesterday we were driven to Theodosia with great pomp: automobiles, supper with the governor. I read, beaming white in my tennis outfit, from the stage of the summer theater.[2] We returned in the morning and spent yesterday resting. This autumn I will definitely take my examinations.[3] Please find out the dates and send me either

Windelband's or Vvedensky's book on ancient philosophy. We have acquired a second room. Darling Mama, write me how you feel about my coming home—whether I might be of use in P. Congratulations on the Polytechnical Institute! Good boy, Zhenya! I kiss Papa!

Osia

No. 15. To N. Ya. Mandelstam,[1] December 5 [1919], Theodosia

My darling child! There is almost no hope that this letter will reach you. Tomorrow Kolachevsky is traveling to Kiev through Odessa. I pray to God that you will hear what I say: my dear child, I cannot live and do not want to live without you. You are all my joy, you are my own. For me that is as simple as God's day. You have become so dear to me that I constantly talk to you, call you, complain to you. It is only to you that I can tell everything, everything. My poor darling! You are your mama's *kinechka*[2] and you are my *kinechka* as well. I rejoice and thank God that He gave you to me. With you nothing will be frightening, nothing will be difficult.

Your childish little paw, all charcoal-smeared, your dark-blue smock—I remember everything, I haven't forgotten a thing...

Forgive me my weakness and for not always being able to show how much I love you.

Nadyusha! If you should suddenly appear here this minute, I would cry for joy. Forgive me, my beastikins! Let me kiss your dear little brow. Your plump, childish, dear little brow! My daughter, my sister, I smile with your smile and I hear your voice in the silence.

Yesterday I deliberately and wittingly spoke "for you." I said: "I *must* (in the feminine form) find it." That is, you said it *through* me... You and I are just like children—we do not look for important words but just say what must be said.

Nadyusha, we shall be together at any cost. I shall find you and live for you because you give me life, without knowing it yourself—my darling—"by your immortal tenderness..."

Nadenka! I received four letters all at once, in one day, only just now... I telegraphed many times, I called.

Now there is only one route open from here[3]: Odessa, all the closer to Kiev. I'll leave in a few days. My address: *The Odessa Sheet*, in care of Mochulsky.[4] From Odessa I may somehow make my way through: somehow, somehow I'll reach you...

I have already been in Theodosia, for five weeks. Shura has been with me all the time. Panya was here. He left for Evpatoria. Katyusha Ginzberg is living in the Astoria Hotel. There is one copy of *Crocodile*[5] in the city!! Also Mordkin and Froman.[6] (It is cold and dark. The "Fountain." Speculators.) I cannot forgive myself for leaving without you. Goodbye, my friend! May God preserve you! My little child! Goodbye!

Your O.M.: "freak"

Kolachevsky is coming back. I will beg him to take you to Odessa. Take advantage of the opportunity!!

No. 16. To N. Ya. Mandelstam, March 9, 1921

Nadyusha, dearest!

I received your note. I'll be in Kiev in a few days. Do not lose heart, darling. We'll think of a way to make things comfortable for you. We'll see each other very soon, darling! I'm all ready for my departure. Just don't go anywhere, but wait calmly for me to come!

Yours,
O. Mandelstam

No. 17. To. V. Ya. Khazina[1] [May-June] 1921

Dear Vera Yakovlevna!

I am glad to inform you that everything is going well for us. On Saturday Nadya and I will probably go to Tiflis under favorable conditions and assured of financial support.

I met my friend here, the Special Commissioner for the evacuation of the Caucasus, and he will take us with him when he goes to Georgia on business. He is the artist Lopatinsky, a very good man: he once worked with me in the Ministry of Education (Narkompros). He is now the head of a huge organization in the Caucasus.[2] We are on very friendly terms and he'll do everything he can for me. I made a trip to Petersburg without Nadya. We didn't have to go hungry. We're living with Zhenya. The carpet will be sold very cheaply for the trip. Carpets aren't at a high premium these days and are very hard to sell; we think we'll get about two hundred thousand. Nadya is well, she doesn't drink unboiled water and she won't eat any raw food on the trip. She is cheerful.

You can reach us at the address: Mandelstam, Central Office of the Special Commissioner of Evacuation in the Caucasus, Rostov. This is the center. We'll travel further from here. Your letter will be forwarded from here according to our itinerary.

When we pass through Kharkov we'll telegraph to Kiev.

Before leaving, we'll submit our application to the Lithuanian mission.[3] The grounds (my papers) have been acknowledged to be *sufficient*. It will take a month and will go through automatically in our absence.

Give my heartfelt greetings to Yakov Arkadievich[4] and Anna Yakovlevna.[5]

With true devotion,
O. Mandelstam

No. 18. To his father [early Spring 1923]

Dear Papa!

Today Shura is leaving to visit you for two or three days. It would be senseless for me to come now because I must wait for Bukharin's answer. I was at his place yesterday. He was very attentive and today he'll call Zinoviev to talk about Zhenya.[1] He promised to do everything possible and suggested that I keep in contact with him regularly.

Incidentally, he said: "I cannot give any commissions... A few days ago the Central Committee forbade its members to do that. Only the roundabout method remains."

Then he said: "You take it as a commission (did he mean me?), you are a famous person(?)."[2] Tomorrow I'll learn from Bukharin how Zinoviev reacted to his request and what his *auspicii* were: his vision of the future (Bukharin's expression). He also asked *which of the (important) Communists know Zhenya;* he was obviously counting on *supporting their action on the side.* If possible, *get a character reference for Zhenya from the Communist Party Organization of the institute: a recommendation about his behavior and attitude over the past year.* I will give it to Bukharin and that will make his work easier. I repeat: he received me exceptionally well. We had a long talk, about twenty minutes. He said that Zinoviev *will still come to Moscow.* He regretted that he had not known yesterday morning when Zinoviev was here. *You must not trouble Zinoviev himself.*

Everything is going well for us. There is just one problem. *Although we have the essentials, lately we have had just barely enough money. Right now* I can't send you a single cent. Don't detain Shura—he must return before the deadline—otherwise he'll lose his job, which for him is *everything.*

It is most advisable for the Pan to come for two or three days (so as not to leave Marya Nikolaevna[3] alone). I myself can leave as soon as there is reason to. No one is detaining me...

No. 19. To his father [Winter 1923-24]

Dear Papa[1]!

We received your last letter-feuilleton and it made us very happy. You really get to the heart of the matter and show a great insight. We answered your letter right away with a telegram. And now, in anticipation of your arrival, I want to answer all your questions in detail.

When we arrived in Moscow we stayed with Evgeny Yakovlevich[2] at Ostozhenka for three weeks. It was quite cozy and cheery thanks to his kind nature and to his recent divorce—but it wasn't very convenient.

I had grown somewhat distraught. I had let go of the reins. We had no work, no money, no apartment. Nadyusha made four trips out of town (we didn't even think of looking in the city). Everything was in vain. Everything there is shacks, rubbish, expensive, slush. A room in the city costs forty chervontsy. We were ready to leave—but to go where? We wanted to stop our account at the *store* in order to live.

And suddenly a man comes and says: go immediately to Bolshaya Yakimanka Street. Twenty minutes later we were in Zamoskvorechie.[3] It is a quiet street. The youse is a "mansion with columns." The apartment belongs to a professor who lives in his summer cottage the year round. The room is enormous—eight square arshins, two windows, light, quiet... Some kind of eccentric lives next to us, he is some sort of music critic or poetry esthete... The house is poverty-ridden, as in 1920.

They are asking fifteen chervontsy for the room and are renting it until autumn. Naturally, we took it. We shall see. Apparently we will buy the room outright. It's already been a month since we moved, registered, and moved the furniture. Our room is warm and incredibly quiet. It takes twenty minutes on the streetcar to get to the center of town. Not a single soul comes to visit us.

Our own kitchen...firewood...quiet... In a word, paradise. Evgeny Yakovlevich was the obstetrician of the move. He borrowed five chervontsy from someone when we needed it. At %%?! I scraped together the remainder. All our things are intact.

What am I doing? I'm working for money. The crisis is grave.

It's much worse than last year. But I've already made some progress. There were more translations, articles, and so forth... World Literature[4] is loathesome to me. I dream of quitting this nonsense. The last time I worked for myself was in the summer. Last year I still worked for myself quite often. This year—not a bit...

We have all the necessities for winter, papa: shoes, galoshes, coats, hats, gloves. I gave Nadyusha nearly a whole new wardrobe (two dresses). I wear an old suit but it's still holding up. The only people who visit us are our brothers, Shura and Evgeny Yakovlevich.

Shura is living with my friend Parnok.[5] Three live in one room. Disorder. Filth. Cold. His room is near the "Union" on Tverskoi Boulevard.[6] He tires very easily. He visits us nearly every day...

No. 20. To N. Ya. Mandelstam [between October 1 and 4, 1925]

My darling Nadenka! Sweetheart!

You're just about to leave Moscow and I'm writing to you at the post office at six p.m. Yesterday on the way back I stopped in to see Vygodsky.[1] A meeting of the Domkom was being held at his place, but later we talked about Priboi,[2] and I suggested Edgar Allan Poe (?). However, at Livshits's[3] house some redhaired man resembling a cook answered the door and told me: "There's no one home." In the evening I even translated three pages. Anya was very humble. Today we got up at eight o'clock, worked until twelve. Later, I went everywhere: to Priboi and to GIZ.[4] They promised to pay sixty rubles at the paper tomorrow... Gorlin[5] submitted some kind of "Billya"[6] —100 lines—50 rubles, and Priboi wanted Edgar Allan Poe (?)...

My darling, I'm writing all this to you because this makes it possible for me to leave, to come to you, and I'm already closer, my bird, my little gloved sparrow. I kiss your little gloves and your dear little hat.

Now listen: I can actually leave on Tuesday and will explain it tomorrow. Tomorrow I'll submit my application to the Finance

Department and send it to Luga.

Sasha cries all the time... Nadyusha, I'm *very happy* and healthy. I don't rush about, but do everything calmly, and I think about you all the time, about my own dear Nadya...

Nadichka! Ah! My sweet child, take care of yourself. Wait for me... I'll telegraph you the day I leave. God be with you, Nadenka. And I'll bring you a little ring...

Osya

My child, we came back home—we were twenty kopeks short, I wrote foolishly about Gorlin: the contract was signed today and what is more—100 lines of "Billya."

Dear child, be calm,—the house is warm and the sun shone today. I want to come to you and be with you...

[My Nadka, Nadyushok, Nanusha! Tomorrow I'll write you twice.

I kiss you, Donya, write every day, if only a postcard. O.E. is in a fine mood. I am anxious without you. How's your health? Anya.] [7]

No. 21. To. N. Ya. Mandelstam, October 5, 1925, 6:00 p.m.

My darling Nanusha!

I came home at four o'clock, dined on the usual meatballs, lit a fire in the fireplace and heated the bathroom. Anya got a letter, but not from her Zhenechka. And, Nadichka, tomorrow I'll pay for the insurance and part of what we owe to Sasha. Today I was at the insurance office on Moskovskaya Street and I was told that everything would be officially arranged there. Today we paid the interest on the watch. Tomorrow the *Leningrad Red News*[1] will give me sixty rubles, and on Wednesday the 21st, Gorlin will give me fifty more rubles for some poems. That means I already have 110 of the 200 rubles. The Priboi problem is nearly solved. I'm looking for Balmont's translation of Edgar Allan Poe to show them. Nadichka, I'll be able to come to you this week without waiting until Tuesday, for there are trains leaving Moscow. I have twenty pages left of *The Thousand and Second Night*,[2] but tomorrow GIZ will give me only 100 rubles, and 125 more on the twentieth.

That's how things stand, my darling. I'll bring you a book without fail: I'll think up something.

Nanochka, why didn't you write from Moscow? Is that really how Niakas behave? Nadik, will there be a telegram from you tomorrow? Marietta[3] has returned and I want to drop in on her tomorrow.

How was your train trip?

Nadik, I'm so anxious to see you that my head is spinning. Rejoice in life, my child, we are fortunate, rejoice as I do in our reunion. God be with you, Nadichka. Sleep soundly. Remember my advice, my little child: 1) go to the doctor, 2) get better lodgings, 3) use arsenic and compresses.

Yesterday I met Vogel[4] on the street; he was looking for an apartment in our area. He says that it's most important for you to stay off your feet. Don't walk anywhere! Take a cab to the post office or send someone else. I kiss your lovely hair, my child. Until our reunion, my darling little bird.

Nadik, I beg you, don't smoke!

No. 22. To N. Ya. Mandelstam [the beginning of November, 1925]

My little pet! I'm writing this five minutes before the post office closes. Thank you for your tender words, darling. What's happening to you there? Don't let them insult you. Everything is going well with me; I'll set out to join you on the fifteenth.[1] That's almost certain... I cannot live without you, my swallow. But be calm—I'm living right and am well. I'm having good luck in my work. I kiss you, my beloved.

May God preserve you, my sunshine.
Your Nanny...

The watch is fixed. I'll redeem it.

No. 23. To N. Ya. Mandelstam [The end of January, 1926]

My beloved joy! I don't want to write you a postcard because I want to tell you how cute you were—my darling in threadbare slippers—standing on the embankment like a dear angel...

I kiss you, kiss you, kiss you and rejoice that you are with me, that you are with me!

I had an excellent trip. It was invigorating... The telegrams have been sent. The ticket is in my pocket.

I was very sleepy and cold. Now I've warmed up and rested.

Good night, Nadichka. Sleep, darling, and wake up wise.

I'll write you throughout the journey. It is now ten minutes to nine.

No. 24. To N. Ya. Mandelstam [Leningrad] February 2, [1926]

My darling little pet!

Hello! Your Nanny is talking to you and kisses your lovely brow. I'm well, my little child. And how are you? Don't be stingy with your letters.

Shura,[1] quixotic and terribly sweet, met me in Moscow. Then I visited Pasternak[2] and saw their little boy. "I'm still little," he said. He's two and a half years old. He insists on taking part in the general conversation.[3] Shura didn't succeed in contacting your Zhenya.[4] He talked with Anya[5] on the telephone. She said: "I have a private position." She didn't want to elaborate. I'll learn the details tomorrow. This is how things stand... (Yes, in Moscow, by the way, Pasternak talked my ear off and I missed the train. My things left at 9:30, and I left on the next train at 11:00, seen off by Shura, after I had sent a telegram to Klin. I arrived, and my luggage was handed to me at GPU. What an adventure!) This, Nadya, is how things stand:

LenGIZ is an upside-down ant-hill. It tends to partly squeeze, partly destroy. No one understands anything or knows anything. Gorlin shrugs his shoulders with a guilty smile. He is surrounded only by his closest colleagues... Women and the general public have stopped coming. Reviews are still done here, but the books are sent to Moscow for approval.[6] The first batch has already been sent. As soon as it is returned there will be another discussion. Their slogan is: be prepared for everything and make use of the last weeks to secure work for yourself. Tomorrow GIZ will enter 125 rubles into my final account. Today I received 100 rubles for "nothing" at the *Star.*[7] Belitsky arranged it. Ionov is leaving. Belitsky is staying, so far... I received three books to review.[8] I'm "included" in Gorlin's request for Saturday. Everything is absolutely calm at Priboi. They do the rewriting and I do the corrections. They promise not to delay. I found a typist and today I'll start dictation.

I found Grandfather[9] in a poor state, all hunched over into a little ball, with a headache. I cheered him up.

But Zhenya is irreproachable. M.N.[10] is as polite as a brick wall. Yesterday they heated the bath for me. Zhenya is offering me 1) the dining room, 2) the well-lighted servant's room, 3) the room next to theirs. I categorically refused the rooms. This is what we'll do: I'll reimburse Nadezhda for 10 or 15 rubles, and she'll move into the dark servant's room for a month. Zhenya assures me that this is the best thing to do, since I need a "house."[11]

The weather is very mild: 3-4 degrees Centigrade. The transition was very easy.

And so, my darling, February is paid for in full[12] (Priboi plus 225 from GIZ). I'll sign one more contract and we'll be free again and can be together starting in March. Today I'll call Vogel about the quartz-lamp treatments and will let you know by telegram.

Remember, by the first of March I can be with you at any moment.

Poor little bird, what's happening to you there? Send a detailed telegram.

No, my little child, I can be with you at any time—just say when!

God be with you, darling... Your friend, brother, husband...

No. 25. To N. Ya. Mandelstam [Leningrad. February 1926]

My darling little bird!

This is how I spent the day: in the morning I wasted three hours at GIZ. The cashier's office was closed. We waited for a banker. Then at two o'clock I went to the telegraph office, then back to GIZ, then to the Gourmet for lunch. Today Gorlin said that as soon as Angert[1] delivers the approved plan we'll conclude the contract. Then I went to The Sower[2] and showed them Gorlin's new books. They'll take them. Gorlin will give them back if I ask him to.

Well, my little child, enough about business. I know how much it upsets you, and that's why I'm writing in advance. You and I have better things to talk about, my swallow! I love you, my beastikins, more than ever before—I can't live without you— I want to come join you... And I will be with you...

My beloved, you're thousands of versts away from me in a big empty room with your thermometer! My life, you must understand that you are my life! What is your temperature? Are you happy? Do you laugh? And do you understand, or do you not, that I'm willing to be separated from you only for the month of February and *not a day* more!

My little child, I'm a swine, I haven't seen Anya yet. I'm busy and so is she. We've only talked to each other on the phone. I've been at the Vygodskys' and the Bens'.[3] David and Emma[4] are imperturbable Spaniards. The Bens complain about their little baby. His name is Kiril (?). He has evil, professorial, yellow eyes. He doesn't smile but gets very angry. They're very *crowded* now, but soon there may be a vacant apartment for us in Vygodsky's house.

Meanwhile, my little child, I sleep in the dining room. *Our* horsehair mattress is on the sofa. I go to sleep at one a.m. and all is very quiet until ten o'clock. It's warm and nice.[5]

I was just at the Punins'.[6] *The old woman*[7] *lives there;* she was lying down on the sofa, she had a cold but was happy. She greeted me with "scandals": 1) Georgy Ivanov[8] is writing "terrible pasquilles" about her and me in the Paris newspapers; 2) *The Noise of Time* provoked a "storm" of ecstasy and enthusiasm in the foreign press, for which we can be congratulated.[9] Another curious thing: today I read in the *Evening News* that "yesterday I went to the Finance Department to complain about taxes."[10] And it never even occurred to me to go! The newspaper is lying—but what's the good. I'll send you the clipping and save the newspaper for the revenue inspector!

I still haven't had any letters from you, my little pet. Do you know where I'm writing? At the Nikolaevsky station, after ten p.m., after the Punins...

Until tomorrow, sweet child! God be with you, my darling! I kiss you tenderly, a long kiss... I kiss your little paws and hair and little eyes...

I'll go get in line with this letter now... Write every day, darling.

Your Nanny.[11]

Nadya, do not hide *anything* from me! Do you hear, darling?!

No. 26. To N. Ya. Mandelstam [Leningrad] February 7, [1926] 6:00 p.m.

My darling!

Today I received your sad letter and by evening I expect an answer to my telegram. Little beastikins, are things really going badly for you there? Tell them to heat your room well. What kind of slippers did you buy? Do you go into the city? How much do you weigh? My darling, I haven't gone out for four days now: I have a "slight case of flu"—my temperature got up to 37.3, but it's already gone down. And incidentally, the weather isn't as cold now. I'll be able to go out by tomorrow. Grandfather doesn't even attempt to lecture me on philosophy: it's all the same to him—I've gotten off the subject... Zhenya is jabbering on the telephone right by me. Modpik[1] is flourishing! Tatka[2] sat on my lap and wrote you a letter all by herself... Today, my little one, I got around to the sheets from your work, and I enjoy leafing through them.

My little bird, sweet little squirrel, every day I go to sleep I say to myself: "Oh Lord, save my Nadenka!" Love shall preserve us, Nadya. We have nothing to fear, my joy! Distance has no meaning for us. But I'm insanely anxious to be with you.

In about ten days I'll finish my business in Petersburg and will come to you by way of Moscow. Sweet child! Beastikins! Don't you dare be alarmed. I've become a man of pre-war strength. Everything comes easy for me now.

It's peaceful and boring at Zhenya's. M.N. suffers from attacks. Grandpa is always offended, as if everyone ignores him and leaves him out and so on... Yes, he's right, my dear, but the family is basically unfriendly... Nanusha, I dream of how I'll go into the city tomorrow, visit Gorlin, see people, fuss about the new contract, send you newspapers and a special delivery letter.

But right now, darling, Papa is taking this letter away from me to mail it. I kiss you, my beloved, I'm with you each night, I do not leave you for a minute.

Your Nanny.

No. 27. To N. Ya. Mandelstam [February 1926]

A letter from you every day... Thank you, my pet. You are my life, yet still you ask... Do you know, my child, these weeks will pass quickly, very quickly. We have been torn away from each other. It's some kind of barbarous absurdity that we can't be together.

I haven't gone out for two days. It's more than twenty degrees below zero (Centigrade) and there is a strong wind. The windows have frozen. I'm sitting in the leather study. It's warm and quiet. Tatka is here. I am working calmly. The whole book has already been copied for me. I can honestly say that you are very smart; your translation is very good, it's not bad at all. You have been a great help to me.[1] Yesterday Zhenya found a typist for me who will work here at home.

Grandfather is an angel. He goes to Priboi and to the post

office for me. They have my reviews but won't pay for them right away: they are being recopied and gathered together. Tomorrow Broide, the head of GIZ, is coming. We're waiting for full clarification.

I still haven't seen Anya, but I talk to her every day. It turns out (I had to twist her arm) that she is working as a governess for two children (the girl is nine years old and the boy seven) in a "middle-bourgeois" family. That is what she calls her "private position." Her voice sounded cheerful, and over the phone I heard the children pestering her. "They want me to go watch their show," she said.

How did you spend the money, Nadyushok? Don't give more than thirty rubles for room no. 8... Keep fifty rubles for your own expenses. In a few days I'll send another hundred.

My child, if only I had your photograph with me! I wrapped your tussah scarf around my neck and wear it like a jabot. Our wool afghan—that's also you.

Write me the truth, only the truth about your health. Punin's wife[2] doesn't recommend quartz-lamp treatments, but says it's better to wait for sunny weather. I've just talked to Shklovsky on the phone. He's here. He'll visit me tomorrow. "I have," he says, "a matter to discuss with you." I think, Nadenka, that when I've finished with Priboi I'll go to Moscow, and from there it's so close to you that I won't be able to resist... What do you say? By the way, I'll be judicious as long as necessary, as long as it's possible to be judicious.

God be with you, my beloved, my joy, my bride without a ring... I love you the only way I can love, that is, I'm growing foolish and can't talk to anyone about anything, my life...

Tomorrow I'll subscribe to the *Evening Red News* for my little child and I'll send off a copy of *Streetcar*.[3]

You won't believe this, but I enjoy living with Zhenya. Tatka goes to kindergarten. She's turned into a "lady." She is a chubby little girl and very naughty. She reads everything. A few days ago she even read the words "abortion" ("Grandma, what's that?") and "government Senate." Anna Andreevna sends her regards. So does Katerina Konstantinova.

Nanusha, don't smoke (me too). Eat eggs and butter and drink cocoa. Make the old woman work harder. Entice her with chervontsy...

No. 28. To N. Ya. Mandelstam [February 1926]

My darling, beloved Nadenka!

Yesterday Papa was late in sending my special delivery letter, so today I'm finishing it. I reached an agreement yesterday with Shklovsky. He suggests that I take a trip to Moscow. His publishing house seems to have realized that I must be fed. I will go as soon as I am finished at Priboi. Right now I'm waiting for the typist who called to say she had already left with the typewriter. I talked to Gorlin late yesterday evening. We have not parted company. The work will continue.[1] Angert[2] has returned from Moscow. And there's still another thing I have to tell you, my pet: I cannot live without you. I'm suffocating. I'm counting the days, but I'm healthy and hardy, as they say. Send me telegrams more often, my little bird. Do you have to scrimp and save? Are they stifling you? I kiss your dear little hands... Your...

No. 29. To N. Ya. Mandelstam [February 1926]

I hear your plaintive voice, my darling little dovekin. Don't cry, my little one. Don't cry, my little daughter. Wipe away your tears and listen to your nanny: in about a month I can start thinking about Kiev. I'll do everything possible to rescue you from the old woman. This week I have 80 rubles from Gorlin... On the third, Priboi will give me the first hundred. The entire month and even next month are quite secure financially. I'll try to get hold of 200 or 250 rubles and send it to you in time for you to move. Is it true that you're not in pain, my child? I beg you not to hide anything from me. And your weight? If for some reason I send less money than expected, then keep some to buy good food, for extra purchases: tangerines, caviar, good butter, pastries, ham. Brighten up your sad life. Go into the city.

Vogel is very pleased with my report. He approves of the quartz-lamp treatments. "Why not?" he says; he advises against spending the spring here, especially March.

You know I can get money for you, darling. The Rybakovs are here. Punin will try to get some from Priboi. I haven't asked yet. I didn't know that things were so bad for you there. So far I've managed to stay independent, but right after today's letter I'll talk to Punin and Zhenya and, naturally, they will help me out.

Anya was here yesterday. You wouldn't recognize her: she is lively and healthier. She is working as a governess for a wealthy Trust executive. She wears her old clothes, her gray overalls and fur jacket from Tiflis. She's jumping right into things. Mama knit her a pink scarf.

And I, my child, go about merrily in papa's Jewish fur coat and Shura's cap with earflaps. I lost my own cap on the trip. I've become used to winter. I read Gorlin's French books on the streetcar.

Nadik, don't you dare not sleep. Order them to heat your place properly every day.

At about eleven p.m. they put our "horsehair" mattress on the sofa in the dining room. I make the bed. Zhenya is never home. It's quiet. Grandfather is out for a stroll. I only manage to say: "Save, oh Lord, my Nadenka," and then I fall asleep.

Gorlin commissioned me to write reviews (pending approval) for Moscow. Whatever is approved will be mine.[1] My first approved book. When I finish with Daudistel[2] (yesterday I submitted all of *our* work), I'll go to Moscow, where Shklovsky has done the groundwork for me.

Draw a picture for me, one of your clumsy pictures, little daughter. I love you, my little girl, and for that reason I'm happy here. Your husband, my pet.

No. 30. To N. Ya. Mandelstam [February 1926]

My darling, beloved little girl!

What's wrong with you? Don't worry, my joy, don't be alarmed. Today I'm awaiting your telegram with a report on your health. This evening I'll consult Vogel (for the second time). So far he believes it would be better for you to wait there before going to Kiev. In any case, I'll take you away from Tarkhova. I have money. I haven't touched Priboi yet. So far only GIZ has given my money (300 rubles). That's good. Priboi will give me an advance.[1] Moscow will give me some, too. There will be a new contract. I can—and I'm very serious—either come to you there or else leave for Kiev to meet you there (if Vogel allows it).

Go on your diet again for a short time, my little bird... That's me speaking, not the doctor. I now have a stenographer (Priboi, of course). I'll write very, very often... I'll write a second letter today. I'm healthy as an ox. The weather is milder. I kiss my beloved...

No. 31. To N. Ya. Mandelstam, February 12 [1926]

My darling little daughter, I happened to drop in on the Vygodskys and am writing this letter at their place. I took a look at our china cabinet and am now sitting in the red armchair.[1] I talked to Vogel and reported all your complaints to him. He thinks that your nausea is gastric and that cooking oil and fat is the major cause. You must find good board in Yalta, whatever the cost. Take Emelyan along as a guide and start searching. You'll have money enough to move by the fifteenth: I know that you need 190 + 100 rubles in the meantime, not counting the 75 that I sent today.

He will at least allow you to go to Kiev now, but he recommends that you spend the spring in Yalta—with good board, of course—and he forbids you to spend spring in the North with us... A local doctor, let's say Tsanov, should have the final say, of course. Has he been to see you, my child?

My sweet child, I'm living serenely and working with all my strength. I've found a way to take shorthand. I do twenty pages in two hours. The stenographer comes here in the afternoon, and in the evening I work for another hour with a typist who lives on the Eighth Line.[2]

LenGIZ is meeting me halfway. By the way, Wolfson,[3] an old fellow from Odessa with whom I'm on very friendly terms, has been sent by Moscow to supervise the editorial department. He's a real bigwig. I dragged him along to meet Gorlin and he's arranged something for me.

Today I had dinner at the Punins. Their little girl Irina is marvelously candid and kind-hearted. She is reading *Streetcar*[4] and reworking it into prose. She draws wonderful pictures. The Rybakovs are offering 200 rubles. If Priboi delays, I'll take it, but perhaps I'll make do. How do you like that! So far I'm not a single kopek in debt.

My darling little sister, you write me very little about yourself and what you write is very vague. How do you spend your days? Are you "bedridden" or "ambulatory"? Do you ever go into the city? Go to perfumeries, go out of your way for your nanny and send me a telegram—even if it's as brief as a commercial telegram.

Nadik, what do you mean by "the usual pains"? I want to know how frequent the pains are, how long they last, when they occur... Do you keep a hot water bottle in bed with you? Who is there with you, darling, when you're not feeling well? Everyone's talking about mesentery glands: it's terribly fashionable. They say there's a good sanitorium in Tsarskoe Selo where one can have a private room and where I'll have visiting rights. Incidentally, they treat glands there by injecting calcium into the veins. I learned that quite by chance. I'll look into it for the summer. But meanwhile, my pet, you're entirely free to choose: Yalta or Kiev. Just think it over carefully and ask Tsanov's advice.

If you stay in Yalta I'll probably come for the month of March, after I've gone to Moscow; then I will have all the more reason to go to Kiev.

Some strange "engineer" has been calling grandfather yesterday and today, asking him to do some leather work. Poor grandfather changed out of his felt boots into good boots and went to the "conference." And Anya really did become a nanny (I'm used to Nanny with a capital letter). Believe me, Nadka, my precious, lovely mouth, I am filled with you and the thoughts of you. How is your golden beard of hair? Let me kiss it. I love you madly, so much that I'm not even aware of the distance separating us. I don't have a picture of you. You have the "till," so have your picture taken. The most difficult separation has passed, my little bird, and we're already close to seeing each other. I'm counting the days. May the Lord preserve you, my pet.

No. 32. To N. Ya. Mandelstam [February 1926]

My beautiful darling, my beloved, when you receive this letter you'll already have a lot of money—the "till"—and then no one can insult you anymore, my dearest.

Punin borrowed 200 rubles for me from Rybakov. I still haven't touched Priboi: in a few days you'll receive the entire amount. I can borrow still more from the Rybakovs. I don't have any deadline to meet. The matter is complicated by some woman being in debt to him...

I'm going out of my mind, my darling: everything is so terrifying from a distance, although I know you write the truth. I implore you to get a permanent doctor and to obey his orders. Vogel insists on it. It's an absolute necessity. Send me all the records of your temperature and weight when you go into the city. How many days have you been in bed? Are you still feeling nauseated? What are you eating—normal food or a special diet? I beg you to write in detail, detail to the point of stupidity and foolishness. *Otherwise I cannot endure it.* When do you feel pains? How many minutes do they last? Write, my darling.

It no longer appears so absurd and impossible for me to come and see you, my little bird. There's a good chance of a contract with GIZ. It seems I'll be able to come, with my work, for the month of March, with a stopover in Moscow. You and I shall prosper once again! And you, my child, will spend April in Kiev. And starting in May, I'll be your nanny in Tsarskoe Selo.

Zhenya's immediate concern about his relationship with Natasha[1] is even more of an immediate concern for M.N.[2] and grandfather. They are both severely opposed to it. M.N. is a kind, intelligent woman (Zhenka is always blaming her). "Let him get married," she says, "no matter how hard it'll be for me!" At night she unburdens her soul to me, and I love to hear her apt, colorful way of speaking. Zhenya looks distraught and guilty. Natasha just looks stupid.

Tatka is too grown up for me. She said to Natasha: "Why do you look upon my papa as if he were your child?"

My child, I'm writing to you at the station again: it's become a habit with me, just as if I were visiting you. And every morning I sit in Nadezhda's kitchen and wait for a letter... Will there be a telegram from you today, dear? I'm taking shorthand and dictating furiously these days. There are seventeen pages left. Hurrah! Hurrah! Tomorrow I'll be done. Then I'll devote all my energy to convincing Gorlin and Wolfson to let me leave sooner to be with you. I kiss your lovely full lips and your beautiful hair... I hear your sweet voice each night...

Niakushka, my little bird, I'm coming to you... May the Lord keep you. Keep happy. I cannot live and do not want to live without you. I love you...

No. 33. To N. Ya. Mandelstam [February 1926]

My darling dummy! What's wrong with you? This morning at ten o'clock I sent you a telegram: I'm completely well, and so on... At six o'clock you still hadn't received the telegram! Amazing! Nanushka, see what my disorganization has led to: you've been suffering for three or four days now while your nanny is quite well and flourishing between Gorlin and Grünberg.[1] My little child, put your dear heart at ease—there is absolutely no reason to be upset. I'm not even exhausted. I feel incomparably better that I did in Yalta. I'm simply ashamed to write about myself.[2] But enough of that, Nadik. I kiss your dear little head, and now I have all kinds of things to tell you... First of all, this phase of my work will be finished in about ten days. Then I'll be left with a big new contract from Gorlin (tomorrow the books and answers will arrive from Moscow) and, of course, then I'll come to join you. Tell me, darling, is it nice in Yalta now that spring is on the way? Surely you'll be glad to live with your nanny by the sea with those dogs[3]? Is the first of May really too late to be in Kiev?

Grandfather was involved in a tragicomedy yesterday: he planned to celebrate Purim[4] at the Jewish watchmaker's and fell into a "trap" which kept him there from nine p.m. until 2:30 p.m. the next day in the company of many people who just dropped by. The poor man was terribly upset whenever someone alluded to the fact that he was the father of "the writer Mandelstam." He was treated considerately and was not insulted. But how sorry I am for Grandfather: just think, he's gone visiting only once all year. He was even smart enough to telephone to say that he would be "staying overnight" (without explaining why). So much for our little adventure.

Nothing has changed at LenGIZ. I call that "stabilization." Belitsky[5] and the new head of the editorial department paid me for my regular work (the last 200 rubles). Very considerate, isn't it? I'm taking shorthand at home again: it's very convenient—I do twenty pages in two hours, then I make corrections, and then I'm free to do whatever I want for the whole day.

Today is the first springlike day. Everything has melted. It's actually quite hot, it was especially warm in Gorlin's office... The tailor mended my trousers for two and a half rubles, but he cut off the prettiest part—the lower cuffs... I'm planning to buy boots. And you, Nadik, don't you need anything? Write to your nanny: she'll bring it to you. That's the truth, Nanushka. I'll bring you a watch, rings, gifts, whatever you say. Tell me, Nanushka, have you settled matters with Tarkhova? Can't you really find someplace else before spring if it's so bad there? Only be careful not to take any risks. I'm basically a conservative, you know. Order the whole menu. Buy some nice things in the city. Don't spare money. There will be enough. My dearest, my precious, send me your temperature curve as soon as you know it, and let me know your temperature each time you write. Okay, Nanushka?

My darling, I can hear you breathing, sleeping, and talking in your sleep—I am always with you. I love you, my precious. God be with you, dearest. Be happy, my little wife. Your husband, your nanny, your foolish Okushka. Well, goodbye, my pet, I love you...

No. 34. To N. Ya. Mandelstam, February 17 [1926]

Nadik, where are you? I haven't heard anything from you for two days, and I haven't written for two days. The day before yesterday I was not quite myself. I was waiting for a telegram from you. I called home every minute and sent you a dandy little telegram. Then I met Shileiko[1] on Liteiny Avenue and he took me to Sower Publishing House where I made a phone call to see if there was a telegram. He was wearing a cap with earflaps and shopping for sixteenth century books. When some old woman read your dear words to me over the phone, I cheered up so much I accepted Shileiko's invitation to have a drink of ale in the bar and I sat with him for half an hour: I had dark ale with ham and listened to his wise words... I'm tenacious, I said, and he said, yes, unfortunately for you...and I told him that I love only you, that is I *didn't say it* that way, of course, and Jews.[2] He understands that I'm a completely different person and that I can't be trifled with like other worldly fops...

Nadik, where are you? I went to visit you again at the station. The Daudistel translation[3] is still suffocating me: I'm revising the last part. It's about two days work.

Nadichka, *I must hear your voice every day*. What was wrong with you, darling? Are you well again? How quickly the last third of this month is passing! In a few days I'll send you enough money to last all of March. You wanted to know what my plans are: Gorlin, with Wolfson's support, is sending me a reject. Marshak[4] is signing a contract for the biography of Khalturin—a carpenter and member of People's Freedom: 1-1½ signatures for 150-200 rubles. That's very easy. I'll be able to write it in five days. Then Fedin[5] included a book of poems in the "plan"—it will be sent to Moscow (only the list of titles and annotations)—and...struck off[6]... The reviews are coming. In a week all these knots will be disentangled. I have no worries about work. If only I could manage to be with you sooner. I so dislike the idea of sending you off to those damned snowplow towns...

Nadik, do you go down to see the dogs on your walks? Down my road above the Armenian cypresses!

Tatyanka has a slight fever today. I'm always complaining to her that I want to go see Aunt Nadya, and she says: "Then go, I'll let you."

Grandfather went to Luga "on business" and came back with a cold. Sasha arrived: she's out of work, she was selling bagels, and she dreams about the "union" constantly.

Nadik! My precious! I was at the Bens'[7]: they took me to the movies. They go every Monday, as if to the bathhouse...

Forgive me, darling, for not writing for two days... Darling little bird, what is your dear face like now? You aren't pale or sad?

My child! They're stamping the letters at the post office now. It's ten minutes before eleven. I must turn in the letter. Till tomorrow, my beloved, my precious. I kiss you. I hear each minute... May the Lord keep you! I love you. Nanny. Nadik! It's me.

Your Nanny

No. 35. To N. Ya. Mandelstam [February 1926]

Nadik, my little girl, hello, little one! Nanny is talking to you. In your letters you don't tell me your temperature and so forth... That's not right, honey. Write every day.

Tatka has chicken pox. She's in bed with a fever but very cheerful: "Write Aunt Nadya that I have a slight cold. I can't think up anything else." She already has a tiny pustule above her lip. It's a mild disease.

Today was my lucky day at GIZ, Nadik. Wolfson has arrived. First he proposed a resolution for the contract, omitting Moscow, then he and Gorlin decided to draw it up in Moscow anyway (it will take ten days), but in the meantime I'll get a small, easy book to do—a French one—about courts and judges: six sheets at thirty-five rubles per sheet. I sit peacefully at home all day. Tomorrow I'll finish Priboi. Last night I longed to go to the station—to you—with *Streetcar* and some newspapers. For me those trips are a vacation—direct route on the "No. 4." Grandfather still keeps company with those Jewish "capons." M.N. (she's really very nice, a very smart woman) insists that he get dentures. That grandmother takes wonderful care of grandfather and Tatka, understands everything, accepted me without the slightest strain—so everything's fine.

(This is terrible paper—I'll buy a new sheet.)

There. Nadik on a new sheet of paper. M.N. is an intelligent woman. Zhenya blames her for everything. She had absolutely nothing to do with the incident about the room (now it's obvious). Zhenya rented the room to some elderly actress and her daughter. He's almost never at home. He has virtually abandoned Tatka. She is offended and jealous.

Sometimes I go to the well-lighted servants' room to work because I love the kitchen and the servants and also because I smoke "a little bit," but smoking isn't allowed in the clean rooms because of asthma...

But just "a little bit," Nadik! You won't believe it: there's not a trace left of my neurosis. I walk up the stairs to the fifth floor purring, without noticing.

This is already the third day of the thaw. Black snow. It's two degrees above zero (Centigrade) during the day. Today Fedin asked me how much I want for the book of poems.[1] I said 600 rubles. We'll see. But this is nonsense.

Priboi will probably start to pay me on Tuesday. You know, Nadenka, our situation will be no worse at the beginning of March than it was in October.

If you are getting along well, don't leave Yalta. You and I will still have our fling. I kiss you, my darling Nadik: it's time to turn in the letter. N... I always remember...

No. 36. To N. Ya. Mandelstam, Friday [February 1926]

My darling! I'm in the small servants' room because it's "cozy" here and I'm finishing up, literally, the last five pages of that accursed German.[1] How this work has suffocated both you and me, my little one. Tomorrow I'll put it all out of my mind. This morning I went to Ligovka to see the typist. Towards 3:00 p.m. I stopped in at GIZ. I stopped in at Fedin's and Gruzdev's[2] room. They just happened to be filling out forms with book proposals. And I just happened to catch: "one of the best modern poets..." They're trying[3]! Among others they're trying to push through Ehrenburg's book *The Grabber*.[4] Nadik, I'm tired of all this pushing through and pulling through! These nannies and guardian-saviors! I'm sad, my little child.

A red lamp is burning and Nadezhda is singing "The Bricks." It doesn't bother me. Grandfather came up to me and revealed his plan about the loan: he must write a "report." Tatuska still has the chicken pox. She tormented her grandmother demanding that she "play!" And she insists that I give *Streetcar* back to her—why did I ever take it from her!—for you, Nadik.

I didn't get a letter from you today. What's wrong with you, Nadik? Answer in your own voice!... I simply can't imagine how you live, Nadik. Does the doctor look after you? That is essential.

This evening after I've sent this letter I'll drop in to see Ben.[5] Everyone is terribly afraid that I'll run off to be with you, and that's not sensible. Don't worry, darling, I'll do that only when it's permissible. Like an adult. I had a slight cold the first week, Nadik. Now there's not a trace of it left. Here I'm talking to you and I don't even know how you are. My little darling, my *kinechka*,[6] don't you want to be in Yalta? No? But tell me, is it spring there? You seem to prefer dampness and snow... That's not good, Nadik, Kiev is nice in April. In a week your nanny will sign the contracts and ask permission to come to you. Isn't anyone there with you, Nadik? What are you thinking about, my precious, my good girl? Is Mitya teaching you wisdom? Are you tormented by card games? The days are probably long and light in Yalta, darling. Nadik, I want to see our lantern-room, to throw a sunbeam at the Bolsheviks, to lie in bed, in a hard, narrow bed. I fall asleep easily now, darling: I don't think about sleep. I go to sleep at one a.m. I wake up at seven a.m. And you, Nadik, are you well? My skinny little beastikins... You won't escape misfortune... There will be telegrams from me... How much money do you need? I'll have a "fair amount." I'll shower you with it...

I always carry all your letters with me, darling. At night I say, "Keep, oh Lord, My Nadenka..." Also, send me your mother's last letter, because I always read them all. I kiss your beautiful hair and paws and brow and eyes. I'm sad without you. Sunny little Nadik, answer me. I'm coming to you, to you... Nanny.

No. 37. To N. Ya. Mandelstam [February 1926]

My darling, I probably alarmed you. It was foolish and stupid of me not to write. I wanted to send a telegram but it came out even worse. Believe me, little child, I am well, that is, as well as I can be without you, that is, terrible. I live peacefully and comfortably. Everything is going well. I'm healthy. No one bothers me, but I can't endure this any longer and will rush to you the first chance I get. Nadenka dearest, with that cute little grimace, I constantly see you squinting in the sunlight... You're so comical and wonderful when you walk alone... Don't be bitter, my child, you must endure just one more week—and then we'll be together again. How could I have survived for a whole month without you, Nadichka? I myself don't understand.

Here's what I'm doing now: I don't even go to Gorlin's very often anymore. Twice a day, at ten and seven, I crawl out slowly at a strolling pace—early in the day I take the First Line to a typist who lives in a philistine apartment with her large family, and in the evening—I take the Fifth Line to a typist who lives in a huge, well-ventilated room. Tomorrow I'll introduce Ben to the staff at Priboi,[1] and in the evening we'll go to a movie. And you, Nadik, come and see your nanny whenever you want to. Okay? In ten days I'll finish the work at hand. Then I'll be free. I won't take any rush orders. Just to be with you, with you... Where is your picture?

Darling, my darling...listen my meek one, my little candle, my little rabbit: I know you don't believe me, but I believe you— I'm not sick and didn't suffer from exhaustion with complications. I live rhythmically, I work willingly. Believe me, it's true. But what can I do with you... Did you walk far to get the snowdrops? Are you tired?

No one is at home. Grandmother went to visit the Radlovs.[2] Tatka came up to me on the sofa and I started to read her *The Balloons* and so forth, but she was singing *The Kitchen*.[3] She uttered various maxims: "Mischief brings nothing but unpleasantness to adults" and so forth. Grandfather walks around looking for cigarettes, but there are none to be found. Today a messenger came to see him from Riga, from "Perman." He's a pharmacist, a childhood friend, also a Mandelstam. Papa is being summoned to Riga seriously. Visas and transportation are unusually easy to get and inexpensive. We decided definitely to send him there this spring... Spring!... Ah, my Nadik, a foreigner from under the spreading Yalta cranberry bush! Ten degrees below zero (Centigrade) feels like ten above. The first of March here is winter through and through—five to six degees below zero, not above. Winter is everywhere, my little child... Spring is still a month away.

Tell me, sweetheart, why don't you report your temperature in every letter? Nadik, why don't you?

When I say your precious name, Nadichka, I am happy. You are mine. I love you as if it were the first day, even before the first day. Thinking of you I breathe easily. I know it was you who taught me to breathe. How I shall run to you up the hill. Now I could even run up a mountain.

On Tuesday I'll explain the problem with the antithyroidin. Tomorrow I'll send you the translation of *The Thousand and Second Night.*[4] It is very cleverly done and a pleasure to reread. Anka[5] and I did it. Grandfather just came up. He says hello to you and gives you his best.

Nadyusha, tell me please, should I rent the little house in Tsarskoe Selo or not? Ben says it must be done in March. I will agree to move to Tsarskoe Selo between the fifteenth and twentieth of May, but no earlier. Are you receiving my newspapers? Don't I paste them together amusingly?

Nadik, darling, my love, goodbye. I kiss you goodnight on your lovely brow and say: "God keep Nadenka..." Love me, Nadik, I am yours...

No. 38. To N. Ya. Mandelstam [February 1926]

Nadenka, my joy, I just sent you a very incoherent telegram, but you'll understand everything. Don't leave Yalta, my darling. I might come to join you there. You don't know, you've forgotten, how cold and damp the world is. Your little place is like a greenhouse. All of Russia and the Ukraine is either cold or muddy or thawing... No one could recuperate after such a transition, Nadik... Even I got sick for the first time. Let's wait at least for the warmth of April so we can clatter along dry sidewalks... Yes, Nadik? Listen, my fair one, you're a brave girl, aren't you? Where is your temperature?

My little child, I want to complain to you and I'll begin by saying that the coffee they serve at Zhenya's house is terrible, it's so vile that no amount of sugar can save it. And there's actually nothing more to complain about. Grandfather insists that I "keep him company," as for Zhenya—he's never home. I spend day after day in the "empty" apartment with Tatka and M.N.... It's so enjoyable to be with her—she's a wonderful grandmother. All my work is ready for the typist, darling. "Uncle" is with me now and then I'll go see Gorlin. Priboi liked our translation very much. They're looking after me, the idiots... They're asking me to work.

Nadik, we call to one another like birds—I can't live, I can't live without you!... Without you my whole life is dreary—I'm a useless stranger to myself. The day before yesterday I put your telegram under my pillow and so in the evening when I was tired I was able to fall asleep... Tatinka's "pox" is going away. I had it some twenty years ago so I won't catch it. I'll do my complaining to Tatka instead of to you, darling. She makes a serious face and says: "Uncle Osya, why don't you go to Aunt Nadya, I can't be of any help to you here."

Do you want to talk business, my little one? I signed a contract with Gorlin for 4½ signatures at 210 rubles... It was terribly easy... Priboi is paying 200 rubles now and the remainder in March. The reviews yield 30 rubles a week. The book of poems is engraved.[1] The contract for the children's book was turned down. I don't like Marshak[2]! The big book will be at GIZ at the beginning of March. Not bad, as you can see. Oh yes, I forgot to say that I took on a strange editing job at Priboi that pays 15 rubles for 6 signatures.

Nadik, my darling, take me away with you. I'm lost here without you. I no longer wear Papa's fur coat. It's cold and dry here. It's even pleasant outside. My child, whenever I look at our stores—Eliseev's[3]—I become sad and dejected. On Nevsky Prospect radios blare down the whole street. Zhenya is going to Moscow today. Those Moscow swindlers are chasing him out.[4] Yesterday the poor fellow spent half the night consulting me.

He's afraid of losing his position, he's terribly upset.

Nadya, your mama's *kinechka*, Anya, called. She's fine.

What do you think, little one, should I bring a lot of work to do when I come? Do you sunbathe on the wicker chair, Nadik? My darling, are you the same as when you saw me off? Do you still wear those patched slippers? Nadik, be there to meet me in a few days, my little bird. Wait for me! I am waiting, but I can't wait...

May God keep Nadenka. The Lord be with you...

No. 39. To N. Ya. Mandelstam [March 1926]

Thank you for your letter, Nadenka. My dear, my sweet-heart, no one writes as you do. So many pages. Thank you for the picture: it's you. I smiled at you, darling. I even laughed while reading your letter.

Today I had quite an adventure: Priboi gave me 200 rubles. I have just sent you the money. I looked for antithyroidin in all the pharmacies and stores. It can't be found anywhere. That batch was completely distributed. I was advised to telephone all the regional pharmacies. There is more of a chance of finding some outside the city... I'll do that this evening.

On March first I got 200 rubles for a new book at GIZ, then another 170 at Priboi. The Sower replied today: they want Gorlin's book very much but are vacillating, and they asked me to come back if GIZ doesn't take it (it's a large book). I decided to rest for three days, my darling, to sit with Tatka, even go to the movies with the Bens, or simply take a stroll. It's ten degrees. I wear Grandfather's fur coat while I make him stay at home. He's hurt, but he's an old man and is better off near the stove. Yesterday Zhenya went to Moscow for five days. Anya called yesterday. Her voice sounds absolutely healthy, confident, determined, and firm. One of her charges, the schoolboy, that is, was taken away to Moscow... Nadka, do you feel that I'll find your wise "thyroidin"?

Today I had coffee with Gorlin at the Gourmet. Is it true that Yalta was a dream come true? Now don't run off to Kiev with the money or I'll *refuse* you! Just sit quietly, little Nadik!

Ben and I decided to write a script based on the "Dzhorygov affair." You can read it in the *Evening News*. It's hard to believe, but Ek[aterina] Konst[antinovna] wants it.[1] I gave her your letter.

Nadyushok, we'll be together again on May first in Kiev and we'll climb that old Dniepr mountain. I'm so glad about this, so glad... By the early part of March we should know whether I'll be able to come (I think I will be). Don't forget there is still Moscow on the way. It will be sheer pleasure. What does Mama write? Send me her letter...

Do you sleep late if there are no letters to wake you up? Where did you have your picture taken—in the garden or at your present place? Tomorrow I'll send you the second *Streetcar* for Panov and I'll buy *The Balloons* for Irina Punina while I'm at it— Punin and Anna Andreevna[2] searched up and down Nevsky Prospect today for that book.

On March first I'll pay back 100 rubles to the Rybakovs. We agreed that the remainder is to be paid at the end of the month. Don't worry, dear. Your nanny is clever.

They say Klychkov[3] is in Yalta, Nadik. Though God only knows what he's like, look him up, you'll enjoy it. Is it a lot worse at Tarkhova's? If it is, leave, but be careful...

No. 40. To N. Ya. Mandelstam, March 5 [1926]

Nadichka, my life, thank you for the photograph. My little child, what a dear face you have. But you seem so sad, so sickly and confused. What were you thinking about, Nadik? What's wrong with you, my precious sweetheart? I won't show anyone your photograph. No one knows that I have it. When I saw your sad little face I rushed to the door—to go to you at once... I know that you would smile at me, but the photograph can't smile. Thank you, gentle Nadik. I kiss your beautiful salient brow. How precious you are, darling. There is no other face like yours. "A reunion?" You are my reunion, you are my whole life. I await a reunion with you, you give me life. Listen to me, my sad angel. It's comical to say it, but only one and a half signatures of translation for Priboi separates us. Then I'll be in Moscow with you. I drag myself around the city, clutching your letters in my briefcase. I won't let them out of my hands, I won't lose them, I won't let them out of my sight. I love you, my darling pet. To love you so makes life worth living, Nadik, Nadik!

Well, now, sweetheart, listen to me! For the last few days I haven't been able to keep track of your condition. I don't know your weight, your temperature, or anything. Nothing but generalizations. I implore you to give me more details. You can send a telegram.

Fool that I was, I didn't understand your telegram. I'm talking about the three days without a letter. *I was overworked then, but healthy.* I would only get exhausted toward evening.

I was physically sound. *My heart trouble vanished without a trace.*[1] I've had no attacks. I feel wonderful. Enough of that! There's no sense talking about it!

Here are the details of how things stand: GIZ is racking its brains trying to give me work. Wolfson (the political editor from Moscow) has invited me to go to Moscow with him next week apologizing that he is traveling in a "second class" railroad car: "We'll think up something for you." *There are many opportunities for work at Priboi and The Sower.*[2] In any case we are already taken care of financially through April twentieth—I can be alone with my darling.

Grandfather is quite well. He left taking his "questionnaire." He plans to go to Riga. I like M.N. more and more. She understands everything: just like a grandmother! My Nadik! No letters from you today? Are you angry? No? Write me, darling. We'll soon be together—so write, my dear, while I'm still far away. Your Nanny.

No. 40a. To N. Ya. Mandelstam[1]

Nanushka, Vaginov's[2] book has been published. It's such an effete book. I'll send it to you. It's worse in print. There's a lot that's funny. A[nna] Andr[eevna] and Punin went to Moscow. I'll take advantage of that and visit Shileiko.[3] After I'd spent some time with you, my Nadichka, I cheered up. Yes, my angel, we shall be together, always together, and God will not abandon us. I kiss you, my happiness. Your lovely brow looks at me. You've tossed your hair back—it won't stay in place... I kiss you. I am yours, darling. Your Nanny.

Nadichka, how are things at Tarkhova's now? When will the rent go up? Do you have somewhere else to move? *What's your weight? Your temperature?*

Nadik, if it gets cold make a *good, hot* fire. Don't spare money. Make a fire every day. Write down your temperature every day. Most important, send me a telegram.

No. 41. To N. Ya. Mandelstam (March 7) [1926]

My darling, if only you knew how worried I am! It has been a whole day and there still isn't any answer to the telegram I sent in reply to yours. I'm insanely afraid for you, my little sunshine, and most important, I don't know what's wrong with you. One word in the telegram was garbled: "if" obviously meant "pains." Are the pains back again? Yes, Nadik? How can I give you advice if I don't know everything? Then I wrote special delivery letters on the 28th, 1st, 3rd, 5th, and today, the 7th. Didn't you really get them? I'll write every day, darling. I'm still afraid that a regular letter will take a long time, but I'm too late to mail it special delivery: that's the reason for the delay in letters.

Nadenka, there's a terrible flu epidemic in the cities now. It's slushy and treacherous outside. Where are you rushing off to? You and anyone else in your condition would fall ill after three days. Wait at least until April if you don't want to spend the spring in Yalta. Don't act like a madman. I wrote you not to spare money. Those were not empty words: I have enough money. Even if you spend 400 rubles in March, there will still be enough money for April. I don't know how, but everything can be taken care of for a price. You're in a better position to judge how. Just don't leave Yalta. If you stay there long enough, I'll come in April. In a few days I'll head out in your direction. I'll take the new commissions and go to Moscow, and from there to you. I implore you to write me about your health in detail. You know how you're supposed to write, darling. It's absurd to worry about me. I've gotten a lot better. If only you knew how good I'm being in my work and in doing all that's necessary. Now Nanny is bragging...

I agree to your moving into No. 8, Nadik. It's all nonsense, just so my Nyakushka isn't given rubbish to eat. Perhaps you'll refuse the boarding house and join the Tyuflins?

Darling Nadik, let me give you some foolish advice—you're in a better position to decide, but don't leave Yalta during this dangerous season.

Listen to your Nanny, my pet. Buy good breakfasts in town. To hell with Tarkhova's stuff. Even pay her the money for nothing. The cold spring weather there is harmless, but here and in Kiev it is treacherous... Obey Nanny and Tsanov, darling. I've been waiting insanely for a telegram all day, my dear... God save my Nadenka...

No. 42. To N. Ya. Mandelstam [March 1926]

I kiss your little garnets, darling. Nadik, what was it? For three days I was out of my mind. Between Saturday and Tuesday there was no answer to my telegram... What's wrong with you, my life? So your cold is gone. But your pains? And your nausea? My Nadik, you still write me too little, not enough detail. I'm waiting for a letter, a letter. You were smart to stay in Yalta. *Now you will be able to wait for me, your nanny!* You know, tomorrow I finish my work. Priboi owes me 300 rubles. I can get the money immediately. March is already passing, my darling. How easy it is for us now...

If only you knew how I have languished these last few days. Yesterday I didn't write—I had no strength left from worrying. You understand. Today I sent a telegram to Mitya, then I wanted urgently to speak to Tarkhova and telephoned her. Your morning telegram was read to me. Did my telegram wake you up? Everyone in the house regards me with tender sympathy, as they would a madman... Grandfather tried unsuccessfully to console me. M.N. tried to influence me, and so on. If only I knew what was wrong with you, my little bird! Now I'm really very close to being with you...but your letters avoid the subject of your health. Where's your temperature *curve*? How is the cooking? You don't talk about anything. That's wrong. Only tiny fragments. What does Tsanov say? Why don't you *buy* some firewood and heat the place well? Who dares to forbid you that! Buy a good wool sweater immediately! If you don't go out, send M[arya] Mikh[ailovna] to do it for you...

You wanted to know about the plans for my departure. As of now I have no new work. But Gorlin is like a relative to me: he'll send me work, and then possibly Moscow will give me something, or Angert and Wolfson might even give me something here. Priboi is offering me *steady* work, but it's still very unpleasant to work there: although accommodating and respectful, Priboi is always in some kind of muddle. If I arrive with 400 or 500 rubles I'll be able to live with you from the fifteenth or twentieth of March until the twenty-fifth of April and do some work without any need to hurry. And even if I couldn't work in Yalta? That's bad? But your nanny will bring some work...

Yesterday I was dragged along to a conference at the Zubov Institute.[1] Tikhonov[2] read. I was received as if I were Sologub, young people offered me their chairs as if I were France Ingres [sic][3] and I was looked upon as some sort of child-oracle. I was some sort of madman thinking of you, only of you, Nadik my pet. Drink a glass of port to your nanny's health. I kiss your little garnets, darling, and your new, horrible (but also Nanny's) sweater. Nothing could keep me from coming to you now. I'll dally here a week longer at the most (and then Moscow!). My dearest, my precious one with your lovely salient brow, my friend, my angel, wait for me... May the Lord keep my Nadenka. Your Nanny is with you.

P.S. I'm *completely* well and always *have been* well.

No. 43. To N. Ya. Mandelstam [March 1926]

My darling, my beloved, you found some snowdrops for me...
I'm a monster, Nadik: I haven't written for three days. I won't
deny it: I've *been working too much* recently, I've made work
into a sport. I was doing two books simultaneously, for GIZ and
for Priboi... I put everything off until evening, intending to write a
"special delivery letter" then, but I *got tired* in the evenings. Forgive me, Nadik, it will never happen again. It's simply *unnecesary.*
Our financial situation is very good. It's curious how Priboi has
become a second GIZ for me, and I now have two Gorlins (one is
Grünberg).[1]

Darling, your telegram of the 26th said you were *well,* but
on the 22nd your temperature was 37.6 (?). What does that mean?
For only one day? Or do you still have a fever? Write in *more de-*
tail, more detail, darling, and don't be angry at my telegrams.
That's the way I am! I'm well, my dear child. That's the truth. I'm
very able-bodied and hardy, physically hardy. I was very upset at
your telegram. We racked our brains around here, Grandfather
especially tried very hard. Does that mean Tarkhova again? That's
good. Keep our little room until my arrival. I love our little beds
"kapotsal."[2] What is it dripping? Nadik, my travel plans are based
on the following:

1) The Crimea is marvelous from March fifteenth until May
fifteenth. These are truly healthful, salubrious months. We're
set up in the Crimea and it would be a pity not to take advantage
of it. Finally, it will simply be *fun.*

2) Besides the 200 rubles I sent to you, I already have 400
which I earned at GIZ and Priboi (the remaining 130 rubles from
the Daudistel translation doesn't count: that goes to Rybakov).[3]

3) By March fifteenth I'll sign two new contracts with GIZ
(big ones) and Priboi. We'll arrange for the money to be sent.

4) I'll stop in Moscow for two or three days and I'll borrow
a little there *in addition to everything else.* So the month will be
financially secure "and more so" and the money for the second
month will be sent to us. Perhaps it will be even better.

If you ran across me in Yalta now, you wouldn't recognize
me. Fool that I am, I sat still like a stay-at-home, like some kind of
maniac. Right now I'm ready to climb mountains, to run into the

city, take walks every day by the sea. Yet I was "afraid" to go to the typist! Wasn't I a fool? Nadichka, is Lev Platonych[4] still around? Have they arrested him? Make inquiries: I need him very much.

Today Zhenya came back from Moscow. Their organization has just gone through a dreadful scandal. The enemies Kugel[5] and Shchegolev[6] are in with them. Svirsky[7] has set up a magnificent restaurant in the basement on Tverskoi Boulevard, where our kind old janitress fed Khlebnikov.

Tatka is all better. Yesterday she was given a bath in a large bathtub. I'm reading *Dead Souls* (with illustrations) for relaxation. I didn't throw away your translation, but kissed it and made some corrections: *it's a very fine translation*.

Have you become the life of the party and the chairman of the club, Nadichka? Yes?

M[arya] N[ikolaevna] gave me some sheets. I'm very comfortable on the sofa with our mattress. I sleep well. I don't go anywhere, Nadichka. I've only been at the Bens' and the Vygodskys' a few times... The poet Komarovsky[8] is "the same." He's wonderful. Get a hold of his poems. Explain to Bezobrazova.

How are you now, Nadichka? You're not sick? I'll send a telegram right away. I won't let a day go by without writing a letter. I'll carry out all your requests. I almost got the medicine on the Avenue of the Young Proletarians (!).

God keep you, my beloved Nadik!

Grünberg just called: he read about me in some English *magazine*.[9] Much praise... A[nna] Andr[eevna][10] read it in *Mercure de France*.[11]

I love you. Your Nanny. I'm with you, darling. Love me, Nadik. I kiss your dear brow and your eyes and your cute little wrinkles!

No. 44. To N. Ya. Mandelstam [March 1926]

My darling Nadenka, Anya and I are writing to you together —I'm at her place visiting (for the first time, unfortunately). She has a clean, tidy room next to the master bedroom. The children have already gone to sleep. Her employer doesn't like her anymore. There's a radio in the house.

I got your angry letter today: is your 37.6 temperature from a cold or just so? I also got the telegram with Mitya's visa. Thank you, my angel. I can hear your sweet voice even in the telegram. So you obeyed me, you smart girl, but make sure you don't spare any money. Make them feed you well... Bribe them every day even if it's at your own expense... The main thing is not to let anyone hurt you until I get there. I think anxiety has a great effect on you: it causes your nausea and even your pains. Don't worry, my gentle little sunshine. And buy some firewood and a sweater.

I terrorized Priboi: they'll pay everything because they're afraid I'll disgrace them. That's what they said. I'm thinking very seriously of leaving for Moscow in a week, that is, on the 17th, and from there going to join you, darling. Today I filled out Grandfather's application for Riga. I had a headache for two or three hours today, but it didn't last a whole day as it used to. M.N.—grandmother—treated me with headache powder and a tasty dinner.

Sleep soundly, Nadik darling. Those are Nanny's orders. The important thing is not to think about sleep while you're trying to fall asleep. Think about the little hill in Kiev and the house in the park at Tsarskoe Selo. Well, my little one, goodbye... I'll give Anya the pen.

[Nadyusha, I'm displeased. O.E. doesn't wear cufflinks; his cuffs are rolled up and in tatters (scold him). Anya]

Nadik, my pet! I'll finish writing at the station (Anka lives nearby). This paper belongs to her charges...

Sleep tight, my darling, and pleasant dreams. Don't think about anything depressing. Dear child, the air I breathe is yours—it's mine, it's mute!

No. 45. To N. Ya. Mandelstam [March 1926]

Nadik, my darling, sweetheart, how quickly we conversed by telegram. I'm really going to Moscow on Tuesday but I don't know how many days I'll stay there. I'm afraid to give you advice concerning Lolanov. Well, how will you manage there all alone? Even without Mitya and the others? If even just a few people will be poking around there, then by all means move. Leave that godforsaken place. After all, Lolanov's place is so pleasant and spacious. Just don't go if you're going to be all alone! The two of us will have enough money for all of April if I come on the 20th. But I want to bring some work when I come—later would be better—so that we'll have a steady income in May. I'll certainly be able to manage that. Priboi guarantees me steady work beginning at the end of April, as GIZ did earlier. And Gorlin advises me to go to Moscow with Wolfson to promote one of the books. It's a *very certain* business venture. In any case, if I have 500 rubles in cash (and I almost have the money already), I'll come to you directly from Moscow. Both Gorlin and Grünberg will send me books and sign contracts in my absence. In May I'll leave for just one little week to go ahead to arrange your trip to Kiev. One more thing: the Children's Department at Priboi wants a children's book. They're very easy and simple to do. If I reach an agreement tomorrow, I'll write you the next day. You must understand, dear, that I'll be able to come be with you for a month at the very beginning of summer. I would have come long ago if I hadn't been concerned about the facility of your return home and about the good life in Kiev and in Tsarskoe Selo... Well, enough about business, my little bird. As you can see, I'm not counting on anything unexpected, although something unexpected might even happen in Moscow.

I'm sending Grandfather to you. He's such a dear, really... And Vaginov's book... You know, there's a line in it: "Oh, sea, gentle brother of Man..."

I'll send you a telegram the day I leave for Moscow, and from Moscow I'll let you know of any further plans. Until you get my telegram, write me at the Petersburg address, and later write care of your Zhenya.[1] If I'm in Moscow for just a couple days I'll stay with Pasternak[2]; if I'm there for a week I'll stay with Shura.[3]

Nadik, the tailor on Nevsky Prospect did a splendid job mending my trousers and I now look "dignified." Now I'll buy some boots. That's a necessity. Nadik, do you really search the Yalta seashore for threads for your Nanny? How considerate you are, sweetheart —what are you thinking of! Do you have a sweater? It's winter again here: dry and snowy. This morning we ate pancakes and had only sour cream to put on them...

No. 46. To N. Ya. Mandelstam [March 1926]

Your Nanny is taking a vacation beginning today: he finished two little books for GIZ and Priboi. I frequently sit in the warm room behind the kitchen, although the whole apartment is empty. But I feel somehow at home there and closer to you. Your dear little face no longer looks so unhealthy to me. It shines brightly on the photograph. I look at it for two little seconds in the morning and in the evening. Do you know why? So that I won't run off to you ahead of schedule. Tomorrow morning I'm going to see Gorlin to get my instructions concerning Moscow and to arrange things with my traveling companion.[1]

My darling, my fair one, my gentle one, take care of yourself. Don't walk so much. Let me kiss your lovely golden hair. No doubt you've taken advantage of my absence and dyed it. I'm coming to you, my Nadik... I sound indecisive because I'm being very cautious. That's the only reason. I am with you. Don't you dare cry, my darling. Sleep well... I am with you. Smile for me and say: "I'm your Nyakushka, come be with me"—and I'll come— your Nanny...

No. 47. To N. Ya. Mandelstam, March 16 [1926]

My darling, I'm writing from Shklovsky's[1] apartment. I arrived in Moscow this morning. I went to GIZ the first thing. They received me very well, no worse than at Gorlin's and Belitsky's.[2] My business, that is, getting the new books approved, is almost settled.[3] There are just a few trifles left to take care of in Moscow: Voronsky[4] and *The Noise of Time,* which is having more and more success. I'll allot a few days to these affairs and then set out for Yalta. I might have to go to Petersburg for two days to sign a contract with LenGIZ. That would be a wise thing to do:

Nadichka, my pet, my bride, I'm just about to go see your Zhenya (I gave you the wrong address by mistake: it's not No. 8, but No. 6 Strastnoi Boulevard). Aren't there any telegrams from you?

Your Nanny is irreproachably healthy. I traveled in a "second class" railroad car and am rushing to be with you. I'm spending the night (such a big choice) at Pasternak's.

I didn't get a chance to write during all the commotion before I left. Priboi will send 500 rubles in two installments to you in Yalta.

Forgive me, my darling, for writing so little. I'm rushing to be with you and am trying to do everything at once. I can't even bear to wait a day. I'm both cheerful and anxious. I'm already closer to you, my Nadik, my love. May the Lord keep you, my darling. Your Nanny is coming to you. I kiss your pathetic little picture. Ah, Nadik...

I'm not going to Petersburg. Livshits will sign the contract. I'll be with my beloved, with my Nadik, all the sooner... But now I'm going to see Zhenya. Tomorrow I'll write in more detail.

No. 48. To N. Ya. Mandelstam, March 17 [1926] Moscow

My darling Nadik, why don't you answer? I've been in Moscow two days and haven't gotten a telegram from you. I managed everything with great ease, my child. I already have GIZ's sanction for the contract. The film press[1] is also paying a fantastic amount: 150-200 rubles for nothing. All I have left to do is talk to Narbut[2] and Voronsky tomorrow. That's no longer even necessary. Our finances are taken care of until summer. On Saturday I'm going to

Petersburg to say goodbyes. On Monday I'll be able to take care of all my business and on Tuesday I'm planning to leave for Yalta.

Yesterday I spent the night at Pasternak's on a horrible sofa-bed in a room with his brother, but today I'll be at your Zhenya's. He's such a wonderful person! True, he quarreled with the old folks, but they don't call Zhenya to the phone or let people in to see him. Lena was in Kiev a few days ago. And you and I will go to Kiev in May. Your nanny is quite well and insanely worried because you haven't sent any telegrams.

I walk along the streets of Moscow, darling, and remember all of our precious, difficult life. Sonya's portrait of you is up in Zhenya's place, my angel. When I visited you for the first time — how happy he made me! How I love you, my sunshine! Shura is with me at the post office. I'm coming to you, Nadik my life...

[I kiss you because I haven't seen you for a long time. Correspondent A. Mandelstam[3] (that's a habit from work).]

No. 49. To N. Ya. Mandelstam, Autumn 1926 [Leningrad]

Friday

My darling little child, my sunny Nadik! Why did I send you away to the sea as if you were some kind of Ovid? Do you want to come home to your Nanny and the cat and Anya? I understand. Just brave it a little longer: then we'll see... I got your telegram. Are you healthy? Yes? And the cyclone has passed? Do you take baths? Do you go to Jung for your walks? That's too far! Don't go there! It would be better to take your walks along the shore in the other direction, where the Turkish fisherman used to be. Most important, don't worry about spending money.

I've had various adventures. First of all, yesterday evening I went to see Anya in Tsarskoe Selo[1] in the Chinese Village: she had been guarding the place all alone for two days—and in a military fashion, in the darkness, I made her pack all her things, then I took her to the Semicircle[2] (the house manager suggested that we come in without waiting for the tenants to leave). The shrew in charge of rooms took offense: "You have Jakobson, but I have Lunacharsky."[3] Nevertheless, I subdued her with politeness and she let us in, that is, she let our things in but *asked* us *to return on Sunday, that is, tomorrow*... (The repairs haven't been completed there yet). Tomorrow Anya and I will get settled. There's electricity there, it's warm and pleasant. They'll give us furniture after another apartment has been vacated. We'll live in two rooms *for the time being.* Another piece of news: Leonov sequestered my GIZ contract.[4] Then I went to Priboi, got all the money, and am laughing about it now, but GIZ has only 30 rubles. However, I'll do enough work to reimburse GIZ within one week.

Anya went into the city with me yesterday and will spend two nights at Uncle's. It's empty in the Chinese Village. No one is there. I turned in the keys. The cat is with the watchman. The guard is on duty, guarding our china that we'll move tomorrow in a basket.

The third piece of news: suddenly, without cause, I've been busy with taxes. I went to inquire. $400 + 66 + ?$ (three receipts). I'm sick of the whole thing.[5]

Fedin and Voitolovsky[6] advised me to go to Smolny[7] to see the chairman of the press department of the Central Committee at the Provincial Committee level. I've just come from there— he's a most courteous gentleman. He *promises* to ask someone from the Financial Department to come over and arrange, *for the time being*, a one- or two-year installment plan. It seems to be very serious. In addition, I promised him a report on copyrights. Right now this whole thing is in full swing and in full bloom, it's like "spring." Misha Slonimsky[8] has been in charge at Priboi since October fifteenth! Just one person like him is enough! We're saved! Davidka[9] is the editor of a foreign literature journal affiliated with the *Red News*! My briefcase is stuffed full of books from Priboi under these exceptionally advantageous circumstances. I've taken a job writing reviews for the newspaper at thirty rubles per book (10-20 pages)...[10] My former rich uncle, Abram Kapeliansky,[11] showed up from abroad in the Children's Department: he's old and shabby. He and his family live in a splendid apartment next to Belitsky's boarding house. His daughter works at *Red News*. She's a friend of Ev[geny] Em[ilievich].

Anna Andreevna[12] went to the Chinese Village a few days ago. She returned your pink shawl, took fright at the prospect of a tête-à-tête, jumped up and ran out.

I didn't get the pebble, Nadik: it fell out of the envelope. The weather here is heavenly: eighteen degrees in the sun. I have a terrible cold from the cold night I spent in Tsarskoe Selo.

I haven't seen the Bens[13] since the move—I don't like them, that is, him, but is she really a person without him? That is, without him in particular... I'd like to keep our things, Nadik, and I think it will be possible.

My sweet Nadik, it's your nameday! Give me your brow and your cheap flannel dress and your little paws... I kiss you... We'll be together at Christmas, Nadka. I've resolved that we will. And you? Yes, Nadik? May the Lord be with you, darling! Be cheerful, my kitten. Nanny wants to be with you. This is your Nanny. You're not cold, darling? Should I send you a knit jacket? Write. Don't spare your "Nyanka."

No. 50. To N. Ya. Mandelstam [1926, Leningrad, after October 15]

My darling wife, I can't go on any longer without you, my sunny Nadik. Why did I let you go? I know that it was necessary, but I'm so depressed, so depressed... Yesterday I brought your watch home. I went to see the pawnbroker's secretary and I was allowed a partial redemption. The watch will stay with us now and never leave, and soon the chain, too, will be returned. I won't go to Tsarskoe Selo until tomorrow, Monday. Anya is staying at Uncle's these days. Yesterday he bought boots for her.

There's been a big change in my work: Slonimsky was appointed at Priboi: *he's offering me a permanent position,* like Gorlin offered Ben. I'll discuss it with him tomorrow. However, I want to do something else, my darling: to obtain work from Priboi and from Marshak and come join you. I don't know if it will be possible without selling some furniture. But it's worth it, dear... What need do we have for things when we're together. Can we really be separated for long?

I think that all of my affairs will be taken care of in the next ten days—and the apartment will be secured by the contract (our trunks are already there) and I'll have lots of work. Then I'll come home, my little one! Or do you want to go home? Dearest, dearest, how are you? Are you really all alone? Whom do you see? Whom do you talk to? At least describe your day to me, whatever it may be like.

Right now I'm at Zhenya's. Last night there was a party at Varvara Kirillovna's with guitar music and it kept me from sleeping. The weather here is always clear, it must be nice in Tsarskoe Selo. I'll buy a lot of firewood so that you'll be warm when you come here and I'll put out a lot of flowers for Nadik.

Did you see Max[1] or not? I can't believe that this time you're in Koktebel without me and in general I don't believe that you went away. Nadik, Nadik, my tattered pet (those wretched coatsleeves)! Are you cold? Tell me that you're waiting for Nanny... The Lord be with you, my little child. I'm your husband, I love you. Nanny.

I don't even have your picture with me here in the city.

No. 51. To N. Ya. Mandelstam [1926, Leningrad]

Darling Nadik, it's the uncertainty more than anything else that torments me—what's wrong with you? Everything you write is too little for me. I haven't heard your voice even once. Nadichka, give me your voice, answer me and tell me if you're all right. I'm not bad, darling, just incredibly depressed as never before. I live like a machine, doing everything that's necessary, and have absolutely no conscious sense of myself. The minute you left everything stopped inside me and it has remained that way ever since. You know, Nadechka, I still haven't been to Tsarskoe Selo. Yesterday I talked to Lavrentiev on the phone. Tomorrow I'll go to sign the contract and pay him. We've reached an agreement. After all, I have only one concern: to be reunited with you, to shelter my poor but radiant beggarwoman. I'm reading all the books—there are so many—both for Priboi and Gorlin.[1] I've almost worked enough to reimburse Leonov the 90 rubles. I'm living in the same room where you and I spent the night. It's heated and not damp there. Anya is already at Uncle's.

Ben got caught in the latest clampdown: distrained by the revenue officer, he ran to Geft claiming that he earns 20 rubles a week. Nika was sick. Do you still love him, Nadik? Nadik, take pity on me and my French books[2] and your watch without its chain (it was left behind—pawned again).

Nadichka, I'm expecting the absolute truth from you: are you healthy? Answer me, little child, don't hide anything. I may go to Moscow in about two days. Konar was promoted: right now he's at GIZ, but he's going to the Ukraine as chairman of the Council of National Economy.[3]

Smile for me, my sunny Nadik, kiss me and say to me: I'm with you, Nanny. The Lord be with you, darling... For we shall soon, very soon, my life, be reunited. Yes? Your Nanny...

No. 52. To N. Ya. Mandelstam [1926]

My darling, I just came back from Tsarskoe Selo and found your angry letter; Grandfather has the other letter. Don't be angry at me, little one—I haven't written for three days because it was extremely difficult for me to write. Everything was happening at once. It *seemed* to me that the editor at GIZ was sabotaging my work, or to put it bluntly, that he was trying to get rid of me. Those idiotic bureaucrats made enigmatic remarks to me such as: "The nature of our relationship in general must change, and so forth," but as it turned out they *were only asking me not to push them, not to "bother" them* about money. You know that I'm mistrustful to the point of stupidity. I even infected Gorlin, who advised me to take a trip to Moscow. Marshak noticed my anxiety and cleared up all this nonsense. *My work is now in full swing.*

That's not all, though. The apartment in the Semicircle turned out to be unsuitable—much too cold! The whole building is settling. The workmen warned me. And here I was rushing back and forth every day between the city and Tsarskoe Selo. The administration was undergoing a large-scale investigation. No one wanted to talk. For two days Anya and I looked for an apartment in Tsarskoe Selo—we followed right in your tracks, Nadik—only the old woman's apartment had already been rented... I was already in despair, but I was saved by that very same Maximich: he secretly showed me apartment No. 7 (you and I didn't see it earlier) on the second floor.

back door

Front door /No. 7/   /No. 6/ Front door

It's just like number six only the rooms are arranged in the opposite order and there are doors and an extra stove. Here's the floor plan:

large room	bedroom	dining room	bathroom	kitchen
no stove	stove	stove	stove	stove

Anya and I were always freezing in the apartment in the Semicircle, but the new apartment is warm and dry like Evgeny Emilievich's, although his place has never been heated. There's an extra stove in the bathroom and a bed for Anya. The walls are clean and white.

When I found out about it I went to see Lavrentiev and (I hadn't expected this at all) he let us have the apartment, gave us the keys, and told Maximich to have it furnished. The beds there are better than those in the Chinese Village, and *he'll get the rest for me as soon as I give him three rubles.* He's coming this evening for a list of furniture.

In no time at all Anya and I had hauled over all our things, called a housekeeper, and I took a bath (we bought firewood). You won't believe how much good it did me to spend just one night next to your bed. We live across from the Kikinaya bell tower, my child. It rings every morning at nine a.m., but on the Orthodox holidays (there aren't many of them) at *six a.m.* But that's no problem. You and I will *go to bed early.* Right, Nadik? It will discipline us... And the boom-boom lasts fifteen minutes.

The day before yesterday I went out to mail you a special delivery letter, and what do you know! I dropped into a store to buy some socks—and bang!—the G.P.U. were there looking for contraband. I was detained for three hours and even had to turn my pockets inside-out—they contained all the usual rubbish. Out of nervousness I interfered with the agents' work and demanded to be released, citing my rank and, for lack of any document, showing them books from Gosizdat. Then, after having suffered such a strong emotional reaction, I went right home, and that's why I never sent your letter. You see, Nadenka, how many adventures your Nanny has.

I think, my little bird, that if you have no temperature you can *come home* for your *birthday, that is, on the 30th. Okay? Just don't conceal your temperature from me. What a reception is awaiting you at your Nanny's!*

My Nadik, how could you get so angry with me! Your telegram got lost on the Third Line (?). Still more delay with the reply... And something is wrong with your cat's eyes. Tomorrow we'll take him to the doctor.

Evgeny Emilievich dragged me along to Moscow (also during this period) to help him at some meeting of Modpik[1] (runoff elections). I almost refused. Grandfather was furious. He wanted me to go to Moscow. Total idiocy! You understand how apropos that is! A repeat of the Granovsky incident...[2]

Nadik, my radiant beastikins by the sea, let the sea pebbles tell you that your nanny is with you. It seems horribly strange to me that you're in Koktebel all alone. Don't be angry with me, just love me, you're my wife and my life. The Lord be with you, darling. That's what I say when I go to bed. Your Nanny.

In a few days I'll send you some extra money. Okay?

No. 53. To N. Ya. Mandelstam [1926]

Nadik, Grandfather and I are at the Nikolaevsky station. I took him to a cafe, and now we're going to Tsarskoe Selo to look at our apartment where Anya has taken charge. I'm terribly sorry for Anya because she wears your gray, Dantean overcoat. I've learned how to treat her: simply, meekly, and tenderly, yet decisively. We quarreled and made up. That was yesterday.

Darling Nadenysh, I'm afraid that you won't survive your exile. How are you? I beg you to write the truth. Everything's going well with me. I have tons of work. I'll send you a hundred rubles this week... Will that be enough to last you till you come home on the 30th?

I gave you a fright with that foolish telegram, my little child. How can I make you believe me? I don't have a single serious problem! You know how I sometimes spin around like a top—I'm suspicious, impatient, foolish... Those three days I didn't write were spent entirely on apartment chores and Gosizdat. How foolish, darling! But I've had my hands full these days. Don't be at all upset on my account. The conditions for your departure have greatly improved. Gorlin has become stronger and livelier, Marshak is flourishing, Angert has been conquered, and Priboi has become like heaven on earth.

Nanushka, write whether I should buy you the fur coat (that one we looked at for 150 rubles) before you come. I want to take it with me to the train station when I go to meet you. Dearest, dearest, my faraway kitten, how is your cheap flannel dress? And your poor slippers? It's warm and damp here. Is it cold there? Soon your Nanny will take you in, Nadik. You're like some poor little animal scratching at my door, begging to come in. Right? Wait, my sweet, my darling wife. The Lord be with you. Love your Nanny.

[My warmest regards. I'm not afraid of the cold and the winds do not frighten me. A big kiss for you. "Grandfather."]

Grandfather wrote about the cold and the winds "allegorically." Nadik, my sunshine, write me a little feuilleton. Your story about "to the right and the left" was so delightfully written...

No. 54. To N. Ya. Mandelstam [1926]

Nadik, it worries me that you don't have enough money. I think I'll send you 50 rubles before you get this letter. In any case, be sure to telegraph if even the slightest difficulty should arise. I didn't sell our things and I'll start getting paid this week. Is November a good time for you to come home, sweetheart? The weather here is very gloomy and cold now. Think about it, darling! Perhaps you'll go to good old Yalta by way of Dzhankoi? (You shouldn't go by sea.) I won't try to persuade you, darling. You're in a better position to decide. But if you do come back, we'll go to the Leningrad clothing store straight from the train station and buy you that fur coat for 150 rubles! Our apartment in the Lyceum isn't ready yet. Lavrentiev is being obstinate about the furniture. Those are trifles: I'll be able to persuade that idiot. The beds are very nice. Meanwhile there is nothing left over. There was some kind of rubbish, but I threw it out. The rooms are quite warm and very dry. If you close off the entrance hall, then half a fireplace and a tiled stove manage for two rooms... Besides the cooking stove there is a good round stove in the kitchen. It's very clean, light, and cozy. Nanusha, I suppose you'll live with your Koktebel landlady in Theodosia? Did I guess right? Yes? And what do you say about my plan to meet you in Moscow? I'm crazy about the idea! Here's how my affairs stand:

1) Priboi has one book (three signatures).

2) A lot of reviews there, too.

3) Marshak suggests I do a *paraphrase* of *Tartarin de Tarascon* at 80 rubles per signature (that's nonsense and empty twaddle).

4) Slonimsky will take an *ordinary* translation of *Tartarin de Tarascon* to Priboi (that's better).[1]

5) An editing job for Marshak at 50 rubles...

6) 220 rubles already earned at GIZ and Priboi (80 of those rubles are for Leonov) which they'll pay me in a few days.

7) The second book (Vildrac) will be at Priboi in a few days (three signatures).

Now you know, darling, how your Nanny is earning his living. I have a good friend—grandfather. He's wonderful and kind. I spend all my time on his green sofa. I feel better there. My little bird! Little sunshine! This separation of ours is not real. It's the most savage separation. I don't believe in it. You are here with me, sweetheart.

No. 55. To N. Ya. Mandelstam [1926]

Hello, Nadyusha! Nanny is homesick: not lonely, but homesick for his homeland, for his life. Were your paltry pennies really enough, dear? Didn't you freeze? You're such a naked little waif carring a basket like some recruit. Do you buy water a dime's worth at a time? Nadichka, I just remembered that you have our cheery Moscow blanket. It's going to come back to me. How I would like to go to Theodosia for the winter! No, I wouldn't, on second thought. It will be better to be in the Lyceum with my Nadichka! Perhaps the South will be very nice in November... There's still a chance I'll come there... But I'm only saying that, Nadenka, because you're counting on coming home and I don't want to distress you... My little child, before you leave you absolutely must let me know your weight and temperature. Aren't there really any large scales in the stores in Koktebel?... I don't believe that your temperature was normal all month. If there was another sudden rise in your temperature like the last one, then it's pretty silly to come for the month of November. I beg you not to conceal anything from me, Nadik. If you have to stay in the Crimea until the first snowfall, then I'll come join you there. This is very serious. In general our financial situation is not bad at all now. Our situation has greatly improved, although the Bens, whom Gorlin has abandoned, fret and complain. Do you recognize your malevolent Nanny? Phoo, this is no good!... Their servant Shura feeds them. Our things are intact (except the mahogany armchair). I kept them for your little house. Tomorrow I'm going to see Anya...to get the furniture from Lavrentiev. I squeezed it out of him with the help of Glavnauka, and that idiot is finally yielding. Our place will be very cozy, but it's still not too late to get an apartment on the third floor: the rooms are smaller, two of them get direct sunlight, and the interior is more elegant: wood paneling, high ceilings, a good stove, and...it's still unclear whether we'll have water in the winter, but most likely we will. I love the winter sun in the rooms and you'll love it, too, but Nanusha, I'm smart. I know that you won't let me change apartments so I'll stay where we are. Everything I do is for you, Nadik, and for us together. You would do the same thing yourself. Remember how in Yalta you...

Today I asked Tatka whether she likes drunkards, but she put an abrupt end to the conversation: "We'd better not talk about them: they're not worth it!"

Grandfather's engineers ruined 1000 pieces of his leather. What a tragedy!

Well, darling, let me kiss you for the whole night and look into your merry, weeping eyes. I love you. The Lord be with you, my woman and my life...

No. 56. To N. Ya. Mandelstam [1926]

Nadik, my distant sunshine! Do you keep your coat on? Are you cold, my darling? I'll warm you, my pet. You'll soon return. How can I live without you? I'm lonely and sad. I'm somewhat afraid that I'll touch you before it's time. It's been a marvelous autumn here so far. Will my letter reach you? Are you well, darling? Make the right decision, my smart girl. I kiss your lovely, salient brow. When you set out I'll meet you in Moscow, okay?

My Nanushka! Your Anya is living in the Lyceum like a fly, but I spent yesterday and today at Tatka's. I obtained a lot of work. I'm well. Nadik, my beloved, I saw Kika yesterday. He has a fantastic, sweet little smile. Nadik, dear! Do you know what I was thinking of just now?... I remember everything. Where are you? How happy we are, Nadik! My joy, my sunshine! Answer me. The Lord be with you, Nadik. I love you. Nanny.

Your watch is intact. The apartment, too. The cat is sick (it's his eyes). Anya is sweet and good.

No. 57. To N. Ya. Mandelstam [1926]

Thank you for your sweet letter, Nadik. I'm writing this in the evening, at the post office, after I sent the telegram. I can hear them tapping it out. Be more careful, darling. It's really autumn now. Slush and rot, even in Tsarskoe Selo. I was there at Anya's today. To my surprise she has acquired a servant. The floors were washed and shining. Something was hissing on the primus stove. Do you know, she lost the cat! That hurts me terribly, since the cat was yours. I'll have the puppy that you wanted waiting for you when you get here. Just don't cry, Nadik. Don't be angry with me, sweetheart, for trying to talk you out of coming. I don't even know how you'll manage to get settled in Theodosia. But joking aside, I have enough money to send you to Yalta. You did get better in the Crimea, after all, and there you could spend half the day outside, even on cold days. Or couldn't you? You need to go there, Nadik. Grab hold of another little piece, make our winter shorter: it's so, so long... *If the weather in Theodosia isn't sharp and biting, stay there in a good boarding house until you get fed up with it.*

I love you and am waiting patiently. You're closer and closer to me. Your sweet voice follows me everywhere, Nanochka. Smart little girl! you want Nanny to make the decision for you. But Nanny wants you to decide! Soon, darling, soon! Bright little bird, you'll soon return.

The Lord be with you, my wife, my friend, my daughter. I'm yours...

No. 58. To N. Ya. Mandelstam (October 15, 1926, Leningrad)

Nadik, my faraway pet! Is this really the last letter? You're just about to leave. So listen to nanny's advice, darling: if your temperature is suddenly very high at the end of the month, don't come back here, but let me know and I'll send you back to Yalta. Your weight is even more important. I'm afraid that you have been going hungry and have lost weight. But if everything is fine, then come and God be with you! The weather here is nice, but cold. It even snowed—how "impractical." The days are sunny. In Theodosia try to buy yourself some plain, warm underwear and stockings for the trip. Those are nanny's orders. And I'll be waiting for you with the material for a coat: we'll take it to a tailor the same day. I don't like the ready-made coat. Don't be cunning, my little one, don't be a sly fox—I'll be very offended if you come back by deceit. My affairs are in order. Priboi was supposed to confirm my new contracts, but the meeting wasn't held.

I didn't get to Tsarskoe Selo today. I'll go tomorrow evening. I'm definitely in favor of the second floor apartment at the Lyceum. It's already been cleaned up and it will be our apartment. I'm waiting for you, darling. I kiss you, my clever little sweetheart. I don't leave you for a minute. Your husband.

No. 59. To Comrade Korobova

Yalta, June 25, 1928

Greatly esteemed Comrade Korobova[1]!

Your letter and the proofs of *The Egyptian Stamp* were delivered to me. What a pity that Lidiya Moiseevna[2] took my address with her. Two months ago I wrote to Lit-Khud and asked them to throw out the *end of The Egyptian Stamp at all costs:* everything except "The Egyptian Stamp" itself and   *The Noise of Time,* which ends with the words: "in the goat milk of the Theodosia moon."[3] I *beg* you to throw everything out between these words and the end. Leave out "The Return"[4] and the like. By including these trifles in the book I committed a most serious *error.* By leaving these trifles in we will *kill* the book. It is worth keeping it alive: *save* it. Consult Gruzdev and Slonimsky. Settle the technicalities of this matter: if it is connected with a financial loss, then I will *make up* for everything, I will *return the money* (I am enclosing a commitment).

Inform me immediately that everything is in order. Until then I will not sleep soundly and I will renounce the book if it is printed in any other form. After all, I requested this *as early as April* (in a letter to Lit-Khud addressed to Varkovitskaya). It is still not too late.

I tried to omit parts of these chapters. It *did not help*. I will simply delete them from the proofs you have sent. I can sign for the book to go to press *only* in such a form. *Nothing* of what is deleted must be printed, but if "Encounter in the Editorial Office" and "Absalom"[5] are printed, nothing remains except for me to hang myself. However, I am sure that I am worrying for no reason. Everything is settled because I admit my fault and am willing to *return immediately the cost of the typesetting for this half-folio and the royalties for it* to the State Publishing House (see the "commitment"). What is more, I call your attention to the fact that the title *The Noise of Time* has *disappeared* from the book. After "The Egyptian Stamp" and before the chapter "Music in Pavlovsk," an insert must be made, a blank page, and after it: *The Noise of Time* the subtitle.

In "The Egyptian Stamp," which consists of fragments, a whole series of "impositions" has been omitted. I am marking them. I requested that the cover be assigned to Mitrokhin.[6]

Please give my regards to Gruzdev, Slonimsky, and Lidiya Moiseevna, if she has returned, and likewise convey my gratitude for the outstanding layout of the *Poems*.[7] I am enclosing a letter to D.N. Angert.[8] It is an extreme measure. It will probably be unnecessary to give it to him. I think that you will be able to settle everything satisfactorily. In this letter I repeat my request to abridge "The Egyptian Stamp" and also to talk about my accounts. Show this letter to Gruzdev or Slonimsky.

Read it yourself and send my questions about financial matters to Comrade Likhnitsky.[9] Show him this letter. Tell him I tried to achieve *maximum clarity* in my accounts with the State Publishing House. I *want to pay up, a little at a time,* if I owe anything. I request that you draw up the *balance after my books have been published*. Tell this to Likhnitsky and Angert. One more thing: a few weeks ago a lawyer from the State Publishing House suggested that I return the money or the forfeit according to some agreement. Meanwhile Likhnitsky and I *balanced* the accounts and entered this in the record. The lawyer's paper *did not reach me*: it was lost in the hands of a third party because it was not addressed to me, so I do not know what is going on. Please have Izmail Mikhailovich make an inquiry and confirm what I have called the "stability of our agreement" in my letter to Angert. If, in accord with this agreement, with all *four* of its points, which I have enumerated in my letter to Angert, it turns out that I am still in debt to the State Publishing House, then please inform me how much and from which account. Please let *The Star*[10] know that I *am working* for it, that I do not expect any money from it, and that I am very sorry I am late. There *will be* a second story in *The Star.*[11]

> I impatiently await your reply,
> With comradely regards,
> O. Mandelstam

No. 60. To A. A. Akhmatova, August 25, 1928

Dear Anna Andreevna,
P.N. Luknitsky[1] and I are writing to you from Yalta where all three of us live our harsh, arduous lives.
I want to go home, I want to see you. You should know that I'm able to conduct imaginary conversations with only two people: Nikolai Stepanovich[2] and you. My conversation with Kolya[3] never was and never will be broken off. We'll return to Petersburg for a short while in October. Nadya[4] is under orders not to spend the winter there. We persuaded P.N. to stay in Yalta out of selfish considerations. Write to us.

> Yours,
> O. Mandelstam

No. 61. To N. Ya. Mandelstam [February 1930]

...everything's just as it was, and it's easier now. Let me bear your grief, my darling. My fearless one, my radiant one...
I hear your voice, Nadenka, and I recognize you once again—

don't cry, my bitter Nadenka, don't cry, little swallow, don't cry, little golden bird.

Take care of Mama, stay home as long as necessary, then bring Mama to live with us.[1] We'll never let her go. Tell her that we'll never let her go.

Write as soon as you arrive to tell me how much money you need. I'll get it all. Christ be with you, my life. There is no death, my joy. No one will take my beloved away. Yours... Yours... I'm going home now, darling—I'll write in more detail later.

Osia.

No. 62. To N. Ya. Mandelstam [February 1930]

...Shashkova is arriving soon (I'm writing at the editorial office), and then I'll send you a mandate for procuring essays.

If you want to talk to me on the phone, find out the hours for calling, then telegraph when you're at Ivanitsky's apartment (Dzhigach's wife).

Shouldn't I drop in at the *Young Pioneer*[1] office to discuss your status? If only we could be together sooner, my Nadik... Just think how it will be... Your brother won't be able to return to Kiev for a long time—you must understand that. A decision must be made, otherwise we'll be ruined: or else I must turn down the apartment and take two rooms near Moscow, and you and Mama must come there. That has to be done no later than the fifteenth of March. Write, darling. I kiss your Mama. The Lord keep you both. Osia.

No. 63. To N. Ya. Mandelstam, February 24, 1930

My darling little bird, little Nadik! It's so difficult for me without you, but I'm ashamed to complain. Never mind, darling.

Here's the major news. My Zhenya is not to be tried for the time being. There was no abuse of power involved, but there was a tremendous amount of harassment and defamation.[1] So far it is just a domestic squabble. The second commission arrived from Moscow to do a more in depth investigation. Here are some of the charges: he deceived the administration about the real state of affairs (false); he manipulated the accounts (false); he applied for a loan for half the amount of his pay (true); and, finally, he "juggled the cash": he and Grigorieva[2] took their wages two days ahead of time. When the investigating commission arrived, Grigorieva childishly tried to conceal it, but he reported it and assumed the responsibility. Furthermore, the Bureau secretly found a replacement, suppressed its employees, started a dispute between Moscow and Leningrad, did an inadequate investigation of the secret service (there was no abuse of power, they say, but there could have been), and that was all. The conclusion of the first investigation: "Exceptional mismanagement" which "will inevitably entail a financial catastrophe." I don't know the results of the more in-depth investigation. A few days ago Natasha told me over the phone: there's no news, no more charges.... He was expelled from Modpik and is now without any source of income. He wants to go into medicine after everything has been cleared up. He was going to go to Sovkino[3] (he was invited *after* the harassment had started—the invitation was a friendly gesture of protest, but was revoked because of pressure from *someone*).

Tanya[4] went to Rostov where she has a job in her field. Natasha is still working (?!?) at Modpik (?!). That's typical of the scandalous nature of the whole affair... The whole gang of writers betrayed Zhenya and then scattered... The members of LAPP are providing very little support. The Party cell is fearful and passive... Grandfather is well. So far I've given him literally *nothing* to help him out. Rent for the room eats up all my pay. How can we survive, Nadik, how...

The next paycheck: 15 rubles on account—a deduction (what's left of the earlier one)—30 rubles (I owe the cafeteria)—the literary fund (?)—What will I do with 90 rubles minus 60 for the room (not counting the debts totaling 25 rubles, they are beginning to mount up). Nadik, Nadik, tell me how to survive.

The situation at the newspaper office has improved. There's a fresh surge of respect for me. They're beginning to understand that the assignment they gave me was worthy of Manilov[5] and impossible to fulfill. Now they want me to teach and uplift the staff. I'm leading a worker-correspondents group at *Evening Moscow*. I'm getting acquainted with the young workers. Yesterday right *after* I'd sent the telegram in reply to yours the secretary showered me with compliments. They expect me to wedge myself into work in the departments and help them from within the system. But I have no comrades at the paper. The bureaucracy and lack of talent is just appalling. I made a huge montage of the Red Army (on February 23rd). That strengthened my already very strong position. It showed that I'm *capable*.

Yurasov is leaving on the first. He insists that I go with him, that is, he'll send for me, with traveling expenses, in a month. He is quite serious. There are good opportunities there. The *Komsomol Member of the East*[6] is at the center of all the regional political work—cotton, Turkic Siberia, and so on... It's very tempting. But are we *able* to bring ourselves to do it? You are also guaranteed a job there. A place to live, too. But we can't abandon the dear old folks! Can we, Nadik? Nadichka, how are we to survive?

Now for the "Dreyfus affair."[7] As soon as I arrived I received a summons to the plenum of the commission. The interrogation, or rather, my uninterrupted speech, lasted four hours. I was terribly dissatisfied with myself. The next morning: "You gave us many valuable hints, don't worry, don't demand the impossible of yourself. We're not planning to drag this affair out." But then the case was divided into segments. Each investigator is now working with me individually. There was a summons from FOSP.[8] The interrogation lasted three hours. The interrogator was a woman, an old Party member, an editor at *Young Guard*.[9] She forced me to confess to certain technicalities. She yanked out the confessions—seventeen of them—like a dentist. She was still not satisfied and she ordered me to finish up the matter at home and send her the remainder in the mail. That's done. Berezner exploded at the commission. "Bear in mind that the feuilleton was *ordered from above*..." The day before yesterday I was interrogated for four hours at ZIF.[10] Their method consisted of making me give written answers on the spot which did not deviate in the slightest from the question. What incredible patience! What is more, until now I've been utterly incapable of saying what is most important! A curious thing happened: I didn't pick up the piece of paper, they sent me home, they waited (I flew home in a taxi). I made two copies of your copy of the K.K. protocol. It's a most important document. They sent the third interrogator back: "You're a very popular item," Berezner said.

So, my darling, there you have the most important facts. I don't go out anywhere (I dropped in on the Shifrins). He spoke to the people at OZET (Society for Property Distribution for Working Jews in the USSR). *They're willing to think about it.* But about what? Would it be nice to go to the Northern Crimea[11]? Yes, My Nadik? I'll pay Nissen another visit. Margulis[12] is here.

Oh, yes, I forgot, one other charge: I refuse to help other writers: Aseev, Aduev, Lidin, etc.[13] Aseev *was not offended.* He was embarrassed. He questioned me for a long time, concluding: "Well, so far we haven't helped each other out." Aduika was inimitable. He ran into Livshits at Zhenya's place and turned his back on him.

I *haven't seen* anyone in Leningrad. It's impossible to circulate the letter right now.[14]

No. 64. To N. Ya. Mandelstam [1930]

Darling Nadenka! I'm at my wit's end. I'm miserable, Nadik: I should have stayed with you the whole time. You are my strong, pale, darling little bird. I kiss your lovely brow, my old woman, my young girl, my beloved. You're working, you're doing something, you're wonderful, little Nadik. I want to come to Kiev to be with you. I won't forgive myself for abandoning you in February. I didn't rush back to you. I didn't go back to you as soon as I heard your voice on the phone—and I didn't write; I wrote almost nothing the whole time. As you walk around our room, darling, all that is precious and eternal is with you. You must cling, cling to this sweet, immortal something till the very end. Don't give it away to anyone at any cost. I'm miserable, darling, I'm always miserable, but now I can't find the words to tell you. They've confused me and they're holding me here as if I were in prison; there's no light. I keep wanting to brush away the lie—and I can't;

I keep wanting to wash away the dirt—and it's impossible.

Should I tell you what a delirium, what a frenzied, dreary nightmare everything is, absolutely everything...

They've been tormenting me with the case,[1] I've been summoned five times, three different interrogations. They lasted for a long time: 3-4 hours. I don't believe them even though they're kind. I only fully believe Ruger from FOSP: she's candid, serious, and filled with human warmth. What do they want with me? Once again I'm a toy. Once again, for no reason at all. The most recent summons was to see some university lecturer: to tell my whole life story. Question: Didn't I once work for White newspapers? What did I do in Theodosia? Did I have connections with Osvag[2]? (??)... This must be someone's delirium. Did I incriminate the Theodosia Communists (?!).[3] I read him poems about Kerensky and others... I myself pointed out all that was wrong in the poems. He had studied *The Noise of Time*.[4] He typed out quotations—he showed them to me, asked for explanations, and spoke in a friendly tone. He said: "We know everything about Ionov[5] and the others. We must also know everything about you..." No later than ten days from now a meeting will be called to make public the conclusions of the commission. Everyone is invited: ZIF, FOSP, etc. They'll let them have their say: "They should know their place in the general plan and make their comments; we don't have a Federation; we won't allow polemics to come between them." But a different committee—the highest one—will pronounce judgement and print it up. He ordered me to send him all my books and a chronological account of my biography. In conclusion: "We have sufficient authority to insure that no one will reproach you with your past." (My past as a writer or something like that?) "To hell with the princess Maria Alekseevna..." But not a word about the case itself. Zenkevich[6] was summoned: not a word about the case ("everything's so obvious"). Only a general character reference and the time spent with the Whites (sheer fabrication). It seems as if they want to negotiate fairly with me: who I am, what I want, and so on—it would be good if that were so. But I know one thing: I'm out of work, I'm growing more uncivilized each day. I'm afraid of my newspaper office—there are no people there, only terrible fish... I can't stand it. I'm scandalized and out of place. I must leave. I should have left long ago... It's too late... I want to rest. Tomorrow I'll go to the outpatient clinic. Shall I try to get a vacation pass[7]? But that won't do. I must leave. And now. But where can I go? There's nothing but emptiness all around. I feel bad about the book that was stopped. It's too bad. Apel is the only person who associates with me. I couldn't pay any rent for the room on the 1st. What will my situation be like on the 15th? 20 rubles are for the cafeteria. That will leave 100 rubles. M. Rom. will take 10 rubles. That leaves 90.

Nadik, darling, I must decide—the time is right! (Today Aseev was questioned at FOSP. Sutyrin is "writing" a resolution. Kanatchikov was removed. Why?)

I'm alone. *Ich bin arm.*[8] Everything is irreparable. The severance is a blessing. I must preserve it. I must not upset it. I think your Zhenya will probably be detained. But don't be in a hurry to come here, my dearest, it *won't change anything.* Take care of your Mama. Just write to tell me what I should do, help me to stand firm, help me to avoid all lies and vile people—I need people, like my comrades at the *Moscow Komsomol Member.* We'll find friends yet, we'll find support. We do not have to go to Tashkent.[9] We'll try living in Moscow. We'll take Mama along. You decide—is newspaper work suited to me? Won't my old brain dry out in the end? But I need work, and *easy* work. I don't want to "parade around as Mandelstam." I don't dare! I must not!

The Lord be with you, darling. He won't abandon you, my precious love. Do you recognize me? Do you hear me? Your Osia.

No. 65. To N. Ya. Mandelstam [1930s]

I went to the outpatient clinic, Nadik. The internist found that my heart muscles were somewhat weakened. "Essentially," he said, "it's myocarditis..."

He found nothing wrong that hadn't already been corrected by normal compensation. He prescribed a stay in the sanitorium pending approval by a neuropathologist, and immediately sent me to a neurologist. The latter behaved very seriously. He knows who I am (?). "A *minimum* of six weeks in a sanitorium," he said, and directed me to a professor of neuropathology for a consultation (after my examination) on the methods of treatment. Tomorrow I'll go see the professor. "Then," said the doctor, "*we'll rock the whole unwieldy machine* in order to get you into a sanitorium quickly."

I told him about the confidential part. He said: "Never mind, we'll take care of everything." I have no reason to complain. *There is no pain.* I'm healthy. My word of honor, Nadik, I'm as healthy as I've always been. My darling! Stay in Kiev. You're better off there! Perhaps, darling, you need a good rest? I kiss you. Your Nanny.

No. 66. To N. Ya. Mandelstam [Spring 1935]

Nadenka, my child!

I'm sending you the revised poems at the beginning of the cycle (2,3,4).[1] Keep the rhyme "coal quarry—voluntary." I ended the final manuscript (without the addition) with the poem "Black Earth"[2] and submitted it to Plotnikov. It was a necessary and natural thing to do.

I miss you, my dearest, but my life is calm. My patience will hold out a *few* more days. I kiss you, my dear, my good friend, Nadik... For some reason, "faithful" usually accompanies the word "friend." Faithfully yours, O.M.

Is all well with the *"zhelezias'"*[3]?

No. 67. To N. Ya. Mandelstam [Spring 1935]

My darling Nadik! I just now spoke to you. It's 8:30 p.m. Here are four fair copies of various things for you which were done without you. How sad it is. Yesterday I did "Haircuts for Children."[1] Today I took a bath. We have bedbugs here. And the

day before yesterday I went to the bath-house too. So...all's
well with me. Yesterday I called Stoichev[2] on the phone. I still
don't know whether I should take the job. It's awkward to quit
when I'm busy writing.[3] What's more, they'll pay me very little.
Oh, how I've been neglecting the radio. Help me. Give me some
material *for Shervinsky*[4] ("Goethe's Youth").[5]

I'm just about to go to the movies. What a little ass I
am.

Nadik, call Akhmatova on the phone and tease her a bit. So,
no one has gone yet. Or, the Metropolitan, for he's also a Jew
terrified of his fate. I kiss you, darling. Your Osia.

No. 68. To N. Ya. Mandelstam, May 26, 1935

Nadiushok! Forgive me for frightening you. The telephone
operator is a raving scoundrel, and she said that "according to instructions *we don't make mistakes.*" Like a fool, I believed her.
What an old hag! She got it from a lady-friend. That night I didn't
go to bed. The devil only knows what it's all about! Forgive me,
Nadenka.

I submitted what was in my typewriter to the journal *Ascent.*[1] They have a tendency there to good-naturedly degrade my
work. I refused to change another letter. All or nothing. In the
meantime I'm not accepting any money. Should I take the job
at the library?

Add "Stanzas"[2] and "Iron"[3] to the "collection." Explain
the typing. *Moscow* must accept my conditions: *all* or nothing.[4]
A broad illustration of the cycle. It would be nice to publish in
the *Literary Gazette.*[5] All the variants are in their final form. A
few changes could perhaps be made at the beginning of "Stanzas," but let it be.

Right now I need a direct literary link with Moscow. Give
the poems to Levin[6] while you're at it. Tell him that it's impossible to write honest prose here in Voronezh in my present
situation. It's absurd!

Here's what I propose: I'll offer to accept a work assignment from the Union of Writers or the Publishing House in the Urals *by way of the old route*. I'll write a remarkable book (according to the old agreement). What a marvelous idea.

Don't worry at all, my pet. I'm living well. Write *the truth about your health*. I kiss you, my darling. Osia.

Think about how to structure the cycle.[7] Tell me on the telephone.

No. 69. To N. Ya. Mandelstam [1935]

I'm well today. I was at Stoichev's[1] place and told him just what I think of my situation. He volunteered to write to Marchenko in his capacity as chairman of the Union of Writers, and for the first time he displayed genuine interest and concern.

I'm sending the certificate from Doctor Glauberman (the best throat specialist around here). He said: "If it doesn't go away in three or four days, come back to my office and I'll scarify your throat." It was only then that I asked for a certificate.

No one can say when I'll have to be operated on or how urgent it is. In any case, the most recent attack was the most severe.

I kiss you, sweetheart. Come as soon as possible. Everything will be fine. Osia.

No. 70. To N. Ya. Mandelstam [1935]

Nadik! I'm already very, very lonesome. I can't say how much I wish you were here. Osia.

> The earth must be maligned
> It needs a brutal brother.
> No lucid shoots of grain will reach it
> From mutants seven times removed.

May

No. 71. To N. Ya. Mandelstam [the end of 1935]

Darling Nadenka! Forgive me for the rude, disgusting telephone conversation. I was fuming and I made certain demands of you. Here's why: only one thing matters to me—to know when I'll see you again. You must tell me immediately: I hope to arrive on such and such a date. If I don't hear that from you I'll lose control of myself.

Nadyusha, don't ask anyone for anything. *No one*. But try to find out how the Union, that is, the Party Central Committee, is responding to my poems and to my letters. A talk with Shcherbakov[1] should be sufficient to establish this.

Nothing else need be done. I don't want you to start looking for work. Is DetGIZ perhaps leading you on? Whatever happened to Efros's offer[2]? If worst comes to worst, we'll meet in Voronezh before January 20th. In Voronezh we'll have nothing to worry about. But what a pity! The two of us together here—it's an indescribably beautiful winter paradise. Let me tell you how I came to be here[3]: you went to the train station and I went to the theater. I gave a business-like "producer's speech." The actors began to crowd around me. The producers were asking me serious questions. I stayed at my post for two or three days. Then I went to pieces. The old, usual "stupor" occurred on the street. A distinguished comic actor picked me up and took me to the theater. I was with Wolf when he called Genken: "So and so is working for us. His health is a cause of serious apprehension for *me personally*... We must etc...." That's Wolf for you! Then I wandered around like a shadow, but quite safely. I held a consultation at the Radio Committee. Goriachev gave me 100 rubles, and Wolf added 50. Half an hour before I was supposed to leave, a car with the deputy director and manager came to pick me up. The driver, a soldier, drove the car to the NKVD. They put me in a railroad car. They carried my suitcase. What touching solicitude. It was awful, that is, absolutely foul in the railroad car. No reserved seats. The conductor took me into his own compartment. In Michurinsk I sent a telegram to you and then immediately changed trains. We reached Tambov at 2 a.m. Crackling frost. Fairytale-like calm and the look of a provincial town. I was taken on an endless trip somewhere in a sled (those are the cabs here) and driven to a palace resembling Kshesinska's mansion, only it is ten times larger and guarded by an old man in a sheepskin coat with a gun. I was led down marble stairs to the basement and given a warm (tepid) bath. Then and there a maid gathered up my clothes to have them laundered, the clock was hissing—then I was taken to an enormous office. Brigade bosses and tractor drivers with bad hearts live here, along with two or three pilots and teachers. All in all, it's not bad. We have pine baths every day and two kinds of electric treatments on alternate days: a "Franklin" treatment and electric massage of the spine. The director permits me (with an investment) to be fastidious. As of now there are only two of us in an empty ward meant for ten people. This happiness is only temporary. Rooms with their quota of people are terrible. Five people is a luxury (there's no ventilation, but there are plate-glass windows. The window in my room opens).

The next morning I rented a marvelous room a short distance away, half a minute's walk: it has a cow, a couch, slipcovers, a gramophone, and cactuses. We live on a steep bank of the Tsna River. It is a wide river, or seems to be wide, like the Volga. It flows into ink-blue forests. The gentleness and harmony of the Russian winter bring me great joy. This is the real countryside. It takes ten minutes on the bus to get to the center of town. Watch-towers, monasteries out of touch with civilization, fat women with moustaches.

I had a letter from Goriachev to Reentovich, the director of the technical museum. Today after breakfast I went into town. Two old men played a dreadful sonata for me (for violin and piano) written by a local composer and intended to be performed in Voronezh. They were crying and complaining. Reentovich is a distinguished performer. Smetanin[4] also showed up—he's the resident composer of this region. He knows me. We made an appointment for this evening. I'm on my way to see him now. I'm writing this letter from *my* room, which I haven't moved into yet.

Nadik, I miss you madly. Do something foolish and come join me. Nadik, I can't say how much I love you! I don't have a picture of you. Where are you darling? Come to me as soon as possible! Okay, little child?

I love you, Nadik. Answer me. Your Nanny.

Tell me if I can call you at 8:30 a.m.

My address: Tambov, Naberezhnaia 9. Psychiatric Sanitorium. My telephone number: 1.55

No. 72. To N. Ya. Mandelstam [the end of 1935]

Darling Nadenka!

Yesterday I just about decided to return to Voronezh. The food here is worse than in some cheap little cafeteria. It's dreary here. Yet all the same I managed to gain a kilo in four days and get a good rest. I must be patient. The main thing is the incredibly active situation I found myself in. Now things are becoming more "static." A consultation was held. The director (he's not a doctor) and two doctors were there. The theme was: "how to make you better" and "how not to make you worse"—having taken into consideration the fact that "we can do very little, but all the same, etc." They'll take X-rays of my heart and lungs. They want to call in a consultant from the city. And they're hesitating about giving me a "certificate" ("we'll wait and see...in about ten days... now's not a good time..."). The same old story! I think I should leave here before January 5th, the date my pass officially begins, after I've arranged to get my money back minus what was spent. If something turns up for you by the 5th you should leave that ugly place.

I got your lovely second letter. Thank you! Write every day. Send a telegram if there's any news. Bear in mind that the Tambov sanitorium is only a palliative. Even Voronezh (without you) would be better—and that's all there is to it.

My temperature is somewhat up again. Yesterday evening it was 37.2. My heart is highly excitable. Sometimes my pulse speeds up. In spite of all this I'm quite cheerful and feel like taking a walk. But seeing people upsets me. Conversations exhaust me. Reading, also. I must pose the question seriously—right up to a special declaration at the NKVD concerning the necessity of treatment in adequate surroundings. Voronezh *isn't able* to give me any more care. They've done *everything in their power*...

I think that after you meet with Shcherbakov you shouldn't

drag out your stay in Moscow. The situation is too simple. Both "yes" and "no" are laid bare. If it's "no," we'll stand firm in the domestic situation. I'll go back to the theater (it's very friendly, protective, and not tiring) and to my own dear radio (just about!),[1] and you will take a little job. The main thing is that we be together. Your coming home is an enormous, immeasurable happiness for me.

But for now, my pet, goodbye.

I got permission to spend the rest hour in the reading room. I wrote this little letter and now I'll take it to the post office.

Goodbye, sweetheart. I kiss Shura and Shurik and V[era] Ya[kovlevna]. Nanny.

P.S. In spite of all my whining, I'm better off here than in Voronezh!

No. 73. To N. Ya. Mandelstam, No. 3 [the end of 1935]

Darling Nadenka!

I got your letter No. 3. Tell me, aren't you cold in that fur coat? Are you having freezing weather there, too? Wear Mama's fur coat when you go out: they're both equally ugly, that is, Mama's fur coat and yours (don't show this to Mama)...

Can it be possible that Shcherbakov won't receive you? Well? The days are going well. I'm getting used to it. There was a blue frost today. I got the Pushkin. It's a rare luxury for me. I can almost never get hold of him, you know.

I had the X-rays taken yesterday. My heart is normal for my age. There are no anomalies, they say. There's an enlarged hilus in my lungs. They inquired if I had recently had the flu or pneumonia.

They're very attentive and observe me very carefully. They listen and tap every day. They put me on a special diet. I get a bath every day. Electric treatments as well. I'm lonesome without you, sweetheart, I can't find the right words. Stop worrying about me. I'm capricious. And how are you faring? Take care of yourself, my joy. Write me every day. And call me on the phone sometimes. Goodbye. Yours...

Do you think I can write 20 lines to Luppol[1] about "Maupassant and the French metaphor and the idiotic editor"? Theoretically? Well?

Greetings to Vishnevsky.[2]

No. 74. To N. Ya. Mandelstam, No. 4 [the end of 1935]

My darling! There was no letter from you today. I received the 40 rubles that were wired. I have fifty (50) in all... (By the way, I made an agreement with the director—he'll "buy" the month's pass from me, keep it for the duration of my stay here, and pay me the difference. That bargain I thought up gave me freedom at once.) Oh, it's so boring here! They don't let me sleep. Tactful young people wearing Russian felt boots start walking through the ward on tiptoe at three a.m.

Yesterday my ears got slightly frostbitten and they were treated with the dark-blue light of a quartz-lamp. That's all the news. I can't bring myself to move into the room I rented: it's cold there. I paid a ten ruble deposit and I'm getting it back in milk. I go there whenever I can't stand it here any longer. At least it's someplace to call my own.

Nadik, don't you think I should contact Shcherbakov or Gorky by letter or telegram and request a reply to my appeal, which was quite serious? That won't interfere with your coming here, my dearest. But whichever way you look at it, the matter is too well-known to chat about it intimately.

If this proposal of mine is not too late, telegraph me immediately and let me know your opinion. I'm speaking only of the question.

I want to tell you once more what happiness it will be for me to be with you. Will we really see each other after the fifth? It seems that we will. Nadik, eternally mine, do you hear me?

No. 75. To N. Ya. Mandelstam, January 1, 1936

My darling little child! Happy New Year, my angel! Here's to our unhappy happiness: to something new, whatever it may be, to the eternally old that is younger than us! Long live my Nadenka, my wife, my eternal friend! Happy New Year, little one!

Like a fool I didn't write to you for two days: the day before yesterday it was because I was so happy after our phone conversation, and yesterday it was out of sheer stupidity.

Last night the military band played here and there were various games: Chekhov in a hopital gown, fishing poles with rings on them. It's so bad here that many people leave before they are released: the unpampered regional workers. All at the expense of the organization. Tea without sugar. Noise. The doctors are like postal officials. Yesterday the head doctor said to me: "You need to be in a private institution where they treat moderate cases of psychopathy" (there, he said, there are only one or two people in a room). On my honor, that's what he said! After he had listened to me for two minutes.

I gained 600 grams in the first ten days (not bad for a baby). Many people lose weight after a month here. It's like a boarding school in a Dickens novel. The other doctor says: "Weight is not a serious problem for neurotics." What's more, the head doctor asked me what clinics I had been in before Tambov. Tomorrow I must formalize the sale of my pass with the director. I'll leave on the fifth or even sooner. What bliss! These last days have been like a bad dream! Some sort of penal battalion... I'll have enough money in Voronezh to last until the 20th. I get my wages from the theater on the 15th and will return to work the same day.

I'm physically healthy (*not only* physically, I believe). I just need to recover my strength. The only reason I *might* become ill is if the *pressure* is not removed!

Stoichev told me that the letter was sent on December 20th. Podobedov confirmed that there was some correspondence about the District Department of the Union in regard to my work ("we won't write anything bad"). Where is the letter? Who received it? Explain it as precisely as you can. If the letter has been lost, send a copy of it to: 1) Marchenko, 2) the Poets' Section, and 3) to the Party Central Committee. In general, it would be a *good* thing to do. In regard to the poems, what is meant by "in principle"? I must have concrete answers about these poems. Why did you turn in all of them indiscriminately? I'm *against* stool pigeons. Marchenko is right.

Remember to tell him that I demand a reply concerning the *effective* poems. They constitute a whole. Some people only dream about quality, for others it is a reality. Write me in Tambov and *send a telegram.* Describe everything in brief. We'll talk when I return to Voronezh.

Goodbye, my darling. Your Nanny.

I spend my time here with a certain young fellow, a tractor driver. He's talented and candid, but he thinks that there are Soviets in France and that France has been renamed Paris. I protect him and he's become very attached to me and calls me a Bolshevik.

No. 76. To N. Ya. Mandelstam, January 2 [1936]

Darling Nadenka!

I received all your letters. I'm sending two applications and the certificate by special delivery. The doctors refuse to keep me here. They say: "you were brought to us because of a technical error." There's nothing terribly wrong with me, but I'm not any better. I'll be objective: it's exactly the same thing, but the conditions here are downright harmful (the opinion of the doctors). If I can get a ticket, I'll leave tomorrow (the 3rd). They'll return my money. I have traveling companions all the way to Voronezh. I'm very satisfied. I rejoice in the thought of Voronezh, as if it were home. One way or another, you'll arrive soon. That's all. Be happy. I'm in a hurry to mail this. I'll write tomorrow. Yours...

No. 77. To N. Ya. Mandelstam, January 3 [1936]

Darling Nadyusha!

Thank you for the lovely phone call. You know it's the easiest thing in the world to calm me down. What's wrong with me? Where is the pain? There is no pain. My intestines are healthier than ever. The catarrh in my throat has gone away. How's my mood? Uneven. The sanitorium depressed me. My anticipation is more intense. The situation here is unbearable. Associations take an unhealthy course (which is usual without you). How do I feel? I have palpitations of the heart after walking (not right away; sometimes my pulse speeds up, but I'm coping with it, consciously fighting it and overcoming it). Yesterday I went to the train station with the letter—I felt refreshed and bought a copy of *Red Virgin Soil*[1] that contained some wretched poems by our dear Zenkevich and Zoshchenko's Talmud. I took my temperature at random twice. It was identical both times: 37.2. Obviously, that's the average. I sleep well if no one disturbs me. Last night, without permission, I moved into an empty room meant to hold five people. I laid my claim on it. It's much nicer. I nap during the day. I can leave *any* day, *and after the fifth* I can leave with my refund (the head doctor confirmed it today).

All the same I might leave on the fifth. In Voronezh I'll be closer to you somehow. And the change will be good for me. Further... My weight has stayed at exactly 66 kilos. The "roomy lightness in my body" is weakness and nothing more, in my opinion. My appearance is quite miserable. There, my Nadik, is the whole truth.

We must always keep in mind, Nadik, that my letter to the Voronezh Union of Writers is eternally binding, that it is not the same as literature. After that letter there's no possibility of my breaking with the Bolshevik Party—no matter what the reply is, even if there is no reply, even if the situation worsens. No feeling hurt. No grumbling. The Party is neither a nanny nor a doctor. Every decision the Party makes is binding for the author of such a letter. It seems to me that you haven't yet drawn sufficient conclusions from my action and haven't learned how to continue it in the future.

At present, no matter what, I'm *already* free. I'm very sorry about Voronezh, but I'm afraid that if I stay there any longer it will prove to be harmful, and *not only* for myself. I'll telephone you on the morning of the fifth. More about Old Crimea: let there be no departure, no running away, no "Cincinnatus tricks." I'm not Pliny the Younger and I'm not Voloshin. Explain that to whomever you must. One other request, insignificant at first glance: freedom of movement *throughout the entire region*. It would be terrible without that freedom. You must make that clear.

Now then, Nadik, I kiss you countless times and rejoice and take pride in my wife. Goodbye, my Nadik!

Your Nanny

No. 78. To N. Ya. Mandelstam [beginning of January 1936]

Nadik my dear, my newborn love! I kiss you ardently. You can't believe how much I want to see you.

Soon, soon, we'll be together. I've never missed you so much or been so anxious to see you. Do you hear, Nadik?

Goodbye. Yours...

I'll still take very, very good care of you, properly, as I used to. I'll protect you and make you happy... Nadik, my pet, come to me...

No. 79. To. E.E. Mandelstam, January 8 [19] 36

Evgeny Emilievich[1]!

You decided long ago what my life is worth and for you it is hardly a first priority item.

But you have children. Someday they will understand just *what* you are doing. They will blush for their father.

Understand the following: in the *final* analysis I have only two alternatives: to be supported by my relatives (?) or to go off to some hospital which will then cast me out into a home for invalids (among vagrants and paralytics).

In order to remain free, *I have recently pleaded for mercy.* Do you understand *what* you are doing?

Osia.

I won't ask you for any money, but I forbid you, wherever you may be, ever to call yourself my brother.

No. 80. To E.E. Mandelstam [beginning of 1936]

Listen, Zhenya: it's not a question of whether you'll send the money or not. Such a form of aid, such negligent indifference is taking on monstrous proportions. Just tell me, don't you give a damn about me? Is that it?

He's far away. You can't see your brother... There's no "visual evidence." You pay 60 rubles to have a candle lit for three months and are still moved by the nobility of your act.

However, you have nothing for me. That means you regard me as superfluous. Let me put it in simple terms: for you my life is not worth a periodic reduction of *your own* budget, your whole family's budget, by 10% or even less. You won't go against the facts. There are brothers and there are brothers. But it's very rare, very rare indeed, when love for one's family (and I mean by family *only* one's wife and children and oneself) finds expression in the form of such a petty and *shameful* convulsive shudder, such frowning. Meanwhile, I must say, you're carrying on like a nasty little boy trying to avoid responsibility. It's not likely that I'll force you to save me from hunger and sickness.* (After all, you are ill yourself and still work hard: I pity you), nonetheless you should know that you have exceeded *simple* negligence.

I'm glad that you have never experienced even a hundredth part of my fate. (How I would help you! Splendidly! You know that. I would *rave* about such help.) But you are a sober-minded man and will be able to justify your actions. It's hard to have a brother who is a doctor. Farewell, doctor.

Osia.

Aren't you going to advise me to make my *destitution* rational? This month the two of us are living on 100 rubles.

*In the doctors' opinion I can still "last" a while longer if conditions are "completely calm." We've been reduced to dire poverty.

No. 81. To E.E. Mandelstam, Voronezh, February 4, [19]37

Greetings, brother. However, it seems you are no longer my brother. What you are is *not* a brother. What you are is something else entirely.

Osia.

No. 82. To V. Ya. Khazina [beginning of 1937]

Dear Vera Yakovlevna!

I have a big favor to ask of you: come and live with me for awhile.[1] Give Nadenka a chance to go [to Moscow] undisturbed on some urgent business. She'll have to be gone a long time on this trip. Why am I asking you to do this? I'll explain.

As soon as Nadya goes away I am stricken with an agonizing psychosomatic illness which has the following symptoms: in recent years I've developed an asthmatic condition. *Breathing is always difficult.* When I'm with Nadya I breathe normally, but when she has to leave I literally begin to suffocate. Subjectively speaking, it is unendurable: I sense the end. Each minute seems like an eternity. When I'm alone I can't take a single step by myself. It's impossible to get used to. The last time she was gone (7 days) I grew worse by the day. There's no one to stay with me. Only *my own* people can comfort me. Moreover, we hardly have any casual acquaintances. Last time I suffered as if I had a critical illness. The day before Nadya returned I was in such a state that I wanted to go to the hospital, any hospital. I clung to people. I would sit for hours on end in strange places (in some office building in the middle of a work day)—just to be near someone. It was then I vowed that I would never endure this anymore. It will leave its mark on me.

There are many deep-rooted causes of this illness. What can I do? My sole hope is in your coming here. In all other respects I'm entirely normal. Believe me, I won't be a burden on you and you can't guess, you can't believe what a favor you'll be doing for me and Nadya.

You'll have to stay with me for a *minimum* of two weeks. The living conditions will be good. The room is very cozy. The landlady is wonderful. There are no stairs. Everything is nearby. There's a telephone next door. We're close to the center of town. Spring in Voronezh is glorious. I'll even take you for a drive in the country.

But without you I'll fall ill and my psychosomatic condition will be unendurably intense.

I implore you not to ignore my letter but to send a telegram in reply immediately. Show the letter to Evg[geny] Yak[ovlevich][2] and Shura.[3] They'll help you get ready for the trip. I firmly believe in your desire to help us.

Yours, Osia.

No. 83. To K. I. Chukovsky [beginning of 1937?]

Dear Kornei Ivanovich[1]!
I must turn to you with a most serious request: *can you send*

me some money?

I no longer have any choice but to ask for help from people who don't want me to perish.

You know that I'm very ill, that my wife looked for work in vain. *I not only can't afford treatment, but I can't afford to live: I have nothing to live on. I implore you, even though you and I are not close friends.* What can I do? My brother Ev[geny] Em[i-lievich] won't give me a cent. It's impossible to do *anything at all* in this place. It's only a place to live and *nothing* more. Do you understand what is becoming of me?

Just one more thing: if you aren't able to help—telegraph your refusal. It's too agonizing to wait and hope.

O. Mandelstam

Voronezh district
27th of February Street, Building No. 50, Apartment No. 1

No. 84. To K. I. Chukovsky [beginning of 1937]

Dear Kornei Ivanovich!

What is happening to me cannot go on any longer. Neither my wife nor I have the strength left to prolong this nightmare. What is more, we are firmly resolved to put an end to it in any way possible. This has not turned out to be a "temporary sojourn in Voronezh," an "administrative exile," or anything of the kind. I'll tell you what it is: a man who has suffered from a very critical mental illness (a bleak and exhausting madness, to be more exact) goes back to work physically maimed, right after this illness, after an attempted suicide. I said those who judged me were right. I have found historical meaning in everything. Fine. I rushed headlong into my work. For this I was beaten, rebuffed, and subjected to a moral trial. All the same, I worked. I denied myself any self-esteem. I considered it a miracle that I was allowed to work. I regarded our whole life as a miracle. After a year and a half I became an invalid. About that time, although I had done nothing else wrong, everything was taken away from me: my right to life, to work, and to treatment. I was put in the position of a dog, a cur... I am a shadow. I do not exist. I have only the right to die. My wife and I are being driven to suicide. It's futile to turn to the Writers' Union for help. They will wash their hands of the whole affair. There is only one person in the whole world to whom I can and must turn for help in this matter.[1] They will write to him only when they consider it their duty to do so. I am not my own warrantor or appraiser. I'm not speaking of my letter. If you want to save me from inevitable ruin—to save two people—help me, persuade others to write a letter. It's amusing to think that it can "strike" those who do so. There's no other way out. This is the solid historical solution. But understand that we refuse to prolong our agony. Each time I send my wife off I have a nervous breakdown. And it's terrifying to look at her, to see how sick she is. Think about it: WHY is she going? What is life clinging to? I will not comply with another sentence of exile. I can't.

O. Mandelstam

The illness. I can't remain "alone" for a minute. My wife's mother, an old woman, has just come to stay with me. If I am left alone they'll have to put me in a madhouse.

No. 85. To Boris L. Pasternak,[1] January 2, 1937

Happy New Year!

Dear Boris Leonidovich,
When one recalls the whole great volume of your life's work, all of its incomparable scope of life—one cannot find words enough for gratitude.

I want your poetry, by which we have all been spoiled and undeservedly gifted—to leap further out into the world, to the people, to children...

Let me say to you at least once in life: thank you for everything, and for the fact that this "everything"—is still "not everything."

Excuse me for writing you as if it were an anniversary. I know myself that it is anything but an anniversary: you nurse life, and in it me, unworthy of you, most affectionately yours.

O. Mandelstam

No. 86. To Yu. N. Tynianov, January 21, 1937, Voronezh.

Dear Yury Nikolaevich[1]!

I want to see you. What can I do? It's a legitimate desire.

Please do not regard me as a shadow. I am still casting off my shadow. But recently I am becoming intelligible to virtually everyone. That's terrifying. It's already been a quarter of a century that I, confusing essentials with trifles, have been steadily encroaching on Russian poetry; but soon my poems will merge with it, thereby altering something of its structure and composition.

It's easy not to answer me,[2] but it's impossible to justify silence. Do as you please.

Yours, O.M.

No. 87. To N. Ya. Mandelstam, April 19 [1937]

Nadyushenka!

This morning I got the letter you wrote at the train station. The postman must have knocked very loudly at my window. Then the kitty chased Toma away. This morning Mama talked about the hereditary characteristics of children. Yesterday the Korngold family had an adventure. Yesterday both Mama and I, relying on each other, went shopping without any money. We arrived only to find that we had to turn right around and go back. Grandmother had turned off the light. I inadvertently turned it back on.

Yesterday Mama and I went to the Red Army building. There, in the luxurious barber shop, I grew young again, for 2 rubles and 50 kopeks. The concert turned out to be free with special passes. I took two—for myself and for Mama. But when Natasha[1] came, they wouldn't give her a pass. Mama went home (having given her pass to Natasha) very reluctantly:, she really took a liking to the Red Army building. Sebastian danced like a Syrian, a Nubian, a Thracian, and a Jew all rolled into one. And the orchestra was splendid.

I just reserved Zhenya's phone for emergency use from morning till midnight and gave them a warning. But even that isn't certain. Nadik, live at our house or else you'll grow tired of visiting people. I'll try to call in the mornings between 8:30 and 9:00. If that's impossible, send me a telegram. Tell Grandfather that I want to see him. Let him write to me. My illness called "being without You" is progressing quite peacefully (thanks to Mama), but it's an illness all the same. I'm counting the days and minutes until Your return. If circumstances indicate, drop in at *The Banner*.[2] But if not? I'll write every morning. And you send a telegram if I don't reach you by phone. You must go to the doctor. I kiss you, my darling. Osia, yours, Nanny...

No. 88. To N. Ya. Mandelstam, April 23 [1937]

Darling Nadenka: this is the second letter. I'm a fool, of course—isn't that so?—but I don't understand what you're waiting for in Moscow. Well, so I don't understand. If you're staying in Moscow then it must be necessary. This time your absence is difficult for me, but I'm more calm. Your Mama is very helpful— with all her being, right down to the irritating moments. All this has a very sobering and down-to-earth effect on me. We don't quarrel. I'm very untalkative and can't do anything, although I know that bothers her. I spend a lot of time out of doors. I walk alone near home. My poems are most likely much worse than the earlier ones. Don't hide it from me. It's not a great misfortune.

We'll skip over them. We will live—so there will be poems. My health is good except for shortness of breath. However, that is so serious that I can only live if I'm with you and near you. Your second trip disturbs me greatly. But when I'm with you my shortness of breath is much less severe. It is also notably alleviated by fresh air, however. I find it almost impossible to read. Every book seems repugnant to me. Reading, too, is possible only if I'm with you. The question is obvious: can we be together? Everything else is unimportant in my opinion. No one comes to see me. Even Natasha[1] was here only twice.

Once again I'm indifferent to everything except your coming back. Describe your illness to me as thoroughly as possible. A week seems like a very long time to me. There aren't any letters from you. You sound as if one week will turn into two, and so forth.

Don't think of my letter as depressing. It's just that you've gone away and I've grown quieter. Everything that you and I talked about is right. We are not weak people by any means. And during difficult times we'll do what we must. Don't rely on the telephone. Moscow is almost impossible to reach. It's pure chance each time the phone rings. If something goes wrong with the phone, telegraph a few words. Tell Shura: "You can't change the fact that he didn't answer my letter—there's no need to worry anymore." Be sure to give him that exact message.

Well, goodbye, my dear friend. I'm waiting for you. I love you. Your Osia... Nanny.

No. 89. To N. Ya. Mandelstam, April 26 [1937]

Greetings, Nadik!
Here's what new with me: this morning I went to take a bath. They've made a cage for the rooster. Mama let me have her pot of tea and promised not to touch the electric mechanism, which is in great danger: it crackles and smells of variegated roast meat. An Armenian nailed the sole back on my shoe. It's holding. Don't believe it when you hear praise of facile verses. Our braggarts are

a petty breed. The gardens are green here. It's very nice to walk through the yard next door. I take a lot of walks there... The severe cold has abated, for the most part. I take short walks by myself. I look like I've just come back from a health resort. As far as money goes, I have 40 rubles left and no debts. I paid Pelagea Gerasimovna 30 rubles in advance. The little girl Raya brought me a plaintive letter, so I gave her 5 rubles. Of the four telephone calls, three were emergencies. Mornings are always an emergency. That's why I have so little money. And another 5 rubles went to the laundress. And 4 rubles to the shoemaker. Well, I admit it, I first borrowed 15 rubles from Emma's mother and haven't paid it back yet. Now that's bad.

Nadik, mix some pleasure with your business while you're in Moscow. Go see some movies—all the ones I want to see. Even go to the theater just to see what it's like. Don't be bored. One way or another, just so you come home enlightened. Why did you write the word "here" and cross it out? Who is it that's here, that is, in Moscow?

Yesterday I took Mama to a concert again. She sat in a box and was very proud. She was surprised to get a pass so easily. She's been completely calm and agreeable lately.

I used up a bottle of cologne (with Mama's help). The sty has dried up. My eyes are fine if I don't wear my glasses. There's no dust now. Earlier there were cosmic clouds of dust over the steppe. Mama mended my trousers today—interesting but ugly. I implore you not to let yourself be deluded by anything. Thank you for the presents. I kiss my little darling and await her. Osia.

I kiss Shurik. I gave him a present. Ask him when you're alone with him. He'll tell you what it is.

Mama is shouting, "I'm fed up with you!" and she's rushing off alone to mail a letter. I'll try and catch her.

No. 90. To N. Ya. Mandelstam, Apr[il] 28 [1937]

Nadik, my little one!
What shall this letter say to you? Will it be delivered in the

morning or will you find it in the evening? Then good morning, my angel, and good night, and I kiss you whether you're sleepy and tired, or clean, fresh, efficient, and bustling with inspiration about your shrewd, clever, good deeds. I envy everyone that sees you. You're my Moscow, my Rome and my little David.[1] I know you by heart and still you are always new and I can always hear you, my joy. Ah! Nadenka!

Peace and harmony reign here. I alone am seething quietly. I'm happy. I'm waiting for you. I don't want anything but you.

I'll show you the handsome rooster that crows three hundred times between 4:00 and 6:00 a.m. And the kitty Pushok that runs around all over the place. And the pussywillows are green.

The sole of my shoe is almost coming off the nails already. But my shoes will last about three more days. We don't have any debts. We're not embezzlers. But the telephone ate up a lot of money. We'll hold out until May 2nd. Yesterday Natasha and I took a walk in the park. We went very far, farther than that pavilion. That's why my sole came loose.

I saw "Uncle Lenia" on the street. He's been resurrected and runs around panting. I gave him some medical advice as a comrade in illness.

In fact, however, I'm uncommonly healthy now and ready for life. We'll begin our life wherever fate may cast us. Now I shall be stronger than the poems. Enough of their ordering us about. Let's mutiny! Then the poems will dance to our pipe and what do we care if no one dares to praise them. I kiss your bright, intelligent eyes, your darling old, young brow. At times Mama is downright witty. She's beginning to like our way of life. What a fright! Nadik, come back to us and we won't let Mama go.

I kiss my little pet and wait. Nanny.

You're not offended that I called your dear brow old?

No. 91. To N. Ya. Mandelstam, April 30 [1937]

My darling Nadenka!
I'm enclosing the excerpt and my statement to be forwarded

to Stavsky.[1]

I'm well and tranquil. Come back as soon as you've done everything you have to. I think it's unnecessary to stay any longer than the 5th. If worst comes to worst, come back without any money. Isn't it all the same? If only so we can send Mama home.

I regard my statement to the Union of Soviet Writers as urgent.

But if Stavsky thinks it's not worth raising a question over such a foolish thing—I agree. I'm not a troublemaker.

Show it to him, in any case. The main thing is that after this it will be *virtually impossible to live in Voronezh*. Explain that to him.

I kiss you, my darling. I'm in a hurry to mail this. Your Osia.

A.

April 30 [19]37

An excerpt from the article[2] by O. Kretova in the Voronezh newspaper *Commune*, April 23, 1937 (Report on the Plenum of the Union of Soviet Writers and an article on the tasks of literature).

" . . . In recent years Trotskyites and other class enemies (Stefan, Aich, O. Mandelstam) have attempted to infiltrate and influence the organization (of the Voronezh District Division of the Union of Soviet Writers), but they were exposed . . ."*

*"The Union adopted an entirely different attitude toward those who have made mistakes in the past but who are trying to correct them by honest work (the Voronezh writers Peskov and Zavadovsky)."

O.E. Mandelstam

B.

April 30 [19]37

Comrade Stavsky:
I ask you to bring to the attention of the leadership of the Union

of Soviet Writers the irresponsible use of my name by the Voronezh District Division of the Union.

The Union credits itself in vain with my denunciation. That denunciation *never* took place.

A year and a half ago the Union refused to cooperate with me, claiming "the absence of instructions."

At the same time it gave me a *public recommendation* (the resolution of the administration: protocol) so that I would be able to obtain work. The attacks (the second one in print) are being carried out by antedating.

For all intents and purposes, the Voronezh District Division of the Union is charging me with seeking, in and through the Union, the opinion and guidance of the Soviet and of the Party.

Furthermore, the inclusion of three names in parentheses, with the aim of making the reader regard them *arbitrarily,* is absolutely inadmissible.[3]

O. Mandelstam

No. 92. To N. Ya. Mandelstam [end of April 1937]

My darling little girl Nadik!

Your hundred rubles just arrived. We had some more money, and everything had already been purchased for the 1st of May. Here's the news: the chicken pecked Mama's cheek and scratched it. Just slightly. Today I stood in line myself for groceries and made Mama sit on a bench nearby. This morning I sent you the excerpt from the article by O. Kretova in the April 23rd edition of *Commune* and my statement to Stavsky regarding the Voronezh Writers' Union.[1] Just in case, I'm sending a second excerpt and an abridged statement to the Union of Soviet Writers in care of Evgeny Yakovlevich.[2]

I don't know what to do about my shoes. I'm asking you. The future does not worry me.

Come back on the sixth at the latest. Without money if

necessary. It's absolutely *all the same*.

I wait for you endlessly.

Your Osia.

No. 93. To N. Ya. Mandelstam, May 2 [1937]

Darling Nadenka!

Forgive me for writing on the back of your lists. Save the sheets of paper and bring them back with you. Publicly, I have had to pretend that Natasha has an older brother and sister and to postulate the character of her future husband. But the fact that I'm trying to persuade her to get married is quite real.[1]

As you see, I'm occupied with trifles and am far from having gloomy thoughts. What's more, each day is different from the next. This morning Mama and I looked for shoes on Siti Street (*sity streat*—right?).[2] I bought some horrible dark-blue ones for 25 rubles. I wanted to buy green socks to go with them (to wear with my brown trousers), but Mama wouldn't allow it. Then an elderly customer (I'm acquainted with him from concerts) engaged me in a conversation about music. Were there really amateurs in *The Soldier*[3]? I want to thank those good souls personally. The plug to the "machine" broke[4] and Adrian Fyodorovich attached a complicated pendant to it, which is also breaking. But the light is fading and I'm writing by the light of a lamp and a candle.

Darling, forgive me for chattering idly while you're on the verge of being over-strained, etc. It seems to me that we must stop *waiting*. Our ability to do that has run short. Anything you please but waiting. Nothing is frightening for you and me. (The light just went on.) We are together eternally, and that fact is growing to such a degree and growing so formidably, that there is *nothing* to fear.

I kiss you, my bright eternal friend. I'll see you soon, I'll see you and embrace you.

Your husband

No. 94. To N. Ya. Mandelstam, May 4 [1937]

Nadik Darling!
Come back as soon as possible. I have trouble breathing without you. The spring brings no joy. Come back quickly. Today I
got two of your letters from the 29th and 30th. You have three
visitors all at once. Almost like home. I did too, it seems? Yes?
And why do I scold Emma? Don't you scold me, sweetheart: I
understand everything—I'm just very foolish. My little child, don't
stay an extra minute. If worse comes to worst you will go again
(?). *No, you won't!* You shouldn't stay indefinitely if the nego-
tiations[1] start getting disorderly. I think what they can do and
want to do, they will do *immediately*.
Last night I ran away from Mama like a Spanish girl running
away from her old duenna. At midnight Natasha and her Boris[2]
knocked at the window. Mama was sleeping. I sneaked out secretly
and went to the Bristol. Boris served the three of us one pork
chop, three oranges, and a bottle of bordeaux. I bought Mama an
orange and put it under her pillow. She woke up and said: "I'm
a little girl." She *hadn't even noticed* that I had gone out.
I just got a letter from Rudakov.[3] I deciphered it with great
difficulty. He writes (apparently?) that the poems are uneven in
quality and that it's only possible to convey that by talking in
person. The latest thing is poems about Russian poetry. Really!
I just came back from a bookstore—a huge one. The amazing
Sassanid Metals from the Hermitage collection is there for 50
rubles. The kind saleslady set it aside for me. As you see, I'm a
mad fool. But we'll buy those Persian saucers anyway. We're such
monsters. Come back as soon as you can, my pet—your Nanny will
suffocate without you. He can't be kept dangling and waiting any
longer. Ah! Nadik! Quickly!

Nanny

No. 95. To N. Ya. Mandelstam, May 4 (second letter) [1937]

Nadik—my sunshine! I just came home and composed a little trifle, which I'm enclosing. I find it bitter and empty to write without you. Mama is indifferent to the "froggies,"[1] praises "Natasha,"[2] and ignored "The Bird-cherry."[3]

About ten days ago I had a quarrel with the landlady over the rooster (I yelled about the rooster to no one in particular and she thought I was yelling at her... She was very tactful, but still said some caustic words). It's all forgotten now. Her tact is amazing. They didn't take any money. They're immensely tolerant.

As for Mama's being attacked by the chicken, there are no serious scratches. The scar is healing. The devil only knows what nonsense I'm writing! Gogol himself couldn't think up such stuff!...

If you should fail, my sunshine, I implore you to come back cheerfully. Remember, it's shameful for us to despair. Who knows what lies ahead... Anything could happen... We'll survive. So there, my child. I implore you once more: if you are detained, don't deny yourself anything, don't spoil us.

I kiss you, my darling...

No. 96. To N. Ya. Mandelstam, May 7 [1937]

Nadik, my darling little child!

Yesterday I got your letter of the 4th, and today your letter of the 2nd. Dearest, there's really nothing for you to do there. Your Moscow is empty! Where are you poking about? How do you drag out the time? Meanwhile, I've gone completely sour. I quit work on the poems. I can't even find my place. This evening the telephone was taken away to put in a radio, otherwise I would have been able to hear your voice. I don't want any news. I want my Nadya's voice. These last few days I've been able to go out alone almost freely, astounding the Voronezh inhabitants with my solitary figure. Yesterday I even made it to Natasha's.

Only I had somewhat of a scare on the No. 3 streetcar. Natasha says the matchmaking poems[1] are "somehow familiar—reminiscent of Lermontov," that is, they're second-rate literature. She appreciates the little park. But "Iron"[2] is just that, iron. She is working ten hours a day now and almost never stops by. Mama and I are all alone. Us, the cat and her kitten. Mama has gotten out of the habit of quarreling with me. The scratch from the chicken claw has almost disappeared. Mama washed my dark-blue shirt and your underwear. I, too, am licking my lips in anticipation of the Persians.[3] I don't believe anything good. It's better that way. And your little star—ooh—how very nice. It keeps getting bigger. Nadik, bring my prose back with you. If we live, teach me English.[4] 75 rubles came today. Last time the telegraph operator had tea with us. Your letter made me feel better, Nadik: I've started chattering and smiling. I'm waiting for you, my wife, my daughter, my friend, quickly, quickly. Your Nanny.

No. 97. To his brother Alexander Emilievich Mandelstam (and to his wife) [October 20-30, 1938]

Dear Shura! My address: Vladivostok, USVITL, barracks No. 11.[1]

I got five years for counterrevolutionary activity by decree of the Special Tribunal. The transport left Butyrki Prison in Moscow on the 9th of September and we arrived on the 12th of October. I'm in very poor health, utterly exhausted, emaciated, and almost beyond recognition. I don't know if there's any sense in sending clothes, food, and money, but try just the same. I'm freezing without proper clothes.

Darling Nadenka, are you alive, my precious? Shura, write me at once about Nadya. This is a transit point. I wasn't picked for Kolyma. I may have to spend the winter here.

My dear ones, I kiss you. Osia.

Shurochka, one thing more. We've gone out to work these last few days. That has lifted my spirits. People are sent from our camp, as from a transit point, to regular camps. I was apparently "sifted out" so I must get ready to spend the winter here. So please send me a telegram and wire me some money.[2]

V. Ya. Khazina's letters to her daughter—N. Ya. Mandelstam

I

[1935-1936?]

Dear Nadenka!

We got your letters today.[1] And it's nice to hear that you'll be closer to us. I don't remember how many hours the trip takes, but it's possible to make the trip often even to Voronezh. It's nice that you have a samovar. It will come in handy. We spend most of our money not on food, but on tobacco: 2 or 3 rubles a day for the two of us. If I bake *pirozhki* or something else, it uses up all the money for the day's budget. 200 rubles a month is probably our entire budget. Because of such expenses—and the telephone conversations—it's impossible to cut down the budget. He's already talking about borrowing money—and it can't be otherwise— Osia is upset to the point of tears. Today (the 6th) we had no money left, but I always have a small reserve on hand—groats, flour, sunflower-seed oil—everything that Osia doesn't like. He went to visit Emma's mother, she cut up a chicken on credit, made a marvelous broth—enough to last us two days—and marvelous chicken; that incredible little Emma takes an interest in everything and is always running around here and there. I knit a little bag and a collar for her, but I should give her a children's book—she's seven years old and her parents read to her but they still haven't taught her how to read. Confiscate a couple of books for her from Zhenya.[2] But get a cheaper book for Vitka—he's not worth it. But you must bring some for the little girl, perhaps Osip's *Primus Stove* or *Streetcar*, or ask Zhenya for some. It seems he has a free supplement [*Bug*?]. I was so worried that you were wearing your pink coat there, but the landlady said that it's in her closet, which made me very happy. It's hellishly cold here, no more than 5 or 6 degrees, I think. Grandmother predicts a crop failure for the fruit trees which are in full bloom. Osip is in a good mood today, and so am I. He hasn't scolded me once yet, and I haven't scolded him either. I kiss Zhenya—has he done what I wrote him to do?

I kiss you heartily and wish for a spell of good times. We have endured so much these last years—illness and adversity—perhaps better days await us?

II

April 19 [1937]

Dear Nadenka!

Nothing special happened today. We take walks and go shopping—we're in a state of armed neutrality. We don't agree on money matters. But Osia is sure that he's just as good an economist as he is a poet. He likes everything that is more expensive, and so do I, but I always glance into my purse and take an oath of restraint... He won't give in, but he'll be humbled when he sees the bottom of the purse.

It's cold, like early winter, and there's enough dust for all of Moscow. We don't have enough plates. Take the worst ones from the cupboard, leave the best ones. I can't live without potatoes: 2 rubles for ten. Bring back at least 10 kilos in the black and pink sack, though Osia will moan if he just touches it.

He wanted us to go to a concert, but I preferred that the lame young lady[3] go...

There's a bottle of cooking oil in the kitchen cupboard—wrap it in twenty pieces of paper and bring it back with you. Yesterday I baked half a chicken that cost 4 rubles and 75 kopeks. He liked it very much.

Perhaps you can re-sew your white coat? Consult Lena.

I kiss you and Zhenya.

[A collective letter from a group of writers to the Division of Press and Publications of the Central Committee of the RKP(b)] [1]

We, the writers, having learned that the Division of Press and Publications of the Central Committee of the RKP is organizing a Conference on literary politics, consider it necessary to bring the following to the attention of the Conference:

We believe that the course of modern Russian literature, and consequently our course, is tied to the course of post-revolutionary Soviet Russia. We believe that literature must reflect that new life which surrounds us, in which we live and work. On the other hand, however, literature must be the creation of an individual author who perceives and reflects the world in his own way. We believe that the two fundamental values of a writer are his talent and his being in touch with the times: a wide range of Communist writers and critics share our view of authorship. We welcome the new writers—workers and peasants—who are presently entering the field of literature. We are not opposed to them in any way and do not regard them as hostile or alien to us. Both their labor and ours are the united labor of contemporary Russian literature which follows a single course and has a single aim.

The new course of the new Soviet literature is a course of labor which will inevitably entail mistakes. And our mistakes hurt no one so much as ourselves. But we protest the groundless attacks against us. The tone taken by journals such as *On Guard*[2] and the criticism contained in them, which is purported, moreover, to be the opinion of the RKP as a whole, takes a deliberately prejudiced and incorrect attitude toward our literary work. We feel it necessary to declare that such a treatment of literature is worthy neither of literature nor of the revolution, and it has a demoralizing effect on the masses—both readers and writers. We, the writers of Soviet Russia, are convinced that our labor as authors is both necessary and beneficial for our country.

P. Sakulin, N. Nikandrov, Valentin Kataev, Alexander Yakovlev, Mikhail Kozyrev, Bor[is] Pilnyak, Sergei Klychkov, Andrei Sobol, Sergei Esenin, Mikhail Gerasimov, V. Kirillov, Abram Efros, Yury Sobolev, Vl[adimir] Lidin, O. Mandelstam, V. Lvov-Rogachevsky, S. Polyakov, I. Babel, Al[exei]

Tolstoi, Efim Zozulya, Mikhail Prishvin, Maximilian Voloshin, S. Fyodorchenko, Peter Oreshin, Vera Inber, N. Tikhonov, M. Zoshchenko, E. Polonskaia, M. Slonimsky, V. Kaverin, Vs[evolod] Ivanov, N. Nikitin, Vyach[eslav] Shishkov, A. Chapygin, M. Shaginyan, O. Forsh.

—May 1924—

NOTES

1. FRANÇOIS VILLON

Mandelstam's earliest extant essay was written in 1910, but was first published in 1913, in the St. Petersburg magazine, *Apollon* (No. 4), along with Nikolai Gumilev's translation of fragments from Villon's *Grand Testament*. It was republished in Mandelstam's collection of essays, *On Poetry (O poezii)*, in 1928. See O. Mandel'shtam, *Sobranie sochinenii v trekh tomakh* (Inter-Language Literary Associates, 1967-69, 2nd ed.) II, 644 for variants in the 1928 text.

This essay should be read in conjunction with the essays of 1913, "Morning of Acmeism" and "On the Addressee," which share several common images and motifs. This essay also benefits from a comparison with the essays begun in 1915, "Remarks on Chenier" and "Pushkin and Scriabin," and suggests the genesis of several ideas and images worked out two decades later in "Conversation about Dante."

Mandelstam's interest in Villon is not surprising. Having grown up in St. Petersburg, in an intellectual milieu strongly influenced by French literary currents, he expressed his personal interest in French literature by pursuing studies in Old French at Heidelberg. He also translated fragments from Old French epic poetry and, in 1923, a note published in the magazine *Russia*, announced that he was preparing an anthology of Old French epic poetry for the publishing house, World Literature (SS, I, 554-5). The anthology never appeared, and we do not know if it was ever "prepared."

François Villon was not only resurrected by the French Symbolist movement, but was named by Nikolai Gumilev, leader of the Russian Acmeists, as one of the four Acmeist "ancestors." See my notes to "Morning of Acmeism."

This essay is also of great interest for being much more biographically and historically grounded than any of Mandelstam's subsequent essays, which suggests that it was at least begun as a student paper in Heidelberg (1909-10); Mandelstam only enrolled as a student in the Faculty of History and Philology at the University of St. Petersburg in 1911. Furthermore, while biographical and historical details are rare in Mandelstam's later essays, they assume a prominent role in his literary prose, namely in *The Noise of Time*, "The Egyptian Stamp," and "Fourth Prose." There, as in the essay on Villon, living human beings emerge, if but momentarily, as dynamic figures out of a few shrewdly chosen autobiographical and historical details. Indeed, this essay foreshadows Mandelstam's literary prose in its concentration on pictorial effects and portraiture, as well as in its use of biographical data to depict concrete space and historical time.

What is more, "François Villon" raises most of the great themes presented in the course of Mandelstam's literary career:

1) Man's interaction with history, more specifically, the poet's powers to challenge and conquer time.

2) The poet as *raznochinets* aided only by his "sharp irony" to attain the unattainable, a theme most clearly worked out a decade later in *The Noise of Time*.

3) The source of poetic impulse.

4) The relationship of the reader's experience to the poet's.

5) The ultimate role(s) of the poet.

6) The organic nature of poetry, expressed, among other places, in his famous poem "Notre Dame" (1912), in the essays of the 1920s, and in his later works, "On the Naturalists" and "Conversation about Dante."

1. François Villon, the penname of François de Montcorbier or François des Loges, born in Paris c. 1431; the date of his death is unknown. He is best known for his *Grand Testament* which includes a number of ballads and rondeaux, and for his *Petit Testament*. Both works are written in eight-line stanzas with eight syllables to the line, known as *"huitains."*

2. Paul Verlaine (1844-1896). French Symbolist poet. His early works, including *Poèmes saturniens* (1866) are characterized by the anti-Romanticism of the Parnassians. But by 1884, with the publication of *Les Poètes maudites,* a work of criticism, and *Jadis et Naguère,* a collection of verse including the famous Symbolist poem, "Art poétique," Verlaine became a leading figure in the French Symbolist movement.

It is possible that Mandelstam's comparison of Villon and Verlaine was suggested by Paul Valéry's essay, "Villon et Verlaine." Furthermore, Mandelstam's comparison of their poetry must have been based primarily on Verlaine's collection of 1874, *Romances sans paroles.*

3. This reference may be to the Belgian poet and dramatist Maurice Maeterlinck (1862-1949), who published a collection of poetry expressing Symbolist ideals and techniques entitled *Serres chaudes* (1889). However, since most of Verlaine's poetry preceded that publication, Mandelstam was undoubtedly using *serres chaudes* merely as a general metaphor for the prescribed formulae of Symbolism. The Russian poet, Alexander Blok, began a translation of Maeterlinck's volume in 1908, but never completed it.

4. *Roman de la Rose* is a lengthy allegorical poem written in the 13th and early 14th centuries, begun by Guillaume de Lorris and completed by Jean de Meung. It was one of the most popular works of the 14th and 15th centuries.

5. Alain Chartier (c. 1385-c.1433). French poet, prose writer and diplomat at the court of Charles VII. "La Belle Dame sans merci," one of his most famous love poems, set a literary fashion in his day and served as a source of poetic inspiration well into the 20th century.

6. *Grand Testament,* st. 26. Translation by Peter Dale: *The Legacy, The Testament, and Other Poems of François Villon* (New York, 1973), p. 43.

7. Sainte Geneviève: a district on the Left Bank and site of the student quarters.

8. "The Devil's Fart"—because of its name this marker became the subject of endless student pranks; the other marker may be translated as "The Silent Fart."

9. The University (and Church) authorities versus the Government (and Police).

10. Verlaine's famous line from "Art poétique," which became a Symbolist motto, reads: "De la musique avant toute chose." Mandelstam's variant transforms it into an Acmeist slogan: "Du mouvement avant toute chose." See my notes to "Morning of Acmeism."

11. *Grand Testament,* st. 42, Peter Dale translation, *op. cit.,* p. 51-52.

12. This addendum is from SS, III, 143.

2. MORNING OF ACMEISM

Although written in 1913, this essay was not published until 1919 in the Voronezh bi-monthly, *Sirena,* edited by Vladimir Narbut, a fellow Acmeist. It was reprinted in Moscow in 1929 in the collection, *Literary Manifestoes. From Symbolism to October (Literaturnye manifesty. Ot simvolizma k Oktiabriu. Sbornik materialov),* edited by N.L. Brodsky, V. L'vov-Rogachevsky and N.P. Sidorov. For details, see SS, II, 647.

Acmeism has been variously discussed and characterized [See, for example, H. Chalsma, "Russian Acmeism: Its History, Doctrine, and Poetry," Unpublished Ph.D. dissertation, University of Washington, 1967; S. Driver, "Acmeism," *Slavic and East European Journal,* No. 2, 1968) pp. 141-56; and a reappraisal of Acmeism and Mandelstam's essay, "On the Morning of Acmeism," by C. Brown, *Mandelstam,* pp. 135-158.] but basically, it grew up as a Symbolist heresy, as an attempt to revaluate and re-establish modernist poetics as verbal craft, as "art" rather than as a vehicle for a mystical (otherworldly or escapist, religious or esthetic) experience. That heresy became a full-fledged, if short-lived, movement, with manifestoes, a membership, and a canon of its own, persisting until about 1915. However, certain Acmeist values were to transcend time and continue to influence the poetry of its members throughout their lives. Indeed, Mandelstam persisted in redefining Acmeism throughout his poetic career.

As opposed to the Symbolists, the Acmeists sought their inspiration in the world of Man and in man-made culture, in the dynamism of the phenomenal world as opposed to the relative stasis of the noumenal or divine world. Acmeism strictly opposed abstract otherworldly or mystical subject matter, and concentrated instead on the depiction of objects of divine and human creation; people, places, monuments, things of beauty visible, tangible, and physiological. In this sense, Acmeism, as opposed to Symbolism, may be considered both more objective than subjective, more concrete than abstract.

Like the Symbolists, the Acmeists placed a high value on technique and craft. However, the favorite techniques of the latter included irony, poetic distance, and a sensitive use of visual and psychological imagery, indeed, psychophysiological imagery, while the former showed a general preference for a more ideological (theoretical, philosophical, religious) vision, immersion in "the moment of transcendence," and an emphatic, often superimposed or artificial use of musical and religious imagery.

Nevertheless, like the Symbolists, the Acmeists did not forgo thematic content in favor of technique as Mandelstam accused the Futurists of doing. They never advocated "throwing Pushkin overboard," but on the contrary, created a cult of the great nineteenth century poet and his Russian neo-classical style. Furthermore, like the Symbolists, Gumilev, Mandelstam and their fellow Acmeists retained the idea of the "word" as an autonomous entity, the sacred "Logos," which had to include both content and form. Gumilev recalled Oscar Wilde's statement about "the word": "The material used by musicians and artists is poor in comparison to the word. The word contains not only music, tender music like that of the alto or lute; not only colors, vivid and luxurious colors like those which enchant us on Venetian and Spanish canvases; not only plastic forms, more lucid and distinct than those forms revealed to us in marble or bronze—those which contain thought and passion and spirituality. Words contain all of these qualities" (Gumilev, "The Life of Verse," 1910). Most significant, perhaps, Mandelstam advocated raising the "word" to the position of honor held by "music" in the Symbolist canon: "For the Acmeists the conscious sense of the word, the Logos, is just as magnificent a form as music is for the Symbolists" ("Morning of Acmeism"). In this way, Mandelstam emphasized the semantic value of words, the basic "verbal fabric" of poetry, in contrast to the Symbolist ideal which called for obscuring the denotative values of words, of making words as "vague" as possible so as to transcend meaning and achieve metaphysical "harmony."

The first issue of *Apollon* for 1913 contains both Gumilev's Acmeist manifesto, "Acmeism and the Heritage of Symbolism" (translated in *Russian Literature Triquarterly*, No. 1, 1971) and Gorodetsky's anti-Symbolist polemic, "Some Currents in Contemporary Russian Poetry." Mandelstam's essay "On the Addressee," at least in part a rebuttal to Ivanov's "Thoughts on Symbolism," appeared in the second issue. And the third issue contained not only Mandelstam's essay, "François Villon" (accompanied by Gumilev's translation of fragments of Villon's *Grand Testament*), but a fine sampling of Acmeist verse, including Mandelstam's "Notre Dame" and "Aiia-Sofiia," Gorodetsky's "Adam" and "Stars," Akhmatova's "Cabaret artistique" and "I came to take your place, sister..."), Gumilev's "Iambic pentameters," Narbut's "She is ugly..." and "How swiftly the roofs dry out."

It remains a puzzle as to why Mandelstam's "Morning of Acmeism" was not published along with Gumilev's "Acmeism and the Heritage of Symbolism" and Gorodetsky's more polemical essay, "Some Currents in Contemporary Russian Poetry" in the first issue of *Apollon* for 1913. All three were obviously intended as Acmeist manifestoes. In the 1929 volume both Gumilev's and Mandelstam's manifestoes appear, but

Gorodetsky's is absent. It is also somewhat puzzling as to why Mandelstam's "Morning of Acmeism" did not appear in his collected essay, *On Poetry* published in 1928. The commonly accepted political reason (see, for instance, C. Brown, *Mandelstam*, p. 153) is insufficient when we realize that not only Mandelstam's, but Gumilev's, manifesto was published but one year later. I would like to suggest that, perhaps, by 1928 Mandelstam considered himself to have outgrown Acmeism in its formative conception. The essays "François Villon" and "On the Nature of the Word" contain a more mature and more generalized Acmeist credo than the manifesto. They reflect a deeper concern with the general problems of defining the poet's esthetic vision as opposed to the more specific, limited and even dogmatic and aggressive platform (characteristic of any manifesto) presented in "Morning of Acmeism." (See my comparison of the poetic "I" in "Morning of Acmeism" and "Conversation about Dante" in the Introduction.) The imagery of "Morning of Acmeism" revolves around the ideals of mathematical logic and the stone-mason's craft, while the imagery of "On the Nature of the Word" is much less concrete, less precise. It is Mandelstam's most "Bergsonian" essay in intent and content; it is more philosophically oriented, concerned as it is with the poet's relationship to time and history. Its concern is not with proving the poet a skilled craftsman or professional, but with explaining poetics or "philology" ("love of the word") as an "organic" phenomenon. He says: ". . . such an interpretation of philological ideas opens up broad new perspectives, allowing us to dream about the creation of an organic poetics, a poetics of a biological rather than juridical nature, a poetics which would destroy the canon in the name of the internal unity of the organism, which would master all aspects of biological science." Nevertheless, in conclusion, Mandelstam ambiguously contrasts these two views through the images of Mozart and Salieri; Mozart he rejects as "the idealistic dreamer," while Salieri is praised for his capacity to hear "the music of algebra as vibrantly as living harmony." For a fuller discussion of the Mozart-Salieri theme in Mandelstam's work, see: Nadezhda Mandelstam, *Mozart and Salieri* (Ann Arbor: Ardis, 1973).

On a somewhat less ambiguous note, the imagery of "Morning of Acmeism" reinforces its predominant tone of self-confidence, of the poet's sense of being "right," to the point of sharing the egoism of the Futurist manifestoes of the 1910s. See my notes to Mandelstam's 1913 review of Severyanin's *The Thunder-Seething Goblet*. This youthful sense of poetic self-confidence as a necessary criterion for art is reasserted in "On the Addressee," but with less fanfare. However, by the 1920s, Mandelstam recognizes in himself (or at least in his lyrical persona) feelings of worthlessness as well as lack of confidence (see the poems of the early 1920s), and by the 1930s, in his essay on Dante, he specifically discusses the poet's need to experience both attitudes. In the later essay, he refers to the great Italian poet as an "internal *raznochinets*," as one who experiences the feelings of the "tortured and outcast man. . . inner anxiety" and lack of self-confidence. Of Dante he said: "Alighieri underwent fever and chills all the way from marvelous fits of self-esteem to feelings of utter worthlessness." Thus, I would also suggest that another possible reason for omitting "Morning of Acmeism" from the 1928 volume of essays had something to do with its overbearing egotistical tone. By 1928 Mandelstam had a rather less resolute conception of the poet's ego. (See my Introduction, and Brown, *Mandelstam*, for more biographical details and for another view of these essays, pp. 151-158.)

1. The Russian word is *biriul'ki*, the name of a game played with rules much like our "pick-up-sticks." Instead of sticks, the players use tiny hooks to pick up tiny replicas of household objects, such as pots and pans, etc., spilled from a tiny barrel. This image emerges again in Mandelstam's magnificent poetic cycle, "The Octets" (Vos'mistishiia) of 1933-1935, which contains his last poetic effort to define his esthetic vision.

2. The Gothic element is discussed in the essays on Villon and Dante, as well as in

"Humanism and the Present." In the latter, the esthetic element is elevated to an essential aspect of Mandelstam's ideal vision of social architecture.

3. Vladimir Sergeevich Soloviev (1853-1900). Outstanding Russian philosopher and mystic. He also wrote poetry explicitly intended to convey his mystical and religious experiences. His poetry, in particular, "Three Meetings" in which he describes his three mystic visions of Sophia —the incarnation of Divine Wisdom —inspired and encouraged the Russian Symbolists to develop their own poetics. Soloviev had stated that poetry is the supreme instrument of vision, both the vessel and vehicle of the "prophetic dream" or revelation which he considered the means "to discover eternal truth." His acclaim of the poet, Tyutchev (see next note), in 1895 was echoed by the universal acclaim of the Modernists and Symbolists. Soloviev was the first to praise Tyutchev's mystical and metaphysical insights, to declare that Tyutchev's verse expressed the older poet's attempts to reveal the chaotic and mystical essence of existence. See "Poeziia F.I. Tiutcheva" in *Sobranie sochinenii Vladimira Sergeevicha Solov'eva,* ed. S.M. Soloviev and E.L. Radlov, VII, 117-34.

4. Fyodor Ivanovich Tyutchev (1803-1873). One of Russia's finest poets, despite the fact that he spent a good portion of his life as a career diplomat in Germany. His poetic output was very small. His influence on the course of Russian poetry was also very slight until the Symbolists rediscovered him. The first references to Tyutchev were those of Merezhkovsky in 1893 and Vladimir Soloviev in 1895 (see note No. 3, above). See D. Blagoi, "Tiutchev, ego kritiki i chitateli" in *Tiutchevskii sbornik* (Petrograd, 1923), pp. 63-105. According to Blagoi, it was not really until the publication of Tyutchev's collected works in 1912-1913 that he finally acquired a broad reading public. Merezhkovsky ("Dve tainy russkoi poezii") considered Tyutchev "not only a poet, but a prophet, a teacher of life;" A. G. Gornfeld in his *History of Russian Literature of the Nineteenth Century* (M. 1909, Vol. III), stated that Tyutchev was not only the greatest philosopher in Russian lyric poetry, but the most powerful Russian political poet. And Blagoi noted that Tyutchev's influence went far beyond the Symbolist movement, affecting such diverse poets as Mandelstam and Severyanin: "The Acmeist Mandelstam has written a number of poems bearing the same titles as Tyutchev's poems and inspired by his themes; the Ego-Futurist, Igor Severyanin used Tyutchevian language for the title of his first book of poetry—*The Thunder-Seething Goblet"*(see Mandelstam's 1913 review of this book). Furthermore, Georgette Donchin points out in her excellent study, *The Influence of French Symbolism on Russian Poetry* (The Hague, 1958, pp. 92-93), that several Symbolist poets considered Tyutchev a forerunner of Baudelaire in Russian poetry. Merezhkovsky and Balmont, she says, "did everything to credit Tyutchev alone with the theory of correspondence . . . the second generation [of Symbolists] truly discovered Tyutchev at the same time as Baudelaire. But, on the whole, Baudelaire's "Correspondances" was instrumental in the appreciation of Tyutchev as a forerunner of Russian Symbolism."

Basically, the Symbolists found in Tyutchev a Russian metaphysical poet who expressed the isolation of the individual, emphasized the mysteries of the universe, and taught that the universe is divided into two worlds, that of Cosmos (the world of life, order, and beauty) and Chaos (nothingness, or the abyss), the latter being the ultimate reality, for it alone animates the Cosmos. (Mandelstam's own use of the word "chaos" in *The Noise of Time* was undoubtedly Tyutchevian in inspiration.) The ultimate mystery of the universal life-giving force is presented in the poem cited in this paragraph: Tyutchev's "Having rolled down the mountain" ("S gory skativshis' " Jan. 15, 1833). Another reference to this poem and related themes is found in "For the Anniversary of F. K. Sologub." For more information on Tyutchev, see Richard A. Gregg, *Fedor Tiutchev: The Evolution of a Poet* (New York: Columbia University Press, 1965).

5. See "François Villon" for a more detailed statement of this theme.

6. See "The Nineteenth Century" for further development of this idea.

7. See the poem "Notre Dame" (1912) for an illustration of this thesis in verse. These works should be read together. See C. Brown's illuminating treatment of this theme in the chapter "Stone" in his *Mandelstam*.

8. A reference to Baudelaire's poem "Correspondances," a major "doctrinal" source for the Symbolists:

> La nature est un temple où de vivants piliers
> Laissent parfois sortir de confuses paroles;
> L'homme y passe à travers des forêts de symboles
> Qui l'observent avec des regards familiers.

Both Mandelstam's poem, "Notre Dame," and this essay may be read, at least in part, as an answer to Baudelaire and his Russian heirs.

9. *Author's note:* Vyacheslav Ivanov's formula. See his "Thoughts on Symbolism" in the volume *Furrows and Boundaries (Borozdy i mezhi). Translator's note:* An English translation of Ivanov's essay may be found in *Russian Literature Triquarterly*, No. 4 (1972) devoted to Symbolism, pp. 151-158. Mandelstam's essay is, at least in part, a rejoinder to this essay of Ivanov's.

10. See "On the Addressee" for a similar comment on the esthetic nature and value of "astonishment."

11. Mandelstam must have been familiar with the Charter of the Romanic school, published by Jean Moréas in 1891 and with the work and esthetic values of the Romanic and neo-Romanic poets. His interest in the French Middle Ages, in Villon, Racine, and Chénier must have been, at least in part, inspired by his studies of French literature and culture, while many of the Acmeist ideals which he shared with Gumilev were undoubtedly influenced or at least stimulated by Bryusov's interests: the latter's editorship of *The Scales (Vesy)* made French literary and cultural values readily available to the Russian intellectual elite, especially during Mandelstam's student years.

These ideas are also expressed in the essays on Villon, Chénier and Dante.

See also Marcel Raymond, *From Baudelaire to Surrealism* (New York, 1950), for an excellent discussion of the Romanic school, its doctrines and influence.

3. ON THE ADDRESSEE

This essay was first published in 1913 in the second issue of *Apollon*. It was republished with certain omissions in Mandelstam's *On Poetry* in 1928. This translation follows the original text; variants are given in SS, II, 629-31.

"On the Addressee" was written, at least in part, as an Acmeist answer to Vyacheslav Ivanov's "Thoughts on Symbolism." Nevertheless, while it is obviously Acmeist in inspiration, this essay is much more universal in its appeal than "Morning of Acmeism," and therefore could easily be included in the collection of essays republished in 1928. See notes to "Morning of Acmeism."

1. Alexander Sergeevich Pushkin (1799-1837). Russia's greatest poet and Mandelstam's ultimate reference. Pushkin's career has generally been divided into four stages. His youthful period (1814-1821) and most neo-classical phase exhibits the influence of the Russian poets Zhukovsky and Batyushkov, as well as strong stylistic bonds with the French poets, Parny, Voltaire and Andre Chénier. His second period (1820-1823) has often been called "Byronic" since many of the poems of this period reflect highly romantic subject matter, portray a socially alienated, self-centered "Byronic hero," and show a great interest in the dynamics of non-urban, non-civilized existence. More important stylistically, however, is Pushkin's developing interest in the narrative poem as a more flexible and personal genre than the earlier neo-classical forms. The narratives of this period include "The Prisoner of the Caucasus" (1820-21)

and "The Fountain of Bakhchisarai" (1822). Pushkin's third period (1823-1830) includes his magnificent novel in verse, *Eugene Onegin* (1823-1831), "The Prophet" (1826), one of his most popular and influential lyric poems, his attempts at drama–*Boris Godunov* and the so-called "Little Tragedies." These include "Mozart and Salieri," "The Stone Guest," "The Covetous Knight" and "The Feast During the Plague." The poem, "Poet" (1827), referred to here is also from this period. Pushkin's last creative period (1830-1837) included most of his prose fiction and emphasized his deep interest in Russian history and Russia's historical destiny. It also included his superb narrative poem, *The Bronze Horseman* (1833), his fairytales in verse, and much of his remarkable critical prose.

2. See Pushkin's poem, "The Bird" (1822) and lines 105-145 of his longer narrative poem, *The Gypsies* (1824).

3. Evgeny Abramovich Baratynsky (1800-1844). A contemporary of Pushkin and the most original member of the so-called Pushkin Pleiade. Pushkin characterized him as "original in Russia because he thinks." See, in particular his poems of the end of the 1820s when his poetry is most intellectual and analytical. At his best in the elegiac genre, Baratynsky's major themes include death, eternal recurrence, and immortality through artistic creativity. "My gift is humble, and my voice is not loud " (1828) is a beautiful statement of his faith in the saving grace of art. The moral force of his poetry made a deep impression on Mandelstam.

4. Konstantin Dmitrievich Balmont (1867-1943). One of the first Russian Symbolist poets, known primarily for the "musicality" of his verse. He was also one of the most important disseminators of foreign poetry in Russia, the result of his extensive travels, tireless activity as a translator, and intense interest in other cultures. Egotism as a conscious attitude was expounded not only by Balmont, but by most of the Symbolist poets, dedicated as they were to expressing through art their own innermost experiences. The poem "I do not know wisdom..." was written in 1902 and published in the collection *Only Love (Tol'ko liubov')*. A positive evaluation of Balmont's contribution to modern Russian poetry appears in "Storm and Stress."

5. Balmont's poem "I am the exquisite voice of our broad Russian speech" ("Ia–izyskannost' russkoi medlitel'noi rechi," 1902).

6. Pushkin's poem "The Poet and the Mob" (1828)

7. Nekrasov's poem, "The Poet and the Citizen." On Nekrasov, see note No. 11, "Badger Hole."

8. This is a major tenet of Mandelstam's esthetic vision. See "Morning of Acmeism" and "Conversation about Dante"; See also, *The Noise of Time,* and the poetic cycle, "The Octets."

9. Semyon Yakovlevich Nadson (1862-1887). One of the most popular of the pre-Symbolist poets. He continued the idealistic and socially-conscious "civic poetry" of the 1880s, but also reflected the disillusionment of the intelligentsia. In his portrayal of the 1890s in *The Noise of Time,* Mandelstam singles out Nadson as the "key to the epoch," seeing him basically as a social, rather than literary, phenomenon. The passage is worth quoting:

> "Would you like to know the key to the epoch, the book which had positively become white-hot from handling, the book which would not under any circumstances agree to die, that lay like someone alive in the narrow coffin of the 1890s.... whose first page bore the features of a youth with an inspired hairdo, features that became an icon? Gazing into the face of young Nadson, I am astonished by the genuine fieriness of those features and at the same time by their total inexpressiveness, their almost wooden simplicity. Does this not describe the whole book? Does it not describe the era? Do not laugh at Nadsonism: it is the enigma of Russian culture."–(Slightly revised version of C. Brown's translation in *The Prose of Mandelstam,* Princeton, 1967).

10. Fyodor Sologub (penname of Fyodor Kuzmich Teternikov: 1863-1927). One of the most original of the Russian Symbolist poets and prose writers. His poetry belongs rather to the esthetic-decadent than the religious-mystical trend in Russian Symbolism. For him Beauty is the only Salvation. Individual isolation and metaphysical emptiness are major themes of his poetry. Although his lexicon is quite restricted, as Mandelstam points out, it is remarkably controlled and is used to create a sense of incantation, of magic and sorcery, rather than the "musicality" associated with Balmont or the "music" of correspondences towards which Bely and Ivanov were striving. His first *Collected Works* were published in St. Petersburg: Shipovnik, 1909-13. Sologub is one of the few Symbolist poets whom Mandelstam nearly always perceived in a positive light. See his tribute to Sologub, "For the Anniversary of Fyodor Sologub," and his letters to Gippius, 1908, and to Sologub, 1915. The poem to which Mandelstam refers appeared in Sologub's *Collected Works* in 1909, but it had been written earlier, in the 1890s. In that edition it begins "My silent friend" ("Drug moi tikhii") and ends "And so wordless and mournful." Hence, Mandelstam saw fit to emphasize the "mysterious" element rather than the "silent" or "wordless" aspect of Sologub's mood.

11. Mandelstam is drawing a major distinction between Symbolism and Acmeism. The Acmeists accused the Symbolists, for instance Soloviev and Ivanov, of valuing a poem merely as the record of an experience, or at best as a means to attaining a transcendent experience, while the Acmeists emphasized the intrinsic value of each poem as an "event" in itself. Indeed, this essay seems to be a direct answer to Ivanov's "echo theory" propounded in his "Thoughts on Symbolism."

4. REMARKS ON CHENIER

This essay first appeared in Mandelstam's *On Poetry*, 1928, although it had been announced as "proposed for publication" in *Apollon* for 1914 or 1915. See SS, II, 644.

The immediate reason for writing this essay may have been the publication of Chénier's own *Essai* in 1914. The *Essai*, which was first published in 1899, was republished in Abel Lefranc's *Oeuvres inédites* in 1914. Chenier's poetry was very popular and readily available in the first decades of the twentieth century. Hérédia himself produced a fine edition of the *Bucoliques* (1907), and Paul Dimoff edited Chénier's *Oeuvres complètes* in three volumes between 1908 and 1912. The impact that Chénier's *Essai* must have had on Mandelstam, in particular with regard to the role of the poet in society, is reflected in his essay, in its ideas, values, and even in its fragmented style.

Chénier never lost sight of the fact that the writer is both an individual with his own individual capacities, as well as a social creature, responsive to his society. Moreover, he was careful not to allow his views of contemporary society and the arts to falsify his historical sense. He sees the artist's role in society as related to the health or corruption of its institutions balanced by the moral consciousness of the artist himself. Thus, the artist's role is posited as an active force in society through its opposition to, as well as through its reflection of, social values and institutions. Chénier also had an exaggerated idea of the power of the word. He believed that literature was an integral part of the accepted way of life in young societies, but that as soon as a society began to fail, the writer was thrust into a defensive position; hence, only great writers had the courage to protest.

Such ideas are reflected time and again in Mandelstam's work, in his essays and literary prose, in particular in the essays on Chénier and Dante, and in *The Noise of Time* and "Fourth Prose," where he asserts the poet's or artist's right to challenge the values of a particular age in the name of the eternal verities. This theme is also expressed in his meditative poems of the early 1920s and in his poetry of the 1930s.

It should also be mentioned here that Mandelstam's conception of the role of the poet in society is morally determined, that this was a focal problem for him long before the Revolution of 1917, and that it is not merely a narrowly focused political issue reflecting temporal political duress. See the 1910 essay on Villon, for instance, wherein he first raises the issue by juxtaposing poetic "dynamism" to "morality."

1. Andre-Marie de Chénier (1762-1794), often considered the best poet of 18th century France, died on the scaffold at the age of 31. His martyrdom resulted in his becoming a symbolic figure, whose legendary reputation as the romantic ideal of the "poet as hero" (Carlyle) inspired such poets as Larmartine, Hugo, etc. to assert that the poet must also be a man of action. Although at the end of his life he wrote mostly political poetry *(Iambes),* the pure lyricism of his *Bucoliques* contains an original dramatic quality setting Chénier apart from the poets of his day, and explaining his appeal to the Romantic age. He was equally adored by the Parnassians and the Romanic school *(École Romane).*

In his *Iambes,* he fuses the pure lyrical impulse and Classical background with robust irony and extreme contrasts in language, at times creating deliberately ugly verse. His celebration of the three qualities of Justice, Truth and Virtue, his ultimate appeal to the conscience, serves as an ironical substitution for the values of Liberty, Equality and Fraternity bandied about and destroyed by the Revolutionists and the subsequent Reign of Terror. While many of his *Iambes* are no better than poeticized journalism, his last *Iambes,* composed in prison, are genuine works of art, rising above the topical events which inspired them.

In addition to poetry, Chénier is known for his prose writings, the most significant being the *Essai,* first published only in 1899. It includes, among other things, Chénier's theoretical statements about the relations between literature and society, including his belief that great literature can come only from free men living in a free society. For further information, see Francis Scarfe, *André Chénier, His Life and Work* (Oxford, 1965).

Mandelstam maintained his admiration for Chénier throughout his life. See, for instance, references to Chénier in his 1923 essay on Barbier, or again, in "Fourth Prose" (1929-30). Mandelstam's attack against the artificiality and false values of the 18th century *philosophes,* against the abstraction of basic virtues into meaningless rhetorical principles, against the mechanical repetition of pompous phrases as a last attempt to make them effective or meaningful, combined with praise for the "absolute character of Classical morality" which he sees as "pure," "naive" and "hygienic," seems to echo various thoughts expressed in Chénier's poetry and in his *Essai,* and to reinforce the ideas expressed by the spokesmen of the Romanic school.

For instance, Chénier's admiration of the Greeks and Classical literature caused him to scorn much of the work of his contemporaries. He claimed the Greeks were *"nés pour les beaux-art plus que nul peuple au monde. Eux seuls, dans les égarements de l'enthousiasme, suivent toujours la nature et la vérité."* The Greeks could write with *"une sensibilité intéressante et douce qui vous émeut, qui vous pénètre.... Leurs expressions sont vraies, humaines, nées dans l'homme et doivent toucher tous les hommes* (p. 47)." Those statements are in direct opposition to his comments on Voltaire or Pascal. About the latter he wrote in a chapter entitled "Influence d'une mauvaise littérature": *"Ceux qui ne peuvent se résoudre a penser, et qui croient et répètent sans examen ce qu'ils ont jadis oui dire, nous les vautent sans cesse comme un livre admirable. Il y a en effet des endroits éloquents, mais combien c'est peu de chose que de l'éloquence employée à soutenir du ton le plus arrogant, les plus impitoyables sophismes"* (p. 87).

Furthermore, such ideas as Chénier's interesting comments on originality and invention may have made an impression on Mandelstam, or at least have reinforced his own views and values. For example, Chénier's stress on the communication between writer and reader through universal sentiments and truths, expressed simply, directly, in human terms, and his perhaps exaggerated idea of the power of the word: *"Il y a des sentiments si purs, si simples, des pensées si éternelles, si humaines, si notres, si profondement innées dans l'âme, qui les âmes de tous les lecteurs les reconnaissent a l'instant; elles se réunissent à celle de l'auteur, elles semblent se reconnaître toutes et se souvenir qu'elles ont une origine commune"* (p. 110). *"Souvent un bon livre est lui-même une bonne action; et souvent un auteur sage et sublime, étant la cause lente de saines révolutions dans les moeurs et dans les idées, peut sembler avoir fait lui-même tout ce qu'il fait faire de bien"* (p. 3).

Or, his statements about the continuity of eternal truths, values, and ideas, especially the idea that writers can express their own originality through the reinterpretation of works of the past, appear throughout Mandelstam's work: *"Et d'abord je demanderai s'il n'y a pas un grand nombre de pensées fécondes et universelles qui, étant liées par leurs rapports à une multitude de choses, étant la suite, l'origine ou le noeud d'une multitude de notions, doivent entrer nécessairement dans beaucoup de matières diverses, et par consequent se trouver sur le droit chemin de tous les divers auteurs qui les traitent.... cette sorte d'imitation inventrice... enrichit les auteurs les plus justement renommés pour leur originalité"* (p. 117).

And, in particular, the idea that the poet is certain of meeting his poet-ancestors, if they are reborn, because he will recognize them immediately: *"Je suis sur de connaître des hommes morts depuis des siècles comme si j'avais vécu avec eux; s'ils renaissaient, je les reconnaitrais dans la rue..."* This idea is beautifully captured in Mandelstam's poem No. 261, "Batyushkov" (1932).

And last, but not least, Chénier's statement about every work having its own "physiognomy" seems to echo in Mandelstam's essay "On the Nature of the Word" and, much later, in the essay on Dante. *"Les ouvrages ont une physiognomie; ils font connaître non seulement les humeurs et le caractère, mais même la figure"* (p. 123).

2. See the development of this image of the golden sphere in Mandelstam's remarkable poem, "The Horseshoe Finder" (No. 136).

See: Stephen J. Broyde's excellent article, "Osip Mandelstam's 'Nashedshii Podkovu' " in *Slavic Poetics: Essays in Honor of Kiril Taranovsky* (The Hague, 1973), pp. 49-66.

The similarity in imagery as well as the similarity in thematic interests of this essay and other essays and poems of the early 1920s suggests that "Remarks on Chénier" may well have been finished about 1923, although it was obviously begun as early as 1914-15.

3. See the essays, "François Villon," "Morning of Acmeism," and "Conversation about Dante."

4. See the essay "Nineteenth Century."

5. Chénier's *Bucoliques* were written in Alexandrine couplets. Later, however, his *Iambes* superceded this popular meter.

6. See *Addendum* to this essay for Mandelstam's more detailed analysis of a Chénier poem.

7. A reference to the ideals of the French Romanic school

8. Bion, Greek Bucolic poet born near Phlossa, near Smyrna, in the first half of the first century B.C. The "Epithalamium of Achilles and Deidameia" referred to here, which had been ascribed to Bion's authorship, has subsequently been proven not to be of Bion's authorship. There was no reason for Mandelstam to have been aware of this.

9. Clément Marot (1496-1544). French poet who combined the poetic traditions of the French Middle Ages with the newly emerging values of secular and humanis-

tic culture dominating the Renaissance. His most interesting work is found in his early collected poems, *L'Adolescence Clémentine* (1532-34), his witty satirical Épigrammes and occasional Épîtres, his poem *L'Enfer* (1542) inspired by the rigors of imprisonment, as well as in his editions of *Le Roman de la Rose* (1529) and of Villon (1532), and in his metrical version of the Psalms. Marot was not the father of the Alexandrine. The Alexandrine was actually popularized somewhat later by Ronsard. See: G. Guiffrey, R. Yve-Plessis (eds.), *Ouevres complètes* (5 vols., 1875-1931).

10. A significant element in Mandelstam's esthetic. See note No. 8 to "On the Addressee."

11. The next five paragraphs are based on Mandelstam's reading of Pushkin's poem, "To the Courtier" ("K Vel'mozhe," 1830), addressed to N.B. Yusupov, in which he contrasts the courtier's life in the age of the Enlightenment with the changes wrought by the French Revolution.

12. A reference to Chénier's bitter denunciation of the Reign of Terror in his *Iambes* of 1794, written while in prison.

13. "Jeu de paume" is a lengthy political poem, an ode on "Le Serment du Jeu de Paume," celebrating Louis David's painting of the historic occasion of the Tennis Court Oath. The ode is divided into two main parts. The first describes the circumstances of the Tennis Court Oath and the fall of the Bastille. The second part is a warning "to the people" against the abuse of power. It contains a scrupulously careful statement of political doctrine, while its fundamentally didactic tone links it to the later *Iambes*.

14. This is another reference to Pushkin's poem to Yusupov, who also served in London. Chénier served as secretary to the French Ambassador in London from 1787 to 1790. See note No. 11 above.

15. This "Addendum" to "Remarks on Chénier" is dated 1922, see SS, III, 144-45, based on its recent Soviet publication in *Voprosy literatury* (IV, 1968, 200-201). This date seems much more realistic than 1914-15 for the essay itself, judging from the thematic content and imagery alone. Nevertheless, the inspiration for the subject must have originally come in 1914-15, hence its placement in this volume. It deserves to be read along with both the early essays and with the essays of the early 1920s.

16. The opening line of Chénier's "La Mort d'Hercule" from his *Bucoliques:*

O Eta, mont ennobli par cette nuit ardente,
Quand l'infidèle époux d'une épouse imprudente
Reçut de son amour un present trop jaloux,
Victime du Centaure immolé par ses coups.
Il brise tes forêts. Ta cime épaisse et sombre
En un bûcher immense amoncelle sans nombre
Les sapins résineux que son bras a ployés.
Il y porte la flamme. Il monte; sous ses pieds
Étend du vieux lion la dépouille héroïque,
Et l'oeil au ciel, la main sur sa massue antique,
Attend sa récompense et l'heure d'être un Dieu.
Le vent souffle et mugit. Le bûcher tout en feu
Brille autour du héros; et la flamme rapide
Porte aux palais divins l'âme du grand Alcide.

Pushkin did a free version of this poem which Mandelstam undoubtedly knew. See "Iz A. Shen'e."

It is significant that precisely "Mort d'Hercule" became a model for the Parnassian style in French verse. Hérédia, in his edition of Chénier's *Bucoliques*, ranked this poem among Chénier's finest. Its stress on the ideals of heroism and stoicism in the face of adversity and ultimate destiny reinforced by its terse narrative style and severity of tone, appealed in France to the members of the Parnassian movement and Romantic school and in Russia, to Bryusov and later to Gumilev and his fellow Acmeists.

Mandelstam's interest centers on the poem's internal variety and dynamism. He interprets the variety of grammatical, syntactical, and rhythmical relations as providing the source of the poem's dynamism within the confines of the traditionally strict form of the Alexandrine, in keeping with the ideals of his French predecessors and his Russian Acmeist companions. Mandelstam's interest in, and analysis of, the inner relations of verse elements developed into an art of reading, an art best presented in his essay on Dante.

17. See the essay on Dante for a more developed discussion of verbal tense forms and inner dialogue, in particular, the section treating Canto X of the *Inferno*.

18. This is a good example of Mandelstam's attempts to analyze Chenier's manipulation of syntax discussed in the main body of the essay.

19. "L'Aveugle" is also from *Bucoliques*. The following lines are at issue:

—Les barbares! J'etais assis pres de la poupe.
Aveugle vagabond, dit l'insolente troupe,
Chante: si ton esprit n'est point comme tes yeux,
Amus notre ennui; tu rendras grace aux Dieux.
J'ai fait taire mon coeur qui voulait les confondre;
Ma bouche ne s'est point ouverte a leur repondre.
Ils n'ont pas entendu ma voix, et sous ma main
J'ai retenu le Dieu courrouce dans mon seine.

This paragraph is obviously related to the main theme of the essay, the problem of the artist and society, also discussed with reference to the same Pushkin poem, "The Poet and the Mob," noted in "On the Addressee." See Note No. 6 to that essay.

5. Peter Chaadaev

This essay first appeared in *Apollon* in 1915 (No. 6-7), under the title "Chaadaev." It was reprinted in 1928 with several changes; the entire fifth part was quite obviously omitted for political reasons. This translation is based primarily on the *Apollon* text. For omissions in the censored 1928 version, see SS, II, 642-43.

1. Peter Yakovlevich Chaadaev (1794-1856). Western-oriented Russian philosopher. His major work, *The Philosophical Letters,* began to circulate in manuscript when Chaadaev was in his late twenties. While the original was written in French, the *First Letter* appeared in a Russian translation in *The Telescope* in 1836. Public outrage and the censorship under the regime of Nicholas I caused Chaadaev to be declared officially insane and placed under house arrest for a year and a half; it caused the permanent suspension of *The Telescope* and the exile of the editor, N.I. Nadezhdin. *Four Letters* and the "Apology of a Madman" (1837, Chaadaev's last philosophical essay) finally appeared in a bi-lingual Russian-French edition in Russia in 1913-14: M.O. Gershenzon (ed.), *Sochineniia i pis'ma P.Ia. Chaadaeva* (Moscow, 1913-14). This was undoubtedly Mandelstam's text. Only in the early 1930s did D. Shakhovskoy (a distant relative of Chaadaev's) discover the remainder of Chaadaev's *Letters* and publish them in a Russian translation in *Literaturnoe Nasledstvo*, Vols. 22-24, 1935. For more information and an English text of the *Letters* and the "Apology," see Mary-Barbara Zeldin, *Peter Yakovlevich Chaadayev* (Knoxville, 1969). *The Letters* present a devastating critique of Russia's cultural evolution based on a quasi-Catholic world view.

Mandelstam's essay on Chaadaev is both an expression of his interest in the intellectual issues of his day as well as a personal attempt to define his own conception of Russia's place in the history of European culture. The essay appeared just one year after Gershenzon's edition of Chaadaev's writings made the philosopher's work available to the Russian reading public for the first time (the exception being the *First Letter*). The post-1905 intelligentsia was busy evaluating its own past, tracing the legacy of its 19th century intellectual heritage, witness the extreme popularity of Ivanov-Razumnik's *The History of Russian Social Thought,* which first appeared in 1906 and went through four editions by 1914. See also, Mandelstam's own discussion of this period in Chapter 7 of *The Noise of Time.* Furthermore, Mandelstam's singular interest in Chaadaev seems to be at least in part attributable to his reverence for Pushkin, on the one hand, and his admiration for Herzen, on the other, both being great admirers of Chaadaev.

With the interest in Russia's intellectual and cultural heritage, Pushkin, of necessity, became the focus of scholarly studies, beginning with S.A. Vengerov's Pushkin Seminar at Petersburg University organized in 1908. The Seminar was begun with the intention of doing a systematic study of Pushkin's work, of compiling a dictionary of Pushkin's language, and training young scholars in the traditional methods of ideological criticism and academic biographism. Indeed, the study of Pushkin became a phenomenon of the period by attracting some of its very best minds. The seminar became one of the centers of the incipient Formalist movement: it included Boris Eikhenbaum, Boris Tomashevsky, Yury Tynianov, among others. It is not known if Mandelstam participated in any of its sessions, although he was admitted to the Faculty of History and Philology at the university in 1911 and was still concerned about taking his exams in July 1916. In *The Noise of Time,* Mandelstam is scornful of his distant relative, Academician Vengerov, for his excessive academicism.

Chaadaev considered himself Pushkin's intellectual mentor, and Pushkin attributed all his political ideas to Chaadaev. Pushkin dedicated not one but three epistles to his friend, and it has been suggested that many character traits of Pushkin's hero, Eugene Onegin, are based on aspects of Chaadaev's personality. (For more details on the relationship between Pushkin and Chaadaev, see Charles Quenet, *Tchaadaev et les Lettres philosophiques* [Paris, 1931], pp. 31-51).

Alexander Herzen was also immensely popular at this time. Between 1897 and 1910, numerous works on Herzen appeared, including studies by V. Smirnov (1897), S.N. Bulgakov (1906), Ovsianiko-Kulikovsky (1908), A. Veselovsky (1909), and his *Complete Works,* edited by M.K. Lemke, was published between 1915 and 1923 in Petrograd. In chapter seven of *The Noise of Time,* Mandelstam describes the political debates of this post-1905 period as follows: "Here in the deep and passionate strife of the SR's and SD's one could sense the continuation of the ancient feud of the Slavophiles and Westernizers. This life, this struggle received the distant blessings of men so far apart as Khomiakov and Kireevskii, on the one hand, and on the other the eloquently Western Herzen whose stormy political thought will always sound like a Beethoven sonata." Herzen had called Chaadaev "an embodied veto, a living protest," and had even compared him to Dante. He welcomed Chaadaev's *First Letter* as "a shot that rang out in the dark night... it forced everyone to awaken.... such is the power of the word in a silent land unaccustomed to free speech, that Chaadaev's *Letter* shook all thinking Russia to its very foundations... suddenly, quietly, a mournful figure arose and demanded the floor in order calmly to voice his *lasciate ogni speranza*" (See A.I. Herzen, *Byloe i dumy* (Minsk, 1957), pp. 378-80. The English translation by Constance Garnett is called *My Past and Thoughts* [New York, 1968]).

Chaadaev emerges in Mandelstam's eyes as the national embodiment of the union of morality and the intellect. To Mandelstam, Chaadaev expressed and defined the Russian national ideology as "national individuality."

By daring to admit that Russia had nothing to offer but itself, that it was separated from the West and the Western cultural heritage, Chaadaev recognized that Russia was also "free" from the West's legacy of stagnation and petrified ideas and forms, and that Russia was therefore free to choose between joining the West or the East, or remaining independent and following its own individual national path. According to Mandelstam, Chaadaev had gone to the West and returned, and in so doing had come to understand and value Russia's role in determining the future course of the modern world:

> Chaadaev was the first Russian who had actually lived in the West ideologically, and found the road back. His contemporaries... could point to him with superstitious respect, as they once pointed to Dante: 'He was there, he saw—and he returned.'

> Chaadaev signifies a new, deepened understanding of nationality... of Russia as the source of absolute moral freedom.

> For Chaadaev, Russia had only one thing to offer: moral freedom, the freedom of choice.

> Having endowed us with inner freedom, Russia offers us a choice, and those who make this choice are true Russians, no matter what they affiliate themselves with.

According to Mandelstam, Chaadaev created his own myth of the West and judged Russia against it. He found Russia lacking, because it was cut off from the "unity" of Western European culture, cut off from the Church represented on earth by the Papal succession which gave continuity and unity to all the Western European nations. However, Russia was endowed with its own "national individuality" expressed, in Mandelstam's words, as "moral freedom," which is "worth the majesty petrified in architectural forms, it is as valuable as everything the West has created in the realm of material culture, and I see that the Pope. . . has raised himself to greet this freedom."

2. The idea of the organic union of esthetic, ethical, and intellectual values had a profound appeal for Mandelstam. And the idea of the organization of those values in some harmonious, structured whole, e.g., a work of art, was to him a source of freedom and spiritual release.

3. Pushkin and Chaadaev were lifelong friends. See Note No. 1, above.

4. M.B. Zeldin's concise explanation of Chaadaev's philosophical views is given here for those who do not know or remember the essential points made in the *Philosophical Letters:*

> The categories on which Chaadaev bases his philosophy are now clear: the unity of reality through the principle of the transmission of primitive ideas, divinely introduced when man was first created and expressed concretely in history in individual men and nations. These men and nations play, by the combined force of free will and Providence, their role in the progress of Christian society toward the achievement of the Kingdom of God on earth, that is, the achievement of the completely harmonious system of every man and of his cognitive, esthetic and moral faculties. Reality is one through history, which itself is a history of ideas working through men and of which the principle is identical with that of the physical world, namely motion originating from a divine impulse. History is meaningful and therefore truly history only insofar as it embodies the fundamental divine idea, hence, insofar as it is Christian: neither history nor Christianity can be understood without the other. Christianity is thus the reality and the truth and the unity of the world. The historical focus of unity is Christ, its institutional expression is the [Roman Catholic] church centered in the papacy, and its embodiment, which provides the union of the mental and material realms, is the sacrament of the Eucharist.

> Egoism, a result of the perversion of the free will man received from God, shatters the unity and leads to isolation, both in the individual and in nations, and to error both logical and moral. This, as grounded in the schism of Orthodoxy and Roman Catholicism, is the cause of Russia's present nature, its backwardness, its insignificance, its immorality. All reality is united by shared tradi-

tional ideas: Russia has refused its share and thus, Chaadaev implies, is not part of reality at all.

Later in his "Apology of a Madman," Chaadaev expressed a kind of "enlightened patriotism," in which he came up with a new and significant role for Russia in the history of Western civilization. M.B. Zeldin defines it as follows: "A proper understanding of history would make it clear that Russia, by being a latecomer in the development of history, can, from its objective, dispassionate position, arbitrate and resolve all social problems and thus lead the West. This... is its destined role" (Zeldin, *op. cit.,* pp. 26-27).

5. "Apology of a Madman" was Chaadaev's last attempt to express his thought in philosophical essays. It was written in 1837, while he was living under house arrest and being observed for "insanity." It was also an attempt to temper and explain some of the ideas presented in his *Letters.* Chaadaev was freed in 1838 on the condition that he not write again. However, this prohibition did not prevent him from actively frequenting Moscow's intellectual circles, including the English Club, or from being admired and sought after for his keen opinions.

6. Note the similarity of imagery in "Morning of Acmeism": "The handsome arrow of the Gothic belltower rages because it is dedicated entirely to stabbing the sky, to reproaching it for its emptiness" (Part 3). Mandelstam's work is an integral whole, and should be read chronologically, since he builds on, develops and transforms his own images and thoughts, e.g., "gothic thought" refers to the intellectual and moral protest of the dynamic or creative mind.

7. This is undoubtedly a reference to the more subdued presentation of ideas in "Apology of a Madman." See Note No. 4, above.

8. Here we can see Mandelstam's unique mind in operation, distorting, juxtaposing, and transforming the traditional interpretation of Chaadaev's *Philosophical Letters* to fit his own thought processes, to express his own aspirations for Russia, his own "nationalism." Mandelstam essentially admits that what interests him is not Chaadaev's thought *per se,* but the "cause of Chaadaev's thought": Russia, the history of Russia, and the perception of Russia by historians, critics and intellectuals in general; the myth of Russia.

9. From Ershov's fairytale, "The Little Humpbacked Horse."

10. Chaadaev sought unity in the form of the Catholic Church and the Papacy. Mandelstam, in his essays of the 1920s, including among others, "Government and Rhythm" and "Humanism and the Present," sought a social architecture based on what he called Gothic balance and harmony. He was not a proponent of the destruction of the State or the Church or the Law; rather he saw "structure" as essential to man's existence. However, he believed that it would be possible to define more clearly separate and particular functions for the Church and the State. See the essays for more details.

11. For a more detailed presentation of this idea, see "The Word and Culture."

12. According to Chaadaev's first *Letter,* Russia was cut off from history and, therefore, tradition, for Russia did not participate in the historical continuum which began with the Divine creation of Man and developed down through the ages in Western Europe under the laws of the Papal succession. Russia had followed Byzantium instead. However, according to Mandelstam's interpretation, now that Western European cultural tradition had become petrified—"its majesty petrified in architectual forms— Russia had something to offer the West: "moral freedom," or perhaps, "national individuality" as opposed to the traditional tendency toward "unity." Thus, Mandelstam, at least in this essay, sees the Russian nation as morally unique, as a "national individuum" amidst a world of nations participating in a unified but stagnant cultural heritage.

13. Mandelstam evidently bore this image of Chaadaev's "holy staff" of "moral freedom" with him until he could use it as an autobiographical reference a decade and

a half later; see "Fourth Prose," Part Seven. In "Fourth Prose," however, this image is presented in the conditional mode; the holy staff of Russia's moral freedom, of Russia as a "national individuum," now incorporates Mandelstam's Jewish consciousness— a revised self-image; and he dreams of setting off for Erevan, capital of Armenia, the "younger sister of the Jewish nation," rather than for Chaadaev's Rome, capital of "the West" in Chaadaev's imagination.

6. PUSHKIN AND SCRIABIN (FRAGMENTS)

This essay comes down to us only in fragments. It was never published in any form in Russia. Nadezhda Yakovlevna Mandelstam (*Hope Abandoned,* trans. by Max Hayward, New York, 1974, pp. 104-13) states that it was originally read to the Religious-Philosophical Society in St. Petersburg, whose secretary, Sergei Platonovich Kablukov, was entrusted with the text. When Mandelstam "returned from his second visit to Georgia [1921] . . ., he learned that Kablukov had died and that his archives had been turned over to the Public Library... Several times M. went to the library to inquire about his paper on Scriabin, but it had disappeared. 'I have no luck,' he said, 'this was my most important article'." In 1923, in going through Mandelstam's father's trunks, Nadezhda Yakovlevna came across part of the manuscript: "M. was overjoyed, looked through all the pages, found it was about half of what he had given to Kablukov, and instructed me to keep it. He never came back to it again, since publication would have been absolutely out of the question." Nadezhda Yakovlevna also states: "There were two first pages, completely identical except for the title. On one the title was: 'Pushkin and Scriabin,' and on the other: 'Scriabin and Christianity'." This fact may be a clue to the contradictory nature of the "fragments" as we have them. Mandelstam may have had two themes in mind and have begun two separate articles. This is only speculation on my part, but it helps to explain the confusion in logic and thought found in the text as it now exists. I have not attempted to rearrange the fragments in a different order for I do not feel up to the task. However, I have tried to point out some of the discrepancies in the notes accompanying this translation. I share Clarence Brown's humility before the complexities of these fragments, even though we do not always agree on interpretation (see C. Brown, *Mandelstam*).

It seems that some of the fragments attempt to compare Pushkin and Scriabin along the lines of V.V. Gippius' pamphlet, "Pushkin and Christianity," also dating from 1915 (see Note No. 11, below), and in so doing praise Scriabin's contribution to art as "pre-Christian" or the work of a "Mad Hellene." (See Introduction). Other fragments, however, have nothing at all to do with Pushkin, and are, apparently, intended to question the sources of Scriabin's inspiration, condemning him not only as a Symbolist, but as an emblem of modern Russian history, as Mandelstam interprets it, an emblem of the movement away from Christianity toward Theosophy and Buddhism. The latter is discussed in more detail in "The Nineteenth Century."

According to the editors of Mandelstam's collected works, this essay was begun in 1915, soon after Scriabin's death (April 25, 1915). However other information gives the date of its completion as 1919 or 1920, when it was incorporated in some collection which remained unpublished. It is also suggested that "its completion in 1919 was connected with the publication that year of the collection, *Russian Propylaea* (Vol. VI), edited by M.O. Gershenzon." Materials about Pushkin and Scriabin appear in that volume. Later, however, while preparing his essays for publication in *On Poetry,* Mandelstam searched again in the Leningrad archives for his manuscript and could not locate it. See SS, II, 646.

Nevertheless, Brown (*Mandelstam,* pp. 230-37, 244-45) indicates that Mandelstam may have completely altered his view of the importance of this essay, for he "even satirized the whole business in the episode of "The Egyptian Stamp" where Parnok, the hero, is said to have been thrown out of some literary society for having read such a paper." For more details on why Mandelstam may have altered the views expressed in this essay, see my Introduction.

Nadezhda Yakovlevna has pointed out that, "The lecture on the death of Scriabin, despite its fragmentary form... is in every sense a companion piece to the *Tristia* volume, for 'Phaedra' right through to the last poem about the granaries in which 'the grain of faith profound and full' is stored" *(Hope Abandoned).* Brown proves the validity of this statement in his account of the relationship of the essay to Mandelstam's poem "Solominka" (1916) and in his discussion of Mandelstam's conception of Pushkin in this volume, in particular, in "We shall gather again in Petersburg," 1920. In addition, Brown carefully interprets one of the major themes of the essay, Mandelstam's "definition of Christian art."

While I find myself in basic agreement with the "definition," I am perturbed by the fact that Brown does not seem to go far enough in his interpretation of the poem or in his interpretation of the relationship of the "definition of Christian art" to the latter parts of the essay (as they are now arranged). Although this is very understandable due to the confusion, ambiguity, and contradictory nature of several of the essay fragments, I would like to try to pursue this discussion a bit further, bearing in mind Lidiya Ginzburg's remarks about Mandelstam's "single semantic system" (see her remarkable essay, "Poetika Osipa Mandelstama" in *Izvestiia Akademiia Nauk SSR,* seriia literatury i iazyka, July-August 1972, pp. 310-327. A good English translation by Sona Hoisington is found in V. Erlich (ed.), *Twentieth Century Russian Criticism,* New Haven: Yale University Press, 1975). Ginzburg states: "[In 1933] Mandelstam read the essay [Conversation about Dante], read his poems, and talked copiously about poetry and about painting. We were struck by the remarkable affinities between the essay, the poems, and the table talk. Here was a single semantic system, a single stream of similes and juxtapositions. The image-bearing matrix from which Mandelstam's poems emerged became strangely tangible. The same semantic principles are operative in Mandelstam's prose, including his essays. Paradoxical as it may seem, Mandelstam's prose is often more metaphorical than his poetry.... Within this overall pattern pivotal or key words acquire special impact. Mandelstam's insight into the nature of these words owes a great deal to Annensky's poetry with its psychological symbolism. Mandelstam accepts the notion of life refracted through poetic symbols, but he cannot accept the abstract nature of 'professional symbolism'." Thus, Mandelstam's poem No. 118, "We shall gather again in Petersburg," appears to work as an explanation of the essay, "Pushkin and Scriabin," as much as the essay works to elucidate the poem (No. 117 should also be read in conjunction with the "definition of Christian art"). Above all, No. 118 contains one of Mandelstam's incredibly optimistic statements about the immortality of art; it emerges almost as a polemic against those who sought to interpret it as an admission of the poet's failure, of the victory of politics over poetry. (See also, "The Horseshoe Finder" another remarkable poem on this theme.)

In "We shall gather again..." the immortality of "the word" is assured through the imagery affirming the life-death-rebirth cycle as well as through the theme of the return. The "return to Petersburg" where the sun (read: Pushkin, the word, or art) was buried is now cause for the rebirth of poetry, of the "blessed meaningless word" (variously interpreted as "poetry" or "love"—see, respectively, Brown, Ginzburg). The opening stanza of the poem echoes, almost literally, the opening two paragraphs of the essay:

> We shall gather again in Petersburg,
> As if we had buried the sun there,
> And we shall utter for the first time
> The blessed meaningless word.

In the black velvet of the Soviet night,
In the velvet of the universal void
The kindred eyes of the blessed women still sing,
Immortal flowers are still in bloom.

V Peterburge my soidemsia snova,
Slovno solntse my pokhoronili v nem,
I blazhennoe, bessmyslennoe slovo
V pervyi raz proiznesem.
V chernom barkhate sovetskoi nochi,
V barkhate vsemirnoi pustoty,
Vse poiut blazhennykh zhen rodnye ochi,
Vse tsvetut bessmertnye tsvety.

Perhaps I am wrong, but I do not think one has to go much further than this. Not only are the images strikingly similar, but the thought process and the very patterns of image formation and transformation reinforce each other. Mandelstam's beloved devices of "transformation" (see, "Conversation about Dante") and "astonishment" (see, the Acmeist essays, especially "Morning of Acmeism" and "On the Addressee") are presented in "Pushkin and Scriabin" as an effort on Mandelstam's part to reconcile his esthetic vision with a major intellectual-poetic trend of his day—the attempt to reconcile the myths of Christianity and Hellenism (see V.V. Gippius, "Pushkin and Christianity"—*Pushkin i khristianstvo*, 1915, V. Ivanov's play "Prometheus"—*Prometei*, 1916, and the above-mentioned Gershenzon collection of 1919).

While the poem is complex and ambiguous, it certainly lacks the confusing demands of the religious-philosophical context of the essay fragments into which Mandelstam seems to be forcing his esthetic vision. In the poem, "transformation" and "astonishment" are both obvious and natural, if one puts aside secondary political considerations which only serve to further confuse the reading of the poem's basic theme. Almost all the images—"the blessed meaningless word," "the blessed women," "the immortal roses," and Pushkin's (the poet's) spirit—and their reiteration in slightly different forms (transformations) seem to be intended to "astonish" us, to force us to recognize Mandelstam's faith in the immortality of art and in the immortality which art confers through "poetic symbols" in reiterating the idea of the return, of rebirth, or in Christian terms, of the Resurrection.

What is more, the poem's subtext is surely Hérédia's "Sur le Livre des amours de Pierre de Ronsard," a poem commemorating the immortality that Ronsard bestowed on his three beloved (blessed) women through his poetic art. Hérédia's sonnet cleverly juxtaposes the ephemeral beauty of Marie Dupin, Hélène de Surgères and Cassandre Salviati to the permanence woven from poetic craft and creative vision. The poet's skill and creative power are extolled in the following tercets:

Tout meurt. Marie, Hélène et toi, fière Cassandre,
Vos beaux corps ne seraient qu'une insensible cendre,
—Les roses et les lys n'ont pas de lendemain—

Si Ronsard, sur la Seine ou sur la blonde Loire,
N'eut tressé pour vos fronts, d'une immortelle main,
Aux myrtes de l'Amour le laurier de la Gloire.

Mandelstam's essay, then, read in conjunction with this reading of the poem "We shall gather again in Petersburg," appears to be merely a more mystical-religious-philosophical statement of his basic esthetic tenets, indeed of his Acmeist views juxtaposed against the esthetic tenets of Symbolism.

Indeed, the essay seems to contain yet another Mandelstamian refutation of certain Symbolist values. Mandelstam simultaneously attacks the ideas of art as "sacrifice" and art as "redemption." In his efforts to declare art (or "the word") autonomous (not merely the means to a religious or philosophical end), he seems to be attempting to turn Symbolist concepts and the extremely popular Symbolist musician, Scriabin, to his own purposes. In the later fragments, "Death" is identified with "Divine Grace," thus becoming a means of "transformation" or a fundamental "source" of art. In other words, if to the Symbolists art is but a vehicle for a religious experience, to Mandelstam "the divine illusion of redemption" makes possible independent, autonomous art: "Christian art . . . condenses grace into magnificent clouds and empties them out as life-giving rain." Mandelstam focuses on the experience of "illusion" or esthetic consciousness and poetic craft as opposed to the religious experience and "pure music." Here he seems to be invoking Annensky's tradition while opposing V. Ivanov's.

However, to fully understand this essay, we need several preliminary studies, including a study of the thematic and symbolic images of Pushkin, Christianity and Hellenism in the first two decades of the 20th century, of Scriabin's influence on, or relations with, Russian poets in the early 20th century, of ideological and symbolic uses of the concepts of "Buddhism," "Theosophy" and the "occult" and their impact on the poets of the late 19th-early 20th centuries in Russia.

For more details with special reference to the text of the essay, see the notes below.

1. On Pushkin, see Note No. 1, "On the Addressee."

2. Alexander Nikolaevich Scriabin (1871-1915). Russian modernist composer and pianist. Approximately ninety per cent of Scriabin's compositions involve piano parts. According to his biographers, E.A. Hull and A. Swan, Scriabin's mystical-philosophical values played an extremely important part in his music: "Art as Religion and Religion as Art is the fundamental idea of Scriabin's music" (Hull). Furthermore, Swan maintains, that when Scriabin took up Theosophy in 1905 (on Buddhism, Theosophy, etc. in Russian cultural life, see Mandelstam's views in "The Nineteenth Century"), his grand project—the incorporation of the ultimate Mystery in music—"dominated Scriabin's mind." James Billington in his summation of Scriabin's complex orchestral works, claims that they reflected "the inner aspirations of the age." He divides the orchestral works into four stages: " 'The Divine Poem' of 1903, his third and last symphony; 'The Poem of Ecstasy' of 1908; 'Prometheus: The Poem of Fire' of 1909-10; and his 'Mystery,' which he had only begun at the time of his sudden death in 1915." Scriabin was extremely popular with the Symbolist poets of his day. It would also seem, from the fragmentary evidence of this essay, that Mandelstam was very favorably impressed by the first two "Poems." The first is said to express "the spirit's liberation from its earthly trammels and the consequent free expression of purified personality" (Hull); the second is said to "voice the highest of all joys, that of creative work. [Scriabin] held that in the artist's incessant creative activity, his constant progression towards the Ideal, the spirit alone truly lives" (Hull).

However, Scriabin's later work, "Prometheus" and the projected "Mystery," were undoubtedly too Symbolist and too theosophical in orientation for Mandelstam, for in those instances art was merely a vehicle for fundamentally religious ends. It is these latter works that Mandelstam had in mind when he accused Scriabin of "breaking with the voice... with the Christian sense of individuality."

On Scriabin and his work see E.A. Hull, *A Great Russian Tone-Poet: Scriabin* (London, 1921), Alfred Swan, *Scriabin* (London, 1923), James Billington, *The Icon and the Axe* (New York, 1966, pp. 481-3), M. Cooper, "Scriabin's Mystical Beliefs" in *Music and Letters,* XVI (1935).

3. "Transformation" is a ·major element in Mandelstam's esthetic. See "The Word and Culture" and "Conversation about Dante" for a discussion of its role in poetic creation.

Indeed, the lives of both Pushkin and Scriabin were transformed into myth. Belinsky's comment on Pushkin is exemplary: "Pushkin was called upon to be the living revelation of the mystery of poetry in Russia." See also Pasternak's comments on Scriabin in his autobiography *Safe Conduct*.

4. *Sobornyi* refers to the religious term *sobornost',* – the sense of spiritual fellowship in the Russian orthodox church. Nadezhda Yakovlevna Mandelstam discusses the distinction between *sobornost'* and "collectivism": "*Sobornost'* is a term relating to religion and the church which not only has nothing in common with collectivism, but is even used in a contrary meaning. *Sobornost'* is the brotherhood of people who are a part of the *sobor* (cathedral; assembly of God) as children of the same Father.... *Sobornost'...* is unthinkable without full freedom of the personality" (*Hope Abandoned*, p. 407).

5. See Note No. 19.

6. A.E. Hull states: "Immediately after his death [Scriabin's] fame increased doubly. Memorial concerts were given in many cities, and his works appeared in concerts all over the globe. Especially remarkable was the cycle of orchestral concerts organized in Moscow by the famous conductor Kussevitsky..." (p. 76).

7. That is, Scriabin is not a Christian symbol of God's grace, of redemption, and hence, of artistic celebration, but is rather a pre-Christian Hellenistic symbol of tragedy, of pathos. He expresses passion, but not redemption; thus he is not a "free" artist. As V. Asafyev stated of Scriabin's "Prometheus: Poem of Fire," "Scriabin's [fire brings about] rebirth... the creation of that new world which opens up in the presence of man's spiritual ecstasy... His fundamental condition is ecstasy, flight. His element is fire . . . Fire, fire, fire, everywhere fire" (cited in Billington).

8. Of this paragraph Nadezhda Yakovlevna writes: "The most important passage is where M. says what he understands the chief sin of the epoch to be, the one for which we would all have to pay: the whole of modern history, he writes: 'has turned away from Christianity to Buddhism and Theosophy' "(*Hope Abandoned*, p. 106).

9. These particular negatives should be read in conjunction with the essay on Chaadaev, especially parts II and V.

10. See the similar image in the poem "The Horseshoe Finder."

11. See V.V. Gippius' "Pushkin and Christianity" (1915). Vladimir Gippius, fellow member of the Poet's Guild, and friend or "companion" as Mandelstam presented him in the last chapter of *The Noise of Time,* might have been one of the original stimuli behind this lecture. See also, Mandelstam's letter to Gippius (*Letters*, No. 1, April, 1908).

In his pamphlet, Gippius attempts to show how Pushkin, although not consciously a Christian artist, unconsciously expresses the Christian experience. On the one hand, according to Gippius, Pushkin's esthetic is essentially pre-Christian–"the tragic pathos" of Hellenism: "If I were asked to define the essence of Pushkin's poetry I would say... that it was sensuality with regard to everything... If I were asked to define Pushkin's soul as it was expressed in his poetry, it would be necessary to define it as a Christian soul in its most fundamental aspect,–sin aspiring toward sanctity... The depth of [Pushkin's] sinfulness was in his sensuality and, insofar as his sensuality was that of a suffering man, it was the passion of the Christian experience. The Greeks understood the interrelationship of sensuality and passion in just this way, in their tragic consciousness which identified passion and suffering as Pathos.... In his consciousness Pushkin always remained within the limits of estheticism. The highest expression of Pushkin's passion was artistic–the tragic pathos." Mandelstam seems to be following this line of reasoning when he depicts Scriabin as still a "Hellene," that is, not yet the recipient of divine (Christian) grace, and therefore not yet capable of expressing the Christian esthetic, "joy"–"the joyous communion with God," the freedom associated by Mandelstam with the "divine illusion of redemption" which secures the true Christian artist his calling. See below.

12. See C. Brown's interpretation of Mandelstam's "definition of Christian art" in

Mandelstam. Brown concentrates on this section of the essay. It seems to be consistent in itself. However, the reader should be aware that it is not consistent with all the later fragments of the essay. See the introductory remarks to this essay, above.

13. Terpander: the first lyric poet to set poems to music. These were primarily liturgical hymns to Apollo.

14. This is a reference to Scriabin's famous orchestral tone-poem, "Prometheus: Poem of Fire," which was first performed in Moscow on March 2, 1911, under the baton of Sergei Kusevitsky, with Scriabin playing the piano part himself. Its reception was extremely divided. It was also performed abroad that summer in Holland and Germany, and in 1913-1914 in London. See also, Note No. 7, above.

On Scriabin's "pianism," it is interesting to note E.A. Hull's impressions: "Everyone was struck by what appeared to be a new kind of Pianism.... It appeared as though this new music had brought along with it a new kind of playing." Moreover, Mandelstam's recognition of "the loss of the Christian sense of individuality" is also *de facto* recognition that the composer achieved his aim, which was theosophical, not orthodox Christian. Hull states of this work: "[Scriabin] is apparently striving to obtain by means of his music that state of ecstasy which the true mystic realizes can only be obtained when a perfect union with the divine has been achieved.... Scriabin comes closest to this in his 'Prometheus.' There theosophy has provided the tone-poem with a strong story or 'programme'." Even more significant, perhaps, this paragraph is crucial to an understanding of Mandelstam's essay. In direct contrast to the opening two paragraphs of the essay (as we have it), in which Scriabin's "achievement" of "death" is praised as "the supreme act of his creative activity," Mandelstam here links Scriabin with the turning point in modern history, with its anti-Christian direction: "with terrible speed [modern history has] turned away from Christianity to Buddhism and Theosophy." Mandelstam is speaking here as a prophet of doom and is singling out Scriabin as the emblem of that doom, as the emblem of modern history. This section must be read in conjunction with the essay "The Nineteenth Century" which develops this theme more clearly.

These two paragraphs are also fascinating with regard to how Mandelstam contrasts his interpretation of the Christian with the pre-Christian (or Hellenic) myth of Prometheus. Mandelstam perceives Christianity as that which frees the poet to experience and celebrate the "divine illusion of redemption," that is, man's consciousness of individual freedom. On the other hand, in Mandelstam's view, the pre-Christian myth of Prometheus celebrates man's eternal tragedy, his perpetual struggle against the Gods (not his freedom). Here Mandelstam counters Vyacheslav Ivanov's ideas. No words are capable of expressing such tragic pathos; only "pure music" or pure passion. Scriabin's "Mute Chorus" is thus the ultimate expression of man's impasse, of his tragedy. Hence, according to Mandelstam, Scriabin is *not* a Christian artist and his music is *not* "Christian music," for it does not even approach the expression of Christian joy exemplified in Beethoven's Ninth Symphony—"Beethoven's Catholic joy."

Furthermore, in Mandelstam's view, this antithesis of Christian and pre-Christian art raises a major esthetic issue—it questions the ideal of artistic control, of craftsmanship. According to Mandelstam, since the true Christian artist is "free from the burden of necessity," that is, free from all ideological concerns (religious, philosophical, moral, social), he is free to devote himself completely to perfecting his craft (see also, the last paragraphs of "On the Nature of the Word"). Thus, Symbolism and its values as exemplified by Scriabin—the attainment of "pure music" and transcendence—are attacked here on esthetic as well as religious grounds. The artistic expression of pure passion, ecstasy or the mystical experience is condemned as not being Christian art or genuine art, for it lacks artistic control. Even the Classical Greeks made the "word" the guardian of music, while the Acmeists emphasized craft over "pure music" and demanded harmony and balance between "the voice" and "music" as in Beethoven's Ninth Symphony. Theosophy and Buddhism are condemned on social, moral and religious grounds, as leading mankind away from Christianity.

It is also interesting to note that many years later, in his Voronezh exile, Mandelstam wrote a poem treating the Prometheus theme, see No. 356.

15. For a discussion of Mandelstam's essay with reference to his and Tyutchev's poems, "Silentium," see Ryszard Przybylski, "Osip Mandelstam i muzyka," *Russian Literature* (The Hague, No. 2, 1972). See also, Kiril Taranovsky, "Dva 'Molchaniia' Osipa Mandelstama," *ibid.,* in which Mandelstam's poem is considered as a polemic against Tyutchev.

16. This section is rather incomprehensible unless it is read in conjunction with "The Slate Ode" (1923, No. 137). See D.M. Segal's fine discussion of this poem, "O nekotorykh aspektakh smyslovoi struktury 'Grifel'noi ody' O.E. Mandelstama," in *Russian Literature,* No. 2, 1972. Mandelstam seems to be saying here that memory rather than invention is the essence of art, for "to conquer oblivion" is to conquer death; hence, genuine art is immortal. The theme of the relative significance of "memory" and "invention" or "inventiveness" is also raised in "Literary Moscow" and elsewhere in Mandelstam's work.

17. This fragment must be read in conjunction with the following fragment.

18. Scriabin embraced World War I enthusiastically as the beginning of the long-awaited "cataclysm." See Hull, Swan, *op. cit.*

19. "Death" here in the sense of "Grace."

20. Christianity thus supports "memory" in its efforts to triumph over death, for Christianity offers the artist "the divine illusion of redemption." See above.

21. V.V. Gippius' pamphlet (see note No. 11, above) also helps to explain this passage. As Mandelstam (and Gippius) seem to perceive it, the Hellenes were prepared for Christianity, while the Romans were not. Gippius associates "the sensuality of the suffering man" with the "passion of the Christian experience," and claims that the Greeks understood "the interrelationship of sensuality and passion in just this way, in their tragic consciousness which identified passion and suffering as *Pathos."* (Gippius, p. 10).

22. That is, the reckoning of time from the birth of Christ; all that preceded being rendered as "B.C."

23. Mystical revelation can occur only when the individual merges with the eternal, divine, or Nirvana.

7. SERGEI GORODETSKY. *OLD NESTS: TALES AND STORIES*

This review first appeared in the newspaper, *The Day* (*Den',* October 21, 1913). See SS, II, 670.

1. Sergei Mitrofanovich Gorodetsky (1884-1967) began as a Symbolist poet; his first book, *Spring Corn* (*Iar',* 1907) was welcomed by both Bryusov and Blok, bringing him immediate fame. By the end of 1911, however, he had broken with the Symbolist movement and became one of the original founders of the Acmeists, joining Nikolai Gumilev in organizing the Guild of Poets. Gorodetsky's Acmeist manifesto, "Some Currents in Contemporary Russian Poetry," in fact an extremely partial comparison of Symbolist and Acmeist poets, appeared along with Gumilev's manifesto, "Acmeism and the Heritage of Symbolism," in the first issue of *Apollon* for 1913. And two of his poems, "Adam" and "The Stars," appeared in the third issue with poems by Gumilev, Akhmatova, and Mandelstam, as examples of Acmeist practice.

2. *Old Nests (Starye gnezda)* was published in St. Petersburg by A.S. Suvorin in 1913 in 3,100 copies. It is listed as No. 26914 in the *Knizhnaia letopis'* for 1913.

3. This story, at least, has much in common with Turgenev's more mystical tales,

such as "In the Region of Dead Calm."

8. JACK LONDON. *COLLECTED WORKS*

This review first appeared in the magazine *Apollon* (No. 3, 1913). It has never been reprinted.

1. Jack London (1876-1916). One of the most popular American writers in Russia. His work was translated into Russian as early as 1905, see *The Call of the Wild*. By 1913, when this review appeared, numerous novels and stories had already been translated, including: *The People of the Abyss* (trans. 1906), "Love of Life" (trans., 1907), *The Sea Wolf* (trans. 1911), *Martin Eden* and *The Iron Heel* (both trans., 1912).

2. On Andreev, see, "Literary Moscow: The Birth of Plot." Mandelstam was very hostile to Andreev, see also his comments in *The Noise of Time*.

3. Mandelstam's negative attitude toward cinematography is also expressed in his ironic poem of 1913, "The Cinematographer" (No. 50).

4. Jack London was known as an active American Socialist for many years. This may be one of the reasons behind his continued popularity in the Soviet Union, especially in the 1920s when a complete collection of his works was published: see *Polnoe sobranie sochinenii*, 24 volumes (M-L., 1928-1929).

9. J. K. HUYSMANS. *PARISIAN ARABESQUES*

This review first appeared in *Apollon* (No. 3, 1913). See SS, II, 670.

1. *Parisian Arabesques* is a translation of *Croquis parisiens*, dating from 1880. It is one of Huysman's earliest works. His first prose poems and sketches, *Le drageoir aux épices* (1874) and his first novel, *Marthe, histoire d'une fille* (1876), established Huysmans with Zola and his Médan group of Naturalist writers. His second novel, *Les soeurs Vatard* (1879) and his second collection of sketches, *Croquis parisiens* (1880), were also welcomed by them. Indeed, in 1880, he was asked to contribute a story to their collection of war stories, *Soirée de Médan*.

2. Joris Karl Huysmans (1848-1907). French novelist of Dutch descent. In Russia and elsewhere his name became a synonym for "decadence." His first recognition in a published article in Russia, in Zinaida Vengerova's collection, *Literaturnye kharakteristiki* (St. Petersburg, 1897, Vol. I) and his influence on Sologub and Bely are noted by G. Donchin in *The Influence of French Symbolism on Russian Poetry* (The Hague, 1958). Huysmans' work was reviewed in the Symbolist organ, *The Scales* and in *The Golden Fleece*, 1906.

Huysmans' literary work is best divided into two periods. From 1876 to 1884 he was associated with Emile Zola and his Naturalist school. During this time he also wrote *L'Art Moderne* (1883), in which he expressed one of the first positive evaluations of Impressionist painting.

His despair at the limitations of the Naturalist school apparently drove him to find other outlets for his talents. His second phase (1884-1907) led to his renown as a "decadent." His search for spiritual values in both art and religion made him extremely popular with the Symbolists. The chief interest and importance of his later novels resides in their autobiographical character, in their intensely personal tormented style which focuses on the vacillating, anguished spiritual odyssey of the hero.

3. Des Esseintes is the hero of Huysmans' extremely popular novel, *A Rebours* (1884), first reviewed in Russia in *The Golden Fleece*, No. 11-12 (1906). Des Esseintes

is the prototype of the decadent, the frail scion of an old family seeking to overcome his boredom through refined taste and extraordinary sensations. He is an esthetic idealist, morally ambiguous and drawn to occult religions.

4. *Là-Bas* (1891). In his later autobiographical novels, Huysmans followed the career of his hero, Durtal, who like himself, reconverted to Roman Catholicism through Satanism, was drawn to the physiological and spiritual world of the Middle Ages, to a Trappist monastery, and then to Chartres Cathedral. Durtal eventually became an oblate in a Benedictine monastery in the last novel of the series, *L'Oblat* (1903). For more details, see R. Baldick, *The Life of Joris Karl Huysmans* (1955).

5. Mandelstam's comments on the "physiological" and "organic" nature of Huysmans' early work and his attraction to the "real Middle Ages" should be compared with similar comments in his essays, including "François Villon," "Morning of Acmeism," and "Conversation about Dante" as well as with his poem "Notre Dame."

6. Simeon Stylites (c. 390-459). A Syrian monk who originated a dreadful form of asceticism which demanded standing continuously, day and night, and in any kind of weather, on top of a column. His tallest column, where he spent about 20 years, was about fifty feet high. Twice a day he would preach to an assembly of pilgrims below who gazed up at him as a superhuman example of piety and penitence.

10. I. ANNENSKY. *THAMYRIS THE CITHARA PLAYER*

This review first appeared in the newspaper, *The Day* (October 8, 1913). See, SS, II, 671.

1. Innokenty Annensky (1856-1909). Russian modernist poet, classical scholar, literary critic and inspired teacher. Greatly admired by the Acmeists. Akhmatova and Gumilev were also privileged to be his students. While Director of the Tsarskoe Selo Lyceum (1896-1906), Annensky translated the complete tragedies of Euripides and wrote four classical tragedies of his own, *Melanippa-Filosof, Tsar Iksion, Laodamiya,* and *Thamyris, the Cithara Player* (1906). The latter was his only tragedy to have been staged (1916). In 1904, he published his first book of verse, *Quiet Songs,* under the pseudonym, "Mr. Nobody." This volume contained about fifty original poems and a like number of translations, mainly modern French poets. However, this slight volume went almost unnoticed. Between 1906 and his death, he served as Inspector of the Petersburg School District, a job which allowed him more time for scholarship and poetry. His creative power reached its peak with the essays printed in his *Books of Reflections* and the poetry of *The Cypress Chest* published in 1910. In 1923, Annensky's son published another volume called *Posthumous Poems.*

In 1909, only about eight months before his sudden death, Sergei Makovsky and Gumilev, having obtained funds to establish a new modernist magazine, *Apollon,* offered Annensky a leading, although unofficial, editorial role. The reevaluation of Symbolism had begun in earnest, and Annensky, opposed to the turn French Symbolism had taken in Russia—the gradual replacement of the esthetic emphasis by mystical, religious and nationalistic tendencies—was pleased to be able to state his "esthetic point of view." He did so in his essay entitled "On Contemporary Lyricism" (*Apollon,* No. 1-3, 1909), an ironic and erudite attack on Russian Symbolism. This article was very influential on the young Acmeist movement. For more details, see Vsevolod Setchkarev, *Studies in the Life and Works of Innokentij Annenskij* (The Hague, 1963).

2. The best statement of Annensky's approach and intentions in creating this work is found in his letter to A.V. Borodina, August 2, 1906: "About six years ago I conceived a tragedy. I do not remember whether I told you the title. I dropped the idea; it was wiped away by other plans, poems, articles and events—then it flared up again.

In March I firmly resolved either to write my *Thamyris* by August or to give up the task.... Now, listen to the myth, which was little known over the ancient world and which apparently has not fascinated anyone in recent times. Thamyris... the son of the Thracian King, was a cytharoed, i.e., a player upon the cithara. He was born of the nymph Argiope. Thamyris' pride and success led him to challenge the Muses to a contest but he was blinded and deprived of his musical gifts. Sophocles wrote a tragedy about this myth which was lost, but we know by tradition that he was still a young man because he took the role of Thamyris himself in the play. Something attracted me to this theme a long time ago.... And now the reading of my *Thamyris* has already taken place...." (Setchkarev, pp. 36-37). Nevertheless, Annensky treated this legend quite freely. For instance, Argiope was turned into a bird, to punish her for her love. She perches on Thamyris' hand.

3. These are Thamyris' last words, representing his final despair.

4. Mandelstam's attitude toward music and its relationship to Classical drama is further discussed in the extant fragments of the essay "Pushkin and Scriabin," in particular the power of "pure music" and its relationship to "the word."

11. PAVEL KOKORIN. *THE MUSIC OF RHYMES: POESOPIECES*

This review first appeared in the newspaper, *The Day* (October 21, 1913). See SS, II, 671.

1. Pavel Kokorin. Vladimir Markov, in his excellent account of the Futurist movement, *Russian Futurism* (Berkeley and Los Angeles, 1968), characterizes Kokorin as follows: "Pavel Kokorin was a peasant encouraged by Severyanin in his poetic ventures. From 1909 to 1913 he published in St. Petersburg four books of very mediocre poetry, full of clumsy and illiterate lines, folksy in form and content, but occasionally betraying Severyanin's influence... Kokorin's first real attempt to appear 'modern' did not come until his fourth book, *Muzyka rifm: Poezopiesy (Music of Rhymes: Poesopieces)* whose subtitle is definitely ego-futurist. Despite its poor quality, the book is rather unique in concentrating heavily on two- and one-foot line poems and on poems filled with internal rhymes. His previously announced plan to publish eight more books of verse never materialized, and nothing was heard of him after 1913" (p. 207).

12. IGOR-SEVERYANIN. *THE THUNDER-SEETHING GOBLET*

This review first appeared in the Acmeist magazine, *Hyperboreus (Giperborei,* No. 6, March 1913) under the signature, "O.M." See, SS, III, 360.

1. Igor-Severyanin (pseudonym of Igor Vasilievich Lotarev, 1887-1942). Russian poet and creator-inventor of Ego-Futurism, one of several directions taken by the Russian Futurist movement. (See V. Markov, *Russian Futurism.* I am most indebted to Markov for my comments on Futurism and Severyanin.)

Although poorly educated and not very well-read, Severyanin was an extremely energetic and enthusiastic young poet. He began his career very early and published his verse in pamphlet form, in what he called "brochures." His favorite poets were Konstantin Fofanov (1862-1911) and Mirra Lokhvitskaya (1869-1905), neo-romantic poets also known as "impressionists."

Severyanin's first genuinely Futurist brochure, *Brooks Full of Lilies (Ruch'i v liliiakh)* appeared in 1911. It is preoccupied with neologisms, the attainment of variety, and concern to express his modernist drive to recombine, revise and simply revive numerous older genres of lyric poetry. These poems were all republished in his book, *The Thunder-Seething Goblet.*

In the fall of 1911, Severyanin formed his so-called "Ego-group," naming it the "intuitive school of Universal Ego-Futurism" or the "Academy of Ego-Poetry." He published an extremely laconic manifesto, later called "The Tables," which is actually little more than a declaration of unlimited individualism based on individual intuition justified as "theosophy." The basic characteristics of Ego-Futurism include the philosophical ideal of extreme individualism, poetic experimentation, the urban theme as reflecting modern life, eclecticism. The Ego-Futurists were also the only Futurist group seriously interested in ideology and metaphysics. The major Ego-Futurist poets included, besides Severyanin, Konstantin Olimpov (pseudonym of Konstantin K. Fofanov), Ivan Ignatiev, and Dmitry Kryuchkov.

2. The publication of *The Thunder-Seething Goblet* in 1913 by the Symbolist publishing house, Grif, was an enormous success. It represents the apex of Severyanin's popularity, which was to continue for several more years. He emigrated to Estonia in 1919.

3. The fact that Severyanin's book contains an introduction by the famous Symbolist poet, Fyodor Sologub, is significant. Vladimir Markov points out that "Sologub's interest in Ego-Futurism seems to be deeper than a personal enthusiasm for Severyanin's poetry; an essay entitled 'Ia: Kniga sovershennogo samoutverzhdeniia' ('I: A Book of Perfect Self-Assertion') has been preserved among his manuscripts" (p. 393).

4. Mandelstam's hostility to the Futurist movement is variously expressed in his prose writings. However, certain basic accusations frequently recur. As an Acmeist, as an admirer of Pushkinian "Classicism" and of the French Symbolist tradition (and perhaps the *École romane*), as a proponent of such basic Neo-Classical tenets as simplicity of outline and complexity of thematic treatment, Mandelstam sought poetic "dynamism" in efforts to achieve balance and harmony through striking juxtapositions of human, architectural or natural images in verbal constructions which astonish the reader's intellect as well as his senses. However, Mandelstam was hostile to the use of "dissonance," "discord," "fragmentation" for the end purpose of dynamism. He was hardly disturbed by "neologisms" or "foreign words" *per se,* but he was greatly distressed by what he considered "insensitivity to the laws of the Russian language" and to the inherent "aural" qualities of words and verbal relationships. Furthermore, he was disgusted by what he considered "superficial displays" and pretentious emphasis on the lyrical "I" (egoism) and the concomitant enmity shown toward the great poetry of the past—Dante, Pushkin, and Baratynsky among others.

On the other hand, Mandelstam greatly admired the enthusiasm, irony, spirit of vitality, and power or "dynamism" of Futurist poetry, and the insistence on treating themes of "this world." He was never so antagonistic to Futurism that he was unable to recognize and give credit to Futurist achievements. Indeed, his admiration for Khlebnikov is testimony to that ("Storm and Stress," or "Some Notes about Poetry"). In a word, he rejected outright what seemed to him the "confusion" of extremes—juxtaposition for the mere sake of juxtaposition—and the blatantly intentional "non-beautiful," anti-classical poetry of Futurism. But he praised Khlebnikov, for instance, for his deep knowledge of the Russian language, his humble experimentation, and genuine poetic achievements.

13. ON CONTEMPORARY POETRY

Mandelstam's polemical review of the *Almanac of Muses* (*Almanakh muz,* Petrograd: Felana, 1916; 192 pages) was never published in the Soviet Union. It first appeared in SS, III, pp. 27-30, in 1969. Reasons given for its not being published vary, but it was most likely due to Mandelstam's own poems being included (No. 8, 44, 84, 85) in the almanac (SS, III, 355-56) and to the extremely critical statements about Symbolism and its adherents, in particular Bryusov and Ivanov (See Khardziev, below).

In his article "Vosstanovlennyi Mandelstam" (*Russian Literature*, No. 7/8, 1974, pp. 19-22), N. Khardzhiev reproduces the text of "the author's final redaction" found in the poet's personal archive. While the differences between this text and the text included in SS, III are not numerous, they are worth noting in the annotations to this text. Most important, the incorrect or incomplete citations from the poems have all been verified. My translation is based on the Khardzhiev text.

1. This is a theme which runs through Mandelstam's essays. Its clearest statement is found in "On the Nature of the Word."

2. This line was omitted in the SS variant.

3. On Pushkin, see "On the Addressee."

4. Gavriil Romanovich Derzhavin (1743-1816). The most original poet of the Russian eighteenth century. Primarily known as an ode-writer, he completely transformed that genre by gradually introducing elements from the major lyric genres of his day into the panegyric and triumphal odes. His greatest ode is "The Waterfall" (1798). Other famous odes include his "Ode to Felitsa" (1773), "On the Death of Prince Meshchersky" (1779), and "Ode to God" (1784). His last (incomplete) poem, "The River of Time" (1816), left a deep impression on Mandelstam; indeed, it serves as the major subtext of his own magnificent poem No. 137, "The Slate Ode." For more details, see my forthcoming book, *G. R. Derzhavin: The Poet in Evolution*. For translations, see Harold B. Segel, *The Literature of Eighteenth Century Russia* (New York, 1967).

5. Mikhail Vasilievich Lomonosov (1711-1765). Famous eighteenth-century Russian poet, literary theorist, academician, and scientist. While Lomonosov's odes are uneven in poetic quality, individual lines and passages left their mark on many later Russian poets. His greatest odes are his "Morning Meditations" (1751) and "Evening Meditations on God's Majesty" (1748), although he is equally well-known for his triumphal odes and panegyrics as well as odes on scientific themes, such as his "Epistle on Glass" (1752) dedicated to Shuvalov. For translations, see H.B. Segel, *op. cit.*

6. The word "almanac" is used in Russian to denote "anthology" or "collection." "Almanacs" were extremely popular in the first quarter of the twentieth century. See the fascinating bibliographical reference, *Literaturno-khudozhestvennye al'-manakhi i sborniki* (Moscow, 1957-).

Among the poems included in the *Almanac of the Muses* were: I. Annensky, "Esli liubish'–gori!...," V. Bryusov, "Na zakatnom pole," "Gorod sester liubvi," V. Ivanov, two poems from his cycle *Elevsinskie nochi:* "Vesna," "Drema Orfeia," M. Kuzmin, "Vse dni u boga khoroshi!...," "Sredi nochnykh i dolgikh bdenii," V.V. Gippius (Neledinskii, V.), "Vliublennost' (poema)," A. Akhmatova, "Ty mne ne obeshchan ni zhizn'iu, ni bogom...," "Pod kryshei promerzshei pustogo zhil'ia...," "Iz pamiati tvoei ia vynu etot den'," "Muza ushla po doroge...," and M. Tsvetaeva, "S bol'shoiu nezhnost'-iu –potomu," "V tumane, sinee ladana...," "Otkuda takaia nezhnost'," "Otmykala larets zheleznyi."

7. Valery Yakovlevich Bryusov (1873-1924). Russian Symbolist poet, prose writer, translator, literary critic, and scholar. Founder of *The Scales (Vesy)*, the organ of the Russian Symbolist movement and the most important magazine of the epoch (1904-1909), both in terms of keeping abreast of the French literary scene and publishing the best Russian Symbolist works. Bryusov may properly be included among the founders of Russian Symbolism since he not only helped to edit and publish three small books or almanacs entitled *Russian Symbolists* (1894-1895)–considered the formal beginning of Russian Symbolism, but to write his own modernist poems (poor imitations of French *fin-de-siècle* poetry) rather than merely translate French originals.

In addition, most of the contributors to these volumes were Bryusov's fictitious creations intended to impress the reading public that there was indeed a Symbolist movement in Russia.

Bryusov was profoundly influenced by French Symbolism, in particular by Baudelaire and Mallarmé. His Symbolism is predominantly esthetic (rather than religious) in orientation, international (rather than nationalistic) in scope, and is dedicated to experimentation, to the craft of poetry as "the supreme form of art." Following Baudelaire, Bryusov asserted the dictum: "Poetry has no end but itself" (the antithesis of V. Ivanov's belief, and that held by the second generation of Russian Symbolists, that art cannot be severed from religion). Following Mallarmé, Bryusov considered poetry a "sacred duty," art being a rite, an esoteric practice, whose priest and seer is the poet.

Bryusov was extremely prolific as a poet, translator, scholar, and prose fiction writer. He was very bookish in his thematic interests, and fascinated by remote historical epochs, legends, languages, and "high" culture, as well as by modernist erotic and urban themes and images. English translations of some of his best and most influential poems are found in Vladimir Markov's anthology, *Modern Russian Poetry* (Indianapolis, 1967). For more details on Bryusov and his role in bringing French Symbolist values to Russia, see Georgette Donchin's excellent book, *The Influence of French Symbolism on Russian Poetry* (The Hague, 1958). See also Volume 21 of Bryusov's *Collected Works* (SS, St. Petersburg: Sirin, 1913) for his translations of 19th century French poets and his "Foreword" to Ellis' translation of Baudelaire's *Les Fleurs du mal* (M, 1908). On Bryusov, see M. Rice, *Valery Briusov and The Rise of Russian Symbolism* (Ardis, 1976) and K. Mochulsky, *Valerij Briusov* (Paris:YMCA Press, 1962). Mandelstam's more positive view of Bryusov's contribution to Russian poetry appears in "Storm and Stress."

8. Vyacheslav Ivanovich Ivanov (1866-1949). Major poet and theoretician of the religious-mystical direction of the Russian Symbolist movement as well as a professor and scholar of Classics and Ancient History. After the publication of his first volume of poems, *Guiding Stars* (*Kormchie zvezdy*, 1902), Ivanov became the spiritual leader of the St. Petersburg Symbolists and was known to them as "Vyacheslav the Magnificent." From 1905 on, his pent-house apartment, "The Tower," became the central meeting place of the Petersburg modernists. His other collections of poetry include *Transparency* (*Prozrachnost'*, 1904), *Eros* (1907), *Cor ardens* (1909-1911), *Winter Sonnets* (1919), and *Roman Sonnets* (1924-25, written in Rome).

He is also author of a tragedy, *Prometheus* (1916), which is an attempt to present the theme of human freedom combining the idea of Prometheus as a Dionysian hero with the Christian concept of sacrifice. (See notes to Mandelstam's essay "Pushkin and Scriabin").

Ivanov's theoretical ideas and critical essays are presented in several volumes, including *Toward the Stars* (*Po zvezdam*, 1909) and *Furrows and Boundaries* (*Borozdy i mezhi*, 1916). In his fascinating *Correspondence between Two Corners* (1921) written in conjunction with the philosopher, essayist, and literary historian, Mikhail Osipovich Gershenzon (1869-1925), Ivanov emerges as a defender of humanism and the Classical tradition as against the values of the Revolution.

Ivanov's essays "Two Elements in Contemporary Symbolism" (1908) and "Thoughts on Symbolism" (1912) include his most lucid attempts to explain his beliefs that the highest calling of the poet is to serve God and help the reader experience a sense of union with the Divine Spirit. In the latter essay, he simultaneously attacks the defenders of the autonomy of art as having "no knowledge of Symbolism." Mandelstam's attempts to refute the latter essay appear in "On the Addressee" and "Morning of Acmeism." A more positive revaluation of Ivanov appears in "Storm and Stress." For further discussion of Ivanov's theoretical work, see James West, *Russian Symbolism:*

A Study of Vyacheslav Ivanov and the Russian Symbolist Esthetic, (London, 1970).

9. In the SS variant, this line is followed by:

> The poet feels so much at home with his own images that he is too lazy to create anything and utters instead incantations completely devoid of all magic:
>> But to me the phenomena... of spring
>> Are as sorrowful as forgotten dreams.
>
> (he has apparently attained such sublimity that he is able to touch the cithara even as he drowses, barely fingering its strings.)

10. From Ivanov's "Spring."

11. In the SS variant, this line is followed by: "the poet feels himself a Magus composing stanzas of verse."

12. From Bryusov's "On the Field at Sunset" ("Na zakatnom pole").

13. From Bryusov's "City of the Sisters of Love" ("Gorod sester liubvi").

14. This line is followed in the SS variant by: "(it is now located in the venerable archives along with Nadson's 'Baal')."

15. Mikhail Alekseevich Kuzmin (1875-1936). A Russian modernist poet and prose writer claimed by both the Symbolists and Acmeists. He exemplifies one kind of poetic transition away from Symbolism experienced by the St. Petersburg poets in the inter-revolutionary years. His best known collections of poetry include his pastoral *Seasons of Love* (1907), stylized in accord with the traditions of the eighteenth century and set to Kuzmin's own music, and his *Alexandrian Songs* (1908) modelled on Pierre Louys' *Chansons de Bilitis.*

His later collections of poetry include *Parabolas* (1923) and *The Trout Breaks the Ice* (*Forel' razbivaet led,* Leningrad, 1929). Unfortunately, very little of Kuzmin's work is available in English translation. For some idea of the early Kuzmin, see M. Kuzmin, *Wings: Prose and Poetry,* translated by N. Granoien and M. Green (Ardis, 1972).

Kuzmin is also famous for his essay "On Beautiful Clarity" (*Apollon,* 1910) which foreshadowed several of the Acmeist tenets.

16. This is a major tenet of Mandelstam's esthetic. See its clearest statement in "Tristia" (1918):

> All was before, all will be repeated again,
> And only the moment of recognition is sweet.

17. Anna Andreevna Akhmatova (penname of Anna Gorenko, 1889-1966). One of the most outstanding Russian poets of the twentieth century, a member of the Acmeist movement, erstwhile wife of Nikolai Gumilev, its founder, and long-time friend of Osip Mandelstam and his wife, Nadezhda Yakovlevna (see N. Y. Mandelstam's two books of memoirs, *Hope Against Hope* and *Hope Abandoned, op. cit.*).

Akhmatova's best known collections of poetry were published between 1912 and 1922, after which time she was silent for two decades. These collections include *Evening* (1912), *The Rosary* (1914), *The White Flock* (1918)—the verses cited below are in this collection—*Road Grass* (1921), *Anno Domini MCMXXI* (1922). Her later poetry includes the famous longer poems, *The Requiem* and *A Poem without a Hero.* (Translations of these and other poems are in A. Akhmatova, *Selected Poems* (Ardis, 1976).

Akhmatova is best known as an accomplished master of the small and intimate personal drama in verse. Her style is spare, terse, and precise, endowing her poetry with an intensity of feeling associated with Annensky's "psychologism." Her descriptive poetry is perhaps the most Acmeist in inspiration. Her models are Pushkin, Annensky and to a certain extent, Kuzmin. During her "silent years" Akhmatova completed scholarly studies of Pushkin. Her memoirs of Mandelstam are extremely perceptive. For an English translation of those memoirs, see *Russian Literature Triquarterly,* No. 9 (Spring, 1974). For more details about Akhmatova and her poetry, see the fine studies by Sam Driver, Kees Verheul, and Boris Eikhenbaum.

18. See Note 1 to Mandelstam's review of Annensky's *Thamyris, the Cithara Player*.

19. The last two lines of Akhmatova's "Under the icy roof of the empty dwelling" ("Pod kryshei promerzshei pustogo zhil'ia").

20. This paragraph was omitted in the SS variant.

21. Pushkin's line from "I remember the school at life's beginning" ("V nachale zhizni shkolu pomniu ia").

14. GOVERNMENT AND RHYTHM

This essay first appeared in *Paths of Creation (Puti tvorchestva)*, Kharkov, 1920. See SS, III, 363-364.

1. For Mandelstam's major statements about social organization, see "A Revolutionary in the Theater," "Humanism and the Present," as well as the last section of "Morning of Acmeism."

2. For other apprehensive statements pertaining to decreasing interest in esthetic values in the new society, specifically, in "philology" or "the word," see the essays of the early 1920s, in particular, "The Word and Culture" and "On the Nature of the Word." This theme is also very much present in the poetry of the early 1920s, if in a more ambiguous form.

3. Émile Jacques-Dalcroze (1865-1950). Swiss composer and educator. A pioneer in the teaching of Eurhythmics, a term used to designate the representation of musical rhythms by bodily movements. His goal was to "create by the help of rhythm a rapid and regular current of communication between the brain and the body"; his pupils were taught to indicate note-values by movements of the feet, and time-values by arm movements. The training was intended to develop the power of concentration and rapid physical reaction. See his *Méthode Jacques-Dalcroze* (1907-1914). It has been pointed out by the editors of Mandelstam's *Collected Works* that: "At the beginning of the 1920s Mandelstam often frequented the studios of rhythmic movement (gymnastic dancing according to the Dalcroze system) on the Petrograd Side of Leningrad, where Mikhail Kuzmin, Yury Shaporin and others were also frequent guests..." Furthermore, not only Mandelstam, but Blok, Piast, Kuzmin and Vsevolod Rozhdestvensky "even participated in the masquerade organized by the schools of rhythmic gymnastics" (SS, III, 363-365).

Clarence Brown (*Mandelstam*, p. 72) points out that when Mandelstam was employed in Lunacharsky's Ministry of Education in 1918, he organized "something called the Institute of Rhythmics." I have not succeeded in obtaining any information, but this essay seems to indicate that that was a rather positive experience. Indeed, the essay may be an outgrowth of that experience.

4. Hellerau, Germany, near Dresden was the site of Jacques-Dalcroze's first institute, established in 1910. In 1914, he transferred his school to Geneva, where it became known as the Institute Jacques-Dalcroze. Meanwhile, the Dalcroze method became very fashionable, and other schools were set up in London, Paris, Berlin, Vienna, Stockholm and New York.

5. Mandelstam's cautionary statements are reminiscent of I.A. Aksenov's premonitions for the future expressed in his fascinating book *Picasso and the Environment* (*Pikasso i okresnosti*, M.: 1917, p. 6): Aksenov's words are worth quoting:

> If we have reason to suppose that art is fundamentally rhythm which is perceptible subject only to the material which gives the rhythm its flesh, and if we allow, moreover, the correctness of the opinion about the progressive paralysis of the visual arts, we arrive at the possibility of defining this process as the

development of rhythmic susceptibility which rejects as useless the crudest coverings of rhythm. The evolutionary interpretation of the above process must eventually lead to a recognition of the necessity to get rid of the last intermediate vestiges of the veritable substance of art. The need for a verbal expression of rhythm will pass just like the requirement (let's say) for its sculptural verisimilitude. After poetry, it will be the turn of music: there are already those who tire us out with their talk of the uselessness of sound effects. For our progeny in the far distant future, for those highly developed rhythmical beings, art will cease to exist: it must die. Rhythmical needs will be met by the contemplation of mathematical formulas which will establish the functional dependence on every kind of rhythmical process. In the future, we will probably be confined to inhaling air through our right nostrils and exhaling it through our left. How unbounded the perspectives of mystics!

15. THE WORD AND CULTURE

This essay first appeared in the Guild of Poets' almanac, *The Dragon* (Petersburg, 1921) and was reprinted (with no change except the elimination of the misprints) in the almanac, *Guild of Poets* 1(Berlin, 1922). However, when it was published in Mandelstam's collection of essays, *On Poetry* (1928), several changes were made, most of which were connected with the religious theme, the imagery of Christianity, and the political theme of the French Revolution. For details, see SS, II, pp. 625-27. These changes were undoubtedly the result of censorship, but how much was externally enforced and how much self-invoked remains unknown. After writing "The Word and Culture," which is in many ways closely related to "Pushkin and Scriabin," at least in its attempts to reconcile Christian mythology with classical or neo-classical esthetics, Mandelstam ceased to include much Christian imagery in his work, in particular, that of Death, Grace, and Resurrection, that is, until his *Journey to Armenia* (published 1933).

1. The esthetic tenets of "astonishment" and "metamorphosis" (or "transformation") as well as the Christian imagery associated with culture and the cultured person relate this essay to "Pushkin and Scriabin." However, while in the latter, the definition of Christian art was applied only to the artist, here (in keeping with Mandelstam's interest in the theme of art and society, more specifically, with the role of the esthetic forces in the new social structure) it is applied to the relationship of the State and Culture.

2. From Pushkin's narrative poem *The Gypsies,* lines 194-97.

3. The relationship of the old world to the new is one of the dominant themes of Mandelstam's work during this period (1921-25). See, for instance, such poems as No. 135, "My Age, My Monster," No. 140, "Jan. 1, 1924," *The Noise of Time,* as well as the essay "The Nineteenth Century," among others.

4. Ovid's *Tristia,* Book I, No. 3, lines 1-4, a literal translation being: "When I remember the fearful image of that night which marked my last moments in Rome, when I recall that night when I left so many precious things behind, even now tears flow from my eyes."

5. See "Pushkin and Scriabin." There only the poet obtained a sense of freedom as a result of the "divine illusion of redemption." Here "every cultured person" has gained "inner freedom . . . joy," and is a "Christian."

6. While the Revolution of 1917 is seemingly equated in this essay with "redemption," with providing "every cultured person" with "inner freedom . . . joy," the new State is not. The State must be tempered by culture (the Church).

7. See poem No. 108, "Sisters—heaviness and tenderness" (1920).

8. Reference to Jacques Louis David's paintings of scenes from the French Revo-

lution. See Note 13 to the essay on Chénier discussing David's painting of the "Tennis-Court Oath."

9. From Catullus' "Carmen No. XLVI." Boris Eikhenbaum's comments on Catullus and Blok are pertinent here: "In speaking of Catullus, Blok was alluding to himself: Catullus' personal passion, like the passion of any poet, was filled with the spirit of his age; its fate, its rhythm and measure, just as the rhythms and measures of the poet's verses were inculcated in him by his time; because in the poetic experience of the world there is no break between the personal and the universal; the more sensitive the poet, the more inseparable he feels what is "his" and "not his"; because in epochs of storms and alarms, the most tender and intimate yearnings of the poet's soul also express the same storms and alarms" (B. Eikhenbaum, "Blok's Fate" [1921], in *Skvoz' literaturu* (L. 1924, p. 223.)

10. See Mandelstam's poem No. 104, "Tristia" (1918). Furthermore, Pushkin's "presentiments" may be read, at least in part, for this poem and its greater references, as Pushkin's early (1812) poems "O Delia dear" and "Delia." These poems are mentioned by Gippius in his pamphlet *Pushkin and Christianity* as essential to understanding Pushkin's creative development and the evolution of his creative process.

11. See No. 6, above.

12. This is an implicit attack on the poetics of the Futurists, and, indeed, on the polemics raging between the various literary groups of the time.

13. See the essay "Pushkin and Scriabin" for Mandelstam's discussion of the relationship between Christian art and death.

14. Baudelaire's *Les Fleurs du Mal* (1857), was extremely influential on the Symbolist movement in France, Russia, and elsewhere, in particular in providing examples of "decadent" themes. [See Note 8 to "Morning of Acmeism," referring to the poem "Correspondances." Also Ellis' Russian translations of *Les Fleurs du Mal* (M. 1908), with a foreword by Bryusov.] "Une charogne" was one of Baudelaire's most popular poems.

15. Suprematism in Russian painting paralleled the Futurist movement in Russian poetry. Suprematism was most closely connected with the names of the painters Kasimir Malevich (1878-1935) and Ivan Puni (1894-1956), both of whom were associated with the Futurists, in particular, Ego-Futurism. The best definition of Suprematism is, perhaps, that expressed in a handout distributed at the famous avant-garde "0.10" exhibition (advertised as "The Last Futurist Exhibition of Paintings") in the winter of 1915. The handout was signed by Puni and his wife K. Boguslavskaya: "An object is the sum of real units, a sum which has a utilitarian purpose . . . A picture is a new conception of abstracted real elements, deprived of meaning. . . An object (a world) freed from meaning disintegrates into real elements—the foundation of art" (From I. Puni and K. Boguslavskaya's *Manifesto of Suprematism*, P. 1915, cited in John E. Bowlt's "Artists of the World, Disunite," Catalogue for the exhibition *Russian Avant-Garde: 1908-22*, Leonard Hutton Galleries, N.Y., 1971, pp. 10-14). In Malevich's later Suprematist works, culminating in his famous "White on White" series of 1917, even color was completely eliminated, and emphasis given to "The Infinite Whiteness." Malevich's ideal of painting, to which he referred as the "pure sensation of infinity," triumphed. No human measure is present; and even his earlier attempts to contrast new and old space (or concepts of space) is gone. Thus, as Camilla Gray states in *The Great Experiment* (N.Y., 1962), p. 140: "Form in the purest, most de-humanized shape of the square has been reduced to the faintest pencilled outline."

16. Here Mandelstam more explicitly contrasts Futurist techniques and intentions with the "decadent" themes of their Symbolist predecessors. For the Symbolists, death and destruction were often presentiments of life and resurrection, of the coming Milennium, of the New Age. The Symbolists in this interpretation, were martyrs for a cause—for the future. The Futurists, however, as Mandelstam sees them here, were interested

in negating phenomena for the sake of negation alone. Hence, the following paragraph, that "the word" itself is endangered, in particular, if the State determines to support Futurism.

17. This theme is further developed in "The Nineteenth Century" and in the last chapter of *The Noise of Time.*

18. See Note 12, "The Nineteenth Century," and Note 3, "On Contemporary Poetry." Also Mandelstam's "The Slate Ode" and an excellent commentary on it by D. M. Segal, *op. cit.*

19. Mandelstam's poem No. 103, "Twilight/Dawn of Freedom" written in May, 1918, has been variously interpreted. Basically, it expresses Mandelstam's ambiguous attitude toward the Revolution and the role of the State in the new society. Stephen J. Broyde points out how ambiguous and untranslatable this poem is, for both meanings of "sumerki" are intended: the ominous "twilight" and the rousing "dawn's early light," see *Osip Mandelstam and His Age* (Cambridge, Massachusetts: 1975, pp. 46-61).

20. This is a reference to Stanza 6 of Verlaine's "Art poétique." Verlaine retains Mandelstam's admiration.

21. This is a basic tenet of Mandelstam's esthetic. See its statement in his "Octets" in particular No. 281.

22. See Note 10, above.

23. See Note 20, above. Verlaine's poem, "Écoutez la chanson bien douce."

24. See Mandelstam's poem No. 124, "I love the gray silence under the arches" (1921), in which "grain" and "granaries" are associated with spiritual culture and, hence, the "word" (Logos).

25. "Classical" and "revolutionary": in the sense of that which lives to be "transformed" and to "astonish."

16. ON THE NATURE OF THE WORD

This major essay first appeared as a separate booklet in Kharkov in 1922. It was commissioned by Madame Rakovskaya (sister of the Premier of the Ukraine, K.G. Rakovsky) who had established a small publishing house, *Istoki,* in the Ukrainian capital. She also commissioned Mandelstam's first piece of prose fiction, "The Fur Coat" ("Shuba"), which has yet to be found. Significantly, it was Rakovskaya, and not Mandelstam, who chose as the epigraph for this essay stanzas from Nikolai Gumilev's poem "The Word" ("Slovo," 1921). This essay was subsequently included in Mandelstam's collection, *On Poetry,* without the epigraph, without the entire last section (see Note 42, below), and with a number of other changes and omissions. See SS, II, 631-636. See also comments on the publication of this essay in N.Y. Mandelstam, *Hope Abandoned,* pp. 72-74, and C. Brown, *Mandelstam,* p. 97.

1. The epigraph comprises the last two stanzas of Gumilev's "The Word." Nikolai Stepanovich Gumilev (1886-1921). poet, literary critic, instructor, and co-founder (with Sergei Gorodetsky) of the Guild of Poets (November, 1911), and subsequently of the Acmeist movement, and husband of Anna Akhmatova (until 1918). Gumilev's masters were Bryusov and Annensky. After the Revolution and before his assassination for alleged counter-revolutionary activities (1921), Gumilev served as an instructor in creative writing (poetry) in the Studio for Literature sponsored by the House of the Arts in Leningrad where Zamiatin and Shklovsky were instructors in prose.

Gumilev is best known for his poetry of masculine heroism and romantic adventure, although such themes are virtually absent from his most mature, later collections. His earliest books, including *The Path of the Conquistadors* (1905), *Romantic Flowers* (1908), and *Pearls* (1910) are Symbolist in inspiration and orientation. His books of

1912-1916 are his most Acmeist in their concreteness and precision of style, in their man-centered thematic material, and non-mystical ideology: *Foreign Skies* (1912), *The Quiver* (1916). His later poetry, however, is characterized by a new mystical and religious tendency, a more personal element, and an interest in fantasy, see for instance, "The Word" and "The Streetcar Gone Astray" from his last and most mature collection, *Pillar of Fire* (1921). See M. Maline, *Nicolas Gumilev* (Brussels, 1964).

    2. Simeon Polotsky (1629-1680). Seventeenth century poet at the court of Tsar Alexei Mikhailovich, tutor of the Tsar's children, church leader, and literary innovator. He introduced the syllabic system of versification into Muscovite Russia along with a variety of new literary forms from southwest Russia.

    3. Mandelstam's reverence for mathematics and his consequent use of mathematical metaphors in depicting the poet, poetry and "the word," appear in several essays, beginning with "Morning of Acmeism": "The spectacle of a mathematician who, without seeming to think about it, produces the square of some ten-digit number, fills us with a kind of astonishment. But too often we fail to see that a poet raises a phenomenon to its tenth power, and the modest exterior of a work of art often deceives us with regard to the monstrously condensed reality [the word as such] contained within." In "The Nineteenth Century," Mandelstam singles out mathematics as the only science allowing for "genuine cognition." His interest in mathematics is undoubtedly related to his poetic quest after the "principle of unity" in the universe best expressed through his preoccupation with the theme of time. See, for instance, such poems as No. 54 (1913), No. 108 (1920), or the entire collection *Second Book* (1921-1925). Nevertheless, as opposed to Khlebnikov who devoted an extraordinary amount of energy to the study of mathematics for the intent purpose of discovering the mathematical laws of time (history), Mandelstam was a poet above all else, and his actual knowledge of mathematics was limited. However, Mandelstam's recognition of mathematical laws as a means to understanding time (history), presented in this essay, may in some way have been influenced by Khlebnikov's work, or both may have been ultimately influenced by Henri Bergson whose attempts to perceive time "being made" as opposed to static, "ready-made" time, are found throughout his work. Bergson's interest in "modern mathematics" is worth quoting here: "Modern mathematics is precisely an effort to substitute the *being made* for the *ready-made*, to follow the generation of magnitudes, to grasp motion no longer from without and in its displayed result, but from within and in its tendency to change; in short, to adopt the mobile continuity of the outlines of things..." (from T.E. Hulme's translation of "Introduction à la métaphysique," 1903, New York, 1949, p. 52). See also Mandelstam's "Octets."

    As early as 1915, Khlebnikov had lamented that no one had bothered to explore the laws of time, while the laws of space had been carefully analyzed. See his "Bugi na nebe," as well as Vladimir Markov's comments on it in *Russian Futurism* p. 294 . Mandelstam's relationship with Khlebnikov remains to be studied. However, his admiration for Khlebnikov's contributions to Russian poetry is expressed in numerous essays (see Index). Although Nadezhda Mandelstam tends to downplay Mandelstam's interest in Khlebnikov's poetry (one suspects that this is as much her own taste as his), she emphasizes his interest in Khlebnikov the man. In 1922, just before Khlebnikov's death, the Mandelstams helped to feed him and attempted to find him a permanent room in Herzen House: "[Mandelstam seemingly] looked upon him as a 'man of God.' He never showed as much care and concern for anyone as he did for Khlebnikov. As regards Khlebnikov's verse, he liked bits and pieces of it . . . In Samatikha [the sanatorium where Mandelstam was arrested for the last time] in the spring of 1938, we had two volumes of Khlebnikov with us . . ." (*Hope Abandoned*, pp. 89-97). Furthermore, Nadezhda Yakovlevna notes: "In Kharkhov [1921] we were told about certain new developments already known to a lot of people: news of the theory of relativity and of Freud, delayed because of the war, had only now reached Russia. Everybody was talking about them, but actual information was vague and amorphous" (*Hope Abandoned*, p. 74).

4. Henri Bergson (1859-1941). French philosopher of evolution whose work exerted an enormous influence on European intellectual circles. In the first two decades of the twentieth century, Bergson's teachings were extremely popular in Russia, affecting among others, Pasternak, Mandelstam, Mikhail Gershenzon, and probably, Khlebnikov. Bergson's major works include: *Essai sur les données immédiates de la conscience* (1889), *Matière et mémoire* (1896), "Introduction à la métaphysique" (1903), *L'Evolution créatrice* (1907), *Les Deux sources de la morale et de la religion* (1932). Bergson's collected works were published in Russia between 1910 and 1914.

Popular interpretations of Bergson's philosophy often reduced it to nothing more than a defense of biological vitalism, which aspect of Bergsonianism is emphasized in Pasternak's *My Sister, Life*, for example. However, even in his earliest work, Bergson's emphasis on spiritual and moral freedom obviously transcended his biological critique of freedom and human nature. It is interesting to note this conflict between the spiritual and physiological character of freedom in Mandelstam's earliest essay, "François Villon," wherein the poet questions the relationship between Villon's poetic dynamism and morality. However, in "Peter Chaadaev" (1915), Mandelstam already regards freedom as "moral freedom," indeed, as Russia's contribution to the West (this may very well be Mandelstam's response to the Russian intellectual tendency to regard Western freedom as predominantly "amoral," see Dostoevsky, Rozanov, et al.). By the early 1920s, when Mandelstam wrote "On the Nature of the Word," Bergson already represented the philosophical possibility of uniting physiological and moral freedom. Toward the end of his essay, Mandelstam specifically comments on the limitations of a purely "biological canon" of poetics, the "organic school of Russian poetry" (Acmeism), and asserts the need to transcend all schools and movements for poetry, for "philology," for the love of "the Word as such"—notice the peculiarly Khlebnikovian-Mandelstamian play on wordroots which colors this entire essay ("philia" + "logos"). He defines the word in Bergsonian terms as a "verbal representation": "The verbal representation is a complex composite of phenomena, it is a connection, 'a system'." By "system" he means: "a system in the Bergsonian sense of the term which man unfolds around himself like a fan of phenomena freed of their temporal dependence, phenomena subjected by the human 'I' to an internal connection."

In this essay, Mandelstam views language as the unifying force of history (temporally related phenomena of perception) and culture (spatially related phenomena which endure outside of time). "Philological" or verbal freedom (what he calls the "philological system") thus supersedes "physiological" freedom (the biological "system") in Mandelstam's canon. Nevertheless, Mandelstam's esthetic vision (as represented in its fullest form in his "Octets") contains three major aspects: the esthetic, the historical and the biological. Mandelstam perceives the poet's role as rediscovering, recognizing, preserving and passing on to posterity the eternal verities, morality being one of the eternal verities. Mandelstam obviously found support for his esthetic views in Bergson's theory of the system of phenomena, in particular, in the concept of time as "duration" (la durée) and in the concept of the continuity or "creative evolution" *(l'évolution créatrice)* or eternal recurrence and metamorphosis of eternal values.

Mandelstam's interest in Bergson thus centers around the French philosopher's attempts to find the unity, or unifying force behind the two basic aspects of the human essence. Bergson defines these aspects as the "material-vital aspect" (animal instinct or the life force) and the "spiritual-vital aspect" (human aspiration or the moral and spiritual force expressed in art, ethics, religion and science). Furthermore, Bergson endeavors to distinguish between two fundamental modes of cognition, one which can perceive the unity of the two aspects of the human essence, the other which cannot. The "simple intellect," which is ordered and bound by Time, which is expressed through the "static" abstractions of logic, cannot achieve such unity because it merely analyzes and thereby decomposes all phenomena in accord with the physical demands of the principle of time, with the laws of causality. On the other hand, "intuition," the act or series of acts of direct participation in the immediacy of experience, demands expression in "fluid concepts" or metaphors. Of these two modes of human cognition, "intuition" is capable of grasping the "duration" *(la durée)* of reality, the mobility or flow of life and time, "becoming" (or process) and "evolution" (or change), that is, "intuition" perceives reality as a continuous, spontaneous and creative evolutionary process *(l'évolution créatrice)* rather than as a series of linked or connected impulses or phases interrupted by intermediary transitions. Reality or human action perceived as "duration" can never be reduced to mere precedents, to the laws of causality; reality is essentially perceived as outside of, or beyond Time. However, cosmic development must not be viewed as a linear development, for there is no "radical finalism," or as Mandelstam states it, there can be no vulgar "theory of progress."

Following Bergson's esthetic theories, Mandelstam views the poet as the master of "intuition." The poet seeks to perceive the unity and continuity of life and to preserve that unity and continuity for posterity by shaping it, by giving it artistic form. He can do so, however, only by mastering the craft of poetry. In this way, the poet acts both spontaneously, in accord with his intuition, and rationally, in accord with the demands of poetic craft (posited autonomous esthetic criteria) to give form (eternal shape or structure) to the objects ("object-words") of his spontaneous intuition, thereby "extending a hand to the master craftsman of things and material values, to the builder and creator of the material world."

Thus, in "On the Nature of the Word," Mandelstam endeavors to synthesize the basic tenets of Acmeism with a broader, more metaphysically oriented esthetic vision. Moreover, Mandelstam's essay may be read as a defense of Bergson and "creative evolution" against the Futurists, who posited the idea of the destruction of "the past," the complete antithesis of the idea of continuity or "creative evolution"; against the materialists, who would not recognize the autonomous nature of "the word"; and against the various popular interpretations of Bergson, which viewed the French philosopher as no more than a proponent of biological vitalism.

A monograph on Bergson's impact on Mandelstam (and on Russian poetry and culture of the first two decades of the twentieth century) is sorely wanting.

5. See, in particular, Mandelstam's "Slate Ode" for a poetic vision of the power of "internal connections," unities in the face of Time. Poetry and poetic genius is capable of perceiving and perpetrating this power (Derzhavin, Lermontov, Pushkin, Mandelstam himself). Or, as Lidiya Ginzburg has so carefully expressed the central theme of this remarkable poem: "In the complex semantic instrumentation of "Slate Ode," *water* is an emblem of time. Water-time erodes *flint*—that which resists time, while *slate*,—the vehicle of creativity—interprets time" ("Poetika Osipa Mandelstama," *Izvestiia Akademii Nauk SSSR.* Seriia literatury i iazyka, July-August 1972, 310-327).

6. See the opening paragraph of "The Word and Culture" for a statement of Mandelstam's poetic vision of genuine "progress" as the "recurrence" of Classical or eternal values. He terms St. Petersburg the most "progressive city" because signs of eternal values (green grass) rise up through the pavement of the present technological age, that is, genuine progress is expressed in the "recurrence" of the eternal verities, whatever form their metamorphoses may take. As such they act as a kind of check on temporal and temporary technological expressions of false or pseudo-progress.

7. See also "The Nineteenth Century" for a development of these ideas.

8. See "The Nineteenth Century," especially Mandelstam's use of "Buddhism" as a term of abuse,—this ultimately goes back to Alexander Herzen's essay, "Buddhism in Science."

9. Undoubtedly, Mandelstam's response to Soviet Marxist and non-Marxist

theorizing about literary evolution. While discussions of literary evolution such as those of the Formalist critics, Yury Tynianov (*Dostoevskii i Gogol'*, 1921) and Viktor Shklovsky (*Rozanov*, 1921), recognized "evolution" as extremely irregular, admitting of mutations, deviations, transformations, the attempts of Soviet historical materialists to formulate laws of literary historical development could only have aroused Mandelstam's ire. Tynianov's major statement on literary evolution as "mutation" as opposed to progressive development was not published until 1927 (see "On Literary Evolution" in *Na literaturnom postu*, No. 4, 1927).

10. See "Literary Moscow" for a further discussion of poetic originality—"inventiveness" versus "memory"—as well as "Slate Ode."

11. Nikolai Ivanovich Lobachevsky (1792-1856). The Russian creator of non-Euclidean geometry. See also, Letters, No. 3, to Vyacheslav Ivanov, August 1909.

12. Here is Mandelstam's major theme, of course. From the point of view of schematic structure and Mandelstam's cognitive approach to his thematic materials, it is interesting to compare this essay with many of his poems: the poet begins with a direct statement introducing the theme, he then veers off in several directions (related tangentially, but not directly to the main theme), and only at the end does he return again to the main theme in earnest. It is almost as if he desired to warm up his cognitive faculties with exercises in free association. See, among others, such poems as No. 54, "The bread is poisoned and the air is all drunk up" (1913), No. 92, "The stream of golden honey flowed from the bottle" (1917), No. 118, "We shall gather again in Petersburg" (1920), and even his cycle of "Octets."

13. Russia's medieval epic. For an English translation, see *Medieval Russia's Epics, Chronicles, and Tales,* edited by S.A. Zenkovsky (New York, 1974).

14. See Note 3, above.

15. Before the ninth century, Latin was the literary language of France. Fragments of the "Cantilene de Sainte Eulalie," dating from the ninth century, are the earliest extant literature written in the vernacular.

16. On Bely, see Note 26, "Badger Hole."

17. Qualities Mandelstam ascribes to great works of poetry. See, for instance, "Conversation about Dante."

18. From Tyutchev's poem, "Silentium."

19. For a more positive, but critical analysis of Futurism and certain Futurist poets, see "Storm and Stress." For an excellent study of the Futurist movement in Russian literature, see Vladimir Markov, *Russian Futurism.*

Imagism or Imaginism, on the other hand, was a short-lived poetic movement, organized in 1919 and lasting more or less until 1924, which emphasized imagery, in particular, the metaphor as the foundation of poetry. Many of the Imaginist poems were little more than catalogues of images, however ingenious. The best study of this subject is *The Russian Imaginists* by Nils A. Nilsson (Stockholm, 1970). Sergei Esenin (1895-1925), the most successful poet of the group (although he was not a member for long), expressed the group's Bohemianism and celebrated its rowdy cafe life and so-called "hooliganism" in his famous "Tavern Moscow" (1924) and "Confession of a Hooligan" (1925). However, Esenin showed little enthusiasm for the stylistic exploits of Imaginism.

20. See "Peter Chaadaev."

21. Mandelstam's thesis that language *is* history clarifies his basic definition of history as cultural history. This is even more clearly reflected in his autobiographical fiction, see *The Noise of Time* and "Fourth Prose." See also "Conversation about Dante."

22. Vasily Vasilievich Rozanov (1856-1919). Major Russian writer, critic and philosopher. He is best known for his profound critical studies of Dostoevsky (see in particular, *The Legend of the Grand Inquisitor*). In these studies he was undoubtedly aided by

his marriage to Dostoevsky's former mistress, Apollinaria Suslova.

Although never officially a member of the Symbolist movement, Rozanov was considered a modernist writer both in terms of his literary style and his unconventional views on religion, society, and sex. He is well known for his naturalistic religion of sex and procreation, for his sincerity and even naiveté in questioning religious, social, and sexual beliefs. Morality, for Rozanov, derived from spontaneity, from the religion of life, not from what he regarded as the ascetic ideals of Christianity. He criticized Christian metaphysics for deviating too far from the Old Testament. Christianity, he believed, was no longer capable of understanding life for it had become a religion of suffering and death. Rozanov's ideas on religion, family life, and sexuality are presented in a number of books, including *The Family Question in Russia* (1903), *By Cathedral Walls* (1906), and *The Dark Countenance* (1911).

Rozanov's literary genius found its outlet in his highly original meditations structured around a kind of interior monologue. He uses a variety of short forms, including aphorisms, maxims, anecdotes, quotations, and various elements of small talk, through which he performs fascinating experiments with language usage. He attempts to capture actual speech patterns, including intonations and voice rhythms, through the violation of standard literary syntax, the use of unconventional grammar, typographical distortions, colloquial diction, and the fragmented form. The best examples of his literary style are *Solitary Thoughts* (1912), and *Fallen Leaves,* 2 volumes, (1913-1915).

Mandelstam's intense interest in Rozanov at this particular juncture was undoubtedly stimulated by Viktor Shklovsky's fascinating study, *Rozanov* (Petrograd, 1921).

On the other hand, Mandelstam's ideal of Hellenistic culture seems to be more closely related to Annensky's views on art and the problems of creation than to Rozanov's views. See the quotes below from Annensky's verse, and see, in particular, Annensky's essays dealing with Greek tragedy or Greek culture in general, plus his comments on, and interest in, the Hellenistic trend in nineteenth century French poetry.

23. On this poem, which Rozanov discusses in his *Solitary Thoughts,* D.S. Mirsky commented: "Lastly, among [Nekrasov's] very earliest poems (1846) there is that veritably immortal poem which so many people (Grigoriev, among others, and Rozanov) have felt and experienced as something more than poetry, that poem of tragic love on the brink of starvation and moral degradation . . ." (*A History of Russian Literautre,* New York, 1958, p. 242).

24. Vladimir Ivanovich Dal (1801-1872). Ethnographer, lexicographer, and short story writer. His four volume *Dictionary of the Russian Language* (1861-1868) still forms the basis of our knowledge of popular spoken Russian before the standard language of the educated classes became widespread. It includes numerous dialectalisms, colloquialisms, and even vulgarisms, idioms, sayings and proverbs, and jargon.

25. On Annensky, see Index. The citations here are from: (a) a free adaptation of Verlaine's "Pensées du Soir" (1887)—"In the Evening" (1901), and (b) "Nightmares." Both poems are found in Annensky's *The Cypress Chest.*

26. A reference to the lines from Pushkin's poem *The Gypsies.*

27. On *The Scales* (1904-1909), see Index.

28. On Vyacheslav Ivanov, see "On Contemporary Poetry."

29. From Pushkin's *The Gypsies,* lines 198-201.

30. This is a significant aspect of Mandelstam's poetry, the idea that words and images are essentially equal, even interchangeable; *how* they are used then determines their values, their differences. Hence, part of Mandelstam's attack against the Symbolists is directed against the creation of static symbols, for he sees this tendency as leading ultimately to the creation of an inflexible, immobile language. See also, Note 4 above, on Henri Bergson.

31. This is a reference to the closing lines of Goethe's *Faust,* often taken as the

credo of the Symbolists, especially by their critics: "Alles vergängliche ist nur ein Gleichniss."

32. A reference to Baudelaire's poem "Correspondances" from *Spleen et Idéal.*

33. The beginning of the Symbolist movement in Russia is usually regarded as dating from 1893-95, with the publication of *Symbols* by Dmitry Merezhkovsky and three collections entitled *Russian Symbolists* by V. Bryusov, as well as a number of theoretical works by N. Minsky, Merezhkovsky, and A. Volynsky. For further details, see Georgette Donchin, *The Influence of French Symbolism on Russian Poetry.* The end of the movement is dated from the so-called "crisis" of Symbolism marked by the closing of *The Scales* in December 1909 and the mass of articles and discussions of "the crisis" produced between 1909 and 1912.

34. An extremely important tenet in Mandelstam's esthetic. See also, "The Word and Culture" in which Mandelstam asks: ". . . . why equate the word with the thing . . .? Is the thing really master of the word? The word is a Psyche. The living word . . . freely chooses for its dwelling place, as it were, some objective significance, material thing, or beloved body. And the word wanders freely around the thing, like the soul around an abandoned, but not forgotten body."

35. Here Mandelstam seems to be at one with a basic doctrine of Formalist theory, the revulsion against the traditional separation of "form" and "content" in analyzing a literary work. However, Mandelstam was unprepared to accept the "scientism" of the Formalists, their terminology, or the early Formalists' resolution of the problem of the relationship of art to society, which must have struck him as a kind of *de facto* elevation of "form" over "content" in its almost total concentration on the device. Nevertheless, Mandelstam was an admirer and personal friend of certain of the Formalist critics, including Boris Eikhenbaum (see "Badger Hole") and Viktor Shklovsky (see "I Write a Scenario").

36. Likewise, Mandelstam's use of Bergson's term "system" is not consistent. Mandelstam's critical terminology is eclectic and unscientific. See Note 4, above.

37. See "Morning of Acmeism."

38. On Gorodetsky, see Index.

39. See "Morning of Acmeism."

40. See "Remarks on Chénier."

41. The Romantic movement.

42. The English historian, Henry Thomas Buckle (1821-1862), author of the *History of Civilization in England* (1857-1861), was at least partly responsible for suggesting that history should be regarded as a "science." He maintained that environmental factors form the character of a people.

43. This is a significant aspect of Mandelstam's esthetic reflected, in particular, in his "Octets" and in "Conversation about Dante." Here we encounter Mandelstam the teacher as well as Mandelstam the artist, for his esthetic vision demands that the poet teach no mere "civic" virtue, but human values, morality being one of the eternal verities.

44. Bryusov's poem, "Z.N. Gippius," was written in December, 1901 (V. Bryusov, SS, I, M., 1973).

45. This should be considered in conjunction with the essay, "The Word and Culture."

46. See his earlier essay "On the Addressee," which contains the statement that poetry must be addressed to "the reader in posterity."

47. The 1928 republication of "On the Nature of the Word" omits the section beginning "But I can already see..." to the end (SS, II, 636). The reasons for this omission are not completely clear, but must have been at least in part the result of politically inspired self-censorship. This section suggests a possible negative evaluation of Acmeism in the future, a possibility which, by 1928, Mandelstam would not have cared to express himself. See my introductory notes to "Morning of Acmeism." Indeed, by 1928,

Acmeism was more in need of a defense than Bergson. Furthermore, by the end of the 1920s, Salieri could no longer have appeared to Mandelstam as a hero; the reality of circumstances in which geniuses were being hounded by hacks had come too close to home. See, for instance, the poet-hero of "Fourth Prose."

48. See Mandelstam's poem "Notre Dame."

49. For an interesting discussion of the Mozart-Salieri theme in Mandelstam's work, see Nadezhda Mandelstam, *Mozart and Salieri* (Ardis, 1973). Mrs. Mandelstam suggests that Mandelstam really had Bach in mind when he contrasted "the stern and strict craftsman" to Mozart. See his adulation of Bach in the early essay, "Morning of Acmeism."

17. BADGER HOLE

This essay on the first anniversary of Blok's death was first published in I. Lezhnev's magazine *Rossiia,* 1922, under the title "A. Blok." It was subsequently republished with major changes in Mandelstam's collection *On Poetry* in 1928. Page 1 and the entire second section were omitted. The essay began with the paragraph "Establishing the literary genesis of the poet . . ." Minor changes in the text are also noted in SS, II, p. 639.

1. Alexander Alexandrovich Blok (1880-1921). Russia's greatest Symbolist poet. While Blok expressed a harmonious mystical vision, a yearning after the "Beautiful Lady"—a cosmic, feminine soul based on V. Soloviev's mystic, erotic concept of the Divine Feminine, Sophia—in his earliest collection, *Verses about the Beautiful Lady* (1901-2), by the end of 1903, an enigmatic, unidentifiable "femme fatale"—see such poems as "The Stranger" (1906) or "Humiliation" (1911)—came to replace the Divine Feminine in his verse, and the rather Romantic poetry of yearning gave way to a more metaphysically oriented Symbolist poetry of quest. Blok's harmonious vision of the cosmos was replaced by an enigmatic and Symbolist vision of the "terrible world," which eventually provided the title for his collection, *The Terrible World* (1909-16). Blok's Symbolist quest took him on a nightmarish journey through a fantastic urban underworld, a world of physical debauchery and metaphysical loneliness and despair—revelations of sordid human misery and ugliness as well as experiences of superhuman spiritual torment and suffering. While this mystical journey never really ended, Blok was also to seek and to express a sense of renewed spiritual faith in poems dedicated to the third incarnation of his feminine image, Russia. These poems are included in his collection *Homeland* (1907-16).

As Mandelstam recognizes, Blok combined numerous and various sources of poetic inspiration in his work, including early 19th century German Romantic poetry, Baudelaire, and Apollon Grigoriev's Russian gypsy songs; his poetry included both metaphysical and historical motifs, both windswept spaces and confined urban landscapes, but all the images and themes were informed by his mystical Symbolist sensibility which viewed everything through metaphysical lenses and heard everything through the powerful rhythms and sounds of music.

Blok's mystical intuition of Russia's destiny reached its peak in his dramatic narrative masterpiece, *The Twelve* (1918) which actually combines elements from most of his major poetic cycles. Around 1910, Blok began working on a long autobiographical narrative poem about his own cultural past, called "Retribution." Planned as a portrait of Russian social and cultural life, it was divided into three cantos, each treating a different historical period and cultural generation: the 1880s, the 1890s, and the first decade of the twentieth century. Unfortunately, only fragments of this fascinating work remain, primarily from the first and third cantos, for Blok was still working on it when he died in 1921. Blok also tried his hand at several verse dramas, including the popular *The Puppet Show* (1907) and *The Rose and the Cross* (1913). He also wrote numerous ideological and political essays, most of which were collected in the volume, *Russia and the Intelligentsia* (1908-18), and literary essays collected in *About Symbolism* (1921).

2. Ivanov-Razumnik (pseudonym of R.V. Ivanov, 1878-1945). A social historian, literary critic, and political thinker, member of the Left Social Revolutionary party. Leader of the Scythian movement whose major doctrine envisioned the Russian masses as building not only a new society (hence, their welcome of the 1917 Revolution) but a new religion, a new city of man and a new city of God. The 1917 Revolution, the Scythians believed, would sweep away the harmful influences which European tradition had left on Russia, leaving Russia free to develop her own national history. Author of the extremely popular *History of Russian Social Thought,* which went through four editions between 1907 and 1914. He exerted a strong influence on both Blok and Bely: see Blok's poems, "The Scythians" (1918) and "The Twelve."

3. Yury Isaevich Aikhenvald (1872-1928). Russian literary critic best known for his *Silhouettes of Russian Writers* (1906-1910), "lyrical essays" rather than literary historical portraits. He was very critical of "literary history" as a discipline.

4. Wilhelm Alexandrovich Zorgenfrey (1882-1938). Poet and translator, much influenced by Blok. He left memoirs of Blok, "A. A. Blok (po pamiati za 15 let)" in Bely's periodical *Notebooks of Daydreamers (Zapiski mechtatelei,* No. 16, 1922).

5. Boris Mikhailovich Eikhenbaum (1886-1959). Leading Russian Formalist critic. In the early twenties, he published several works on poetry, including *The Melody of Verse* (1921) and *Through Literature* (1924); the latter contains "Blok's Fate" (1921), Eikhenbaum's memorial speech on Blok's death given at the House of Writers. It was also during these years that he wrote *Anna Akhmatova* (1923). In later years he concentrated primarily on prose fiction, in particular, on the work of Lev Tolstoy. His essay "Theory of the 'Formal Method' " (1926) is an excellent overview and defense of the Formalist approach.

6. Victor Maximovich Zhirmunsky (1899-1972). A fellow schoolmate of Mandelstam's at the Tenishev Commercial school. Outstanding Russian literary scholar and critic. In the early twenties, Zhirmunsky published several studies of Russian Symbolism and its relationship to the Russian poetic tradition, including *The Poetry of Alexander Blok* (1921), *Valery Bryusov and Pushkin's Literary Heritage* (1922). He also completed two major works on versification, *Rhyme, Its History and Theory* (1923) and *Introduction to Metrics: Theory of Poetry* (1925).

7. Mandelstam is interested here primarily in determining the poet's cultural-historical sources, not merely the details of his biography. See, in particular, *The Noise of Time,* Mandelstam's attempt to present his own philological or cultural-historical "Ancestry" or autobiography. *The Noise of Time* is very closely connected with, indeed inspired by, what Mandelstam terms "Blok's historical sensibility" and his unfinished narrative poem "Retribution." See below.

8. As Mandelstam returned to the decade of his birth, the 1890s, in *The Noise of Time.*

9. Apollon Alexandrovich Grigoriev (1822-1864). Best known for his autobiographical memoirs, *My Literary and Moral Wanderings,* a personal record of Russian cultural life in the 1830s, although he wrote literary criticism, short stories, and verse, and published a weekly almost single-handedly. In 1916, Blok rescued Grigoriev's verse from oblivion, and his gypsy songs gained great popularity.

10. From Stanza 10 of Blok's poem "The Scythians." The stanza actually begins: "We remember everything."

11. Nikolai Alexeevich Nekrasov (1821-78). Russian poet of the mid-19th century. Many of Nekrasov's poems are written in a folk manner based on the adoption of various folklore devices, in particular, freer accentual rhythms. His most famous poems include

such narratives as "Vlas" (1854), "Red-Nosed Frost" (1863), and his lengthy poetic satire, *Who Can Be Happy in Russia?* (1873-6).

12. Sophia Perovskaya (1853-1881).Daughter of a former governor-general of St. Petersburg, who began her revolutionary career as a peaceful propagandist for the populist cause. She became one of the fanatical leaders (along with Andrei Zhelyabov) of the People's Will party, which concentrated its activities on a single objective, the assassination of Tsar Alexander II. Perovskaya was involved in all seven of the known attempts on the Tsar's life. She contributed her entire fortune to the organization. She might easily have escaped abroad, but chose to remain in Russia and share the fate of her lover, Zhelyabov. She was arrested March 10, 1881. (See Michael T. Florinsky, *Russia: A History and Interpretation,* II, pp. 1076-1084.) Turgenev's prose poem, "The Threshold," is an apotheosis of this woman terrorist's life.

13. Nikolai Ivanovich Kostomarov (1817-1885). Historian of Russia and the Ukraine, in particular, of the 16th to 17th centuries. A Ukrainian nationalist profoundly interested in the customs and culture of the Ukraine.

14. Sergei Mikhailovich Soloviev (1820-1879). Known as the father of modern Russian historical scholarship. Also, the father of Vladimir Soloviev, poet and philosopher.

15. Vasily Osipovich Klyuchevsky (1842-1911). Prominent and popular Russian historian, known best in the West for his *History of Russia.* Other books in English include: *The Rise of the Romanovs, Peter the Great, A Course in Russian History: The Seventeenth Century.*

16. References to Pushkin's "little tragedy": "The Feast during the Plague" (1830) and to his poem "To Mary's Health" (1830), both inspired by English works. "To Mary's Health" is also mentioned in the last chapter of *The Noise of Time.*

17. Prosper Mérimée (1803-1870). French novelist, whose most famous work, *La Venus d'Ille. Carmen,* was transformed by Bizet into one of the most popular romantic operas of all time, *Carmen.* In 1827 he published a fake translation of Illyrian national songs and poems, *La Guzla,* which was so good it deceived Pushkin. After the latter discovered it was a hoax, Mérimée and Pushkin developed a friendly correspondence which led to Merimee's fine translations of Pushkin's tales and their subsequent introduction to the French reading public. Mérimée is famous for his treatment of Romantic and historical themes; his objective style tempers tales of savagery and extremes of passion.

18. The remarkable poem "Steps of the Knight Commander" (1910-12) is dedicated to V.A. Zorgenfrey (see Note 4, above) and is included in Blok's collection *Retribution* (1908-13), not to be confused with his longer poem of the same title. Zorgenfrey states that the poem was inspired by the horn of a distant car. Here Blok truly combines the Don Juan myth with imagery of the modern age. The lines cited are from Stanzas 2 and 6. The quiet, heavy footsteps of the Knight Commander are compared to the "quiet, black... motorcar..."

19. See the similar reference to the English model of Revolution, in "Humanism and the Present."

20. See Note 3, "Morning of Acmeism."

21. Afanasy Afanasievich Fet (1820-92). A major 19th century Russian poet, known as the foremost Russian exponent of "art for art's sake," and for his astonishing ability to capture the most ineffable states of mind and moments of spiritual experience. While his earlier poetry (1840s) is most often inspired by nature and themes from classical antiquity, his poetry of the 1880s, *Evening Fires (Vechernie ogni),* a series of small collections of poems, published from 1883 to 1891 is more metaphysical in inspiration and, consequently, exerted a strong influence on two of the leading Symbolist poets, Sologub and Blok. Fet also translated the writings of the German philosopher, Schopenhauer, into Russian.

22. See Note 11, above.

23. See Notes 16 and 17, above, and 1, "On the Addressee."

24. An essential tenet of Mandelstam's esthetic. See, in particular, his most Bergsonian essay, "On the Nature of the Word."

25. The *chastushka* is a relatively new and extremely popular form of folk song, dating from the mid-19th century. It usually consists of four rhymed lines and is much more regular than its older, freer poetic predecessors. A *chastushka* may be freely and easily composed on any subject, although love and politics seem to dominate.

26. Paper money issued in 1917 by the short-lived Kerensky government.

27. See Note 4, "On the Addressee."

28. See Note 6, "On Contemporary Poetry."

29. Andrei Bely (1880-1934, pen name of Boris Nikolaevich Bugaev). Leading Symbolist prose writer, poet, and literary scholar, and by some considered the "most representative figure of Russian Symbolism" because of the variety of his work and life experience. He is best known for his prose fiction, including his novels, *Petersburg* (1913) and *Kotik Letaev* (1918), and for his highly original study of *Gogol's Craftsmanship* (1934). His prose fiction and poetry are both theoretically oriented, the result of personal efforts to create a firm theoretical foundation for his Symbolist vision. Indeed, his early novel, *The Silver Dove* (1909) can be read, at least on one level, as the record of a young student's gradual involvement and disillusionment with the occult, while *Petersburg* is strongly influenced by the anthroposophical teachings of Rudolf Steiner, presented both seriously and in parody. Bely's lyrical poetry is included in the collection, *Gold in Azure* (1904), *Ashes* (1909), and *The Urn* (1909). The ecstasy and joy of mystical celebration found in the earliest volume is replaced by tense, mournful despair in the second, and by a rather more reflective tone in the third. After 1910, he essentially gave up poetry for prose. However, in 1921 he wrote what many consider his finest verse, a lengthy autobiographical narrative poem, *The First Meeting,* an attempt (much like Blok's *Retribution*) to recreate the cultural environment of his youth. He also wrote (and rewrote) several books of memoirs and reminiscences, including the rather biased *Recollections of Alexander Blok.* And he edited the Petrograd periodical *Notebooks of Daydreamers* (1919-22).

Although Mandelstam is very hostile to Bely in most of his essay and reviews, he radically altered his attitude toward the older poet in 1933 when they met for the first time at the Writer's Union Rest Home in Koktebel, in the Crimea. Upon Bely's death in 1934, Mandelstam composed several poems of tribute, including No. 279 and Nos. 288-294. Furthermore, Bely may have been Mandelstam's "interlocutor" in "Conversation about Dante." See my notes to that essay.

30. Quote from Dante, *Paradiso, XXXIII, 145. See "Conversation about Dante" for more details regarding the ideas stated in the following paragraph.

18. THE NINETEENTH CENTURY

This essay was first published in the Imaginist magazine, *Hotel for Travelers in the Land of the Beautiful* (*Gostinitsa dlia puteshestvuiushchikh v prekrasnom,* M., No. 1, 1922) and later republished in Mandelstam's *On Poetry.* The text of our translation is based on the latter publication (SS, II, pp. 276-83). Variants are given in SS, II, 639-42.

1. From his twentieth century vantage point, Mandelstam applies Baudelaire's metaphor of the poet to the fate of the entire nineteenth century. The last stanza of Baudelaire's "L'Albatros" reads:

Le Poète est semblable au prince des nuées
Qui hante la tempête et se rit de l'archer;
Exile sure le sol au milieu des huées,
Ses ailes de géant l'empêchent de marcher.

Mandelstam shares Baudelaire's horror of being unable to move, of being confined, closed in, unfree, and he blames this state of paralysis on the nineteenth century reaction against the Age of Reason, which he sees manifest in "Buddhism."

2. Derzhavin scratched this fragment of his last poem, "The River of Time" on his slate just before he died. See also Mandelstam's "The Slate Ode," in which he refers to Derzhavin's slate and the poem scratched on it.

3. On Lomonosov, see Index.

4. For another statement on the eighteenth century, see "Remarks on Chénier."

5. For other statements on social architecture, see "Government and Rhythm" and "Humanism and the Present"; on Medieval equilibrium and social order, see "François Villon," "Morning of Acmeism," and "Conversation about Dante," or the poem "Notre Dame." Here, Mandelstam seems to be expressing the values of his generation (1890s-1910s) as against the values of social Darwinism dominating the thinking of the preceding age, and then revived again in the discussions of social life in the new Soviet society. In his fascinating book, *Consciousness and Society: The Reorientation of European Social Thought, 1890-1930* (New York: 1958), H. Stuart Hughes states: ". . . in the perspective of a cultural scene dominated by Social Darwinism, the young thinkers of the 1890s can be regarded as aiming at precisely the opposite of what they have usually been accused of doing. Far from being "irrationalists," they were striving to vindicate the rights of rational inquiry. Alarmed by the threat of an iron determinism, they were seeking to restore the freely speculating mind to the dignity it had enjoyed a century earlier."

6. See Mandelstam's poem No. 135, "The Age," which depicts the nineteenth century as a beast whose spine has been broken.

7. From Pushkin's "Epigram" of 1827, beginning with the cited lines.

8. Mandelstam's sensitivity to the "theatricalization of life and politics" is beautifully illustrated in his historical vignette, "The Bloody Mystery of January Ninth," see below.

9. See "Remarks on Chénier."

10. This image is taken from Pushkin's poem "To the Courtier" ("K Vel'mozhe") and cited in "Remarks on Chénier." See, in particular, Note 11 to that essay.

11. Unidentified poem.

12. "Buddhism in Science" is the title of an essay by Alexander Herzen. It is available in an English translation in *Russian Philosophy,* edited by J.M. Edie, J.P. Scanlan, M.-B. Zeldin, and G.L. Kline, Vol. I, pp. 328-337 (Chicago, 1965). Mandelstam was a great admirer of Herzen (see notes to "Peter Chaadaev"), and such statements as the following obviously left a deep impression on him: "The fault of the Buddhists is that they feel no need for egress into life, for the real realization of the idea. They mistake the reconciliation in science for *all possible* reconciliation. To them it is not a stimulus to action but a pretext for complete, self-sufficient contentment. For the world beyond the covers of their books, they care nought. They are prepared to suffer anything for the vacancy of the universal. It is thus that the Indian Buddhists strive to purchase liberation in Buddha at *the price of existence.* To them Buddha is an abstract infinity, mere nothing. But science has conquered the world for man, it has in fact conquered history for him, and it has not done all this to enable him to rest content. The universality kept within its abstract sphere must always lead to the somnolence destructive to activity—to Indian quietism" (pp. 336-7, *Russian Philosophy*).

Mandelstam develops Herzen's idea of "Buddhism in science," seeing manifestations of "Buddhism" everywhere, in art, religion, indeed as the dominant spiritual and intellectual force of the nineteenth century. This essay develops the idea already presented in passing in connection with Scriabin (see "Pushkin and Scriabin," in particular, Notes 8 and 14). By 1922, however, it emerges as a full-blown polemic against the turning away from reason, the turning away from the active, energetic pursuit of knowledge of the real world, away from "active cognition." It is an attack against static, self-contained contemplation, against the negation of the world and the self, and hence, a condemnation of what appears to be a kind of abstract science for science's sake or art for art's sake, wherein both scientists and artists (intellectuals in general) show no concern for reality or for "individual phenomena," and therefore cannot even recognize traditional humanistic values.

13. The brothers Goncourts, Edmond (1822-1896) and Jules (1830-1870). French novelists and originators of the so-called "roman documentaire." Edmond did much to help make Japanese art fashionable in French cultural life.

14. Gustave Flaubert (1821-1880). French novelist noted for his slow and painstaking literary labors: for instance, *Madame Bovary* took five years to complete. Flaubert stated his artistic goal was to find through style alone that beauty which does not exist in reality.

15. The "tanka" may be called the classic Japanese poetic form, having originated ca. 7th century A.D. It is a lyric of 31 syllables, written in lines of 5, 7, 5, 7, 7 syllables respectively. Western interest in the "tanka" developed in the early twentieth century in France (1905-10, or so) and in America and England (1910-15) among the so-called Imagists. Mandelstam could easily have been familiar with the French experiments in "tanka," or may have based his judgment on Samuil M. Vermel's *Tankas* (*Tanki*, M., 1915), which, according to V. Markov (*Russian Futurism*, p. 285), "was perhaps the first attempt to introduce this Japanese form into Russian—an achievement slightly diminished by the fact that the poems had little merit." Mandelstam's strong attack on the "tanka" may also be part of his general attack on the Russian Futurists who continued and expanded the Eastern orientation of many of the Symbolists. For example, the Eastern-oriented late Hylaea group. (See V. Markov, *Russian Futurism*.)

16. For further discussion of Mandelstam's views on the novel as a historical literary form, see "The End of the Novel."

17. See Mandelstam's poem No. 140, "Jan. 1, 1924."

18. This is the first verse of Mandelstam's poem No. 133, "The wind brought us consolation" (1922).

19. LITERARY MOSCOW

This essay was published in Lezhnev's magazine *Rossiia*, No. 2 (1922), in the issue immediately following the one containing the essay "Badger Hole," while the third issue contained "Birth of Plot." It has never been republished in Russia. See SS, II, 647.

1. Fyodor Yaseevich Dolidze (1883- ?). An organizer of poetry readings in the capital and tours in the provinces. In particular, he arranged the famous "election of the King of Poets," held in February, 1918 at the Polytechnical Museum, at a poetry reading dominated by Severyanin's followers, hence Severyanin, rather than Mayakovsky, was elected "King." Dolidze also organized an evening devoted to women poets at which Marina Tsvetaeva read her verse (SS, II, 647-48).

2. Velimir Khlebnikov (pen-name of Viktor Vladimirovich Khlebnikov, 1885-1922). The most original poet of the Futurist movement. His most important collections include *Selected Poems* (*Izbornik stikhov*, 1914), *Works I* (*Tvoreniia I*, 1914), and *Poems* (*Stikhi*, 1923). His collected works appeared in Leningrad in five volumes be-

tween 1928 and 1933. He is probably best known in this country for his early poem "Incantation by Laughter" (1910), constructed from neologisms derived from the root "smekh" (laughter), and for his longer poems discussed in Vladimir Markov's superb study, *The Longer Poems of Velimir Khlebnikov* (Berkeley and L.A., 1962); also see *Snake Train*, trans. by Gary Kern (Ardis, 1976).

Khlebnikov was fascinated by Slavic word-roots and the pre-history of the Slavic language or proto-language. He created and employed neologisms with the purpose of exploring the inner life, the inner meanings, of language, thereby compelling his readers to think and respond etymologically. In addition, his philological interests were founded on naive hope and ideological commitment: he was a utopian pacifist who sought to create a new, universal language which would eliminate the idea of war, and thus help return mankind to the simple values of primitive life, to the state of natural harmony. He believed he could reveal the essence of primitive existence through the study of language and myth, and discover fundamental laws of history through the study of mathematics. But while the former study led to magnificent poetic creations, the latter led primarily to his being considered a "madman."

He welcomed the Revolution but was not unaware of its negative features. The last five years of his life (1917-22) were his most creative and most prolific, the period when he wrote the majority of his longer poems. According to Vladimir Markov, "it was in his poems on civil war and revolution that he achieved a new dimension and showed the rare ability that was his, a direct poetic vision of events and things." (V. Markov, *Russian Futurism, op. cit.* p. 306). Of all the Futurists, Mandelstam was most partial to Khlebnikov; he was keenly aware of his genius. See Index for references to him.

3. Ivan Alexandrovich Aksenov (1884-1935). A Futurist poet (member of the Centrifuge group which included Pasternak, Aseev, and Bobrov, among others), literary scholar, theoretician, and translator. He published *Invalid Foundations* (*Neuvazhitel'-nye osnovaniia*) in 1916, which V. Markov characterizes as "one of the few genuinely avant-garde works published by Centrifuge" (*Russian Futurism*, p. 271). Also according to Markov, Aksenov saw the "foundation of art in rhythm," not beauty, and therefore envisioned "a complete disappearance of art, because people would be so highly organized rhythmically that a mere contemplation of mathematical formulas would give them esthetic satisfaction" (p. 273). See Note 5, "Government and Rhythm." He also wrote about Picasso and the Elizabethans, and was deeply interested in the theater.

4. Marina Tsvetaeva (1892-1941). One of the finest and most unique Russian poets of the twentieth century. Her poetic craft has much more in common with the Futurists, such as early Pasternak and even Khlebnikov, than with the Symbolists or Acmeists. She is best known for her remarkable verbal invention, compressed lyrical style, original use of syntax and rhythm, all of which give her poetry its sense of spontaneity, dynamism and brilliance. Indeed, her style makes her more traditional subject matter appear "Futurist."

Although 1917-1922 was a period of terrible physical hardship for Tsvetaeva, it was the time of her major creative development: see, *Mileposts II* (1917-1922), *The Camp of the Swans* (1917-1922), and *Craft* (1921-1922). Simon Karlinsky mentions this period as the time when Tsvetaeva "extended her range and, in addition to lyric poetry, turned to larger epic forms. . ., to the theater, and eventually to prose" (p. 46). In 1922, she emigrated from Russia, living first in Berlin and Czechoslovakia, and later in Paris. The collection, *After Russia*, published in 1928, is considered her finest and most mature work. This was the period of the magnificent longer poems, including "Poem of the End" (1923-24), "Poem of the Hill" (1923-24), and "The Pied Piper" (*Krysolov*, 1925). The end of the 1920s to 1939, when she returned to the Soviet Union, were tragic years, combining physical hardship with personal literary ostracism. Prose dominates her writing in the 1930s.

Mandelstam had been infatuated with Tsvetaeva in 1916, and had dedicated three poems to her, see Nos. 84, 85, 90 (Karlinsky, p. 39). However, Mandelstam's views of Tsvetaeva as a poet expressed in his essays were biased and unfair. For an interesting account of Tsvetaeva's own opinion of her friendship with Mandelstam, see her "The History of a Dedication" (in SS, III, 306-44).For further details about Tsvetaeva and her craft, see Simon Karlinsky's fine study, *Marina Cvetaeva: Her Life and Art* (Berkeley and Los Angeles, 1968).

5. Anna Dmitrievna Radlova (née Darmolatova, 1891-1951). Minor Russian poetess and translator. Mandelstam's "relative" by marriage, the sister of his brother Evgeny's wife. See N. Y. Mandelstam, *Hope Abandoned,* pp. 120-121, and Mandelstam's letters which refer to her in passing, e.g., No. 37.

6. For a fine discusssion of the Formalist movement, its history and member-ship, and for a discussion of the pioneering efforts of Potebnya and Bely in the study of poetics, see V. Erlich, *Russian Formalism: History-Doctrine* (Mouton, 1965, 2nd revised edition).

7. Adelina Efimovna Adalis (penname of Adelina Efron, 1900-1969). Minor Russian poetess, translator and critic. During the winter of 1921, Bryusov organized a special Evening of Women Poets at which Adalis, Tsvetaeva, and many others read their verse.

8. Sofya Yakovlevna Parnok (1885-1933). Minor Russian poetess and translator, extremely well-known in her day.

9. While no one could ever accuse Mandelstam of being a "feminist," this is both unfair and outrageous.

10. This paragraph is a direct attack on Futurism. However, this theme is of major interest to Mandelstam and is presented in a most unique manner in his "The Slate Ode."

11. Vladislav Felitsianovich Khodasevich (1886-1939). Considered one of the major Russian émigré poets and critics. Khodasevich emigrated from the Soviet Union in 1922 and lived the rest of his life in Paris. Three volumes of lyrics appeared in Russia before he emigrated, including *Grain's Way* (1920). *The Heavy Lyre* (1922) and *Col-lected Poems* (Paris, 1927) were published abroad. Khodasevich also wrote a fascinating book of memoirs, *Necropolis* (1935), and many fine critical works, including *Pushkin's Poetic Craft* (1929) and *Derzhavin* (1931).

12. MAF: the Moscow Association of Futurists.

13. The Lyrical Circle refers to a group of Moscow poets who published an al-manac bearing the same title. The first and last issue of *Lyrical Circle: Pages of Poetry and Criticism* appeared in 1922 in 2000 copies and included some poems of Mandel-stam's, hence the snide reference to "guest artists from Petersburg." Mandelstam's poems were: No. 126, "I was washing in the courtyard at night" and No.112, "When Psyche-Life descended to the shades...".

14. Vladimir Vladimirovich Mayakovsky (1893-1930). Major Russian and Soviet poet, playwright and propagandist. Mayakovsky's aggressive, flamboyant style created the dominant stereotype of the Russian Futurist poet. A master of sound effects, hyper-bolic metaphor, and colloquial diction, Mayakovsky's poetry is meant to be declaimed. His first major work, *Vladimir Mayakovsky—A Tragedy* (1913), was written, directed and performed by the author. This was followed by two longer poems which established his reputation: *A Cloud in Trousers* (1914-15) and *The Backbone Flute* (1915). After the Revolution he concentrated on civic themes, although one of his finest poems, *About This* (1923) is also deeply personal. His most interesting post-revolutionary works include the long poems, *150,000,000* (1919-20), *Vladimir Ilich Lenin* (1924) and *Okay! (Khorosho!,* 1927), his play *Mystery-Bouffe* (1918-21) and his satirical dramas, *The Bedbug* (1928-29) and *The Bathhouse* (1929-30), both of which caused extreme official displeasure. Mayakovsky was also the founder and editor of the Futurist

journal, *LEF* (Left Front of the Arts, 1923) and of its successor, *New LEF,* as well as the designer of numerous propaganda posters and political slogans. For more details, see Edward Brown's fine study, *Mayakovsky: A Poet in the Revolution* (Princeton University Press, 1973).

15. Alexei Eliseevich Kruchenykh (1886-1970). A Russian Futurist poet associated with Khlebnikov and the Cubo-Futurists, who is best known for his interest in meta-logical or trans-sense language. He differed from Khlebnikov in his attempts to create a new language: whereas Khlebnikov (see Note 2, above) based his theory on the discovery of etymologically derivable word-roots which expressed their meaning in the most direct way, Kruchenykh based his primarily on sound relationships mostly of his own invention. See, for instance, his poem of 1913, "Heights: Universal Language" in V. Markov's bi-lingual anthology, *Modern Russian Poetry* (Bobbs-Merrill, 1967). See also Markov's edition of his *Selected Works* (*Izbrannoe,* Munich, 1973).

16. Nikolai Nikolaevich Aseev (1889-1963). A Russian Futurist poet associated with the Centrifuge group of Futurists which included Pasternak, Bobrov, and Ivan Aksenov, among others (see V. Markov, *Russian Futurism*). By temperament and in-terest, however, he was much closer to Mayakovsky, with whom he eventually be-came an organizer of LEF (see Note 14, above). Moreover, his best known work is his long poem, *Mayakovsky Begins* (1940), a portrait of Mayakovsky and a paean to the Futurist movement. His best poetry dates from the years 1914-1917, e.g., his collec-tion *Zor* (1914). Like Khlebnikov, he had a penchant for Slavic themes and neologisms. He also adopted Khlebnikov's theory of "internal declension." He continued to publish and exert his influence on the development of Soviet poetry until his death.

17. *Raeshnik* is very difficult to translate because it assumes the reader's familiarity with its historical context. The *raeshnik* or *raeshnyi stikh* is found primarily in folklore and in imitations of folklore and colloquial speech, and especially in the kind of rimed prose shouted by street vendors and hawkers in pre-revolutionary Russia or the kind of rimed, comically inspired commentary developed by itinerant "magic lantern" show-men for their carnival performances. In form, the *raeshnik* is made up of lines of un-equal length (no set number of syllables or stresses are required per line), and is or-ganized phonetically, primarily by odd-rimes which are often paired. A distinctive feature of this verse form is its comic content which stems primarily from its verbal play, its use of catchy colloquial idiom, patter and hyperbole. Hence, its characteristically per-sonal, colorful, flamboyant, topical and comical expression in Mayakovsky's poetry.

18. *Pauznik.* A poetic meter, usually a ternary meter lacking one or more un-stressed syllables, that is, having an uneven number of unstressed syllables between the stressed syllables.

19. Boris Leonidovich Pasternak (1890-1960). One of the finest poets and prose writers of twentieth century Russia. His first collection, *A Twin in the Clouds* (1914) was published by the Lirika group, the nucleus of the Centrifuge-Futurists, with a pre-face by N. N. Aseev. His second book, *Above the Barriers* (1917) was published under Centrifuge auspices, and contains most of the elements defining Pasternak's unique poetic vision. His basic themes of life and nature dominate, and the stylistic traits, in particular, abrupt syntactical changes, personification, dynamic rhythms, conversa-tional diction, and the slightly distorted but extremely precise empirical imagery, of his mature poetry prevail. His subsequent, and more famous collections, include: *My Sister Life* (*Sestra moia zhizn',* Leto; 1917), published in 1922 (see Mandelstam's re-view in "Some Notes on Poetry"), *Themes and Variations* (1923), *Second Birth* (1932). He also wrote four longer narrative poems, several prose tales, including the remarkable "The Childhood of Luvers" (1918), autobiographies, including *Safe Conduct* (1931), and the novel, *Doctor Zhivago* (finished in 1955, and never published in the Soviet Union). For an interpretation of his esthetic vision, see my article, "Pasternak's Vision of Life," *Russian Literature Triquarterly,* No. 9 (Spring 1974). Translations of most of

his prose and poetry are available in English. For discussions of Mandelstam's personal relationship with Pasternak, see Mandelstam's letters for instance, No. 24, and Nadezhda Yakovlevna Mandelstam's *Hope Against Hope* and *Hope Abandoned.*

20. For information on Blok, see "Badger Hole."

21. The reference here is to the publishing house, World Literature, established by Maxim Gorky to carry out his ambitious scheme of translating the entire body of literary classics into Russian (1918-1924). The publishing enterprise was headed by A. N. Tikhonov. Another purpose of the publishing house was to give employment to Russian intellectuals such as Mandelstam and his wife. For more comments on this venture, see Mandelstam's "On Translation" and "Torrents of Hackwork."

20. LITERARY MOSCOW: THE BIRTH OF PLOT

First published in Lezhnev's *Rossiia,* in the issue following "Literary Moscow" (No. 3, 1922). See SS, II, 647.

1. *The Book of Monthly Readings (Chet'i-Minei)* was the official church compilation of hagiography, patristic literature, homiletic and didactic works, even occasional apocryphal works, all arranged according to the days and months of the calendar. In the 16th century, under the guiding spirit of the Metropolitan of Moscow, Macarius, a grandiose twelve-volume compilation of ecclesiastical readings was made, known as the *Grand Chet'i Minei.* This work was based on the old translated Greek *Chetya Mineya,* which had, over the centuries, broadened its scope to include Russian as well as Greek materials. However, it was not until Macarius' project that all the dates were finally filled in. See, N.K. Gudzy, *A History of Early Russian Literature* (New York, 1949).

2. For information on Bely, see Note No. 29, "Badger Hole."

3. Leonid Nikolaevich Andreev (1871-1919). Russian novelist and dramatist interested in delving into pathological states of mind, including insanity, sexual obsession, suicide, and fear of death. Although very popular among middle-brow readers, he was despised by such intellectuals as Mandelstam. The latter's sarcastic remarks about Andreev and his disciples in *The Noise of Time* are not untypical: "the grimy hairy hands of the traffickers in life and death were rendering the very words life and death repugnant . . . *Literati* in Russian blouses and black shirts traded, like grain dealers, in God and the Devil, and there was not a single house where the dull polka from *The Life of Man* [Andreev's 1906 Symbolist melodrama on the vanity and falsity of everything human—JGH], which had become the symbol of tawdry vulgar Symbolism, was not picked out with one finger on the piano." (C. Brown, translation, p. 121).

Andreev's earliest, more realistic stories were published in Gorky's *Anthologies of Knowledge* (e.g., "The Red Laugh," 1904). His later works were more fantastic and symbolist in inspiration. In the West, Andreev is probably best known for *The Seven Who Were Hanged* (1908) and the play, *He Who Gets Slapped* (1914).

4. Maxim Gorky (penname for Alexei Maximovich Peshkov, 1868-1936). Novelist and dramatist of the late nineteenth-early twentieth century, publisher, revolutionary, and literary activist, who wielded enormous influence over literary developments in the USSR. His fame began with the publication of two volumes of short stories in 1898, most of which expressed his keen sympathy for the plight of man as well as his extremely romantic idealism. His popularity brought him great wealth which he invested in the publishing house Knowledge ("Znanie") and in the revolutionary cause. His most popular novel, *Mother* (1907), and his autobiographical trilogy, *Childhood* (1913), *Among the People* (1918), and *My Universities* (1923) have all been made into popular films. Besides numerous novels, stories and plays, he wrote fine *Reminiscences*

of Tolstoy, Chekhov and Andreev (1924-31).

Gorky's relations with the Bolshevik regime were complex and ambiguous, but he devoted great energy to preserving cultural values and to obtaining rooms and livelihood for Soviet writers of all persuasions. One of his most famous projects was World Literature ("Vsemirnaia literatura"), initiating a series of translations to include the literary classics of all time.

5. Ivan Sergeevich Shmelev (1873-1950). Leading Russian émigré novelist. Shmelev's most important works are *The Man from a Restaurant* (1910) published in Russia and *The Sun of the Dead* (1925), published abroad.

6. Sergei Nikolaevich Sergeev-Tsensky (1875-1958). Russian novelist whose earlier thematic interests differed little from Andreev's (see Note 3, above), but whose style placed him close to the ornamentalist tradition of Bely and Remizov. By 1923, with the publication of *Valya*, the first part of his grand epic of contemporary Russian life, his writing tended more in the direction of traditional 19th century themes and his style was tempered accordingly, emphasizing "realism." The collective title of his epic is *The Transfiguration of Russia (Preobrazhenie Rossii)*. It consists of twelve novels, three novellas, and two sketches created over a 35 year period.

7. Evgeny Ivanovich Zamyatin (1884-1937). Novelist, dramatist and critic, best known in the West for his anti-utopian novel, *We* (1920, published abroad in 1924), which strongly influenced George Orwell's novel, *1984*. He also wrote numerous stories and plays, and a study of H.G. Wells (1921-1922). He played a major role in the development of Soviet literature. He was an inspired and original teacher of prose writing in the Petrograd House of the Arts in the early 1920s and a respected literary scholar. He also helped to establish the Serapion Brotherhood, a movement of young Soviet writers seeking to create a vivid and independent literature (see Note 12, below). Their manifesto defined genuine writers as: "madmen, hermits, heretics, dreamers, rebels or sceptics, and not . . . diligent, reliable government employees" (V. Zavalishin, *Early Soviet Writers*, New York, 1958, pp. 224-229). His fiction is dominated by the complex and ornate prose style popular in the early 1920s, inspired by Gogol, Leskov, and Bely, known as "ornamentalism." Zamyatin is a master of dialogue and characterization, of the cleverly devised narrative design, of fantasy and satire.

8. An almanac published by Maxim Gorky under the auspices of the Knowledge Publishing House, which specialized primarily in realistic works of such writers as Gorky himself, Kuprin, Andreev, Veresaev, Chirikov, Shmelev, Bunin, Sugruchev, Skitalets and others. Forty issues were published between 1904 and 1913 (SS, II, 648). In 1907, Andreev began to publish a series of almanacs under the auspices of the Sweetbriar ("Shipovnik") Publishing House in protest against Gorky's emphasis on "realism." See Note 13 to "The Slump."

9. Bely was considered the leader of the "ornamentalist" school of prose writing which dominated much of the fiction of the early 1920s.

10. On Mérimée, Carmen, Blok and Pushkin, see note 15, "Badger Hole." The reference below is to Pushkin's *The Gypsies*.

11. Boris Pilnyak (penname of Boris Andreevich Vogau, 1894-1938). Novelist best known for his novel, *The Naked Year* (1922), a modernist attempt to portray the dynamics and emotions of the Civil War years through narrative means, mainly via fragmentary episodes. While his style was certainly influenced by the "ornamentalist" prose of Bely and Remizov, his ideas are largely his own.

12. The group of young Soviet writers who called themselves The Serapion Brotherhood was formed with Evgeny Zamyatin's assistance in 1921 and included many of his students. The group included Lev Lunts, Mikhail Zoshchenko, Konstantin Fedin, Veniamin Kaverin, Nikolai Tikhonov, Nikolai Nikitin, Mikhail Slonimsky, Vsevolod Ivanov, Ilya Gruzdev, Elizaveta Polonskaya, Vladimir Pozner. Viktor Shklovsky was also closely associated with the group. They took their name from a story by E. T. A.

Hoffmann, "Die Serapionsbrüder," about an individualist who vowed to dedicate his life to imaginative art. The Serapions were all individualists, united primarily by their desire to create literary works free from political ideology. See Gary Kern and Christopher Collins (eds.), *The Serapion Brothers: A Critical Anthology* (Ardis, 1975), H. Oulanoff, *The Serapion Brothers: Theory and Practice* (The Hague: Mouton, 1966) and Viktor Shklovsky *Sentimental Journey* (Cornell University Press, 1970) for more details.

13. See "Badger Hole" for similar ideas about Blok's poetry.

14. The preceding paragraphs owe much to Khlebnikov, in particular, to his interest in unearthing the linguistic and mythological foundations of Slavic culture, and to the Formalists, especially to Shklovsky's interest in "plot-construction." See, for instance, Shklovsky's essays, "Art as Device" (1917), "The Relationship between Devices of Plot-Construction and General Stylistic Devices" and "The Unfolding of the Plot" (1921). See also Boris Eikhenbaum's *The Young Tolstoy* (1922, English trans. Ardis, 1972). However, Mandelstam does *not* adhere to the rigid Formalist distinction between "plot" and "fable" ("siuzhet" and "fabula"), thus the English word "plot" is used here to denote Mandelstam's "fabula."

Mandelstam's own attempts at literary prose date from this period: See, for example, "Sukharevka" and "Cold Summer."

The following citation is from Khlebnikov's popular poem, "The Grasshopper" (Kuznechik, dated 1908-1909 by N. Stepanov), which begins with the lines cited above. This poem appeared in the Futurist manifesto, "A Slap in the Face of Public Taste" (1912).

15. This type of generalization is very typical of the Formalist critics of this period. It is most illuminating to read this essay in conjunction with the above-mentioned essays by Shklovsky and other contemporary Formalist studies. However, Mandelstam never developed his "theoretical principles" beyond this point. He preferred to raise issues, like the fine conversationalist he was, but not to develop them in theoretical terms. See "Conversation about Dante" and my Introduction.

16. This is a reference to Tyutchev's poem, "A dark and rainy eve" (1836). In Russian folklore, the skylark is the harbinger of spring.

21. A LETTER ABOUT RUSSIAN POETRY

First published in the Rostov newspaper, *Soviet South* (*Sovetskii iug,* January 19, 1922) in the same issue as "A Word or Two About Georgian Art." See, SS, II, 695.

1. This is a reference to Balmont's collection, *Burning Buildings* (*Goriashchie zdaniia,* 1900). Rodney Patterson's comments on Balmont are applicable here: "In his youth he sedulously expressed a literary *culte de moi* no less outrageous in public opinion than that of Oscar Wilde's characters... 'to love oneself is the beginning of a life-long romance'."(R. L. Patterson, "Balmont: In Search of Sun and Shadow," *Russian Literature Triquarterly,* No. 4, 1972, p. 242).

2. On Bryusov, see Note 7, "On Contemporary Poetry."

3. On Ivanov, see Note 8, "On Contemporary Poetry" and Index.

4. On Bely, see Note 29, "Badger Hole" and Index.

5. On Fet, see Note 21, "Badger Hole."

6. Count Arseny Arkadievich Golenishchev-Kutuzov (1848-1913). Minor poet of the late 19th century whose major theme was nostalgia for the Russian gentry. He was also known as "the poet of Nirvana" (Mirsky). A number of his poems were set to music by Mussorgsky and Rachmaninov.

7. *The Scales* (*Vesy*, 1904-1909) was the major organ of the Russian Symbolist movement. Under the editorship of Bryusov (1904-07), it dominated the intellectual world. Indeed, it was the first Russian literary magazine to completely ignore political news and to dedicate itself to the arts. *Vesy* expressed a Modernist attitude in both format and content. It was devoted primarily to literature, and above all, to critical material as opposed to *belles-lettres*. It also gave much more space to poetry than to prose, contained articles on the other arts and on philosophy, as well as up-to-date news and reviews of foreign modernist works, including lists of modernist books appearing in France and Scandinavia, and all references to *The Scales* or Russian Symbolism appearing abroad. In the course of its short existence, it created a genuine revolution in popular taste. By 1910, according to A. Bely, the revolution was accomplished. While before 1900, Russians paid no heed to the modernists: "By 1910 volumes of Wilde, d'Annunzio, Ibsen, Strindberg, Przybyszewski, and Hoffmannsthal were on the shelves; people were already reading Verhaeren, Baudelaire, Verlaine, Van Lerberghe, Bryusov, Blok, and Balmont; they were carried away by Sologub; and they were already beginning to talk of Corbière, Gilkin, Arcos, Gourmont, Régnier, Duhamel, Stefan George, and Lilienkron; a distinctive interest became apparent in the poetry of Pushkin, Tiutchev, Baratynsky; and even the old poets of France, Ronsard, Racan, and Malherbe were experienced anew" (From A. Bely, *Nachalo Veka*, quoted in G. Donchin, *The Influence of French Symbolism on Russian Poetry*, Mouton, 1958, p. 66). For more on *The Scales*, see Donchin, *Influence*, pp. 44-68.

8. Ellis (penname for L. L. Kobylinsky). Modernist critic, major contributor to *The Scales*, and specialist in Baudelaire. Best remembered for his book, *The Russian Symbolists* (M., 1910), on Balmont, Bryusov and Bely.

9. Zinaida Nikolaevna Gippius (1867-1945). Major Symbolist poet and literary critic. Married to Dmitry Merezhkovsky. In her articles in *The Scales*, she used the pseudonyms, Anton Krainy and Comrade Herman. Her St. Petersburg salon (1905-1917) was a major gathering place for the younger Symbolists. She is best known for her decadent themes which she treated in a profoundly intellectual manner, and for the complex religious and philosophical ideas informing her poetry. Her poetic craft is interesting for its use of abstract images, and for the stark comparisons and parallelisms which support her religio-philosophical ideas. Her *Collected Poems* were published in 1904. Her interesting book of memoirs, *Living Faces* appeared in Prague in 1925. For more information, see Temira Pachmuss, *Zinaida Gippius: An Intellectual Profile* (Carbondale, 1971).

10. This quote is from Blok's poem "The Scythians."

11. Mandelstam's assessment of Blok in this essay should be read in conjunction with "Badger Hole."

12. On A. Grigoriev and Nekrasov, see Notes 9 and 11, "Badger Hole."

13. On Nekrasov, see Note 11, "Badger Hole."

14. On Kuzmin, see Note 15, "On Contemporary Poetry."

15. Mandelstam is obviously referring to Titian's painting, "The Concert," hanging in the Pitti Palace, Florence. Titian's painting, however, is truly in the style of Georgione, hence the confusion.

16. Nikolai Alexeevich Klyuev (1885-1937). A peasant poet from Olonetsk, idolized in such pre-revolutionary salons as that run by Zinaida Gippius. Klyuev often wrote about the religious sects of northern Russia, his mystical hopes for a new peasant paradise, and idealized pre-Petrine Russia. His best known collection is *Songs of Praise* (*Pesnoslov*, 1919). He exerted a strong influence on Esenin.

17. On Akhmatova, see Index.

18. On Annensky, see Index.

19. From Annensky's poem "It Happened at Vallen-Koski" in *The Cypress Chest*.

22. A WORD OR TWO ABOUT GEORGIAN ART

This essay appeared in the Rostov newspaper, *Soviet South* (*Sovetskii iug,* January 19, 1922) along with "A Letter on Russian Poetry." See SS, II, 695.

1. The poems to which Mandelstam is referring are Lermontov's "Argument" and "Tamara," both dating from 1841, and Pushkin's "Don't sing to me, my beauty." See Mandelstam's own poem No. 115, "I dream of hunchbacked Tiflis" (1920). Mandelstam's translations of Georgian poetry (Nos. 464, 465) appeared in *Novaia gruzinskaia poeziia,* (ed.) N. Mitsisvili (Tbilisi, 1921). See also Note 4 below.

2. Twentieth-century Russian poets, the Futurists in particular, were also captivated by Georgia. According to Vladimir Markov, "Futurism found especially fertile ground in Tiflis... some of the most significant Georgian poets of the time (Paolo Yashvili, Titian Tabidze) then considered themselves futurists and formed their own group, The Blue Horn." (*Russian Futurism,* p. 337). See also, Boris Pasternak's poems in *My Sister, Life* and his *Letters to Georgian Friends* (including Yashvili, Tabidze). On the other hand, see Mandelstam's "Journey to Armenia," and his Armenian cycle of poems, plus his symbolic conception of Armenia in "Fourth Prose" as "the promised land." And both Bryusov and Bely expressed a deeper interest in Armenia than Georgia.

3. Niko Pirosmanishvili (1860-1918?). Talented, self-made artist, who painted signboards and pictures, primarily on oilcloth and wood with home-made paints. His main subjects were landscapes, animals, genre paintings, still lifes (SS, III, 356). A beautiful film depicting the life of this primitive artist was produced in 1971, written and directed by Georgy Shengelaya, entitled *Pirosmani.*

4. Vazha Pshavela (penname of Luka Pavlovich Pazikashvili, 1861-1915). Extremely popular Georgian poet. (SS, I, 556-60). See Mandelstam's translation, No. 466, based on the epic poem, "Gogotur and Apshina" (SS, I, 321-333), originally published in *Poemy,* ed. V. Goltsev and T. Tabidze (M.,1955, pp. 7-21).

5. These lines complement Mandelstam's poem No. 107, "Oh, this air, intoxicated with disorder," which also treats the theme of the preservation of culture.

23. FROM AN INTERVIEW: COMMENTS ON THE LYRIC AND THE EPIC

These comments were first published in the magazine, *On Guard* (*Na Postu,* No. 2, column 250, 1923). See, SS, II, 497. Mandelstam's remarks formed part of an interview entitled "At a Meeting of Writers."

1. A major interest of Mandelstam's during this period, see especially his attempt to recreate the 1890s-1910s in his autobiographical fiction, *The Noise of Time,* and his desire to revaluate the developments in modern Russian poetry and culture in such essays as "On the Nature of the Word," "Storm and Stress," among others.

2. Mandelstam's interest in Old French epic poetry is partly expressed in his translations. See SS, I, 310-319.

24. SOME NOTES ON POETRY

This essay combines two articles, both of which were first published in 1923: the first half of the essay appeared as "Vulgata. Some Notes on Poetry" in *Russian Art* (*Russkoe iskusstvo,* No. 2, 1923); the second (beginning: "When Fet first made his appearance...") appeared as "Boris Pasternak" in *Rossiia* (No. 6, Feb. 1923). In Mandelstam's collected essays, *On Poetry,* the two articles were combined into one. This translation is based primarily on the original journal publications; variants are noted in SS, II, 636-638.

1. One of Mandelstam's primary concerns in the 1920s was determining, showing, and proving the historical continuity of Russian culture. The theme of the continuity of Russian culture, indeed, of Russian history as the history of "the word," or poetry, emerges as both a moral and esthetic force in Mandelstam's essays, poetry, and literary prose. See, in particular, "On the Nature of the Word," the poems, "The Slate Ode" and "The Horseshoe Finder" and *The Noise of Time*.

2. Nikolai Mikhailovich Yazykov (1803-1846). Russian poet, contemporary of Pushkin, known mainly for his verbal art, in particular, for his dynamic rhythms and extraordinary verbal combinations. Although his earliest poetry continues the 18th century tradition of charming and exuberant Anacreontic songs, his later elegies, especially his famous "Waterfall" and "To the Rhine", testify to his place as a truly gifted poet of the early nineteenth century.

3. Militaristic imagery used to emphasize non-military, peaceful themes plus the interest in "word-roots" echoes Khlebnikov here. See, for instance, Khlebnikov's poem, "Eh! eh! ee-eem! All covered in sweat" (E—e! Y—ym! Ves' v potu, 1921), which calls on people to learn "a new war," of springtime, Nature, and the primitive, natural way of life.

4. Saints Cyril and Methodius, Byzantine apostles to the Moravian Slavs in the ninth century A.D. are credited with introducing Christianity, the Church Slavonic dialect, and the Cyrillic alphabet into the Slavic world. Russia was Christianized in 988 or 989, and received the Church language and alphabet at that time.

5. Volapük—an artificially created international language, less successful than Esperanto (SS, II, 645). It was invented about 1879 by J.M. Schleyer of Baden, Germany. Its name is based on "vol" (world) and "pük" (language).

6. Vasily Kirilovich Trediakovsky (1703-1769). Eighteenth century Russian poet and literary theorist. Best known for his treatise, *The New and Brief Method for the Composition of Russian Verse* (1735), in which he advocated replacing the rather artificial syllabic verse then in use with the more natural (to the Russian language) syllabotonic system of versification. His work aided the development of the secular Russian literary language rather than its Church Slavonic counterpart.

7. On Lomonosov, see No. 4, "On Contemporary Poetry."

8. Konstantin Nikolaevich Batyushkov (1787-1855). Major Russian poet of the early 19th century. One of the founders of Arzamas, the semi-humorous literary society which opposed the archaic linguistic demands and language usage of Admiral Alexander Semenovich Shishkov's (1753-1841) conservative literary society. The Arzamas cultivated the genres of pre-Romanticism, in particular, epistles to friends and the lighter verse forms. Mandelstam's admiration for Batyushkov as a poet and man is magnificently expressed in his poem No. 261, "Batyushkov" (1932). This poem refers to Batyushkov's famous elegy, "The Dying Tasso" and his personal relations with his fellow poets of all ages and places. Batyushkov is known for his translations, e.g., Tasso's *Gerusaleme liberata,* and for his free adaptations, e.g., his poem "Istochnik" based on Parny's "Le Torrent. Idylle persanne" (Mandelstam's reference to "Zafna").

9. On Khlebnikov see Note 2, "Literary Moscow." For a number of translations of his work, V. Khlebnikov *Snake Train; Prose and Poetry* (Ardis, 1977).

10. On Pasternak, see Note 19, "Literary Moscow."

11. Khlebnikov's poem "Incantation by Laughter" is based on neologisms derived from every possible or conceivable root of the word "smekh" (laughter), concentrating on consonantal prefixes and suffixes. See Gary Kern's various translations of this poem in Khlebnikov *Snake Train.*

12. Here Mandelstam seems to suggest that Sologub exemplified the type of "deaf"

or "hard of hearing" poet under discussion. Note also that one of Sologub's best known collections is called *The Flaming Circle*.

13. On Akhmatova, see No. 17, "On Contemporary Poetry."

14. On Kuzmin, see No. 15, "On Contemporary Poetry."

15. Both of these citations are from Salieri's speech in Pushkin's little tragedy, *Mozart and Salieri*. For further discussion of the Mozart-Salieri theme in Mandelstam's work, see N.Y. Mandelstam, *Mozart and Salieri*.

16. *My Sister, Life*, although written in 1917, was only published in 1922. It was this work which brought Pasternak to fame. For instance, Marina Tsvetaeva said of it: "What first surprises us in Pasternak's verse (that unbroken chain of first things) is everyday life. Its fullness, its detail and its 'prosiness.' Not just tokens of the day, but of the hour!" (M. Tsvetaeva, "Svetovoi liven'," *Proza*, New York, 1953). See also, Mandelstam's other, still more enthusiastic comments about *My Sister, Life* on the last page of "Storm and Stress."

17. On Fet, see Note 21, "Badger Hole."

18. From Pasternak's "Definition of Poetry" in *My Sister, Life*.

19. From Pasternak's "To Helen" in *My Sister, Life*.

20. See Alexander Herzen's memoirs, *My Past and Thoughts*, translated into English by Constance Garnett.

25. STORM AND STRESS

This essay first appeared in January 1923 in the first issue of the short-lived journal *Russian Art (Russkoe iskusstvo)*, see SS, II, 648-49. Its Russian title, *Buria i natisk* is a Russian translation of the German concept, *Sturm und Drang*.

1. The idea and image of the "knitting together of the spines of two poetic systems, two poetic epochs" is reiterated in poetic form in Mandelstam's poem No. 135, "The Age," also dated 1923.

2. Both Khlebnikov and Kruchenykh developed "trans-sense" or "trans-rational" language. On Kruchenykh, see V. Markov, *Russian Futurism* for Kruchenykh's "Declaration of the Word as Such" (pp. 130-131) and "Declaration of Transrational Language" (pp. 345-346) in English translation.

3. It is interesting to note that by 1923 Mandelstam was linking the Acmeist movement with Symbolism. This is a statement of historical perspective and critical distance; it should be contrasted with his polemical manifesto, "Morning of Acmeism," which clearly disassociated Acmeism from Symbolism. "Storm and Stress" should also be compared with Annensky's essay, "On Contemporary Lyricism," published in *Apollon* (Nos. 1-3), 1909, which was the first historical survey and revaluation of the Symbolist movement. Futurism, of course, was not yet discussed. Mandelstam seems to be taking Annensky's essay as his model.

4. On Balmont, see Note 4, "On the Addressee." That essay contains mainly negative criticism of Balmont.

5. On Bryusov, see Note 6, "On Contemporary Poetry." Also see "Badger Hole."

6. On Bely, see Note 29, "Badger Hole." See also negative criticism in "On the Nature of the Word."

7. For comments on Ivanov, see Index.

8. On Sologub, see Note 9, "On the Addressee." See also comments in other essays, including "For the Anniversary of F. K. Sologub."

9. On Annensky, see Index. See particularly the statement of major importance in "On the Nature of the Word."

10. Alexei Nikolaevich Apukhtin (1840-1893). A popular poet of the 1880s. His

melancholy themes, simplicity of diction, and conversational intonation, as well as the poet's friendship with the composer Peter Ilich Chaikovsky led to many of his poems being set to music.

11. On Kuzmin, see Note 15, "On Contemporary Poetry."

12. On Khodasevich, see Note 11, "Literary Moscow."

13. On Baratynsky, see Note 3, "On the Addressee."

14. On Derzhavin, see Note 3, "On Contemporary Poetry."

15. On Tyutchev, see Note 4, "Morning of Acmeism."

16. A major tenet of Mandelstam's poetry of this period, 1923, and one of his major criticisms of Futurism, which otherwise is treated very positively in this essay.

17. A reference to Tyutchev's poem "Autumn Evening" (1830).

18. On Akhmatova, see Note 17, "On Contemporary Poetry."

19. On Blok, see "Badger Hole," which is devoted to Blok. Comments appear in "Literary Moscow," "A Letter on Russian Poetry," among others.

20. In the early 1920s, Mandelstam was profoundly concerned with the theme of the relationship of art (or poetry) to history, and with the role of "the word" and language with respect to art and history. This theme emerges most clearly in the essay "On the Nature of the Word," in which Mandelstam attempts to show that Russian literature is a unified entity because it is an outgrowth of its national language and partakes of that language; and, furthermore, that that language is inseparable from its cultural history.

In his autobiographical novella *The Noise of Time* Mandelstam confronts "great Russian literature" with the literature of reflection. The latter reflects history and historical forces; the former is allegedly autonomous and paticipates in history, but is free to reject (rather than reflect) particular historical events. His theory of "literary savagery" (*literaturnaia zlost'*) develops out of this juxtaposition. Hence, his assertion in this essay that Blok's poetry, being "great literature," was "at odds with history," and thereby proves the autonomy of "the word."

21. Other valuable comments on Khlebnikov and his poetry appear in "On the Nature of the Word," "Literary Moscow: The Birth of Plot," "Some Notes on Poetry." See also, Mandelstam's very personal poem on this theme, No. 141, "No, never was I anyone's contemporary," written shortly after this essay, in 1924. Both Mandelstam and Khlebnikov were profoundly concerned with the themes of time and history, although they usually treated them from different perspectives, different angles of vision. See notes to "On the Nature of the Word" concerning Bergson and Khlebnikov.

22. Mandelstam's contrast of Mayakovsky and Khlebnikov here must also be intended as a kind of defense of his own (and others), difficult poetry as against the "easy," "didactic," and more direct poetry of post-revolutionary Mayakovsky and his followers.

23. On Mayakovsky, see Note 14, "Literary Moscow."

24. On Klyuev, see Note 16, "A Letter about Russian Poetry." Sergei Alexandrovich Esenin (1895-1925). An extremely popular peasant poet of the early twentieth century. Like Klyuev, he was made much of in the Petersburg salons of Zinaida Gippius and her friends. After the revolution, he joined the Scythians under the leadership of Ivanov-Razumnik and Bely, and a year later the Imaginists, whose leading poet he became. In 1922-23, no longer associated with any particular group or movement, he married and travelled abroad with the famous American dancer, Isadora Duncan. In 1925 he committed suicide. He is known for the remarkable lyricism of his poetry, for his peasant motifs and for his themes of tavern life and hooliganism. See Mandelstam's poignant references to Esenin in "Fourth Prose." On Esenin see Gordon McVay, *Esenin: A Life* (Ardis, 1976).

25. On Aseev, see Note 16, "Literary Moscow."

26. A major theme of Mandelstam.

27. On Pasternak, see Note 19, "Literary Moscow," and "Some Notes on Poetry," the last part of which is Mandelstam's enthusiastic review of *My Sister, Life.*

28. On Batyushkov, see Note 8, "Some Notes on Poetry."

26. HUMANISM AND THE PRESENT

This essay was published in the "Literary Supplement" of the Berlin newspaper *On the Eve* (*Nakanune,* January 20, 1923, No. 240) under the editorship of A. N. Tolstoy and others (SS, II, p. 649).

1. This essay should be read in conjunction with Mandelstam's other essays treating the themes of social architecture, or what the author has also termed "Social Gothic"—"François Villon," "Morning of Acmeism," "Conversation about Dante"; the artist and society—"On the Addressee," "Government and Rhythm," "The Word and Culture," "A Revolutionary in the Theater"; and the nineteenth century—"The Nineteenth Century"—among others. It also demands comparison with Mandelstam's autobiographical prose, *The Noise of Time* and with his poetry of 1921-25.

2. Here, perhaps, the most pertinent chapters in *The Noise of Time* are "The Judaic Chaos" and "The Erfurt Program."

3. See Mandelstam's marvelous image of man's humble human dwelling place in poem No. 127, "To some winter is arrack and the blue-eyed punch" (1922).

4. The passage on the last page of *The Noise of Time* reads: "Looking back at the entire nineteenth century of Russian culture—shattered, finished, unrepeatable, which no one must repeat or dares to repeat—I wish to hail the century, as one would hail settled weather, and see in it the unity lent it by the measureless cold which welded decades together into one day, one night, one profound winter wherein the terrible State, like a stove, is blazing in the ice."

5. See the last section of Mandelstam's poem No. 136, "The Horseshoe Finder," also dated 1923.

27. HENRI-AUGUSTE BARBIER

This essay was originally published in *Searchlight* (*Prozhektor,* No. 13) in August, 1923 (SS, III, 357) accompanied by Mandelstam's translation of Barbier's "La Curée" (SS, II, 465-68, 676-7). Mandelstam translated a number of Barbier's *Iambes* (SS, I, 562) in 1923-1924.

1. Henri Auguste Barbier (1805-1882). Outside of Russia, he is now considered a minor French poet. Best known for his *Iambes* (1831) on the July days of 1830. One might say Barbier was to Chénier as the 1830 revolution was the great French Revolution. Mandelstam's characterization of the July days of 1830 as a "classically unsuccessful revolution" might well apply to Barbier, a "classically unsuccessful poet," as it were. Inspired by the spirit of the July days and Chenier's *Iambes,* Barbier, in a very short period of time, wrote a series of powerful, morally committed poems, denouncing the evils of his day, and then, for all intents and purposes, essentially lost his poetic voice. See also, Mandelstam's essay on Chenier.

However, Barbier's popularity was very great and very real in Russia, where his *Iambes* were translated almost immediately, and continued to be translated well into the twentieth century. See Note 11, below.

Barbier's most popular poems included: "La Curée," "La Popularité," "L'Idole," "Paris," "Dante," "Quartre-vingt-treize," and "Varsovie."

2. The ironic tone of this essay on a historical theme and personage should be noted and compared with Mandelstam's autobiographical novella, *The Noise of Time,* written during the same period. While the essay is serious, much of it is "tongue-in-cheek" mockery, expounded in Mandelstam's theory of "literary savagery" and developed to its highest pitch in "Fourth Prose."

3. On the histrionics of the French Revolution, see the essay "The Nineteenth Century."

4. An ironic reference to the Cathédrale de Notre Dame de Paris. This image is diametrically opposed to the image presented in Mandelstam's poem "Notre Dame," in which the cathedral's powerful, dynamic, masculine qualities (i.e., Adam flexing his muscles) are emphasized; here the feminine (i.e., weak) body is overwhelmed by the insurgents and used as a mere theatrical prop.

5. The serious themes of this essay—the relationship of art to history and of the poet to the event—are developed more fully and more artistically in *The Noise of Time.*

6. See Mandelstam's translation No. 491a. See Nadezhda Mandelstam's comments on Mandelstam's translation of this poem in *Hope Against Hope,* pp. 170, 177, 239.

7. See Mandelstam's essay on Chénier.

8. See Mandelstam's essay on Dante.

9. See Mandelstam's translations of these poems, Nos. 467-471.

10. See Mandelstam's comments on the novel and the Napoleonic myth in "The End of the Novel."

11. Barbier's popularity in Russia began almost immediately with Lermontov's translations of his poems; it continued throughout the nineteenth century and well into the twentieth century. Besides Mandelstam, Barbier was translated in the twentieth century by Bryusov, Antokolsky, and others, and in 1922 an almost complete edition of his work appeared in Odessa: see Alekseev (editor), *Iamby i poemy (Iambes and Poems)* (SS, I, p. 562).

12. A major goal of Mandelstam in *The Noise of Time.*

28. THE MOSCOW ART THEATER AND THE WORD

This essay was first published in *Theater and Music (Teatr i muzyka),* No. 36, November 6, 1923 (SS, III, 361).

1. The Moscow Art Theater (MXAT) was founded in 1898 by Konstantin Sergeevich Stanislavsky (1863-1938) and Vladimir Ivanovich Nemirovich-Danchenko (1858-1943). The theater opened in October 1898 with the production of A. K. Tolstoi 's *Tsar Fyodor Ioannovich.* Chekhov's *The Seagull* was also staged there in 1898, followed by his *Uncle Vanya* in 1899, *The Three Sisters* in 1901, and *The Cherry Orchard* in 1904. Gorky's first plays were also staged there, *The Lower Depths* in 1902 and *Children of the Sun* in 1905. Griboedov's *Woe from Wit* was presented in 1906 and Turgenev's *A Month in the Country* in 1909. There were also several productions of Shakespearian plays, including *Hamlet, Othello,* and *Twelfth Night,* as well as numerous Symbolist dramas, including works by Maeterlinck, Ibsen, Andreev, and Hamsun.

The founders of MXAT were intent on creating a new theater to replace what they regarded as the commercialized and vulgarized theater of the late nineteenth century. The traditional theater leaned heavily on the representation of external forms, on elaborate artifice, and on the genius of a few stars. The new theater was dubbed "the theater of inner feeling," for it was postulated on the idea of revealing man's inner experiences. Furthermore, ensemble acting would replace the unpredictable and uneven quality of the star system. Most important, perhaps, the director's role was revaluated: instead of allowing the stars to do as they pleased and ordering the supporting cast to act in a particular manner to enhance the popularity of the star performers, the director's role was now conceived to focus on helping each of his actors to discover his own role, to reveal the character beneath the actor, and on guiding the ensemble as a whole to reveal the play behind the text, the inner drama.

In its early years, MXAT was truly the theater of the avant-garde. It was devoted to all that was new in acting, directing, staging; its repertoire was very varied, including plays of social and political content, plays of history and manners, as well as Symbolist and impressionist works. After its first tour abroad in 1905, however, it began to concentrate on the Symbolist and mystical drama then dominating Western European theater, a tendency which proved distasteful to the progressive intelligentsia, including Mandelstam. Mandelstam for one was very hostile to such productions as Andreev's *Life of a Man* in which he saw only the negation of life, the preoccupation with abstraction, death, and darkness. However, his major criticism of MXAT was that it reflected the shortcomings of the generation that founded it, that it misinterpreted its own role. Mandelstam was more hostile to the Stanislavsky method or code, presented as *The Actor's Handbook*, than to the repertoire itself. For him the theater represented the incomprehension and misinterpretation of literature itself, of "the word." This essay should be read in conjunction with "The Word and Culture," and with the autobiographical novella, *The Noise of Time*. It is interesting to note here Mandelstam's use of poetic technique in his prose essays and fiction.

2. Just as his essay "Henri-Auguste Barbier" foreshadows aspects of *The Noise of Time* in using a historical personage (Barbier) to represent an historical event (1830 July days) and thereby illuminate the theme of the artist's relationship to history, so this essay foreshadows the autobiographical novella in using a historical institution (MXAT) to represent the shortcomings of the intelligentsia of the 1890s to 1910s and thus illuminate the theme of literary and dramatic interpretation, a major theme in *The Noise of Time*. In both instances, cultural-historical metaphors are developed not only to illustrate thematic statements, but to create the illusion of historical reinforcement for the ideas presented in the text. See, in particular, the chapter "Komissarzhevskaya" in *The Noise of Time*.

3. See the chapter "The Tenishev School" in *The Noise of Time*.

4. This theme is remarkably elucidated in the imagery of the last stanza of Mandelstam's "The Slate Ode."

5. Mandelstam's hostility to the predominant values of the 1880s-1890s—positivism, social Darwinism, and the demand for empirical verification of everything—was reinforced by the emerging values of his own generation expressed, at least in part, in his education at the Tenishev School, his interest in, and study of, French literature, and his reading of Henri Bergson.

6. This is a favorite theme of Mandelstam's, see especially the second half of "The Horseshoe Finder."

7. See Note 1, above for a listing of the various productions of MXAT.

8. An attack on literary interpretation as opposed to reading, also a major theme of *The Noise of Time*, see the last chapter, in particular.

9. See especially, the chapter "Komissarzhevskaya" in *The Noise of Time*.

10. See K. S. Stanislavsky, *An Actor's Handbook: An Alphabetical Arrangement of Concise Statements on Aspects of Acting*, edited and translated by Elizabeth R. Hapgood (N.Y.: 1963). This English translation is used here and below to avoid confusion. This book is a codification of Stanislavsky's method, sometimes known as the "ABC of Feelings."

11. Henryk Ippolitovich Semiradsky (1843-1902). A member of the Russian Imperial Academy who specialized in large-scale canvases and murals treating Biblical, Classical, and historical subjects. Although his compositions are technically competent,

his forms are somewhat awkward, as if intentionally painted for backdrops of a theater. He did the murals for the Historical Museum in Moscow on the life of the ancient Slavs, and he also did theater curtains in Cracow and Lvov.

29. AN ARMY OF POETS

The first section of this polemical essay appeared in the popular magazine, *Ogonek* (No. 33, November 11, 1923); the second section appeared the following week (No. 34, November 18, 1923). Both sections were republished as "Army of Poets" in the Moscow weekly, *Literary Russia (Literaturnaia Rossiia,* No. 34, August 19, 1966). See SS, II, 619-20.

1. The Stray Dog (Brodiachaia sobaka) was perhaps the most popular cabaret in pre-revolutionary St. Petersburg. It was opened by B. K. Pronin on New Years, 1912, and became a gathering place for the literary and artistic elite, indeed a major forum for the Futurists, until it was closed down by the police in March 1915. Pronin reopened it later under a new name, The Actor's Stop (Prival komediantov). Aside from being a popular meeting place, the cabaret served as a center for popular literary readings, celebrations of various types, pantomimes and concerts. See SS, I, 477-79 and V. Markov, *Russian Futurism.*
2. Mandelstam's defense of the poet is primarily a diatribe against the intelligentsia of his day, whom he considered "enemies of the word." See, "The Word and Culture."
3. Cafes and cabarets on Tverskoi Boulevard, where Moscow's literary Bohemia gathered, especially in the years 1919-1921. During these years, one of the favorite themes of the Imaginists was cafe life. See, for instance, Esenin's famous "Tavern Moscow." The audience would pay an admission fee for the privilege of listening to poetry readings and participating in literary discussions.

30. THE END OF THE NOVEL

This essay was first published in Mandelstam's volume of essays, *On Poetry* (1928). It is not known if it had been published earlier. See SS, II, 638. It may have been begun as early as 1923, but seems to have been completed after 1925. More evidence is needed to date it definitively. Mandelstam's emphasis on the individual, on the relationship of biography to the genre of the novel, and on the problem of the artist-writer-biographer's role in society, could place this essay with the works of the second half of the 1920s, rather than with those of the first half. See the concerns of this period as expressed in his letters of 1926-1928, as well as in the literary prose of 1926-1930s. On the other hand, there is no doubt that it is also very closely connected with "Literary Moscow: The Birth of Plot," *The Noise of Time,* and "The Egyptian Stamp," and that its inception belongs to the period of the first half of the 1920s.

1. Interest in the novel and in prose forms in general (in contrast to poetry) increased enormously in the Soviet Union in the 1920s. Shklovsky, Eikhenbaum, Zamyatin, and the Serapion Brothers, to name but a few critics and practitioners, were leaders in this movement, in particular, in Petrograd-Leningrad, but also in Moscow. See "Literary Moscow: The Birth of Plot."
2. See "Literary Moscow: The Birth of Plot."
3. See Mandelstam's review of Bely's *Diary of an Eccentric.*
4. See *The Noise of Time* in *The Prose of Mandelstam* (Princeton, 1967), in parti-

cular, the discussion of biography with respect to the *raznochinets* (the declassed intellectual) and the juxtaposition of biographical and historical detail.

5. Mandelstam seems to have confused "centrifugal" and "centripetal" in this essay (see the original publication of *O poezii,* 1928). The opposite reading seems to be intended.

6. See "Literary Moscow: The Birth of Plot" and "Fourth Prose."

7. See, for instance, Mandelstam's *The Noise of Time,* and V. Shklovsky's novels, *Sentimental Journey* and *Zoo, or Letters Not about Love* (R. Sheldon, trans., Ithaca, 1970, 1971, respectively).

31. THE SLUMP

This essay first appeared in *Russia* (No. 3, 1924), and was republished with numerous changes in Mandelstam's *On Poetry* (1928). The changes were primarily political. See SS, II, 627-628.

1. Like "An Army of Poets," with which this essay should be read, "The Slump" is explicitly directed against those whom Mandelstam designated "enemies of the word" (See "The Word and Culture"). It is a diatribe of a "contemporary," not an objective analysis. Of all his polemical essays, Mandelstam probably chose to include this one in his collection, *On Poetry* because it most clearly concerns the "slump" or decline in the reader's response to poetry.

2. Sweetbriar ("Shipovnik") Publishing House began issuing a series of literary almanacs in 1907, and continued until 1917 (26 issues). Leonid Andreev was the editor. His editorial policy was to a great extent conditioned by his antagonism toward Maxim Gorky and the almanacs issued by Gorky's publishing house, Knowledge, established in 1903. The Sweetbriar almanacs contained mostly prose fiction, but also some poetry and art reproductions. The eclectic nature of these almanacs led to the inclusion of both good and "bad" literature. Among the contributors were: Sologub, Bunin, Sergeev-Tsensky, A. Kuprin, A. Serafimovich, Andreev, M. Dobuzhinsky, B. Zaitsev.

3. Dmitry Nikolayevich Ovsianiko-Kulikovsky (1853-1920). Russian literary historian and Academician, author of the three-volume *History of the Russian Intelligentsia,* a gallery of Russian "socio-psychological types." Of his work on Pushkin, he stated: "My task was not literary-historical in nature, but psychological." Mandelstam opposed Ovsianiko-Kulikovsky's method on the grounds that he concentrated on the psychological motivation behind the text rather than on the text itself—the product of the poet's esthetic vision.

4. Mandelstam was obviously very aware of the various scholarly approaches to the reading of literature, including semiotics, but he was not a member or even fellow-traveller of the Formalist movement. He voiced his hopes, however, for some kind of "objective, scholarly" approach to poetry. See below. See also, "Conversation about Dante" and my Introduction.

5. See *The Noise of Time* for Mandelstam's positive evaluation of the literate "reader" (as opposed to the hostile view of the literary "critic") presented through the characterization of V. V. Gippius, his favorite teacher, mentor, and "companion." See my comments on Mandelstam's "ideal reader" in the Introduction.

32. FOR THE ANNIVERSARY OF F. K. SOLOGUB

This tribute to Sologub originally appeared in the Leningrad newspaper, *Latest News (Poslednie Novosti),* February 11, 1924. SS, II, 649.

1. See the first volume of Sologub's *Collected Works* published in 1909. The poem cited in "On the Addressee" as characteristic of the qualities Mandelstam admired in Sologub's work is from this volume.

2. This may be a reference to the cold relations between the Acmeists and Sologub around 1915, the time of Mandelstam's unpleasant letter to Sologub; see Letter No. 11. Later, the Acmeists, in particular Gumilev, came to greatly admire Sologub's poetry. (SS, III, 376-7).

3. This last section bears comparison with Mandelstam's poem No. 141, "No, never was I anyone's contemporary."

33. A REVOLUTIONARY IN THE THEATER

This review was originally published in *Theatre and Music (Teatr i muzyka,* Nos. 1-2, Jan. 5, 1923). See SS, III, 356-357.

1. Ernst Toller (1893-1939). German poet, dramatist and prose writer, whose plays were staged in the Soviet theater in the 1920s-1930s (SS, III, 356-7). He left Germany in 1932 and committed suicide in New York in 1939. At the beginning of World War I he volunteered for the German Army, but came home an invalid in 1916, having undergone a complete political transformation. In 1919, he was elected to the short-lived Bavarian Socialist Republic, as a result of which he was consequently sentenced to five years imprisonment for revolutionary activities.

He has aptly been called the "most dominant and flagrant genius hatched by the German revolution." This is clearly expressed in his drama; see, for example, *Die Wandlung (Transfiguration,* 1919), in which he reveals in thirteen tableaux, the horror of war as he experienced it, and *Masse-Mensche (Mass Man,* 1929), in which he attacks individualism, militarism, capitalism, mechanistic civilization, and other social phenomena, envisaging common brotherhood as the ultimate salvation of mankind.

Toller is also well-known for his *Die Maschinenstürmer (The Machine Wreckers,* 1922) dramatizing the Luddite riots in England, and *Hoppla, wir leben (Hoppla!, 1927),* a satire on contemporary society. His autobiography *Eine Jugend in Deutschland (I Was A German),* appeared in 1933.

2. Mandelstam thoroughly condemned Andreev and his *Life of a Man* in *The Noise of Time.*

3. These quotations are from Vera Mendel's English translation, *Man and the Masses,* London: The Nonesuch Press, 1923 (Translator's note).

4. Mandelstam's concern with the relationship of humanism and the collective consciousness, with the survival of humanistic values in the new Soviet society emerges in both his poetry and prose of the early 1920s. See, for instance, poems No. 135, "My Age," and No. 140, "January 1, 1924," as well as the essays, "Government and Rhythm," "Humanism and the Present."

34. A. BELY. *DIARY OF AN ECCENTRIC*

This review originally appeared in the magazine, *Red Virgin Soil (Krasnaia nov',* No. 5, 1923). See SS, II, 671.

1. Andrei Bely, see Note 29, "Badger Hole." There are also numerous comments, predominantly hostile, on Bely and his creative work, in Mandelstam's other essays of the 1920s, including "On the Nature of the Word," "Storm and Stress," "A Letter about Russian Poetry." In 1934, on the occasion of Bely's death, however, Mandelstam dedicated several poems to his memory, as a great poet, man and intellect. "Conversation about Dante" may also have been written with Bely as its "interlocutor." See notes to that essay.

2. *Diary of an Eccentric (Zapiski Chudaka)* dates from what is generally termed the third phase of Bely's literary career (1921-1934), a period characterized to a great extent by heterogeneous autobiographical works. This book deals mainly with Bely's spiritual autobiography, in particular, with his interest in theosophy or anthroposophy.

3. See Mandelstam's essay, "The Nineteenth Century," in which his hostility toward "theosophy," "Buddhism," and mysticism is carefully delineated.

4. Mandelstam's dislike of the novel *St. Petersburg* is also expressed in the opening paragraphs of "Literary Moscow: The Birth of Plot."

5. For other interesting comments on the prose style of the 1920s, see "Literary Moscow: The Birth of Plot." See also Mandelstam's own literary prose of this period, "Cold Summer," "Sukharevka," as well as *The Noise of Time.*

35. G. HAUPTMAN. *THE HERETIC OF SOANA*

This review was first published in the magazine, *Press and Revolution (Pechat' i revolutsiia,* No. 5, 1923). See SS, II, 671.

1. Gerhart Hauptmann (1862-1946). German writer best known for his dramatic works. *The Weavers* (1892), perhaps his most popular drama, was extremely successful in Russia. He also wrote poetry and novels. His novella, *Der Ketzen von Soana (The Heretic of Soana)* dates from 1918; it was translated into Russian in 1920. As is true of much of Hauptmann's work, this novella is a blend of fantasy and stark realism, the fantasy being at least partly erotic in inspiration, treating an ambiguously sensual-spiritual situation—in keeping with the Symbolist traditions of the end of the 19th century-early 20th century. In this novella, a priest is transformed into a pagan-poetic representative of Nature.

36. AN. SVENTITSKY. *A BOOK OF TALES ABOUT KING ARTHUR...*

This review first appeared in the magazine, *Press and Revolution (Pechat' i revoliutsiia,* No. 6, 1923). See SS, II, 671. I did not succeed in locating any information about Sventitsky.

1. Chrétien de Troyes. French medieval poet. Author of the best and earliest extant courtly romances dealing with the semi-legendary English King Arthur. His works include, among others, *Percival, or the Story of the Grail, Lancelot, or the Knight of the Cart,* and *Erec and Enide.*

2. Tatiana Lvovna Shchepkin-Kupernik (b. 1874-d.?). Writer of sentimental stories and poetry dealing primarily with the experiences of women in love. Granddaughter of the famous serf-actor, Mikhail Shchepkin.

3. Mandelstam's view of the Middle Ages is developed in several of his essays, including "François Villon," "Morning of Acmeism," and "Conversation about Dante." His interest in French medieval literature goes back to his student days at the University of Heidelberg.

4. Charles-Marie Joseph Bédier (1864-1938). Renowned French medievalist, appointed professor of medieval French language and literature at the Collège de France in 1903. His famous reconstruction of the *Roman de Tristan et Iseult* was published in 1900, and his critical edition of the *Roman de Tristan* by Thomas in 1902-1905; the latter proved that the earliest Tristan poem was the work of an individual poet, not the result of popular tradition. Between 1908 and 1921, he published *Les légendes épiques*, a work in which he details his theory that the great French medieval epics did not arise out of popular tradition.

37. THE RETURN

This autobiographical vignette was published for the first time in SS, III, 20-24. Osip Mandelstam and his brother Alexander (Shura) left the Crimean port of Theodosia in August 1919 to return to their family in Moscow. "Mensheviks in Georgia" is the account of their misadventures en route. "The Return" seems to be an earlier version or draft of the latter, and should be read along with it. (SS, III, 353-354). See Clarence Brown, *Mandelstam,* for more biographical details about this period. See also, Mandelstam's Letter No. 59, in which this vignette is mentioned as originally having been a part of the volume of prose fiction issued in 1928 as "The Egyptian Stamp."

1. *Burka:* a felt cloak worn primarily by the mountain people of the Caucasus, such as the Daghestanis.
2. Tiflis, now Tbilisi, is the capital of Georgia. Between 1918 and 1921, Georgia was an independent state under Menshevik rule. Deportation back to the Crimea from Georgia was regarded as evidence of complicity with the enemy and deportees were usually shot. Hence, the severity of the situation.
3. Riurik Ivnev (pseudonym of Mikhail Alexandrovich Kovalev), Russian poet born in Tiflis in 1893, member of the Futurist group, Mezzanine of Poetry, and later of the Imaginists. *Self-Immolation (Samosozhzhenie,* 1913) is considered his most typical work. His imaginist works include *Sun in the Grave (Solntse vo grobe,* 1921), a collection of poetry, and *Four Shots (Chetyre vystrela,* 1921), criticism. He later became a secretary to the first Soviet Minister of Culture, Anatoly Lunacharsky, for whom Mandelstam worked in 1918 (see Note 3, "Government and Rhythm"). Most recently he published a book of prose fiction and memoirs entitled *At the Foot of the Mtatsminda (U podnozhniia Mtatsmindy,* M. 1973), under his given name.
4. Vladimir Alexandrovich Mazurkevich (1871-1942). Russian poet and author of popular romances (SS, III, 355).

38. MENSHEVIKS IN GEORGIA

These memoirs were first published in the weekly magazine, *Ogonek (The Flame,* No. 20, August 12, 1923). See SS, II, 617. This is one of a number of memoirs, vignettes and reportage that Mandelstam wrote for *The Flame* between July and December of 1923. His other pieces include: "Cold Summer," "Sukharevka," "Army of Poets," "The First International Peasants' Conference," "Nguyen Ai Quoc (Ho Chi Minh)..."

1. See "The Return," undoubtedly an earlier version of this piece. See also "Batum," a kind of companion piece.
2. Karl Johann Kautsky (1854-1938). A leader of the German Social Democratic Party and prominent figure in the Second International, a personal friend of Karl Marx and Friedrich Engels (in their last years), an opponent of the Soviet Bolshevik regime.

(SS, II, 618)

3. Emil Vandervelde (1866-1938). Leader of the Belgian Workers' Party, member of the Second International. In 1925-1927 he was Minister of Foreign Affairs for Belgium. Also an opponent of the Soviet Bolshevik regime (SS, II, 618).

4. Between 1918 and February 1921, Georgia was an independent republic under Menshevik leadership. See "The Return."

5. A reference to Mandelstam's arrest and imprisonment in Theodosia. He was arrested by the Whites on charges of working for the Bolsheviks. His friends managed to secure his release, see N. Y. Mandelstam, *Hope Abandoned,* pp. 86-87, for details. For a fascinating fictionalized account of Mandelstam's impressions of Theodosia and its inhabitants, see "Theodosia" in Clarence Brown, *The Prose of Mandelstam.*

6. See Note 2, "The Return."

8. See "Batum."

9. See "The Return."

10. For more on Mandelstam's views of such "independent" states as Switzerland, see his 1923 review of Bely's *Diary of an Eccentric.*

11. Noe Nikolai Zhordania (1868-1953). The leader of the *Mesame dasi* or "third group" interested in national revival, an illegal Social Democratic party, founded in 1893. This group was led by Zhordania, Karlo Chkheidze and others. (In 1898 Stalin also became a member, but fled the Caucasus to join Lenin and the Bolsheviks when the Mensheviks gained control of Georgia). The original groups of national revival—the "first group" and the "second group"—were predominantaly literary and social in orientation, rather than political. On May 26, 1918, the Georgians set up an independent state under the leadership of Zhordania. A Soviet mission headed by S. M. Kirov, was sent to Tbilisi in 1920; it prepared the way for the Bolshevik coup which took place there the following year, led by Stalin and G. K. Ordzhonikidze. On February 25, 1921, a Soviet regime was established in Georgia, with Tbilisi, formerly known as Tiflis, as its capital city.

12. *Russian Word* (*Russkoe Slovo,* published 1895-1918), a liberal Russian newspaper published in Moscow by I.D. Sytin (SS, II, 618)

39. BATUM

This piece first appeared in the newspaper *Soviet South* (Rostov), January 17, 1922; part two first appeared in *Kommunist* (Kharkov), Feb. 9, 1922. See SS, II, 695.

1. Traditional Turkish flat bread.

2. An extremely popular Russian opera whose leading role was sung by Chaliapin.

3. Sazandari—a band of native Georgian musicians playing on ethnic instruments.

4. A reference to the double windows used in Russia against the winter cold, the outer one of which may be opened or removed for the summer months.

40. THE BLOODY MYSTERY-PLAY OF JANUARY NINTH

This dramatic historical commemorative was first published in the newspaper, *Soviet South* (January 22, 1922) to commemorate the January 9, (Old Style) massacre which triggered the 1905 Revolution. See SS, III, 365.

1. The relationship of art to history is a major theme in Mandelstam's work. Here, the emphasis seems to be on the question: What gives order or structure to a major historical event?

2. The date of publication of this piece is based on the New Style calendar; thus January 9, Old Style, is the same as January 22, New Style. This article commemorates the January 9 massacre of the Petersburg workers led by Father Gapon to air their grievances before the Tsar. The massacre is considered the beginning of the 1905 Revolution. See next note.

3. Father Georgy Apollonovich Gapon (1870-1906) and "Bloody Sunday." Little is known about Father Gapon except that he was a St. Petersburg priest of peasant origin who worked primarily among the lower classes, and that he was a charismatic figure, endowed with enormous energy and a gift for oratory. His popularity with the working classes made it possible for him to organize and preside over the Society of Industrial Workers of St. Petersburg, formally established on April 11, 1904; its purpose was "to teach the members (1) self-respect and moral conduct; (2) a healthy national spirit; (3) a social consciousness of citizens; (4) peaceful pursuit of material improvement" (Mazour).

Although the Society failed to secure the support of the intelligentsia or the progressive workers since it was headed by a priest, the masses placed their faith in Gapon, still trusting in the Tsar as the ultimate authority. Simultaneously, national involvements, in particular, the Russo-Japanese war, added to the workers' difficulties. A petition was finally suggested, a direct appeal to the Tsar, which would list the workers' grievances and request "the summoning of the Constitutional Assembly elected by universal, equal and secret voting [to consider] universal education, amnesty for all political victims..., inviolability of personal freedom, a responsible cabinet, equality before the law, and separation of Church and State. The immediate social legislation urged was the abolition of redemption payments,... income tax as well as the various forms of indirect taxes, the right of labor to organize an eight-hour working day, a minimum wage law, and a number of other alleviating measures" (Mazour). The petition had been read to the Society before the day of the political Manifestation. The Tsar and his family had left the Winter Palace for Tsarskoe Selo, leaving the military in charge. "On Sunday, January 9, 1905, columns of workers bearing [their] petition... converged from distant suburbs upon the [Winter Palace] square. The authorities were aware of the proposed demonstration. The marchers were peaceful and orderly, some [carrying] portraits of the Tsar and sacred icons. They were stopped, nevertheless, by cordons of troops, and when they refused to disperse were fired upon" (Florinsky). The tragedy produced an extraordinary impression in Russia and abroad, to become known as "Bloody Sunday," the first violent episode of the 1905 Revolution.

Following the massacre, Gapon strongly censured the Tsar, the administration and the army. He was immediately defrocked and forced to flee abroad, where he subsequently joined the Social Revolutionaries (SRs). However, Gapon apparently also had ties with the security police, so when he finally returned to Russia, he was sentenced to death and hung by the SRs in 1906. Father Gapon's actual role is still being debated by historians. (SS, III, 365-367).

Most of the above information is taken from A. Mazour, *Russia Past and Present,* pp. 352-357, and M. T. Florinsky, *Russia: A History and Interpretation,* II.

4. Evgeny Viktorovich Tarle (1875-1955). Russian historian and publicist close to Marxist circles.

5. Mandelstam's interest in the theatre and in the imagery of the theatre, is indicated in his discussions of theatre in his prose fiction, *The Noise of Time,* in his essays such as "A Revolutionary in the Theatre," "The Art Theatre and the Word," ' "Mikhoels," "Berezil," and "Yakhontov," and in such poems as No. 82 (based on Racine's *Phaedre*), No. 114, No. 118.

6. See the imagery of Psyche and St. Petersburg in "The Word and Culture."

41. COLD SUMMER

This vignette of Moscow was first published in *The Flame* (No. 16 July 15, 1923). See SS, II, 591. It should be read along with "Sukharevka," and also in conjunction with Mandelstam's other depictions of urban life: "Batum," "Kiev," and the evocation of St. Petersburg in *The Noise of Time*.

1. A large department store near the Bolshoi Theatre, now known as *TsUM* The Central Department Store.
2. "Neskuchnyi Sad" may be translated here as "Pleasure Gardens." It is now called the Gorky Park of Culture and Rest.
3. See "Henri-August Barbier."
4. Gogol's influence on Mandelstam's prose takes various forms and demands serious study.
5. *Vkhutemas (Vysshie gosudarstvennye khudozhestvenno-tekhnicheskie master-skie),* Studios for the Applied Arts of the State Ministry of Higher Education, 1921-1926.
6. See Mandelstam's poems of the early 1930s about Moscow, in particular, No. 265, "Today's the day to make decalcomanias."
7. This church was torn down to make room for the Palace of Soviets (SS, II, 591).
8. See similar imagery in Mandelstam's "The Slate Ode."

42. SUKHAREVKA

This vignette was first published in *The Flame,* No. 18 (1923). See SS, II, 591. It should be read in conjunction with "Cold Summer," as part of Mandelstam's series of Moscow vignettes.

"Cold Summer" and "Sukharevka" are actually the results of Mandelstam's third attempt to write and publish literary prose. His first attempt—"The Fur Coat" ("Shuba")—was written in Kharkov and printed there in a local newspaper. An expanded version was later sold to Madame Rakovskaya for publication by her newly established publishing house, "Istoki," where "On the Nature of the Word" first appeared. The manuscript was lost, however, and a copy of the newspaper has yet to be found. Mandelstam's second attempt concerned "a tapestry found in a Moscow hovel" near the Smolensk market. It too is lost. For further details, see N. Mandelstam, *Hope Abandoned,* pp. 188-190.

1. Sukharevskaya Square had served as a marketplace until the Sukharevka tower was razed during the Stalin era. (SS, II, 592). The tower was originally built in 1692-1695 as part of a fortification system and named after the Sukharevka regiment stationed there. The tower stood between the Sretenka (now Dzerzhinskaya Street) and First Meshchanskaya Street (now Peace Prospect). It was also the site of a school of Navigation under Peter I. (SS, II, 591).
2. Kholmogori cows. Kholmogori, a village located at the mouth of the Northern Dvina river, just southeast of Archangelsk, was formerly a center for dairy cattle. It was a market center in the fifteenth and sixteenth centuries for Novgorod merchants.
3. See "Batum," for Mandelstam's discussion of the difference between European and Oriental commerce.
4. See the opening paragraphs of "Literary Moscow."

43. THE FIRST INTERNATIONAL PEASANTS' CONFERENCE

This news item was first published in *The Flame,* (No. 31, October 28, 1923). The conference was held in October. See, SS, II, 618.

1. Clara Zetkin (1857-1933). One of the founders of the German Communist Party.

44. A VISIT WITH NGUYEN AI QUOC (HO CHI MINH)

This interview was published in the Soviet weekly, *The Flame* (No. 39, December 23, 1923). The interview was conducted in French. See, SS, II, 619.

1. Nguyen Ai Quoc (1890-1970) is best known in the West by his Communist Party pseudonym, Ho Chi Minh, and as leader of the North Vietnamese. At the time of this interview, both Mandelstam and Ho Chi Minh were in their early thirties. Ho Chi Minh was then a representative of the Annamese people and a Comintern member.

2. Rene Maran (1887-1960). Originally from Martinique, he was the author of a novel about African life, *Batouala,* which attained great popularity in Soviet Russia in the 1920s.

45. KIEV

This piece first appeared in the *Evening Red News* (*Vechernaia krasnaia gazeta* [Leningrad] May 27 and June 3, 1926). See SS, II, 695. It should be read in conjunction with Mandelstam's other pieces on his Kievan experiences, the theatre and Jewish life, published in the same newspaper; see "Mikhoels," "Berezil," and "Yakhontov," as well as his letters of 1926.

1. Kiev is known as the "Mother of Cities." First mention of it is perhaps Ptolomeus' indication of a town on the Dniepr river called "Metropolis" (2nd century A.D.). Kiev was the capital of the Varangian principality in the ninth century, a trading center of major cultural and political significance on the route from Scandinavia to Constantinople. It was a constant object of princely rivalry, was ruined by the Tatar invasion of 1240, annexed by Lithuania in the fourteenth century, transferred to Poland in 1569, incorporated into the Russian empire in 1654 (after being seized by Boghdan Khmelnitsky), and officially annexed by Russia in 1686. Its twentieth century battle scars include occupation by German troops during both World Wars, and being at the center of violent fighting during the Russian Revolution and Civil War (1917-20).
In 1934, Kiev replaced Kharkov as the capital of the Ukraine. In addition to its historical and political significance, Kiev is also one of the most beautiful of Soviet cities, with numerous parks and gardens, historical buildings and churches, including the eleventh century Pechersk monastery.
2. Simon Vasilievich Petlura (1877-1926). Controversial Ukrainian nationalist leader. Hetman of the Ukraine and head of Kiev's reactionary government (1919-1920), notorious for its atrocities. Defeated by the Bolsheviks, Petlura concluded a treaty with Poland's Marshal Pilsudski and participated in the Polish-Soviet war of 1920, an abortive attempt to free the Ukraine from Soviet domination. Petlura emigrated to France where he was assassinated by Shalom Schwarzbard in retaliation for the perpetration of pogroms against the Jews by his army.
3. Main street in Kiev popular for promenades.

4. Jewish elementary school.

5. Jewish prayer shawls.

6. Marc Chagall (1889-). Outstanding twentieth century painter and graphic artist, reknowned for his vivid portrayals of Russian-Jewish life, and for the humor and fantasy with which he treated his subjects. He was director of the Vitebsk Academy of Art in 1918-1919, and between 1919 and 1922 acted as art director of the Jewish State Theatre in Moscow, (see "Mikhoels"). He emigrated to France in 1922.

7. Mikhail Moiseevich Botvinnik (1911-). Popular Russian chess player, Grand Master of Chess, and world champion.

8. City in the Southwestern Ukraine situated òn the Bug river.

9. *The Mandate* (1925) was an extremely successful comedy by Nikolai Erdman (1902-1970) which opened at the Meyerhold Theatre in Moscow on April 20, 1925, and toured the Soviet Union between 1925 and 1928. Erdman's second play, *The Suicide* (1928) was accepted by the Moscow Art Theatre and was almost produced at the Meyerhold Theatre when permission was refused. Both plays are now availalbe in English, see Nikolai Erdman, *The Mandate and The Suicide* (Ardis, 1975). For more information, see Marjorie Hoover, "Nikolai Erdman: A Soviet Dramatist Rediscovered," *Russian Literature Triquarterly* (No. 2, 1972).

10. On the Jewish Chamber Theatre and Solomon Mikhoels, see Note 2, "Mikhoels."

11. Vsevolod Emilievich Meyerhold (1874-1942). An extremely gifted, influential, and controversial theatre director, active both before and after the Revolution. He is best known for his theatrical experimentation, his taging of highly satirical productions (e.g., Erdman, Mayakovsky), his use of grotesques, and for the hyperbole of his mask images. He was fascinated by constructivism at first and later by so-called "biomechanics," a system involving special physical training for actors. He also introduced elements of the revue, the circus and the cinema into the traditional dramatic theatre. His productions of the Classics were all highly original. For more information, see V.E. Meierkhol'd, *Stat'i, pis'ma, rechi, besedy* (M., 1968), K. Rudnitsky, *Meyerhold The Director* (Ann Arbor: Ardis, 1979), M.L. Hoover, *Meyerhold: The Art of Conscious Theatre* (Amherst, 1974), E. Braun's anthology, *Meyerhold on Theatre* (New York, 1969).

12. Vladimir Leonidovich Durov (1863-1934). Famous clown and animal trainer who traveled widely in Russia and Western Europe (SS, III, 351-52).

13. A pre-revolutionary elementary school in Kiev corresponding to the last four years of the gymnazium (SS, III, 352).

14. Traditional Jewish braided bread made of egg dough.

15. Kiev is built principally on hills overlooking the Dniepr River and has three main sections: the oldest part, built on hills surrounded by ancient fortifications, dates back to the 11th century; the Pechersk hill, the site of the famous Pechersk monastery (one of the most sacred monuments of the Orthodox Church); and the Podol, the commercial section, built on lower ground adjoining the river.

46. BEREZIL

This article first appeared in the Leningrad newspaper, *Evening Red News* (*Vecherniaia krasnaia gazeta,*, No. 140, July 17, 1926), a month before the article on Mikhoels and the Jewish State Theatre (see below). SS, III, 361.

1. The Berezil Theatre Company, organized in Kiev in 1922, was an outgrowth of the Ukrainian Young Theatre ("Molodyi teatr"), an experimental theatre-studio which operated in Kiev in 1916-1919. The Young Theatre, which included all the outstanding actors and directors of the Ukraine, including Les' Kurbas, who was to be-

come the Berezil's director, was originally founded with the purpose of revitalizing the Ukrainian theatre, as a protest against its traditional historic-ethnographic emphasis. The Berezil Theatre Company took its name from the Ukrainian word designating March or the beginning of spring. This organization included not only the Berezil Dramatic Theatre located in Kiev until 1926, when it moved to Kharkov, but also several theatrical workshops and studios throughout the Ukraine.

Les' (Alexander Stepanovich, 1887-1942) Kurbas, the Ukrainian actor, director, producer and organizer of the Berezil, gained fame for his experimental productions, e.g.,for staging such Expressionist works as Ernst Toller's *Masse-Mensch* and *Die Machinenstürmer,* and Georg Kaiser's *Gas II,* for his ability to synthesize conventional and psychological forms, e.g.,Taras Shevchenko's *The Haidamaks (Haidamaky,* 1920), Upton Sinclair's novel, *Jimmy Higgins* (1923), and for his profoundly philosophical interpretations, e.g., Ivan Mikitenko's *The Dictatorship (Diktatura,* 1929). Kurbas understood theatricality not as an end in itself, but as a medium for expressing ideas and emotions. The goal of his productions was synthesis: words, gestures, movement, music, light and color were all called upon to create a rhythmic whole. He was especially interested in such theatrical problems as mass stylized motion, accentuation of word rhythms, and the combination of a Ukrainian style with modern dramatic techniques. In December 1933, after being criticized for "formalism," Les' Kurbas was relieved of his post as theater director, deprived of his title of "Peoples' artist," arrested and sent to his death in a labor camp. The theater was radically reorganized as the Shevchenko Ukrainian Theater of Kharkov.

Some of the Berezil's most outstanding actors included Joseph Hirniak (b. 1895), Ambros Buchma (1891-1956), Olimpia Dobrovolska (b. 1895), Marian Krushelnystsky, (1897-1963), Valentyna Chystiakova (b. 1900), and many others.

For more information, see *Theater-Studio of Joseph Hirniak and Olimpia Dobrovolska* (in Ukrainian), edited by Bohdan Boychuk (New York: The Ukrainian Academy of Arts and Sciences in the U.S., 1975), *Ukraine: A Concise Encyclopedia* (Toronto: University of Toronto Press, 1971, vol. II), and J. Hirniak, "Birth and Death of the Modern Ukrainian Theatre" in *Soviet Theatres: 1917-1954* (New York, 1954).

2. Prosper Mérimée (1803-1870). *La Jacquerie* (1828) is set in feudal times and comprises thirty-six dramatic tableaux focused around a peasant insurrection. Its romantic plot was inspired by the vogue of historical romances popularized by Sir Walter Scott.

3. *Tsar Maximilian.* One of the most elaborate Russian theatrical productions. It was composed of elements borrowed from a variety of dramatic forms, including popular folk drama, the puppet show, nativity tableaux, etc. Its plot consists in linking together loosely related episodes and fragments.

4. *Jimmy Higgins.* See Note 1.

5. On Toller, see notes to "A Revolutionary in the Theatre." Kurbas was evidently fascinated by Max Reinhardt's experimental theater, and thus staged the Expressionist works of Toller and Kaiser (see Note 1, above). These dramatic works played an important role in establishing Kurbas' concept of an active "thinking" theatre.

6. *Commune of the Steppes (Komuna v stepakh)* by Mikola Kulish.

7. Haidamak. A Ukrainian Cossack insurgent who fought against the Poles. See Note 1, above.

8. *The Rabble* (Shpana), a comedy by Volodimir Yaroshenko.

9. Charlie Chaplin was extremely popular in the Soviet Union. See, for instance, *Chaplin: A Collection of Articles* (Chaplin: sbornik statei; Berlin, 1923) including articles by P. Bogatyrev, V. Shklovsky. See also, one of Mandelstam's last poems, No. 386, is entitled "Charlie Chaplin."

10. Apparently Buchma and Hirniak shared this role. See Note 1, above.

11. *The Mandate,* a popular comedy by Erdman (see Note 9, "Kiev").

12. *The Meringue (Vozdushnyi pirog,* 1924), a comedy by Boris Sergeevich

Romashov.

47. MIKHOELS

Part I of this essay appeared for the first time in the Leningrad newspaper, *Evening Red News* (*Vecherniaia krasnaia gazeta*, August 10, 1926). The remaining part(s) remained in rough copy, unpublished. See SS, III, 361-362.

1. This is one of several essays Mandelstam wrote in 1926 touching on Jewish life, Kiev and the theater. See also, "Kiev," "Yakhontov," and "Berezil," as well as his letters from 1926.

2. The Jewish State Theater (GOSET) was originally founded in Petrograd-Leningrad in 1918 as a theatrical studio. In 1921, under the leadership of Alexander Granovsky, it was reorganized as the Jewish Chamber Theater and moved to Moscow; from 1925 to its demise it was known as the Jewish State Theater of Moscow. Its guiding light was Solomon Mikhoels (See Note 5, below). Marc Chagall served as art director from 1919 to 1922. The theatre was closed down in 1949 as part of Stalin's campaign against Soviet Jewish cultural life.

3. Alexander Granovsky (pseudonym of Abraham Azarch, 1890-1937). Founder of the Jewish drama studio in Leningrad in 1918, reorganized as the Jewish Chamber Theater in 1921 in Moscow, and from 1925 on known as the Jewish State Theater. Granovsky staged works by all the leading Jewish writers, including: Shalom Aleichem's *Agents* and *Tevye, the Dairyman*, I.L. Peretz' *Night in the Old Market*, Goldfaden's *The Witch*, Mendele Mokher Seforim's *The Travels of Benjamin the Third*. Granovsky toured Western Europe in 1928-29 and decided to remain in Berlin. There he worked for the Habimah Theater, staging both Yiddish and non-Jewish works, including *Trouhadec* by Jules Romains.

4. *Lapserdak* is the long black overcoat worn by orthodox Jews.

5. Solomon Mikhailovich Mikhoels (pseudonym of Vovsi, 1890-1948). Foremost Yiddish actor and director. Director of the Jewish State Theater, succeeding Alexander Granovsky. Mikhoels was also Chairman of the Jewish Anti-Fascist Committee, from which position, from 1941 on, he launched fervent appeals to Jews abroad to help the Soviet war effort against the Nazis. In 1943, he and Itzik Fefer travelled on the Committee's behalf to the U.S.A., Canada, Mexico, and England. After the war, Mikhoels remained an active spokesman and protector of the Soviet Jews, in particular, in helping those returning to their homes after being evacuated to Central Asia or from prison camps. He was also apparently connected with the "Crimean Project," aimed at resettling homeless Jews. He was brutally murdered in January 1948, on Stalin's orders, the first step in Stalin's campaign to liquidate all Jewish cultural institutions and most of the outstanding Jewish writers, artists and actors.

Mikhoels first entered the Jewish Dramatic Studio in Petrograd in 1919. He quickly became a professional actor, moving to Moscow with the theater in 1921. During the eighteen years of the theater's existence, he played thirty roles, ranging from vaudeville parts to King Lear. A master of the expressive theatrical gesture, Mikhoels was profoundly opposed to any naturalistic reproduction of reality. Rather, he is famous for having imbued his acting with a philosophical, spiritual tone and an almost sculptural plasticity. Some of Mikhoels' best known roles include: Shimele Soroker in *Two Hundred Thousand*, Hotsmakh in Goldfaden's *The Witch*, Benjamin in Mendele Mokher Seforim's *The Travels of Benjamin the Third*, Tevye in Shalom Aleichem's *Tevye, the Dairyman*, and King Lear in Sergy Pavlov's 1935 production of Shakespeare's drama. One of his most outstanding roles was as the Jester in I.L. Peretz' *Night in the Old Market*.

For more information on Mikhoels, see K.L. Rudnitskii (editor), *Mikhoels* (in

Russian; [1965]). On Mikhoels' death, see his daughter's article, Nataliya Mikhoels-Vovsi, "The Murder of Mikhoels" ("Ubiistvo Mikhoelsa"), in *Vremia i my* (No. 3, 1976).

6. This is probably a reference to Mikhoels' performance of the Jester in I.L. Peretz' symbolic verse drama, *Night in the Old Market* (*Baynacht oyfn Altn Mark,* 1907; first staged in 1925), one of Granovsky's most famous productions. This work attempts to portray all of Polish-Jewish history in an operatic and panoramic style, in which all the characters, except the Jester, appear briefly and exit. It relied heavily on music, movement, and lighting as well as on the "art of silence."

7. A reference to the role of Shimele Soroker in *Two Hundred Thousand.*

8. Homel is a Belorussian town on the Sozh River, about 100 miles northeast of Kiev, in the Jewish Pale of Settlement. Founded in the twelfth century, it was under alternate Polish and Russian domination until 1772 when the Russians took over. It is an important railroad and riverboat junction.

9. This section of the essay remained unpublished in the Soviet Union.

10. Narkompros was the National Commission of Education.

11. See Mandelstam's own magnificent poem on this theme, dedicated to Anna Akhmatova, No. 235 (1931), in which he begs her: "Preserve my words forever for their aftertaste of misfortune and smoke."

48. JACQUES WAS BORN AND DIED

This essay first appeared in the Leningrad *Evening Red News* (July 3, 1926). See SS, II, 695.

1. One of Mandelstam's major activities in 1926, see the letters of that year, and his major means of support in the 1920s. See his other essays on the subject, "On Translations," "Torrents of Hackwork," as well as his literary prose, "Fourth Prose."

2. *Ukhazhivat'* and *ukhodit'* are two different aspects of the same verb, the former containing the meaning "to make advances on, to court," the latter containing the colloquial meaning "to do someone in, to get rid of someone."

3. See "Sukharevka."

4. Copper coins.

5. See essays "On Translations" and "Torrents of Hackwork."

6. Irinarkh Ivanovich Vvedensky (1813-1855). Russian translator, teacher, and literary historian. Known primarily for his translations of English novels, in particular, for his translations of Dickens and Thackeray, and also of James Fenimore Cooper.

7. See Mandelstam's essay on Barbier.

8. *Apraksin dvor*—a large shopping arcade in St. Petersburg.

9. Pavel Ivanovich Chichikov, the shadowy merchant and dealer in "dead souls" in Gogol's novel, *Dead Souls.*

49. YAKHONTOV

This tribute to Yakhontov first appeared in the magazine, *The Screen* (*Ekran,* No. 31, Moscow, 1927). See SS, III, 362.

1. Vladimir Nikolaevich Yakhontov (1899-1945). Actor and professional reader ("Chtets") from 1922 until his suicide in 1945, and one of the founders of the literary-stage genre known as *Litmontage* (literary montage), extremely popular with amateur performers in Soviet social clubs. Between 1924 and 1926, Yakhontov acted with

Meyerhold's theater, but in the following year he created his own *Contemporary Thea-tre* (*Teatr sovremennik*, closed in 1935), known as the "theater of one actor." After 1935, he was forced to give more conventional literary readings.

Yakhontov's earliest *litmontages* included *On the Death of Lenin* and *October* (both 1924), *Lenin* (1925), *Pushkin* (1926). The first production of Yakhontov's *Contemporary Theater* was a work called *Petersburg* (1927). It was followed by *The War* (1929), *Evgeny Onegin* (1930), *Evenings with Mayakovsky* (1931), and *Nastasya Filipov-na* (1933, based on Dostoevsky's *Idiot*). From 1927 on, Yakhontov worked with two special producers, S.Y. Vladimirsky and E.E. Popova-Yakhontova, with a composer and, on occasion, with a few supplementary actors.

For further details, see V. N. Yakhontov, *The Theater of One Actor* (*Teatr odnogo cheloveka*, M., 1958).

2. The conceptualization of "space" is of major significance in Mandelstam's esthetic vision, see, in particular, his poetic cycle, "The Octets."

3. S.Y. Vladimirsky and E.E. Popova-Yakhontova were special producers of the *Contemporary Theater* (SS, III, 362).

4. "Madman Evgeny" refers to Pushkin's *The Bronze Horseman*.

5. Reference to Gogol's "The Overcoat."

6. See Note 2, above.

7. *Petersburg* was the first production of Yakhontov's *Contemporary Theater* and one of its most popular works. It was based on Pushkin's *The Bronze Horseman*, Gogol's "The Overcoat," and Dostoevsky's "White Nights." Although extremely popu-lar, it came in for criticism by some as "too formalistic."

8. For similar remarks on "the reader," see the last chapter of *The Noise of Time*. Nadezhda Yakovlevna Mandelstam states: "... M. liked Yakhontov's rendering of Gogol and Dostoevsky, and thought of him as a 'family retainer of literature' rather than as an actor—he had made himself so familiar with Akaky Akakievich and Makar Devushkin that he was their living reincarnation in the modern world. M's friendship with him dated from their first meeting, and from then on he never ceased to work with him on his poetry readings" (*Hope Abandoned*, p. 316).

50. JULES ROMAINS: FOREWORD TO A VOLUME OF TRANSLATIONS

This piece was originally published without a title as a foreword to Mandelstam's translation of Jules Romains' poetic drama, *Cromedeyre-le-Vieil (Kromedeir-staryi)*, which appeared in 1927 (Moscow-Leningrad, GIZ). See OM's letters of 1926. See SS, II, 649.

1. Jules Romains (1885-1972). French novelist, dramatist, and poet. He was the apostle of the French literary movement and doctrine known as Unanimism. The doc-trine postulated that man must not be regarded merely as an individual, but must be con-sidered a social creature. Jules Romains and a group of like-minded writers, including Georges Duhamel and René Arcos, attempted to put this doctrine into practice in an early endeavor to apply group psychology to literature. In his book of poems, *La Vie unanime* (1908) and in his book of precepts, *Manuel de déification* (1910), he praised the "group soul" as far superior to the individual soul and suggested methods for culti-vating it. His monumental study in 27 volumes of the evolution of French life and thought during the period 1908-1933, *Les Hommes de bonne volonté* (1932-1947), gives the most comprehensive illustration of his philosophical doctrine. Other works by Jules Romains mentioned in Mandelstam's foreword include his early novel, *Mort de quelqu'un* (1911) and his play, *L'Armée dans la ville*, performed at the Paris Odéon in 1911. Both of these preceded *Cromedeyre-le-Vieil* which was first published in 1920

but had been written earlier. In the 1920s, Jules Romains' major successes were in the theatre, but in the 1930s he returned to the novel.

2. Unanimism. See Note 1.

3. On Georges Duhamel, see Mandelstam's review of his *Géographie Cordiale de l'Europe*. Mandelstam's translation of Duhamel's "Ode to a Few" appeared in *The Contemporary West* (*Sovremmenyi zapad*, No. 3, 1923). See SS, II, 469-472; also II, 677.

4. See "Conversation about Dante" and my Introduction for more details on Mandelstam's interest in the relationship of the human gait, breathing, rhythm and poetics.

5. According to Nadezhda Mandelstam, *Hope Abandoned* (p. 318), Mandelstam was not very interested in the theater. However, it would seem from his essays concerning the theater and from his poems in which theatrical imagery appears, that he had a great love of Classical drama, and that any drama in which he perceived Classical elements or forms greatly impressed him, see for instance, "Mikhoels." His hostility to the theater appears to be limited primarily to Symbolist drama, in particular, to Leonid Andreev. See "A Revolutionary in the Theater" and the review of Gerhardt Hauptmann's *The Heretic of Soana*.

51. FROM THE AUTHOR

This impersonal, didactic and laconic foreword is more characteristic of Mandelstam's polemical essays of the second half of the 1920s than of the essays included in the volume it introduces. Hence, the placement of this statement in its chronological rather than "logical" position in the present volume. This foreword introduced Mandelstam's collection of essays, *On Poetry (O poezii)* which was being prepared for publication as early as 1926 (see his letters of 1926-1928), but was not published until 1928.

1. The table of contents of the 1928 volume includes eleven essays, half of which date from before 1920, the other half from the early 1920s. The only exception may be "The End of the Novel," which, from internal evidence only, may have been completed after 1925. It first appeared in 1928, in this collection. Most of the other essays were revised, at least in part, for the 1928 volume.

The order in which the essays were presented in the 1928 volume was not chronological, but, again, more in keeping with Mandelstam's mood or attitude of the latter half of the 1920s: the most polemical essays tending to be first; the more literary, and more contemplative, last. The following order was used: "The Word and Culture," "The Slump," "On the Addressee," "On the Nature of the Word," "Some Notes on Poetry," "The End of the Novel," "Badger Hole," "The Nineteenth Century," "Peter Chaadaev," "Remarks on Chénier," "François Villon."

52. A POET ABOUT HIMSELF

These comments were printed in the magazine, *Reader and Writer* (*Chitatel' i pisatel'*, No. 45, 1928), in response to a questionnaire entitled "The Soviet Writer and October." See SS, II, 260.

1. Other comments of major interest on biography and the autobiographical act are to be found in Mandelstam's literary prose, *The Noise of Time*, "The Egyptian Stamp" and "Fourth Prose," in his essay "The End of the Novel," and in his letters. More indirect remarks appear throughout his poetry and essays.

2. See, for instance, Mandelstam's magnificent poem No. 116, "Take from my palms..." (1920), in which he offers up a "Wild gift" of a "dry necklace/Of dead bees, who once transformed honey into sun."

53. A STATEMENT ABOUT "THE BASSOONIST"

It is not known whether Mandelstam ever actually wrote this story. It is possible that he only contemplated it. In Letter No. 59, to Comrade Korobova, Mandelstam mentions that he will have a second story for the magazine, *The Star (Zvezda)*, very possibly a reference to his proposed "The Bassoonist." See, SS, II, 680.

1. Peter Arkadievich Stolypin (1862-1911). Russian Prime Minister assassinated in Kiev in 1911 during a special performance at the Kiev Opera House to honor the royal family. Stolypin's assassin was a former revolutionary opposed to the Prime Minister's agrarian reforms and iron rule, both of which were intended to stem the tide of revolution after 1905 by encouraging rich peasants to expand their landholdings and poor peasants to sell their land and resettle in the cities or on the vast eastern lands of the Russian empire.

2. "The Egyptian Stamp" ("Egipetskaia marka," 1928), one of Mandelstam's most intriguing pieces of literary prose. See Clarence Brown's fine English translation in *The Prose of Mandelstam.*

54. THE DOLL WITH MILLIONS

This essay movie review originally appeared in the newspaper *Kievan Proletariat (Kievskii proletarii,* 1928). See, SS, III, 362.

1. *The Doll With Millions (Kukla s millionami),* a Soviet film-comedy shown in 1928, produced by Sergei Komarov (1891-1957), written by Oleg Leonidov (1893-1951) and F. Otsep. The film's cameraman was Konstantin Kuznetsov (1899-), its artistic director, Alexander Rodchenko (1891-1956)—a member of LEF and constructivist artist, and its major actors included the illustrious film stars, Igor Ilinsky (1901-) and Vladimir Fogel (1902-1929). SS, III, 362.

2. *The Flame (Ogonek),* a popular Soviet weekly magazine which started publication in April, 1923. Mandelstam did a number of pieces for the magazine between July and December of 1923. See notes for "Mensheviks in Georgia."

3. Pathé Frères. Of this film company Jay Leyda states: "The first film companies represented in Russia were Pathé Frères (1904) and Gaumont, and these pioneers held onto the entire market.... Pathé particularly occupied a strategic position through he entire period of the pre-revolutionary cinema, developing from the chief Russian distributor to one of the chief Russian producers" (*Kino,* New York, 1960, p. 24).

4. *Mezhrabpom (Mezhdunarodnaia rabochaia pomoshch'),* International Workers' Relief Fund, founded in 1921 by the International Congress in Berlin. At first dedicated to helping the famine-struck Soviet population in 1921, later on it began directing its activity toward aiding workers of all nations during strikes and lockouts. It also came to the aid of children and wives of workers and disabled workers. Soviet trade unions joined *Mezhrabpom* in 1924.

5. Alexei Konstantinovich Gastev (1882-1941). Poet, publicist, and one of the leaders of Proletkult. In 1920, he formed the Central Institute of Labor of the *VTsSPS* (All Union Central Council of Professional Unions). He preached the Taylor method of the scientific organization of labor in his books. See SS, III, 362.

6. Max Linder (pseudonym of Gabriel Leuvielle, 1883-1925). French comic actor who achieved world-wide fame in Pathé films beginning in 1905. 1910-1913 saw the peak of his career. Linder's films were still extremely popular in Russia in the 1920s.

7. Glupyshkin ("Dopey"). A French film comedian, Andre Deed, whose French name was forgotten for his Russian role. Glupyshkin's situation comedy became extremely well-known in Russia until Max Linder surpassed him in popularity. (See Jay Leyda, *Kino,* p. 52.).

8. Herzen House. Moscow headquarters of the Writers' Union. See notes and references to Herzen House in Mandelstam's "Fourth Prose." "It was first organized in 1920. In its early years it had 222 members and 114 candidate members" (SS, III, 363).

55. CHILDREN'S LITERATURE

This piece was first published only posthumously by the poet's widow, Nadezhda Yakovlevna Mandelstam, in the magazine *Children's Literature (Detskaia literatura,* No. 6, 1967). During the period when it was written, undoubtedly 1928-1930, the traditional fairytale and its modern variants were officially out of favor. N. K. Krupskaya, Lenin's wife, led an official propaganda campaign against the fairytale, in general and against Kornei Chukovsky's delightful stories, in particular. Mandelstam's article is an ironic response to that campaign [SS, III, 357-59]. Mandelstam also tried his hand at children's stories in verse. Four volumes were published, including: *Primus,* 1925, *Two Trams (Dva tramvaia),* 1925, *Balloons (Shary),* 1926, and *The Kitchen (Kukhnia),* 1926. See his letters of 1926 for more details about publication of these volumes.

1. The anthropomorphization of animals was not considered scientifically correct; children's literature was meant to educate, not merely to entertain. See Mandelstam's own statements to this effect in his positive review of Louis Pergaud's animal stories.

2. State Academic Council: "Gosudarstvennyi uchenyi sovet" (GUS).

3. See Mandelstam's essays on "literary work," for example, "Torrents of Hackwork," "On Translations," "The Duchess' Fan."

56. TORRENTS OF HACKWORK

This essay was originally published in *News (Izvestiia),* No. 7 (3616), April 7, 1929. (It should be read in conjunction with "Jacques was Born and Died," "On Translations," and "The Duchess' Fan".) See SS, II, p. 671.

1. GIZ refers to the State Publishing House which is located in Moscow. Its Leningrad branch is known as LenGIZ. See Mandelstam's letters of 1926 for a sense of his personal involvement with GIZ, LenGiz, their editors, problems of translation, publication, reviews, payments, etc.

2. Land and Factory ("ZIF: Zemlia i fabrika") Publishing House was located in Leningrad.

3. Young Guard ("Molodaia gvardiia") Publishing House is the organ of the Central Committee of the All-Union Lenin Communist Union of Youth, better known as the Komsomol. See "On Translations" for Mandelstam's attack on this publishing house.

4. In the 1920s Mandelstam did a lot of this kind of reviewing. See his "internal reviews" (1926-1930s) as examples. See also his letters of 1926-28 for comments on such work, in particular, no. 19.

5. See "Fourth Prose" and the scandal over Mandelstam's "revision" of earlier translations of *Till Eulenspiegel.*

6. See note 2, "On Translations."

57. ON TRANSLATIONS

This essay originally appeared in the magazine *On Literary Guard* (*Na literaturnom postu,* No. 13, July, 1929). See SS, II, 671.

1. Dmitry Ivanovich Pisarev (1840-68). Literary critic, political journalist, ideologist of nihilism, and idol of the radical youth of the 1860s. Arrested in 1862 for speading revolutionary propaganda, he spent four and a half years in the Petropavlovsk Fortress writing brilliant essays which were avidly read by his radical followers. Although a nobleman by birth, he shared the values and ideas of the *raznochintsy,* Russia's non-gentry intellectuals, usually the sons of teachers, clergymen, professionals, etc. who generally espoused radical social and political views.

2. See Mandelstam's references to these appendices in *The Noise of Time* (Chapter I, "Music in Pavlovsk") [C. Brown (trans.), *The Prose of Mandelstam*].

3. Vladimir Mikhailovich Sablin (1872-1916). Russian book publisher and respected translator of German, Flemish, and Scandinavian literature, including G. Hauptman, M. Maeterlinck, and H. Ibsen. Soikin and Sytin were run-of-the-mill translators.

4. World Literature, the publishing house established by Maxim Gorky to publish the classics of world literature in translation and simultaneously provide support for the impoverished intelligentsia. It existed from 1918 to 1924. See also "Jacques Was Born and Died."

5. TsEKUBU (*Tsentral'naia komissiia po ulushcheniiu byta uchenykh*), Commission for the Improvement of the Living Conditions of Scholars, created in 1921. See "Fourth Prose."

6. Academia was the successor to the World Literature Publishing House. Although begun as a private publishing house in Petrograd in 1922, it was taken over subsequently by the State Institute for the History of Art in Leningrad, and then transferred to Moscow. Gorky was chairman of its editorial board for a time. Toward the end of the 1920s, Academia began to publish a series of translations of the Classics (along the lines of Gorky's earlier scheme, World Literature) entitled "Treasures of World Literature." In this way, Academia seems to have been the "esthetic" arm of Land and Factory (ZIF), at least according to Mandelstam (see p. 293). By 1938, Academia was merged with GIZ (State Publishing House) and lost its independence. However, GIZ continued to publish translations of the Classics.

7. See "Torrents of Hackwork."

8. A youth newspaper, published by the Komsomol organization.

9. Reference to "Torrents of Hackwork."

10. See Note 3, "Torrents of Hackwork."

11. Mayne Reid (1818-1883). American novelist who specialized in adventure stories for boys, many of which deal with America's Wild West. Extremely popular among Russian readers.

12. See "Children's Literature."

13. See Mandelstam's review of Duhamel's travel book.

14. Acronym for the Moscow Union of Industries for the Processing of Agricultural Products.

15. This is discussed in "The Duchess' Fan."

58. THE DUCHESS' FAN

This essay appeared originally in the newspaper, *Kievan Proletariat* (*Kievskii proletarii*, 1929). See, SS, III, 359. Other critical pieces of Mandelstam's which also appeared in that paper include: "Jacques Was Born and Died," "The Doll with Millions."

1. Alexei Vladimirovich Lipetsky (1887-1942). Soviet hack writer.

2. Veniamin Alexandrovich Kaverin (1902- , pseudonym of V.A. Zilberg). Soviet novelist and critic. Author of the fantastic portrayal of Leningrad's underworld during NEP (the New Economic Policy), *The End of a Gang* (1925); of *The Scandalist, or Evenings on Vasilievsky Island* (1928), a vivid and not-too-flattering portrayal of the polemics of the literary world, with a parodic depiction of Victor Shklovsky and the Formalists; and of the fine novel, *Artist Unknown* (1931). Kaverin was one of the original Serapion Brothers.

3. N. Berkovsky. A Soviet literary critic who also wrote on Mandelstam's prose. See "On Prose Writers" ("O prozaikakh," *Zvezda,* No. 12, 1929, 147-52), and "On Mandelstam's Prose" ("O proze Mandelstama," *Tekushchaia literatura. Stat'i kriticheskie i teoreticheskie,* M., 1930, 155-181).

4. Valentin Petrovich Kataev (1897-) Soviet novelist and playwright. Author of the very amusing picaresque novel about two embezzlers and their adventurous journey through the USSR during the NEP period, *The Embezzlers* (1926).

5. Ilya Arnoldovich Ilf (1897-1937, pseudonym of Fainzilberg) and Evgeny Petrovich Petrov (1903-1942, pseudonym of Kataev). Soviet satirists who collaborated on the picaresques novels *Twelve Chairs* (1928) and *Little Golden Calf* (1931), in which the exploits of the hero, Ostap Bender, the "smooth operator" satirize Soviet life during the NEP period.

59. I WRITE A SCENARIO

This amusing piece never appeared in the Soviet Union. See SS, II, 684. It must date from the very late 1920s or early 1930s when Shklovsky, according to Nadezhda Mandelstam (*Hope Abandoned,* pp. 339-342), advised his closest friends to write scenarios: "[Shklovsky] took refuge in a film studio, rather as a Jew in occupied Hungary might have hidden in a Catholic monastery. He strongly recommended M. to seek salvation in the same way, and urged him to write something for films. . . The point was that film studios always paid for everything they commissioned, even if it was only a few pages long. Shklovsky gave the same advice to everyone he thought well of, suggesting they write a script together. Coming from him, a proposal of this kind was tantamount to a declaration of love or friendship." Indeed, in 1931 Shklovsky published a guide to writing scenarios, entitled *How to Write Scenarios; a Guide for Beginning Scenarists with Examples of Different Types of Scenarios* (M-L.,1931).

1. Victor Borisovich Shklovsky (1893-). Outstanding Soviet-Russian literary figure: literary critic, theorist, writer, scenarist and film critic. Known primarily as one of the founders of the Russian Formalist movement, he was also an extremely prolific writer, and the author of numerous film scripts and articles on film and the film industry. Among his best known film scenarios is *Bed and Sofa* (1927), written in collaboration with Abram Room, and *By the Law* (1926), written with Lev Kuleshov, based on Jack London's "The Unexpected." He also authored the guide, *How to Write Scenarios.* For a listing of his screen plays, film commentary, articles, and other works see Richard Sheldon (comp.), *Viktor Shklovsky: An International Bibliography of Works by and about Him* (Ardis, 1977).

Shklovsky exerted a major influence on the cultural values of his generation as a writer, as a founder of Russian Formalism, as a teacher of the Serapion Brothers in the House of the Arts in Petrograd, and as a member of LEF, the Left Front for the Arts (a post-revolutionary union of Formalists and Futurists organized by Mayakovsky in 1923, whose stated purpose was to counter the re-emergence of conservative literary tendencies and to advocate and produce a new documentary literature).

Shklovsky's earliest formalist statement, "The Resurrection of the Word" (1914), in Richard Sheldon's words, "stimulated the formation of OPOIAZ in 1914 and outlined, in inchoate form, the concerns to be pursued by the group during its initial period" (*Slavic Review*, March 1975). Other well-known critical studies include *On the Theory of Prose* (1925), the more recent *Lev Tolstoy* (1963) and *Tales about Prose* (1966). His numerous autobiographical works include *Mayakovsky* (1940), memoirs of the twenties, and the more recent *Once Upon a Time* (*Zhili-Byli*, 1964). His remarkable autobiographical novel, *A Sentimental Journey* (1923) and his epistolary novel, *Zoo, or Letters Not about Love* (1923) are now available in fine English translations by Richard Sheldon (Ithaca, 1970, 1971, respectively).

Mandelstam's personal relations with Shklovsky must have been quite complex. For some information on this, see Mandelstam's letters No. 27, 28, 47, and Nadezhda Mandelstam's memoirs. It would be nice to know more.

2. Sergei Mikhailovich Eisenstein (1898-1948). Internationally renowned Soviet film producer. Director of the First Workers' Theater in Moscow, 1921-24, Professor at the All-Union State Institute of Cinematography, 1937. Best known for his cinematographic innovations, in particular, his use of montage, fantasy, close-ups, and striking technical virtuosity. His best known films include *Potemkin* (1925), *Strike* (1925), *Ten Days that Shook the World* (1928), *Alexander Nevsky* (1941), *Ivan the Terrible* (Part I, 1944, Part II, 1946).

3. Primus Stove. Trade name for a kind of portable oil burning cookstove popular in Russia.

60-63. INTERNAL REVIEWS

These four reviews were written as "internal reviews," that is, as in-house evaluations for particular publishers. Foreign books considered for possible translation into Russian were referred to "experts" for their opinions as were Russian manuscripts considered for potential publication. Furthermore, the "experts" responsible for the "internal reviews" were normally given first choice at translating or editing the works under consideration. For more details, see M's letters, especially No. 19, and the essays, "On Translations" and "Torrents of Hackwork." See also, SS, III, 360.

60. JEAN RICHARD BLOCH: *DESTIN DU SIECLE*

1. Jean Richard Bloch (1884-1947). French Jewish essayist, novelist, playwright, and journalist. Founder of the magazine, *l'Effort libre* (1910-1914), editor (with Romains Rolland) of the magazine, *l'Europe* (1923 on), and later collaborator on the weekly, *Clarte*. Prominent member of the French Communist Party, Bloch originally came to the Soviet Union in 1934 to attend the first meeting of the Union of Writers held that year (SS, III, 361). In the spring of 1941 he returned to the USSR, and from 1942 through the war served as the Moscow announcer for Radio-France. His essays express the belief that a new civilization and a new art could unite democratic traditions and proletarian culture. From 1910 to the late 1930s Bloch issued several collections of "essais pour mieux comprendre mon temps," including the one under review: (1) *Car-*

naval est mort (1920), (2) *Destin du siècle* (1930), (3) *Offrande à la politique* (1933),
(4) *Naissance d'une culture* (1936). He also wrote prose fiction, including *Lévy* (1912),
Et Cie (1914), and *La Nuit Kurde* (1925).

2. Although not mentioned in the text, Mandelstam is undoubtedly reviewing
Destin du siècle, seconds essais pour mieux comprendre mon temps (which includes
essays written in the 1920s), Paris, 1930. These essays were not published in the USSR.

3. See Mandelstam's essay, "The End of the Novel."

61. GEORGES DUHAMEL: *GEOGRAPHIE CORDIALE DE L'EUROPE*

1. Georges Duhamel (1884-1966). French poet, novelist, and essayist. A member
of Jules Romains' Unanimist circle before World War I (see, "Jules Romains"), wherein
he developed his ideas of brotherhood and social responsibility. One of his major themes
is the problem of individual freedom in the modern world. He is best known for his
two large novel cycles: *Vie et Aventures de Salavin* (1930-1932) and *Chronique des
Pasquier* (1933-1941). Although his travel literature was very popular in its day, it is
hardly the basis for his election to the Académie Française in 1935. Mandelstam obviously disliked it both for its chauvinism and for its cloying style. On the other hand,
he admired some of Duhamel's poetry; see "Ode to a Few," which he translated in 1923
(SS, II, 469-72). Duhamel's collections of verse include: *Des Légendes de batailles*
(1907), *La Lumière* (1911), *Compagnons* (1912), *Élégies* (1920). Much of Duhamel's
work was translated into Russian, see for instance, Y. Tynianov's translation of *Civilization, 1914-17: Stories* (M.,1923).

2. The Duhamel book under review, although not mentioned in the text, is his
travel book, *Géographie Cordiale de l'Europe,* published in Paris in 1931. It is composed
of four sections which had appeared earlier as separate booklets: (1) Introduction,
(2) Suite Hollandaise, (3) Images de la Grèce, (4) Chant du Nord.

62. LOUIS PERGAUD: STORIES FROM THE LIVES OF ANIMALS

1. Louis Pergaud (1882-1914). French writer who began his literary career with
two collections of verse, *L'Aube* (1904) and *L'Herbe d'avril* (1908). His talents are best
illustrated, however, in his humorous tales of animals and rural life. His animal stories,
De Goupil à Margot (1910) and *Le Roman de Miraut, chien de chasse* (1914), are both
sensitive studies of anthropomorphized animal psychology against a background of
scenes from realistic rural life. His *La Guerre des boutons* (1912) was made into a film
in 1962. For more information, see *Dictionnaire universel des noms propres* (Paris,
1974).

63. ABEL ARMAND: *THE SCEPTRE*

1. I was unable to locate a reference to this work. While Mandelstam basically
praises it, it does not seem to have been published in the Soviet Union.

2. Figaro—Beaumarchais' hero in *The Barber of Seville* and *Marriage of Figaro*.
Beaumarchais is noted for his lampoons of the French ruling class.

64. FOURTH PROSE

"Fourth Prose," according to Nadezhda Mandelstam's memoirs, *Hope Against*

Hope (HAH), was written mainly between the culmination of the "Eulenspiegel affair" in 1929 and the Mandelstam trip to Armenia in 1930, but may have been altered as late as 1931. In *Hope Abandoned* (HA), Nadezhda Yakovlevna states that it was begun the winter of 1929: "M. went to work for the newspaper *Moscow Komsomol* in the autumn of 1929. He lasted there until February of the following year. In December, 1929, or thereabouts, he began to dictate 'Fourth Prose' " (P. 526).

The Eulenspiegel affair, the events which provoked Osip Mandelstam to write "Fourth Prose," occurred in 1928-1929. According to the editors of Mandelstam's *Collected Works* (SS, II, 604-617), G.P. Struve and B.A. Filipoff, the ZIF (Land and Factory) Publishing House had commissioned Mandelstam to revise two earlier translations of *Till Eulenspiegel,* one by A.G. Gornfeld dated 1915 and one by V.N. Kariakin dated 1916, for a new edition. However, in 1928 when the new edition appeared, Mandelstam alone was given credit on the title page as translator. This was done without the knowledge or consent of either Mandelstam or the original translators. Mandelstam was quickly accused of plagiarism and the whole affair assumed the proportions of a scandal.

In a letter to the editor of *Evening Moscow* (see Addenda, below), Mandelstam hastened to state that he "considered [himself] morally reponsible before his colleagues in the translating profession," and that he was ready "to answer for his honorarium with the entire body of his literary work." Nevertheless, Gornfeld insisted on criticizing Mandelstam in public, in the *Red Evening News.* In May of 1929, Mandelstam wrote a letter to the *Literary Gazette* (see Addenda, below) venting his rage against the wretched state of Soviet translations and translators. The notorious hatchet man, David Zaslavsky, "answered" the same month with a crude attack on Mandelstam. The latter was so crude, however, it served as an occasion for Mandelstam's defense in the form of a strongly worded letter signed by such leading Moscow writers as Pasternak, Zoshchenko, Fadeev, Kataev, Averbakh, etc., published in the *Literary Gazette.* The whole affair was finally somewhat ambiguously resolved by FOSP (The Federation of the Unions of Soviet Writers) which adopted a resolution stating that although on the one hand, Mandelstam may have been subjected to unfair attacks, on the other hand, he was morally at fault since no proper contract had been drawn up between him and the original translators. Nevertheless, the affair and its repercussions were not really forgotten until Nikolai Ivanovich Bukharin intervened by arranging for a trip to Armenia (see "Journey to Armenia" and my notes).

Nadezhda Mandelstam reviews the affair and the resultant "Fourth Prose" in a rather positive light, asserting that it "released" Mandelstam once more to write poetry: "The 'Fourth Prose' was based on the episode of the Eulenspiegel translation, which, with all its ramifications, would have died down sooner if M. had not insisted on keeping 't alive. It was this that really opened M.'s eyes to what was happening around us. As Bukharin had said, the atmosphere in Soviet institutions was indeed like that of a cesspool. During the Eulenspiegel affair we felt as though we were watching a film about literature at the service of the new regime, about the fantastic bureaucratic apparatus... about the Soviet press with its Zaslavskys, about the Komsomol, in whose newspaper M. worked for a year after breaking with the writers' organizations, and so forth. The two years spent on this business were rewarded a hundred times over: the 'sick son of the age' now realized that he was in fact healthy. When he started writing poetry again, there was no longer a trace of the 'drying crust.' M.'s was henceforth the voice of an outsider who knew he was alone and prized his isolation. M. had come of age and assumed the role of witness. His spirit was no longer troubled" (HAH, 178).

"Fourth Prose," according to his widow, was literally Mandelstam's fourth piece of prose writing, following *The Noise of Time,* "The Egyptian Stamp," and his numerous critical articles: "This title was our private way of referring to it: it was literally his fourth piece of prose, but there was also an association with the 'fourth estate' which so much preoccupied him, as well as with our 'Fourth Rome.' It was this work which cleared the way for poetry again, restoring M.'s sense of his place in life and his rightness. In it he spoke of our bloodstained land, cursed the official literature, tore off the literary 'fur coat' he had momentarily donned and again stretched out his hand to the upstart intellectual, 'the first Komsomol, Akaki Akakievich.' At a certain dangerous moment we destroyed the opening chapter, which dealt with our idea of socialism" [there is a reference to this in part III. JGH] (p. 177-78). See also, *HA*, p. 360.

"Fourth Prose" was also considered Mandelstam's most dangerous work, for as Nadezhda Yakovlevna stated, "they would not have patted M. on the head for this prose." Obviously, it was never published in the Soviet Union.

"Fourth Prose" is an extremely clever feuilleton directed against the idea and actuality of the literary establishment, a masterful polemic against "authorized" literature, and a diabolical exorcism of the "death trust," directed against all those who willed the destruction and defamation of "Mother Philology." Simultaneously, it is a glorious tribute to genuine Truth in literature embodied in the work of such masters as Gogol, Esenin, and Zoshchenko, and to faith in humanity as expressed in the section devoted to Bukharin and his secretary. And no less significant, it is a rather formidable attack on anti-Semitism, anti-intellectualism, and anti-individualism. But, above all, "Fourth Prose" is the expression of an uncompromised and uncompromising poetic conscience, which takes as its scourge the Truth, Justice, Morality, and Irony embodied and expressed in the esthetic ideal of "literary savagery" ("literaturnaia zlost' ") which Mandelstam had defined in his first major work of autobiographical fiction, *The Noise of Time*. In that work, he characterizes "literary savagery" as the ethical and esthetic values which the literary consciousness confers on history or on life itself: "Literary savagery . . . you are the seasoning for the unleavened bread of understanding, you are the joyful consciousness of injustice, you are the conspiratorial salt transmitted with a malicious bow from decade to decade in a cut-glass salt cellar, with a serving cloth!"

Furthermore, Mandelstam compares the relationship of "genuine literature" to history with the response of the *raznochinets* (the non-gentry intellectual rebel of nineteenth century Russia) to his environment: "Literature rages. . . and glowers at the event with the slant-eyed gaze of a *raznochinets* and chronic failure, with the savagery of a lay brother . . . dragged to be a witness in the Byzantine court of history." This response is instinctual, uncivilized and unsocialized, free and independent. Thus, the esthetic process itself is established not as mere reflection or imitation, but as a cognitive act invoking the poet's potential challenge to history in the name of the literary consciousness or the universal creative spirit.

While *The Noise of Time* poses the issue of the poet's challenge to society and history, "Fourth Prose" takes up that challenge and invokes it in the form of a supreme curse hurled against the forces of death and destruction (the literary establishment, in particular). Indeed, "Fourth Prose" may be read as a form of poetic exorcism. According to Nadezhda Yakovlevna, its power derives from the poet's renewed faith in himself and in the "creative spirit" following a long period of doubt and despair. Mandelstam's renewed faith was brought about to a great extent by a personal revaluation of himself as a poet, as a man, and as a Jew. What is more, it is most illuminating to note how in both its autobiographical and esthetic structures, "Fourth Prose" seems to resort to the thunder and all-consuming moral passion of Old Testament prophecy, in particular, to the Mosaic Law: "Thou shalt not kill!" established in this work as a fundamental esthetic precept. Indeed, it is in this piece of autobiographical fiction that the esthetic process is affirmed in Mandelstam's esthetic vision as a moral, intellectual and cognitive act. For more details, see my Introduction.

1. Benjamin Fyodorovich Kagan (1869-1953) was a well-known mathematician. After many years at Novorossisk University in Odessa (1897 to 1923), he became a

Professor of Mathematics at the University of Moscow. His credentials include popularizing the work of N.I. Lobachevsky, and receiving a Stalin prize in 1943. It is suggested that he may have been called into the Mandelstam "case" as a translation "expert" (SS, II, 609).

    2. Isaiah Benediktovich Mandelstam. A namesake, but not a relative of Osip Mandelstam, best known for his translations from French and German. I.B. Mandelstam's translations included: (1) Jean-Jacques Brousson's *Anatole France in a Dressing Gown,* 1925; (2) Marcel de Goff's *Anatole France in the Years 1914-1921, Conversations and Memoirs,* 1925; (3) Goethe's *Sorrows of Young Werther,* edited and introduced by A.G. Gornfeld 1922, (4) works by Arthur Schnitzler and Gerhardt Hauptmann, among others. "In 1928 Mandelstam had learned from a chance conversation in the street with his namesake Isaiah Mandelstam that five bank officials, specialists left over from the old regime, had been sentenced to death by shooting for embezzlement or negligence. Much to his friends' and his own surprise, and despite the rule against intervening in such matters, Mandelstam raised such a hue and cry all over Moscow that the five old men were spared. He mentions this episode in his 'Fourth Prose' " (HAH).

    3. The light cavalry. According to the *Great Soviet Encyclopedia,* the light cavalry was the name given to "Komsomol groups (or brigades) helping the Communist Party and the Soviet government struggle against bureaucracy and mismanagement in cooperatives, unions, businesses and Soviet organizations. . . The activity of the light cavalry was greatly expanded in 1928. . . [as] one of the forms of mass control and criticism from below." According to Struve and Filippov, "The light cavalry" was used not only to verify the work of organizations but to check up on the personal lives of individual citizens, especially the intelligentsia, persons accused of being "alien elements" and *byvshie liudi*–people owing allegiance to the pre-revolutionary way of life... "Very often Komsomol organizations assigned cripples, failures or people expressing hostility to the entire world to work in the light cavalry so they would work more maliciously and fundamentally. . ." (SS, II, 610). See the cripple in Andrei Platonov's *The Foundation Pit (Kotlovan)* for an example of this type.

    4. About "hooves" Nadezhda Yakovlevna says: "On leaving for Armenia, M. resigned his job with the newspaper and was given a favorable reference. It was said he was one of those members of the intelligentsia who could be allowed to work, provided it was under the guidance of Party supervisors. He was somehow upset by this, but I made fun of him for taking offense at his 'hooved' friends: long before he got his reference from them, he had decided they had hooves instead of feet" (HA, p. 531).

    5. This reference is clarified by Nadezhda Yakovlevna: "During our *Moscow Komsomol* days, we had to live on our salaries. The editorial offices were in an arcade on Tverskaya street (now Gorky Street) and bore the general name of 'The Combine.' They were run by a 'daredevil manager' . . .called Giber. ... Giber was simply Giber, a manager or commercial director with an exuberant imagination. The structure of 'The Combine' was really something of a mystery. It . . . spread in some way to the whole of the arcade and, besides editorial offices, included a miniature theater, a restaurant, and perhaps a few other things, of no interest to us" (HA, p. 530).

    6. *Moscow Komsomol.* Nadezhda Yakovlevna states: "M. went to work for the newspaper *Moscow Komsomol* in the autumn of 1929. He lasted there until February of the following year. . . On leaving for Armenia, M. resigned his job with the newspaper and was given a favorable reference" (HA, pp. 526-531).

    7. TsEKUBU or the Commission for the Improvement of the Living Conditions of Scholars. It was created in 1921 (SS, II, 612).

    8. "I do samoi kosti raneno/ Vse ushchel'e krikom sokola."

    9. Herzen House on Tverskoy Boulevard, the official headquarters of the writer's organizations in the 1920s, e.g., Unions of the Federation of the Soviet Writers (pre-

decessor of the more centralized Union of Writers formed in 1934). Herzen House was also used to house homeless writers. The Mandelstams lived there for a while in 1922, at which time Mandelstam valiantly attempted to obtain a room for the homeless poet Khlebnikov, but was refused. Dmitry Blagoy received the room in his stead. For more information on the Mandelstam's life in Herzen House, see *Hope Abandoned,* pp. 90-97, 114.

10. Arkady Georgievich Gornfeld (1867-1941). Well-known critic and literary scholar, a student of Potebnya. Before the revolution he was the major critic for the populist journal, *Russian Wealth (Russkoe bogatstvo),* and author of a number of books about Russian and foreign literature. Known generally for his independent ideas and respected even by his opponents. Consequently, his conflict with Mandelstam is "one of the unhappier episodes in the history of Russian literature." (SS, II, 612). His book *Torments of the Word (Muki slova)* was very popular.

11. Askanaz Artemevich Mravian (1886-1929). Peoples' Commissar of Foreign Affairs for the Republic of Armenia (1920-21), Peoples' Commissar of Education and Deputy Chairman of the Soviet Peoples' Commissariat of Armenia (1923-1929). (SS, II, 612). The reference to "ant" and "anthill" is a pun on the Russian word for "ant"—"muravei"—which is quite close to Mravian. So Mandelstam added "Muravian." "Like all the good things in our life, the trip to Armenia was eventually arranged by Bukharin. He had first tried to send us there at the end of the twenties, when the Armenian Peoples' Commissar for Education was Mravian. He had invited M. to Erevan University to give a course of lectures and a seminar. Nothing came of this—partly because of Mravian's sudden death and partly because M. was scared to death at the thought of giving lectures" (HAH, p. 250). It is also interesting to remember that Vyacheslav Ivanov held the post of Deputy Peoples' Commissar for Education of the new Soviet Republic of Azerbaidzhan from 1921-1924. He held the University Chair of Classical Philology in Baku at the same time. The Mandelstams met Ivanov there in 1921. In 1924, Ivanov emigrated to Italy.

12. See the essay "Peter Chaadaev," in which Mandelstam speaks of Chaadaev descending with his "holy staff" of "moral freedom" in Rome.

13. This line is from Esenin's poem "I will not begin to deceive myself," from his cycle of poems known as *Moscow Taverns* (1922). The line in Russian reads: "Ne rasstrelival neschastnykh po temnitsam" (st. 2).

14. Dmitry Dmitrievich Blagoy (1893-). Soviet literary critic best known for his *History of Eighteenth Century Russian Literature* which he revised along party lines. See also, Note 9, above.

15. See Note 10, above, and references in the introductory remarks to this work.

16. See Addenda, below.

17. Nikolai Ivanovich Bukharin (1888-1938). Member of the Communist Party since 1906. Major theoretician of Bolshevism. Editor of *Pravda (The Truth),* the central organ of the Party, and later, of *Izvestia (The News),* the government paper. Dismissed from Party posts in 1929 and executed in 1938 after being forced to participate in the Great Purge Trials. He was Mandelstam's major Party benefactor. Nadezhda Yakovlevna characterizes him as being "as impulsive as M.": "We had first started 'going to see' Bukharin in 1922 when M. had asked him to intercede for his brother, Evgeny, who had been arrested. M. owed him all the pleasant things in his life. His 1928 volume of poetry would never have come out without the active intervention of Bukharin, who also managed to enlist the support of Kirov. The journey to Armenia, our apartment and ration cards, contracts for future volumes (which were never actually published but were paid for—a very important factor, since M. was not allowed to work anywhere)—all this was arranged by Bukharin. His last favor was to get us transferred from Cherdyn to Voronezh" (*HAH,* p. 112-13).

18. Bukharin's secretary, Korotkova, the "squirrel" of the "Fourth Prose," is

characterized further in *HAH*, p. 251.

19. Angelina Bosio, an Italian opera singer. According to Clarence Brown's notes to *The Prose of Osip Mandelstam*, she sang four seasons in St. Petersburg before she died there in 1859. Her death is the subject of a poem by Nekrasov, "On the Weather." Mandelstam refers to her twice in his story; "The Egyptian Stamp" where in each case she is associated with a beginning or an end, an overture or finale: "But in the flickering consciousness of the dying singer this bedlam of feverish, official clamor. . . this armful of noises, arrested and driven off under guard, was transformed into the appeal of an orchestral overture. In her tiny, homely ears she clearly heard the final measures of the overture to *I due Foscari,* the opera of her London debut " (Part VII).

20. Eternal Memory *(Vechnaia Pamïat').* Perhaps the most powerful part of the entire Requiem Mass of the Russian Orthodox service. It is the second to last part, and is repeated three times.

21. The arbitration board of the Federation of the Unions of Soviet Writers (FOSP) decided Mandelstam's "case" in the Eulenspiegel affair in a rather ambiguous manner. See my introductory remarks above.

22. It is interesting to notice here how Mandelstam transfers all the traits associated with anti-semitic remarks about Jews to Gypsies. Furthermore, he opposes the positive images of Jew, poet, outcast (and *raznochinets* in *The Noise of Time* and "Conversation about Dante") to the negative images of gypsies, (hack) writers, and the Literary Establishment. The former create genuine poetry, the latter produce "Literature."

23. On Andrei-Marie Chénier, see the essay, "Remarks on Chénier." His younger brother, Marie-Joseph-Blaise Chénier (1764-1811), achieved great popularity with a number of propagandist historical dramas. It is said that he remained silent when he might have saved his older brother's life.

24. Obviously, Mandelstam was already reading Dante's *Divina Commedia.*

25. ZIF refers to "Zemlia i Fabrika," the Land and Factory Publishing House.

26. Herzen House. See Note 9, above.

27. Ivan Moiseich. A reference to another poem by Nekrasov, "Hey, Ivan," and Nekrasov's poetry which was often dedicated to the "fourth estate." The lines to which Mandelstam refers include the following: ... "Ei, Ivan! Cheshi sobak!/ ...Pil detina erofeich,/ Plakal da krichal:/ "Khot' by raz Ivan Moiseich/ Kto menia nazval!..." (SS, II, 616-17).

28. A reference to Mayakovsky's play, *Mystery-Bouffe* in which the following lines appear (SS, II, 617): "What's up?/ We promised to divide everything equally:/ One will get the doughnut, the other—the hole./ That's democracy for you!"

29. Mikhail Mikhailovich Zoshchenko (1895-1958). Outstanding Soviet Russian humorist, best known for his extremely short stories told by a stylized narrator-participant in the vernacular of the uneducated urban proletariat. The narrator's language and language usage, his capacity for observation and reasoning, as well as his techniques of analysis and evaluation give these stories a dual perspective not unlike that of the fable. Perhaps that is why Mandelstam juxtaposes Zoshchenko with Krylov, the master of the Russian fable, suggesting that the twentieth century humorist is a modern fabulist.

Most of Zoshchenko's themes, characters and situations concern ordinary everyday life in the Soviet Russia of the 1920s and 1930s. His humor arises primarily from the disjuncture between the narrator's experiences of everyday reality and the perceptions, dreams, and values expressed by the individuals, groups and organizations which comprise Soviet society and/or govern it, between everyday reality and "some splendiferous future life." For a fine introduction to Zoshchenko, see Hugh McLean (trans.), Mihail Zoshchenko, *Nervous People* (Bloomington: I.U. Press, 1977).

During World War II, Zoshchenko began an autobiographical novel, *Before Sunrise*, which was not published complete until an emigre edition came out in 1973. It is a work of fearful reminiscences. In 1946, Zoshchenko and Akhmatova were singled out for political criticism and expelled from the Union of Writers. Zoshchenko never fully recovered his creative inspiration. During the last twelve years of his life he published a number of banal stories for the Soviet humor magazine, *Crocodile*.

30. M.S.P.O. Initials of the Moscow Union of Consumer Organizations.

31. Viy, in Gogol's words, is the name of the "chief of the gnomes, whose eyelids droop down to the earth." In Gogol's tale, Viy is called upon to point out the sinful philosopher, Khoma. Viy says: "Lift up my eyelids, I do not see." Once his eyelids have been raised, he can point out the source of evil.

32. The last verse of Mandelstam's poem No. 354, "Yes, I am still alive..." written in January 1937 in Voronezh exile, reads:

> Unhappy is he who like his own shadow
> Fears a barking dog or the wind after dark,
> Poor is he who half-alive and callow,
> Begs for alms of the shadows in the park.

64. ADDENDA TO FOURTH PROSE

These two letters were written in response to the "scandal" created over Mandelstam's revision of the translations of Charles de Coster's *La Légende d'Uhlenspiegel*. See my introductory notes to "Fourth Prose," above. Since these are both open letters pertaining to "Fourth Prose," it was decided to include them with that work, rather than with the remainder of Mandelstam's letters.

1. Letter to the editorial staff of *Evening Moscow*, No. 288, 1928 (SS, II, 477-480). This letter should be read in conjunction with Mandelstam's polemical essays, "On Translations," "Torrents of Hackwork," and "The Duchess' Fan," written during this same period.

2. Letter to the editorial staff of the *Literary Gazette*, May 10, 1929 (SS, II, 480).

3. David Iosifovich Zaslavsky (1880-1965). Hack journalist and notorious apologist for Stalinism. Not only did he savagely attack Mandelstam, but thirty years later, in 1958, he launched a similar vicious attack on Pasternak, following the latter's nomination for the Nobel Prize for literature.

65. ON THE NATURALISTS

This essay first appeared in the Moscow newspaper, *For a Communist Education* (*Za kommunisticheskoe prosveshchenie,* April 19, 1932) on the Fiftieth Anniversary of Darwin's Death. See SS, III, 368. Nadezhda Mandelstam worked at that newspaper in the early 1930s. This essay should be read in conjunction with its Addenda, as well as with "Journey to Armenia" and its Addenda, and with the poetry of the 1930s such as poem No. 254 "Lamarck," and 266 "To the German Language." This essay was also known as "Darwin's Literary Style." Of Mandelstam's interest in the naturalists, Nadezhda Yakovlevna writes: "Later interests represented in M.'s bookcase were the Armenian chronicles... and biology: he was lucky enough to be able to buy Linnaeus, Buffon, Pallas and Lamarck, as well as Darwin *(The Voyage of the Beagle)* and some of the philosophers, such as Driesch, who take biology as their starting point" (*Hope Against Hope,* p. 241).

1. "Darwin's literary style" was one of the titles of this essay. See Addenda to "On the Naturalists": *The organization of scientific material is the naturalist's style.*

2. Charles Robert Darwin (1809-1882). English naturalist and originator of the theory of evolution now known as Darwinism. From December 1831 to October 1836, Darwin circumnavigated the world on the HMS *Beagle* as a naturalist for a surveying expedition. He published his work on the geology and zoology of various regions of the world in his *Journal of Researches* (1839) and in *The Zoology of the Voyage of H.M.S. Beagle* (1839-1843). This work paved the way for his most famous and influential book, *On the Origin of Species by Means of Natural Selection or the Preservation of Favored Races in the Struggle for Life* (1859), the first edition of which was sold out the first day it appeared. For more information, see C. Darwin, *Autobiography: 1809-1882*, edited by Nora Barlow (1958).

This quote is from Charles Darwin, *Journal of Researches* (New York, 1902, pp. 43-44)—translator's note.

3. Peter Simon Pallas (1741-1811). German naturalist and explorer, who travelled and studied the length and breadth of the Russian empire; he was appointed Professor at the St. Petersburg Academy of Sciences from 1768. From 1769 through 1774, as a member of a scientific expedition, he explored the upper Amur River, the Caspian Sea, and the Ural and Altai Mountain Ranges. His account of this expedition, *A Geological Journey Through the Various Provinces of the Russian Empire* appeared first in German in 1768-1774, but was soon translated into Russian (*Puteshestvie po raznym provintsiiam Rossiiskago gosudarstva*, St. Petersburg: 1773-1788). Pallas was extremely prolific, and his writings include studies of natural history, geology, topography, botany, zoology, languages, and even Bering's discoveries. For more information, see the entry on Pallas in the *Brockhaus Enzyklopadie, 1972*.

4. Carolus Linnaeus (Latinized penname of Carl Von Linne, 1707-1778). Swedish botanist and founder of the modern system of the classification of organisms known as the "binomial system of nomenclature." His *Species Plantarum* (1753) is the first scientific work to undertake the naming of vascular plants. He was appointed both Professor of Medicine in 1741 and Professor of Botany in 1742 at the University of Uppsala.

5. Georges Léopold Chrétien Frédéric Dagobert Cuvier (1769-1832). French naturalist and geologist. Mandelstam is incorrect in representing Cuvier as an evolutionist. He adamantly rejected all the various theories of evolution in favor of the doctrine of catastrophism, of which he became a most prominent proponent. According to the thesis of catastrophism all living things are destroyed at intervals in the earth's history by floods, earthquakes, or other cataclysms, only to be subsequently replaced by entirely new populations. This doctrine was long accepted by geologists for it was easily reconcilable with Biblical dogma. Moreover, Cuvier as the leading geologist of his day, defended it vigorously and could not be easily opposed.

In 1803, Cuvier was made a permanent member of the French Academy of Sciences. He was also a pioneer in the field of comparative anatomy and originated a classification system in zoology which consisted of four phyla based on differences in the structure of the skeleton and organs. He also made a major contribution in paleontology by deducing and reconstructing the soft parts of fossils from their skeletons.

6. Compte Georges Louis Leclerc de Buffon (1707-1788). French naturalist best known for his monumental *Histoire Naturelle*, published in 44 volumes between 1749 and 1804. In 1739, he became the keeper of the Royal Botanical Gardens (Jardin du Roi, later Jardin des Plantes) in Paris, which he eventually transformed into a famous biological research center. Buffon was the first naturalist to compile current knowledge about nature in a manner appealing to the general reader. Certain suggestions in his work anticipated the theories of evolution subsequently held by such naturalists as Lamarck and Darwin. For instance, Buffon believed that climate was a major factor in determining variations in heredity, and thus suggested that many species were created or eliminated due to climatic conditions. Buffon was also the first European scientist to

suggest that the earth was older than the 6000 years postulated in the Bible, and thus paved the way for the future study of geological eras.

7. Jean Baptiste Pierre Antoine de Monet, Chevalier de Lamarck (1744-1829). French naturalist and associate of Buffon (see above Note 6), member of the French Academy of Sciences, and curator of the Royal Botanical Gardens (1779). He is noted for his study and classification of invertebrates, in particular, for his division of the animal kingdom into the invertebrate and vertebrate subkingdoms. His work in classification naturally led him to speculate on the origin of species and to develop a theory of evolution based on the postulate of the inheritance of acquired characteristics. Lamarck believed that specific needs created by the environment caused organisms to respond and develop in particular ways. This theory was eventually supplanted by Darwin's theory of evolution which attributed adaptations to the selection of successful types. Although Lamarck's concepts have been rejected by most modern biologists, they strongly influenced Soviet biology, namely, the work of the plant breeder, Trofim Denisovich Lysenko (1898-) and his predecessor, Michurin. This concept was partially responsible for the failures of Soviet agriculture and for the backwardness of Soviet genetics until 1965. For more information, see D. Joravsky, *The Lysenko Affair* (Harvard, 1970).

Nevertheless, Lamarck's doctrine was important as a forerunner of Darwin's work. Darwin called Lamarck "the first man whose conclusions in the subject [of the transformation of the species] excited much attention. In his [*Philosophie zoologique* (1809) and *Histoire Naturelle des Animaux sans Vertèbres* (1815-22)] he upholds the doctrine that all species, including man, are descended from other species. He first did the eminent service of arousing attention to the probability of all change in the organic, as well as in the inorganic world, being the result of law, and not of miraculous interposition." From Charles Darwin, "An Historical Sketch: of the Progress of Opinion on the Origin of Species."

8. See Addenda to "On the Naturalists": "Darwin's work is prosaic. Popular. It is aimed at the average reader. Its tone is conversational."

9. See Addenda to "On the Naturalists": "Dickens performed the very same role in debunking contemporary English society."

10. Translator's note: Quoted from Charles Darwin, *On the Origin of Species* (a facsimile of the first edition, Harvard University Press, 1966, p. 180). Darwin is speaking here of the difficulty of determining the means of transition from one form to another owing to the rarity or absence of transitional forms.

11. See Mandelstam's "Journey to Armenia" in which he partially adapts this technique of "correspondence." A good part of his "Journey" is "written" to Boris Kuzin (BSK), the biologist to whom poem No. 266, "To the German Language" is dedicated as well. See my Introduction.

12. A similar claim might be made for a good portion of Mandelstam's prose of the 1930s. See "Journey to Armenia" and "Conversation about Dante," in particular.

65a: ADDENDA: "DARWIN'S LITERARY STYLE"

These materials are translations of Mandelstam's *Notebooks of 1931-1932.* This translation is based on the text of the *Notebooks* prepared for publication in *Problems of Literature* (*Voprosy literatury*, No. 4, pp. 194-199) by Irina Semenko and supplemented by a text based on the author's typescript. This combined text was first published in SS, III, 169-178.

1. See Mandelstam's *The Noise of Time* for a discussion of what he read, and how he responded to the adult reading matter popular during his childhood.

2. For more information on the various scientists mentioned in these Addenda, see notes to the essay "On the Naturalists."

3. See note 2, "On the Naturalists" for more information on Darwin, his travels, and his works.

4. See the transformation of this imagery in the "The Octets," in particular, poem No. 285, second quatrain.

5. Compare with Mandelstam's own use of quotes, references, and subtexts.

6. See Mandelstam's essays, "On the Nature of the Word" and "Conversation about Dante."

7. See "On the Addressee" and "Conversation about Dante."

8. See similar imagery in "Conversation about Dante."

9. See similar ideas expressed in "Conversation about Dante" as the basis of Dante's success.

10. See similar imagery in "Conversation about Dante."

11. Again, a statement pertaining to Mandelstam's own methodology.

12. See "Conversation about Dante" on illumination.

66. JOURNEY TO ARMENIA

"Journey to Armenia" was originally published in the Leningrad literary magazine, *The Star* (*Zvezda,* No. 5, 1933), edited by Caesar Volpe, who lost his job as a result. It was later published in revised form in *Literary Armenia* (*Literaturnaia Armeniia,* No. 3, 1967) with both addenda to, and omissions from, the original version, and with an introduction by Gevork Emin. Nadezhda Yakovlevna's memoirs of the trip are also included (pp. 99-101). Mandelstam's *Collected Works* contains a combined version, on which this translation is based (See SS, I, 592). See N.Y. Mandelstam, *Hope Abandoned,* p. 410, for more details on Caesar Volpe and the original publication, as well as SS, III, 369-72.

Mandelstam had long been interested in Armenia, in its language and history, and in its symbolic value as a source of humanistic and Judaeo-Christian values. N.Y. Mandelstam in *Hope Abandoned* asserts that Mandelstam associated Armenia with the beginning of the "historical world" (pp. 468-69), that he viewed Armenia as an "outpost" "not of 'culture' but of Christianity, of the Hellenistic and Judaic world" (p. 491). Mandelstam discusses Armenia as early as 1922 in "A Word or Two About Georgian Art," and evokes it in "Fourth Prose" as a symbol of individual freedom, of national, spiritual, and personal independence. The Mandelstams finally visited Armenia, the result of Bukharin's aid and support, between May and November 1930 (See *Hope Against Hope,* p. 250). Of this period in Mandelstam's life, N.Y. Mandelstam states: "The journey to Armenia restored the gift of poetry to M., and a new period of his life began" (*Hope Against Hope,* p. 180).

Moreover, Mandelstam was not alone in his love for Armenia. Valery Bryusov had not only mastered the Armenian language enough to do linear translations for a collection of Armenian poetry which he edited in 1916, but did a historical study of Armenia as well: *The Chronicle of the Historic Events of the Armenian Nation* (*Letopis' istoricheskikh sudeb armianskogo naroda,* Moscow, 1918). Mandelstam must have known these works. N.Y. Mandelstam mentions how: "Our small hotel room in Erivan was soon full of books on Armenia: Strzigovski, the Armenian chronicles, Moses of Chorene, and much more. The general description of the country that impressed M. most of all was by Shopen, an official under Alexander I" (*Hope Against Hope,* 227).

1. Sevan. An island in Lake Sevan formerly known as Lake Gokcha, the largest lake in Armenia. Lake Sevan is especially famous for its abundance of trout. The island

of Sevan is famous for its monastery which dates from the Arab conquest in the mid-7th century. Several ancient Armenian churches lie along the lake shore.

2. Lake Gokcha. See Note 1.

3. Urartu (or Urardhu), is the Assyro-Babylonian name of a kingdom which flourished between the Aras and Upper Tigris Rivers from the 9th to 7th centuries B.C. Although the people are of uncertain ethnological origin, their kingdom was known to the Assyrians as Urartu and to the Hebrews as Ararat. During the 9-8th centuries B.C., this kingdom had considerable power in the Near East, but it was eclipsed by the Assyrians in the late 8th century and conquered by the Scythians and Babylonians in the 7th century B.C.. The Armenian people (of Indo-European origin) are said to have entered the Urartu area during the time of the Assyrian incursions. An independent Armenia was established in the 2nd century B.C., but became a buffer state between the Roman and Parthian empires. After the 13th century A.D., it was dominated by one or another of its powerful neighbors. However, a fierce sense of independence was retained giving impetus to the nationalist movement in the 19th century.

Urartian, also known as Chaldean or Vannic, was an ancient language spoken in NE Anatolia. It is not Indo-European in origin. Its texts were written in a cuneiform script called neo-Assyrian.

4. Possibly Professor Astvadsatur Khachaturian (1861-1937). Archaeologist and specialist in cuneiform writing. Repatriated to Soviet Armenia in 1921, given a chair at Erevan University, but killed in the purges of 1937.

5. Nikolai Yakovlevich Marr (1864-1934). Specialist in Caucasian archaeology and linguistics, whose significant contributions to those fields have obscured his eccentric theories regarding language as a phenomenon of social class rather than nationality. He developed a general theory of language based on the proposition that all languages are related and will finally merge after thousands of years of differentiation. He believed that differentiation was based on social rather than national divisions. What is more he claimed to be able to derive the vocabulary of all languages from four primordial roots. Ironically enough, Marr's name became famous in the West, when in 1950, on the pages of *Pravda*, Stalin himself contributed to a discussion of Marrist linguistics, attacking his social theories and advocating a return to traditional linguistics. See, *Marxism and Problems of Linguistics* (M., 1950).

6. See Addenda to "Journey to Armenia" (known subsequently in these notes as J.A.)

7. See Addenda (J.A.), section on "Sevan."

8. See N.Y. Mandelstam, *Hope Abandoned*, pp. 543-44.

9. Ivan Stepanovich Mazeppa (1644-1709). Ukrainian Cossack Hetman and nationalist leader, who deserted Peter the Great's forces for those of Charles XII of Sweden during the Great Northern War in the hope of liberating the Ukraine from Russian domination. He was defeated along with the Swedes at Poltava. See Pushkin's romantic account of Mazeppa's love for Maria and of his military involvements in his historical narrative poem, *Poltava*.

10. See Addenda (J.A.), section on "Sevan."

11. See Addenda (J.A.), section on "Sevan." This may be a reference to "the Armenian version of *Les Misérables*. An elderly man, who having obtained a military education..." etc.

12. The Khlysts, also known as "God's People" *(Bozhie liudi)* comprised a religious sect of "flagellants" which first appeared in Russia in the 17th century. This sect was related to other dualistic heresies of Christendom with its claims to be a secret elect group and its demands for self-mortification. The Khlysts would congregate in secret meeting places (not churches) known as "Jerusalem" or "Mt. Zion" to perform a "rejoicing" *(radenie)* or "spiritual bath." The congregation, known as a "boat," was led by a "pilot" who took them on a "voyage" from the material to the spiritual world.

This journey was accomplished by intense, semi-hypnotic singing and incantations intended to produce spiritual ecstasy and liberation from the material world. A "circle procession" which attained a frenzied circular motion as the flagellants beat themselves and each other, chanting "Khlyshchu, khlyshchu, Khrista ishchu" (I flagellate, I flagellate, seeking Christ) provided the means of ascent into the seventh heaven where men could become one with God.

13. The Molokans or "Milk drinkers" comprised another Russian religious sect which developed in the Tambov region in the 18th century, so named for their practice of drinking milk during Lent. They accepted the name, claiming that it meant they were already drinking the milk of Paradise or dwelling by rivers of milk and honey. They practiced communal and egalitarian living, and believed that man was capable of attaining direct communion with God outside all established churches. In place of the liturgy and church ritual, they worshipped with "spiritual songs," believed in flagellation, and called themselves "spiritual Christians." The Molokans settled in several villages in Northern Armenia.

14. See Addenda (J.A.), "Sevan." This is undoubtedly a reference to Margot Vartanian: "but Margot quite obviously had no feel for the mysterious and sacred charm of her own native language."

15. In Rusisian "glukhota" means "deafness," "remoteness," the adjective being "glukhoi." The Russian word for "head" is "glava" or "golova."

16. *Zamoskvorechie* literally means "beyond the Moscow river." It is the name of the old merchant quarter of Moscow on the opposite bank of the Moscow River from the Kremlin. Another reference to this section of the city appears in one of Mandelstam's Moscow poems, No. 265 (Summer, 1932), written while he was living in Zamoskvorech'e on Yakimanka Street.

17. Paul Signac (1863-1935). French Impresionist painter who, with Georges Seurat, developed the technique known as Pointillism. He wrote *D'Eugène Delacroix au néo-impressionisme* (Paris, 1899), an exposition of Pointillism.

18. Eugène Delacroix (1798-1863). Considered the greatest French Romantic painter. His use of color was extremely influential on the development of Impressionist and Post-Impressionist painting. Delacroix' visit to Morocco in 1832 provided him with numerous exotic subjects.

19. See Addenda (J.A.), section on "Moscow."

20. Ivan Fyodorov, known as The First Printer (?–d. 1583). He is known to have set the first printed book in Russia in 1563, *The Gospels (Apostoly)* in Moscow. He also put out the first printed grammar of Russian in 1574 in Lvov. In 1909 a statue of the First Printer by S.M. Volnukhin was erected in Moscow in front of the Government Printing Office (*Gosudarev pechatnyi dvor*).

21. See "Fourth Prose," section 7.

22. Notice how Mandelstam combines present tense narration with reminiscences of the past and projections of the future. His mixture of tenses and styles makes the "Journey to Armenia" seem like a letter, a memoir and a dream simultaneously. He seems to be attempting what he claims Dante achieves. See the last pages of "Conversation about Dante."

23. See Addenda (J.A.), "Moscow," beginning: "My neighbors in our communal apartment..."

24. See Addenda (J.A.), "Moscow," same as no. 23, above.

25. See Addenda (J.A.), "Moscow," beginning: "I was forever plagued by the mysteries of the stables and sheds, and by two ancient and barren linden trees."

26. Another reference to "pike's teeth" appears in the poem, "January 1, 1924."

27. *Tsentrosoiuz* is the Central Union of Consumer Cooperatives. See "Batum."

28. B.S. or B.S.K. are the initials of Boris Sergeevich Kuzin, a young biologist, the Curator of the Moscow Zoological Museum, and one of the first to hear Mandel-

stam's poetry of the 1930s, when "poetry returned" to him. It was to Kuzin that Mandelstam dedicated poem No. 266, "To the German Language." See SS, II, 596-600. See also, N.Y. Mandelstam, *Hope Against Hope* (226-228): "It was Armenia that took M. back to Goethe, Herder and the other German poets. If his meeting with the young biologist Kuzin—whose enthusiasm for literature and philosophy was somewhat in the Bursche tradition—had taken place in Moscow, it might have made little impact, but in Armenia he and M. hit it off at once. . . M. was interested in what he had to say about the application of biology to the things that concerned him, such as the perennial question as to how new forms arise. . . Kuzin was very fond of Goethe, which was also relevant to M's concerns at the moment. Later on, in Moscow, when M. "met" Dante, his friendship with Kuzin and the other biologists in his circle was reduced to a mere acquaintanceship over an occasional glass of wine."

29. See Addendan (J.A.), "Moscow." See also, "Tristia" (1918).

30. The Pamir mountains form a highland region in Central Asia mostly located in Tadzhikistan.

31. Undoubtedly, a fond reference to Nadezhda Yakovlevna Mandelstam. See also the section of this work, "On the Naturalists," for notes on Linnaeus, Lamarck, and scientific discussions.

32. Vasily Vaslilievich Vereshchagin (1842-1904). Russian painter known best for his canvases of military scenes. Wounded himself in the Balkans during the Russo-Turkish Wars, he painted many scenes from his own experience. The painting referred to here hangs in Moscow's Tretyakov Gallery: "The Apotheosis of War" (1871).

33. Abkhaziya (today known as the Abkhaz Autonomous Soviet Socialist Republic) was formed in the 8th century as an independent kingdom, later it became a part of Georgia. It was annexed as part of the Russian Empire in 1864. It borders on the eastern shores of the Black Sea and the crestline of the Caucasus Mountains. The Abkhazian people are Caucasians related to the Circassians. Abkhaziya's capital is Sukhum. Its largest inland city is Tkvarchel, a coal-mining center.

The Abkhazian language is part of the Abkhazo-Adyghian or Northwest Caucasian language group. These languages are noted for their limited number of distinctive vowels and for the great diversity of consonants in their sound systems.

34. Erevan. The capital city of Armenia. (Sometimes transcribed as Erivan or Yerevan).

35. Mt. Ararat is an extinct volcanic massif located in extreme eastern Turkey, overlooking the point at which the borders of present-day Turkey, Armenia and Iran meet. Its snow-capped conical peak reaches 14,000 feet above sea level. Ararat is associated traditionally with the mountain on which Noah's ark is said to have landed. The name Ararat, as it appears in the Old Testament, is the equivalent of Urartu (see Note 3, above). Ararat is sacred to the Armenians who believe themselves to be the first race of men to appear after the Deluge. A Persian legend names Ararat as the cradle of the human race.

36. See Note 28, above. See also, Mandelstam's Radiodrama: *Goethe's Youth,* written in exile in Voronezh.

37. Professor Alexander Gavrilovich Gurvich (1874-?). Biologist. "Dualism is characteristic of Gurvich's work. On the one hand, he recognizes the possibility of empirical research into the processes of life, on the other hand, he indicates a conviction of the impossibility of uncovering their essence." See SS, II, 602, which quotes the *Bolshaia Sovetskaia Entsiklopediia.*

38. See Addenda (J.A.), "Moscow," beginning: "The calico-colored luxury of field flowers . . . Flowers are a great nation and thoroughly literate. Their excited language consists only of proper names and dialects."

39. Author's footnote: M.E. Kozakov (SS, II, 154).

40. See "Conversation about Dante."

41. See Mandelstam's poems No. 137, "The Slate Ode," and "The Octets," and the essay, "On the Nature of the Word."

42. Capital of Abkhaziya.

43. See Note 33, above, on the Abkhazian language.

44. See Addenda (J.A.), "Sukhum," opening paragraphs.

45. See Note 33, above.

46. A *verst* is approximately 2/3 of a mile.

47. Lavrenty Pavlovich Beria (1899-1953). Head of the Soviet secret police from 1938.

48. Characters from Alphonse Daudet's burlesque novel, *Tartarin de Tarascon* (1872). Daudet was strongly influenced by his upbringing in the Provençal region of France.

49. Nikolai Nikolaevich Evreinov (1879-1953). Extremely talented Russian playwright, director, and theorist, who emigrated to Paris in 1925. Perhaps best known in the West for his fabulous spectacle, *The Taking of the Winter Palace,* which was performed on November 7, 1920 with 8000 actors, 500 musicians and 150,000 spectators. For more information and a selection of his plays, see Christopher Collins (ed.) Nikolai Evreinov, *Theater as Life: Five Modern Plays* (Ardis, 1973).

50. Alexander Ilytich Bezymensky (1898-). Prolific Soviet poet, active member of RAPP (Russian Association of Proletarian Writers), and major contributor to the RAPP journal, *On Guard (Na postu).*

51. See Addenda (J.A.), "Sukhum," where the painful experience of Mayakovsky's death is ironically juxtaposed to Bezymensky's carefree cheeriness.

52. See Addenda (J.A.), "Frenchmen," beginning: "such delicious boldness of colors are found only at the races..." See also, poem No. 258, "Impressionism."

53. Paul Cézanne (1839-1906). French post-Impressionist painter. He exerted a major influence on the stylistic and esthetic development of twentieth century art, especially on the Cubists.

54. Henri Matisse (1869-1954). Leading Fauvist painter, regarded by many as one of the most significant French painters of the twentieth century. He also designed sets for Diaghilev's ballet, *Le chant du rossignol.*

55. Vincent van Gogh (1853-1890). Often considered the best Dutch painter after Rembrandt, although his last years were spent in France. He exerted enormous influence on the Expressionist movement in modern art.

56. See Addenda (J.A.), "Frenchmen." This line is followed by many lines omitted in the final text.

57. Claude Monet (1840-1926). Major French painter who evolved the characteristic technique of Impressionist painting. Between 1900 and 1926, he worked on a series of large and small paintings of his water-garden at Giverny.

58. Auguste Renoir (1841-1919). Major French Impressionist painter, repeatedly used the same motifs as Monet in his early years, but achieved his best work in figure paintings.

59. On Paul Signac, see note 17, above.

60. Amédée Ozenfant (1886-?). With the architect Le Corbusier, he led the art movement known as Purism. Le Corbusier (1888-1965) and Ozenfant announced the death of Cubism in their publication, *Après le cubisme* (1918), offering in its stead a reform program opposing dissection, and based on a reassertion of the integrity of individual objects. Their still-lifes emphasized architectural clarity and ascetic exactitude, detachment and almost sterile perfection.

61. Pablo Picasso (1881-1977). Spanish-born painter, renowned as one of the parents of Cubism. Although much of his early work is concerned with the allegorical, steeped as it is in compassion for humanity and concern with morality, there is a foreshadowing of the cubist dialectic between the representation of objects in space and the

assertion of the reality of the flat surface of the canvas. Mandelstam is referring to a famous portrait of his early Blue period.

62. Camille Pisarro (1830-1903). A master of French Impressionism.

63. See Addenda (J.A.), "Frenchmen," for much more detailed directions: "Move back. The eye demands a bath..."

64. See Mandelstam's essay, "On the Naturalists," published in 1932 and the Addenda to that essay.

65. On Lamarck, see Note 7, "On the Naturalists."

66. See Mandelstam's earlier essay, "The Nineteenth Century."

67. See Mandelstam's earlier attack on "evolution" in "On the Nature of the Word."

68. See Addenda (J.A.), section "Pallas": "Reading this naturalist [Pallas—JGH] has a marvellous effect on your disposition; it straightens out the eye and communicates to the soul a mineral quartz calm." On Linnaeus and Pallas see Notes 3 and 4, "On the Naturalists."

69. See Addenda (J.A.), "Pallas": "[Look at the picture of Russia's enormity as Pallas shapes it out of its magnitudes...]"

70. See Addenda (J.A.), "Pallas": "He distills dyes out of a mixture of birch leaves alum."

71. See Addenda (J.A.), "Pallas": "... from the Chuvash countryside to the distillery..."

72. See Addenda (J.A.), "Pallas": "Pallas whistles tunes from Mozart. He hums Gluck. Whoever does not admire Handel, Gluck and Mozart..."

73. See Addenda (J.A.), "Pallas": "The physiology of reading still remains to be studied. Moreover, this subject differs radically from bibliography, and must be related to the organic phenomena of nature." "A book in use, a book established on a reader's desk, is like a canvas stretched on its frame."

74. See Addenda (J.A.), "Pallas": same paragraph, but preceded by: "We read books, in order to refresh our memory, but therein lies the problem, for you can read a book only during the process of remembering."

75. See Addenda (J.A.), "Pallas": similarity.

76. Mandelstam's friend, Boris Kuzin, was curator of the Zoological Museum. See Addenda (J.A.).

77. On Mandelstam's views of Darwin and Dickens, see the opening and closing pages of his essay entitled "On the Naturalists." See also, the opening paragraph to the Addenda for "On the Naturalists," which begins: "I have been accustomed since childhood to regard Darwin as no more than a mediocre mind." On Dickens, see also Mandelstam's poem No. 53, "Dombey and Son" (1913).

78. See the essay "On the Naturalists," beginning: "This new variety of curiosity about nature was radically different from Linnaeus' thirst for knowledge or Lamarck's intellectual inquisitiveness..."

79. See "Conversation about Dante."

80. See Addenda (J.A.), "On the Naturalists."

81. See Addenda (J.A.), "On the Naturalists."

82. A reference to Lamarck's work in which he explained his theory of evolution by citing the then generally accepted theory of acquired characteristics, that is, the concept that an organism develops in response to a specific need produced by the environment. Ironically enough, it is this thesis of anti-genetics which began to gain strength in the Soviet Union in the early 1930s (represented by Michurin and his followers, including Lysenko). See David Joravsky's excellent book on Soviet biologists, *The Lysenko Affair* (Harvard, 1970). Mandelstam's friendship with B.S. Kuzin and other biologists in the early 1930s would have made him very aware of this problem. Kuzin was a neo-Larmarckian.

83. See "Conversation about Dante." See also "The Octets" in particular, poem No. 281, "And Shubert on the water."

84. See Addenda (J.A.), "On the Naturalists."

85. See Addenda (J.A.), "On the Naturalists."

86. Notice Mandelstam's emphasis on narrative, narration and literary style in discussing all of the biologists, from Lamarck and Linnaeus to Darwin. Lamarck is compared to Shakespeare, Darwin to Dickens (See essay, "On the Naturalists"). See Addenda to "On the Naturalists" for a discussion of Darwin's "literary style."

87. See Linnaeus' descriptions in the first pages of the Addenda to the essay, "On the Naturalists."

88. N.Y. Mandelstam claims that this is a reference to herself. See *Hope Against Hope*, p. 189.

89. Firdusi (also transliterated: Firdousi, Firdausi). Outstanding Persian poet, author of the *Shah-namah* (The Epic of Kings), the national epic of Persia, translated into Armenian.

90. Ashtarak. One of the oldest settlements in Armenia, and an ancient cultural center, about 30 kilometers from Erevan. A few ancient basilicas and churches dating back to the 5-8th centuries still remain in addition to a church from the 13th century.

91. See similar references to the variety of sounds and the mythical quality of primitive, infantile and unpronounceable sounds in "The Octets" (*Vos'mistishiia*), in "Conversation about Dante" and elsewhere in Mandelstam's poetry and prose. See also poems No. 216, 218 calling the Armenian tongue a "wildcat" and "prickly speech."

92. See poem No. 278 of "The Octets."

93. See Addenda (J.A.), "Ashtarak."

94. Undoubtedly a reference to the little 7th century church, Karmravor. (SS, II, 603).

95. See Note 5, above.

96. A not so subtle attack on Collectivization.

97. Mandelstam seemed to have a predilection for the Sentimental novel. See also his essay, "The End of the Novel."

98. Alagez is an extinct volcano and natural barrier between Northern Armenia and the valley of the Araxes River about Erevan.

99. See Addenda (J.A.), "Alagez": "The horizon emerges in the form of a Latin gerundive." See also the magnificent image of the "one-eyed song... sung on horseback" in poem No. 365 (February, 1937).

100. See the essay, "Word and Culture," especially the reference to Catullus and poetry as imperative.

101. See the cycle of poems, "Armenia," Nos. 203-215.

102. See Addenda (J.A.), "Alagez."

103. Arshak, King of the Arshakide dynasty which ruled in Armenia from 63 to 428 A.D. In the 4th century, the kingdom was divided into two spheres of influence, the Persian and the Roman. Nadezhda Yakovlevna Mandelstam states that this section was published against the censor's orders (*Hope Abandoned,* p. 410). See also Gevork Emin's introductory remarks to the 1967 publication of "Journey to Armenia" in *Literary Armenia* (pp. 82-83), in which he states: "Not only did Mandelstam write a cycle of poems dedicated to Armenia, but he studied the Armenian legend, 'Arshak and Shapukh,' very seriously, thinking, perhaps, of eventually writing poetry on this theme or of reworking this sage ancient tale himself."

66a. ADDENDA TO "JOURNEY TO ARMENIA"

These Addenda to "Journey to Armenia" are from Mandelstam's *Notebooks* dated 1931-1932 (*Zapisnye Knizhki,* 1931-1932 godov). See SS, III, 369. This translation is based on SS, III, 147-178, which in turn is based on the author's typescript plus Irina Semenko's text published in *Problems of Literature (Voprosy literatury,* 1968, No. 4, pp. 189-194). All words, phrases, etc. in square brackets are omissions from the Semenko text reinstated by the editors of the *Collected Works.* See SS, III, 368.

1. Comparative references to the "Journey to Armenia" will not be made in these notes. The reader is referred back to the notes of the essay itself.
2. Armenian nationalists.
3. Ivan Ivanovich Shopen (1798-1870). A Frenchman by birth who served as a government official in Russia. He was sent to the Caucasus by General Paskevich, Commander of the Russian Army in the Caucasus (with whom Pushkin travelled in 1829—See Pushkin's fascinating *Journey to Arzrum,* 1836). Shopen is best known as a Russian ethnographer and historian of the Caucasus. His major work is *An Historic Testimony to the Vicissitudes of the Province of Armenia during its Annexation as Part of the Russian Empire* (St. Petersburg, 1852). Mandelstam probably also read his *New Commentary on the Ancient History of the Caucasus and its Inhabitants* (St. Petersburg, 1866) which contains the history of Moses of Chorene, Czar Vagtang, Moses of Kagkantov, and detailed notes on linguistic and phonetic variations of words and word-roots. See also my introductory notes to *Journey to Armenia.*
4. See "Fourth Prose," Part 7.
5. Head of the Armenian church.
6. See Mandelstam's Moscow poems of the early 1930s, in particular, No. 265, "Today's the day for making decalcomanias."
7. Here Mandelstam probably had in mind the colloquial idiom: "to count ribs" ("pereschitat' rebra"), meaning "to want to beat someone up," "to want to kill someone for something," and the numerous idioms based on the words for "devil," implying cynicism, disbelief, distrust and disgust. See, in particular, the last stanza of poem No. 265.
8. A reference to his wife, Nadezhda Yakovlevna Mandelstam.
9. See "Fourth Prose," Part 7.
10. Boris Kuzin.
11. See poem No. 365, "I sing with a damp throat and dry soul" (1937).
12. Raboche-Krest'ianskaia Inspektsiia—A Soviet Monitoring agency known as The Worker-Peasant Investigating Commission (SS, III, 373).
13. The Council of Peoples' Commissars (*Sovnarkom* or *Sovet Narodnykh Komissarov*) was renamed in 1946 as the Council of Ministers (*Sovet Ministrov*).
14. Nestor Ivanovich Lakoba (1893-1936). Old Bolshevik. In 1918, he was one of the leaders of the uprising against the Menshevik government in Abkhaziya; in 1922 he became Chairman of the Council of Peoples' Commissars; and between 1930 and 1936, he was made Chairman of the Central Executive Committee of the Caucasian SFSR and a member of the Central Committee of the Georgian Communist Party, only to be shot in 1936 as an "enemy of the people." (SS, III, 373).
15. See Boris Pasternak's novel, *Dr. Zhivago,* in which this concept is fully developed. The two poets shared many ideas in the late 1920s-early 1930s.
16. Mandelstam's use of the intimate form of "you" here probably results from his addressing much of the "Journey to Armenia" to Boris Kuzin.
17. Mandelstam's increased usage of Biblical imagery in the late 1920s and 1930s is noteworthy. See also "Fourth Prose," "Conversation about Dante."
18. This fragment bears the same title as the published essay "On the Naturalists."

However, the latter concentrates primarily on Darwin and his literary style.

19. Akhmatova stated in her memoirs that Mandelstam's only friends during these years were "natural scientists."

20. The monument to the famous biologist, K. A. Timiryazev (SS, III, 374).

21. Irina Semenko, in publishing Mandelstam's *Notebooks for 1931-1932*, decided to call this section "Pallas," since it is mainly concerned with him.

22. See similar imagery of "infinitesimal magnitudes" in "The Octets" especially poem Nos. 284, 285.

23. See similar image of hooks in "The Octets," poem No. 284.

24. See also "Conversation about Dante."

25. Emelyan Pugachev. Leader of the last of the great peasant revolts, against the rule of Catherine the Great (1773-1775). See Pushkin's sympathetic portrayal of Pugachev in his historical work, *The History of the Pugachev Rebellion* (1830s).

26. Mandelstam's great interest in the "reader" and reading goes back to the last chapter in *The Noise of Time* and is a major theme of "Conversation about Dante."

27. See *Other Notes and Jottings:* "For 1932: On Apollon Grigoriev."

28. On prose, see "The End of the Novel," "Literary Moscow: The Birth of Plot."

29. In math, the "characteristic" of a logarithm is the whole number, while its "fractional remainder" is on the right side of the decimal point, e.g., 4.1976: 4 = the characteristic.

30. John Tyndall (1820-1893). British physicist.

31. See Mandelstam's early statement of this basic idea in his essay, "Morning of Acmeism." There he expresses his awe before both the mathematician who almost miraculously produces the square root of some ten-digit number, and the poet for whom the "word" is "monstrously condensed reality."

32. For an early statement on the differences between the prose writer and the poet, see "On the Addressee." For an example of Mandelstam's latest prose, see "Fourth Prose."

33. An idiom meaning approximately: "Here's a fine how-do-you-do!"

34. For the ultimate statement on poetic perversity, see "Fourth Prose."

35. See also, "Humanism and the Present."

36. On Goethe, see notes to "Goethe's Youth: Radiodrama."

37. See "Word and Culture."

38. See SS, III, 169.

67. CONVERSATION ABOUT DANTE

This essay, although written during the spring-summer of 1933 in Koktebel, in the Crimea, was not published in the Soviet Union until 1967. Mandelstam gave his authorized typescript to N.I. Khardzhiev in 1937. Three decades later, Khardzhiev was instrumental in seeing to the publication of *"Razgovor o Dante"* ("Conversation about Dante," M., Iskusstvo, 1967), edited and annotated by A. A. Morozov, with an afterword by L.E. Pinsky. This translation and most of my information and notes are based on that authorized text. Ironically enough, the first publication of "Conversation about Dante" was an English translation by Clarence Brown and R. P. Hughes (*Books Abroad*, May 1965, pp. 25-48), based on an earlier, less complete version of Mandelstam's text. For more information on the other versions of this essay, see the above-mentioned Moscow, 1967 edition and SS, II, 649-50.

Mandelstam's interest in Dante is underscored by Nadezhda Yakovlevna: "Anticipating his arrest—as I have said before—everybody we knew did this as a matter of course—M. obtained an edition of the *Divine Comedy* in small format and always had it

677

with him in his pocket" (*Hope Against Hope,* p. 228). Indeed, in the 1930s, Mandelstam came to regard Dante as his "ideal" poet, even assigning to him the epithet *raznochinets,* a metaphor which he had used earlier to characterize the ideal poet and the ideal reader or interpreter of poetry in *The Noise of Time.* According to Akhmatova, it was only in the 1930s that Mandelstam began his intensive study of Italian and developed his love of Italian poetry. In the opening pages of the Addenda to this essay, Mandelstam discusses the unfortunate dearth of knowledge among Russian poets and readers of Italian poetry, possibly including himself.

Mandelstam's first meeting with Bely took place in 1933, in the Writers' Union Rest home in Koktebel, in the Crimea. Although it is purely conjecture on my part, it seems to me that just as Boris Kuzin serves as Mandelstam's primary addressee in "Journey to Armenia," sharing his views on everything from the nature of language and poetic creation as a biological process to German poetry and French Impressionist painting, so Bely seems to serve as Mandelstam's somewhat less audible interlocutor in "Conversation about Dante." Mandelstam obviously altered his formerly negative opinions of the older poet during this time, and the two poets undoubtedly shared many hours of literary conversation. Mandelstam's only direct reference to Bely, however, appears in the "Rough Drafts" to "Conversation about Dante." See Note 6, Addenda to "Conversation about Dante."

At the time of their meeting in Koktebel, Bely was working on his fanciful critical study *Gogol's Craftsmanship (Masterstvo Gogolia,* M., 1934). Both Bely and Mandelstam are primarily concerned in their criticism with the dynamics of the poetic text, with how the original creative impulse is transformed in the mind of the creative artist into living poetic material. What is more, they are both keenly interested in the effects of a great master's work on themselves as both readers and poets. Although Bely's study of Gogol is far more detailed than Mandelstam's essay on Dante, they share many similar impulses and inspirations. How frustrating not to know more about this relationship.

1. This epigraph appears in the Moscow 1967 publication but is absent from the authorized final typescript. However, it is included in Part V of the authorized text. According to A. A. Morozov, it was intended to be part of the final redaction.

2. This essay as a whole, and, in particular, this section defining "poetic speech," should be read in conjunction with Mandelstam's "Octets." It is another attempt to rephrase his views on the relationship of poetic craft, philology (see "On the Nature of the Word") and "the word as such" or poetry as an autonomous force in the universe. Mandelstam's use of critical terminology here is striking. A. A. Morozov's comments are very appropos, indicating a possible source in Yury Tynianov's *Problema stikhotvornogo iazyka,* Leningrad, 1924, p. 10. Bely may be another more immediate source of Mandelstam's critical terminology.

3. Ryszard Przybylski (*Slowo i kultura,* Warsaw, 1972) points out that this is a paraphrase of Turgenev's polemic with Nekrasov. Turgenev said of Nekrasov's verse that "poetry never spent the night there."

4. Morozov carefully points out that the explanation of Mandelstam's use of "images" and "instruments" here is found in the lengthy section of his "rough draft" (see Addenda to "Conversation about Dante," p. 444), which begins: "What is an image? An instrument in the metamorphosis of hybridized poetic speech..." and concludes: "which spits out culture like water used for gargling, is revealed and brought to light."

5. Mandelstam was never keen on films, and indeed, rather hostile toward films and film-making. See, "I Write a Scenario," as well as his early poem, No. 50, "The Cinematograph."

6. See also Mandelstam's emphasis on "process" or the "creative process" in "Octets."

7. Morozov compares this statement with Mandelstam's *Notes and Jottings*. See "For 1932: On Apollon Grigoriev": "Our memory, our experience, including its gaps, the tropes and metaphors of our sense perceptions and associations, all become uncontrolled possessions."

8. See the "Octets" especially No. 278, 281.

9. Morozov compares this paragraph with Mandelstam's "rough draft" (see Addenda, p. 5), beginning: "There exists an intermediary activity between the act of listening and the act of speech delivery," and ending: "Material is not matter."

10. In other words, a "pattern," as Mandelstam uses it here, can be repeated time and again, for it is based only on mastering a skill. "Ornament," unlike a "pattern," is variable and changing, for it both preserves and transforms, like "poetic discourse."

11. Morozov compares this with the first redaction (see Addenda, first version, from *IRLI*, p. 1), which begins: "That Russian readers are unacquainted with the Italian poets..." and ends: "... not yet having been inoculated against Dante."

12. The imagery of the mouth especially of "moving lips," is a very positive image in Mandelstam's Voronezh poetry. See, for instance, poem No. 306, "Yes, I lie in the earth..." and No. 307, "Having deprived me of seas..."

13. See the "Octets" especially Nos. 281, 283.

14. Morozov points out that "Dadaism" is a word derived from juvenile lexicon, popularized by a Modernist group of artists, including Tristan Tzara, Jean Arp, and Hugo Ball. The dadaists emphasized that the basis of the creative process stems from alogisms, that "thought is formed in the mouth" (see SS, II, 663).

15. Similar imagery occurs in Mandelstam's poem No. 278 from the "Octets."

16. See the "Octets."

17. Morozov compares this statement with Dante's *Purgatorio*, XI, 103-108. Also, compare with Mandelstam's omission from the text (see Addenda, p. 445), which begins: "To Dante a child is an infant, *il infanciullo...*" and ends: "... rescuing her child from a fire." The distinctive natural or primitive quality of juvenile expressions also appears in Mandelstam's poetry of the early 1920s, see No. 136, "The Horseshoe Finder."

18. See Mandelstam's statements comparing Dante's work with the fine arts below, in section IV of this essay. Morozov points out that Mandelstam uses "sculptural" to mean "form which reflects a given content."

19. Morozov claims that Mandelstam intends here "the possiblity of the dual existence of matter: in its material form and in the form of its emanation (light waves)..." (p. 75).

20. Note Mandelstam's emphasis on reading and creating as physiological (biological) as well as intellectual acts. See also, "On the Nature of the Word" and the last chapter of *The Noise of Time*.

21. See Mandelstam's use of the imagery of teacher and apprentice in poem No. 137, "The Slate Ode."

22. Morozov compares this paragraph with Mandelstam's rough draft (see Addenda, p. 446), which begins: "The reason they were offended by the seminarist's nickname for the 'classics'..."

23. Morozov points out that in *Inferno*, Canto XV, 121-124, Dante's meeting with his teacher Brunetto Latini is described. Latini is condemned to "eternal flight."

24. Mandelstam's interest in the sciences was very strong during this period in his life. See "On the Naturalists" and "Journey to Armenia," for examples.

25. See similar imagery in the "Octets."

26. The imagery of the orchestra introduced in this essay goes far beyond the imagery of "Morning of Acmeism," although the essentials are already present in the earlier essay.

27. Morozov compares this to the rough draft (see Addenda, p. 446) which begins: "... Dante's question is itself already bursting forth in Virgil's answer..." and ends: "... Such

pleasures await Epicurus and his disciples."

28. A reference to Mikhail Bakhtin's famous and controversial book on Dostoevsky, *Problems of Dostoevsky's Poetics* (*Problemy poetiki Dostoevskogo;* first edition, 1929, as *Problemy tvorchestva Dostoevskogo*, revised and re-published only in 1963 under the above title), English trans. by R.W. Rotsel, Ardis, 1973.

29. Mandelstam's use of the word *raznochinets* begins to develop as an image in *The Noise of Time*, where it is first used in reference to his mentor and friend, V. V. Gippius, and to himself, the poet, in the last chapter. In "Fourth Prose," "Jew" substitutes for *raznochinets* and broadens the image of the poet as "outsider." *Raznochinets* and "Jew" also have the moral power to oppose the authorities be they the disciples of Nadson in the earlier work, or "The gypsies of Tverskoy Boulevard" in the latter. See the above-mentioned works. See also Mandelstam's poem No. 260, "Midnight in Moscow" (1932).

30. Another reflection of Bakhtin's possible influence (see Note 28 above). In his book on Dostoevsky, he emphasized what he called "polyphony" and the polyphonic nature of the novel's structure. This is simply another example of Mandelstam's capacity to transforms the ideas of his age and turn them to his own use. Bakhtin's work could also have been a major topic of conversation with Bely in 1933.

31. From the first line of Tyutchev's poem "Twilight" ("Sumerki," 1836).

32. Morozov is the first critic I have come across who recognizes the fundamental esthetic significance in Mandelstam's concept of "literary spite/savagery" (*literaturnaia zlost'*)—for further details, see my notes to "Fourth Prose" and my Introduction. Morozov points out that Mandelstam's statement about the "stop mechanism of an organ" and its "psychological priming" relate to those "expressive forms" of a work of art which reveal the organization of an author's spiritual material (his "laboratory of spiritual qualities"). In Mandelstam's own work, this expressive source is termed "literary spite/savagery." See, the last chapter of *The Noise of Time*.

33. Here Morozov states: "For O. Mandelstam, involved in a polemic against the theory of evolutionary progress (uninterrupted development), everything which comes to pass assumes the form of a happening, an event, a 'storm'." Morozov compares Mandelstam's statement beginning, "the storm in nature serves as the prototype of the historical event. The movement of the hour hand... The prototype of the non-event." See *Notes and Jottings for the 1930s:* "Undated Notes and Fragments." See also the passage from the first version of this essay (Addenda, p. 12), beginning: "But the compositional roots of the tenth Canto of the *Inferno* lie in the gathering of the storm which matures like a meteorological phenomenon..." Also see section XI of this essay, below.

34. See the less-developed geological imagery of poem No. 137, "The Slate Ode," used to denote the creative power and creative process.

35. See "Morning of Acmeism." Morozov points out that Mandelstam's earliest collection of poems is called *Stone* (*Kamen'*, 1913) and that as early as 1913, in "Morning of Acmeism," Mandelstam had located the structural principle of his art in the material itself; see the lines beginning: "Tyutchev's stone, which 'having rolled down the mountain, lay...' "

36. Here Mandelstam both reflects and projects the ideas of the "structuralist critics" of his generation, in particular, Tynianov and Bakhtin. Furthermore, he advocates that the reader's involvement in the author's text must be one of total immersion, not only in the text itself, but in the language and culture out of which the text is created: "an enormous journey to which we are so accustomed that we travel in our sleep." See below. Again, this section may reflect an actual "conversation" with Bely in 1933.

37. Morozov suggests the comparison with Mandelstam's definition in "On the Nature of the Word" of the word as a "verbal representation," a "complex composite

of phenomena, it is a connection, a 'system'."

38. Morozov points out Mandelstam's aversion to poetic cliches and states: "For Mandelstam's poetics sharp semantic shifts are characteristic, shifts emerging from the combination of semantically distant words, but also from his sensitivity to the historical life of the word." As an example, he cites the third stanza of poem No. 113, which reads (in W.S. Merwin's and C. Brown's translation): "And it [the word—JGH] rises *slowly like a pavilion or a temple,/ performs the madness of Antigone,/ or falls at one's* feet, a dead swallow,/ with Stygian tenderness and a green branch."

39. Morozov compares this with section VIII of the essay, a comparative analysis of the phonetic and semantic levels of Canto XXXII, *Inferno*.

40. Morozov compares this with the "Rough Notes" (see Addenda, p. 446), beginning: "What was previously said about the plurality of forms is equally applicable to lexicon."

41. See "On the Nature of the Word" for Mandelstam's earlier statements on the internal relationships of phonetic and semantic meaning, for example: "The significance of the word may be viewed as a candle burning inside a paper lantern, and conversely, its phonetic value, the so-called phoneme, may be located inside the significance, just as that candle may be inside that lantern."

42. Morozov points out the source of this thought in the "Rough draft" (See Addenda), beginning: "Here is an example, Canto XXXII of the *Inferno* is suddenly taken ill with a barbarian Slavicitis.." I would also point out the similarity of this comparison between literary criticism and medicine with the organic comparison between poetics and physiology drawn in "On the Nature of the Word," beginning: "However, the extremely rapid humanization of science, including the theory of knowledge, forces us to move in another direction. We can consider representations not only as objective data of consciousness, but also as human organs, just like the liver and the heart.

In its application to the word, such an interpretation of verbal representations opens up broad new perspectives, allowing us to dream about the creation of an organic poetics, a poetics of biological rather than legislative nature, a poetics which would destroy the canon in the name of the internal unity of the organism, a poetics which would exhibit all the traits of biological science."

43. Morozov points out that the exact number of lines in the *Divina Commedia* is 14233.

44. Compare with "Morning of Acmeism," in which Mandelstam states: "Too often we fail to see that a poet raises a phenomenon to its tenth power, and the modest exterior of a work of art often deceives us with regard to *the monstrously condensed reality contained within.* In poetry this reality is the word as such (my italics).

45. See the "Octets."

46. See Kiril Taranovsky's fascinating article on the imagery of bees and wasps in Mandelstam's poetry: "Pchely i osy v poezii Mandel'shtama...," in *To Honor Roman Jakobson* (The Hague, 1967, pp. 1973-1995). A revised version appears in his new book, *Essays on Mandelstam* (Cambridge, 1976).

47. Mandelstam is still fighting the Symbolists and the Imaginists here, whose images were often self-sufficient. For Mandelstam, images must be innate elements of the poem's overall structure, "architecture." See "Morning of Acmeism" or the poem No. 39, "Notre Dame" (1912); see also, "On the Nature of the Word," or such poems as Nos. 136, 137.

48. Mandelstam's continued attack on Symbolism.

49. Morozov mentions Gustave Doré as an example.

50. From Blok's poem "Ravenna."

51. Morozov illustrates this statement with a reference to Mandelstam's "rough notes" (See Addenda, p. 447), beginning: "Dante never regarded human speech as an island of isolated rationality. Dante's lexical groupings were thoroughly barbarianized."

52. Morozov states that Mandelstam's source is unknown. However, he suggests the catalogue of L. Volkmann, *Iconografia dantesca* (Florence-Venice, 1898, p. 16, 18).

53. Morozov notes that remarks about Dante are scattered through Oswald Spengler's *Decline of Europe,* the first volume of which was translated into Russian in 1923 (*Zakat Evropy,* I, M.P., 1923).

54. Morozov gives as an example the work of A. Dzhivelegov, *Dante* (M., 1933, p. 170): "There is a peculiarity about Dante's images which is very typical. They are for the most part extremely pale in their colors."

55. Morozov points out that Spengler associated brown with a striving toward otherworldliness.

56. See the weaving/textile images in the "Octets."

57. See also the desert imagery in the "Octets," especially No. 283.

58. This idea is presented in poetic form several times in Mandelstam's poems about the creative process. See, in particular, No. 137, "The Slate Ode" and the "Octets."

59. Morozov explains that Mandelstam has in mind the identification of the grammatical and logical forms of thought, for instance, the grammatical subject is often taken for the subject of a thought.

I might add here that Mandelstam had long been interested in poetic experiments with syntax and meaning, see, for instance, his interest in the work of Khlebnikov and Pasternak in "Some Remarks on Poetry."

60. On Mandelstam's pejorative conception of Buddhism, see "The Nineteenth Century" and "The End of the Novel."

61. On the need for the creation of a new syntax, see "Storm and Stress," pp. 179-80 above.

62. See similar ideas pertaining to Khlebnikov and Pasternak in "Some Notes on Poetry" and "Storm and Stress."

63. See Mandelstam's own "rough drafts" and "notes" under Addenda.

64. See the "Octets."

65. Morozov points out that Mandelstam has in mind here a part of the text which he excluded from the final version (See Addenda, p. 447), beginning: "The questions and answers of the 'journey with conversations,' otherwise known as the *Divina Commedia...*"

66. This is the same citation as the epigraph to the essay.

67. Similar kinds of metaphors exist in Mandelstam's poetry, especially in those poems treating the creative process: see, for instance, No. 137, "The Slate Ode" and the "Octets."

68. A similar kind of structure might be used to describe some of Mandelstam's own verse, see such diverse poems as No. 78, "Insomnia. Homer..." (1915) or No. 127, "To some winter is nut-stains and blue-eyed punch" (1922), or No. 265, "Today's the day for making decalcomanias" (1932).

69. Mandelstam's attack on literary critics goes back at least as far as *The Noise of Time* (see the last chapter) and "On the Nature of the Word." Hence, his ideal reader is one who participates in, or experiences, a work of art, not one who "distances it" by whatever means. This juxtaposition is vividly presented in *The Noise of Time,* in which V.V. Gippius, is opposed to the Literary Fund's commemorative readings held in the Tenishev School auditorium. For a major polemic against "the reader," see "The Slump."

70. See Mandelstam's poem No. 104, "Tristia."

71. See the similar imagery in "Storm and Stress": "syntax, the circulatory system of poetry has been stricken with sclerosis." See Note 60, above.

72. Morozov points out that in the "rough draft" (see Addenda, p. 447), this paragraph is followed by: "The power of culture lies in our incomprehension of death.

This is one of the essential qualities of Homeric poetry. That is why the Middle Ages had a weakness for Homer and a fear of Ovid."

73. R. Przybylski (*Slowo i kultura*) points out the difficulty in translating this passage adequately. The original reads: "... *soderzhanie* istorii est *so*vmestnoe *derzhanie* vremeni—*so*tovarishchami, *so*iskateliami, *so*otkryvateliami ego. (My italics—JGH). The prefix *so*—meaning "all/everyone together" is reiterated five times, emphasizing the contents *(soderzhanie)* of history as all-inclusive, all-encompassing. *Soderzhanie* is formed from *derzhanie,* the noun form of *derzhat'* (to hold/contain/keep/own/possess). Its qualities are emphasized by isolating it, breaking it down into its component parts, and relating it through its phonetic and semantic relationships to the other elements in the passage.

74. On "the word" or poetry and history, see also "On the Nature of the Word" and "On the Addressee."

75. Morozov indicates this quote is from Tsvetaeva's "Under the blueness of Moscow copses" ("Nad sinevom podmoskovnykh roshch"), from the cycle of *Verses about Moscow,* 1916. I would add that the poem cited is "From my hands a city not made by human hands" ("Iz ruk moikh nerukotvornyi grad") dedicated to Mandelstam, a reference to Pushkin's famous "I built myself a monument not made by human hands" ("Ia pamiatnik sebe vozdvig nerukotvornyi").

76. Morozov reminds us that the combination of theology and Aristotelian logic characterized much of the Scholastic thinking of Dante's age.

77. This, of course, is also most applicable to Mandelstam and his use of "texts."

78. Morozov points out that Dante (in *Paradiso,* II, 95-96) called experience the "source of science."

79. Morozov indicates that in the original text (see Addenda) this was followed by a passage beginning: "The true privy councillors of the Catholic hierarchy were the apostles themselves, and the school boy facing them..."

80. Morozov points out that Dante, in *Paradiso,* XIV, compares himself with a student preparing for his Baccalaureate exams.

81. See Mandelstam's earlier comments on "cognition" and perception in "The Nineteenth Century," "On the Nature of the Word," among others.

82. Morozov points out this reference is to *Paradiso,* Canto II, 97-105.

83. Morozov compares this with *Paradiso,* XXVI, 71-72.

84. Towards a definition of the ideal reader. However, the following paragraph would indicate that the ideal reader and ideal creator had more in common than could be easily defined.

85. Mandelstam's own footnote here is: Kars, *History of Orchestration (Istoriia orkestrovki,* Muzgiz, 1932).

86. The image of the baton, its birth, and its role in the creative process, is closely related to one of Mandelstam's earliest statements about the relationship of the different elements of poetry. See, "Morning of Acmeism": " 'The word as such' was born very slowly. Gradually, one after another, all the elements of the word were drawn into the concept of form. To this day only the conscious sense, the Logos, has been mistakenly and arbitrarily taken for the content. . . The Logos demands nothing more than to be considered on an equal footing with the other elements of the word."

87. Valery Yakovlevich Kirpotin (b. 1898). "Orthodox" critic, professor, and Party member; between 1932 and 1936 he headed the Literature Section of the Central Committee. Author of many books on classics.

88. According to Mandelstam the essence of poetic material is its "transmutability" or "convertiblity" (obratimaia i obrashchaiushchaiasia poeticheskaia materiia).

89. On Mandelstam's statements about the concepts of time and space, see the essays "On the Nature of the Word," "Nineteenth Century," "On the Addressee," and "Morning of Acmeism," among others, as well as his poems of the early 1920s, especially

No. 135, 136, 137, 140, and the "Octets."

90. Notice the significance of autobiography in Mandelstam's conception of poetic creativity. For other statements on autobiography, see *The Noise of Time*, the essays "Literary Moscow: The Birth of Plot" and "The End of the Novel."

91. The theme of the poet addressing "the reader in posterity" harks back to the early essay, "On the Addressee." See my Introduction.

92. Another major aspect of Mandelstam's own poetry. See SS, I. See also Mandelstam's comments on auditory coloration with reference to the work of Fet and Pasternak, in "Some Notes on Poetry."

93. Morozov points out that Mandelstam substitutes "grasshopper" ("kuznechik") here for Dante's "stork" ("cicogna"). I would like to add that the sounds of the "grasshopper" held much greater significance for modern Russian poets, see Khlebnikov's famous poem on the subject, "The Grasshopper" ("kuznechik"), which Mandelstam cites in his essay, "Literary Moscow: The Birth of Plot."

94. See Mandelstam's own poems of the early 1930s on Moscow, expressing his "love," "passion," and "hatred" for that city.

95. Morozov suggests that this passage is associated with the passage in Mandelstam's *Notes and Jottings* (see, "1932: On Apollon Grigoriev"), beginning: "In this way 'the purpose of catharsis and the purpose of self-creation' of which our Apollon Grigoriev once spoke, is achieved." He also mentions that these notes refer to Grigoriev's poem, "The Comet" ("Kometa").

96. See the "Octets," especially No. 279, 284.

97. Morozov suggests that "copious riches" is a common poetic cliche, giving examples from Batyushkov and V. Ivanov.

98. On Mandelstam's view of "invention and money," see "Literary Moscow." See also "The Slate Ode."

99. Morozov points out that "red vests" became fashionable among the French romantics in the 1830s. One should add that Théophile Gautier, one of the leading Romantics helped to assure the success of Victor Hugo's *Hernani* in 1830 by scandalizing the audience at the Comédie Française, wearing a bright rose-colored doublet.

100. The Romantic age emphasized "invention," "fantasy," "imagination," over "craft" or "art." Mandelstam and his Acmeist colleagues emphasized "craft" and "form" over "invention."

101. Dante was elected one of the six priors of Florence in 1300—Morozov. It should be added, however, that he served as prior for only two months. Two years later, he was banned from the city.

102. "Chiostro" means "monastery"—Morozov.

103. See the "Octets," especially No. 278, 280, 281.

104. From Rimbaud's famous sonnet "Vowels"—Morozov.

105. Morozov points out that Mandelstam is here returning to the theme of ornamentation connected with fabrics or textiles, "inasmuch as the constructive characteristics of the depicted object appear in the ornamentation."

106. Here Mandelstam is playing with verbal sound coloration himself: *Tkachestvo* (weaving) and *kachestvennost'* (qualitativeness) and *kachestvo* (quality) are as much related by sound as by semantic meaning. See also, the imagery of "weaving" and "fabric" in "Tristia" (1918), and the "Octets." Most significant, however, Mandelstam must have had in mind the poetic cliche, *slovesnaia tkan'* ("verbal fabric").

107. Here again, Mandelstam's connections are based on verbal sound coloration. His baton is performing the same "conductorial flight" as Dante's. "Net sintaksisa— est' namagnichennyi poryv, *toska* po *korabel'noi korme, toska* po cherviachnomu *kormu, toska* po neizdannomu *zakonu, toska* po Florentsii." (My italics.) His words are linked primarily by their phonetic rather than semantic relationships. The similarity to his poetry is striking, for instance: "Kto ia? Ne kamenshchik priamoi,/ Ne krovel'-

shchik, ne korabel'shchik:/ Dvurushnik ia, s dvoinoi dushoi" ("The Slate Ode").

108. Mandelstam's work is filled with images of rock, stone and references to the fields of architecture, archaeology, geology and meteorology. In his earliest work, "stone" is seen primarily as a "building block" or foundation stone of art, see "Morning of Acmeism" and his first collection of poems, *Stone*. In the early 1920s, he views his own autobiography through archaeological imagery—*(The Noise of Time)* and uses images of "slate"/"stone" to represent the creative process. In the 1930s, he seems to combine the earlier images with geological and meteorological imagery to represent culture—past, present and future, as well as elements in the creative process, see below. Also see "Octets" and "Journey to Armenia." It should be recalled that Mandelstam wrote this essay in Koktebel in the Crimea.

109. The reference is to Novalis' unfinished novel, *Heinrich von Ofterdingen*, Chapter 5 (the Russian translations appeared in Moscow in 1914)—Morozov.

110. This theme is also very prominent in "The Slate Ode."—Morozov.

111. See "The Slate Ode" for another presentation of this theme.

112. "Glossolalia" refers to the pronunciation of unrelated sounds, a practice common to the customs of certain mystical sects.

113. See "On the Nature of the Word"—Morozov. See also Mandelstam's comments on "personality" in "François Villon" and "The End of the Novel," as well as his poem, "Batyushkov."

114. See "On the Nature of the Word," in particular, Mandelstam's interpretation of Bergson's concepts of time and space, and "causality."

115. Morozov compares this statement with "rough jottings" (See Addenda, p. 451), beginning: " 'I compare, therefore I am,' so Dante might have put it. He was the Descartes of metaphor..."

116. See reference in Note 115, above, conclusion: "... because there is no existence outside of comparison, because existence itself is comparison."

117. See Index for references to V.V. Gippius.

118. For examples in Mandelstam's verse, see the "Octets."

119. See No. 281 of the "Octets."

120. R. Przybylski *(op. cit.)* points out that this passage may be a reference to Mozart's *Magic Flute.*

121. Morozov notes that this refers to Canto VI, quoted above.

122. An image from Batyushkov's poem, "The Shade of a Friend" ("Ten' druga")—Morozov.

123. Morozov compares this major statement with Mandelstam's "rough draft" (see Addenda, p. 451), beginning: "Allow me to give an obvious example involving nearly the entire *Commedia* taken as a whole."

124. See Note 88, above.

125. See the "Octets," especially No. 280 (November, 1933), and No. 281 (January, 1934).

67a. ADDENDA TO "CONVERSATION ABOUT DANTE"

These addenda are from Mandelstam's first version of the "Conversation about Dante," from Rough Drafts and Notes, which were first published in the commentary to the 1967 Moscow publication of "Conversation about Dante," *op. cit.,* as well as in SS, II and III, and in the magazine *Problems of Literature (Voprosy literatury,* No. 4, 1968). It was not considered necessary to provide extensive annotations for these Addenda since references to almost all the addenda are to be found in the annotations to the essay itself.

Mandelstam's own sense of the value of "rough drafts" is clearly stated in the essay: "The safety of the rough draft is the statute assuring the preservation of the power behind the literary work."

1. SS, III, 180. "In another version this is followed by a citation: Dawn is breaking. Tattered old Dante drops from my hands..."

2. While these comments on Pushkin are interesting to us for what they tell us about Mandelstam's admiration for the older poet, they were obviously omitted from the Final Version of the essay because they had little to do with the comments on Dante.

3. On Pushkin and Batyushkov, see the last page of "Some Notes on Poetry."

4. SS, III, 181: "In another version, this was followed by: 'Egyptian culture' is essentially Egyptian propriety, Medieval culture—Medieval propriety. Those opposed to the cult of Amon-Ra or to the thesis of the Council of Trent were drawn willy-nilly into the circle of so to speak, 'improper proper behavior.' It is precisely this context of culture worship..."

5. See the use of the imagery of childhood in "The Octets" (Vos'mistishiia, 1933-35).

6. Author's footnote: "This idea belongs to B.N. Bugaev" SS, III, 184.

7. See also "Storm and Stress" and "Some Notes on Poetry."

68. GOETHE'S YOUTH: RADIODRAMA

This radio script was written by Mandelstam in the spring of 1935 (April-June) during his Voronezh exile. This translation is based on the text which was first published in SS, III, 61-80. See also, Mandelstam's Letters, in particular, No. 67, dated spring 1935, in which the poet begs his wife for material for Shervinsky, e.g., for his radio program (SS, III, 359).

Nadezhda Mandelstam provides the most informed commentary on this work. See *Hope Abandoned:* "In Voronezh we worked together on the script for a broadcast about the young Goethe, using Goethe's own autobiography as our main source. All the connecting passages and other technical parts written by me have been left out of Mandelstam's text as published. I noticed that he chose those episodes in Goethe's life which he thought typical for the development of any poet—insofar, that is, as he himself had experienced something similar... When Goethe talks about his meeting with Klopstock he describes how the young people who came to see the maestro were respectful and irreverent at the same time. This was exactly the attitude of M. and Akhmatova toward their elders. Only Bely provoked a different reaction in M.—he was so tragic that he aroused compassion and respect. By the time he met Bely, however, M. was no longer all that young himself" (pp. 240-241).

1. Johann Wolfgang von Goethe (1749-1832). Mandelstam expressed a deep interest in Goethe's life and work throughout his lifetime. *Wilhelm Meister* and the role of (auto)biography in the genre of the novel is mentioned in "The End of the Novel"; *The Sorrows of Young Werther* is mentioned in several essays, including the Addenda to "On the Naturalists": "Darwin's Literary Style." Mandelstam was re-introduced to Goethe and German poetry, according to Nadezhda Mandelstam, by Boris Kuzin (see Index).

Much of Mandelstam's radio text was based on Goethe's autobiography, *Dichtung and Wahrheit,* in which he provides a fascinating picture of a happy, sensitive childhood and youth as well as his profound sense of the cross-fertilization of life and literature which he recognized as essential to human development. See, for instance, Mandelstam's discussion of Goethe's childhood years in Frankfurt; his first passionate love for the barmaid Gretchen: his interest in the theater inspired by his grandmother's gift of a puppet theater; life in Leipzig (Mandelstam confuses this with Goethe's stay in Strasbourg, however) where he was sent in 1765 to study law.

2. Strasbourg. Mandelstam probably confused this city with Leipzig where young Goethe was first sent to study law at his father's alma mater in 1765. In *Faust,* Goethe calls Leipzig "little Paris," a world of cosmopolitan elegance and fashion as opposed to provincial Frankfurt: it was in Leipzig that he met Gottshed and Klopstock. However, Goethe had to break off his studies in Leipzig in 1768 because of a severe illness. He returned home to Frankfurt for a long convalescence. Upon his recovery, it was decided that he should pursue his legal studies in Strasbourg. His stay in the German capital of a French province proved a turning point in his life, for he experienced a strong nationalistic reaction against the cosmopolitan atmosphere of Leipzig. Indeed, it was under the great Strasbourg cathedral that he proclaimed his conversion to the German Gothic ideal. And it was in Strasbourg during the winter of 1770-1771 that he met J.G. Herder, leader of the German *Sturm und Drang* movement. (See Note 12 below on Herder and Herder's influence on Goethe).

3. See "Morning of Acmeism" and "Conversation about Dante." Goethe, apparently, was also interested enough in architecture to contribute a theoretical piece to Herder's *Von deutscher Art und Kunst* in 1773 which marked him as a theoretician of the *Sturm und Drang* movement.

4. See Goethe's *Dichtung und Wahrheit.*

5. Johann Christoph Gottshed (1700-1766). German literary critic who dominated the theater with his French classical values while providing it with a repertory of the best plays of contemporary Europe, in particular, Racine. Professor of poetry and philosophy at the University of Leipzig and virtual dictator of intellectual life in the city of Leipzig. His rationalistic *Versuch einer kritischen Dichtkunst* (1730) rejected poetic fancy, emphasizing purity of language and classical construction.

6. Friend of Goethe.

7. Friedrich Gottlieb Klopstock (1724-1803). German poet, best known for his lyrics and his influence on Goethe, the Göttingen poets, and the *Sturm und Drang* movement. His epic *Messias,* published in four volumes between 1748 and 1773, created a literary storm when it appeared. Many of his odes were set to music by Gluck, C.P.E. Bach, Beethoven, Schubert, and Mahler, and strongly influenced the development of the German *Lieder.*

8. Kätchen refers to Käthe Schönkopf, Goethe's great love when he was eighteen.

9. Shakespeare's works were rarely performed in the Soviet Union during the dark years of Stalin's power. Goethe's chaotically Shakespearean *Göetz von Berlichingen,* published in 1773, is credited with launching the cult of Shakespeare in Germany and with providing the *Sturm und Drang* movement with its first major dramatic work. Indeed, the movement's manifesto issued two years previously in 1771, had been heralded by Goethe's *Rede zum Shakespeare Tag.*

10. Johann Bernhard Basedow (1723-1790). German educator. His methods of elementary education are outlined in his *Elementarwerk,* published in 1774, based on the writings of Locke and Rousseau. His model school emphasized practical education, e.g., courses in physical education, manual training, nature study.

11. Johann Heinrich Merck (1741-1791). German writer and critic who supported the young writers of the *Sturm und Drang* movement including Goethe and Herder. Merck helped to found the journal *Frankfurter Gelehrte Anzeigen* in which some of Goethe's early works appeared.

12. Johann Gottfried von Herder (1744-1803). German philosopher, literary critic, and leader of the *Sturm und Drang* literary movement which sought to liberate German literature and culture from the then dominant French Classicist movement. Herder developed the idea of *Volkgeist* (national character or spirit of a people) which

emphasized the differences and peculiarities of individual peoples in contrast to the traditional Classicist stress on universal truths and values. Herder's interest in folk customs and the vernacular led to his collection of popular poetry and folk songs, *Stimmen der Völker in Liedern* (2 volumes, 1778-1779). His major ideas are found in his four-volume philosophical study, *Ideen zur Philosophie der Geschichte der Menschheit* (1800).

Goethe met Herder in Strasbourg during the winter of 1770-1771. From him Goethe learned a new theory of poetry—that poetry is the original and most vital language of man; a new view of the artist—that of the creator as fashioning forms expressive of feeling; the virtues of a new literary style—of the *Volkslied* and the poetry of what Herder called "primitive" peoples, his examples being the Hebrew Bible and the Homeric epic. Herder's influence on Goethe was first clearly expressed in the latter's love lyrics of the early 1770s, which mark the beginning of a new era in German lyric poetry.

13. Frederike Brion, the Pastor's daughter of Sesenheim, one of Goethe's early loves, was the stimulus behind his love lyrics of the early 1770s which mark the beginning of a new epoch in German lyric poetry. (See Note 12, above)

14. Lotte, or Charlotte Buff, the girl with whom Goethe was passionately in love in Wetzlar, and a major stimulus behind the composition of his extremely popular novel, *The Sorrows of Young Werther* (1774). Lotte was betrothed to Christian Kestner, who was apparently most tolerant of Goethe's passion, until he found their affair publicized on the pages of *Werther*.

15. Lili Schönemann, the daughter of a rich banker, betrothed for a while to Goethe. With his departure for Weimar in 1775, the engagement was permitted to lapse.

16. Translator's note—This translation is from *Wilhelm Meister's Apprenticeship* (trans. R. Dillon Boylan, London, 1855, p. 123).

17. See "The End of the Novel," in which Mandelstam discusses the issues of biography and prose fiction, the genre of the novel, and more specifically, the Napoleonic myth and the 19th century novel.

18. *Wilhelm Meister* or *William Meister's Apprenticeship* (*Wilhelm Meisters Lehrjahre,* 1795-1796) was the product of Goethe's "mature years," written during that period when "mastery of life" became his major concern. The title of this autobiographical novel suggests the lengthy apprenticeship such mastery requires. This novel was succeeded by *Wilhelm Meisters Wanderjahre* (1821-1829), which indicates that "mastery of life" is not the result of an apprenticeship, but the ceaseless wandering associated with that life, in which the goal and the road to the goal are constantly interacting. See also Mandelstam's fascinating comments on biography, autobiography and the genre of the novel in "The End of the Novel."

19. In September 1786, Goethe departed secretly for Italy, where he remained until April 1788. It has been said that this flight was both "a death and a rebirth" (See Goethe's *Letters*). He sought his own rebirth as man and as artist. This period is said to have influenced the creation of *Faust,* one of the masterpieces of world literature, as well as *Egmont, Torquato Tasso, Iphigenie auf Tauris* (1787), and the *Römische Elegien* (1788-1789).

20. Torquato Tasso (1544-1595). Italian poet of the Renaissance. His masterpiece *Jerusalem Delivered* is an epic devoted to the exploits of Godfrey of Boulogne during the First Crusade. Goethe wrote a psychological drama based on Tasso's life, his recurring insanity and confinements, and his doomed love for Leonora d'Este: *Torquato Tasso* (1789). It is basically the study of a poet or the poetical character, of an artist whose medium is the ordinary vehicle of communication between men. Somewhat later, Goethe is said to have stated that Tasso was "an intensified Werther." Tasso become a Romantic hero as a result of works by Goethe, Byron and other poets of the Romantic age. See Mandelstam's poem No. 261, "Batyushkov" in which Tasso is men-

tioned. Batyushkov was Tasso's Russian translator.

69. NOTES, JOTTINGS, AND FRAGMENTS

These translations are all based on the materials in SS, III. Some of the notes, however, also appeared in the journal, *Problems of Literature* (*Voprosy literatury,* No. 4, 1968, pp. 181-204). For more information, see SS, III, 368-69.

Most of Mandelstam's Notebooks for 1931-1932 pertain to "On the Naturalists" and "Journey to Armenia." These have been included in the Addenda to these two items. See, above.

1. On Nekrasov. See Note 11, "Badger Hole."
2. "The Poor Knight" refers to Pushkin's "There Was a Poor Knight" (1829).
3. On Pasternak, see Index. Mandelstam's meaning here is complicated by being bound up with his pun on an idiom in which he substitutes one of the key words. The idiom, *nabrat' vody v rot* (literally: to take so much water into one's mouth that one dare not speak) means: "to keep mum." Mandelstam substitutes "universe" for "waters," thus his literal meaning is something like: "to take so much of the universe into one's mouth that one dare not speak."
4. The pun on *vyvod* and *vykhod* is much more striking in Russian, for the verbal play involves both phonetic and semantic relationships.
5. Compare "Literary Moscow: The Birth of Plot."
6. For more on this theme, see "On the Nature of the Word." These notes may very well date from 1922-1923.
7. See similar statements in "An Army of Poets."

THE LETTERS

All the translations of the Letters included in this volume are based on their publication in the Struve-Filipoff *Collected Works* (SS, II and III) unless otherwise noted. The numbering system has been altered to allow for a chronological ordering of the letters included in both volumes. Dating and most of the annotations are based on the *Collected Works* (SS I, II and III), on Nadezhda Yakovlevna's memoirs, *Hope Against Hope* and *Hope Abandoned,* and on Clarence Brown's *Mandelstam.* This supplemental information is given within square brackets in the text. Dates separated by a slash mark (/) indicate old and new calendar dates. For further details reference to the above mentioned works is highly recommended.

NO. 1: TO VLADIMIR GIPPIUS

1. Vladimir Vasilievich Gippius (1876-1941). Poet, literary critic, and Director of the Tenishev Commercial School which Mandelstam attended in St. Petersburg. Brother of the literary historian, Vasily Vasilievich Gippius, author of *Gogol* (Leningrad, 1924). As a poet, Gippius published under two pseudonyms: Vladimir Bestuzhev and Vladimir Neledinsky. Gippius also wrote the long poem, *The Human Visage* (*Lik chelovecheskii,* 1922). He began publishing as early as 1895 and was best known as a "decadent" poet. He later joined Gumilev's Guild of Poets. His critical works were devoted to Pushkin (see his *Pushkin and the Journalistic Polemics of his Day* [Pushkin i zhurnal'naia polemika ego vremeni], 1900 and *Pushkin and Christianity* [Pushkin i khristianstvo], 1915). On the latter, notes to "Pushkin and Scriabin."

Mandelstam's love and admiration for his teacher and later friend-companion in the Guild of Poets is best expressed in the last chapter of *The Noise of Time*. His profound influence on the younger poets of the early twentieth century is also mentioned by Gumilev in his *Letters on Russian Poetry* (*Pis'ma o russkoi poezii*, 1923) and by Bryusov in his *Diaries: 1891-1910* (*Dnevniki: 1891-1910*, 1927). See Index.

2. The concept of "literary spite" or "literary savagery" *(literaturnaia zlost')* is discussed in reference to Gippius in the last chapter of *The Noise of Time*.

3. See "Pushkin and Scriabin," and notes, for further discussion of Mandelstam's religious-philosophical-esthetic quest.

4. Nikolai Maximovich Minsky (pseudonym of Vilenkin, 1855-1937). Russian poet, philosopher, editor and translator. In 1884, Minsky issued the first manifesto of the Russian Decadents in his article "The Ancient Dispute" ("Starinnyi spor"). He called for individualism which strives after "self-deification of the personality" in both life and art. Minsky stated: "One moment of dazzling, intense consciousness of being is more comforting and desirable than many years of decaying and vegetating." Man's striving after the ideal, the immaterial, his desire to seek knowledge of the Divine presence in the Universe and, consequently, to comprehend the incomprehensible or the immaterial, forms the basic paradox of Minsky's philosophical theory, *Maeonism* (from Plato's *Meon*). This theory was sharply criticized both by Marxist (Plekhanov) and non-Marxist philosophers (Soloviev, Berdyaev).

Minsky's extremely eclectic philosophy, which included his profound belief in a kind of "social humanism," in a union of intelligentsia and workers based on equal rights, at least partially explains his capacity to organize both religious-philosophical meetings and to edit Lenin's Bolshevik newspaper, *New Life* (*Novaia zhizn'*, 1905), for which he was subsequently arrested and forced to emigrate.

Other books by Minsky are *In the Light of Conscience: Thoughts and Dreams about the Purpose of Life* (*Pri svete sovesti...*, 1897), *Religion of the Future* (*Religiia budushchego*, 1905), and *On Civic Themes* (*Na obshchestvennye temy*, 1907). See also his statement on Meonism: " 'Meonism' N.M. Minskogo v szhatom izlozhenii avtora," in S.A. Vengerov, *Russian Literature of the XX Century* (*Russkaia literatura XX veka* [1890-1910], Vol. I, pp. 364-68, Moscow, 1914).

5. Mandelstam did enroll in the Department of Philology at the University of St. Petersburg in 1911. For more biographical details, see Clarence Brown, *Mandelstam*.

NO. 2: TO VYACHESLAV IVANOV

1. On Ivanov, see Index.

NO. 3: TO V. I. IVANOV

1. The reference to Ivanov's book is probably *By the Stars* (*Po zvezdam*) which was published in 1909, a collection of critical essays and sayings.

2. Swiss resort in Bern Canton.

3. See Mandelstam's poem No. 118, entitled "We will gather again in Petersburg" ("V Peterburge my soidemsia, snova," 1920).

4. *Apollon* (1909-1917). Russian periodical founded in 1909 by Gumilev (see Note 1, "On the Nature of the Word") and Sergei Makovsky (see Letters: No. 12, to Makovsky) which eventually became the organ of the Acmeists (see my Introduction). Mandelstam's early essays, book reviews, and poetry appeared in this magazine, beginning in 1913.

5. *The Island (Ostrov)* was a literary magazine edited by A. N. Tolstoi and

Gumilev, which appeared in only 2-3 issues (SS, II, 679).

6. Richard Dehmel (1863-1920). German poet and prose writer. His two-volume collected works appeared in a Russian translation in 1911-12. (SS, II, 679).

7. The poems included No. 147 (see C. Brown, *Mandelstam* pp. 38-39).

NO. 6

1. It is not clear which poems accompanied this letter.

NO. 7

1. These poems are found in SS, II, 446, poems No. 457b, 457v: "There is no other path," and "What is the music of my tender eulogies."

NO. 8

1. A reference to Verlaine's *Romances sans paroles*. A rare comment, indeed, on M's own poetry. See SS, II, 445, poem No. 457a: "In the darkened skies, like a pattern."

NO. 9

1. The "Academy of Verse" or *Akademiia stikha* (also known as The Society of the Adepts of the Artistic Word or *Obshchestvo revnitelei khudozhestvennogo slova*) was organized by V. Ivanov. Meetings were held in his penthouse apartment.

NO. 11: TO FYODOR KUZMICH (TETERNIKOV) SOLOGUB

1. On Sologub, see Note 9, "On the Addressee" and Index.

2. The magazine *Hyperboreus* was published in St. Petersburg in 1912-13. Only ten issues appeared. Mandelstam's early poems, Nos. 34, 37, 42, 45, 49, and 173 appeared in it. It was edited by M. L. Lozinsky and served as the organ of The Guild of Poets and the Acmeists.

3. These were all Acmeist publishing houses. *Hyperboreus* also issued books under its imprint from 1913 to 1918, after the magazine was closed.

4. Sologub's wife.

5. We do not know the circumstances or reasons for this letter and its tone. Mandelstam was generally positive in his evaluations of Sologub's poetry, see no. 1, above. As indicated in SS, III, 376-7, Gumilev wrote a letter to Sologub in August of 1915 praising Sologub, and declaring Sologub to be an important influence on his own poetry.

NO. 12: TO SERGEI MAKOVSKY

1. Sergei Konstantinovich Makovsky (1877-1962). Poet, art and literary critic, editor and publisher of the monthly magazine *Apollon* from October 1909 to 1917. He is best known for his books, *Silhouettes of Russian Artists (Siluety russkikh khudozhnikov), The Folk Art of Subcarpathian Rus' (Narodnoe iskusstvo podkarpatskoi*

rusi), Contemporary Portraits (Portrety sovremennikov, New York, 1955), and *On Parnassus of the Silver Age (Na Parnase serebrianogo veka,* Munich, 1962). The latter two works contain reminiscences of Mandelstam.

2. The essay "Peter Chaadaev" was published in *Apollon* in 1915 simply as "Chaadaev."

NO. 13: TO HIS MOTHER

1. Shura: Mandelstam's middle brother, Alexander Emilievich Mandelstam. See Letters: Nos. 14, 15, 18, 19, 24, 45, 48, 87, 96. See Nadezhda Mandelstam, *Hope Abandoned,* pp. 508-509. Shura worked as a minor clerk in the sales department of the State Publishing House (GIZ) in Moscow. Mandelstam often stayed with him when he was in Moscow, and was generally fond and protective of him.

2. Maximilian Alexandrovich Voloshin (1878-1932). Russian poet and artist who resided in the fashionable resort of Koktebel, near Theodosia in the Crimea, from 1917 until his death. His summer house was a gathering place for fellow poets, writers and artists, including Mandelstam and Tsvetaeva. Later, after his death, Voloshin's residence was turned into a rest home for Moscow writers. For more details about Voloshin and his guests, see M. Tsvetaeva, "History of a Dedication" (*Istoriia odnogo posviashcheniia,* SS, III, 306-344), and C. Brown, *Mandelstam,* pp. 63-66.

3. Zhenya: Mandelstam's younger brother. Evgeny Emilievich Mandelstam (1898-). Although he had obtained a medical degree, he gave up medicine to become a kind of literary agent. Later on, he became a film editor and consultant as well as scenarist for several popular scientific films. Mandelstam's father lived with Evgeny and his family. See Letters: No. 14, 18, 24, 26, 32, 35, 38, 43, 50, 63, 79, 80, and Nadezhda Mandelstam *Hope Abandoned,* pp. 104-6, 508-9, and *Hope Against Hope,* 115-16, 307-8. Basically, it seems that the Mandelstams had a poor opinion of Zhenya as a man and as a brother.

NO. 14: TO HIS MOTHER.

1. Little is known about Mandelstam's mother except that she was well-educated, played the piano well, came from the milieu of the civic-minded Vilno intelligentsia, spoke faultless Russian and according to Nadezhda Mandelstam, "tried to protect" her sons from their father. See *Hope Abandoned,* pp. 507-508.

2. Mandelstam's first book, *Stone,* was published in 1913; a second edition appeared in 1916. His reading undoubtedly included poems from this volume and perhaps poems for his next book, *Tristia.*

3. Notice Mandelstam's intentions to complete his University studies. There is no record, however, that he ever did. See C. Brown, *Mandelstam,* for more biographical details.

NO. 15: TO NADEZHDA YAKOVLEVNA MANDELSTAM.

1. Nadezhda Yakovlevna Mandelstam, the poet's indomitable widow, was born N.Y. Khazina in Saratov in 1899. After many years of wandering, condemned to the life of a "politically suspect wife," she was given an apartment in Moscow in the Cheremushki suburb, the southwestern sector of the city. Not only was Nadezhda Yakovlevna able to miraculously preserve the major portion of her husband's work for posterity, but she has written two brilliant testaments to the poet and his age, both of which are

available in Max Hayward's fine English translations: *Hope Against Hope* (1970) and *Hope Abandoned* (1974) [*Vospominaniia*, 1970; *Vtoraia kniga*, 1972] published in New York by Atheneum Publishers. Needless to say, these books never appeared in the Soviet Union except in *samizdat*. These memoirs not only contain the biographical details of Mandelstam's life in the 1920s and 1930s, but capture the dauntless spirit of the poet reflected and dramatized against the backdrop of Soviet cultural and intellectual life. See also Brown's fine volume, *Mandelstam,* the best "biography" of the poet, and a generous tribute to Nadezhda Yakovlevna.

2. An intimate pet name which is untranslatable.

3. This letter was written during the Civil War, when travel, especially in the Ukraine and areas south of Moscow, was almost impossible.

4. Konstantin Vasilievich Mochulsky (1892-1948). Highly esteemed Russian literary critic and scholar, who emigrated from the Soviet Union in the 1920s. Author of books on Blok, Bely, Bryusov, Dostoevsky, Gogol and Soloviev.

5. Soviet humor magazine.

6. Mikhail Mikhailovich Mordkin (1881-1944). Ballet dancer at the Bolshoi Theater. Emigrated in 1924, and organized the Mordkin Ballet in the United States. Margareta Petrovna Froman (b. 1890-   ). Ballet dancer originally with the Bolshoi Theater. Emigrated to Yugoslavia in 1921, to the USA in 1950 (SS, III, 378-9).

NO. 17: TO VERA YAKOVLEVNA KHAZINA

1. Nadezhda Yakovlevna Mandelstam's mother with whom Mandelstam seemed to be on excellent terms. See also, Letters No. 82, and Other Letters I-II, From Vera Y. Khazina to Nadezhda Y. Mandelstam.

2. Nadezhda Yakovlevna writes of this trip in *Hope Abandoned*, pp. 33-34.

3. At one point Mandelstam thought about becoming a Lithuanian citizen: "His having been born in Warsaw and his father's origin from Kurland were a help. The Symbolist poet Yurgis Baltrushaitis, a Lithuanian himself and that country's ambassador in Moscow from 1921 to 1939, had urged him to take the step" (C. Brown, *Mandelstam,* p. 92).

4. Nadezhda Yakovlevna's father and Vera Yakovlevna Khazina's husband.

5. The "Anya" of many of the Letters of 1926, see, below: No. 20, 21, 24, 25, 27, 29, 44, 49, 51, 52, 55, 56, 57. She was Nadezhda Yakovlevna's sister, and a major help to the Mandelstams.

NO. 18: TO HIS FATHER

1. Mandelstam's younger brother, Evgeny Emilievich, was arrested in 1922 as a warning to his fellow students.

2. On Bukharin, see Note 15 to "Fourth Prose." Part of "Fourth Prose" is a tribute to Bukharin, to whom, in Nadezhda Yakovlevna's words, Mandelstam owed "All the pleasant things in his life." (*Hope Against Hope,* p. 113).

3. Marya Nikolaevna Darmolatova, Evgeny Mandelstam's mother-in-law, who remained with Evgeny to take care of his daughter, Tatka (her granddaughter) when his first wife died, staying on even when he remarried. She was also very kind to Mandelstam's father who lived in Evgeny's household as well from 1923 on. See Letters below, Nos. 24, 26, 32, 36, 43, 44.

NO. 19: TO HIS FATHER

1. Emil Veniaminovich Mandelstam (? - d. 1938). Nadezhda Yakovlevna Mandelstam discusses him in her memoirs: "He was something completely unique, utterly unlike a *shtetl* philosopher, a Jewish craftsman or merchant, or anybody else under the sun. As a manufacturer of suede leather he apparently knew his job very well, but felt frustrated by an inner restlessness and craving to express himself. He used to quote Spinoza, Rousseau, and Schiller, but in such incredible combinations that people could only gasp. Not just a dreamer, but a spinner of fantasies—or, rather phantasmagorias—he was the sort of person of whom one could not say whether he was good or bad, mean or generous, because the main thing about him was his quality of being totally abstract... As far as I could make out [the] mother had tried only to protect [the sons] from him. She took them out to dachas in the country, or to holiday resorts, arranged for them to go to high school (choosing very shrewdly—she got M. into the Tenishev school), hired governesses for them, and in general did her best to provide a normal intellectual background in their home life" (*Hope Abandoned*, p. 507-8).

2. Evgeny Yakovlevich Khazin, Nadezhda Yakovlevna's beloved brother, who lived in Moscow. As of the writing of her memoirs, *Hope Abandoned*, she did not know "where and how he had perished" (p. 225). He was Nadezhda Yakovlevna's main helper in preserving Mandelstam's work (*Hope Against Hope*, p. 275) and was among the first to hear Mandelstam's death "certified."

3. References to this address are made in "Journey to Armenia": this is also where Mandelstam's friend, B.S. Kuzin lived.

4. See the essays "On Translation," or "Torrents of Hackwork." See lists of some of Mandelstam's translations in SS, II, 699, and III, 426-27. See also Mandelstam's poems of this period, such as "January 1, 1924."

5. Parnok. Poet whose real name was Valentin Yakovlevich Parnakh. He returned to the Soviet Union in 1922 (having emigrated to Paris before the Revolution). Author of several collections of poetry and a book about dance: *Histoire de la Dance* (Paris, 1932). (SS, III, 389). For more information, see SS, II, and notes to "The Egyptian Stamp."

6. The Union of Writers was located in Herzen House on Tverskoy Boulevard.

NO. 20: TO N. Y. MANDELSTAM

1. David Isaakovich Vygodsky (Davidka: d. 1939 "in one of Beria's camps"— see Slonimsky, below). Poet, Hispanic scholar, translator, literary critic and close friend and associate of Mandelstam. They had known each other in the House of the Arts (DISK) in Leningrad in 1921. Author of *Poetry and Poetics* (*Poeziia i poetika,* 1917). Associated with the Priboi Publishing House in 1925, editor there in 1926. Also editor of a literary magazine which published translations of foreign literature, associated with the newspaper, *Evening Red News (Vechernaia krasnaia gazeta),* see Letter No. 49. In May-August, 1926, Mandelstam published several essays in that paper, including "Kiev" and "Mikhoels." See above. His wife, Emma Vygodsky, was a well-known author of children's books. See also Letters No. 25, 31, 49. For a very kind, but not very detailed memoir, see Mikhail Slonimsky, *Book of Memoirs* (*Kniga vospominanii,* 1966, pp. 194-198). Slonimsky called Vygodsky "wise and witty, kind, straightforward, and correct in his judgments of our first efforts"[the Serapion Brothers in the House of the Arts, in Leningrad 1920-1921—JGH].

2. Priboi Publishing House. A major Leningrad publishing house, 1922-1927. In 1926 it was headed by Mikhail Sergeev. Mandelstam translated numerous works for Priboi, including A. Daudet's *Tartarin de Tarascon* (1927, in two editions), and A.

Daudistel's *Das Opfer* (1926). Most significant, Priboi published Mandelstam's volume of prose fiction entitled *The Egyptian Stamp* (*Egipetskaia marka*) in 1928. This volume also included a second edition of *The Noise of Time* and "Theodosia."

3. Benedikt Konstantinovich Livshits (1886-1939). Poet, translator, and author of a book of memoirs, *One-and-a-Half-Eyed Archer* (*Polutorazyi strelets*, Leningrad, 1933), which contains numerous references to Mandelstam. Livshits, Mandelstam and A.N. Gorlin worked together at the ZIF (Land and Factory) Publishing House editing and reworking Sir Walter Scott's *Collected Novels* (*Sobranie romanov*, Leningrad, 1928-29). See also, Letters No. 25, 63.

4. GIZ (State Publishing House, Moscow; LenGIZ, Leningrad bránch).

5. A.N. Gorlin. In 1923-24, Nadezhda Yakovlevna writes, "The main center for translating had shifted to Leningrad, and the big man in charge of it all was Gorlin, whose headquarters were in Book House, opposite the Kazan Cathedral" (*Hope Abandoned*, pp. 206-207). Gorlin is mentioned in numerous letters as a "kind relative," "helpful," etc. See Letters, No. 24, 25, 28, 29, 31, 34, 37, 40, 42, 43, 44, 45, 46, 52.

6. "Billya"—reference unclear.

7. Anya is Nadezhda Yakovlevna's sister.

NO. 21: TO N.Y. MANDELSTAM

1. *Leningrad Red News,* a newspaper with a morning and evening edition (SS, III, 380). Vygodsky had some connections with this paper. See Letter No. 20.

2. F. Heller, *A Thousand and Two Nights,* translated by Mandelstam for GIZ, 1926. (See SS, III, 380).

3. Marietta Shaginyan (?) (b. 1888-   ). Soviet novelist known for her Western-style detective fiction. Also a minor Symbolist poet.

4. Medical doctor.

NO. 22: TO N.Y. MANDELSTAM

1. Mandelstam did finally join his wife in Yalta in mid-November, but he was obviously detained in the process of finding enough translation work to support them. Nadezhda Yakovlevna was sent south to recuperate from tuberculosis.

NO. 24: TO N.Y. MANDELSTAM

1. Mandelstam's brother. See note 1, Letter No. 13.

2. On Pasternak, see No. 45, 47, 85.

3. Mandelstam evidently enjoyed children. See also his comments in the Letters on his niece, Tatka, daughter of brother Evgeny Emilievich Mandelstam. See Letters No. 26, 27, for example. The Mandelstams never had any children of their own.

4. Evgeny Yakovlevich Khazin.

5. Anna Yakovlevna Khazina, Nadezhda's sister.

6. A tightening of the censorship is indicated.

7. A Leningrad monthly, begun in 1924.

8. Mandelstam will do "internal reviews" for the magazine. See, for example, his internal reviews of the late 1920s and early 1930s on Bloch, Duhamel, Pergaud, Armand.

9. Mandelstam's father was living with brother Evgeny in Leningrad. See Letters Nos. 18, 19: to his father.

10. M.N. is Marya Nikolaevna Darmolatova. See Letter No. 18.

11. Mandelstam will live in his brother's apartment in Leningrad until he finds an apartment in Tsarskoe Selo for both of them.

12. They are living, seemingly, from month to month, mostly on his translations.

NO. 25: TO N.Y. MANDELSTAM

1. D. N. Angert. Someone more senior than Gorlin, undoubtedly connected with GIZ in Moscow, from whom LenGIZ awaited orders, approvals, etc. See Letters No. 53, 59.

2. Leningrad Publishing House which commissioned Mandelstam's translation of P. Mill's *The Chinese* in 1926 (SS, III, 427), and two volumes of *Barbusse's* stories in 1925 and 1926 (SS, II, 699). Of the latter, Nadezhda Mandelstam writes: "In Moscow we were coming to the end of our earnings on Barbusse (whose dreary stories literally poisoned our existence), and also on Barbier. . . We hence began to prepare to move to Leningrad... Such was the beginning of our Petersburg idyll, with visits to Gorlin and occasionally to Benedikt Livshits." This was at the end of 1924 when they moved to Leningrad; Nadezhda Yakovlevna's tuberculosis became so bad in early 1925 she had to be sent south to Yalta.

3. Benedict Livshits and his wife.

4. David and Emma Vygodsky. See Letter No. 20.

5. See Letter No. 24.

6. Nikolai Nikolaevich Punin (1888-1953). Art historian and critic, at one time connected with the magazine *Apollon,* later close to the Futurists. Husband of Anna Akhmatova at this juncture.

7. "The old woman" —Anna Akhmatova.

8. Georgy Vladimirovich Ivanov (1894-1958). Poet, originally close to the Acmeists, member of Gumilev's Guild of Poets and contributor to *Apollon*. Emigrated in 1923. His "terrible pasquilles" refer to articles in newspapers and magazines later collected in his book, *Petersburg Winters* (Peterburgskie zimy, Paris, 1928; New York, 1953).

9. *The Noise of Time* received numerous positive reviews, for example, D. Mirsky's review essay in *Contemporary Notes* (*Sovremennye zapiski,* Paris, No. 25, 1925, p. 542). See SS, III, 381.

10. Foreshadows problems which emerge in the Letters.

11. Mandelstam often referred to himself by this "title."

NO. 26: TO N.Y. MANDELSTAM

1. Evgeny worked as some kind of literary agent for this organization. See Letters No. 52, 63.

2. Tatka is Evgeny's daughter, M.N.'s granddaughter, and Osip Mandelstam's niece. See Nadezhda Mandelstam's memoirs for kinds words about her.

NO. 27: TO N.Y. MANDELSTAM

1. Nadezhda Yakovlevna often helped her husband with his translations.

2. Anna Akhmatova.

3. *Tramvai.* One of his collections of children's verse, published by GIZ.

NO. 28: TO N.Y. MANDELSTAM

1. See Letters below; Gorlin treats Mandelstam like a "relative," looks after him, offers to send him work down South so he can be with his wife.
2. D.N. Angert. See Letters No. 25, 53, 59.

NO. 29: TO N.Y. MANDELSTAM

1. See "On Translations," "Torrents of Hackwork," "The Duchess' Fan."
2. A reference to A. Daudistel's *Das Opfer* (1925) which Mandelstam translated for Priboy (1926). See note 2, Letter No. 20. Obviously, Nadezhda Yakovlevna had helped him with this translation—"*our* work." The novel is an autobiographical account of the German author's adventures as a mutinous sailor in a naval mutiny of 1915.

NO. 30

1. Probably an advance for his translation of Daudet.

NO. 31

1. On David Vygodsky, see Letter No. 20. The Mandelstams, being perpetually homeless, still without a permanent address in 1926, were often forced to leave their various belongings with friends: hence, the "china cabinet" and "red armchair" at the Vygodskys'.
2. Eighth line—the name of a street on Vasilyev Island on which one of the streetcars ran.
3. Wolfson—an important figure in the publishing world whom Mandelstam had known previously. See Letters No. 32, 35 and 40 as well.
4. *Streetcar* (or as published: *Two Streetcars, Dva Tramvaia*) was one of Mandelstam's books of children's verse, published by GIZ in 1925. His other volumes of children's verse include: *Balloons* (*Shary*, 1926), *The Primus Stove* (*Primus*, for which the artist M.V. Dobuzhinsky did the illustrations, 1925), and *The Kitchen* (*Kukhnia*, 1926). See SS, I, No. 406, 407-14, 396-405, and 415, respectively.

NO. 32: TO N.Y. MANDELSTAM

1. Natasha Grigoriev, sister of Tanya Grigoriev, who became Evgeny Mandelstam's second wife. See Letter No. 63.
2. On M.N. [Darmolatova], Evgeny's mother-in-law, see Letter No. 18.

NO. 33: TO N.Y. MANDELSTAM

1. Between Gorlin (editor of GIZ) and Grunberg (editor at Priboi). At this point, both are treating Mandelstam "like a relative," offering him plenty of work.
2. Interesting autobiographical comment.
3. Undoubtedly, a personal reference.
4. Jewish holiday celebrating Queen Esther's victory over the wicked Haman.
5. Belitsky. Also mentioned in Letter No. 24, where he obtained "internal re-

views" for Mandelstam. Connected with the magazine, *The Star (Zvezda)*. See also Letter No. 49.

NO. 34: TO N.Y. MANDELSTAM

1. Vladimir Kazimirovich Shileiko (1891-1930). Poet and Professor at the University of Leningrad, specialist in ancient Assyria and Asia Minor. Second husband of the poet, Anna Akhmatova (1918-1924). See also Letter No. 40a.

2. The subject of Jews becomes very important from 1926 on, culminating in "Fourth Prose," wherein "Jew" becomes Mandelstam's metaphor of the poet, *par excellence*. Another interesting autobiographical comment.

3. His translation of *Das Opfer*.

4. Samuil Yakovlevich Marshak (1887-1964). Poet and translator, best known for his children's books and translations of Shakespeare. Editor of the Children's Division at LenGIZ. See also Letters No. 38, 52, 54.

5. Konstantin Alexandrovich Fedin (1892-1977). Soviet prose writer, one time member of the Serapion Brothers, member of the literary establishment at LenGIZ, later cursed in "Fourth Prose." See also Letters No. 35, 36, 49. Fedin helped to include a book of Mandelstam's poetry in the new "Plan." This was the volume, *Poems (Stikhotvoreniia)*, finally published by GIZ in 1928 along with his book of essays, *On Poetry*.

6. Mandelstam is very pessimistic as to the outcome of this publishing venture.

7. On Benjamin Livshits, see Letter No. 20, Note 3.

NO. 35: TO N.Y. MANDELSTAM

1. On Fedin and "the book of poems," see Letter No. 34.

NO. 36: TO N.Y. MANDELSTAM

1. Daudistel.

2. Ilya Gruzdev and Fedin were both original Serapion Brothers. Ilya Alexandrovich Gruzdev (1892-1960). Writer, literary critic and scholar.

3. Faith in Fedin at this point. Contrast with comments in "Fourth Prose" about the literary establishment.

4. Ilya Grigorievich Ehrenburg (1891-1967). Soviet novelist and journalist, extremely prolific. His best known novels include *The Extraordinary Adventures of Julio Jurenito* (1921) and *The Thaw* (1954). His memoirs, *People, Years and Life* available first in an English translation published in the mid-1960s, were instrumental in promoting a review of Soviet cultural values in the post-Stalinist era. Ehrenburg remained a friend to the Mandelstams even in their darkest days, and later in the 1960s, helped to make the poet's "rehabilitation" a reality. Nadezhda Yakovlevna Mandelstam says of him in *Hope Abandoned:* "He was always the odd man out among Soviet writers, and the only one I maintained relations with all through the years. He was as helpless as everyone else, but at least he tried to do something for others."

5. Benjamin Livshits.

6. An untranslatable diminutive.

NO. 37: TO N.Y. MANDELSTAM

1. Obviously jobs were to be had only through introductions for they were already at a premium for a certain segment of the intelligentsia—especially those writers and poets who could not always count on having their creative work published.

2. Relatives. Marya Nikolaevna Darmolatova's family. Her daughter, Anna Radlova (née Darmolatova) was a poetess and translator. See "Literary Moscow." Sergei Ernestovich Radlov (1892-1958) was a film director and theater manager. Evgeny Emilievich Mandelstam's first wife was Anna Radlova's sister, Marya Nikolaevna's other daughter (SS, III, 383).

3. Mandelstam's children's verse books.

4. Mandelstam translated F. Heller's *The Thousand and Second Night* from the German for LenGIZ (1926). (See SS, III, 380).

5. Obviously, Mandelstam did not like translating for the sake of earning a living. He was always happy to have help, either from Nadezhda Yakovlevna or from her sister, Anna Yakovlevna. Anna Yakovlevna Khazina was very kind and helpful to Mandelstam when Nadezhda Yakovlevna was away. See other Letters of this period.

NO. 38: TO N.Y. MANDELSTAM

1. Mandelstam's book, *Poems,* was actually only published in 1928.

2. On Marshak see Letter No. 34.

3. An architectural monument of the early 20th century, a major grocery store on Nevsky Prospect built in the Art Nouveau style, now known as Gastronom Number 1 officially, but still referred to as the Eliseev Store by Leningraders.

4. With Soviet cultural life becoming more and more centralized, Evgeny Emilievich's job as a literary agent located in Leningrad became more difficult. Major competition obviously came from Moscow.

NO. 39: TO N.Y. MANDELSTAM

1. I have been unable to find any information on this script.

2. A reference to Akhmatova and her husband, Punin.

3. Sergei Antonovich Klychkov (Leshenkov, 1889-1937). Russian poet and novelist, member of the group of "Peasant Poets." Nadezhda Yakovlevna writes of him in *Hope Against Hope,* p. 259.

NO. 40: TO N.Y. MANDELSTAM

1. Mandelstam had a weak heart which was not helped by the life he led. It finally got so bad that he could not go out alone. See Nadezhda Yakovlevna's memoirs.

2. Mostly translations. Some internal reviews.

NO. 40a: TO N.Y. MANDELSTAM

1. It is unclear whether this is a separate letter or an addition to the preceding one. See SS, III, 385.

2. Konstantin Konstantinovich Vaginov (1900-1934). Poet (author of three books) and prose writer, very popular among the literary youth of Leningrad in the

1920s and 1930s. His collection *Konstantin Vaginov* was published in 1926.

3. Shileiko was Akhmatova's former husband; it was apparently difficult for Mandelstam to continue to see both of them. See Letter No. 34.

NO. 42: TO N.Y. MANDELSTAM

1. The Zubov Institute of the History of Art. It became a center for non-Marxist literary and art criticism. Besides instructional and research work, the Institute sponsored literary readings and lectures; the Literary Division was headed by Zhirmunsky. See SS, III, 389-86.

2. Nikolai Semyenovich Tikhonov (1896). Russian poet and prose writer who eventually wrote for the state. Secretary of the Union of Writers, 1944-56.

3. This reference is unclear. It probably refers to Franz Jung, the German writer, dramatist, and revolutionary (1888-1963). In 1920, he was sent to Moscow by the German Communist Party. Between 1924 and 1928, he lived illegally in Germany under the assumed name, Franz Larsz, running a publishing concern specializing in Communist party literature and history.

NO. 43: TO N.Y. MANDELSTAM

1. See Letter No. 33.

2. The meaning of this remains unclear.

3. To repay debts—see earlier Letters.

4. Unidentified.

5. Alexander Rafailovich Kugel (1864-1928). Theater critic, playwright and director. Founded the theater of satire and literary parody known as the "Crooked Mirror" in 1908 along with Z.V. Kholmskaya, which he directed until his death in 1928. (SS, III, 387).

6. Pavel Eliseevich Shchegolev (1877-1931). Literary critic, film writer, and dramatist. His criticism focused on Pushkin (SS, III, 387).

7. Alexei Ivanovich Svirsky (1865-1942). Short story writer, and neighbor of the Mandelstams when they lived in Herzen House. He evidently also set up a restaurant for the Union of Writers.

8. Count Vasily Alexeevich Komarovsky (1881-1914). Poet and contributor to *Apollon*. One book of his poetry was published in St. Petersburg in 1913, *First Wharf* (*Pervaia pristan'*). Admired in Acmeist circles. (SS, III, 387).

9. This may refer to Prince D.S. Mirsky's review of *The Noise of Time*.

10. Akhmatova.

11. A reference to reviews of *The Noise of Time* which was very favorably received abroad.

NO. 45: TO N.Y. MANDELSTAM

1. Nadezhda Yakovlevna's brother, Evgeny Yakovlevich Khazin.

2. Pasternak was always very kind to the Mandelstams. See Nadezhda Yakovlevna's memoirs.

3. Mandelstam's brother, Alexander Emilievich.

NO. 46: TO N.Y. MANDELSTAM

1. Wolfson. See references in preceding Letters, No. 45, etc.

NO. 47: TO N.Y. MANDELSTAM

1. Shklovsky had been living in Moscow since 1923, when he returned from abroad. The Shklovskys always welcomed and helped the Mandelstams even in the worst of times. See Nadezhda Yakovlevna's memoirs.

2. Mandelstam did reviews for the *Star* where Belitsky was editor.

3. Usually, when someone was offered work reviewing a book, he was given first option on translating it as well, if the review was positive. This may be what Mandelstam is referring to here in "getting the new books approved." See his essays on translating, reviewing and publishing practices: "On Translations," "Torrents of Hackwork," "Duchess' Fan," "Jacques was Born and Died."

4. Alexander Konstantinovich Voronsky (1884-1943). Literary critic, writer, and journalist. Editor of the magazine, *Red Virgin Soil* between 1921 and 1927 and of *Searchlight (Prozhektor)* between 1923 and 1927, and head of the Circle (Krug) Publishing House. He was expelled from the Communist party in 1927 for his "liberalism," for his advocacy of the "fellow travelers," and for his alleged "Trotskyite leanings." Mandelstam's work appeared in both of his magazines in 1922 and 1923.

NO. 48: TO MANDELSTAM

1. Shklovsky was undoubtedly the source of this windfall for Mandelstam. See notes to "I Write a Scenario."

2. Vladimir Ivanovich Narbut (1888-1938). Poet associated with the Guild of Poets and with the Acmeists. He joined the Communist Party after the Revolution, but was expelled in 1928. In 1919-1920, he published the Voronezh Almanac, *Sirena,* in which poems of Blok, Akhmatova and Mandelstam appeared. He was editor-in-chief of the state publishing house, Land and Factory (ZIF) until 1928, when Ionov took over and Mandelstam's troubles began: see references to the "Dreyfus affair."

3. Alexander Emilievich Mandelstam, the poet's brother, Shura.

NO. 49: TO N.Y. MANDELSTAM

1. In the spring of 1926, Mandelstam had joined his wife in Yalta, where she had been recuperating from tuberculosis. From there, they had returned via Kiev and Moscow to live in Tsarskoe Selo. When Nadezhda Yakovlevna fell ill again, Mandelstam sent her back south, to the Crimea—to Koktebel first, and then Theodosia.

2. The reference to different buildings at Tsarskoe Selo. The "Chinese Village" is in the Palace Park; the "Semicircle" refers to the semicircular part of the Main Palace. (SS, III, 388).

3. Jakobson versus Lunacharsky—a reference to conflicting views of literature and criticism, Jakobson being the outstanding Formalist linguist who emigrated from the Soviet Union; Lunacharsky being the Soviet ideologue in charge of the Ministry of Education.

4. Apparently Mandelstam owed GIZ some money, thus his next contract was held up until he paid it.

5. See "Fourth Prose." There are references there to all Mandelstam's financial

difficulties with contracts, documents, etc.

6. Lev Naumovich Voitolovsky (1876-1941), Marxist critic, literary historian, and writer.

7. Headquarters of the Communist Party in Leningrad.

8. Mikhail Leonidovich Slonimsky (1897-). Prose writer and one-time member of the Serapion Brothers. See note 12, "Literary Moscow: The Birth of Plot." See Slonimsky's *Book of Memoirs* (*Kniga vospominanii*, 1966). Appointed Editor at Priboi in 1926.

9. David Vygodsky.

10. These were undoubtedly "internal reviews." See above.

11. See reference to Kapeliansky in "The Egyptian Stamp," Section 8.

12. Akhmatova.

13. Benedikt Livshits and his wife. See above.

NO. 50: TO N.Y. MANDELSTAM

1. Maximillian Voloshin.

NO. 51: TO N.Y. MANDELSTAM

1. A reference to "internal reviews." See above.

2. A reference to reviews and translations of French books. One of these may have included Mandelstam's translation of Bernard Lekash's novel, *Radan the Magnificent*, which GIZ published in 1927, and which was harshly criticized when it appeared as "anti-semitic" and "decadent." GIZ also published in 1926 Mandelstam's translation of *The Government and the Press of France* (SS, II, 699).

3. The central or regional economic management board in the Soviet Union.

NO. 52: TO N.Y. MANDELSTAM

1. See Letters No. 26, 63.

2. See Letters No. 38, 43, 63.

NO. 54: TO N.Y. MANDELSTAM

1. Mandelstam's translation of Daudet's novel was published by Priboi in 1927. An 85 page book, it was issued in two editions.

NO. 59: TO COMRADE KOROBOVA

This letter was obtained by the editors of the *Collected Works* from Nikita A. Struve. See SS, II, 680.

1. Comrade Korobova was evidently the editor at Priboy in charge of Mandelstam's prose fiction, "The Egyptian Stamp" and *The Noise of Time*. Both works were eventually published under the common title, *The Egyptian Stamp* (1928).

2. Lidiya Moiseevna Varkhovitskaia, editor at GIXL (Gosudarstvennoe Izdatelstvo Khudozhestvennoi Literatury) or Lit.-Khud. the State Publishing House for Belles-

Lettres.

3. This is now the ending of *Theodosia* which was printed in 1928 as a separate work from *The Noise of Time.* In the 1925 edition, published by Vremia, it was included as a "chapter" in *The Noise of Time.*

4. See "The Return" in our collection. Apparently this was one of the causes of Mandelstam's intensive interrogation mentioned in Letter No. 64.

5. These have been lost. "Encounter..." may very well refer to Mandelstam's abortive encounter with A. Tolstoi written up by G. Ivanov in his memoirs, *Petersburg Winters,* see above.

6. D. I. Mitrokhin did the cover for *Poems* (see No. 10, below) instead. He had also done illustrations for the collections published by the House of the Arts (DISK) in 1921. Mandelstam was living at DISK at that time. Mitrokhin also did the cover for the *Jewish Almanac* published in Petrograd in 1923.

7. The 1928 edition of Mandelstam's *Poems,* published by GIZ (State Publishing House).

8. See Letters, No. 28, 53.

9. Izmail Mikhailovich Likhnitsky. Editor at GIZ.

10. *The Star (Zvezda),* a Leningrad monthly magazine edited by Caesar Volpe, which, printed Mandelstam's last published work, "Journey to Armenia" in the spring of 1933 (No. 5).

11. This is unclear, but it may refer to Mandelstam's plans for the story, "The Bassoonist." See above, SS, II, 680.

NO. 60: TO ANNA AKHMATOVA

1. Pavel Nikolaevich Luknitsky (b. 1900-   ). Novelist and short story writer. According to Nadezhda Yakovlevna Mandelstam, a copy of this letter was preserved by Luknitsky and is quoted by Akhmatova in her article "Mandelstam," first published in 1965 in the almanac, *Aerial Ways (Vozdushnye puti).* See *Hope Abandoned,* p. 47.

2. Gumilev.

3. Gumilev.

4. Nadezhda Yakovlevna Mandelstam.

NO. 61: TO N.Y. MANDELSTAM

1. Nadezhda Yakovlevna is in Kiev with her mother, Vera Yakovlevna Khazin. She moves to Moscow eventually and lives with the Mandelstams after her husband's death.

NO. 62: TO N.Y. MANDELSTAM

1. *Young Pioneer* is a youth magazine where Nadezhda Yakovlevna had been working.

NO. 63: TO N.Y. MANDELSTAM

1. See Letters, Nos. 38, 43, etc.

2. Natasha Grigorieva, Evgeny Emilievich's sister-in-law. She was the sister of Tanya Grigorieva, Evgeny's second wife. See *Hope Against Hope,* pp. 307-312.

3. He eventually *did* get a job in the film industry.

4. Tanya Grigoreva Mandelstam, Evgeny's wife. See Note 2, above.

5. The optimistic dreamer in Gogol's *Dead Souls*.

6. Newspaper.

7. See notes to "Fourth Prose." The scandal surrounding Mandelstam's revision of two translations of *Till Euhlenspiegel* was referred to by the Mandelstams as their "Dreyfus affair."

8. See notes to "Fourth Prose."

9. Komsomol magazine published in Moscow.

10. See notes to "Fourth Prose." ZIF was the publishing house which put out the revised translation.

11. There was a movement to resettle working class Jews in agriculture. Property was being offered to them if they would settle in the Northern Crimea and work the land.

12. Alexander Margulis. A good friend of the Mandelstams, about whom Mandelstam made up numerous impromptu humorous verses. See *Hope Abandoned,* pp. 124-126. Nadezhda Yakovlevna refers to their friendship as one of "the most durable" because it was "playful."

13. On Aseev, see Index, also *Hope Abandoned* (pp. 119, 335, 465).

14. A reference to a letter in his defense?!

NO. 64: TO N.Y. MANDELSTAM

1. For more details on "the case" or "the Dreyfus affair," see notes to "Fourth Prose." See also, Letter No. 63, above.

2. Osvag (Osvedomitel' noe agentsvo)—The Intelligence unit of the White Army.

3. See Letter No. 59 and the notes to it. There is an English translation of "Theodosia" in Brown, *The Prose of Osip Mandelstam.*

4. The 1928 edition of Mandelstam's prose fiction published under the title *The Egyptian Stamp* included a second edition of *The Noise of Time* and "Theodosia."

5. Ilya Ionovich Ionov (pseudonym of Bernstein, 1887-1942). Editor in charge of the Leningrad State Publishing House (LenGIZ) in the 1920s. He also took over as head of ZIF (Land and Factory Publishing House) in 1928, after Narbut was dismissed and expelled from the Communist Party. He was partially responsible for letting the Mandelstam scandal ("Dreyfus affair," see Letter No. 59 and "Fourth Prose") over the revision of *Till Euhlenspiegel* get out of hand. Also a "Proletarian" poet. See also, N.Y. Mandelstam, *Hope Abandoned* (p. 54): "He was noted for his vile temper. He was. . . not quite right in the head . . . I believe Ionov eventually met with the same end as everyone else."

6. Mikhail Alexandrovich Zenkevich (1891-1969). One of the original Acmeist poets. See N.Y. Mandelstam, *Hope Abandoned,* esp. pp. 51-52. See also Letter No. 77.

7. Bukharin eventually arranged for the Mandelstams' trip to Armenia and the Caucasus in May 1930. They remained out of the capital until the following winter.

8. See the end of "Fourth Prose."

9. See Letter No. 63, about Yurasov inviting him to work on the newspaper, *Komsomol Member of the East.*

NO. 66: TO N.Y. MANDELSTAM

1. Mandelstam is working on a new volume of poems in his Voronezh exile, now known as his "Voronezh Notebooks," and never to be published during his lifetime.

2. See SS, I, 210-11, Poem No. 299, April 1935.

3. Unclear references. It might possibly refer to the attempt to publish poem No. 313, which he calls "Zhelezo" (Iron) in Letter No. 68. See Note 3, to that letter, below.

NO. 67: TO N.Y. MANDELSTAM

1. See note 1, to Letter 66. See SS, I, 212, poem No. 302, April 1935.

2. Chairman of the Voronezh branch of the Union of Writers. See Letter, No. 69.

3. In 1935, Mandelstam was still able to find work. Later on, when he wanted work, none was to be had.

4. Sergei Vasilievich Shervinsky (b. 1892- ?). Poet and translator. (SS, III, 390). A number of his poems were published in the same issue of the almanac, *Lyric Circle* (*Liricheskii krug*, M., 1922) in which Mandelstam's poems appeared.

5. See "Goethe's Youth: A Radiodrama," and the notes to it.

NO. 68: TO N.Y. MANDELSTAM

1. A Voronezh literary magazine.

2. See SS, I, 217-18, Poem No. 312, May-June, 1935.

3. See SS, I, 219, Poem No. 313. This is dated June, 1935 in SS. If the letter is correct, it should be May, 1935. It is a companion poem to No. 312, *Stanzas (Stansy)*, mentioned above, No. 2. The word "iron" refers to the line: "Where are you, three brave boys from the iron gates of the GPU?" (Gde vy, troe slavnykh rebiat iz zheleznykh vorot GPU?) Neither of these poems, No. 212, nor 213 could have pleased the authorities or publishers in Voronezh or Moscow. Both concern the Mandelstam's trip East after Mandelstam's first arrest in 1934.

4. Mandelstam, the perpetual optimist, could not possibly have known how bad his situation was, if he was dreaming of publishing No. 312 or 313 in Moscow, let alone in the *Literary Gazette*.

5. Major Moscow literary newspaper.

6. A reference to Fyodor Markovich Lenin (b. 1901 -), literary critic and editor, or to Boris Mikhailovich Levin (1898-1940), prose writer and satirist. See SS III, 390. Unclear reference.

7. A reference to Poem No. 312, "Stanzas." See notes No. 2-3 above. Or to The "Octets" poems Nos. 275-285 (?), the first of which was revised in Voronezh in 1935.

NO. 69: TO N.Y. MANDELSTAM

1. Stoichev. See Letter No. 67.

NO. 71: TO N.Y. MANDELSTAM

1. Alexander Sergeevich Shcherbakov (1901-1945). Became a member of the Central Committee in 1932, and was appointed Secretary of the Union of Writers in 1934, despite the fact that he had no connection with literature of any kind.

2. Abram Markovich Efros (1888-1954). Noted art historian and translator. According to Nadezhda Yakovlevna Mandelstam, Efros never forgot a slight and "the celebrated schemer" was behind many of his troubles. See for instance, *Hope Abandoned*, pp. 199-200. The work in question was a joint translation of Petrarch's sonnets

(SS, III, 390).

    3. At the Tambov Psychiatric Sanitorium.

    4. Grigory Aleksandrovich Smetanin (1894-1952). Composer. One of the founders of the Tambov Proletkult and its Choir. He taught musicology at the Tambov Music School from 1922 to 1950 (SS, III, 390).

NO. 72: TO N.Y. MANDELSTAM

    1. See "Goethe's Youth: Radiodrama."

NO. 73: TO N.Y. MANDELSTAM

    1. Ivan Kapitonovich Luppol (1896-1943). Marxist literary historian, critic, and editor. Head of Gorky Institute of World Literature from 1935 to 1940, and elected member of The Academy of Sciences in 1939. According to Nadezhda Yakovlevna in *Hope Against Hope* (p. 281), as Editor-in-Chief of the State Publishing House in 1937, he refused to give Mandelstam work.

    2. Vsevolod Vitalievich Vishnevsky (1900-1951). Prose writer and playwright, best known for his successes in transforming *agitprop* theatre into genuine drama. According to Nadezhda Yakovlevna in *Hope Against Hope* (p. 181), the Mandelstams' last year in Voronezh was supported completely by money sent them by Vishnevsky and Shklovsky through Nadezhda's brother.

NO. 77: TO N.Y. MANDELSTAM

    1. Soviet literary journal, founded in 1921 and ceased publication in 1942. This journal "represented the first serious attempt in nearly half a century to create and shape an entire generation of writers, readers and critics through the energy and authority of a journal." For a fine study of this journal and its impact on Soviet literature, see Robert Maguire, *Red Virgin Soil* (New York, 1968).

NO. 79: TO HIS BROTHER, EVGENY EMILIEVICH MANDELSTAM

    1. See Letters, No. 14, 18, 24, 26, 32, 35, 38, 43, 50, 63, 80, 81.

NO. 82: TO VERA YAKOVLEVNA KHAZINA

    1. Mandelstam's request to his mother-in-law is answered quickly. She comes to live with him in Voronezh while Nadezhda Yakovlevna goes to Moscow to seek work and financial aid. See Vera Yakovlevna's letters to Nadezhda Yakovlevna about her life with Mandelstam: Nos. I and II. See also, Mandelstam's own account in Letters No. 86, 87, 88, 89, 91, 92, 93, 94, 95.

    2. Nadezhda Yakovlevna's brother, Zhenya.

    3. Alexander Emilievich Mandelstam, Mandelstam's brother. See earlier Letters.

NO. 83: TO KORNEI CHUKOVSKY

1. Kornei Ivanovich Chukovsky (pseudonym of N.I. Korneichuk, 1882-1969). Eminent Russian writer, critic, and translator, best known for his memoirs and portraits of Russian writers, his children's literature, and his critical study of Nekrasov. His knowledge of English allowed him to translate not only Dickens, Kipling, Wilde, Twain, Whitman, and O. Henry, but numerous English nursery rhymes and tales for children. He was also a persistent fighter for the preservation of literary Russian, while his fascination with problems of language is expressed in the charming collection of anecdotes about Soviet children and children's language called *From Two to Five* (in English translation). He was well respected both by the pre-Revolutionary intelligentsia and by Soviet literati as extremely knowledgeable, generous, and kind.

NO. 84: KORNEI CHUKOVSKY

1. The reference is to Stalin himself. Stalin's intervention alone could have saved Mandelstam at that time. Mandelstam obviously felt that Chukovsky was one of the few writers who could, or might, dare to write to Stalin in 1937.

NO. 85: TO BORIS LEONIDOVICH PASTERNAK

1. The original of this letter is reprinted in *Russian Literature Triquarterly*, No. 6 (Spring, 1973), page 620. The translation is by Ellendea Proffer.

NO. 86: TO YURY NIKOLAEVICH TYNIANOV

1. Yury Nikolaevich Tynianov (1894-1943). Outstanding Formalist literary critic and author of historical-biographical novels. At the age of twenty-nine, he was a university professor and distinguished scholar. Along with Eikhenbaum, Shklovsky, and Jakobson, he was one of the founders and most creative members of the Formalist movement in literary criticism. His best known works include *Problems of Poetic Language (Problema stikhotvornogo iazyka,* 1924), *Archaists and Innovators* (Arkhaisty i novatory, 1929), and (with R. Jakobson) "Problems in the Study of Literature and Language"("Voprosy izucheniia literatury i iazyka," in *Novyi Lef,* 1928, No. 12 [available in English translation in R. and F. DeGeorge, *The Structuralists*]). Mandelstam and Tynianov were fellow students in the Philology Faculty of Leningrad University, Mandelstam first registering in 1911, Tynianov in 1912. Besides their doubtless contact at the University, they both spent time in the Leningrad House of the Arts (DISK) in the early 1920s. Mandelstam was undoubtedly impressed by Tynianov's *Problems of the Poetic Language,* which includes a chapter on "Rhythm as a constructive factor in verse." See Mandelstam's "Remarks on Chénier" and "Conversation about Dante," in particular, with reference to Tynianov's subsection, "The function of rhythm in verse and in prose." See also the subsections, "Rhythmical signification and semantic signification" and "The influence of rhythm on the meaning of words" in Chapter II: "The Meaning of the Poetic Word."

Both men also expressed deep interest in, and sensitivity to problems of the relationship of literature and history, and the use of (auto-)biographical and historical data in their prose fiction as elements of theme and basic structure. See, for example, Tynianov's novel, *Kiukhlia: The Tale of a Decembrist* (Leningrad, 1925), based on the biography of the poet Kiukhelbeker.

2. Of this letter, Nadezhda Yakovlevna wrote in *Hope Abandoned* (p. 336); "Toward the end of his life, M. could contain himself no longer and accorded himself recognition in a letter to Tynianov. . . I do not know whether this letter has survived among Tynianov's papers. Most likely not . . . Natasha Shtempel made a copy before mailing it for M., and in this form it still survives among my papers. Tynianov never replied to it, but one cannot hold this against him: it was a terrible time and nobody replied to letters." Nadezhda Yakovlevna's disparaging remarks on Tynianov in *Hope Abandoned* caused a polemic with V. Kaverin (see *New York Review of Books,* Feb. 21, 1974).

NO. 87: TO N. Y. MANDELSTAM

1. Natasha Shtempel. A Voronezh schoolteacher, and one of the only truly devoted friends the Mandelstams had in Voronezh. She helped to preserve Mandelstam's papers, and in 1966 published some of his poetry for the first time in a local Voronezh journal, *The Ascent (Pod"em,* Jan-Feb. 1966): see poems Nos. 296, 299, 311, 314, 328, 364, 375, 376, 388, 393. Of her character, Nadezhda Yakovlevna stated in *Hope Abandoned:* "... a woman of rare spiritual grace. She came late into our life, but will always be part of it" (p. 280). On Mandelstam's poems to Natasha Shtempel, see *Hope Abandoned,* pp. 242, 248, 256, 488.

2. A monthly Moscow literary magazine.

NO. 88: TO N. Y. MANDELSTAM

1. Natasha Shtempel. See Letter No. 87.

NO. 90: TO N. Y. MANDELSTAM

1. Reference to Mandelstam's poem No. 381, "Rome." See also Letter No. 95.

NO. 91: TO N. Y. MANDELSTAM

1. Vladimir Petrovich Stavsky (Kirpichnikov, 1900-1943). Prose writer. Appointed Secretary of the Union of Soviet Writers in 1936, upon Maxim Gorky's death. He denounced numerous writers for their "Trotskyite leanings" and for other "crimes" during the Stalinist purges. Nadezhda Yakovlevna accuses him in *Hope Against Hope* (p. 367-369) of being a "respectful assistant to the executioner."

2. With Mandelstam's term of exile in Voronezh drawing to an end, those who wished to keep him in exile or do away with him completely, must have planted this article. In 1937, charges of "Trotskyite leanings" normally led to the labor camps.

3. Few were the writers who even dared to answer charges of "Trotskyite leanings," let along bring their own cases to the attention of the top authorities.

NO. 92: TO N. Y. MANDELSTAM

1. See Letter No. 91.
2. Nadezhda Yakovlevna's brother, Zhenya.

NO. 93: TO N. Y. MANDELSTAM

1. A reference to Natasha Shtempel and poem No. 389. See Letters No. 94, 95.

2. Nadezhda Yakovlevna has an excellent command of English, but Mandelstam's second languages were French and German.

3. Reference is unclear.

4. Reference is unclear; perhaps, he means the room light, which can be turned on and off by pulling a chain.

NO. 94: TO N. Y. MANDELSTAM

1. With the Union of Writers. See also, Letter No. 91.

2. See Letters No. 88, 93.

3. Sergei Borisovich Rudakov. A fellow exile in Voronezh, who at first seemed to be faithful and trustworthy. Nadezhda Yakovlevna gave him many of Mandelstam's poems for safekeeping. He returned to Leningrad in 1936. He was killed during World War II in a penal battalion. His wife inherited his manuscripts, including Mandelstam's papers. Furthermore, according to Nadezhda Yakovlevna, Rudakov may have planned to use Mandelstam's poems and pass them off as his own. See her account of their strange relationship in *Hope Against Hope* (pp. 271-275).

NO. 95: TO N. Y. MANDELSTAM

1. A reference to Mandelstam's poem No. 381, "Rome." See also, Letter No. 90.

2. A reference to Mandelstam's poem No. 389, "The new buds are fragrant with sticky oaths." A poem proposing Natasha Shtempel's marriage. See Letters No. 93, 94.

3. A reference to poem No. 393, "A pear stuck to me, and the birdcherry." This may also be an indirect reference to Pasternak's poem, "Definition of the Soul" from the collection *My Sister Life*.

NO. 96: TO N. Y. MANDELSTAM

1. See especially poem No. 389.

2. A reference to poem No. 313. See Letters No. 68 and 66.

3. A reference to the book of *Sasanid Metals* mentioned in Letter No. 94.

4. See Letter No. 93—"sity streat."

NO. 97: TO HIS BROTHER, ALEXANDER EMILIEVICH MANDELSTAM (AND TO HIS WIFE)

1. This is Mandelstam's last communique, after his second and final arrest.

2. For the fullest commentary on the meaning of this letter, read Nadezhda Yakovlevna's memoirs, *Hope Against Hope* and *Hope Abandoned*. I can add nothing.

NOS. I and II: FROM VERA YAKOVLEVNA KHAZINA TO NADEZHDA YAKOVLEVNA MANDELSTAM

1. Nadezhda Yakovlevna's mother came to stay with Osip Mandelstam in Voronezh while she tried to secure financial aid and political assistance in Moscow. See Mandelstam's Letter No. 82.

2. Nadezhda Yakovlevna's brother, Vera Khazina's son.

3. A reference to Natasha Shtempel. See Letter No. 87.

A COLLECTIVE LETTER TO THE DIVISION OF PRESS AND PUBLICATIONS OF THE COMMUNIST PARTY CENTRAL COMMITTEE, SIGNED BY OSIP MANDELSTAM, AMONG OTHERS

1. First published in the book, *Toward the Question of the Communist Party Position on Literature (K voprosu o politike RKP(b) v khudozhestvennoi literature,* M., 1925), and reprinted subsequently.

2. The letter is directed against the campaign of such magazines and newspapers as *On Guard,* criticizing "fellow travelers" and non-party writers. See SS, III, 392.

INDEX

714

717

Mandelstam, Osip
Streetcar (cont.): 697
"Sukharevka": 644, 647
"Theodosia": 645, 695, 703, 704
"Torrents of Hackwork": 629, 656-57
Tristia: 45, 597, 609 ("Tristia"), 693
"Voronezh Notebooks," poetry from: 546, 547, 548, 572
"The Word and Culture": 12, 45, 595, 610, 611-13, 616, 619, 637, 639, 640, 641, 646, 654
"A Word or Two about Georgian Art": 631, 633
"Yakhontev": 646, 652-53
Mandelstam, Tanya: 704
Manet, Edouard: 359
Manilov (*Dead Souls*): 542
Manshtein: 292
Maran, Rene: 249, 648
Marchenko: 548, 554, 555
Marco Polo: 389
Margulis, A. 543, 704
Markov, V. 605, 608, 614, 617, 625, 626, 628, 633, 635, 640
Marot, Clement: 77, 590
Marr: 345, 350, 373, 670
Marshak, S.Y. 506, 512, 527, 529, 532, 533, 698
Marx, K. 254, 304, 361 (*Kapital*), 361
Marxism: 388, 475
Matisse: 363, 673
Maupassant, Guy de: 283, 296, 553
Mayakovsky, V. 145, 147-48, 178-79, 196, 202, 385-86, 625, 627-28, 636, 659, 665, 673
Mazeppa, I.S. 346, 670
Mazour: 646
Mazurkevich: 644
Mdivani: 223
Mendel, Vera: 642
Mephisto Waltz: 423
Merck, Johann Heinrich: 462, 687
Mercure de France: 520
Merezhkovsky: 585, 619, 632
Merimée: 151, 257, 622, 630, 650
Merwin, W.S. 681
Methodius — See Cyril
Meung, Jean de: 582
Meyerhold: 253, 258, 267, 649, 653
Michurin: 668, 674
Mikhoels: 260-63, 651-52

Mikhoels-Vovsi, N. 652
Mikitenko, I. 650
Mill, P. 696
Minsky, N. 476, 619, 690
Mirsky, D.S. 618, 631, 696, 700
Mitrikhin, D.I. 538, 703
Mitsisvili: 633
Mochulsky, Konstantin: 485, 608, 693
von Mohl: 370
Molière: 259, 305
Molokans: 671
Mommsen: 127
Monaco: 309
Monet, Claude: 331, 359, 364, 388-89, 673
Monmouth, G. de: 217
Montcorbier, G. de: 54
Montenegro: 309
Montesquieu: 80, 249
Mordkin, Mikhail: 485, 693
Moreas, Jean: 586
Morozov, A. 677, 678, 679, 680, 681, 682, 683, 684, 685
Moscow Komsomol: 315, 661, 663
Moscow Komsomol Member: 545
Moses: 440
Moses of Chorene: 676
Moses of Kagkantov: 676
Mozart: 132, 359, 366, 392, 478, 584, 620, 685
Don Juan (opera): 135
Mravian, A.A. 317, 664
Musset: 80, 175
Mussorgsky: 631

Nadezhdin, N. 592
Nadson: 72, 174, 609
Napoleon: 198, 199, 304, 369, 464
Narbut, Vladimir: 130, 524, 582, 583, 701, 704
Nationalism: 88-89
Negro: 307
Nekrasov: 117, 124, 134, 136, 158, 173, 186, 468 ("Vlas"), 587, 618, 621-22, 632, 665, 678, 689, 707
Nemirovich-Danchenko: 638
Netherlands: 306
New Life: 690
News: 293, 656
Nicholas I: 592
Nietzsche, Friedrich: 478 (*Zarathustra*)
Nikandrov, N. 576
Nikitin, V. 153, 154, 577, 630

Pushkin (cont.): 586-87, 592, 593, 594,
596, 597, 598, 599, 600, 606, 607,
609, 610, 611, 612, 616, 618, 622,
624, 630, 632, 633, 634, 635, 641,
653, 670, 676, 677, 683, 686, 689
Boris Godunov: 119
Eugene Onegin: 80-81, 178
Feast during the Plague: 135
"The Poet and the Mob": 82
"The Poor Knight": 468

Quenet, Charles: 593

Rabelais, 77, 131, 151,
Rabinovich, Grishka: 252
Rocan: 632
Rachel: 440
Rachmaninoff: 631
Racine: 77, 131, 305, 586, 646, 687
Radishchev: 14
Radlov, Sergei: 510, 585, 699
Radlova, Anna: 146, 510, 627, 699
Rakovskaya: 613, 647
Rakovsky, K. 613
Raymond, Marcel: 585
Reader and Writer: 654
Red Evening News — See *Leningrad
Red Evening News*
Red Fields: 470
Red Virgin Soil: 556, 642, 701
Reentovich: 550
Régnier, Henri de: 295, 298, 632
Reid, Mayne: 294, 657
Reinhardt, M. 650
Rembrandt: 673
Remizov: 630
Renoir: 364, 389, 673
Rice, Martin: 608
Rimbaud, Arthur: 437, 684
Robespierre: 390
Rodchenko, A. 279, 655
Roland: 450
Rolland, Romain: 143, 200, 303, 304,
306, 659
Romains, Jules: 270-73, 306, 651, 653-
54, 660
Roman de la Rose: 53, 582
Romanov, P. 259 (*The Meringue*)
Romantic: 80, 135, 141, 157, 170-71,
186, 195, 217, 436
Romashov, B. 650-51
Ronsard: 591, 598, 632

Room, A. 658
Rossiia: 620, 625, 629, 633
Rostopchina, Countess: 175
Rotsel, R.W. 680
Rousseau, J.-J. 249, 687, 694
Rozanov, V. 14, 122-24, 476, 615, 617,
618
Rozhdestvensky: 610
Rudakov, S.V. 571, 709
Rudnitsky: 649, 651-52
Ruger: 544
Russia: 581, 641
Russian Art: 633, 635
Russian Literature: 602, 607
Russian Literature Triquarterly: 583,
586, 609, 628, 631, 649, 707
Russian Wealth: 664
Russian Word: 645
Rybakov: 500, 502, 503, 514, 519

Sablin: 290, 657
Sabua: 384
Sagatebian, I.Y. 346
Saint-Just: 390
Sakulin, P. 576
Salieri: 132, 584, 620, 635
Salviati, Cassandra: 598
Saturn: 432
Savanarola: 448
The Scales: 127, 129, 156, 203, 586,
603, 607, 618, 619, 632
Scanlon, J. 624
Scarfe, Francis: 589
Scheherazade: 150
Schelling, F. 131
Schiller: 694
Schnitzler, A. 663
Schonemann, Lili: 463, 688
Schonkopf, Katchen: 462, 687
Schopenhauer: 622
Schubert: 276, 675, 687
Schwarzbard, Shalom: 648
Scott, Walter: 288, 291, 650, 695
The Screen: 652
Scriabin: 90-95, 596-97, 599, 600, 601
Searchlight: 470, 637, 701
Seforim, M. 651
Segal, D.M. 602, 613
Segel, H. 607
Semenko, I. 668, 676, 677
Semiradksy: 190, 639-40
Serafimovich: 641
Serapion Brothers: 131, 151-54, 630-31,

722

Vygodskaya, Emma: 495, 694, 696
Vygodsky, D.I. (Davidka): 490, 495, 501, 520, 526, 694, 695, 696, 697

Wagner: 145, 411
Walter: 426 (*Musical Dictionary*)
"Wanda Warenina": 230
Wells, H.G. 630
West, James: 608
Whitman, Walt: 125, 271, 707
Wilde, Oscar: 583, 631, 632, 707
William Tell: 327
Wilson, Woodrow: 304
Windelband: 484
Wolf: 549
Wolfson: 501, 504, 506, 507, 515, 518, 522, 697
Wrangel: 225

Yakhontov: 267-69, 652-53
Yakovlev, A. 576
Yashvili: 633
Yazykov, N. 84, 165, 166, 194, 634
Young Guard: 542
Young Pioneer: 703
Yurasov: 704

Yusupov, N.B. 592
Yve-Plesis: 591

Zaitsev, B. 641
Zamyatin, E. 151, 613, 630, 640
Zarathustra: 280
Zaslavsky: 329, 661, 666
Zavadovsky: 568, 569
Zavalishin, V. 630
Zeldin, M.-B. 592, 594, 595, 624
Zenkevich, M.A. 130, 544, 556, 704
Zenkovsky, S. 617
Zetkin, K. 248, 648
Zeus: 415
Zhelyabov, A. 622
Zhirmunsky: 133, 146, 621, 700
Zhordania, N. 645
Zhukovsky, V. 265, 586
Zinoviev: 487
Zjuntan: 251
Zola: 199, 603
Zorgenfrey: 133, 621, 622
Zoshchenko: 280, 318, 324, 325, 556, 630, 661, 662, 665-66
Zozulya, E. 277, 577